ROUTLEDGE COMPANION TO PROFESSIONAL AWARENESS AND DIVERSITY IN PLANNING EDUCATION

The *Routledge Companion to Professional Awareness and Diversity in Planning Education* engenders a discourse on how urban planning as a discipline is being made attractive to children and youth as they consider their career preferences. It also provides a discourse around the diversity challenges facing the institutions for training urban planning professionals.

This *Companion* is an impressive collection of initiatives, experiences, and lessons in helping children, youth, and the general public appreciate the importance of, and the diversity challenge confronting, the urban planning profession and education. It comprises empirical, experimental, and case study research on initiatives to address the professional awareness and diversity challenges in urban planning. It has uniquely assembled voices and experiences from countries in Africa, Asia, Europe, and North America. Contributors are educators, practitioners, and activists of urban planning as well as policymakers in their respective countries.

This *Companion* is intended as a resource for urban planning schools and departments, foundations, non-profit organizations, private sector organizations, public institutions, teachers, and alumni, among others to learn and consciously drive efforts to increase planning education awareness among children, youth, and the general public.

Stephen Kofi Diko is Assistant Professor at the Department of City and Regional Planning at the University of Memphis, Tennessee (USA). He holds a PhD in Regional Development Planning from the University of Cincinnati, Ohio (USA). His research interests and experiences encompass urban green spaces, climate change, flooding, informality, community economic development, plan quality assessments, and urban planning awareness. He explores these interests through the lens of sustainable urban development and policy both at the local and global levels.

Leah Marie Hollstein is Assistant Professor in the School of Planning at the University of Cincinnati's College of Design, Architecture, Art, and Planning. She holds a Master of Landscape Architecture from the University of Michigan and a PhD in Urban Planning from the University of Texas at Austin. Her research interests are in the areas of environmental planning, green infrastructure, land use planning, planning practice and education, and planning research methods.

Danilo Palazzo is Professor and Director of the School of Planning at the University of Cincinnati, USA. Prior to moving to Cincinnati, Palazzo was on the faculty at the Polytechnic University of Milan, Italy. Palazzo has authored, with Frederick Steiner, *Urban Ecological Design: A Process for Regenerative Places* (2011), as well as contributing a chapter on "Pedagogical Tradition" to the *Companion to Urban Design* (2011). He is the author, with Vikas Mehta, of *Companion to Public Space* (2020).

ROUTLEDGE COMPANION TO PROFESSIONAL AWARENESS AND DIVERSITY IN PLANNING EDUCATION

Edited by Stephen Kofi Diko, Leah Marie Hollstein, and Danilo Palazzo

NEW YORK AND LONDON

Designed cover image: Curtis Goldstein, *Envision Cincinnati,* acrylic on birch panels, 96" X 96", 2013

First published 2023
by Routledge
605 Third Avenue, New York, NY 10158

and by Routledge
4 Park Square, Milton Park, Abingdon, Oxon, OX14 4RN

Routledge is an imprint of the Taylor & Francis Group, an informa business

© 2023 selection and editorial matter, Stephen Kofi Diko, Leah Marie Hollstein, and Danilo Palazzo; individual chapters, the contributors

The right of Stephen Kofi Diko, Leah Marie Hollstein, and Danilo Palazzo to be identified as the authors of the editorial material, and of the authors for their individual chapters, has been asserted in accordance with sections 77 and 78 of the Copyright, Designs and Patents Act 1988.

All rights reserved. No part of this book may be reprinted or reproduced or utilised in any form or by any electronic, mechanical, or other means, now known or hereafter invented, including photocopying and recording, or in any information storage or retrieval system, without permission in writing from the publishers.

Trademark notice: Product or corporate names may be trademarks or registered trademarks, and are used only for identification and explanation without intent to infringe.

Library of Congress Cataloging-in-Publication Data
Names: Diko, Stephen Kofi, editor. | Hollstein, Leah Marie, editor. | Palazzo, Danilo, 1962– editor.
Title: Routledge companion to professional awareness and diversity in planning education / edited by Stephen Kofi Diko, Leah Marie Hollstein, and Danilo Palazzo.
Description: New York, NY : Routledge, 2023. | Includes bibliographical references and index.
Identifiers: LCCN 2022054226 (print) | LCCN 2022054227 (ebook) | ISBN 9781032183121 (hardback) | ISBN 9781032183138 (paperback) | ISBN 9781003254003 (ebook)
Subjects: LCSH: City planning—Vocational guidance. | Career development. | Diversity in the workplace.
Classification: LCC HT166 .R6939 2023 (print) | LCC HT166 (ebook) | DDC 307.1/216023—dc23/eng/20230113
LC record available at https://lccn.loc.gov/2022054226
LC ebook record available at https://lccn.loc.gov/2022054227

ISBN: 978-1-032-18312-1 (hbk)
ISBN: 978-1-032-18313-8 (pbk)
ISBN: 978-1-003-25400-3 (ebk)

DOI: 10.4324/9781003254003

Typeset in Bembo
by Apex CoVantage, LLC

To our families.

CONTENTS

List of Figures   *xi*
List of Tables   *xiii*
List of Contributors   *xiv*
Foreword   *xxi*
Acknowledgments   *xxiv*

    Introduction: The Urban Planning Profession and Diversity Challenge   1
    Danilo Palazzo, Leah Marie Hollstein, and Stephen Kofi Diko

SECTION I
Diversity in Planning   **11**

1   Racial Diversity and Accredited Planning Programs at Historically Black Colleges and Universities: Contributions, Challenges, and Prospects   15
    Jeffrey S. Lowe and Siddhartha Sen

2   The People That Represent the Region and the Year of Change   26
    Ivis García, April Jackson, Andrew J. Greenlee, and Benjamin Chrisinger

3   More Than an Invitation: Setting the Rhythm of Planning Programs Through DEI Statements and Plans   35
    Sean Angst, Lindsay Oluyede, Jocelyn Poe, and Dylan Stevenson

4   More Than a Job: Building Opportunities for Undergraduate Professional Development in a Minority Serving Institution   47
    Laura Keyes, Lauren Ames Fischer, and Abraham David Benavides

5 Deconstructing Diversity in Urban Planning Education in Italy: Implications for the Future of a "Practical Knowledge" 58
Bertrando Bonfantini and Carolina Pacchi

6 Diversifying Urban Planning and Architecture Programs Through International Education Experience: Lessons From Ferdowsi University of Mashhad, Iran 65
Parsa Pahlavan and Hossein Maroufi

7 A Path to Racial Equity: Representation and Youth Planning Education 75
Giovania Tiarachristie and Daphne Lundi

8 Building Planning Education at a Hispanic-Serving R1 Institution: Challenges in Diversity and Recruitment 88
Lauren Ames Fischer, Laura Keyes, and Abraham David Benavides

SECTION II
Planning Awareness Among Children and Youth 97

9 Becoming Activated: Professional Awareness Through the Activate Community Empowerment Outreach Program 101
Leah Marie Hollstein, Stephen Kofi Diko, and Danilo Palazzo

10 Why Plan? A Two-Decade Exploration Into How and Why to Engage Young People in City Planning and Diversify the Planning Pipeline 117
Deborah McKoy and David Hernandez Garcia

11 Engaging Elementary School Pupils in Community Awareness and Planning: Insights From the Kaizuka Machizukuri Club, Osaka 129
Seth Asare Okyere, Lisa Ueno, Mowa Ebashi, Motoki Shimoda, Hiroshi Tsuji, and Michihiro Kita

12 Learning Environmental Planning With Geodesign: A Case Study in Cache Valley, Utah 139
Bartlett Warren-Kretzschmar and Carlos V. Licon

13 Planning With Children: Implications for the Planning Profession and Active Citizens 149
K. Meghan Wieters

14 Promoting Urban Planning Awareness for Children: An Overview of Multifaceted International Case Studies and Community Outreach Initiatives 158
Aya Elkhouly and Doha Eissa

15 For Mutual Benefit? Introducing Urban Planning to High School
    Geography Students in NSW, Australia   172
    Isabel Virgona and Simon Pinnegar

16 Can Children's Participation Inspire a New Generation of Planners?   184
    Robyn G. Mansfield

17 Town and Gown Partnerships for Youth Engagement and Diversity
    in the Planning Profession   197
    Evangeline Linkous, Melissa Zornitta, and Melissa Dickens

SECTION III
Planning Education Awareness   **209**

18 Shaping Awareness About Planning by Helping Planners to Become
    More Mindful and Critical About Their Identity, Role, and Context   213
    Savis Gohari

19 Undergraduate Urban Planning Students' Awareness of and Motivations
    for Planning Education and Profession   224
    Dohyung Kim

20 Increasing Planning Education Awareness and Addressing Enrollment
    Challenge in Urban Planning Schools: The Iowa State University Experience 235
    Carlton Basmajian and Francis Owusu

21 Factors Influencing Considerations for Urban Planning as a Field of Study
    and/or Career Choice Among Environmental Science Students   246
    Kwame N. Owusu-Daaku and Mackenzie Devine

22 Alabama City Year Program   257
    Binita Mahato, Sweta Byahut, and Jay Mittal

23 Career Choices in the Century of Urbanization: A Comparative Study
    of Student Enrollments in Nigerian Universities From the Urban
    Planning Perspective   272
    David S. Osiyi and Victor U. Onyebueke

24 Enhancing Planning-Education Awareness in Sub-Saharan Africa: Lessons
    From Namibia   289
    Eric Yankson

25 Raising Urban Planning Awareness in India 299
    Bhargav Adhvaryu and Bhavesh Joshi

    Conclusion: A Clarion Call to Act Intentionally 311
    Stephen Kofi Diko, Danilo Palazzo, and Leah Marie Hollstein

Index 317

FIGURES

4.1	UPOP Practice-Oriented Continuum of Professional Exposure	51
4.2	Responses on Career Preparation by Course Type	53
6.1	Vernacular Documentation Workshop	68
6.2	Modern Documentation Workshop	70
7.1	High-School Students in Cobble Hill	83
7.2	Overview of *Speak Up for Your Neighborhood!*	84
9.1	HSTEMHS, Coy Field, and the University of Cincinnati	109
9.2	Students Working and Final Presentation	110
10.1	Y-PLAN Roadmap	121
10.2	Skyline Y-PLAN Students Presenting Final Projects to Civic Partners	123
11.1	Images Depicting the Three Main School Club Activities	134
11.2	Location of Pupil's Proposals: (a) Water Park (b) Specialty Market	135
12.1	Evaluation Models Developed for the Cache Valley Geodesign Workshop	142
12.2	Students Working in "System" Teams to Develop Planning Proposals	143
13.1	Symbols Used for Mapping Field Audits	154
14.1	Examples of Workshop Outcomes	160
14.2	Samples of Children's Activities and 3D Models	161
14.3	Real-Practice Activities for Community Renewal	164
14.4	Structure of In-Class Education, DIY City	166
14.5	Structure of Professional Co-Learning, Mingdong Community Development	167
14.6	Suggested Model Promoting Planning Awareness for Children	169
15.1	HSC Enrolments in Humanities Courses 2000–2021 as Percentage of Cohort	173
15.2	Do You Enjoy Learning About Planning Issues in Your Local Area as Part of Your Geography Class?	177
17.1	FLiP Participants Tour Tampa's Historic Ybor City	199
17.2	FLiP Participants at ULI Tampa Bay-Led Charette Activity	200
17.3	FLiP Jr. Participants Share Their Model Cities	201
19.1	Students' Motivation in Selecting Urban Planning as Major by Ethnicity	228
19.2	Subjects That Prospective Students Are Expected to Learn From the Department	229
20.1	CRP Enrollment Trends Before, During, and After Enrollment Management	238

Figures

21.1a, b, c, d	Survey Outcomes on Course Lectures and Discussions, Readings and Reading Reflections, Planning Pathways and Theory Assignment, and Real-Life Team-Based Project	250
21.2a, b, c	Interest in Taking Additional Planning Due to Course Work, Potential Application on What Learned to Other Situations, and Gains Obtained in This Course to Help Address Real World Issues	251
22.1	Graduate and Undergraduate Planning Enrollment (Full-Time and Part-Time) by Gender and Race	259
22.2	Spring 2020 Urban Design Studio Field Visit, Montgomery	262
23.1	Elements of the Social Cognitive Career Theory	274
23.2	Ahmadu Bello Way and Democracy Avenue, Abuja, FCT, Nigeria	281
23.3	Planning Students Busy With Studio Work	283
23.4	Enrollment Shortfalls in the Faculty of Environmental Studies, UNN (2015–2020)	283
25.1	Planning Degree Programs Launched in India (1950–2020)	303

TABLES

1.1	Black/African American Bachelor of Planning Enrollment in PAB-Accredited Programs: All Schools vs. HBCUs	20
1.2	Black/African American Master of Planning Enrollment: All Schools vs. HBCUs	21
3.1	Percentage and Change in Overall Student Populations	36
3.2	Range of Population Percentages and Changes Across Schools	37
3.3	DEI Statement and Plans	38
3.4	Planning Programs' Best Practices	44
4.1	UPOP Courses: Practice-Oriented Learning Objectives and Pedagogical Approaches	50
4.2	Perceptions on Professional Development in the Classroom	54
7.1	2020 Race/Ethnicity in Overall Population Compared to Urban Planners	76
7.2	General Questions With Urban Planning Themes	82
12.1	Students' Evaluation of the Software (n = 53)	144
12.2	Content Analysis of the Post-Workshop Survey Reveals Five Themes (n = 53)	144
12.3	New Ecological Paradigm Survey Statements That Show a Change in Response (n = 53)	145
12.4	Students Rated the Importance of Planning and Development Issues in Cache Valley	145
13.1	Study Schools Race/Ethnicity Profile	151
13.2	Eligibility for School Lunch Programs	152
14.1	Enabling and Inhibiting Factors of Planning-Awareness Workshops	165
14.2	Comparison of ICE and PCL	168
19.1	Profile of Survey Respondents	226
20.1	CRP 200-Level Course-Enrollment Trends Post EMS	243
22.1	Types of Initiatives, Alabama City Year Program	261
22.2	Framework Demonstrating ACYP's Goals and Objectives for Planning Awareness and Recruitment at the Levels of Students, Program, and Communities	264
23.1	Determinant Factors in Career Choice and Development	275
23.2	Tools and Techniques for Increasing Professional Awareness and Student Enrollment	277
23.3	Ratio of Registered Planners to Population in Selected Countries (2011 and 2021)	278
23.4	Applications to Ten Most-Popular Courses vs. Planning in Nigeria (2012–2017)	279
23.5	Enrollment Shortfalls at UNN (2015–2020)	282

CONTRIBUTORS

Bhargav Adhvaryu is a professor of urban science at the Amrut Mody School of Management, Ahmedabad University, where he teaches urban and transport planning and quantitative research methods. He is an urban and transport planner and modeler trained at Imperial College London, University College London, and Cambridge University. His research includes LUTI models and public transport accessibility measurement and mapping to enhance the plan-making process. He has several publications in these areas with an emphasis on applications to enhance the plan-making process and planning policy. He was earlier a professor at CEPT University (2011–19), a Fulbright Visiting Professor at UCLA (2012), and a British Chevening Scholar (2002–03).

Sean Angst is a postdoctoral scholar at the University of Southern California's Equity Research Institute. His research focuses on housing, community development, and racial justice. Sean is a graduate from the USC Price School of Public Policy where he earned a PhD in public policy and management. During that time, he also participated in organizing graduate student workers and served on the department's Teaching Excellence Committee.

Carlton Basmajian is an associate professor of community and regional planning at Iowa State University. His research focuses on the history of bureaucratic institutions in the planning and building of the American landscape. His teaching focuses on undergraduate courses in the history of city planning design thinking.

Abraham David Benavides is a faculty member at the University of North Texas. He has served in various leadership positions and received awards for his teaching. His research interests include local government, cultural competency, ethics and leadership, and community health issues. He has published in a number of scholarly journals.

Bertrando Bonfantini is a full professor of urban planning, former chair of the master's degree program in urban planning and policy design at Politecnico di Milano (2013–2020), and editor of the journal *Territorio* (issn 1825–8689) after being deputy editor of the journal *Urbanistica* (issn 0042–1022) of the Italian National Institute of Urban Planning. As a planner, he took part in the drafting of the Plan for Bergamo Alta (2002–2004) and the municipal urban plan of Jesi (Ancona, 2003–2006); he was a collaborator in the general scientific advice of the municipal plan of Bologna (2006–2009) and co-responsible for the methodological advice for the new general urban plan of that city (2018–19). His research topics focus on planning tools and techniques, the cumulative and diachronic dimension of urban planning and design practical knowledge, and heritage in urban planning. Among his publications: *Dentro l'urbanistica. Ricerca e progetto, tecniche e storia* (2017), *Progetto urbanistico e città esistente* (2002).

Sweta Byahut brings 23 years of experience. Her research focuses on built-form analysis, development regulations, and urban land management. She has worked for a decade in India in planning consultancy and applied research. She teaches courses in quantitative methods, introduction to planning, climate planning, sustainable transportation, and synthesis studio.

Benjamin Chrisinger is an associate professor of evidence-based policy evaluation at the University of Oxford and member of the POCIG research team.

Mackenzie Devine earned dual undergraduate degrees in environmental science and ecology/evolutionary biology from Piedmont College and her Master of Science in environmental science from the University of West Florida in December 2021. She has interests in environmental justice and assisting underserved communities.

Melissa Dickens, AICP is the strategic planning and policy manager for the Hillsborough County City-County Planning Commission. She has approximately 15 years of planning experience in the public and private sectors of the Tampa Bay area. In her current role, she manages a team responsible for policy updates to local government comprehensive plans, the agency strategic plan, and planning for capital improvements and water resources. Ms. Dickens has extensive leadership experience in APA, including Chair of the Sun Coast Section of APA Florida, Vice Chair of APA National's Women and Planning Division, VP of Communications for APA Florida, and service on the Steering Committee of APA National's Water and Planning Network. Ms. Dickens holds a master's in city planning and a Bachelor of Arts in urban studies, both from the University of Pennsylvania. She has written and presented extensively on mentoring and leadership development in planning.

Mowa Ebashi is a PhD candidate at the Division of Global Architecture, Osaka University. She holds a Master of Engineering from the same university. Her current research focuses children's mapping of their local environment as a Machizukuri practice.

Doha Eissa is an assistant professor of architecture at Cairo University and a design practitioner. She graduated in 2005 from Cairo University with a major in architecture engineering, acquired her MSc from Italy in 2007 in landscape design, and finally obtained her PhD from Cairo University in 2015 in urban sociology. Doha's research interests and publications revolve around design education, human-centered design, creative concept generation, and socio-spatial practices in space. In 2012, she developed her own program, "enlighten," to introduce teenagers to the design discipline with applications to architecture, product design, and urban design. Doha has delivered multiple workshops both in Egypt and Dubai, UAE, helping many of her participants discover their passion for design and regard it as a career option.

Aya Elkhouly is a community development expert on many international projects and workshops—working with organizations such as Cairo University, GIZ, ISOCARP, and NUPI. She is also an assistant professor and a part-time instructor at the American University in Cairo, CHI, and Al-Ahram Canadian University. She earned a PhD in quality of child urban life in 2020 and a master's degree in urban education development in 2014. For the last ten years, she has been an advocate for promoting urban community awareness and residents' quality of urban life. Her research fields are urban education, community-based development, cities for children, quality of life, sustainable planning, brownfields, creativity, scientific thinking, and participatory community design tools.

Lauren Ames Fischer is an inaugural faculty member in the University of North Texas bachelor's in urban policy and planning program. Her research examines the spatial equity of land use and transport planning, and her work has appeared in peer-reviewed journals, books and popular media.

David Hernandez Garcia is a city planner, educator, and youth advocate who works to further equitable planning in cities across the San Franciso Bay Area. He received his master's in city planning from UC Berkeley and served as a co-instructor for the Y-PLAN Studio.

Ivis García is an assistant professor at the University of Utah and co-chair of POCIG.

Andrew Greenlee is an associate professor at the University of Illinois at Champaign–Urbana, former POCIG co-chair and co-chair of ACSP Committee on Diversity.

April Jackson is an associate professor at the University of Illinois at Chicago and co-chair of POCIG.

Bhavesh Joshi is a general manager (civil) at Gujarat Metro rail Corporation Ltd., Surat since June 2021. He was earlier general manager at Rajkot Smart city development Ltd (2018–21) and additional city engineer (Projects) (2008–21) at Rajkot Municipal Corporation. He has 26 years of experience in the field of urban planning and infrastructure development, and he has prepared several town planning schemes for Rajkot city. His research includes enhancing the urban planning process with a focus on land use zoning.

Laura Keyes is an AICP certified planner and holds a position of Lecturer and Undergraduate Coordinator for the Department of Public Administration at the University of North Texas. She has authored and co-authored peer-reviewed publications and book chapters covering topics on local governments, public services, nonprofit management, and organizational theory.

Dohyung Kim is a professor of urban and regional planning at California State Polytechnic University, Pomona. Serving on ACSP's Committee on Diversity, he has put efforts into inclusiveness and diversity in planning education. Serving the department as a graduate coordinator and chair, he promoted faculty and student diversity as well as student recruitment. His teaching and research also focus on transportation planning including GIS applications in transportation, sustainable transportation, and public health and environmental justice in conjunction with transportation planning.

Michihiro Kita is a professor of architectural and urban planning. He currently serves as the deputy director of the Social Solutions Initiative at Osaka University and also the head of the architectural and urban planning laboratory in the Division of Global Architecture, Osaka University. His current interest is the area of school-based community development as a bottom mechanism to address urban planning challenges in distressed communities.

Savis Gohari is an urban planner, a researcher at the Norwegian Institute of Urban and Regional Studies (NIBR) at OsloMet, and an associate professor at the Department of Civil and Environmental Engineering at NTNU, Norway. My research interest includes urban governance, planning, citizen participation, co-creation, and planning education.

Carlos V. Licon is an associate professor in the Department of Landscape Architecture and Environmental Planning at Utah State University. His interests focus on planning for sustainability information and decision making. He has an undergraduate degree in architecture and graduate degrees in environmental design and planning.

Evangeline Linkous is the program director and an associate professor in the master's program of urban and regional planning at the University of South Florida. She studies the fiscal, legal, and institutional instruments and frameworks used to rationalize the management of land resources in rapidly growing areas. She has published extensively about transferable development rights programs and Florida growth management policy in journals including the *Journal of the American Planning Association, Land Use Policy, Urban Affairs Review*, and the *Journal of Environmental Planning and Management*. She previously worked as Director of the University of Florida IFAS Sarasota County Extension and as a planner for the Delaware Valley Regional Planning Commission. She is currently a planning commissioner for the Hillsborough County City-County Planning Commission and serves on the Executive Board of ULI Tampa Bay. She has a PhD and master's in urban and regional planning from the University of Pennsylvania, and a Bachelor of Arts in English from New College of Florida.

Jeffrey S. Lowe is an associate professor in the Department of Urban Planning and Environmental Policy at Texas Southern University. Previously, he was a faculty member in the Department of Urban and Regional Planning at Jackson State University. Lowe earned a master's in city and regional planning from Morgan State University and chaired ACSP's Committee on Diversity, 2016–2018.

Daphne Lundi (she/her) is an urban planner, climate adaptation specialist, self-taught garment maker, and the child of Haitian immigrants. From 2016–2020, she served as the vice-chair of the Diversity Committee of the New York Metro Area American Planning Association and a youth programming coordinator. She is a member of BlackSpace, a collective of Black urbanists that works to bridge the gaps between policy, people, and place to address inequality and injustice in the built environment. She also serves as an advisory board member for the Octavia Project, a science-fiction summer program for teen girls and non-binary youth that uses the lens of science fiction to explore computer science, writing, and city-making.

Binita Mahato is an urban designer and planner with a background in architecture. Her research interest lies in investigating the relationship between space and society using qualitative and interpretive research methods. She teaches urban form, sustainable urbanism, geographic information systems, and urban design studio.

Robyn Mansfield is an international humanitarian settlement design, livelihoods, and community consultation specialist. Robyn's focus is on amplifying the voices of marginalized groups in urban planning processes in communities facing hardship, particularly after disasters or conflict. She has an extensive background in local government and has consulted on a range of international projects in Asia and the Pacific region, Europe, South America, Africa, and the Middle East. Robyn is a qualified landscape architect and holds master's degrees in international and community development, and disaster, design, and development. Robyn has lectured at Monash University, RMIT, and Griffith University in disaster and urban resilience studies. Robyn is due to complete a PhD at Monash University in 2022 focusing on mainstreaming the participation of children in urban planning processes for vulnerable settings.

Hossein Maroufi is an assistant professor of urban planning at Ferdowsi University of Mashhad, Iran. He holds a Master of Science in urban planning and policy design and a PhD in spatial planning from Politecnico di Milano, Italy. Since 2015 he has been the representative of FUM's International Academic Relations Department at the Faculty of Architecture and Urban Planning. In 2016, he was appointed by Ferdowsi University of Mashhad to launch the graduate program of urban design, and in 2020, he became a chief coordinator for the revision of the urban planning curriculum at the undergraduate level. He has organized and coordinated an international congress and a workshop in collaboration with Politecnico di Milano, Italy.

Deborah McKoy is the executive director and founder of UC Berkeley's Center for Cities + Schools and adjunct professor. Her research focuses on the intersection of education, city and regional planning, and public policy. Central to her work is the critical role young people play in urban and metropolitan change and transformation.

Jay Mittal brings 23 years of professional experience in private consulting, research, and academic settings. His research focuses on local economic development, land value capture, land markets, real estate valuation, and urban plan-making processes both in the United States and India. He teaches land and urban economics, geographic information systems, real estate principles, real estate market analysis, and synthesis studio.

Seth Asare Okyere is a multidisciplinary development planner working at the intersection of international development, sustainable urbanism, and community resilience. He is currently a visiting assistant professor at the University of Arizona, USA. He holds a PhD in engineering (urban development planning) from the Osaka University. Seth has multidisciplinary interests at the intersection of social, spatial, and environmental inequities in everyday urban experiences and collaborative solutions for building sustainable cities and communities.

Lindsay Oluyede is a postdoctoral scholar at the School of Geographical Sciences and Urban Planning at Arizona State University. Her research focuses on transportation equity and collaborative decision-making. Lindsay completed a PhD in city and regional planning at the University of North Carolina at Chapel Hill (UNC). While at UNC, she served as an inaugural member of her department's Racial Equity Committee.

Victor U. Onyebueke is a senior lecturer in the Department of Urban and Regional of the University of Nigeria, Enugu Campus (Nigeria), where he is involved in teaching, research, and consultancy. Onyebueke holds a PhD in geography and environmental science from Stellenbosch University, Matieland, South Africa.

David S. Osiyi is a principal lecturer at the Federal Polytechnic, Nasarawa, Nigeria. His research interests include planning education, land delivery, land reform, social service delivery, housing, and infrastructure planning.

Francis Owusu is a professor and chair of the Department of Community and Regional Planning at Iowa State University. He teaches courses on international development courses, world cities and globalization, economic and urban planning, and planning methods. His research engages with issues related to globalization, development policy, public sector reforms, capacity building, and urban development and livelihood issues.

Kwame N. Owusu-Daaku teaches courses related to human geography, environmental management, planning, and sustainability. He earned his PhD in geography from the University of South Carolina, master's in urban and regional planning from the University of Iowa, and bachelor's in development planning from the Kwame Nkrumah University of Science and Technology.

Carolina Pacchi has a PhD in urban and environmental planning and is an associate professor at the Department of Architecture and Urban Studies, Politecnico di Milano, where she teaches planning theory and practice and local conflict resolution, and she is Chair of the master's degree program in urban planning and policy design (since 2021). She has been part of the Polimi2040 Rector's Roundtable on future strategies for technical education since 2017. She has done research on the transformation of urban governance in European cities and on forms of alternative politics, urban conflicts, and grassroots activism at the local level, and she is engaged in research on different forms of urban and spatial inequalities, looking at segregation, stratification, and unequal access to space and services for different social groups. She has published extensively on those topics at the national and international levels. She has spent research periods at MIT, Cambridge (visiting PhD candidate), Kingston University, London (2010), and Technical University, Berlin (2016).

Contributors

Parsa Pahlavan is a conservation architect, material designer and assistant professor of architecture at Ferdowsi University of Mashhad, Iran. He graduated with a master's in architectural engineering at Politecnico di Milano, PhD in material design for restoration of the built environment from DICAM (Department) from the University of Bologna and has experience in the valorization of restorative materials for conservation of some world heritage sites. He has organized and co-directed several workshops, summer schools, and curriculum revisions in the fields of documentation and design in Iran and Italy.

Simon Pinnegar is a professor and director of the City Planning Program and associate director of the City Futures Research Centre, in the Faculty of Arts, Design and Architecture, UNSW Sydney. He teaches strategic planning and urban policy and has published extensively on metropolitan planning, urban renewal, and housing policy issues.

Jocelyn Poe is an assistant professor in the Department of City and Regional Planning at Cornell University. Inspired by her experiences as a planning practitioner, her research focuses on place-based trauma and reparative planning. She earned a PhD in urban planning and development from the Sol Price School of Public Policy at the University of Southern California (USC), where she was involved in student activism and organizing among graduate students.

Siddhartha Sen is a professor and associate dean of the School of Architecture and Planning at Morgan State University. He has written extensively about planning education at historically Black colleges and universities (HBCUs), diversity, and multiculturalism. From 2013 to 2015, he chaired the Committee on Diversity of the Association of Collegiate Schools of Planning (ACSP).

Motoki Shimoda is a registered architect, interior designer, and landscape planner with a PhD in creative arts. He is currently a lecturer at the Faculty of Architecture and Arts, Otemae University, Japan. He researches the topics of architectural planning, urban and landscape design within the spatial context of fishing villages.

Dylan Stevenson is a PhD candidate in city and regional planning at Cornell University. His research examines the intersections between environmental planning and public health, focusing on planning approaches that promote Tribal sovereignty in the United States. He is of Prairie Band Potawatomi descent, born in San Jose, California.

Giovania Tiarachristie (they/them) is a queer, non-binary, South East Asian American urban planner, racial justice facilitator, coach, bodyworker, and illustrator who is dedicated to a vision of more equitable neighborhoods and the healing and liberation of oppressed peoples. They are Co-Founder and former Co-Chair (2015–2020) of the Diversity Committee of the New York Metro Area American Planning Association. In 2016, they authored "Elephant in the Planning Room"–a master's thesis on overcoming the barriers to recruitment and retention of planners of color. Giovania worked in the participatory planning field via the non-profit and public sector for eight years in New York City. They currently reside on the ancestral homelands of the Kizh people (Los Angeles, CA), where they are running a private practice dedicated to the wellness, healing, and liberation of Queer, Trans, Black, Indigenous, People of Color. Visit healingasresistance.com for more info.

Hiroshi Tsuji is a specially appointed assistant professor at Osaka University. He has previously taught Machizukuri practices, a citizen-led community improvement initiative in Japan. His research interests are in the areas of regional studies, from the perspective of community ties and networks, including mechanisms to support such community networks.

Lisa Ueno is an urban planner with Urban Renaissance (UR), a housing development and management agency in Japan. She holds a Master of Engineering from the Division of Global Architecture in the Graduate School of Engineering at Osaka University, Japan.

Isabel Virgona is an adviser to the New South Wales (NSW) Minister for Planning and Public Spaces and a graduate of the Bachelor of City Planning (Hons) at the University of NSW. Her honours thesis focused on planning education in the NSW school geography curriculum and was awarded the Planning Institute of Australia's NSW Presidents Award in 2019.

Bartlett Warren-Kretzschmar is a lecturer and researcher at Leibniz Universität Hannover, Germany. Her research interest focuses on environmental planning methodologies, visualization, and technological support for participation and decision making in planning. She has degrees in landscape architecture and environmental planning.

K. Meghan Wieters was formerly an assistant professor at the University of Oklahoma in regional and city planning and now has moved to the Pacific Northwest to pursue independent research and planning practice work. Her primary research is on how physical activity and planning intersect. Her background prior to academia includes being a practicing planner for 10 years in transit planning, neighborhood planning, and bicycle and pedestrian planning.

Eric Yankson is a senior lecturer and the associate dean for research and innovation of the Faculty of Engineering and Spatial Sciences of the Namibia University of Science and Technology. He obtained his PhD in urban and public affairs from the University of Louisville in Kentucky. His research and teaching interests include planning education, sustainable urbanism, land use planning, political economy, and policy analysis.

Melissa Zornitta, AICP, is the executive director of the Hillsborough County City-County Planning Commission. In this capacity, she manages the long-range, comprehensive planning for unincorporated Hillsborough County, City of Tampa, City of Temple Terrace and Plant City. Ms. Zornitta has over 20 years of experience working in land use planning, comprehensive planning, and community planning for local governments in Florida. Before becoming Executive Director, Ms. Zornitta held a number of progressively responsible planning positions with the Planning Commission, including serving as Assistant Director for three years. Prior to working at the Planning Commission, she worked for the City of St. Petersburg, Charlotte County and the City of Tallahassee. Ms. Zornitta holds a bachelor's degree in government from the College of William and Mary and a master's degree in urban and regional planning from Florida State University. She is a certified planner with the American Institute of Certified Planners.

FOREWORD

A recent study of the built environment professions in Commonwealth countries found that the fastest-growing countries have the smallest planning workforce.[1] In some countries, the city planning profession struggles for recognition while architects or engineers are deemed capable of planning. Even in countries where planning is a well-recognized profession, recruitment and retention of planners, especially planners of color, is challenging. This begs the question, who will plan for the future we want for our urban areas?

Half of the world's population lives in urban areas—a percentage expected to increase to two-thirds by mid-century.[2] We need to create environments that enable them to live, thrive, and sustain their everyday activities. But as much as urban living can offer opportunities for prosperity, it also leads to a high concentration of human problems—poverty, unemployment, increased demand for decent and affordable housing, education, and healthcare, among others—including whether our urban areas can withstand the emergent shocks and impacts from climatic hazards such as hurricanes, flooding, rising heat, and increased exposure to environmental contaminants associated with human activities.

Harnessing the opportunities of our urban areas and addressing the challenges that they present to residents is necessary for the future of human civilization. It demands intentionality, centering of humanity in our actions, and, more importantly, charting the future we want to live in. This is the role and function of the urban planning profession—a profession dedicated to making the urban areas and communities that we live in better. But who will make up this profession in the future if people do not know about it and are not trained to become urban planners? For a profession that is primarily community-facing, it lacks diversity among faculty, students, and practitioners.

Although planners have mounted numerous programs aimed at building diversity among the planning corps, the published discourse about the future of the urban planning profession scantly addresses how the urban planning discipline and profession can be a desired career preference for children and youth. The *Routledge Companion to Professional Awareness and Diversity in Planning Education* engenders an important discourse to bring attention to the urban planning professional awareness challenge and the need for urban planning schools to increase the awareness of children, youth, and the public about urban planning education and its career prospects and, moreover, directing these efforts to underrepresented communities.

While some of the best and brightest in their generations are attracted to urban planning by its promise of meaningful social, economic, and environmental change, student recruitment and retention of planning professionals are such that schools and agencies are choosing from a limited pool of applicants. In the competition among professions for young talent, planning is not an especially well-known profession—in part because planners are seldom spotlighted in the media. When planned interventions are successful, credit is often given to elected officials rather than the planning professionals directly responsible—that is when there are planning professionals involved at all. In many countries, planning is perceived as a specialty of either architecture or engineering or carried out by *urbanists* of varied backgrounds rather than as its own profession. All these factors contribute to making the planning profession less known among children, youth, and the public.

To be successful in their endeavors, urban planning agencies must understand and communicate with those who live in cities. Professional theories, methods, and values learned in school and on the job are vital components in preparing planners to engage effectively with those they serve. Still, the makeup of the profession is also important. If planners matched communities demographically and economically, we might expect communication to be easier, but this is seldom true. While urban populations are often diverse racially, ethnically, and with respect to education and socioeconomic status, in Western industrial countries, the urban planning workforce is overwhelmingly white, highly educated, and middle class. As the values of diversity, equity, and inclusion have grown in importance in the USA and elsewhere, the underrepresentation of minorities in the planning workforce has only become more important.

The three problems of the small size of the professional corps, limited applicant pool, and skewed demographic/economic makeup are long-standing issues that professional associations have struggled to address. Yet today, only 6 percent of Royal Town Planning Institute members,[3] 13 percent of American Planning Association members,[4] and 19 percent of Canadian Institute of Planners members[5] are persons of color. Educational expectations for entry into the profession and planner salaries, of course, virtually eliminate less-educated and lower-income residents from the planning workforce.

This Companion lays out the dimensions of the planning awareness challenge. After presenting key variations in how diversity is understood globally, chapters examine awareness of the planning profession among children and adults; relay the experiences from pilot programs to increase awareness among secondary school students, college students, and the general public; and review programs to boost planning student retention in the profession through changes in curriculum and connections with practitioners.

Experiments underway by planning schools, sometimes in partnership with agencies, firms, and/or NGOs, are truly exciting. Planning student, academic staff, and practitioner engagement with high school teachers and counselors engender familiarity with our profession, enhance understanding of how city planning affects resident lives, and improve understanding of what skills are useful to future planning education. Using processes as different as lectures, field trips, and design charrettes, and ranging in time from a few hours to semester series, they show the possibility of sparking interest in built environment professions at a life stage when career aspirations are first formed. Inaccurate understandings of professional opportunities and requirements by counselors are also identified.

Chapter authors ask how planning schools can influence career awareness of planning among school children through effective collaborations with primary and secondary schools, social media outreach, after-school and summer short courses, and broad-scale marketing. The answers are sometimes surprising. Personal experiences are important, of course, as are the work models available to children. Still, opinions about what careers are accessible to specific target groups are also significant influences, as are messages about what work makes a difference to issues that children and their families care about. Public participation efforts in planning agencies are shown to be critical—when participation is done right, it can build interest in the profession; when done poorly, it can decrease interest. The unmistakable conclusion is that the organized planning profession, its organizations, and its schools can greatly influence and increase decisions by school-age youngsters to choose planning as a career.

Other chapter authors report on changes to college planning programs on campus aimed at recruiting majors, retaining students to graduation, and successfully placing graduates in planning jobs. Success is shown to flow from introductory courses that acquaint pre-majors and non-majors with the planning profession (at colleges without planning schools, too), curricula that are practical and that engage with practicing professionals, financial aid resources that make it possible for young people of modest means to attend planning schools, and mentorship and field work initiatives that bring planning students in contact with the real work of the profession.

Reflections resulting from these many experiments raise important questions about the nature of our profession and about the structure of planning schools. The overlap of urban planning with allied professions is argued to demand action to better clarify how planning adds value that other professions miss. The nuanced interplay of race and ethnicity with national origin calls into question the way some regimes for tabulating diversity provide incentives that actually reduce diversity. The powerful ability of cross-national comparative planning studies is argued to improve the critical abilities of planning graduates to understand how planning operates in their own countries. Parallels in the recruitment and retention challenges across the countries examined suggest that there is a great deal to be learned by greater international exchange among planning educators.

There is another lesson in these pages, albeit not explicitly stated. It is about the interlinked futures of planning practice and planning education. Recruitment, retention, and successful education of planning students are vital to the future of the profession. Visibility, effectiveness, and impact of the planning profession are vital to the success of planning schools. Yet, to listen to us talk, it often seems that the two workforces, at best, have differing world views and, at worst, are at odds with one another over key issues of field definition, skills needed, and research objectives. The experiences reported in this volume, spanning twelve countries, are a testament to the power of cooperation between practice and academy in advancing the shared goals of the urban planning profession.

Bruce Stiftel, FAICP
Atlanta, USA

Notes

1 Commonwealth Association of Architects, Commonwealth Association of Planners, Commonwealth Association of Surveyors and Land Economists, and Commonwealth Engineers Council. Planning for Climate Change and Rapid Urbanization: Survey of the Built Environment Professions in the Commonwealth. 2020. https://commonwealthsustainablecities.org/survey/ Accessed 15 July 2022.
2 United Nations, Department of Economic and Social Affairs, Population Division (2019) *World Urbanization Prospects 2018: Highlights* (ST/ESA/SER.A/421)
3 Royal Town Planning Institute (n.a.). *Membership survey*. www.rtpi.org.uk/membership/about-rtpi-membership/about-our-members/ Accessed 25 September 2022.
4 American Planning Association (2018). *Planners salary survey*. www.planning.org/salary/planner/. HRx Technology Inc. Equity, Diversity and Inclusion Insight Survey. Accessed 25 September 2022.
5 Canadian Institute of Planners (2021). www.cip-icu.ca/Files/EDI-Insight-Survey/20211019_Equity-Diversity-Inclusion-Insight-Survey.aspx Accessed 25 September 2022.

ACKNOWLEDGMENTS

Words cannot express our appreciation to all the contributors of this book who found value in its themes and continued to show interest and patience over the almost two-year period of its development. Their research, experiences, and actions to address the diversity and professional awareness challenges of the urban planning profession form the basis of this book, and we are very grateful to them for willingly sharing them with us.

We are also thankful to Routledge and their editors as well as the anonymous reviewers who provided insightful and constructive feedback to improve the book. We are indebted to Pamela Wissman who copy-edited and proofread the entire book manuscript before our submission to Routledge. We want to also acknowledge the University of Cincinnati's School of Planning for providing funding to support the copy-editing of this book and our Graduate Assistants Simon Donkoh and Olivia Hill.

Our eternal thanks to Curtis Goldstein for his 2013 painting "Envision Cincinnati," which graces the cover of our book.

Finally, to Bruce Stiftel, who gracefully accepted our invitation to write the forward to this book—thank you.

INTRODUCTION

The Urban Planning Profession and Diversity Challenge

Danilo Palazzo, Leah Marie Hollstein, and Stephen Kofi Diko

Today, planners, academics, activists, and scholars who teach in planning schools and in particular those who have contributed chapters to this book are aware of the immense professional awareness and diversity challenges within urban planning. As planners and academics, we teach and believe that planning should be equitable (Krumholz & Hexter, 2018), multicultural (Burayidi, 2015), intercultural (Wood & Landry, 2008), and done by those who empathize with community and residents who can advocate for—and represent—their interests. The best advocates will be those who hold similar values and come from similar backgrounds, who are situated within a community and trusted by their neighbors. To use an efficient rendition by Sweet and Etienne: "without diversity, planners lack legitimacy in the communities where they work" (2011). For this goal to be achieved, planning schools must educate more students who reflect all of the residents in a city, region, state, and/or nation. Attracting to our planning schools a diverse composition of students, developing awareness of the profession, increasing interest in the profession, and matriculation into planning education are all barriers to overcome. García et al. (2021) have summarized the measures, suggested by various authors, that should be taken to inspire young people to pursue an education in planning: (1) hire a workforce (regardless of race and ethnicity) that can interact positively with colleagues and communities from diverse backgrounds; (2) introduce relevant non-Eurocentric curricula and alternative pedagogies (e.g., community-university partnerships); (3) improve classroom climate through activities addressing everyday racism in the classroom; and (4) increase positive interactions that address inequities within African American and Latinx communities. A further step for planning education in reaching for diversity in academies and the profession is to realize that planning needs to come to terms with its past of supporting exclusionary zoning, residential racial segregation, redlining, and structural racism.

Importance of Diversity in Planning

In the United States, the challenge of diversity is particularly acute. In 2019, White (Non-Hispanic) urban and regional planners represented (according to Data USA, 2022) 75.9% of the workforce (15.8% more than the share White Non-Hispanics contribute to the US population according to the 2020 US Census). Asians were 7.82% (while representing 5.9% of the US population), Hispanic and Latino planners were 2.75% (though they are 18.5% of the population), and Black planners were only 5.42%, even though African Americans comprise 13.4% of the US population (US Census Bureau, 2021). Similarly, urban planning education is largely chosen by White students. In 2020, the

Planning Accreditation Board (2020a) reported 62.8% of full-time graduate students (and 60.7% of undergraduates) in accredited programs were White, while Black students represented 9.6% (10.6% of undergraduates), Asian students 8.2% (8.8% of undergraduates), and Hispanic/Latino were 15.5% (18.2% of undergraduates). These statistics seemingly confirm the historical and current role of White affluence and Whiteness in urban planning as recently described by Goetz et al. (2020). The slight change in the demographic distribution of current students and planning practitioners seems to follow a national trend registered by the Pew Research Center: "the number of Black adults with a college degree or more education has more than doubled since 2000" (2021), nonetheless this change should not promote optimism, since the road to equity is still a long one in schools (Jackson et al., 2018) and the profession (Solis, 2020; García et al., 2021).

In reality, there are multiple barriers to recruiting and retaining people of color in urban planning education and the profession. Educational barriers, especially for Black and Latino students in the United States, are correlated (though not exclusively in urban planning programs) with precarious finances (Bozick, 2007; Cox, 2016; Perez & Farruggia, 2022), family income (Belley & Lochner, 2007), investment (Charles et al., 2007), aspirations (Ovink, 2014; Langenkamp, 2019), social-class differences (Goldrick, 2006), and aftereffects of student loan debts, with significant disparities between Black and White students (Scott-Clayton & Li, 2016). Barriers to planning education are more specifically related to lack of clarity and fuzzy boundaries for what planning is (McClendon, 2003; Forsyth, 2022), and this awareness (Palazzo et al., 2021) is a topic that is central to this compendium. Professional barriers have been investigated by Tiarachristie (2016) and include an absence of opportunity for African Americans to act as active change agents for their communities, lack of exposure to urban planning through lived experience of good planning, "the late, or lack of, exposure of the planning profession in communities of color, largely due to limited social capital," and low diversity in urban planning education (p. 49).

Diversity, while having a precise definition in the United States, at least at the federal level—"The term 'diversity' means the practice of including the many communities, identities, races, ethnicities, backgrounds, abilities, cultures, and beliefs of the American people, including underserved communities" (White House, 2021)—does have different translations and interpretations, especially outside the United States. Diversity can be seen as a balance of genders in student populations or practitioners' settings, from a socioeconomic viewpoint, or as a challenge—or an advantage—when it comes to dealing with international students.

Two contributing factors to this lack of diversity are, according to the editors and the authors of this book, the declining enrollment at US planning schools as well as the general deficit of awareness of the profession among the larger public and hence, among high-school teachers and counselors, family members, and high-school students. These two factors are at the center of this book, for which the main goals are to (1) provide a wider global view of these issues and (2) collect examples of good practices designed to overcome them.

Decline of Planning Students

The Planning Accreditation Board (PAB) notes that the number of students—US and international—in PAB-accredited bachelor's degree programs declined by 19% between 2008 and 2019. This occurred in conjunction with an increase in the number of programs from 14 to 16 over the same period (PAB, 2020b). PAB-accredited master's program enrollment declined 21% over the same period of time, while the number of programs increased from 67 to 74 (ibid.). These data are even more dramatic than those pictured in 2016 by the American Planning Report (Joint Task Force of American Planning Association et al., 2016), when the decline from 2008 to 2014 in undergraduate programs was 16% and 5.4% in master's programs. The Joint Task Force also emphasized the decrease was predominant among domestic students (a decline of 12.8% from 2008 to 2014 that reached 28%

when more recent data—PAB, 2020b—were considered), populations of color, and underserved communities, which "portends a serious challenge for the pipeline of professional planners into the future" (Joint Task Force of American Planning Association et al., 2016, p. 5). Some tiny optimistic changes were recorded in an updated PAB Diversity Task Force Report (Ozawa et al., 2019): "about two-thirds (34/53) of the programs showed an increase in non-White students. Moreover, 24 of those 34 programs showed an increase of more than 10% in non-White students between 2010–2014" (ibid., p. 1). In comparison to the PAB data, in the period 2009–2020, data from the National Center for Educational Statistics (NCES, 2022a) shows that the total undergraduate enrollment in degree-granting postsecondary institutions in the United States decreased by 9%, and in the same period White enrollment decreased by 25%, Black enrollment decreased by 21%, while Hispanic enrollment increased by 42% (from 2.4 million to 3.3 million). The NCES also recorded that post-baccalaureate enrollment in the period 2009–2020 increased by 10%. In the same period of time, White enrollment decreased by 7%, Hispanic enrollment increased by 86%, Asian/Pacific Islander enrollment increased by 26%, and Black enrollment increased by 14% (NCES, 2022b). From this data, it is clear that planning programs have suffered more than overall university enrollment both in decline of students and in racial/ethnic composition.

Planning Awareness Deficit

The lack of awareness similarly has multiple causes. Children's future careers are influenced by many factors in their environment—high-school counselors, teachers, and their own families play very important roles (Kenny & Bledsoe, 2005; Hurwitz et al., 2012; Hutchison et al., 2014; Strom et al., 2014; Howard et al., 2015; Stritch & Christensen, 2016). High-school students are very rarely exposed to urban planning concepts during their education (Education Commission of the States, 2020) at least in the United States. When coupled with a general unfamiliarity with urban planning among high-school guidance counselors, teachers, and the public, many of whom fail to recognize the results of planning as deliberate activities, the lack of proximal and distal influences has resulted in low professional awareness (Hutchison et al., 2014; Howard et al., 2015; Gleye, 2015; Palazzo et al., 2021). A Gallup-Strada [college] *Major Influence* report (Gallup-Strada, 2017) revealed that the highest percentage of respondents (55%) choose their majors based on informal social networks (family representing 42% and friends 23%). The report was based on 22,087 responses from US adults ages 18–65 responding to the question: "From what resources or people did you get advice about the major or field you were going to study during your [degree program]?" College and high-school counselors—under the larger category of formal Sources—counted for 28% and 11%, respectively.

Planning as a potential, and solidly white-collar, career might seem, based on the declining enrollment numbers in undergraduate and graduate programs, an unusual choice, especially for first-generation college students in inner-city high schools and their parents. This might result from a common misconception: the perceived lack of professional opportunities once the program is successfully completed. Indeed, a comparison amongst urban and regional planners, architects, and landscape architects using the Bureau of Labor Statistics' 2020 Occupational Outlook Handbook (Bureau of Labor Statistics, 2022a, 2022b, 2022c) shows that even if the median pay per year (in 2021) was a little higher for architects ($80,180) than planners ($78,500 or 2% less) or landscape architects ($67,950), the BLS 2020–2030 Job Outlook (2022a, 2022b, 2022c) indicates that the potential job sector growth for urban planners is 7%, while the number is lower (3%) for architects, and stagnant (0%) for landscape architects.

Yet, on the education side of these related professions, enrollment in their programs seems to be less problematic than planning. In fact, in architecture programs accredited by the NAAB (National Architectural Accrediting Board), according to data organized by the National Council of Architectural Registration Boards (NCARB, 2021), the total enrollment has slightly decreased from

2011 to 2017 by 3,296 students (or -13.6%) with a steady increase of 2,868 students from 2017 to 2020. Landscape architecture programs accredited by Landscape Architectural Accreditation Board (LAAB) show a positive net change of .07% from 2015 to 2019 (LAAB, 2019). The LAAB document compares, for the same five-year period, landscape architecture, planning, and architecture enrollments, showing a net change for planning of -6.85% and +4.75% for architecture. This shows that common perceptions are largely misplaced, while the lack of information and knowledge of planning as a potential profession is real. Misperception or misrepresentation of what urban planning is from outside sources is also reflected in the decisions that families and prospective students make. Some examples might help to clarify this point.

The Urban Planner article on *Wikipedia*—the seventh most visited website according to Semrush (2022) in April 2022 with 1.21 billion visits—associates urban planning with engineering: "An urban planning *engineer* may focus on a specific area of practice and have a title such as city planner, town planner [. . .] Urban Planning is an interdisciplinary field closely related to *civil engineering*" (Wikipedia, 2022, italics added). This misperception from a largely accessed user-generated source adds to the confusion of prospective students and their families if, on top of that, other sources on the Internet present urban planning as a college major in muddled ways. In fact, urban planning is associated with different disciplinary families, ranging from being considered a creative arts profession to being associated with architecture, public policy, or social services. A search of popular websites for students and families looking for some information to support their college major choices brings confusing results. College Majors 101 (2022), for instance, places Urban and Regional Planning under Visual and Performance Arts together with Dance, Theater, Music, Film, and Web Design. ACT (2022), the nonprofit organization that administers the namesake test for accessing undergraduate programs in the United States and Canada, lists City/Urban/Regional Planning under the larger category of Architecture, while Urban Studies/Urban Affairs are under Social Sciences and Law. City/Urban, Community and Regional Planning is listed under Architecture and Related Services at MyMajors (2022) and at PrepScholar (2022). Niche (2022), instead, places Urban, Community and Regional Planning under Public Policy and Social Services, together with Urban Studies and Affairs (and others such as Human Services or Social Work and Youth Services). While none of these classifications are totally incorrect per se, these unclear messages might contribute to prospective students and their families dealing unnecessarily with insecurity about their academic choices and future careers.

Not surprisingly, the role of the urban planning profession has been at the center of debates on both its relevance and impacts on society (Wildavsky, 1973; Alexander, 1981; Klosterman, 1985; Campanella, 2011). Many professionals and academicians can relate to how difficult it is to explain what urban planners do to the general public or, even more, to children and youth who are often unaware that urban planning is a noble discipline and profession dedicated to the transformation of the lives of the people and places they hold dear.

Appreciation of the profession and the role urban planners play in societies, or at least an understanding of their roles, or limits, won't happen without explicit dedication and intervention to increase awareness about it. Since the profession isn't well known by children, youth, and the general population (Rodriguez, 2009), and planning regularly requires rationalization even among planners and scholars (Klosterman, 1985; Mazza, 1993; Guzzetta & Bollens, 2003; Wyatt, 2004; Campbell & Marshall, 2006; Tunström, 2017; Moroni, 2020; Forsyth, 2022), promoting awareness about the profession and addressing its diversity challenges—both in practice and education—requires tremendous effort. These interventions need to start with the agents who provide the space for urban planning knowledge to be imparted to the next generation—city and regional planning departments and their regulating bodies such as national associations and accreditation boards. At the same time, universities and individual planning schools should do their part to reach and engage youth in their own surrounding communities as a service to them as well as for the sake of their enrollment.

Introduction

Planning Awareness Efforts

In order to overcome the lack of exposure to planning as a profession, or planners as recognizable figures—while, paradoxically, the outcomes, cities, and their changes and transformations, are under everyone's eyes—urban planning professional organizations or institutions of higher education are undertaking career awareness programs, here termed Design and Planning Language Programs or DPLPs. Generally, a large number of career awareness programs are related to careers in science, technology, engineering, and mathematics (STEM) fields. While it seems that STEM educators have realized that the potential role that higher education institutions can play in shaping the career choices of youth is immense (Good et al., 2002; Tsui, 2007; Santo et al., 2010) and have acted accordingly, this is still a nascent movement in urban planning (Palazzo et al., 2021). The American Planning Association, the Canadian Institute of Planners, the Royal Town Planning Institute, non-profits, and planning schools, recognizing that there is a professional-awareness challenge, have dedicated some, but as we argue not enough, resources and programs to raise awareness of the planning profession and its related concepts among youth. There are, indeed, some universities, foundations, non-profit organizations, and individuals that have picked up the baton and are working to raise awareness among K–12 and even early-year university students (Palazzo et al., 2021). However, most schools of planning are not addressing the national decline in enrollment in urban planning programs by focusing directly on awareness.

Professional awareness isn't a problem for law, medicine, education, sports, and so forth. Television, movies, and advertising are teeming with role models in these professions. Children in the United States today would have to work very hard to avoid being exposed to, and unaware of, these professions. Unfortunately, the same cannot be said of urban planners. There are urban planners here and there in some television shows, but even if their characters are central, it is not due to their education or their professional activities as planners.

Some examples might help to illustrate the point. Thomas Kirkman (Kiefer Sutherland), the US Secretary of Housing and Urban Development, is the *Designated Survivor* for the country in the eponymous ABC and Netflix show. After an explosion that kills everyone in the presidential line of succession, he becomes the president of the United States. Kirkman is an urban planner educated at Cornell and Stanford Universities, engaged in teaching and the profession at different moments of his career. Seldom, during the three seasons of the show, does President Kirkland refer to his career as an urban planner. Likewise, Beth Pearson (Susan Kelechi Watson) is the wife of Randall Pearson (Sterling K. Brown), one of the three Pearson children in the NBC TV drama *This Is Us*. Beth, after the death of her father, left ballet—her passion—to pursue a career in urban planning (even if she studied architecture). After showing us some rarely represented urban planning activities in private firms, she decides to go back to her first passion, dance and ballet. Another recent television depiction of an urban planner was the character of Mark Brendanawicz (Paul Schneider) on NBC's *Parks and Recreation*, who was dropped after the series' second season. In retrospect, this change may have been a blessing for perceptions of real-life urban planners, as the show's director said that he had based the character on a real person he knew who

> worked for the government for a long time as a city planner and he got so fed up with the lifestyle and the red tape and the bureaucracy, that he . . . moved into the private sector. Then he got so fed up and tired of how gross corporations are that he moved back into the government. He oscillated back and forth multiple times.
>
> *(Martin, 2010)*

There are also TV shows dealing with urban projects where planners are represented, but not as heroes. *Utopia*, produced in Australia by ABC, is a comedy series about a fictional National Building Authority, a newly created government organization responsible for overseeing major infrastructure projects. The show is compared to the famous BBC and NBC programs *The Office*. The show, with an 8.4/10 IMDb rating, has been available on Netflix for a few months, but it does not seem to have created much attention around the planning profession, similarly to, it can be supposed, the way the highly rated and widely broadcast *The Office* did not attract people into the paper distribution industry. If planning cannot depend on the media to widely advertise planning to US society, then the field must use other methods to increase awareness and interest and develop a new, diverse generation of students who are curious about design, community, and the built environment.

The Need for This Discourse

The relevance of the urban planning profession in this current era cannot be overemphasized. Since 2007, when it became apparent that more than 50% of the world's population now lives in urban areas and that "the future of the world's population is urban" (UNDESA, 2018, p. 3), cities have been center stage in debates, policies, and research. No profession is better positioned to handle this situation, and the accompanying changes in cities and urban areas, than the urban planning profession. With emerging climate-change patterns, urbanization, migration, and implementation of economic and community development measures, it is more apparent than ever that the future of humanity will be an urban future. It is crucial there are enough professionals, as well as a broad appreciation of what planners do, to deal with the challenges cities face today and those that will emerge in the future. Indeed, the opportunities and challenges that confront cities transcend technical fixes, exposing societal weaknesses and injustices entangled within cities presently and into the foreseeable future. A combination of engagement with residents through genuine participation and co-production of solutions, multidisciplinary perspectives that embrace the interrelationships and unity among different disciplines, and the appreciation of Anthropocene complexities and forces like climate change and pandemics that undermine human progress are all called for. While planning schools expose students to planning as a discipline that creates knowledge about how we understand and address challenges in our cities (Pinson, 2004), the greater public is left oblivious about what planners do. For those who are aware, their experiences with the planning profession are often entangled with historical missteps and negative consequences of its practices (Rothstein, 2017).

Parallel to the decline in enrollment, or the lack of diversity and awareness, we should also add the following to the previous questions and issues: Are there enough planners to face the future of our cities? What is, in fact, the ideal ratio between planners and inhabitants? Is there a carrying capacity of planners in every country? How can this be measured? Have we already reached the maximum capacity? Is this one of the reasons for the decline in enrollment? Preliminary research suggests that this ratio is different, and sometimes extremely different, from country to country. The number of urban and regional planner jobs in 2020 (Bureau of Labor Statistics, 2022b) in the United States is 39,100, or one planner for every 8,476 inhabitants (based on US Census Bureau, 2021). In the United Kingdom, there are around 27,000 planners (RTPI, 2022), or one planner for every 2,485 inhabitants (based on ONS, 2022). In Canada, there are more than 7,947 planning professionals (CIP, 2021), or one out of every 4,786 inhabitants (based on Statistics Canada, 2021). In Australia, there are 18,800 planners in 2020 (RTPI, 2022), or one for every 1,367 residents (based on Australian Bureau of Statistics, 2021). On the other end of the spectrum, India has one planner for every 75,000 urban residents (*The Economic Times*, 2015). In some African countries (Osiyi and Onyebueke, in this compendium), the ratio goes from one for every 186,000 residents in Kenya, to one in 44,500 in Nigeria, one in 33,630 in Zimbabwe, and one planner for every 22,400 residents in South Africa.

Conclusion and Organization of the Book

Motivated by the 2021 paper *Urban Planning as a Career Preference for Students: Efforts to Improve Awareness About the Profession* (Palazzo et al., 2021), the editors—who were also the authors of the publication—aim to enrich a discourse that will take planning scholarship beyond capturing the existing paucity in the literature on how to increase awareness about the urban planning profession among children and youth so that they consider it as a professional career and also to contribute to its recognizability by the public. With contributions from authors from North America, Europe, Asia, Africa, and Oceania, we hope to engender momentum and motivation to actively ensure that urban planning schools and departments—along with their community, regional, and national partners—contribute to enhancing the awareness of children, youth, and the public about urban planning education and its career prospects.

Divided into three sections, the contributors to this book explore concerns related to diversity and awareness issues in urban planning. The first section includes the topic of diversity—with its multiple definitions—in planning enrollment, among faculty, and how schools have worked to improve diversity in both groups. The second section's contributions look into activities and programs with children and youth to raise planning awareness. It contains case studies from a wide range of urban planning focused DPLPs, from academic institutions and outside academia. Section three collects chapters about awareness of planning as a field among both students and the larger community.

It is our firm belief that raising awareness about the planning profession and addressing its inherent diversity challenges can only be achieved if we move beyond mere acknowledgment of the challenge to understanding what can be done to address it. To this end, we recognize that the contributions from the various authors provide both understanding and recommendations that can inform practical approaches that can be successfully implemented to address the urban planning professional awareness and diversity challenge. We hope that this book will provide a resource for urban planning schools and departments, community-based organizations, and individuals to learn from each other; to inform and consciously drive efforts to increase planning education among children, youth, and the general public; and to address the diversity challenges in planning schools and the profession.

References

ACT. (2022). *List of college majors and occupational choices*. Retrieved February 23, 2022, from www.act.org/content/act/en/research/reports/act-publications/college-choice-report-class-of-2013/college-majors-and-occupational-choices/college-majors-and-occupational-choices.html

Alexander, E. R. (1981). If planning isn't everything, maybe it's something. *The Town Planning Review, 52*(2), 131–142. www.jstor.org/stable/40103791

Australian Bureau of Statistics. (2021, September). *National, state and territory population*. Retrieved November 18, 2021, from www.abs.gov.au/statistics/people/population/national-state-and-territory-population/latest-release

Belley, P., & Lochner, L. (2007). The changing role of family income and ability in determining educational achievement. *Journal of Human Capital, 1*(1), 37–89. https://doi.org/10.1086/524674

Bozick, R. (2007). Making it through the first year of college: The role of students' economic resources, employment, and living arrangements. *Sociology of Education, 80*(3), 261–284. https://doi.org/10.1177/003804070708000304.

Burayidi, M. (Ed.). (2015). *Cities and the politics of difference: Multiculturalism and diversity in urban planning*. Canada, University of Toronto Press, Scholarly Publishing Division.

Bureau of Labor Statistics. (2022a). *Architects: Occupational outlook handbook*. Retrieved June 8, 2022, from www.bls.gov/ooh/architecture-and-engineering/architects.htm

Bureau of Labor Statistics. (2022b). *Urban and regional planners: Occupational outlook handbook*. Retrieved June 8, 2022, from www.bls.gov/ooh/life-physical-and-social-science/urban-and-regional-planners.htm

Bureau of Labor Statistics. (2022c). *Landscape architects. Occupational outlook handbook*. Retrieved June 8, 2022, from www.bls.gov/ooh/architecture-and-engineering/landscape-architects.htm

Campanella, T. (2011, April). Jane Jacobs and the death and life of American planning. *Places Journal*. Retrieved February 28, 2021, from https://doi.org/10.22269/110425

Campbell, H., & Marshall, R. (2006). Professionalism and planning in Britain. *Town Planning Review*, 76(2), 191–214. www.jstor.org/stable/40112641.

Charles, C. Z., Roscigno, V. J., & Torres, K. C. (2007). Racial inequality and college attendance: The mediating role of parental investments. *Social Science Research*, 36(1), 329–352. https://doi.org/10.1016/j.ssresearch.2006.02.004

CIP. (2021). *2020 Annual report*. Canadian Institute of Planners. Retrieved November 18, 2021, from https://2020-cip-icu.ca/

College Majors. (2022). *College Majors 101—discover college majors, jobs and college offerings*. Retrieved June 8, 2022, from www.collegemajors101.com

Cox, R. D. (2016). Complicating conditions: Obstacles and interruptions to low-income students' college "choices". *Journal of Higher Education*, 87(1), 1–26. https://doi.org/10.1080/00221546.2016.11777392

DataUSA. (2022). *Urban and regional planners*. Retrieved June 8, 2022, from https://datausa.io/profile/soc/urban-regional-planners#demographics

The Economic Times. (2015). India has one planner for 75,000 urban people. *The Economic Times*. Retrieved November 18, 2021, from https://economictimes.indiatimes.com/news/politics-and-nation/india-has-one-urban-planner-for-75000-urban-people/articleshow/47027985.cms?from=mdr

Education Commission of the States. (2020). *50-State comparison: High school graduation requirements*. Retrieved June 8, 2022, from http://ecs.force.com/mbdata/mbprofall?Rep=HS01

Forsyth, A. (2022). What is planning? A guide for submitting authors. *Journal of the American Planning Association*, 88(1), 1–2. https://doi.org/10.1080/01944363.2021.1995286

Gallup-Strada. (2017). *Major influence: Where students get valued advice on what to study in college*. Retrieved February 23, 2022, from https://news.gallup.com/reports/219236/major-influence-students-advice-study.aspx?thank-you-report-form=1

García, I., Jackson, A., Greenlee, A. J., Yerena, A., Chrisinger, B., & Lee, C. A. (2021). Feeling like an "odd duck." *Journal of the American Planning Association*, 87(3), 326–340. https://doi.org/10.1080/01944363.2020.1858936

García, I., Jackson, A., Harwood, S. A., Greenlee, A. J., Lee, C. A., & Chrisinger, B. (2021). Like a fish out of water. *Journal of the American Planning Association*, 87(1), 108–122. https://doi.org/10.1080/01944363.2020.1777184

Gleye, P. H. (2015). City planning versus urban planning: Resolving a profession's bifurcated heritage. *Journal of Planning Literature*, 30(1), 3–17. https://doi.org/10.1177/0885412214554088

Goetz, E. G., Williams, R. A., & Damiano, A. (2020). Whiteness and urban planning. *Journal of the American Planning Association*, 86(2), 142–156. https://doi.org/10.1080/01944363.2019.1693907

Goldrick Rab, S. (2006). Following their every move: An investigation of social-class differences in college pathways. *Sociology of Education*, 79(1), 67–79. https://doi.org/10.1177/003804070607900104

Good, J., Halpin, G., & Halpin, G. (2002). Retaining black students in engineering: Do minority programs have a longitudinal impact? *Journal of College Student Retention*, 3(4), 351–364. https://doi.org/10.2190/A0EU-TF7U-RUYN-584X

Guzzetta, J. D., & Bollens, S. A. (2003). Urban planners' skills and competencies: Are we different from other professions? Does context matter? Do we evolve? *Journal of Planning Education and Research*, 23(1), 96–106. https://doi.org/10.1177/0739456X03255426

Howard, K. A. S., Flanagan, S., Castine, E., & Walsh, M. E. (2015). Perceived influences on the career choices of children and youth: An exploratory study. *International Journal for Educational and Vocational Guidance*, 15(2), 99–111. https://doi.org/10.1007/s10775-015-9298-2

Hurwitz, M., Smith, J. I., Howell, J., & Pender, M. (2012). *The role of high schools in students' postsecondary choices*. Retrieved June 8, 2022, from College Board Advocacy & Policy Center. https://eric.ed.gov/?id=ED541972

Hutchison, B., Spencer, N. G., & Trusty, J. (2014). Career development in schools: An historical perspective. In G. T. Eliason, J. L. Samide, & P. John (Eds.), *Issues in career development: Career counseling across the lifespan: Community, school, and higher education*. Information Age Publishing.

Jackson, A., Garcia-Zambrana, I., Greenlee, A. J., Lee, C. A., & Chrisinger, B. (2018, April). All talk no walk: Student perceptions on integration of diversity and practice in planning programs. *Planning Practice & Research*, 33(5), 574–595. https://doi.org/10.1080/02697459.2018.1548207

Joint Task Force of American Planning Association, American Institute of Certified Planners, Association of Collegiate Schools of Planning & Planning Accreditation Board. (2016). *Joint task force on enrollment *report*. American Planning Association. Retrieved June 8, 2022, from https://cdn.ymaws.com/www.acsp.org/resource/collection/055FFFC1-636E-4B9C-9587-6D4FED91A23C/Planning_Enrollment_Trends_2015.pdf

Kenny, M. E., & Bledsoe, M. (2005). Contributions of the relational context to career adaptability among urban adolescents. *Journal of Vocational Behavior, 66*(2), 257–272. https://doi.org/10.1016/j.jvb.2004.10.002

Klosterman, R. E. (1985). Arguments for and against planning. *Town Planning Review, 56*(1), 5–20. www.jstor.org/stable/40112168.

Krumholz, N., & Hexter, K. (Eds.). (2018). *Advancing equity planning now*. Cornell University Press.

LAAB. (2019). *Summary of annual reports 2015–2019*. Retrieved June 8, 2022, from www.asla.org/uploadedFiles/CMS/Education/Accreditation/LAAB2015_2019SUMMARYSHEET.pdf

Langenkamp, A. G. (2019). Latino/a immigrant parents' educational aspirations for their children. *Race Ethnicity and Education, 22*(2), 231–249. https://doi.org/10.1080/13613324.2017.1365054

Martin, D. (2010, March 12). '*Parks and recreation*': *Mike Schur tells us why Paul Schneider is leaving the show, plus more details on Adam Scott and Rob Lowe*. Retrieved June 8, 2022, from https://latimesblogs.latimes.com/showtracker/2010/03/parks-and-recreation-mike-schur-talks-about-why-paul-schneider-is-exiting-the-show-plus-more-details.html

Mazza, L. (1993). Attivista e gentiluomo. *Archivio di Studi Urbani e Regionali, 48*, 29–62.

McClendon, B. W. (2003). A bold vision and a brand identity for the planning profession. *Journal of the American Planning Association, 69*(3), 221–232. https://doi.org/10.1080/01944360308978016

Moroni, S. (2020). The role of planning and the role of planners: Political dimensions, ethical principles, communicative interaction. *Town Planning Review, 91*(6), 563–576. https://doi.org/10.3828/tpr.2020.85

MyMajors. (2022). *Architecture and related service*. Retrieved June 8, 2022, from www.mymajors.com/college-majors/

NCARB. (2021). *Education*. Retrieved June 8, 2022, from www.ncarb.org/nbtn2021/education

NCES. (2022a). *Undergraduate enrollment. Condition of education*. U.S. Department of Education, Institute of Education Sciences, National Center for Education Statistics. Retrieved June 8, 2022, from https://nces.ed.gov/programs/coe/indicator/cha

NCES. (2022b). *Postbaccalaureate enrollment. Condition of education*. U.S. Department of Education, Institute of Education Sciences, National Center for Education Statistics. Retrieved June 8, 2022, from https://nces.ed.gov/programs/coe/indicator/chb/postbaccalaureate-enrollment

Niche. (2022). *College majors*. Retrieved June 8, 2022, from www.niche.com/colleges/majors/

ONS. (2022). *Overview of the UK population: 2020*. Office for National Statistics. Retrieved September 29, 2022, from www.ons.gov.uk/peoplepopulationandcommunity/populationandmigration/populationestimates/articles/overviewoftheukpopulation/2020

Ovink, S. M. (2014). 'They always call me an investment': Gendered familism and Latino/a college pathways. *Gender and Society, 28*(2), 265–288. https://doi.org/10.1177/0891243213508308

Ozawa, C., Schwartz, S., & Johnson, J. (2019). *Diversity task force report*. Planning Accreditation Board. Retrieved November 18, 2021, from www.planningaccreditationboard.org/wp-content/uploads/2021/03/2019DiversityReport.pdf

Palazzo, D., Hollstein, L., & Diko, S. K. (2021). Urban planning as a career preference for students: Efforts to improve awareness about the profession. *Planning Practice & Research, 36*(2), 174–192. https://doi.org/10.1080/02697459.2020.1782056

Perez, N., & Farruggia, S. P. (2022). Pathways to early departure from college: The interrelated and precarious role of finances among black and Latinx students. *Race Ethnicity and Education, 25*(2), 155–172. https://doi.org/10.1080/13613324.2021.1890561

Pew Research Center. (2021). *The growing diversity of Black America*. Retrieved May 27, 2022, from www.pewresearch.org/social-trends/2021/03/25/the-growing-diversity-of-black-america/#a-growing-share-of-black-adults-have-a-college-degree

Pinson, D. (2004). Urban planning: An 'undisciplined' discipline? *Futures, 36*(4), 503–513. https://doi.org/10.1016/j.futures.2003.10.008

Planning Accreditation Board-PAB. (2020a). *Student and faculty composition in PAB-accredited programs. 2020 Annual report*. Retrieved June 3, 2022, from www.planningaccreditationboard.org/wp-content/uploads/2022/06/2020AR.pdf

Planning Accreditation Board-PAB. (2020b). *Student enrollment in PAB-accredited programs 2008–2019*. Retrieved June 3, 2022, from www.planningaccreditationboard.org/wp-content/uploads/2021/05/StudEnroll2019.pdf

PrepScholar. (2022). *The ultimate college majors list: 295 degrees to consider*. Retrieved June 8, 2022, from https://blog.prepscholar.com/college-majors-list

Rodriguez, M. A. (2009, September 24). Let's teach children planning. *Planetizen*. Retrieved June 8, 2022, from www.planetizen.com/node/40827

Rothstein, R. (2017). *The color of law: A forgotten history of how our government segregated America*. Liveright Publishing.

RTPI, Royal Town Planning Institute. (2022). *RTPI goes from strength to strength as it grows to 27K members*. Retrieved September 29, 2022, from www.rtpi.org.uk/news/2021/december/rtpi-goes-from-strength-to-strength-as-it-grows-to-27k-members/

Santo, C. A., Ferguson, N., & Trippel, A. (2010). Engaging urban youth through technology: The youth neighborhood mapping initiative. *Journal of Planning Education and Research*, 30(1), 52–65. https://doi.org/10.1177/0739456X10366427

Scott-Clayton, J., & Li, J. (2016). *Black-White disparity in student loan debt more than triples after graduation. Economic studies reports*. Brookings Institution. Retrieved June 3, 2022, from www.brookings.edu/research/black-white-disparity-in-student-loan-debt-more-than-triples-after-graduation/

Semrush. (2022, April). *Top websites in the US by traffic*. Retrieved June 8, 2022, from www.semrush.com/blog/most-visited-websites/

Solis, M. (2020). Racial equity in planning organizations. *Journal of the American Planning Association*, 86(3), 297–303. https://doi.org/10.1080/01944363.2020.1742189

Statistics Canada. (2021). *Population estimates, quarterly*. Retrieved November 18, 2021, from https://www150.statcan.gc.ca/t1/tbl1/en/tv.action?pid=1710000901

Stritch, J. M., & Christensen, R. K. (2016). Raising the next generation of public servants? Parental influence on volunteering behavior and public service career aspirations. *International Journal of Manpower*, 37(5), 840–858. https://doi.org/10.1108/IJM-12-2014-0249

Strom, P. S., Strom, R. D., Whitten, L. S., & Kraska, M. F. (2014). Adolescent identity and career exploration. *NASSP Bulletin*, 98(2), 163–179. https://doi.org/10.1177/0192636514528749

Sweet, E. L., & Etienne, H. F. (2011). Commentary: Diversity in urban planning education and practice. *Journal of Planning Education and Research*, 31(3), 332–339. https://doi.org/10.1177/0739456X11414715

Tiarachristie, G. G. (2016). *Elephant in the planning room: Overcoming barriers to recruitment and retention of planners of color* (Thesis). School of Architecture, Pratt Institute. Retrieved June 8, 2022, from www.nyplanning.org/wordpress/wp-content/uploads/2016/08/Tiarachristie-Thesis_Elephant-in-the-Planning-Room_080716.pdf

Tsui, L. (2007). Effective strategies to increase diversity in STEM fields: A review of the research literature. *The Journal of Negro Education*, 76(4), 555–581. www.jstor.org/stable/40037228

Tunström, M. (2017). A spider in the web or a puppet on a string? Swedish planning students' reflections on their future professional role. In T. Taşan-Kok & M. Oranje (Eds.), *From student to urban planner: Young practitioners' reflections on contemporary ethical challenges*. Routledge. https://doi.org/10.4324/9781315726854

UNDESA. (2018). *World urbanization prospects: The 2018 revision*. Department of Economic and Social Affairs. United Nation. Retrieved June 8, 2022, from https://population.un.org/wup/Publications/

US Census Bureau. (2021). *Quick facts. United States*. Retrieved November 18, 2021, from www.census.gov/quickfacts/fact/table/US/POP010220#POP010220

White House. (2021). *Executive order on diversity, equity, inclusion, and accessibility in the federal workforce*. Retrieved May 27, 2022, from www.whitehouse.gov/briefing-room/presidential-actions/2021/06/25/executive-order-on-diversity-equity-inclusion-and-accessibility-in-the-federal-workforce/

Wikipedia. (2022). *Urban planner*. Retrieved June 8, 2022, from https://en.wikipedia.org/wiki/Urban_planner

Wildavsky, A. (1973). If planning is everything, maybe it's nothing. *Policy Sciences*, 4(2), 127–153. www.jstor.org/stable/4531522

Wood, P. L. C. (2008). *The intercultural city: Planning for diversity advantage*. Earthscan.

Wyatt, R. (2004). The great divide: Differences in style between architects and urban planners. *Journal of Architectural and Planning Research*, 21(1), 38–54. www.jstor.org/stable/43031058

SECTION I

Diversity in Planning

"Nothing about us without us" is a mantra used in the disability rights movement to express the desire for full participation in society. It is also an ideal goal for urban planning processes—full and genuine participation by all members of a community regardless of age, race, ethnicity, ability, or gender. However, as Sherry Arnstein's ladder of citizen participation holds about participation versus the real power of the "have-nots," participation is not enough. What is needed is a "strategy by which the have-nots join in determining how information is shared, goals and policies are set, tax resources are allocated, programs are operated, and benefits like contracts and patronage are parceled out" (1969, p. 216). Power, representation, and leadership are vital factors in genuine citizen-centered advocacy and leaders of planning processes, decision-makers, and even citizen planners derive legitimacy and validate planning processes when they represent the groups involved. For this to happen, a more diverse range of individuals need to be planning practitioners, given knowledge of planning's ethical values, and informed about the importance of planning for local communities.

Supporting and incentivizing increased diversity among individuals involved in planning should be an activity undertaken by many organizations from both the public and private sectors. Obvious organizations are universities, specifically schools and departments of planning. In this first section, activities undertaken by universities in the United States and globally are profiled. For many of them, increasing racial diversity is the primary goal of their activities. However, other types of diversity are also driving forces, particularly in non-US universities where different interpretations of diversity are paramount.

Concerns about racial equity and justice became mainstream discussions in the wake of the 2020 murder of George Floyd and the impact of the COVID-19 pandemic. Even prior to these events, the American Planning Association (APA) published their Equity, Diversity, and Inclusion Vision, Mission, and Strategy, a key part of which was to increase representation within the planning profession (American Planning Association, 2019). As a certified profession, the standard entryway to urban planning is through graduation from an accredited planning program; contributing significantly to this diversity are the five accredited planning programs at US historically Black colleges and universities (HBCUs). In the opening chapter, Jeffrey S. Lowe and Siddhartha Sen review and establish the contribution that these programs make to both the planning profession as well as the racial diversity of professional planners in the United States. While the desire to increase representation within the profession has been a longstanding concern, diversity has yet to be institutionalized as an accreditation criterion by the Planning Accreditation Board (PAB).

The importance of diversity to the pedagogical purposes of planning education is taken up in the next chapter as Ivis García, April Jackson, Andrew Greenlee, and Benjamin Chrisinger detail the changes that occurred in a US planning program when new faculty of color were hired. Their chapter is based on findings from a 2015 study done for the PAB by the Planners of Color Interest Group (POCIG) regarding the climate for diversity within planning classrooms (Association of Collegiate Schools of Planning, 2018). However, just as there is a need to go beyond participation as a metric of representation within planning practice, there is a need to go beyond hiring, or even enrolling, diverse individuals in planning programs. In this chapter the authors detail the need to make all faculty and students feel included and valued, speaking to specific actions that can be taken to improve the climate of diversity within our academic programs. Their findings demonstrate the importance of recruiting a student body composition reflecting regional representation for purposes of diverse recruitment, community engagement, and long-term stability of the regional-planning job market. They also report on the importance and opportunity associated with diverse faculty membership, calling it a "revolutionary act."

Sean Angst, Lindsay Oluyede, Jocelyn Poe, and Dylan Stevenson pick up on this topic in their chapter reviewing the diversity, equity, and inclusion (DEI) statements of US planning programs. In the 2010s, there has been growing recognition that accredited programs need to focus on diversity, equity, and inclusion concerns and activities more actively. As a result, planning programs have created more of these statements in the past couple of years, responding to national movements, student demands and expectations, and following the lead of the APA. The authors note that many programs in the United States are still majority White, although distinct increases in non-White students and faculty have grown significantly since 2010. The authors, current PhD students, look at this topic from a student-centered perspective, inquiring into the possible conflicts between programs and students, as well as rhetoric and action. Here they distill best DEI practices from their analysis of programs' plans, resulting in suggestions which respond to calls for guidance to increase diversity, such as that of the previous chapter.

In a chapter documenting the efforts of the University of North Texas (UNT) to address many of the aforementioned diversity-related issues, Laura Keyes, Lauren Ames Fischer, and Abraham David Benavides's contribution details steps that can be taken. A key concern recognized at UNT, with a student body that is primarily first-generation Hispanics, is the need for students enrolled in planning programs to be mentored and exposed to professional practices. They also tackle issues associated with recruitment and retention through the development of professional networks that reflect the demographic diversity of the student body, including suggestions for other programs.

In a contribution from Italy, G. Bertrando Bonfantini and Carolina Pacchi demonstrate ways diversity can be defined or interpreted in a global context. In Italy, diversity is being explored within a constrained academic framework where flexibility, openness, and evolution are coming up against history and tradition. Ideas about gender, language of instruction, and prior training and education of students are now part of the conversation regarding the future of the degree—and therefore the profession of planner—in Italy.

Parsa Pahlavan and Hossein Maroufi's chapter from Iran documents Ferdowsi University of Mashhad's organization of two intensive workshops for international students of architecture and urban planning programs. Diversity in this context is interpreted in yet another way, associated with the national origin of students. The authors find that these types of experiences enhance students' cognitive learning and their competencies to compare field experiences to value systems in their home countries. They conclude with a number of recommendations and policies that can be used to diversify pedagogy focusing on internationalization of education.

The last two contributions in this section serve as a bridge between the topics of diversity and awareness—as they are discussed in the next section of this book. Giovania Tiarachristie and Daphne Lundi detail barriers to fostering racial diversity in the profession. Noting the racial disparity in exposure to planning as a career, they outline existing roadblocks and potential antidotes to the recruitment of Black, Indigenous, and People of Color (BIPOC) in the planning profession. They also argue for the critical role of youth engagement as a part of recruitment and equity, providing a framework for developing effective youth planning education models.

In the final chapter, Lauren Ames Fischer, Laura Keyes, and Abraham David Benavides discuss the development of a new undergraduate degree in urban policy and planning at the University of North Texas. Their contribution is centered on their experience as a public R1 research university, a Hispanic-serving institution (HSI), and a minority-serving institution (MSI) in the Dallas–Fort Worth metroplex. They share strategies employed by faculty and university leadership to recruit students, lessons learned from the first two years of the planning program, and recommendations on how to augment faculty hiring processes to enhance diversity. An important contribution here regards mistaken assumptions about employment prospects and financial remuneration in professional design fields that can deter student enrollment. Reflecting these concerns, the authors focus on the challenges of appealing to and attracting primarily first-generation Hispanic students to planning.

The breadth of universities and organizations profiled in this section demonstrates that there has been a true shift in the concept of who is fit to be a planner. No longer is the technocrat, expensively educated and trained, assumed to be best able to provide leadership and translate community needs into plans, policies, and action. There is growing attention to the ability of HBCUs and minority- and Hispanic-serving institutions to educate a heretofore unreached segment of planners able to significantly contribute to the representation of the profession. Globally, similar realizations are happening as planning programs look to broaden their pool of incoming students, as well as the experiences they have during their planning education.

We also see in this section how larger organizations, such as the US-based American Planning Association, are embracing ideals associated with diversity—and how these ideals are being transmitted down to individual universities. While many academic programs are still at the beginning of this process, wrestling with what DEI means on a daily basis, the high number of programs at any point in the process is a very positive sign. A final positive sign coming out of these chapters is the number of young people—early career academics and PhD students—involved with this topic. As they become leaders in their own departments, we can hope that DEI initiatives become ingrained, resulting in planning education and a planning profession that more closely reflects our communities.

References

American Planning Association. (2019). *APA equity, diversity, and inclusion vision, mission, and strategy*. Retrieved June 7, 2022, from https://planning-org-uploaded-media.s3.amazonaws.com/document/APA-Equity-Diversity-and-Inclusion-Strategy-2020.pdf

Arnstein, S. R. (1969). A ladder of citizen participation. *Journal of the American Institute of planners*, *35*(4), 216–224. https://doi.org/10.1080/01944366908977225

Association of Collegiate Schools of Planning—Planners of Color Interest Group. (2018). *ACSP-POCIG student climate study: Summary of findings*. Retrieved June 7, 2022, from https://cdn.ymaws.com/www.acsp.org/resource/resmgr/docs/pocig/pocig_climate_survey_summary.pdf

1
RACIAL DIVERSITY AND ACCREDITED PLANNING PROGRAMS AT HISTORICALLY BLACK COLLEGES AND UNIVERSITIES

Contributions, Challenges, and Prospects

Jeffrey S. Lowe and Siddhartha Sen

Race issues endure in planning education and the profession. Because of this fact, *diversity*, defined by the US Planning Accreditation Board (PAB) as encompassing racial diversity, remains an important accreditation criterion amid declining enrollments nationwide (PAB, 2017). However, we contend that racial diversity has been largely relegated to the margins for most of planning's history concerning the academy, as well as planning pedagogy, and that the critical role historically Black colleges and universities (HBCUs) in the United States play in diversifying the planning profession receives little attention. Accordingly, this chapter seeks to change that by bringing into focus the importance of PAB-accredited HBCU planning programs in ensuring racial diversity and Black representation in the field.

The remainder of the chapter is divided into an additional five sections. The section to follow summarizes specific actions influencing or undertaken by the Association of Collegiate Schools of Planning (ACSP) over the past 30 years to racially diversify the planning academy in the United States. The section after that provides a historical overview of the origins of HBCUs and more detailed synopses regarding the only HBCU PAB-accredited programs: Alabama Agriculture & Mechanical University, Jackson State University, Morgan State University, and Texas Southern University. These synopses highlight the programs' contributions to diversity undergirded by a mission to endow students with the human capabilities of resisting structural racism, subjugation, and exclusion, and the professional competencies to help improve quality of life within the Black community and society at large. The next two sections discuss the influences accredited HBCU planning programs have on racial diversity in planning education and challenges they face in making such contributions, respectively. The final section concludes the chapter and offers recommendations for ACSP, PAB, and HBCU involvement that will lead to greater diversity outcomes by these accredited planning programs.

Racial Diversity in the Planning Academy

Intentional efforts on the part of the ACSP to racially diversify planning education in the United States span more than three decades. In 1988, ACSP President Donald Krueckeberg established the Committee on the Recruitment and Retention of Women and Minorities in Planning Education. At the time of final reporting, the committee found the number of faculty of color so small that any further breakdown by sex and race would have eliminated confidentiality (Ritzdorf et al., 1990). Only 32 Black faculty existed in the planning academy, 25 in PAB programs. These 25 faculty members represented roughly 4% of total faculty in accredited programs. Little has changed over the years despite PAB approving accreditation standards on diversity in 1989 (PAB, 1989). In 2006, another effort to diversify planning education and the profession took shape at a dinner meeting sponsored by the Planning and the Black Community Division (PBCD) of the American Planning Association (APA) at the 47th Annual Conference of the ACSP in Fort Worth, Texas. Faculty and PhD students of color, along with accompanied allies, sought ways to advocate for the interest of people and communities of color within the planning academy and profession, including PAB. Subsequently, the following year the ACSP Governing Board recognized the Planners of Color Interest Group (POCIG) as an official interest group within the organization (POCIG, 2021). In 2010, ACSP President Cheryl Contant appointed a task force to offer a model that member schools could adopt for improving recruitment, retention, and tenure of underrepresented faculty of color (Hibbard et al., 2011). Based on the task force's findings and recommendations, the ACSP Governing Board approved the creation of a Special Committee on Diversity in 2011. Throughout the 2010s, POCIG advocacy helped propel the Committee on Diversity's actions. For example, the committee, in collaboration with POCIG, convenes the Pre-Doctoral Workshop for Underrepresented Students of Color to recruit students into planning doctoral programs as well as the Junior Faculty of Color Workshop that provides early career tenure-track faculty with the skills and knowledge to flourish in the planning professoriate.

Concerns about racial diversity within the ACSP, initially expressed by the Committee on the Recruitment and Retention of Women and Minorities in Planning Education (Ritzdorf et al., 1990) up to the present, and often driven by faculty of color and allies, continuously call for PAB accreditation standards to address the issue. Catherine Ross (1990), who would later become the first Black ACSP president (1993–1995), recommended that ACSP should adopt a policy statement that favorably captures an increase in a program's representation of faculty and students of color. She also recommended that ACSP should support the inclusion of this issue as part of accreditation. Around the same time, Hill (1990) proposed a program for increasing minority faculty representation in ACSP member schools. Thomas's (1996) seminal article criticized planning education for disjointed pluralism, citing the separation between advocacy and equity planning, feminism, and international movements; and called for unified diversity. Since then, many scholars have added their views to the debate, including individual accounts of innovative approaches to teaching issues of diversity (Harwood & Zapata, 2014; Sen et al., 2017). One of the salient points that emerges from the literature is that issues of diversity and social justice must be an integral part of the curriculum and not taught in separate courses that often remain on the margins of the core planning curriculum. There is, however, no evidence that planning schools are following such a path, although the separation between advocacy and equity planning, feminism, and international movements has been narrowed (Sen et al., 2017). Also, nothing specific to HBCUs exists in the PAB accreditation standards, despite their significant role in increasing representation and incorporating diversity in their curricula.

Origins of HBCUs and Their Respective Accredited Planning Programs

A federal designation, HBCUs are institutions of higher learning in the United States founded from 1837 to 1964 to provide an education primarily for Black formerly enslaved people and their descendants (Brown & Davis, 2001; Ashley & Williams, 2004). At least four paths led to establishing most HBCUs: Black church self-help; religious societies and abolitionist or philanthropic efforts; federal intervention through the Bureau of Refugees, Freedmen, and Abandoned Lands, commonly known as the Freedmen's Bureau; and the Morrill Act of 1890, which allowed for the creation of land-grant colleges for African Americans. Nonetheless, virtually all paths commenced through and built upon self-help efforts of the Black church.

Scholarship abounds about the history and legacy of the Black church in pursuit of a social mission to create the means for African Americans to survive and overcome oppression and racial disparities for a better quality of life (Lincoln & Mamiya, 1990; Franklin, 1997; Owens, 2007; Lowe & Shipp, 2014). The Black church—African American Christian denominations or individual congregations—is the oldest institution controlled and operated by Black people in the United States, and from the beginning has offered mutual aid along with religious teaching, educational literacy, and industrial training. For example, the Bethel African Methodist Episcopal Church (AME) movement, beginning in the late 1700s, made teaching and schools a priority among the provisions provided to those who escaped slavery (Mukenge, 1983). Wilberforce University would become the first institution of higher learning to be owned and operated by the AME church as well as a Black church denomination in 1856, while the oldest HBCU, Cheyney University of Pennsylvania, founded in 1837, maintains roots in Quaker abolitionist philanthropy. The American Missionary Association, a Protestant-based abolitionist group primarily sponsored by northern Congregationalist churches, formed approximately two decades before the Emancipation Proclamation to abolish slavery, promoted racial equality, spread Christian values, and educated Black people (Fitzgerald, 2018). After the Civil War, the US federal government established, under the auspices of the Department of War, the Freedmen's Bureau. The Freedmen's Bureau managed all relief and educational activities related to newly emancipated men and women (Anderson, 1988). Accordingly, Black churches, often with support from the American Missionary Association and the Freedmen's Bureau, established the first critical mass or cohort of HBCUs.

The second group of HBCUs came into being with support from the Morrill Act of 1890. Former Confederate states refused to admit Black people into public institutions of higher learning, and state support for educational training remained virtually non-existent for Black people. Subsequently, the federal government, through the Morrill Act of 1890, required, mostly, the former confederate states to provide land grants for the establishment of HBCUs (Anderson, 1988).

With these two cohorts taken together, more than 90 HBCUs existed by 1900, and the vast majority were publicly funded institutions. However, state support for HBCUs remained minimal. Not until the 1972 *Adams v. Richardson* decision did federal enforcement of Title VI of the Civil Rights Act of 1964, which declared states could not maintain separate and unequal public higher-education systems, become a reality (Brown, 1999). The effect of the Adams ruling was that it spurred similar lawsuits by Black people and civil-rights groups for HBCU benefit or preservation at the state level.

While HBCUs never enacted racial-exclusionary policies, the majority focused on undergraduate teaching and public research benefitting communities surrounding main campuses rather than graduate or professional education that would include most urban planning programs (Lowe, 2008; Mayes, 1992).[1] Of the 101 HBCUs, four maintain planning programs accredited by the PAB: Alabama Agriculture and Mechanical University (Alabama A&M), Jackson State University, Morgan State University, and Texas Southern University. The growth of planning and planning-related programs at HBCUs reflected broader societal change. For example, the growth of urban-studies programs at HBCUs in the 1960s and 1970s was a response to the need for quasi planners for anti-poverty programs under the Kennedy and Johnson administrations. By the late 1960s, it had become obvious that Black-studies programs, which were the forerunners of urban-studies programs, did not equip African Americans with the skills needed to gain metropolitan parity. Black architectural educators also started an initiative to establish planning programs around the same time at select urban

HBCUs. The rationale for such schools was for Black people to themselves formulate an urban theory of development to alleviate the problems of inner cities. Unfortunately, the initiative never fully materialized, as only Howard University had a viable planning program from 1967 to 1986 (Sen, 1997). Nevertheless, HBCUs experienced some growth in the diversity of their schools and colleges, which housed planning and allied programs to respond to societal changes. The following discussion describes the development and growth of the four existing planning programs at HBCUs.

Alabama A&M University

Urban planning at Alabama A&M originated out of a response to the mid-20th-century civil rights movement, as well as significant population growth and development of cities and regions. Alabama A&M established a Bachelor of Science in Urban Studies in 1969. Desiring to meet the demand for educational programs that would increase racial diversity among professionally trained planners in the United States, particularly across the state of Alabama, the program transitioned to a Bachelor of Community Planning (BCP) program in 1975. That same year, having accepted and matriculated approximately 50 students, the BCP program became a feeder for the newly established Master of Community Planning (MCP) program (Yin, 2021). Now housed in the Department of Community and Regional Planning, College of Agricultural, Life and Natural Sciences, and renamed from BCP to Bachelor of Science in Regional Planning (BSRP) and from MCP to Master of Urban and Regional Planning (MURP), both programs have retained accreditation for more than four decades. For most of that time, the BSRP and MURP stood as the only accredited undergraduate (1986) and professional (1976 American Institute of Planners, National Education Development Committee [AIP-NEDC] recognition and 1986 PAB) planning programs in Alabama (Yin, 2021). Currently, BSRP stands alone as the only accredited undergraduate planning program at an HBCU.

Jackson State University

Like *Adams v. Richardson*, the 2002 *Ayers v. Musgrove* settlement concluded that the state of Mississippi could no longer maintain separate and unequal institutions of higher learning. Moreover, the Mississippi legislature, anticipating the impending 2002 settlement, would mandate some academic programs non-existing at the eight state-funded universities be established at the three state-supported HBCUs, including an urban planning program at Jackson State, and began to approve funding allocations for their formation in the late 1990s (Mitchell, 2001; Harris, 2021). At the request of Jackson State, ACSP convened approximately 15 faculty from member institutions to travel and spend three days advising the Mississippi Institutions of Higher Learning—the governing body responsible for policy and financial oversight of the state's public universities and colleges—that wanted to accelerate the establishment of an urban planning program (Reardon, 2021). Subsequently, in 1999, Jackson State established the Department of Urban and Regional Planning (DURP) with a Master of Arts in Urban and Regional Planning program in the School of Liberal Arts. Desiring to expand the visibility of Jackson State as a nationally recognized scholarly institution, DURP commenced the Doctor of Philosophy (PhD) in Urban and Regional Planning program in 2000. The professional program received accreditation a decade after its founding, and the PhD in Urban and Regional Planning program was the first at an HBCU. In 2018, DURP became one of very few planning units nationwide to be housed in a school of engineering.

Morgan State University

The planning program at Morgan State maintains roots in the institution's desire to tackle the urban crisis (broadly defined as racial polarization, class alienation, physical decay, and deterioration of race relations in inner cities) through extension work in Black Baltimore neighborhoods dating back to the mid-1950s. The socioeconomic conditions at that juncture of US history influenced then president of the university Martin D. Jenkins' efforts to carry out community development. Jenkins strongly believed that as a Black institution of higher learning, Morgan State should be a pioneer in alleviating the urban crisis (Sen, 1997). These institutional interests converged with allied support from the Baltimore Chapter of the American Institute of Planners (AIP) and the Ford Foundation. In 1969, the Baltimore AIP chapter adopted a resolution that endorsed establishing undergraduate urban studies and master of planning programs. At the time, no graduate-level planning program existed in the state of Maryland. Subsequently, in 1970, Morgan State established a Master of Arts in Urban Planning and Policy Analysis—the first graduate-level planning program in the state of Maryland. In 1974, it became the first at an HBCU to receive degree recognition from AIP-NEDC. Such recognition preceded the 1984 establishment of the PAB. The Master of Arts in Urban Planning and Policy Analysis was reconstituted as the Master of City and Regional Planning (MCRP) and gained PAB accreditation in 1986. When coupled with AIP-NEDC recognition, it is the longest continuously accredited planning program at an HBCU. Over the years, the planning program has had many administrative homes: the Center of Urban Affairs (1970), the School of Urban Affairs and Human Development (1975), the School of Education and Urban Studies (1981), and the Institute of Architecture and Planning (1991), which was established as a free-standing unit also housing the architecture and landscape-architecture programs. In fall 2008, Morgan State elevated the Institute of Architecture and Planning to the School of Architecture and Planning (SA+P), and the program attained departmental status. In fall 2014, the department became a program under a larger Department of Graduate Built Environment Studies, which also houses the graduate programs in architecture and landscape architecture.

Texas Southern University

Established in 1974 as an integral part of the newly created School of Public Affairs, the Master of City Planning program materialized to help realize the prior-year designation by the Texas State legislature of Texas Southern as a special purpose institution for urban programming (Lash et al., 1975). Beginning in 1976, students could also enroll and earn a joint MCP and Juris Doctorate through Texas Southern University Thurgood Marshall School of Law. In 1984, MCP became a department within the newly created School of Management. After the dissolution of the School of Management in 1986, MCP moved to the newly formed Department of Public Affairs in the School of Arts and Sciences. A 2001 Office of Civil Rights agreement with the state of Texas to address federal concerns over systemic racial discrimination in higher education funding led the state of Texas Higher Education Coordinating Board to approve funding that included reconstituting the non-accredited MCP program into the Master of Urban Planning and Environmental Planning program and establishing the PhD in Urban Planning and Environmental Policy program by 2003 (Nissimov, 2001). In 2005, the department of Urban Planning and Environmental Policy (UPEP) came to be, consisting of both master's and PhD programs. Since its founding, UPEP has been housed in the Barbara Jordan–Mickey Leland School of Public Affairs.[2] The Master of Urban Planning and Environmental Policy program received initial PAB accreditation in 2009.

Influence of PAB-Accredited HBCU Planning Programs on Diversity

Accredited HBCU planning programs' influence on diversity in the academy gets realized primarily in curriculum development, conveyance of knowledge, and representation within planning from an

African American perspective. HBCUs' most significant influence is in the number of Black students receiving entry-level and higher-order preparation for professional planning careers. Table 1.1 depicts Black/African American Bachelor of Planning PAB-accredited program enrollment in all schools in comparison to HBCUs from 2010 through 2019. As the table indicates, student enrollment in accredited bachelor's programs declined from 1,545 in 2010 to 1,177 in 2020. The lowest enrollment was in 2017 when the numbers dwindled to 942. While the enrollment of Black/African American students decreased from 135 in 2010 to 117 in 2020, reflecting the overall trend, the percentage of enrollment saw a marginal increase from 8.74% to 9.94%. It is striking that the only accredited undergraduate planning program at an HBCU, Alabama A&M University, had the largest share. The program's enrollment of African American students remained steady from 2010 to 2019 with 30 students enrolled in 2010 and 36 in 2019. It decreased to 23 in 2020; however, the contribution of Alabama A&M to all PAB-accredited bachelor's programs enrollment remained high at 19.66%. The program contributed to 22.22% of such enrollment in 2010, which reached its peak in 2017 when it climbed to 40.79%.

Table 1.2 depicts Black/African American Master of Planning PAB-accredited program enrollment in all schools vs. HBCUs for the same 2010 through 2020 period. As the table shows, accredited masters programs also saw a decline from an enrollment of 5,675 in 2010 to 5,371 in 2020, with the lowest enrollment in 2018 of 4,106. While the number of Black students increased from 447 in 2010 to 506 in 2020, their proportion marginally increased from 7.88% to 9.42%. While not as high as at the bachelor's level, the four accredited master's programs at HBCUs contributed significantly to such enrollment throughout the decade. Though the percentage contribution of HBCUs to total enrollment for Black students dropped from 24.38% in 2010 to 18.18% in 2020, it reached as high as 27.51% in 2017. The significance of these numbers can be further understood from the fact there are 15 accredited bachelor's and 78 accredited master's programs in total, in comparison to the one accredited bachelor's and four accredited master's programs at HBCUs. Clearly, HBCUs are making a significant contribution to educating Black planners and increasing their representation in the profession.

Table 1.1 Black/African American Bachelor of Planning Enrollment in PAB-Accredited Programs: All Schools vs. HBCUs

Enrollment	Year										
	2010	2011	2012	2013	2014	2015	2016	2017	2018	2019	2020
All Schools Black/African American Enrollment	135	127	97	82	94	93	86	76	104	115	117
All Schools Black/African American Enrollment Percentages (%)	8.74	8.66	8.19	7.35	8.59	7.74	8.54	8.07	8.56	10.20	9.94
All Schools Total Enrollment	1,545	1,467	1,184	1,115	1,094	1,201	1,007	942	1,215	1,128	1177
HBCUs Black/African American Enrollment	30	29	30	28	27	33	30	31	30	36	23
HBCUs Black/African American Enrollment Percentage (%)	85.71	87.88	93.75	93.33	96.43	97.06	100	88.57	96.77	97.30	95.83
HBCUs Total Enrollment	35	33	32	30	28	34	30	35	31	37	24
HBCUs Black/African American Enrollment as Percentage of All Schools (%)	22.22	22.83	30.93	34.15	28.72	35.48	34.88	40.79	28.85	31.30	19.66

Source: Planning Accreditation Board, Student and Faculty Composition in Planning-Accredited Programs (Annual Reports, 2010–2020)

Table 1.2 Black/African American Master of Planning Enrollment: All Schools vs. HBCUs

Enrollment	Year 2010	2011	2012	2013	2014	2015	2016	2017	2018	2019	2020
All Schools Black/African American Enrollment	447	438	399	366	386	407	382	418	368	381	506
All Schools Black/African American Enrollment Percentages (%)	7.88	8.06	7.64	7.23	7.74	8.70	8.64	9.55	8.96	9.01	9.42
All Schools Total Enrollment	5,675	5,436	5,222	5,063	4,985	4,678	4,421	4,375	4,106	4,229	5,371
HBCUs Black/African American Enrollment	109	104	88	74	85	87	81	115	80	77	92
HBCUs Black/African American Enrollment Percentage (%)	77.86	77.04	75.86	80.43	80.19	79.82	75.70	82.14	78.43	75.49	76.03
HBCUs Total Enrollment	140	135	116	92	106	109	107	140	102	102	121
HBCUs Black/African American Enrollment as Percentage of All Schools (%)	24.38	23.74	22.06	20.22	22.02	21.38	21.20	27.51	21.74	20.21	18.18

Source: Planning Accreditation Board, Student and Faculty Composition in Planning-Accredited Programs (Annual Reports, 2010–2020)

The four HBCU PAB-accredited planning programs have incorporated diversity into their curricula since their inception. At Morgan State and Texas Southern, those instrumental to the establishment and growth of the programs were dedicated to working with students and community groups to address issues of inner-city neighborhoods. This has left a legacy of serving the underprivileged and integrating diversity issues into the curricula (Sen et al., 2015). Historically and currently, the planning program at Morgan State employs underserved areas of Baltimore as its laboratory for many of its courses, thereby exposing students to diversity. At Texas Southern, students and faculty come together to gain an understanding of greater Houston and the Southwest region with a primary interest in its diverse urban setting. To cite another example, the curriculum at Jackson State was set up to orient students and faculty toward developing appropriate responses to the challenges that racial history posed for planning in general and the city of Jackson in particular. This historic tradition is still reflected in their current curriculum. Studio courses offer opportunities to create plans that often emerge from active community engagement in disadvantaged communities (Sen et al., 2015).

The presence of many African Americans in HBCU programs makes the discussion on race and justice an integral part of all classes. Students are often concerned with community development by virtue of their residence in the inner city, ethnic backgrounds, social concerns, or employment. Even non-Black faculty members are transformed by an HBCU student body and institutional culture and get engaged in issues of diversity through their teaching (Sen et al., 2015).

HBCU planning programs also exhibit diversity in the generation of knowledge. For example, most faculty in planning programs at HBCUs make students cognizant of biases in knowledge construction within urban planning as well as how race, ethnicity, and class influence how knowledge is created. Some courses not only include alternative reading material, but also ask students to critically reflect on the readings given their racial and ethnic origins. At Texas Southern, for instance, the history course requires readings by Black intellectuals and non-planning activist scholars including Ida B. Wells, W.E.B. Dubois, and John Hope Franklin. Discussion on the reform movement includes Jacob Riis, Jane Adams Hull House, or the settlement house movement more broadly, along with the woman's club movement, Urban League, and Universal Negro Improvement Association. Students reflect on questions about and are challenged to go deeper in their own understanding of the role of immigrants, minorities, and women at the 1893 World's Columbian Exhibition to challenge the mainstream perspective of the spectacle's contribution to the 1909 Plan of Chicago. Field trips and site visits encourage students to construct first-hand alternative knowledge about urban spaces and urban planning. Knowledge construction generally takes place within the context of planning practices in the cities where these programs are located (Sen et al., 2015; Lowe, 2008).

Knowledge construction and equity go hand in hand at HBCUs, recognizing that people learn differently and that teaching styles must acknowledge and adapt to these differences (Banks, 1995, 2001). For example, at Texas Southern, usually in any given year, approximately 50% of students are non-traditional, as they are older, employed full time, or have children. The faculty recognize that they are instructing adults with histories, and, perhaps, an inside perspective on the communities in which they reside. Another technique employed is storytelling, a highly appreciated art form in communities of color. At Morgan State, small class sizes, nurturing by the faculty, and cooperative learning are integral to the program.

Helping to advance racial diversity among faculty may be where HBCU impact is less visible. Black/African Americans made up 8% of full-time planning faculty (PAB, 2019). Roughly one of every nine Black planning-faculty members earned an undergraduate degree from an HBCU. A more minute number earned the professional degree or the PhD from one of the four HBCU planning programs. Having earned the PhD, only three joined the ranks of tenured faculty within the planning academy—all at Jackson State.

Challenges HBCUs Face in Diversifying the Planning Academy

HBCU PAB-accredited planning programs mainly face university-administrative challenges to stay alive and maintain accreditation. All four programs are small and face pressure from upper levels of administration to increase enrollment. Furthermore, absence of administrative staff makes preparation of self-studies and arrangements for site visits a difficult task. Often, the faculty, especially the program leader, must undertake this effort. Faculty resources also become a problem, as upper levels of administration often frown on providing the support necessary to maintain accreditation.

Some of the administrative challenges HBCUs face in diversifying the planning academy can be explained by the teaching-research university paradigm. None of the HBCUs with accredited planning programs hold distinction as top research universities; they are better known to be teaching institutions. Teaching institutions place more emphasis and resources on classroom instruction and pedagogy rather than faculty involvement in the creation of knowledge prone to the publish-or-perish aphorism befitting research-one institutions (Irons & Buskist, 2009). HBCUs focus primarily on undergraduate teaching and public research, responding to problems and opportunities in their communities through such forms as direct service, civic engagement, technical assistance, and reports (Smith, 2017; Mayes, 1992). Public research undertaken by HBCU academicians, however, rarely becomes published in peer-reviewed outlets or secures funding. Furthermore, lacking decades of administrative support or understanding, HBCUs maintain an environment and a legacy whereby faculty, overwrought with teaching and service responsibilities, have little time for fostering relationships with colleagues or students that could enable opportunities for research (Gasman et al., 2010; Minor, 2004; Branson, 1984; Bacon, 1974). These difficulties facing teaching universities, particularly HBCUs, impose limitations on how (and to what degree) planning programs tackle challenges to diversity.

Marketing and outreach present another challenge for HBCUs' PAB-accredited programs. As previously mentioned, research or flagship universities tend to house urban planning units. These institutions maintain significant marketing strategies and resources where the small professional programs, such as planning, receive support for recruitment. In turn, none of the HBCU PAB-accredited planning programs are located at a research-one institution, and they receive little-to-no recruitment resources from their administrations. For example, full-time recruiting staff, crucial for such programs, are literally non-existent. The burden of recruiting often falls on faculty and program administrators.

Alabama A&M maintains an undergraduate program that may attract students from other programs on campus. Morgan State's program cross lists many of its courses with the undergraduate interdisciplinary program as well as offers a general education course as a recruitment strategy. In general, faculty and administrators across the four programs carry out activities such as attending college fairs, contacting applicants, and disseminating information to alumni, local APA chapters, and other professional organizations or networks that could attract students.

HBCUs market themselves primarily to potential undergraduate students and more traditional or higher-income professions (i.e., education, law, social work) often pursued by African Americans. This reality manifests in the fact that just half of HBCU accredited planning programs have existed for several decades. As a result, many alumni from these programs may find few others with similar experiences with whom to bond, lack engagement in extensive professional-planning networks, or occupy positions of influence that would enhance marketing and outreach.

Conclusion and Recommendations

This chapter brings attention to the importance of HBCU accredited planning programs in ensuring racial diversity and Black representation in urban planning. The significance of their contribution can be understood from the fact that four HBCUs have provided almost a quarter of the entire supply of PAB-accredited African American master's planning students over the last decade, and just one PAB-accredited HBCU program does so at the undergraduate level. Accredited HBCU planning programs demonstrate how to operationalize and incorporate diversity in planning education, yet survival and maintaining accreditation remains a concern for these programs.

Changes to PAB standards that make achieving accreditation for HBCU planning programs less difficult are necessary. For example, in the 2017 PAB standards, Criteria 1.C.3 (Student Retention and Graduation Rates) requires programs to report student retention and graduation rates. Though the criteria state that these rates should be relative to the program enrollment and to targets set by the program, in reality, only two-year and four-year graduation rates are taken into consideration. Many HBCU programs have part-time students, which prolongs the time taken to graduate due to work and family obligations. Also, most HBCUs have limited financial aid for student recruitment and retention, which affects the time taken to graduate. The HBCU tradition of admitting students with high motivation, who may be somewhat underprepared for graduate work, extends students' time to graduate. Other criteria that negatively impacts HBCU planning program accreditation include Criteria 1.C (Programmatic Assessment) and Criteria 1.D (Student Learning and Outcome Assessment). Both require development of rigorous methodology and data collection that is difficult for HBCU programs because of limited resources (PAB, 2017).

In summary, a concerted effort needs to be undertaken not only on the part of the PAB, but by both the ACSP and the HBCUs, who should be vigorously engaged in order for these programs to thrive and continue their contribution to diversifying planning. The PAB should increase efforts to include diversity as an accreditation standard. There should be some flexibility in letting HBCU programs compile anecdotal and qualitative data, and determine what kind of data they can collect to document program and learning outcomes. Alternative means for assessing student and program outcomes, such as cohort-dependent graduation rates, can accurately reflect the true graduation rates for HBCU programs. Graduation rates should also consider the context of overall HBCU graduation rates, which are generally low. ACSP attempts to increase racial diversity in planning academia ought to include measures not merely directed at Predominantly White Institutions (PWIs). As pointed out by Black faculty, ACSP "does not have effective representation of its Historically Black Colleges and Universities members" (Black Faculty Response to the ACSP Statement, 2020). The ACSP could also reach out to higher-level administration at HBCUs with HBCU planning faculty to drive home the importance of HBCUs in diversifying the planning profession and academy. Last but not least, HBCU planning faculties should become more proactive and engage with the ACSP, local APA chapters, and the PAB. Faculties should, furthermore, forthrightly speak truth to power and develop strategies targeting university upper-level administrations for more resources, including federal resources, while emphasizing the importance of their programs, as well as HBCUs more generally, in planning academia. These recommendations, if implemented, will help better sustain HBCU efforts toward racial diversity within the planning discipline, particularly in the United States.

Notes

1 For example, Hampton University, founded to provide a normal education for Blacks, established a formal education program for Native Americans in 1878 (Lindsey, 1995), and, according to Logan (1969), four White women were the first students to attend Howard University, which was planned to educate a sizable portion of Black men and women as well as White men and women.
2 Similar to UPEP, the Department of Public Affairs was reconstructed into the Barbara Jordan–Mickey Leland School of Public Affairs in 2002 through additional funding from the US Office of Civil Rights Agreement.

References

Anderson, J. D. (1988). *The education of blacks in the South, 1860–1935*. University of North Carolina Press.
Ashley, D., & Williams, J. (2004). *I'll find a way or make one: A tribute to historically black colleges and universities*. HarperCollins.
Bacon, A. (1974). Research in traditionally black schools. In R. Johnson (Ed.), *Black scholars in higher education in the 1970's*. Educational-Community Counselors Associates Publications, Inc.
Banks, J. A. (1995). Multicultural education: Historical development, dimensions, and practice. In J. A. Banks & C. A. Banks-McGee (Eds.), *Handbook of research on multicultural education*. Simon and Schuster MacMillan.
Banks, J. A. (2001). Multicultural education: Historical development, dimensions, and practice. In J. A. Banks & C. A. Banks-McGee (Eds.), *Handbook of research on multicultural education*. Jossey-Bass Inc.
Black Faculty Response to the ACSP Statement. (2020, June 18). Retrieved May 27, 2021, from www.acsp.org/page/ACSPStatement
Branson, H. (1984). Research in the historically black colleges. In A. Garibaldi (Ed.), *Black colleges and universities: Challenges for the future*. Praeger Publishers.
Brown, M. C. (1999). *The quest to define collegiate desegregation: Black colleges, title VI compliance, and post-Adams litigation*. Bergin & Garvey.
Brown, M. C., & Davis, J. (2001). The historically black college as social contract, social capital, and social equalizer. *Peabody Journal of Education*, 76(1), 31–49. https://doi.org/10.1207/S15327930PJE7601_03
Fitzgerald, N. (2018, September 8). American missionary association (1846–1999). *BlackPast.org*. www.blackpast.org/african-american-history/american-missionary-association-1846-1999/
Franklin, R. M. (1997). *Another day's journey: Black churches confronting the American crisis*. Fortress Press.
Gasman, M., Lundy-Wagner, V., Ransom, T., & Bowman, N. (2010). *Unearthing promise and potential: Our nation's historically black colleges and universities*. Jossey Bass.
Harris, W. M. (2021, April 22). *Personal communication*.
Harwood, S. A., & Zapata, M. A. (2014). Changing racial attitudes. In M. Bose, P. Horrigan, C. Doble, & S. Shipp (Eds.), *Community matters: Service-learning in engaged design and planning*. Routledge.
Hibbard, M., Irazábal, C., Thomas, J. M., Umemoto, K., & Wubneh, M. (2011, November). *Recruitment and retention of underrepresented faculty of color in ACSP member programs: Status and recommendations*. Diversity Task Force Report Submitted to the Governing Board of the Association of Collegiate Schools of Planning.

Hill, E. (1990). Increasing minority representation in the planning professoriate. *Journal of Planning Education and Research*, 9(2), 139–142. https://doi.org/10.1177/0739456X9000900211

Irons, J. G., & Buskist, W. (2009). Preparing a career at a teaching institution. In S. F. Davis, P. J. Giordano, & C. A. Licht (Eds.), *Your career in psychology: Putting your graduate degree to work*. Wiley-Blackwell.

Lash, J. S., Dixon, H. W., & Freeman, T. F. (1975). *Texas Southern university: From separation to special designation*. Report to the U.S. Department of Health, Education & Welfare, National Institute of Education.

Lincoln, C., & Mamiya, L. (1990). *The Black church in the African American experience*. Duke University Press.

Lindsey, D. (1995). *Indians at Hampton university, 1877–1923*. University of Illinois Press.

Logan, R. (1969). *Howard University: The first hundred years, 1867–1967*. New York University Press.

Lowe, J. S. (2008). A participatory planning approach to enhancing a historically black university-community partnership: The case of the e-city initiative. *Planning Practice and Research*, 23(4), 549–558. https://doi.org/10.1080/02697450802522897

Lowe, J. S., & Shipp, S. (2014). Black church and black college community development: Enhancing the public sector discourse. *Western Journal of Black Studies*, 38(4), 244–259.

Mayes, M. (1992). Status of agricultural research programs at 1890 land-grant institutions and Tuskegee university. In R. Christy & L. Williamson (Eds.), *A century of service: Land-grant colleges and universities, 1890–1990*. Routledge.

Minor, J. T. (2004). Decision making in historically black colleges and universities: Defining the governance context. *The Journal of Negro Education*, 73, 40–52. https://doi.org/10.2307/3211258

Mitchell, M. L. (2001). A settlement of Ayers v. Musgrove: Is Mississippi moving towards desegregation in higher education or merely a separate but more equal system. *Mississippi Law Journal*, 71, 1011.

Mukenge, I. (1983). *The Black church in urban America: A case study in political economy*. University Press of America.

Nissimov, R. (2001, June 8). Prairie view, TSU getting big increase in funds. *Houston Chronicle*. Retrieved May 3, 2021, from Prairie View, TSU getting big increase in funds (chron.com)

Owens, M. L. (2007). *God and government in the ghetto*. University of Chicago Press.

Planners of Color Interest Group (POCIG). (2021). Retrieved April 19, 2021, from www.acsp.org/page/POCIG_History

Planning Accreditation Board (PAB). (1989, May). *The accreditation document*. Criteria and Procedures of the Planning Degree Accreditation Program. PAB.

Planning Accreditation Board (PAB). (2017, March). *PAB accreditation standards and criteria*. PAB.

Planning Accreditation Board (PAB). (2019). *Student and faculty composition in planning-accredited programs*. Annual Report. PAB.

Reardon, K. M. (2021, April 22). *Personal communication*.

Ritzdorf, M., Fischer, P., Greer, M., Harris, W. M., Ross, C., Siembeida, W., White, S., & Wirka, S. (Committee on the Recruitment and Retention of Women and Minorities in Planning Education). (1990, April). *The recruitment and retention of faculty women and faculty of color in planning education: Survey results*. Prepared for the ACSP Executive Board.

Ross, C. (1990). Increasing minority and female representation in the profession: A call for diversity. *Journal of Planning Education and Research*, 9(4), 135–138. https://doi.org/10.1177/0739456X9000900210

Sen, S. (1997). The status of planning education at historically black colleges and universities: The case of Morgan state university. In J. M. Thomas & M. Ritzdorf (Eds.), *Urban planning and the African American community: In the shadows*. Sage Publications.

Sen, S., Kumar, M., & Smith, S. L. (2015). Educating planners for a cosmopolitan society: Selective case study of historically black colleges and universities. In M. A. Burayidi (Ed.), *Cities and the politics of difference*. University of Toronto Press.

Sen, S., Umemoto, K., Koh, A., & Zambonelli, V. (2017). Diversity and social justice in planning education: A synthesis of topics, pedagogical approaches, and educational goals in planning syllabi. *Journal of Planning Education and Research*, 37(3), 347–358. https://doi.org/10.1177/0739456X16657393

Smith, M. P. (2017). *Historically black college and university presidents' perceptions of their role in the civic engagement of their institutions and students* (Doctoral dissertation). University of Pennsylvania.

Thomas, J. M. (1996). Educating planners: Unified diversity for social action. *Journal of Planning Education and Research*, 15(3), 171–182. https://doi.org/10.1177/0739456X9601500302

Yin, J. (2021, April 12). *Personal communication*.

2
THE PEOPLE THAT REPRESENT THE REGION AND THE YEAR OF CHANGE

Ivis García, April Jackson, Andrew J. Greenlee, and Benjamin Chrisinger

The importance of diversity in planning education is not new, but there are deep divides in the United States that, in recent years, higher-education institutions are trying to address. As a result of our society's prioritization of diversity, universities, like most institutions today, are interested in recruiting and serving a diverse student body, faculty, and staff (Chen, 2017; APA, 2018). In part, university programs respond to a changing composition of enrolled students (García et al., 2020). In addition, secondary educated students are often a reflection of demographic changes across the nation (Frey, 2014; Livingston, 2015; Cohn, 2012). Still, even as we become a minority-majority nation, planning departments struggle to recruit people of color and transform the culture of their institutions.

This chapter is embedded in Amara and Brandon's accounts, two graduate students, one Asian, one White, to provide more of an in-depth narration. Authors use these planning students' voices to understand why diversity and representation are essential and how a planning program can move in the right direction. Specifically, Amara supports the idea that program diversity should reflect the region. Brandon witnessed a landmark event in the history of his planning program when the department hired two African American professors who delivered important changes to the curriculum and extracurricular activities and transformed the culture of the department as a whole.

Authors write this chapter as members of the Planners of Color Interest Group (POCIG)—a coalition within the Association of Collegiate Schools of Planning (ACSP)—whose mission is to advance people's interests, concerns, and communities of color within planning academia and the profession. This chapter is based on a climate study POCIG researchers conducted in 2015 based on two out of 50 interviews that authors conducted with students in planning-accredited schools (García et al., 2020; Greenlee, Jackson, García-Zambrana, Lee et al., 2018; Greenlee, Jackson, García-Zambrana, Lee, 2018; Jackson et al., 2018; Lee et al., 2020).

Since November 2020, POCIG has been involved in Planning Accreditation Board (PAB) advocacy by attending meetings, sending surveys to POCIG members, and writing letters. As part of that process, authors collected more than two dozen comments from our members. This chapter also reflects the analysis and wisdom of all the faculty engaged with POCIG leadership and the concerted efforts planning departments can incorporate. The authors reflect on how PAB can address the way programs might increase diversity and representation based on suggestions from Amara, Brandon, and those involved in PAB advocacy.

The first sections of this chapter provide a review of how PAB currently measures ethnic and racial diversity, why student composition reflecting regional diversity matters, and how the single act of recruiting faculty of color could be beneficial to programs. A methods section then explains our process for interviewing. A findings section then lays out the stories of Amara and Brandon, highlighting the importance of the student composition reflecting that of the region and how recruiting faculty of color could be a revolutionary act. The recommendations section summarizes some of the comments we have provided to the PAB based on our interviews, surveys to members, and informal conversations. Finally, the conclusion offers a summation of the arguments and their implications.

How PAB Measures Ethnic and Racial Diversity

In 2020, anti-racism—actively seeking to name and eliminate racism at the individual and institutional level—became part of a national conversation. Conceptualizations of anti-racism, in a way, started to poke holes in the idea of diversity, which is an all-inclusive umbrella under which all historically underrepresented groups have been gathered. The PAB sees diversity and inclusion as one of their goals:

> Among the foremost responsibilities of the Program is to reject discrimination, including discrimination based on race, color, national origin, sex, disability, age, and other classes protected by law—within the program itself—and to advance diversity and a culture of inclusion among the planning profession's future practitioners in the program, particularly concerning historically underrepresented racial and ethnic minorities.
>
> *(Planning Accreditation Board, 2017, p. 6)*

PAB accreditation standards and criteria require programs to collect and analyze data. Accreditation occurs every five to seven years, and administrators must submit a self-study report that includes student and faculty racial, ethnic, foreign-born, and gender composition with the "intent to achieve and maintain diversity" (Planning Accreditation Board, 2017, p. 4). But committee reports from Association of Collegiate Schools of Planning (ACSP) members have noted that PAB categories to measure diversity are simplistic and problematic (Hibbard et al., 2011; Lee et al., 2021; Tewari et al., 2018). As pointed out in the accreditation standards and criteria, PAB collects data to uncover the presence, or lack thereof, of historically underrepresented racial and ethnic minorities. PAB gathers data for the following racial categories for US citizens and permanent residents only: White, Black or African American, American Indian or Alaska Native, Asian, Native Hawaiian and Other Pacific Islander, Some Other Race, Two or More Races, and Unknown. Outside of race, the two other diversity measures are Foreign and Ethnicity or whether one is or is not Hispanic or Latino (US citizens and permanent residents only).

Based on POCIG's advocacy work with the PAB, it appears that these categories aim to have the program emphasize domestic students and faculty of color that historically have been underrepresented in academia. However, as the Global Planning Educators Interest Group (GPEIG) noted, "it is unclear whether schools are submitting international students [to improve] their shares of racial minorities" (Tewari et al., 2018). We would add that the category of Latino or Hispanic is especially problematic. We know of many instances where reporters include Latinx international students in the category of ethnicity—which explicitly states that the box should include "US Citizen and Permanent Residents Only." This could be because reporters don't understand the difference, but could also be due to personal interactions with students or faculty and self-identification.

For example, a student could assume a US Latino, Black, or Asian identity but be an immigrant. Good data collection would require programs to distinguish between those who are and are not US citizens or permanent residents in an objective way. Hibbard et al. (2011) and Lee et al. (2020) also noted that the category Asian American in general presents issues because it lumps diverse groups of students into one category. Some Asian groups are overrepresented in academia (e.g., Chinese, Japanese,

Korean, Indian), while others are underrepresented (e.g., Burmese, Bhutanese, Hmong, Malaysians, etc.). It might be worth adding, for both domestic and international students, their nationality.

Regional Diversity

Regional diversity plays a role in how diverse programs are. Most undergraduate students go to a local university or college (Kodrzycki et al., 2001; Mak & Moncur, 2003), implying that there is a relationship between how diverse a city is and how diverse their universities are. However, this does not entirely explain variation in the student body (Franklin, 2013). Some graduate programs do a good job recruiting from historically Black colleges and universities (HBCUs), tribal schools, community colleges, or creating high-school programs (Sen et al., 2014).

Within PAB standards, there is no consideration of the relationship between the admitted student body and the region's demographics. Planning research has previously discussed that diversity is highly desirable because it's related to innovation and general economic growth (Florida, 2011, 2014). However, this research hasn't directly linked how universities and colleges can increase the number of students from diverse backgrounds and benefit the region economically. As Rachel Franking, Associate Director of Spatial Structures in the Social Sciences at Brown University noted:

> possession at the regional level of a diverse workforce is a source of economic advantage and if regions are successful at retaining the diverse—and educated—postgraduation, then areas with more diverse student bodies may reap the long-term economic rewards associated with both ethnic diversity and increased human capital.
>
> *(Franklin, 2013, p. 31)*

It is well understood that programs partner with local planning offices and firms for their studios, internships, and other applied curricula. Research shows that students who graduate locally appeal to local employers (Sentz et al., 2018). In addition, many graduates choose to stay in the state where they conducted their studies. About 40% of graduates who went to state schools stayed within 50 miles of the university, but on average, they stayed within 300 miles—working in the general region (Sentz et al., 2018).

Hiring Faculty of Color as a Revolutionary Act

Though attracting students from the region who would also stay in the region is essential to diversity, one of the most significant changes a department can undertake is to hire faculty of color. This single revolutionary act can attract and retain more students of color, train students to work with diverse publics, potentially add issues of social justice and community engagement to the curriculum, and push the envelope with new scholarship areas (Turner et al., 2008).

A report from the ACSP Committee on Diversity recommended that programs proactively create a strategic plan for how they might recruit and retain faculty of color "including the formulation of goals and measurable outcomes" (Hibbard et al., 2011, p. 17). The program should educate themselves on the benefits for students of hiring faculty of color, the challenges they face in predominately White institutions, and the best practices to create a welcoming and stimulating environment (Turner, 2002).

Overall, the idea of diversity doesn't necessarily support a commitment to eradicating "the bad policy decisions of the past" as the American Planning Association (APA) stated in their George Floyd statement. The APA statement, however, did reaffirm a commitment to racial equity (APA, 2020). Racial equity starts from the premise that recruiting and retaining students and faculty of color that are of diverse backgrounds or represent the demographics in the region might be a good start.

Climate-for-Diversity Interviews With Students

The ACSP Planners of Color Interest Group proposed a student-focused climate interview to the ACSP Governing Board in 2015. The interviews focused on the climate for diversity within urban-planning educational programs, including student views on the value of diversity and interactions with peers, faculty, and the community. Interviews were conducted in person or via recorded videoconference, then transcribed. In-depth interviews were conducted with 50 respondents, and each interview lasted between 20 and 45 minutes.

We decided to base this chapter on the stories of two interviewees, Amara and Brandon, exploring how they speak directly to how we might change PAB guidelines. Though this chapter relies on a very small sample, we defend this strategy when producing ethnographic research (Small, 2009). We have heard similar accounts from many students, including students of color, which can be found in previous publications (García et al., 2020; Greenlee, Jackson, García-Zambrana, Lee et al., 2018; Greenlee, Jackson, García-Zambrana, Lee, 2018; Lee et al., 2020). In many ways, the stories told by Amara and Brandon reflect these broader experiences and perspectives.[1]

Digging Deeper Into Amara and Brandon's Accounts

In our climate study, we asked students to define diversity. We ask students about how diverse the current student body in their department was and how diverse the faculty was. We also asked how their department accomplished the goal of diversity and what it could do to improve. Of the 50 interviews we conducted with students of different backgrounds, we chose two student accounts to dig deeper in their answers. Amara is an Asian female student, and Brandon is a White male student.

In the following narrative, Amara provides programs with a simple idea: make your school accessible for diverse people living in your region, and if you can't find them there, attract them. Above all, remember to seek to represent your region's diversity within the diversity of your student body. This is how you make sure that planning serves your community. In the next section titled "Amara: The People That Represent the Region," Amara makes a clear argument to support a fundamental PAB change—that is, match[2] your diversity goals to where you are located.

Brandon remembers the year that everything changed in his program when two African American professors were hired together. They created a cascading effect in new courses, practicums, and outside-of-the-classroom events. The later section titled "Brandon: The Year of Change" supports the idea that if programs can change one thing, it might be hiring faculty of color who care about equity, inclusion, and how to engage people from diverse backgrounds.

Amara: The People That Represent the Region

Amara, a Fulbright female master's student born in India, "came to the city for undergrad and decided to stay." Based on her own experience, Amara spoke about how student diversity could be achieved by recruiting from the region. Now a US resident, she had finished her bachelor's degree and was working in the field of planning. After working for a few years, she decided to apply to a master's program. In her work, Amara had connected locally with Neysa, a woman from her country who had gotten her PhD in urban planning, whom she admired deeply.

With admiration in her voice, Amara said,

> And her methods and the work that she does—a lot of community planning and advocacy planning in Mumbai now (even though she lives in the United States) . . . that was more the kind of work I wanted to end up doing.

This quote also shows that much of the admissions' advertisement is from word of mouth. Students connect locally with alumni that "had done the program and had good things to say." If people of color go to that program, they would likely tell others—building diversity incrementally.

Amara assumed that most planners, like Neysa, her role model, would end up getting a planning job in the city where they went to school and interact with people of their national, racial, or ethnic identity. Amara noted that some planning schools, unfortunately, operate "without any acknowledgment of how dangerous it can be to send a bunch of planners out into a city, especially when your student body doesn't line up with the demographics of the city where they work." She also assumed that residents who are people of color perhaps were unlikely to be admitted into the program. "There's never any acknowledgment that maybe people from the community would be in this program if you made the program accessible to them." Her assumption is probably correct, recognizing that accepting people from the community, including practitioners connected to regional issues, could be of great value, but also recognizing that there's a lack of accessibility. For example, community members who have never been in a university context expressed that the university is for people who are more educated than them. This belief discouraged them from applying, thinking it's "hard to be admitted." Other barriers are finances—it is highly competitive to obtain scholarships or graduate assistantships to cover tuition. A US-resident low-income Asian student admitted to a program without funding may turn down admission hoping for a better outcome in the future.

Another way of increasing diversity that would benefit the community is by recruiting from other regions but still seeking to reflect the city's diversity—knowing that many of those students are likely to stay in the area after graduating. This also applies to faculty. Amara specifically said about her professors:

> We do have a very diverse faculty body. Like, people are coming from a lot of different backgrounds. But not necessarily from the backgrounds of the people in the city who they work for. And it's the same thing with the student body where people have a lot of backgrounds—but even then, we're still not kind of adequately representing the kids who go through the local public schools.

For Amara, recruiting students who live in the region or diverse students with similar backgrounds to the local community who stay after graduation is vital to serve and represent communities adequately. This strategy could improve "relationships with the neighborhood and communities around it." Right now, in her program, this was not happening. "Doing public outreach, there was always this implicit assumption that everyone in the room—like, everyone in the program, part of this class was not also a community member. Like, those things never intersect or overlap."[3]

Amara was frustrated because the studio courses were creating an inequitable situation. Not having students who live in the community resulted in a process that was "very top-down even the way we imagine an inclusive process." In her view, theory and practice did not meet because the program was about how to be inclusive, but at the same time, it was exclusive in a way. It's tough to make those things match. Still, Amara's thought was that if students from these communities were directly recruited into the program or at least students of the same identity, these equity efforts would be more than lip-service. In her analysis, Amara questioned "who has been able to access the program or even how we think about 'serving communities'."

Brandon: The Year of Change

Many of our interviews demonstrated that attracting faculty of color interested in addressing social justice issues and doing community engagement work might be the best tactic that programs could take to create immediate change. We chose to illustrate this fact by highlighting a conversation we had with Brandon, a White graduate student. When asked to define diversity, like most of our interviewees, he emphasized race over income or other categories: "Where I grew up is not diverse. Well, it wasn't diverse racially." He spoke about how he didn't have any African American or Black professors in his first year, and in his second year, the department hired two—a Black male and a Black female. Brandon saw this as a positive change—that he saw as part of a larger movement—by stating that the reason for these hires seems intentional. It was "definitely the national culture at the time . . . also the school culture changing too." It is important to note that this shift happened prior to the 2020–2021 Black Lives Matter movement and global racial reckoning initiated by George Floyd's murder in police custody. This illustrates that there has been an ongoing movement for racial equity in higher education that has deepened over time. When thinking about the overall experience of having faculty members from different backgrounds, Brandon said:

> I enjoyed this. Let's talk about how you talk about race and planning because people were saying, you know like we got White planners here; we got Black planners here; we got Asian planners here, like, and we know they are racial issues out there. We know we're going to be facing different, you know, community groups one day and audiences. We know we're going to be working in these different diverse cities, so how are we supposed to talk about that?

Brandon thought exposure to people from different backgrounds could be beneficial to him and his colleagues once out in the real world and planning with racially diverse communities. How to interact with people from different backgrounds is not always obvious. Brandon appreciated being taught and practicing listening, respecting others, and working toward a common goal with individuals from various racial backgrounds—classmates, professors, and members of the public.

Brandon noted that once these two Black faculty members were hired, everything changed. For example, that same year a conference was put together by the African American Student Association with the assistance of the new faculty members. One of the new professors from a predominately Black city created a class to "do more urban planning research there." There was a symposium "to kick off the multiple years of research." Furthermore, there was a "planning studio that looked at Martin Luther King Boulevards across the country." In regard to theory, "There was one class hosted by the new Black female professor about justice in the community and was just a whole semester on that topic justice in the community and what that means."

Brandon experienced these changes in his second year after Black faculty were hired. Community engagement as a faculty skill was also highlighted; talking about professors who didn't do this kind of work, Brandon said, "it's really safe because you don't have to ever interact with the public at all." He knew that not interacting with the public wasn't a realistic option once students found jobs as planners.

Overall, Brandon's story tells us that if programs could make one change that trickles down and becomes transformative, it is to hire faculty of color. To this suggestion, we might add the need to support those faculty who address social justice issues and engage in community work (e.g., revising tenure guidelines to value community engaged scholarship).

Recommendations

The following recommendations were derived from what we found in the interviews and our POCIG conversations during the PAB revision period, Fall 2020 and Spring 2021. These recommendations were also presented to the PAB for their consideration before they drafted their proposed changes to the PAB accreditation standards and criteria. Next, we discuss the ways in which a program can diversify its student and faculty body.

Use Racial Composition of MSAs to Determine Underrepresented Groups

Require programs to use the racial composition of their metropolitan statistical areas (MSAs) as a general metric of what percentage of Hispanic/Latino/a/x, Black people, and so on. should be admitted in their schools and offered positions as faculty because they are underrepresented. Some schools may not want to follow MSA proportions. It might be more realistic if schools can identify for themselves how to address diversity issues, depending on policies that allow them to recruit and hire, their financial resources, sizes of their programs, and so forth. Still, POCIG favors the PAB at least require programs to develop definitions of who is underrepresented in their local contexts and plans to recruit, hire, retain, and so on. Programs can identify which groups are underrepresented and which could change over time (Lee et al., 2021). For example, a program may determine that American Indians and Native Hawaiian and Pacific Islanders are underrepresented the most, followed by Alaska Native, Black (not of Hispanic origin), Hispanic or Latino/a/x (including persons of Mexican, Puerto Rican, Cuban, and Central or South American origin). Some groups of Asians are underrepresented as well, including those who are Burmese, Bhutanese, Hmong, Malaysian, and so forth.

Allow Specific Goals for Particular Groups

As Lee et al. (2021) noted, using broad categories like Asian has been criticized because it hides Southeast Asian or first-generation students' needs by purely using a pan-ethnic grouping. Rather than pit underrepresented groups against international students and Asian Americans, the PAB should advocate for specific goals and objectives for each group in a way that redresses historical problems unique to each community (Lee et al., 2021). POCIG agrees with separating the categories of international vs. domestic, which is how the PAB currently does its reporting. However, goals should be set for international *and* domestic students. Many programs rely on international students to show overall diversity, while ignoring domestic diversity (Lee et al., 2020). We recommend a more nuanced definition of what diversity means. A Filipino student born in the United States is culturally different from a Filipino student who is moving to the United States to study. Furthermore, a Filipino student born in the United States would be considered underrepresented, while an international Filipino student would not. Therefore, diversity could not be met solely through strategic international recruitment. We recommend adding nationality or origin for both domestic and international students to be more representative and transparent regarding how diversity goals are being met and whether underrepresented groups are being recruited and retained.

Prioritize Diverse Faculty

As discussed, diversifying the faculty could be a revolutionary act that trickles down to include issues of social justice and community engagement in the curriculum both to recruit and retain students of color and to move research in new directions. Programs should create strategic goals to increase racial and ethnic diversity within their faculty and educate themselves about attracting, supporting, and retaining people of color in a primarily White institution (Turner, 2002; Hibbard et al., 2011). This can be done by not only hiring faculty of color but also creating a culture of inclusion. Hiring faculty of color is a first step, but to obtain tenure, mentorship is necessary. Ways that a department can support faculty include paying fair wages, providing research funds, institutionalizing formal mentorship programs, hiring graduate assistants to help with teaching and research, valuing community engagement and activist-based research in tenure guidelines, and hosting open conversations about inclusion, among others.

Engage in Additional Data-Collection Efforts

The PAB must engage in more data collection efforts to determine the most important categories of diversity and make the data public so that researchers can use it. POCIG has used PAB data to complete several studies. We have also collected more nuanced identity data and may be willing to help PAB in regard to categories (Greenlee, Jackson, García-Zambrana, Lee et al., 2018; Greenlee, Jackson, García-Zambrana, Lee, 2018b, Jackson et al., 2018; García et al., 2020; Lee et al., 2020; García et al., 2020).

Conclusion

In "Amara: The People That Represent the Region," Amara recognized that recruiting students from the region would result in many staying locally. Research suggests that programs must find ways to make admissions accessible for ethnically and racially diverse individuals in the region. The admissions committee also needs to take steps to recruit from outside the region and think about how these applicants might reflect the local population. Two clear ways of making the program more accessible would be to (1) introduce the program to the communities that think university is for people more educated than themselves and (2) provide scholarships to attract young community members in the programs. These changes to the way admissions are considered would improve the likelihood of a good yield of new diverse students for the upcoming year.

In "Brandon: The Year of Change," Brandon helps us understand that a program can change many things when they change one aspect. He was mainly talking about hiring two new Black or African American faculty members. Brandon witnessed massive changes inside and outside of the classroom. His arguments were compelling, notably how these faculty taught things that other faculty might have a hard time teaching, like how to communicate and plan with, and for, Black or African American residents.

There is much more that we could have said from our 50 interviews. We chose Amara and Brandon's stories because they match many of the narratives that faculty members and students at POCIG talked about during the PAB proposed-changes period. We believe that if these changes are implemented, ACSP, APA, and the planning community would greatly benefit because student and faculty ethnic and racial diversification is a direct contribution to our communities, cities, and regions.

Notes

1 We have heavily written using underrepresented students. As a result, in this chapter, we use two students whose identities are not underrepresented in planning schools, one South Asian (Indian) and one White. Furthermore, they both match the arguments that we heard from the PAB survey we sent to members, as well as other conversations.
2 It is important to not reify this statement in exact terms. For example, it could be that Native Americans only represent 1% or less of the population in your region. However, the program would benefit greatly from adding a Native American faculty member (see Lee et al., 2021).
3 We used this quote in Jackson et al. (2018).

References

APA. (2018). *Diversity efforts*. American Planning Association. www.planning.org/diversity/forum/
APA. (2020). *APA statement on righting the wrongs of racial inequality*. American Planning Association. www.planning.org/policy/statements/2020/may31/
Chen, A. (2017). Addressing diversity on college campuses: Changing expectations and practices in instructional leadership. *Higher Education Studies*, 7(2), 17–22. http://doi.org/10.5539/hes.v7n2p17

Cohn, D. (2012, May 17). Explaining why minority births now outnumber white births. *Pew Research Center's Social & Demographic Trends Project (blog)*. www.pewsocialtrends.org/2012/05/17/explaining-why-minority-births-now-outnumber-white-births/

Florida, R. (2011). How diversity leads to economic growth. *CityLab*. www.theatlanticcities.com/jobs-and-economy/2011/12/diversity-leads-to-economic-growth/687/

Florida, R. (2014). *The rise of the creative class-revisited*. First Trade Paper Edition. Basic Books.

Franklin, R. (2013). The roles of population, place, and institution in student diversity in American higher education. *Growth and Change*, 44(1), 30–53. https://doi.org/10.1111/grow.12001

Frey, W. H. (2014). *Diversity explosion: How new racial demographics are remaking America. Advance reading copy edition*. Brookings Institution Press.

García, I., Jackson, A., Harwood, S., Greenlee, A., Lee, A., & Chrisinger, B. (2020). "Like a fish out of water": The experience of African Americans and Latinx in U.S. Planning programs. *Journal of American Planning Association*, 87(1), 1–15. https://doi.org/10.1080/01944363.2020.1777184

Greenlee, A. J., Jackson, A., García Zambrana, I., & Lee, C. A. (2018, December). *ACSP-POCIG student climate study: Summary of findings*. https://cdn.ymaws.com/www.acsp.org/resource/resmgr/docs/pocig/pocig_climate_survey_summary.pdf

Greenlee, A. J., Jackson, A., García Zambrana, I., Lee, C. A., & Chrisinger, B. (2018, December). Where are we going? Where have we been? The climate for diversity within urban planning educational programs. *Journal of Planning Education and Research*. https://doi.org/10.1177/0739456X18815740

Hibbard, M., Irazábal, C., Thomas, J. M., Umemoto, K., & Wubneh, M. (2011). *Recruitment and retention of underrepresented faculty of color in ACSP member programs: Status and recommendations*. Diversity Task Force Report. https://cdn.ymaws.com/acsp.site-ym.com/resource/resmgr/files/CoD/ACSP_Diversity_Task_Force_Re.pdf

Jackson, A., García-Zambrana, I., Greenlee, A. J., Lee, C. A., & Chrisinger, B. (2018). All talk no walk: Student perceptions on integration of diversity and practice in planning programs. *Planning Practice & Research*, 33(5), 574–595. https://doi.org/10.1080/02697459.2018.1548207

Kodrzycki, Y. K., Clayton-Matthews, B. A., Testa, W., Triest, R., & Zaretsky, A. (2001). Migration of recent college graduates: Evidence from the national longitudinal survey of youth. *New England Economic Review*, 13–34.

Lee, A., Chrisinger, B., Greenlee, A., García, I., & Jackson, A. (2020). Beyond recruitment: Experiences and recommendations of international students in U.S. Urban planning programs. *Journal of Planning Education and Research*. https://doi.org/10.1177/0739456X20902241

Lee, C. A., Flores, N., & Hom, L. (2021). Learning from Asian Americans: Implications for planning. *Journal of Planning Education & Research*. https://doi.org/10.1177/0739456X211006768

Livingston, G. (2015, June 24). Today's multiracial babies reflect America's changing demographics. *Pew Research Center (blog)*. www.pewresearch.org/fact-tank/2015/06/24/todays-multiracial-babies-reflect-americas-changing-demographics/

Mak, J., & Moncur, J. (2003). Interstate migration of college freshmen. *The Annals of Regional Science*, 37(4), 603–612. https://doi.org/10.1007/s00168-003-0130-4

Planning Accreditation Board. (2017). *PAB accreditation standards and criteria*. www.planningaccreditationboard.org/wp-content/uploads/2021/01/2017Standards.pdf

Sen, S., Edward, H., Forsyth, A., Lowe, J., Sandoval, G. F., Alicea, M., & Unemoto, K. (2014). *Suggested outcome measures for PAB standards and criteria related to diversity and social justice*. ASCP Diversity Committee.

Sentz, R., Metsker, M., Linares, P., & Clemans, R. (2018). How your school affects where you live. *Emsi (blog)*. www.us.ccb/how-your-school-affects-where-you-live/

Small, M. L. (2009). How many cases do I need?' On science and the logic of case selection in field based research. *Ethnography*, 10(1), 5–38. https://doi.org/10.1177/1466138108099586

Tewari, M., Guinn, A., & Chen, Y. (2018). *Globalization of planning education in ACSP programs: A portrait in numbers 1994–2014; 2017 report*. ACSP Task Force on Global Planning Education.

Turner, C. (2002). *Diversifying the faculty: A guidebook for search committees*. Association of American Colleges and Universities, 1818 R Street, NW. https://eric.ed.gov/?id=ED465359

Turner, C., González, J. C., & Wood, J. L. (2008). Faculty of color in academe: What 20 years of literature tells us. *Journal of Diversity in Higher Education*, 1(3), 139–168. https://doi.org/10.1037/a0012837

3

MORE THAN AN INVITATION

Setting the Rhythm of Planning Programs Through DEI Statements and Plans

Sean Angst, Lindsay Oluyede, Jocelyn Poe, and Dylan Stevenson

In 2020, public outcry after the deaths of Ahmaud Arbery, Breonna Taylor, and George Floyd in the United States reignited ongoing civil unrest against racial injustice, compounded by the inequitable toll of the COVID-19 pandemic. This historic moment prompted reflection within many professions about their roles in upholding White supremacy, and the planning field was no exception. Students, faculty, and practitioners produced public denouncements, open letters, and manifestos calling for greater accountability in the planning field to actively pursue anti-racist practices. While the lack of diversity in the field, specifically in academic planning programs, and its lasting impact on perpetuating racial injustice has been central among these calls for action, there is little research examining how programs are approaching diversity, equity, and inclusion (DEI) issues. Various planning programs in the United States have developed strategic and DEI plans addressing these intersectional inequities (race, class, gender, religion, etc.) through curriculum changes, program culture, and faculty and student diversity. In the United States, these efforts are demonstrated by DEI plans developed by planning programs that are accredited by the Planning Accreditation Board (PAB)—the official accrediting body for North America. Plans available online date as far back as 2003; however, 32% of available plans were published in 2020.

In planning education, considerable focus is given to recruitment and retention, as programs struggle to maintain student enrollments reflective of their surrounding communities. Recent literature has shown how the role of Whiteness has been largely ignored within the planning field, limiting the ability to address inequalities and injustices across communities (Goetz et al., 2020). Others have found that students of color in planning programs report experiencing bias and discrimination at higher rates than their White counterparts (García et al., 2021). In academia, leaders turn to DEI initiatives to address these historical inequities in the United States.

Though programs must incorporate DEI goals and objectives in their strategic planning to comply with PAB accreditation standards (Planning Accreditation Board, 2021), the creation of a dedicated DEI plan demonstrates further commitment to racial equity in planning education. As such, this chapter analyzes strategic and DEI plans of PAB-accredited programs to reveal practical ways they're dealing with diversity challenges. Since outreach and recruitment are the primary methods of diversifying, this chapter analyzes recruitment strategies as distinct factors in DEI initiatives. However, meeting DEI goals doesn't occur through recruitment strategies alone but also by focusing on the planning program culture, which can influence student retention (García et al., 2021). While retention involves programming, training, and other services to foster a culture where students feel they belong, we focus on DEI organizational structures and student services as the primary avenues for retaining a diverse student body.

In this chapter, we explore two questions: (1) What is the compositional diversity at accredited planning programs in the United States? and (2) What practices have been identified in PAB programs' DEI plans to meet diverse student populations' needs?

First, this chapter provides an analysis of faculty and student enrollment data from 2010 to 2019 to understand the current diversity landscape of PAB-accredited programs in the United States. Second, using content analysis of publicly available DEI and strategic plans, we provide a national overview of DEI efforts at planning programs. Third, we offer recommendations on how planning programs can be more effective in advancing racial equity, beyond current DEI practices. The findings suggest how planning programs can create a culture in which all students can thrive—both in their academic training and subsequently in professional practice.

Current Diversity Landscape of PAB Programs

Enrollment statistics serve as a primary method for tracking and assessing overall progress on DEI efforts. Examining enrollment data for accredited planning programs reveals improvements in the representation of Black, Latinx, and Asian students in the United States (see Table 3.1).[1] Overall, the representation of non-White domestic undergraduates increased from 27% in 2010 to 38% in 2019—an increase of 45%. For master's students, the non-White domestic student population grew by 38% during that time from 22% to 30%. Additionally, the percentage of non-White domestic faculty increased from 18% to 23%, representing an improvement of nearly 30% (see Table 3.1).

There was considerable variation across programs during the study period (2010–2019). Some programs saw vast improvements in representation while others experienced large declines (see Table 3.2). Though 75% and 75.4% of PAB programs increased representation of Latinx undergraduate and master's degree students, respectively, only 33.3% of programs increased enrollment for Black undergraduates and 60.9% for Black master's students. In addition, 50% increased enrollment of Asian undergraduates and 55.1% for master's students. In contrast, only 8.3% expanded their enrollment of American Indian undergraduates and 20.3% increased enrollment for master's students. Similarly, 8.3% of programs increased the representation of Pacific Islander undergraduates

Table 3.1 Percentage and Change in Overall Student Populations

	Black	Latinx	Native	Pacific Islander	Asian	White	International
Undergraduate							
2010	8.7%	10.6%	0.9%	0.2%	6.0%	72.0%	4.7%
2019	10.2%	18.7%	0.5%	0.2%	8.7%	55.9%	5.8%
Relative Change	16.7%	76.2%	−41.3%	−8.7%	44.3%	−22.4%	22.0%
Masters							
2010	7.9%	7.1%	0.8%	0.2%	5.5%	63.9%	11.0%
2019	9.0%	12.2%	0.9%	0.2%	7.3%	52.7%	15.7%
Relative Change	14.7%	72.6%	13.0%	12.5%	31.5%	−17.5%	43.2%
Faculty							
2010	5.3%	4.2%	0.3%	0.0%	8.1%	76.4%	6.4%
2019	6.8%	6.1%	0.4%	0.2%	9.9%	70.4%	3.7%
Relative Change	22.2%	30.2%	18.9%		18.1%	−8.5%	−42.2%

Table displaying the change in undergraduate, masters, and faculty composition for PAB-accredited programs between 2010 and 2019. This table offers a comparison across racial categories and international populations.

Source: Planning Accreditation Board (PAB)—The Annual Report Online Database (AROD), 2010–2019

Table 3.2 Range of Population Percentages and Changes Across Schools

	Black	Latinx	Native	Pacific Islander	Asian	White	International
Undergraduate							
Max	11.6%	54.4%	1.2%	0.5%	8.1%	21.9%	8.9%
Min	−10.8%	−6.0%	−5.3%	−1.4%	−8.2%	−44.9%	−6.5%
Positive Change	33.3%	75.0%	8.3%	8.3%	50.0%	33.3%	41.7%
Masters							
Max	16.4%	25.8%	11.0%	3.3%	11.4%	34.1%	52.1%
Min	−26.4%	−18.3%	−3.7%	−3.2%	−11.5%	−96.4%	−76.5%
Positive Change	60.9%	75.4%	20.3%	5.8%	55.1%	27.5%	74.3%

Table displaying the variation in population changes across PAB-accredited programs. This table shows the maximum and minimum change observed as well as the percentage of programs that increased enrollment in specific racial categories and international populations.

Source: Planning Accreditation Board (PAB)—The Annual Report Online Database (AROD), 2010–2019

and 5.8% for master's students. For international students, 41.7% of programs exhibited increased enrollment for undergraduates, and 74.3% saw increased enrollment for master's students.

Overall, PAB-accredited programs saw a reduction in enrollment totals during the 2010–2019 period. The only groups to see an increase in absolute numbers were undergraduate and master's Latinx students and Asian undergraduates. For Black, American Indian, and Pacific Islander students, overall enrollment numbers decreased during the study period, even though for some programs their representation increased. These data suggest there may be wide-ranging DEI commitments and strategies at work across PAB-accredited programs. Variation in progress toward PAB's enrollment goals around equity and diversity raises potential concerns. First, we question whether DEI language has been co-opted and whether plans and statements are being used to demonstrate concern after particular events without ensuring meaningful incorporation of the expressed values within the institution. Second, we question whether PAB schools are devoting sufficient resources and attention toward these issues.

Enrollment statistics only tell part of the story. It's also important to explore interventions that move beyond diversity representation and advance racial equity more holistically across the planning field. Planning programs play a crucial role in training students to serve as leaders at multiple levels. These students should be equipped to serve all humanity. In the planning context, this includes serving local residents, providing education to the larger community, and serving as an intermediary between interest groups. A wide variety of DEI strategies are necessary to uphold this responsibility and redress planning's contribution to past harm and—in the long run—influence schools' ability to recruit and retain students (García et al., 2021).

DEI Practices in PAB-Accredited Programs

To understand current strategies and practices at PAB-accredited programs,[2] we compiled a repository of DEI statements and plans produced by US higher education institutions that had a PAB-accredited program in 2020. While we didn't contact programs individually, we searched extensively for materials mentioning diversity, equity, or inclusion by reviewing institutional websites. We separated statements into two types: (1) general alignment with DEI values and (2) acknowledgement of the need for widespread change and commitment to action. We then catalogued those planning programs with specific DEI plans or strategic plans that included significant consideration of DEI for further qualitative analysis.

Of the 80 higher-education institutions that had a PAB-accredited program in the United States in 2020, 69% had a DEI statement, and 40% had a statement with a commitment to deeper action (see Table 3.3). Only 31% of planning programs had a specific DEI plan or detailed DEI section in their strategic plan. We found mixed results comparing PAB schools with DEI plans to those without but have chosen not to present those results due to data limitations and wide variation between schools with plans. Few schools had plans before 2016, which made it difficult to examine the variation between schools in a meaningful way. Additionally, the recent adoption of these plans limited our ability to observe their effectiveness over time—especially since there was a downward trajectory in enrollment numbers during the study period.

The rest of this chapter summarizes findings from a content analysis of the 25 DEI plans that are publicly available,[3] guided by the theoretical thematic approach (Braun & Clarke, 2006). We focused on three themes that emerged in the analysis: recruitment, DEI organizational typology, and student retention. To begin, we undertook an extensive literature review examining diversity in planning education, which explicitly included recruitment, retention, and belonging. From this literature review, we developed a code list (used as the following subheadings) to understand the degree to which best practices were being incorporated within PAB programs' DEI plans.

Recruitment

A literature review of recruitment strategies used to reach DEI objectives revealed seven components: (1) enrollment targets, (2) strategic partnerships, (3) pipeline programs, (4) faculty, (5) admissions, (6) funding, and (7) outreach. Each of these is discussed in more detail later. With an emphasis on racial equity, we highlight key practices for increasing representation and strengthening commitment to DEI. These practices include expanding exposure to the field and access to planning programs as well as ensuring underrepresented students have the resources needed to make higher education a reality.

Enrollment Targets

To improve enrollment numbers of underrepresented groups, planning programs must identify who they are trying to target and set goals to help guide them toward better outcomes. By setting clear metrics, schools can track their progress, build specific strategies to support these goals, and hold themselves accountable over the long run (Cegler, 2012; Dumas-Hines et al., 2001; Quarterman, 2008).

Table 3.3 DEI Statement and Plans

	PAB-Accredited Programs	
	N	%
DEI Statement		
No	25	31.3%
Yes	55	68.8%
With Commitments	32	40.0%
Without Commitments	23	28.8%
DEI Plan	25	31.3%
Total	80	

Table displaying the number and percentage of PAB-accredited programs with and without DEI statements and plans. Statements are categorized by those making specific commitments to DEI and those that more generally speak to DEI values without making commitments to action.

Enrollment goals was the most common theme related to recruitment in the DEI plans, occurring in 16 of 25 plans. Practices ranged from attaching goals to the demographics of their geographic region to broader, less-defined goals of achieving greater diversity. However, state restrictions on what is considered diversity can limit planning programs' capabilities for targeted recruitment.

For example, the planning program at Florida Atlantic University defines its DEI efforts as follows:

> Encourage recruitment of individuals who need financial assistance; Increase international student recruitment; Enroll students who reflect the State of Florida's gender balance . . . developed in the context of the State of Florida Executive Order Number 99–281, which prohibits . . . the use of racial or gender set-asides, preferences or quotas in admissions.
> *(Florida Atlantic University, 2009, p. 12)*

Queerness, disability, and immigration status were only mentioned in a handful of documents. This points to the need for more holistic thinking around how we create an environment where all identity groups are welcomed, respected, and heard (Jackson et al., 2020).

Strategic Partnerships and Pipeline Programs

As others have written, increasing exposure to the profession is crucial to the recruitment of a more diverse student body (Arefi & Ghaffari, 2020; Palazzo et al., 2021). Two ways this may be accomplished is through pipeline programs for high school and undergraduate students as well as targeted partnerships with trusted institutions for outreach assistance. Pipeline programs typically consist of summer intensives allowing potential students to engage with professionals, learn core concepts, and understand how planning shapes the world around us (Baber et al., 2010; Murray et al., 2016).

Pipeline programs appeared in seven of the plans, which discussed summer programs that brought high school students onto campus or pathway programs that incorporate planning topics into high school curriculum. Additionally, six planning programs committed to working with cultural and identity-based institutions to increase representation. This included historically Black colleges and universities (HBCUs), Tribal colleges and universities (TCUs), community colleges, and vocational programs. Schools discussed attending events, asking for assistance in identifying interested students, and using alumni networks to share information about their programs. These institutions help schools reach out to underrepresented groups and build bridges into different communities. Through more inclusive outreach and strategic partnerships with trusted groups, planning programs can recruit students with a wider spectrum of experience and expertise (Cegler, 2012; Dumas-Hines et al., 2001; Quarterman, 2008). For example, the University of Michigan pairs their pipeline programs, ArcPrep and ArcStart, with guaranteed undergraduate admission with the intent to

> continue to develop strategic partnerships with regional institutions and the Equity in Architectural Education Consortium for long term sustainability of ArcPrep as a pathways program to diversify the architecture field . . . 100% of students who went through ArcPrep and ArcStart are accepted to UM
> *(University of Michigan, 2020, p. 15)*

Faculty and Admissions

Faculty are integral to recruitment and retention objectives because they have the most direct interaction with students (Mosholder et al., 2016; Quarterman, 2008). Faculty from diverse backgrounds are especially needed to bring new perspectives and skills into university spaces.

Additionally, faculty training around anti-racism and interpersonal skills are essential to undo discriminatory practices both at the university and in the real world (García & Jackson, 2021; Jackson et al., 2020). In our review, ten plans recognized the importance of faculty and made an explicit connection to their role in recruitment efforts. The University of Pennsylvania discussed inviting diverse alumni and local practitioners into active roles of instruction and recruitment in the program.

Ultimately, robust cultural shifts require everyone in the program working together from the application phase to degree completion. If programs fully internalize the ways structural racism influences access to educational and professional opportunities, then they must reflect this in their admission policies. Schools may collaborate with admissions to set new standards of acceptance that value experience and recognize institutional hurdles students from diverse backgrounds face. The adjustment of these standards varies but may include getting rid of the requirement for standardized testing like the SAT or GRE, identifying local high schools and pipeline programs for guaranteed admissions, and placing greater emphasis on extracurricular activities, life experience, and non-cognitive skills. While only three planning programs discussed working with admissions to accept a more diverse student body, we believe this to be crucial to addressing the impacts of structural racism.

Funding and Outreach

It's essential to support students with funding, allowing them to focus on their studies and allocate resources for the services they need to succeed. The price of higher education is a formidable hurdle for many populations given wealth inequities in the United States. Improving the number of scholarships and the percentage of tuition those scholarships cover is key to making planning programs a realistic option for students from diverse backgrounds (Murray et al., 2016; Quarterman, 2008). The University of Oregon outlines the need for a sustainable revenue stream to keep these programs going through an endowment that covers scholarships and other types of support.

In our review, six planning programs pledged to increase scholarship funding, and only two explicitly mentioned financial resources required to implement other aspects of their plans. Additionally, six programs recognized the need to better communicate availability of these resources and their commitment to DEI values. Schools recognized their websites were important access points for students seeking information on the program's commitment to DEI. Some also mentioned using their websites for transparency and accountability to their goals. For example, the University of Washington used a multi-pronged system for recruitment and outreach by incorporating DEI into their outreach materials, engaging students in conversations with BIPOC (Black, Indigenous, and People of Color) alumni, including their diversity statement in online and print materials, and adjusting strategies based on data from applications, enrollment, and retention.

DEI Organizational Typology

Organizational structures are the blueprints for an institution's internal pattern of relationships, authority, and communication (Thompson, 1967), with deep implications for the effectiveness and longevity of DEI efforts. Each planning program has an internal structure that leverages the formation of an operating unit that not only complements the existing structure but also holds the capacity to meet the DEI needs of the program within its day-to-day functions. Our study found that planning programs either had an existing entity to operationalize DEI efforts within their programs, or they developed a new internal body to implement their DEI plans. Specifically, three general DEI organizational typologies emerged: (1) organizational structuring, (2) staff position, and (3) committees.

Organizational Structuring

Organizational structuring supports DEI implementation through institutionalizing related policies throughout a planning program. By adopting a new organizational structure, program leadership can more easily influence the program, classroom, and individual levels (Guo & Jamal, 2007). We found that many programs incorporated DEI initiatives into teaching approaches, research, and service activities in their respective communities. Others, like the University of Washington and the University of Utah, opted to create specific systems like an in-house ombudsman reporting system within the program where university resources are offered for students, staff, and faculty. Within this capacity, this system can serve as a feedback loop on racial discrimination incidents and can potentially refer individuals to the university ombudsman if needed.

Staff Positions

Dedicated staff positions are another strategy to ensure prioritization of DEI efforts, such as diversity manager, graduate diversity officer, or academic diversity officer (ADO). ADOs can be extremely helpful to update and implement DEI policies, as the work can be centralized through their office, and they can have direct involvement with students. For example, the planning program at the University of Washington strategized to create a diversity staff position to "support the department's work in diversity, equity, and inclusion," by "explor[ing] options and funding sources" (University of Washington, 2018, p. 7). While creating a diversity staff position is an excellent way to institutionalize DEI efforts, it is important to recognize the need for sustained funding for the position to maximize the impact of DEI initiatives.

Committees

Forming a DEI committee was the most common approach and is the third typology that emerged from our analysis. Diversity committees comprise a combination of students, faculty, and staff tasked with designing and implementing DEI strategies within their programs. In the plans reviewed, diversity committees overwhelmingly were involved in creating and updating DEI plans and served in an advisory role to planning program chairs on diversity matters. Implementation roles were equally varied, ranging from curriculum structure and syllabus review to advertising ongoing research and service work. Planning programs' DEI committees were also responsible for holding regular meetings with program members and providing regular progress reports.

Student Services

Student services comprise a range of strategies aimed at enhancing the academic experience and supporting students as they embark on their careers. The student-services strategies that emerged in this review of DEI plans align with findings from a survey of graduate program administrators, which found that dedicated retention efforts—such as mentoring and an inclusive learning environment—are critical for student retention (Quarterman, 2008). Approaches for improving the student experience include enhancing program accessibility, creating an academic environment that's welcoming for all students, and facilitating career growth and development.

Program Accessibility

Four programs addressed their programs' accessibility as an impediment to DEI by including strategies to support the matriculation of non-traditional students (e.g., students who work full time or are caretakers). Actions identified included offering evening and online courses, allowing students to begin the program during the summer semester, making class absence policies more flexible to support students with professional or family obligations, offering remote technology access and software tutorials, and providing computer equipment and Internet access to students facing financial hardship.

DEI-Friendly Environment

Programs can foster a welcoming environment by focusing on physical spaces that are accommodating to a diverse range of people and creating an inclusive program culture (Jackson et al., 2020). A few plans identified strategies to transform their program's physical setting with DEI-friendly upgrades. These strategies included gender-neutral bathrooms, wayfinding signage to improve navigation to regularly used spaces, and wellness spaces for prayer, reflection, meditation, and breastfeeding. The University of Virginia's plan includes an "allies list" with the office locations and email addresses of faculty members who serve as a contact for students from underrepresented groups. Students are encouraged to discuss issues or problems with these faculty allies that they may not feel comfortable sharing with other instructors or advisors.

More plans gave thought to the overarching program culture. While some plans use general language about cultivating inclusive or welcoming environments, other programs offered specific concepts. For example, the planning program at Portland State University seeks to create an environment that "supports students in bringing full intersectional identities to class" (Portland State University, 2018, p. 2). The University of Texas at Austin (2016) program's plan calls for a "climate of inclusion, support, and respect for difference across all types of human diversity" (p. 5).

Another aspect of culture is a sense of belonging. The plans reviewed called for both strategies related to programming and support groups for students and faculty to help cultivate a DEI-friendly academic environment. Programming can serve to support underrepresented groups and reinforce a welcoming culture. Examples found in the plans include cultural competency training during student orientation and offering events customized for specific populations (e.g., first-generation students, etc.). Providing support to DEI-focused organizations is another approach to cultivating a more inclusive planning program culture. Examples found in the plans include creating affinity groups for underrepresented faculty, students, and staff and supporting student groups focused on social justice and diversity.

Career Growth and Development

Several programs emphasize the importance of mentoring in supporting individuals while students and also as they establish careers in planning. In the DEI plans, various programs call for pairing students, particularly from underrepresented backgrounds, with faculty, peer, or alumni mentors to receive ongoing support and guidance as they progress through the program and pursue opportunities for career development and employment. Though few plans explicitly mentioned the importance of mentors reflecting students' identity, Jackson et al. (2020) suggests this reflection is critical. The University of Oregon and the University of Michigan pay students to serve as mentors, underscoring the value and effort of successful mentoring.

In addition, multiple programs facilitate students' career growth and development by identifying opportunities for planning internships, service learning in the local community, and career development programming (e.g., career panels, skills workshops, etc.). Many of these opportunities can also benefit the career development of alumni—ultimately, cultivating a strong professional network among faculty, students, and program graduates that can help strengthen a program's reputation.

Moving Toward Racial Equity

Vernā Myers, a diversity and inclusion expert, said, "Diversity is being invited to the party. Inclusion is being asked to dance."[4] We extend this analogy with, "And belonging is contributing songs to the playlist." Under the current system, the playlist is centered around Whiteness, creating an atmosphere where not everyone may feel welcome. Student activism occurs when "musical tastes" are not being met and are signals to university administration that the playlist needs modification.

Research shows that achieving diverse representation without systemic and systematic solutions perpetuates the pitfalls of DEI work (Byrd, 2021; Horowitz et al., 2019). Creating space for diverse representation in academic settings without a culture of belonging leaves students whose identities are historically affected by oppression susceptible to continued discrimination and other racialized trauma. Without a more transformative, belonging-oriented cultural change among students, faculty, and staff, DEI efforts run the risk of producing results that are the opposite of its intended goals.

The concept of belonging extends to layers of experience and requires resources that construct, claim, justify, or resist forms of socio-spatial inclusion and exclusion (Antonsich, 2010). Since Whiteness has historically been centered within planning education and practice, the spaces where academic training occurs inherently create educational environments where Whiteness is the predominant socio-structural element—which inhibits a sense of belonging by those who are non-White. Without turning a critical eye to a White-centered framework, the complex challenge of fostering a sense of belonging within planning education is undermined.

Any recommendations for improved DEI efforts must cultivate a sense of belonging through a holistic cultural shift that includes participation and power sharing between students, staff, faculty, and administration. Together, programming, training, and student services foster a sense of connection across the program and help create a culture where students feel they are valued and that they belong. This occurs not only through recruitment strategies, but also by focusing on the planning program culture, which can influence student retention (García et al., 2021). Fostering a sense of belonging is based on the needs and preferences of students being included within an academic setting. Higher education literature suggests that student activism is partly a byproduct of unmet student needs (Fisher, 2018). Therefore, student activism has more to contribute toward pushing vital DEI initiatives to move beyond representational diversity and toward greater racial equity.

To create a belonging-oriented cultural change in planning education, we recommend that institutions—not only schools and colleges, but also the PAB and the American Planning Association (APA)—seriously assess their roles in engaging in DEI practices. PAB and APA can encourage a sense of belonging in programs and the profession. Both can strengthen and clarify their definitions of diversity, provide an up-to-date repository of DEI-related materials, and develop policies and processes that cultivate belonging-oriented environments.

Additionally, the PAB has potentially the greatest influence in restructuring planning-education norms given its responsibility to accredit professional planning programs. Requiring programs to establish a diversity strategic plan with some guiding frameworks can provide more uniformity in how diversity plans are constructed and establish recordkeeping for previous iterations of diversity plans that could be made publicly accessible. The PAB could also help in these efforts by gathering and providing more detailed information in published student and faculty diversity statistics. There are many complexities to individual identities that deserve to be considered when developing diversity strategies. Though the current categories found in PAB enrollment data are paramount to studies like this one, including more aspects of diversity within reporting requirements is needed to foster belonging for more people. For example, Portland State University's (2018) concept of diversity includes not only race/ethnicity, but also language, sexual orientation, disability, and class,

Table 3.4 Planning Programs' Best Practices

Recommendation	Explanation	Example
Revisit their definitions of diversity.	If definitions remain abstract, then creating a culture of belonging will remain elusive. As we and others have shown, creating concrete definitions is necessary to strategize and implement plans to achieve meaningful diversity initiatives.	Portland State University (p. 2), New York University (pp. 2–3)
Publicly archive DEI materials on program webpages.	Making DEI materials accessible (e.g., past plans, performance/progress reports, etc.) communicate commitment to DEI and document the evolution of DEI efforts.	University of Maryland (n.p.)
Secure sustainable funding for a diversity staff position.	Diversity staff positions need sustainable funding sources to ensure that the roles have longevity to implement DEI strategies over time.	University of Washington (p. 11)
Develop a program feedback loop for students' input.	Serves as a mechanism to allow students to provide their input regarding their needs, concerns, and opinions regarding the program.	University of Utah (p. 6), University of Washington (p. 6)
Develop pipeline and pathway programs.	Partnerships with HBCUs, TCUs, community colleges, and high schools for outreach and recruitment as well as immersion programs.	University of Virginia (p. 27), Jackson State University (p. 8)
Establish Holistic Admissions Standards	Adjust standards to value experience and recognize institutional inequities. Provide guaranteed acceptance for pipeline students and remove standardized testing requirements.	University of Michigan (p. 15), Portland State University (p. 1)
Stabilize Scholarship Funding and Increase Access	Build sustainable funding sources for scholarships and summer internship support. Improve access to funding for under-represented students, connect them to resources directly, and recognize the unique cost obstacles they face.	University of Oregon (p. 22), Florida Atlantic University (p. 12)
Make the planning program more accessible to non-traditional students.	Identify strategies to make the program more accommodating to students from diverse backgrounds and circumstances (e.g., offer evening courses for working professionals, etc.).	Ohio State University (p. 10), Morgan State University (p. 3)
Offer DEI programming to meet the program's unique needs.	Programming helps to cultivate a culture of belonging. Identify which strategies (e.g., tailored events, affinity groups, etc.) can address the particular needs of DEI students and create an inclusive and welcoming environment.	University of Michigan (pg. 49), Ohio State University (pg. 10)
Provide formal mentoring and career development services to support student retention and early-career success.	Mentoring from faculty, student peers, and alumni can support students throughout their time in the program. Career development services help students navigate their planning careers.	University of Virginia (pg. 23), Jackson State University (pg. 16)

Table displaying recommendations, explanations, and examples of best practices for DEI strategies referencing specific program plans.

emphasizing diverse cultural histories and identities. Similarly, the University of Washington's plan has an expanded definition of diversity:

> Dimensions of difference embrace physical, cultural, intellectual, and economic aspects, and may specifically include (and are not limited to): race, ethnicity, age, nationality, sexual orientation, gender identity, religion, language, (dis)ability, educational background, veteran status, socioeconomic status, immigration status, marital status, parental status, viewpoints and ideas (politics), skills and specialization, personality, learning styles, values, geographical area, life experience, or professional experience.
>
> *(University of Washington, 2018, p. 2)*

Although the PAB can play an important leadership role, ultimately each program is responsible for achieving racial equity through belonging-oriented actions. However, it is important to remember that each program's approach may differ because of context. Regardless, programs should engage affected students in developing DEI strategies to address their own unique needs and challenges. Based on our analysis, we identify current practices that move toward integrating belonging in DEI approaches. Table 3.4 includes recommendations for advancing DEI and fostering a culture of belonging that individual planning schools can use as a guiding framework to build their own contextual plan.

Call to Action

In this chapter, we provided an overview of DEI efforts at PAB-accredited planning programs. We found that programs vary widely in their commitment to DEI. We also note variation across plans as to how schools are thinking about recruitment efforts. Programs should move beyond merely inviting diversity through a focus on enrollment statistics and instead take a more expanded approach to foster belonging both in planning programs and the broader profession.

Tomes of scholarship have shown universities and planning programs how to achieve greater diversity. Yet, our study shows that these interventions are only being applied sporadically and in limited ways across institutions. It is certainly true that schools have specific, local knowledge of the strategies that will be most effective and best serve their students, and these should be prioritized. However, our intent is to bring greater attention to the multitude of practices available in hopes of more widespread adoption and holistic development of DEI. We recommend creating a sense of belonging, defining diversity more holistically, and centering student activism as critical interventions for achieving racial equity. This is not to say that all schools need to be the same or have the same content in their plans, but that all students deserve a baseline of safe and equitable experiences regardless of where they choose to pursue their planning education.

Notes

1. We use PAB designations for racial categories and condense naming for clarity. Per this usage, American Indian includes American Indian or Alaskan Native; additionally, Pacific Islander includes Native Hawaiian or other Pacific Islanders. The remainder of the racial categories are written as found in the PAB database. While there is overlap between these racial categories and international students, international students are characterized as a distinct group and have been included for comparative purposes. For more information specific to international students see Lee et al. (2020).
2. For this chapter, we define programs as schools and departments that offer accredited planning degrees (either bachelors, masters, or both).
3. We have created a repository of the PAB-accredited schools' DEI plans or strategic plans with significant focus on DEI. You can access these plans here: https://tinyurl.com/3h4zthz2.
4. See www.vernamyers.com

References

Antonsich, M. (2010). Searching for belonging—An analytical framework. *Geography Compass*, *4*(6), 644–659. https://doi.org/10.1111/j.1749-8198.2009.00317.x

Arefi, M., & Ghaffari, N. (2020). Five episodes of urban discovery as a student recruitment strategy in planning. *Journal of Planning Education and Research*. https://doi.org/10.1177/0739456x20903362

Baber, L. D., Pifer, M. J., Colbeck, C., & Furman, T. (2010). Increasing diversity in the geosciences: Recruitment programs and student self-efficacy. *Journal of Geoscience Education*, *58*(1), 32–42. https://doi.org/10.5408/1.3544292

Braun, V., & Clarke, V. (2006). Using thematic analysis in psychology. *Qualitative Research in Psychology*, *3*(2), 77–101. https://doi.org/10.1191/1478088706qp063oa

Byrd, C. W. (2021). *Behind the diversity numbers achieving racial equity on campus*. Harvard Education Press.

Cegler, T. D. (2012). Targeted recruitment of GLBT students by colleges and universities. *Journal of College Admission*, *215*, 18–23.

Dumas-Hines, F. A., Cochran, L. L., & Williams, E. U. (2001). Promoting diversity: Recommendations for recruitment and retention of minorities in higher education. *College Student Journal*, *35*(3), 433–442.

Fisher, M. T. (2018). Still fighting the good fight: An analysis of student activism and institutional response. *Public Relations Review*, *44*(1), 22–27. https://doi.org/10.1016/j.pubrev.2017.11.005

Florida Atlantic University. (2019). *Diversity and inclusion plan*. Florida Atlantic University.

García, I., & Jackson, A. (2021). Enhancing the role of government, non-profits, universities, and resident associations as valuable community resources to advance equity, access, diversity, and inclusion. *Societies*, *11*(2), 33. https://doi.org/10.3390/soc11020033

García, I., Jackson, A., Harwood, S. A., Greenlee, A. J., Lee, C. A., & Chrisinger, B. (2021). "Like a fish out of water" the experience of African American and Latinx planning students. *Journal of the American Planning Association*, *87*(1), 108–122. https://doi.org/10.1080/01944363.2020.1777184

Goetz, E. G., Williams, R. A., & Damiano, A. (2020). Whiteness and urban planning. *Journal of the American Planning Association*, *86*(2), 142–156. https://doi.org/10.1080/01944363.2019.1693907

Guo, S., & Jamal, Z. (2007). Nurturing cultural diversity in higher education: A critical review of selected models. *Canadian Journal of Higher Education*, *37*(3), 27–49. https://doi.org/10.47678/cjhe.v37i3.529

Horowitz, J., Brown, A., & Cox, K. (2019). Race in America 2019. *Pew Research Center*.

Jackson, A., García, I., Chrisinger, B., Greenlee, A., Lee, C. A., & Yerna, A. (2020). *Diversity climate survey—moving from aspiration to action: Reorienting planners values towards equity, diversity, and inclusion*. American Planning Association and Association of Collegiate Schools of Planners—Planners of Color Interest Group.

Lee, C. A., Chrisinger, B., Greenlee, A. J., García Zambrana, I., & Jackson, A. (2020). Beyond recruitment: Comparing experiences of climate and diversity between international students and domestic students of color in US urban planning programs. *Journal of Planning Education and Research*. https://doi.org/10.1177/0739456x20902241

Mosholder, R. S., Waite, B., Larsen, C. A., & Goslin, C. (2016). Promoting native American college student recruitment & retention in higher education. *Multicultural Education*, *23*, 27–36.

Murray, T. A., Pole, D. C., Ciarlo, E. M., & Holmes, S. (2016). A nursing workforce diversity project: Strategies for recruitment, retention, graduation, and NCLEX-RN success. *Nursing Education Perspectives*, *37*(3), 138–143. https://doi.org/10.5480/14-1480

Palazzo, D., Hollstein, L., & Diko, S. K. (2021). Urban planning as a career preference for students: Efforts to improve awareness about the profession. *Planning Practice & Research*, *36*(2), 174–192. https://doi.org/10.1080/02697459.2020.1782056

Planning Accreditation Board: Diversity, Equity & Inclusion. (2021). Retrieved April 26, 2021, from www.planningaccreditationboard.org/index.php?id=314

Portland State University. (2018). *Proposed TSUSP (Toulan school of urban studies and planning) strategies to advance diversity, equity, and inclusion*. Portland State University.

Quarterman, J. (2008). An assessment of barriers and strategies for recruitment and retention of a diverse graduate student population. *College Student Journal*, *42*(4), 947–967.

Thompson, J. D. (1967). *Organizations in action: Social science bases of administrative theory*. McGraw-Hill. https://doi.org/10.4324/9781315125930

University of Michigan. (2020). *Taubman college diversity, equity, and inclusion strategic plan*. Year 5, 2020–2021.

University of Texas at Austin. (2016). *2015–2016 strategic plan*. University of Texas at Austin.

University of Washington. (2018). *UDP (Urban design and planning) diversity plan*. University of Washington.

4
MORE THAN A JOB

Building Opportunities for Undergraduate Professional Development in a Minority Serving Institution

Laura Keyes, Lauren Ames Fischer, and Abraham David Benavides

The professional development of planning students requires a balance of theory and practice as well as opportunities to gain direct exposure to the field through coursework and extracurricular activities. Scholars find that planning educators tend to place a stronger emphasis on knowledge development than on developing skills for entry-level planning positions (Greenlee et al., 2015). Students must master academic content that may then be complemented with professional skill development. For accredited planning programs in the United States, the Planning Accreditation Board (PAB) recommends practice-oriented learning opportunities as a theory-to-practice learning objective (Baldwin & Rosier, 2016). The American Planning Association (APA) also prescribes certain knowledge, skills, and abilities to complement the academic knowledge of a future professional.[1] In sum, undergraduate planning education requires a balance of varying sources of faculty and professional input.

Developing planning skills through practice-based approaches can help students appreciate planning theory and learn to frame real-world problems while also forming their own identities as planners (Olesen, 2018). The planning profession also has an expectation that students will attain some level of real-world planning experience before they enter the job market (Baldwin & Rosier, 2016). Scholarship finds that potential employers give high ranking to the importance of advanced oral and written competencies for entry level planners that include report writing and public speaking experiences (Edwards & Bates, 2011). Other equally important practice-oriented competencies include engagement skills related to community development and complex social issues (Baldwin & Rosier, 2016), as well as problem-solving skills illustrating discernment of collected data (Pojani et al., 2018). Generally speaking, students have an expectation that their education will make them employable.

Practitioner-oriented learning considers the direct involvement of practitioners in the student's education (Fischler, 2012), providing opportunities to explore and prepare for professional planning jobs (Dalton, 2007). Baldwin and Rosier (2016) recommend a continuum of exposure that advances with increased student confidence. Engagement with practitioners inside and outside of the classroom must be done strategically with a focus on illustrating a range of diverse experiences and exposure to the professional planning community. The interactions with professional planners provide students with insights into relevant knowledge as well as connecting students with the right people. For underrepresented students, exposure to the continuum of practice is important to expand knowledge of planning and professional opportunities in the field. Developing professional skills in undergraduate education can also help underrepresented students be aware of, and become competitive for, funded graduate programs, which play an important role in diversifying

DOI: 10.4324/9781003254003-6

the profession (Joint Task Force of American Planning Association, American Institute of Certified Planners, and Association of Collegiate Schools of Planning, 2016). Through the design of these experiences, a culturally competent urban policy and planning program should reflect its commitment to diversity and representation.

In this chapter, we discuss the importance of inviting diverse practitioners and stakeholders into the classroom, and we profile the pedagogical strategy used by faculty at an institution with many students who are first generation (FGCS)[2] and identify as belonging to a racial or ethnic minority group. After reviewing the relevant literature on the role of professional networking and practice-oriented education and their intersections with diversity, we provide an overview of how faculty have incorporated different elements into an undergraduate planning degree program and curriculum. Professional networking and practice-oriented education benefit all students. At the departmental level, we explore how a continuum of professional exposure through the use of diverse speakers, materials, and experiences can communicate to FGCS and minority students that they are welcome and represented in a field that is not as diverse as the communities it serves. Retention efforts to create pathways for diverse students to engage in the profession during their academic journeys enhance opportunities to practice the profession after graduation. We then present results of a survey of planning students to understand how their perspectives on the value of networking and professional development align with academic assessments. We conclude the chapter with a discussion of the institutional impediments that unintentionally limit opportunities to diversify the planning profession and insights on how to augment student recruitment efforts in response.

Practice-Oriented Learning: Context and Strategies

A range of practice-based and experiential learning approaches are helpful for increasing student exposure to the planning profession. A continuum of exposure—building blocks of experiences to facilitate a sequence of learning—provides important reinforcement and opportunities for professional socialization throughout a student's academic experience (Long, 2012). Rather than saving professional networking and engagement for upper-level undergraduates searching for post-graduate employment, Baldwin and Rosier (2016) propose a continuum over the four-year undergraduate degree that offers early and ongoing interaction with the professional community. A continuum may start with guest speakers or with students shadowing a practitioner to learn through shared knowledge and experiences. Including practitioners from the field as guest lecturers raises student awareness of the professional dynamics in planning (Guzzetta & Bollens, 2003) and helps build a community of practice for both the academic organization and students (Long, 2012). Students can also benefit directly from access to professionals by establishing interpersonal connections that help them build an employment network for learning about and accessing future employment opportunities.

In a four-year continuum, student exposure to the profession intensifies with progression through course assignments, fieldwork, and an internship, and often culminates in a capstone or urban planning studio partnering with a real-world client. Research with community partners enhances student research skills and the quality of the urban planning educational program (Hart & Wolf, 2006), while the planning studio as a major course requirement creates a platform for experiential learning that provides professional enhancement and skill building (Pojani et al., 2018). Professional participation in planning courses can yield mutual benefits, including employer access to a diverse student recruitment pool and an opportunity for future employers to provide input into the planning curriculum.

To be truly impactful, curricular development and the timing of exposure to the range of practice-oriented approaches must consider student barriers to participating in different learning experiences. Evaluation of student readiness relative to the learning approach safeguards student advancement in interactive experiences with the professional community (Cornell et al., 2013). For instance, initiating student exposure to the profession through guest speakers in the classroom helps students gain confidence through the practice of networking before launching into a planning field-study project that requires them to work closely with a community client. Students may also face equity and access issues such as limitations in available personal transportation to participate in off-campus internships or fieldwork (Barraket et al., 2009). Exposing students to the profession through a range of experiences may help to minimize some obstacles for participation.

Practice-Oriented Learning: Diversity and Inclusion

Practice-oriented pedagogy and learning objectives, if given purposeful attention, can be instrumental to building the cultural competency of students. Cultural competency in higher education requires faculty commitment to cultural understanding in curricular development and classroom support (Kruse et al., 2018). By paying attention to the diversity of guest speakers in the classroom, faculty can foster enhanced connections between students and minority practitioners. Projects can also be structured to encourage students to reflect on their own biases, identifying enhanced opportunities for professional and personal growth (Agyeman & Erickson, 2012). Cultural competency in urban planning programs must also consider the development of student skills and awareness (Agyeman & Erickson, 2012), as well as experience working with individuals of diverse backgrounds to develop a respect for differences (Jackson et al., 2018). Planning students will eventually work in communities with individuals that are different from themselves. The educational journey should foster exploration of issues across a range of social settings, and with respect for a diversity of ideas and experiences. It is necessary for students to learn skills to engage diverse populations and to prioritize the concerns of the most vulnerable populations in planning debates and discourses (APA, 2016). Through service-learning projects, students study complex community problems in the field, helping them to build relationships with community partners and local leaders (Bromley, 2006).

These opportunities are not easily achievable in all educational settings. Institutional barriers may arise. Lowe (2008) found that diverse faculty enhanced learning through community partnerships, but lack of diverse faculty can create barriers to establishing those partnerships. Students of color express a desire for increased exposure to planners of color in their education, but face limitations due to a lack of such perspectives in both the curriculum and classroom preparation to work with different populations in the community (Jackson et al., 2018). Just as positive exposure can lead to improved diversity, similarly, the lack of leadership and role models can inhibit cultural-competency goals.

Pedagogical and Practice-Oriented Approaches to Professional Development

The University of North Texas Urban Policy and Planning (UPOP) curriculum provides students with the fundamental technical skills and substantive knowledge required in the field of urban planning. As a new program launched in the fall term of 2018 with limited faculty (two full-time planning faculty and ten public administration faculty), course design and instructional decisions remain at the discretion of the individual faculty member. A review of syllabi for the major course requirements for the UPOP degree reflects a continuum of student exposure to professional practice that provides professional enhancement activities commensurate with student learning objectives.

Table 4.1 illustrates the practice-oriented learning objectives and pedagogical approaches currently used in the core undergraduate planning curriculum. Guest lecturers visit introductory courses and are used throughout the program. Students in PADM 2120 engage with professionals from the North Central Texas Council of Governments in addition to municipal planners specializing in economic and historic preservation. These students are able to take a field trip to the city of Denton's historic town square for a firsthand examination of planning policies. Classroom interaction with practitioners and local excursions prepare students developmentally for the next level of

Table 4.1 UPOP Courses: Practice-Oriented Learning Objectives and Pedagogical Approaches

Course Name	Practice-Oriented Learning Objective	Pedagogical Approach(es)
PADM 2120 Introduction to Urban and Regional Planning	• Understand the basics of planning • Learn about and leverage tools for planning	• Guest lecturers • Attendance at municipal planning meetings and essay response • Field trip to historic town square • Research project on planning process with oral presentation
PADM 3210 Population and Demographics	• Evaluate various planning interventions related to population change	• Discernment of real-world data • Poster and podcast presentation of findings
PADM 4250 Community Development	• Identify and document community assets for selected community; make policy recommendations	• Guest lecturers • Selection of a real city as their virtual laboratory • Participation in service learning with area nonprofit
PADM 4220 Proposal Writing	• Prepare funding application and proposal for a selected nonprofit agency	• Guest lecturers • Hypothetical grant proposal for nonprofit agency
PADM 4450 Public Policy Analysis	• Apply economic tools to different urban policy areas	• Case studies on urban issues
PADM 4170 Planning Methods	• Conduct analysis using a variety of planning tools through labs and fieldwork	• Guest lecturers • Charrette planning design • Fieldwork participation
PADM 4180 Urban Studio	• Create experiential and constructive learning in active and engaged manner	• Guest lecturers • Planning consultation to community client • Use of ULI Urban Plan[3]

Note: PADM 3220 Land Use and Transportation Planning and PADM 3410 Financial Management of Government not included based on current learning objectives.

learning. In PADM 3210, students present final course projects to a panel of graduate student judges and create podcasts on planning topics to share with the public on a local planning-advocacy website. As students advance to upper level 4000 courses, experiences intensify.

The urban planning studio PADM 4180 is the capstone course for the planning degree program. Students are typically entering the last semester of their degree program, and a core learning objective is the development of work-readiness skills through application of theory to practice. Scholarship suggests that students engage in active participation and collaboration with a community to work on real-world and contemporary issues (Pojani et al., 2018). UNT's Urban Studio course follows this pedagogy and provides an important opportunity to enhance cultural competency by exposing students to communities that are different from their own. The studio includes modules for reflection on assumptions, biases, diversity, and inclusion to understand the importance of building authentic relationships and trust with the communities they serve (Jackson et al., 2018). Learning goals support co-creation of curricular material with students, which empowers them to take responsibility and ownership over their learning and professional development. For example, students in the spring 2021 studio course were expected to invite their own guest speakers to shed light on the issue of affordable housing. Students had to identify, recruit, and host the guest speakers of their choosing; the diversity of speakers enhanced the class discussions, and one student was offered a full-time position from the organization they invited. Studio projects use an experiential approach

More Than a Job

that helps students develop an ethical framework through social interaction with diverse groups and issues (Lo Piccolo & Thomas, 2008) and enhance their cultural competency skills.

Figure 4.1 illustrates the continuum of undergraduate student exposure to professionalism over the four-year degree. Scaffolding student exposure to the field allows students to build knowledge about the profession, learn various strategies through practitioner experience, and gain confidence in their skills before jumping into a client project. There are, however, impediments to implementing the continuum. UNT has a large number of transfer students and uses rolling enrollment. As a result, it is common for students to take courses out of numerical sequence. To ensure flexibility for students, the degree only has a single pre-requisite course, and students who are double majoring or pursuing minors commonly take courses out of numerical sequence. This creates challenges for faculty, who cannot assume that all students have completed activities earlier in the continuum. In response, we have adopted several strategies that provide students with exposure to professional development activities outside the classroom setting.

A core strategy of the UPOP degree is to enhance coursework with extracurricular and professional-development activities, as both a means for supplementing limited course topics and to help students build professional networks to enhance job prospects upon graduation. We profile some of these strategies later.

Faculty Engagement With Professional Associations

The APA is the professional membership organization for the planning profession, and Texas state and regional chapters help connect students to the local planning community. Most state chapters invite planning programs to set up an informational table at conferences, and the department employs an undergraduate coordinator to facilitate these relationships. Faculty membership in professional organizations is important, as faculty often serve as advisors to student presentations and help students learn to navigate a professional conference. Involvement with the APA can also help recruit new guest lecturers into the classroom in addition to providing information about student internships and employment. Faculty have also built close relationships with the Urban Land Institute (ULI) through integration of their Urban Plan curriculum, which asks students to create a development proposal in a constrained scenario. These engagements with professional organizations fulfill the service obligations of planning faculty and provide funding to support faculty and student attendance at state and regional planning conferences.

Student Engagement With Professional Associations

APA and its state chapters offer multiple layers of support for undergraduate planning students, including free student memberships and sponsoring of student planning organizations. UNT's UPOP students set up an American Planning Association Student Organization (APASO) in fall 2019. APASO is open to all UNT students and hosts professional planners to enhance student knowledge on career development and important planning efforts in the field. Led by a diverse

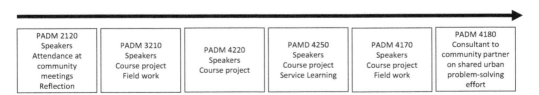

Figure 4.1 UPOP Practice-Oriented Continuum of Professional Exposure

group of students, APASO has purposefully targeted planning professionals who identify as minorities for guest lectures, and organizations that serve minority neighborhoods with volunteer activities. Early professional-development opportunities at the undergraduate level are evolving into leadership opportunities once in the profession. A recent UPOP graduate, representing both first generation and underrepresented students, is now serving on the board of the Midwest Section of the Texas American Planning Association. An underappreciated role of the undergraduate planning program is helping non-planning students become informed and active in community planning.

Student Responses to Professional Development

In fall 2020, we conducted a survey to assess student perspectives on pedagogical strategies related to professional development and networking in UPOP courses. We distributed the survey in four core planning courses and received a total of 76 responses (a 41% response rate). The four-question survey was distributed to students enrolled in two planning-focused courses (PADM 3210 Population and Demographics and PADM 4250 Community Development and Collaboration) and two public policy focused courses (PADM 3410 Financial Management of Government and PADM 4450 Public Policy Analysis) as part of their course evaluation process. The surveys captured perceptions during the university's COVID-19 protocol limiting onsite and offsite events. The substantial number of "No Opinion" and "Disagree" responses to Likert Scale questions reflect limitations for personal contact resulting from the COVID-19 social distancing mandate. Prior to COVID-19, guest speakers were invited to campus for live events. Although the Zoom platform allows students to communicate virtually with professionals, many do not actively take part.

Overall, 65% of students perceived that the UPOP courses prepared them well for a professional career (Figure 4.2). Students enrolled in the urban planning courses were more likely to agree or strongly agree that class activities prepared them for a professional career than those enrolled in the public policy courses.

Our second Likert question showed more ambiguity from students about professional-networking opportunities. Students were asked the extent of opportunities for professional networking presented to them during the courses. A higher concentration of students agreed or strongly agreed that the courses on population demographics and community development (57%) provided more career preparation and networking opportunities than financial management and public policy courses (18%). The analysis of course syllabi (Table 4.1) confirms the specific use of guest speakers, course assignments, fieldwork, and service learning with a community partner in the former courses.

We believe that observed differences across the four courses are, in part, related to faculty discretion and disciplinary training. During the survey period, urban planning courses PADM 3210 and PADM 4250 were taught by instructors trained in urban planning, while the other two public policy courses were taught by instructors with training in public administration. A review of syllabi content in Table 4.1 reflects only the use of case studies as an in-class assignment in the public-policy course and no practice-oriented pedagogical strategies in the financial-management course.

We also asked two open ended questions: (1) What benefits do you receive from applying practical knowledge learned from this class to solving real-world problems? (2) What do you think are the benefits of professional networking as an undergraduate? The findings in Table 4.2 are based on 53 student responses and were analyzed using thematic coding. We identified ten themes in response to the question on practical knowledge and eight themes for the question about professional networking, using two faculty to provide inter-coder reliability.

Most students identified critical analysis and data-driven problem solving as an outcome of applying course knowledge to real-world problems. Some students also drew connections between course material and community action. One student commented, "The benefit of this class . . . is actually being aware of the assets around my community that could help me resolve the issues for me and

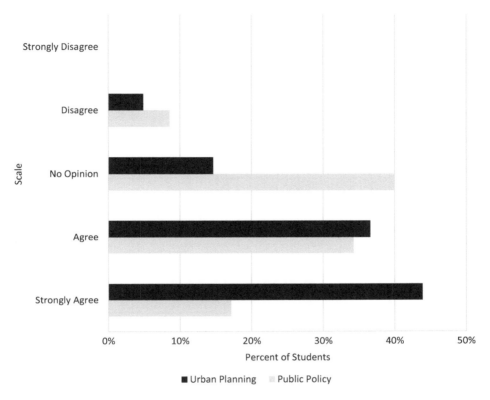

Figure 4.2 Responses on Career Preparation by Course Type

others in need." Another student responded, "Being able to read and interpret data is crucial to urban planning . . . identify the best uses and businesses for new or existing development." Students also perceived professional enhancement and practical application as equally important benefits. For instance, one student commented, "Using Excel is practical. Analyzing data is practical. Creating graphs is practical. The podcast project is practical." Similarly, another student responded, "I can be more informed about relevant things in my government, and I can apply what I have learned regarding economics in minority communities and available resources." Students mentioned how enhanced practical knowledge increased their confidence to make changes in their communities and to pursue a career in urban planning.

A few students also connected knowledge learned in the classroom to enhancing their abilities to be engaged in the community and represent as an informed citizen. As one student noted, "I now have a better understanding of municipal government financially as these decisions and taxes are relevant to my career field in deciding planning projects but also as an informed citizen when it comes to voting and how money is handled." This speaks to students knowing how to hold a government official accountable as a citizen, not just as a professional planner. Findings suggest investment in student development isn't just about training professionals but also educating students to participate in

Table 4.2 Perceptions on Professional Development in the Classroom

What benefits do you receive from applying practical knowledge learned from this class to solving real-world problems?	Total Responses
Skill Building/Data Analytics	5
Critical Analysis/Data Driven Problem Solving	14
Professional Enhancement	8
Practical Application	8
Engagement	1
Knowledge of the Profession	4
Informed Citizen	3
Exposure to the Field	4
Work Ethic	2
Interdisciplinary	4
Total	**53**

What do you think are the benefits of professional networking as an undergraduate?	Total Responses
Active Learning	1
Building Connections	23
Knowledge of the Profession	7
Career Opportunities	14
Professional Enhancement	2
Mentoring	1
Skill Building	4
Limited Access to Networking	2
Total	**54**

the public elements of planning and policy. As a new degree program, UPOP courses tend to serve multiple majors, which increases opportunities to raise awareness about planning among the large first generation and minority student body.

The second part of Table 4.2 highlights 54 perceptions of the benefits of professional networking as an undergraduate. Most students stressed the importance of building connections and career opportunities, a strategy that was reinforced using guest speakers and other practice-oriented learning strategies, even during the pandemic. The use of practice-oriented learning supports professional networking by enabling students to make their own professional contacts and to provide insights on how to be a competitive candidate for various positions.

Surprisingly, many students did not identify knowledge of the profession or mentoring as a major outcome of professional networking. This suggests a need to deepen student engagement with professionals beyond informal interactions at professional conferences, or campus and classroom events. The practice-oriented approaches used in the UPOP degree plan are important, but not required or institutionalized elements of the program's pedagogy. In the state of Texas, all undergraduate syllabi are publicly available to students and serve as an important source of information for students selecting courses. With this information available, students have the opportunity to self-select into courses that integrate professional development into the curriculum.

Lessons Learned

A culturally competent urban policy and planning program should not only foster and respect a diversity of culture, background, ideas, and beliefs; it should also seek out opportunities to bring underrepresented students to the field of planning. The continuum of professionalism presented earlier promotes learning experiences that help expose minority students to the field of urban planning and to diverse planning professionals. UNT's UPOP program uses practice-oriented learning to engage students in real-world experiences and collaborative exercises that give them familiarity with planning methods designed to lift the most vulnerable community voices. One limitation is that our department is not directly responsible for recruitment or enrollment efforts. UNT recruitment and enrollment is managed at the university level by the Office of Admissions. Smaller programs may face similar limitations implementing minority focused recruitment efforts. Strategic priority is given to on-campus events that allow face-to-face discussion about the program and reduce barriers to accessing information. Once the student is enrolled in the UPOP program, our efforts focus on retention by making them feel at home in the program and the profession. To help retain students, we make sure they see themselves represented in the field as they develop necessary skills. Our current UPOP majors mirror the UNT student body relative to racial and ethnic diversity. Planning education programs nationally have struggled to attract and retain minority students. The efforts outlined previously represent a purposeful action by department faculty to reverse this trend. We present our lessons learned from this examination of undergraduate planning education next.

Are Students Making the Right Connections?

An important consideration is whether efforts to introduce students to professionals can help diversify the planning profession, which shows a lack of diversity across race and ethnicity (APA, 2018). Smith (2019) provides suggestions for creating opportunities for equity and diversity in planning education, including creating space to share ideas, paying attention to how invited speakers represent diversity in the practice, and fostering discussion about equity, diversity, and inclusion. When discussing ideas about who to invite to classroom and program-sponsored events, faculty should get students' thoughts on inequities and institutional barriers in the community, then invite speakers with purposeful attention to representativeness—to create environments where students feel comfortable exchanging information and engaging with professionals. The studio course should empower students to create their own capstone experience by reaching out to invite speakers into their network and to have the confidence to take the next step in their development.

Are Extracurricular Networking Activities Benefiting Students?

Similarly, faculty need to consider whether existing networking strategies offered to students, such as attendance at conferences or participation in professional association workshops and events, materialize into substantive benefits for the students. Partnerships with professional associations are important but do not, in and of themselves, address the diversity and representation issues in the field. There are important benefits for student participation in state and local APA chapter conferences and events, many of which focus on diversity and inclusion. Several of our students have secured internships and professionally oriented volunteer opportunities through conference attendance, though we do not track this metric or have data to evaluate whether certain student demographics take advantage of this more than others.

Do Institutional Structures Limit Community Building?

Academic departments may not always be willing to fund faculty membership in professional associations, as the focus of practitioner-based events and conferences typically falls outside the scope of teaching, research, and service for faculty members. Without university support, faculty may be reluctant to engage in partnerships with professional associations because they view it as a distraction from the activities outlined in promotion and tenure guidelines for R1 institutions. To support faculty in building local, professional connections that benefit students, our program employs a full-time undergraduate coordinator that takes the lead on making community contacts and helping new tenure-track faculty build relevant professional networks in the region. This position is currently filled by an AICP-certified planner and has been instrumental in relationship building and professional-networking activities to help faculty incorporate exposure to the field and networking activities into courses.

Can Syllabi Be Used for Marketing and Recruitment?

If practice-oriented learning is central to planning education and a core pedagogical strategy, this should be reflected in the syllabi for major course requirements. Publicly available course syllabi illustrate the program's commitment to the student's professional development over their undergraduate tenure, but also vary by instructor. Syllabi should reflect the urban planning program's commitment to diversity, inclusion, and equity as a policy of the program, but also reflect commitment to representation among its students in its commitment to culturally competent practice-oriented pedagogical approaches.

Conclusion

These insights and lessons learned inform UNT's Urban Policy and Planning degree program's ongoing strategy for addressing student diversity, recruitment, and retention in the coming years. The short-term impact of the UPOP program for diversity and inclusion is evidenced through minority student representation in professional leadership positions. Of the 14 students who graduated in our first cohort in May 2020, five from underrepresented backgrounds received full scholarships to graduate planning and public administration programs. Others are working in planning departments, or advocacy and nonprofit organizations in related areas. In the long term, this program is creating opportunities for underrepresented individuals to engage in the public realm. It's not just about training planners but educating a broader and more diverse group of people to participate in the planning process. Offering a continuum of professional exposure is an important strategy to retain FGCS and minority students. Culturally responsive pedagogical development should pay attention to diversity in the range of professional-development activities to enhance student skills and awareness of issues across a range of social settings. Approaches toward professional development must also help show diverse students they are welcome and represented in the field. The responsibility is on higher education to open the door and invite a broad range of students into the profession.

Notes

1. www.planning.org/choosingplanning/skills/
2. First generation college student (FGCS) is a designation for college students whose parents did not complete a four-year college degree. At the University of North Texas, first generation students comprise 41.5% of the undergraduate student population. https://studentaffairs.unt.edu/first-generation-success-center
3. The Urban Land Institute's Urban Plan is a structured development scenario providing students a simulated hands-on experience in urban development, including site planning, financial feasibility, and community engagement to enhance problem solving. https://dallas-fortworth.uli.org/get-involved/urbanplan-committee/

References

Agyeman, J., & Erickson, J. S. (2012). Culture, recognition, and the negotiation of difference: Some thoughts on cultural competency in planning education. *Journal of Planning Education and Research*, *32*(3), 358–366. https://doi.org/10.1177/0739456X12441213

American Planning Association. (2016). *AICP code of ethics and professional conduct*. Retrieved April 26, 2021, from www.planning.org/ethics/ethicscode/

American Planning Association. (2018). *APA planners salary survey: A portrait of planners*. Retrieved February 12, 2021, from www.planning.org/salary/planner

Baldwin, C., & Rosier, J. (2016). Growing future planners: A framework for integrating experiential learning into tertiary planning programs. *Journal of Planning Education and Research*, 37(1), 43–55. https://doi.org/10.1177/0739456X16634864

Barraket, J., Melville, R., Wright, S., Scott, M., Richardson, S., Carey, G., Thornton, S., & Hodge, P. (2009). *Engaging with learning: Understanding the impact of practice based learning exchange: Final report to Australian learning and teaching council*. Strawberry Hills, New South Wales, Australia. Retrieved July 2, 2022, from https://nova.newcastle.edu.au/vital/access/services/Download/uon:16461/ATTACHMENT01

Bromley, R. (2006). On and off campus: Colleges and universities as local stakeholders. *Planning, Practice and Research*, 21(1), 1–24. https://doi.org/10.1080/02697450600901400

Cornell, R. M., Johnson, C. B., & Schwartz Jr, W. C. (2013). Enhancing student experiential learning with structured interviews. *Journal of Education for Business*, 88(3), 136–146. https://doi.org/10.1080/08832323.2012.659296

Dalton, L. C. (2007). Preparing planners for the breadth of practice: What we need to know depends on whom we ask. *Journal of the American Planning Association*, 73(1), 35–48. https://doi.org/10.1080/01944360708976135

Edwards, M. M., & Bates, L. K. (2011). Planning's core curriculum: Knowledge, practice and implementation. *Journal of Planning Education and Research*, 31(2), 172–183. https://doi.org/10.1177/0739456X11398043

Fischler, R. (2012). Teaching spatial planners: Knowledge, skills, competencies and attitudes—accreditation standards in the US and Canada. In B. Scholl (Ed.), *Higher education in spatial planning: Positions and reflections (HESP)* (pp. 140–148). ETH Press.

Greenlee, A. J., Edwards, M., & Anthony, J. (2015). Planning skills: An examination of supply and local government demand. *Journal of Planning Education and Research*, 35(2), 161–173. https://doi.org/10.1177/0739456X15570321

Guzzetta, J., & Bollens, S. (2003). Urban planners' skills and competencies: Are we different from other professions? Does context matter? Do we evolve? *Journal of Planning Education and Research*, 23(2), 96–108. https://doi.org/10.1177/0739456X03255426

Hart, A., & Wolf, D. (2006). Developing local 'communities of practice' through local community—University partnerships. *Planning Practice and Research*, 21(1), 121–138. https://doi.org/10.1080/02697450600901616

Jackson, A., Garcia-Zambrana, I., Greenlee, A. J., Aujean Lee, C., & Chrisinger, B. (2018). All talk no walk: Student perceptions on integration of diversity and practice in planning programs. *Planning Practice and Research*, 33(5), 574–595. https://doi.org/10.1080/02697459.2018.1548207

Joint Task Force of American Planning Association, American Institute of Certified Planners, and Association of Collegiate Schools of Planning. (2016). *Joint task force on enrollment report*. www.planningaccreditationboard.org/wp-content/uploads/2021/04/2016EnrollmentRpt.pdf

Kruse, S. D., Rakha, S., & Calderone, S. (2018). Developing cultural competency in higher education: An agenda for practice. *Teaching in Higher Education*, 23(6), 733–750. https://doi.org/10.1080/13562517.2017.1414790

Long, J. (2012). State of the studio: Revisiting the potential of studio pedagogy in U.S.-based planning programs. *Journal of Planning Education and Research*, 32, 431–448. https://doi.org/10.1177/0739456X12457685

Lo Piccolo, F., & Thomas, H. (2008). Research ethics in planning: A framework for discussion. *Planning Theory*, 7(1), 7–23. https://doi.org/10.1177/1473095207085663

Lowe, J. S. (2008). A participatory planning approach to enhancing a historical Black University-community partnership: The case of the e-City initiative, planning. *Practice and Research*, 23(4), 549–558. https://doi.org/10.1080/02697450802522897

Olesen, K. (2018). Teaching planning theory as planner roles in urban planning education. *Higher Education Pedagogies*, 3(1), 302–318. https://doi.org/10.1080/23752696.2018.1425098

Pojani, D., Johnson, L., Darchen, S., & Yang, K. (2018). Learning by doing: Employer expectations of planning studio education. *Urban Policy and Research*, 36(1), 11–19. https://doi.org/10.1080/08111146.2016.1221814

Smith, K. (2019). *More and better: Increasing diversity, equity, and inclusion in planning*. PAS Memo, American Planning Association. Retrieved February 12, 2021, from https://planning-org-uploaded-media.s3.amazonaws.com/publication/download_pdf/PASMEMO-2019-05-06.pdf

5
DECONSTRUCTING DIVERSITY IN URBAN PLANNING EDUCATION IN ITALY

Implications for the Future of a "Practical Knowledge"

Bertrando Bonfantini and Carolina Pacchi

Italian planning education, rooted in architecture, has been traditionally characterized by a focus on spatial and morphological dimensions on one side, and on the regulatory aspects of the planning process on the other. The ability to reach out to a global audience of students has thus been limited because regulatory and administrative aspects tend to be deeply country- or context-specific. Against this background, the following chapter critically discusses the experience of the Master of Urban Planning and Policy Design (UPPD) at Politecnico di Milano and how it is widening its scope and diversifying its audience by focusing on emerging urban issues on a European and global scale.

Working with increasingly diverse students—in terms of geographical origin, educational background, and culture—it appears that global outreach is related to the ability to identify and tackle emerging urban challenges (climate change, increasing spatial inequalities, shifting work and housing patterns, etc.) even more than the capacity to train professionals for specific job markets (local, regional, etc.). Moreover, a distinguishing feature of this path has been the capacity to move back and forth between experimental activities on the ground—working with local contexts and communities—and wider policy discourses with an international dimension, all of which characterize studio undertakings. In order to propose and reflect on possible working directions, this chapter highlights teaching strategies, program features, and student–teacher interfaces and critically discusses some recurring pitfalls in this evolution toward a diversity-embracing program.

Diversity in Italian Higher Education and Beyond

In general, few concepts are as fuzzy and contentious as diversity. Reflections and literature on diversity in planning education are still scant, even if they're gaining momentum, in particular in North America (Goonewardena et al., 2004; Sweet & Etienne, 2011; Sen et al., 2017; Greenlee et al., 2018) and in the United Kingdom (Campion & Clark, 2021). If we define diversity in education as the objective to reflect the composition of a population in a smaller unit—be it the university, faculty, students, and so on (Goonewardena et al., 2004; Sweet & Etienne, 2011)—we should first define and qualify which is the reference population, a particularly hard task in the face of global outreach. What is the reference population for planning courses that are addressed to a global audience? Is it the population of the city or region in which the university is located, the population of planning professionals in that area, and/or the population of planning professionals at the global level? Is diversity to be considered as an input or an output measure? Are we considering the population of the possible student audience (younger age groups) or the population of professionals?

Without fully abandoning this perspective, in this chapter, we'll reflect on diversity in Italian planning education as tied to both the composition of the faculty and students. We'll also examine the conceptual basis of the education offered. In this way, we conceptualize the latter as related to the former by considering how differences in terms of gender, origin, competencies, educational background, and so forth may contribute to a rethinking of educational goals, pedagogical approaches, and the redefinition of substantive topics and subject areas. Politecnico di Milano, the university where the UPPD is offered, tackles diversity in its statute: "The University recognizes the dignity of every person in work and study, guaranteeing equal treatment, and promotes initiatives aimed at removing discrimination in training, access to work, orientation and progression of career" (Politecnico di Milano, 2012, art. 3.3, authors' translation). From here stem several university policies aimed at enhancing and valorizing diversity in terms of multiculturalism, gender, different abilities, sexual orientation, and wellbeing.[1]

Understanding diversity from this perspective, we can say that enhanced diversity in terms of gender, national origin, and profile or competencies contributes to pushing the limits of the urban challenges, questions, and teaching approaches applied in planning education. Moreover, the planning discipline, more than other subject areas, is clearly at the forefront of the debate because these topics—that is, the sphere of themes involved in diversity issues—and their effects in the organization of human settlements at different scales are core to planning theory and practice reflections.

Looking more broadly at the Italian higher-education context, concepts of diversity are linked to a broad understanding of the differences in composition of the population (both faculty and students), centered, in particular, on issues of gender, but accounting for aspects of social status, national origin, sexuality, age, and so forth that also affect its composition. Regarding this issue, which is still in an early stage compared to other contexts, many Italian universities have worked on the gender dimension by, for instance, publishing gender budgeting reports to promote equality (Fondazione CRUI, 2019). Other aspects—including attention to intersectionality issues in education (Mitchell, 2014)—while addressed by some universities' projects or programs, are still missing from the wider debate. The gender dimension, in turn, is very frequently understood and conceptualized mainly in terms of a gender gap or inequality, looking at the relatively low levels of participation of female students in STEM (science, technology, engineering and mathematics) degree programs and in ensuing careers (Fondazione CRUI, 2019).

Evolution of a Diverse Master's Degree Program

In Italy, diversity in planning education can hold different meanings and concern different dimensions. The first example occurred in the differentiation of urban planning from architecture education in the 1970s. As in other Mediterranean European countries, and unlike the Anglo-American trajectory, urban planning has traditionally belonged to the university education of architects. Therefore, a first issue of diversity arose in Italy when the degree courses in urban planning were established as distinct from the educational paths in architecture—and engineering as well. In both cases, urban planning continued to constitute a part, but with a minor presence compared to past decades. Considering the current situation at Politecnico di Milano (academic year 2021–22), mandatory courses of urban planning in the Bachelor of Architectural Design program amount to 16 out of the 180 credits required by the European Credit Transfer and Accumulation System (ECTS). At the master's level, in the Architecture and Urban Design degree, course credits reserved for urban planning teaching are about 12 out of 120.

The first autonomous degree course in urban planning in Italy dates to 1970 in Venice. A precious filmed testimony of that event remains in a 30-minute documentary on the founding of that 5-year program—titled "Urbanistica. Un nuovo corso di laurea" (Urban Planning. A new degree program). Created by the national broadcasting service (Giancarlo Ravasio, RAI Radiotelevisione italiana, 1971, see Ciacci, 2014), it's an important document for the historical understanding of the origins and evolution of the Italian educational path in urban planning. Right now, that program is celebrating its 50th anniversary (Musco & Tedesco, 2020). Today in Italy (academic year 2020–21), there are 12 bachelor's degree programs and 8 master's degree programs active in urban planning.

At Politecnico di Milano, a program in urban planning started in the 1996–97 academic year as a four-year degree program for graduation. In the 2000s, it was reorganized into a three-year bachelor's degree and a two-year master's degree. While the bachelor's degree program (now titled Urbanistica: Città Ambiente Paesaggio—Urban Planning: Cities, Environment and Landscapes) continues to be taught in Italian (with a short parallel track in English that lasted five years from 2010–15), the Master of Science switched the language of instruction to English—renaming the degree program from Pianificazione Urbana e Politiche Territoriali to Urban Planning and Policy Design. This was the introduction of another diversity factor, that is, language. Teaching in English opened the program up to international students with different backgrounds.

As anticipated, a real change in the direction of diversity relates to the adoption of English as the language of instruction, opening up the master's degree program to international students. This is apparent when we look at the trend over the last decade at Politecnico di Milano. In the academic year 2010–11, admissions to the Master of Urban Planning and Policy Design program of students with an Italian Bachelor's of Science diploma represented 69% compared to 31% of students with a foreign diploma. In 2020–21, the proportions are reversed; 44% of students have an Italian Bachelor's of Science diploma and 56% a foreign diploma (after peaking at 75% in 2017–18). Every year, with some fluctuation, about 80 students enter the program. In the most recent period, the percentages of incoming students from Europe (EU + non-EU Europe zone) versus the rest of the world were respectively: 52:48% (2020–21), 40:60% (2019–20), 42:58% (2018–19), and 47:53% (2017–18). In 2010–11, class composition was 76:24%. Though international student intake is predominantly Asian, there are classes of students sometimes displaying 20–25 different nationalities of origin—from Africa, North America, South America, Asia, and a range of European countries. The high number of students in the class—quite unusual in planning programs—and students' diversity in terms of national origin has had a direct effect on the methods and content of teaching. This topic will be the subject of the following section.

Efforts to increase diversity in the UPPD program have been even more impressive from a gender perspective. In fact, if one watches the aforementioned movie, made in Venice in the early 1970s, it is striking that professors in that first program in urban planning were all men; no women were part of the faculty. Currently, in the UPPD program at Politecnico di Milano (academic year 2020–21), in the mandatory courses, there are 14 male and 7 female professors. It is also noteworthy that the composition of the student class has achieved gender balance over time. Urban planning education has followed trends previously shown in architecture programs, with the gender gap in class composition progressively reduced to the current state in which the majority of the class is composed of female students (around 63% in the academic years 2018–19, 2019–20, and 2020–21). Indeed, architecture and planning programs at Politecnico di Milano show a composition that is strikingly different from those of engineering degrees (particularly those in mechanical engineering, computer science, and aerospace engineering), in which the gender gap is still acute (less than 20% of the student intake are female). Therefore, urban planning is increasingly seen as a potential job opportunity for women.

Teaching Planning: Between Theory and Practice

In addition to the large number and various international origins of students, their different backgrounds are a further element of diversity. In fact, UPPD admits students not only with undergraduate degrees in urban planning or architecture, but also from urban studies, geography, sociology, economics, political and social sciences, environmental sciences, and engineering—considering such a variety as a great value and potential. Given the average characteristics of the class, on the one hand there is a need to mix and combine skills and build a common ground of knowledge. This is provided by some courses in the first semester of the program that work to blend the class of students. On the other hand, there is the intentional and explicit choice not to specialize the training pathway of the degree according to an exact characterization, leaving students free to combine courses oriented toward urban policies with spatial planning and design. In fact, in such a large class of students—80 students each year—it makes no sense to focus on standardizing their education, but rather on diversifying their vocations, aspirations, trajectories, and possible career paths.

In a schematic overview, the degree pathway ensures an education that ranges between the following two expert practitioner profiles. First, the urbanist/town planner/urban designer has advanced training on the themes and modes of spatial plans and projects that characterize contemporary urban and territorial agendas in Europe and across the world. The study path is aimed at the critical control of themes and tools (e.g., the United Nations' Sustainable Development Goal 11[2] challenges and methods to address them) and toward the acquisition of full professional responsibilities. The second focus is on the planner/policy maker and its roles in the design and management of urban and territorial policies. This student is trained in urban studies and in the definition of policies and programs for the acknowledgement, interpretation, and intervention on complex problems posed by contemporary planning issues. However, between these two profiles, there's no marked separation of the educational pathway—that is, there are not two separate impermeable educational tracks. The curricula are fluid, and students can customize their paths. They can do so primarily through the choice of practical courses—that is, design studios. With this choice, students can accentuate a more specialized trajectory toward urban policies or spatial planning and design, or alternatively opt for more hybrid training. Each year, a different foreign visiting professor, selected through an open call, is invited to teach the course Contemporary City: Descriptions and Projects. It is a further way to keep the degree program open to different perspectives and points of view.

Class composition—its multicultural character—informs a teaching approach based on the discussion of themes, issues, and challenges emerging in urban and territorial agendas around the world. This was an inevitable choice allowing an active exchange of ideas among diverse students. Working in this way has also meant cultivating a planning education aimed at the student's capacity for interpretative judgment and critical autonomy. The aim of the master's degree is not the acquisition of basic technical skills (as at the undergraduate level) but rather the construction of an awareness of leading responsibilities in the development of projects, plans, and policies. In short, toward potential leadership roles instead of executors.

However, working on themes with a strong reflective tension also entails some paradoxes and poses some dilemmas that are not easy to solve. Sometimes it happens that the abstract dimension—a theoretical drift—tends to prevail. In this case, there is a risk of opening a gap between planning scholars dedicated to research and practitioners. This may exacerbate the distance between theory and practice and result in scholarly isolation from the planning profession. It is all a question of balance. Anyway, it should be considered that research and scholarship may only be the working perspective for a small portion of such a numerous class. A second issue lies in what was already mentioned at the beginning of this chapter: planning is an activity strongly rooted in contexts and individual countries—planning is basically a state practice (Mazza, 2006). During recent years' periodic assessment of UPPD by a steering committee composed of various institutional subjects and stakeholders,[3] it has often emerged that there is a demand from some part of public administration for graduate education that is more oriented toward public offices and agencies. This is a need that should not be underestimated, especially now in the face of a generational change in public administration. Recruitment in public agency positions will play a strategic and decisive role in determining the qualification and capacity (or otherwise) of the public administration to meet the challenges posed by evolving contemporary scenarios (including the urgencies of the post-pandemic situation).

Teaching Planning: Processes and Decision Making

Akin to urban planning, the challenges related to diversity reverberate on the subject areas of decision-making processes, policy analysis, and governance. These subject areas, which characterize the master's degree at Politecnico di Milano and set it apart from similar master's programs in other Italian planning schools, engage directly with diversity and intersectionality. Here, intersectionality should be understood and appraised not just as it relates to identity (Mitchell, 2014) but, more appropriately, in its structural aspect and in its ability to unveil recurring structures and patterns of inequality, oppression, and exclusion in the urban space. Attention to policy analysis and design needs to go beyond the understanding of the underlying complexity in decision-making processes related to the planning and design of urban transformation to critically consider such structural aspects.

Seen from this perspective, it is apparent that diversity can be seen as a powerful opportunity to disentangle emerging urban questions, as it can be found at the root of conflicts in the urban realm. This concerns both tractable, negotiable conflicts, as well as increasingly non-negotiable ones (Hirschman, 1994), such as those related to ethics, values, religion, or multiculturalism. Diversity is a key component of the concept of urbanity since it's specific to urban areas as different from other spatial formations; at the same time, contemporary metropolitan regions face unprecedented challenges in this realm, at global and local levels alike. Among many core subject areas that have been the focus of attention in the master's program in the last few years, we have singled out two examples in which a diverse class composition has significantly influenced topics and approaches.

The first is about growing forms of social and spatial polarization increasingly characterizing cities and urban regions, even areas with traditionally lower levels of inequality. There is a complex link between forms of social and spatial polarization (Boterman et al., 2019) that is contextual and related to the co-evolution trajectories linking local economies and societies to the spatial features of each urban context in a non-deterministic way. These connections have been explored in many courses and studios in the UPPD in relation to the position of individuals and groups in society and space (Sen et al., 2017), trying to identify and address emerging patterns of segregation and exclusion. In this context, students coming from different geographical contexts have opened up a dialogue with their peers and with the teaching staff. Such interaction has been conducive to a more precise identification and characterization of emerging phenomena, detectable in their similarities and differences at the global level.

Another area that has been consistently explored, and in which diversity in terms of origins interacts with other lines of division, is that of urban conflicts. The aim is often to unveil the intrinsic contentious nature of space and decisions about its transformation (Mazza, 2015). In this subject area, the complex array of social, political, and cultural aspects, tied on the one hand to the understanding of identity and identity building and on the other to inequality and power imbalances, are extremely sensitive to contexts, perceptions, and the way actors interpret their positions. Here again, the full understanding of the value of a diverse class, and of its implications in terms of intersectionality (Mitchell, 2014), have been at the core of some of the most advanced and promising teaching approaches and experiments in the last few years. The combination and matching of different perspectives, with accompanying possible misunderstandings but also with their openly political implications in terms of feminist or post-colonial approaches, have become visible and a valuable contribution to the development of the educational offerings of the master's degree.

Diversity's Potential for Teaching Planning

This overview of the effects of opening up to a wider diversity of students in the UPPD at Politecnico di Milano enables us to propose some final considerations and to open up paths for further reflection. The first finding is that the increasing diversity along different axes, and at their intersections, has brought with it a new attention and experimentation in terms of educational goals, pedagogical approaches, and substantive topics. It is exactly this novel combination of rethinking educational topics, different pedagogies, and learning objectives that has been, and still is, a constant challenge in the face of more traditional approaches to the teaching of urban studies and planning in the Italian context.

Second, to address some of the dilemmas opened up here, an openness to diversity should also characterize university programs in the teaching of planning. This may include admitting there may be different interpretations of the training path, from the prevailing orientation to environmental questions and challenges, to urban policies and governance issues, or to spatial planning and design. What has been described—the degree in Urban Planning and Policy Design—is not a recipe, but just one way of effectively interpreting the challenges of planning education derived strongly from the choice of opening up to an international class of students—a great opportunity, but also a limitation, for instance, when addressing a planning education more rooted in the institutional framework, inevitably determined by local contextual conditions. Other scenarios, other contexts, other options may arise. It is important that—for an orientation toward diversity—degree programs also differentiate their specific offerings and characterization. It seems profitable to imagine a multi-oriented planning-education system sensitive to contextual conditions and questions operating within a collaborative perspective rather than a standard competitive scenario in which universities race each other for rankings.

Notes

1   See: https://diversityandinclusion.polimi.it/overview/
2   See: https://sdgs.un.org/goals/goal11
3   Pragmatically formed on the initiative of the School of Architecture, Urban Planning and Construction Engineering of the Politecnico di Milano a few years ago, the steering committee is gradually changing its original local and regional composition with the involvement of national and international subjects.

References

Boterman, W., Musterd, S., Pacchi, C., & Ranci, C. (2019). School segregation in contemporary cities: Socio-spatial dynamics, institutional context and urban outcomes. *Urban Studies, 56*(15), 3055–3073. https://doi.org/10.1177/0042098019868377

Campion, K., & Clark, K. (2022). Revitalising race equality policy? Assessing the impact of the race equality charter mark for British universities. *Race Ethnicity and Education, 25*(1), 18–37. https://doi.org/10.1080/13613324.2021.1924133

Ciacci, L. (2014). L'insegnamento dell'urbanistica in Italia. Ricucire lo strappo e . . . andare oltre. *Planum. The Journal of Urbanism, 29.* www.planum.net/planum-magazine/movies/l-insegnamento-dell-urbanistica-in-italia-ricucire-lo-strappo-e-andare-oltre

Fondazione CRUI. (2019). *Linee guida per il Bilancio di Genere negli Atenei italiani.* CRUI Report.

Goonewardena, K., Rankin, K. N., & Weinstock, S. (2004). Diversity and planning education: A Canadian perspective. *Canadian Journal of Urban and Regional Research, 13*(Suppl. 1), 1–26.

Greenlee, A. J., Jackson, A., Garcia-Zambrana, I., Lee, C. A., & Chrisinger, B. (2018). Where are we going? Where have we been? The climate for diversity within urban planning educational programs. *Journal of Planning Education and Research*. https://doi.org/10.1177/0739456X18815740

Hirschman, A. O. (1994). Social conflicts as pillars of democratic market society. *Political Theory*, *22*(2), 203–218.

Mazza, L. (2006). Di cosa parliamo quando parliamo di urbanistica. 'Appunti per le lezioni'. In M. C. Tosi (Ed.), *Di cosa parliamo quando parliamo di urbanistica?* (pp. 167–185). Meltemi.

Mazza, L. (2015). *Planning and citizenship*. London: Routledge.

Mitchell, D. J. (Ed.). (2014). *Intersectionality & HIGHER EDUCATION: Theory, research, & praxis*. Peter Lang.

Musco, F., & Tedesco, C. (Eds.). (2020). 50 anni dall'istituzione del primo corso di laurea di urbanistica in Italia. *Urbanistica Informazioni*, *292*, 36–44.

Politecnico di Milano. (2012). *Statuto del Politecnico di Milano*. Politecnico di Milano.

Sen, S., Umemoto, K., Koh, A., & Zambonelli, V. (2017). Diversity and social justice in planning education: A synthesis of topics, pedagogical approaches, and educational goals in planning syllabi. *Journal of Planning Education and Research*, *37*(3), 347–358. https://doi.org/10.1177/0739456X16657393

Sweet, E. L., & Etienne, H. F. (2011). Commentary: Diversity in urban planning education and practice. *Journal of Planning Education and Research*, *31*(3), 332–339. https://doi.org/10.1177/0739456X11414715

6

DIVERSIFYING URBAN PLANNING AND ARCHITECTURE PROGRAMS THROUGH INTERNATIONAL EDUCATION EXPERIENCE

Lessons From Ferdowsi University of Mashhad, Iran

Parsa Pahlavan and Hossein Maroufi

Diversity in urban-planning education has become a theme of interest among scholars in the past two decades. A thorough review of two main planning journals, the *Journal of the American Planning Association* and the *Journal of Planning Education and Research*, by Sweet and Etienne (2011), indicates that the issue of diversity has been addressed in four main areas: (1) race and gender, (2) master narrative vs. counter narrative, (3) pedagogy and curriculum, and (4) structural barriers to diversity. Over the past two decades, planning education has adopted internationalization and transcultural learning strategies as an avenue to promote diversity. Along with this, the need to internationalize planning education has been recognized by several associations in Europe, North America, and Australasia (Frank, 2006). Urban-planning and architecture schools' efforts and challenges to incorporate diversity into education and the faculty include increasing the number of underrepresented minority academic staff and students (Anthony, 2008; Sweet & Etienne, 2011); incorporating diversity into the planning curriculum and course content (Looye & Sesay, 1998; Kwitko & Thompson, 2002; Jackson et al., 2018; Shilon & Eizenberg, 2020); enhancing awareness of children, youth, and the greater public about urban planning education (Palazzo et al., 2021); promoting an institutional climate for diversity within the university campus (Greenlee et al., 2018); and engagement with transcultural learning experiences via international initiatives (Yigitcanlar, 2013; Jones, 2019).

While there is a growing volume of research on the desirability of promoting diversity in architecture and urban-planning education, there is less discussion about what the term "diversity" means in different locations, as the perception of diversity differs from one context to another. The majority of publications in this area are coming from North America where the issues of race and gender shape the aspirations for bringing and sustaining diversity into architecture and urban-planning education. However, research indicates that diversity is not necessarily solely categorized by race and gender issues. Importantly, as indicated by Sandercock and Forsyth (1992), the increase in the number of female students or students of color in architecture and urban-planning departments does not necessarily lead to the diversification of urban planning in practice.[1]

It is also necessary to mention the efforts at diversifying architecture and urban-planning curricula to include ongoing urban complexities and challenges, especially in the global South. Particularly, with an increase in the number of international students, high mobility of students and academic staff through exchange programs, and shared global visions like the New Urban Agenda, there is a need to focus on major global-planning and sustainable-development issues in the pedagogy (Jones, 2019). For example, in order to develop a global mindset in urban-planning students, Ali and Doan (2006) explore and compare various methodologies in US planning schools to teach global planning issues and diversity of urban development processes to undergraduate students. Similarly, the surveys of Yigitcanlar (2013) and Jones (2019) on planning education in Australia indicate an increase in international learning experiences in which students acquire new knowledge and skills from the Asia-Pacific region through field trips and international planning studios. Today, many architecture and planning schools address this through different plans, programs, and policies that consider their local context and constraints. There appears to be a role for architecture and planning schools to share experiences and good practices in this area.

This chapter focuses on internationalization as a way to promote diversity within the architecture and urban-planning programs at Ferdowsi University of Mashhad in Iran, where diversity is seen as *integration of intercultural/international dimensions into urban planning and architecture pedagogy*. Local Iranian students are included in initiatives not only to benefit from the workshop, but also to benefit from international students' experiences and insights. The aim is to increase students' capacity to become more resilient and innovative in an era of complexity and uncertainty in socio-political and economic conditions. To achieve this, we present here the experience of international students in two intensive workshops organized by the Faculty of Architecture and Urban Planning of Ferdowsi University of Mashhad.

The Faculty: Diversity Gaps in the Mainstream Curriculum

Hosting over ten nationalities, the vision of the faculty[2] is to increase its international status in the field of architecture and urban-planning education in the Middle East and central Asia. This is to be achieved by increasing the enrollment of international students from the region as well as internationalizing education by addressing shared concerns regarding architecture and urbanism in the Middle East region. Several challenges and issues in regard to the built environment—including informal settlements, the aspiration for globalization through large-scale redevelopments, and heritage conservation vs. renovation—are shared between Iran and other neighboring countries, in particular cities in Iraq and Afghanistan.

The official curriculum of architecture and urban-planning programs in Iran is approved by the Ministry of Science, Research, and Technology (MSRT) and is a required component for all higher-education institutions in the country. Reviewing the aims adopted for the two distinct official programs, it becomes clear that the mainstream curriculum does not reflect the *de facto* diversity that is slowly emerging in architecture and urban-planning programs, such as the increasing number of enrolled female students and the increasing demand for internationalization of the two programs. Considering these gaps, the approach to internationalize architecture and urban-planning programs at Ferdowsi University of Mashhad is guided by the following goals:

- To reflect the influence of international intensive workshops on the experience of international students, particularly on how they see themselves integrating these experiences into their own value systems in home countries.
- To recommend programs and policies to the faculty to internationalize the existing curriculum.
- To suggest strategies that create a departmental climate and learning context receptive to international learning experiences.

- To extend the diversity values to other issues: the focus on internationalization as an avenue for promoting diversity in architecture and urban-planning education can be extended to topics such as gender diversity.

To achieve these goals, the experiences of hosting two international workshops at Ferdowsi University of Mashhad are described, in which a group of international students were involved in two different field-work settings. The first workshop concerns exploring a quasi-forgotten vernacular heritage located in a rural setting, where international students experienced three days of living and working in a village camp near Mashhad. The second workshop was held in an urban setting where an abandoned industrial site in Mashhad became a major concern for documentary work. The statements and expressions from international students at the end of each workshop are important for incorporating diversity into the curricula of the Faculty of Architecture and Urban Planning.

The Experience of Organizing International Workshops

The undergraduate programs in architecture and urban planning were launched by the Faculty of Architecture and Urban Planning of Ferdowsi University of Mashhad in 2005. More than 1,000 students (71.36% female), including 33 international students, have completed their studies through the summer of 2021. The international students are mainly from Middle Eastern and neighboring countries: a considerable majority is from Afghanistan, Iraq, and Syria, and others are mainly from Lebanon, Bahrain, Tajikistan, and India.

A large proportion of enrolled international students in the programs (72.72%) are female.[3] This might represent the case of structural barriers to diversity, as female international students are coming from countries where women are typically underrepresented. The faculty has adopted various initiatives addressed to international students in order to guarantee cultural diversity and establish an environment where students of many backgrounds work together. Two examples of these initiatives—documentation-intense workshops—are discussed here.

Vernacular Documentation Intensive Workshop

VERNADOC, a method for documenting vernacular architecture, is a simple, authentic surveying method originating from Finland, later known in various countries thanks to the Survey of Architectural Heritage camps. These workshops rely on on-site measurements and the creation of exquisite, ink-based drawings. In VERNADOC-intensive workshops, scaled drawings with shadow and texture are the sole features fulfilling the documentation (instead of text and specifications) and are followed by an exhibition of the drawings at that community immediately after the workshop. These projects aim to highlight the value of local building tradition (morphology, construction method, and use value), to establish an international network of professionals to cover various disciplines relevant to surveying criteria, and to promote cross-cultural learning in the area of vernacular architecture and urbanism. In September 2019, the Faculty of Architecture and Urban Planning of Ferdowsi University of Mashhad organized a ten-day intensive VERNADOC workshop in collaboration with the Iranian Ministry of Cultural Heritage, Tourism, and Handicrafts and the Iranian VERNADOC association.

Kang historical stepped village is located in northeastern Iran in the center of the greater Khorasan region. The village is estimated to have a 3,000-year history of civilization due to archaeological findings and textual evidence from the holy book of Zoroastrianism. The vernacular architecture of Kang is characterized by the use of only local materials such as wood and stone and an indigenous style commonly created without professional architects and planners. The architecture of Kang is typically practical and simple, without decoration or unnecessary ornaments. Its vicinity to Mashhad (about 40 kilometers or 25 miles), indigenous rural fabric, and continuity of village life made Kang

Figure 6.1 Vernacular Documentation Workshop
Students' activities during the vernacular documentation intensive workshop in Kang historical village and the final exhibition of drawings.

an ideal site for a vernacular documentation intensive workshop chiefly organized to include international students from Afghanistan, Iraq, Syria, India, Lebanon, and Bahrain, as well as Iran. Professional VERNADOC instructors from Finland, Iran, and Thailand joined the crew to document three rustic, original, and vernacularly built houses without considerable restorative interventions. The language barrier in this workshop was not a main concern since all international students study in Farsi, and they have a fair level of proficiency to communicate with local people.

The workshop was divided into two sections. The first took place in the village for five intensive days in which students became involved in surveying and sketching the selected buildings. Students became familiar with local construction techniques, vernacular construction materials, and the local functioning of everyday life in a small-scale rural setting. Instructors also taught various documenting tools and techniques. Through on-site experience, both Iranian and international students got to know different issues from the mainstream curriculum designated for indoor studio work. Indeed, the workshop was an opportunity for students to get familiar with vernacular contexts, cultures, needs, and expectations that can affect their critical and systems-thinking values. Here is a dialogue between an old lady resident in the village questioning one of the Afghan students.

"What are you searching for by drawing my house?" [the old rural lady asked].
"Because your houses are stunning; they are beautiful and to us they have importance; good for you Madame" [the student responded].
"Are we important? Is my house beautiful? This is the first time I am hearing such a thing"[replied the old lady].

The Afghan student witnessed how the atmosphere created by the workshop affected the confidence of the local people and their appreciation of their living environment. Later, she explained to the workshop instructors that Afghanistan and Afghan cultural heritage is suffering from not being appreciated; if people receive appreciation from outsiders about their tangible and intangible belongings, they are less likely to reconstruct or leave their vernacular homes.

The second section of the workshop took place in the Faculty of Architecture and Urban Planning where students were asked to ink and finalize their scaled final sketches. In this section, students learned various methods of drawing, texturing, and inking to present what they documented during the first on-site section.

The VERNADOC workshop adopted very basic, simple techniques and tools for documentation. However, the intercultural experiences during the workshop and over the exhibition of the final works highlighted the vernacular values[4] that are shared by participants' place of origin. Considering that the tangible and intangible heritage of a local community can be appreciated through simple and accessible methods, the VERNADOC camp inspired international students coming from countries with deep traditional roots to look differently at the question of heritage conservation. The organization of similar workshops in Iraq, Afghanistan, and Syria were suggested right after the final exhibition by authorities and academic institutions in these countries.

Modern Documentation Intensive Workshop

The Faculty of Architecture and Urban Planning organized a second international documentation workshop, this one documenting modern architectural heritage, with the collaboration of DOCOMOMO (International Committee for Documentation and Conservation of Buildings, Sites and Neighborhoods of the Modern Movement) Iran, Petroleum Museums and Documents Center of Iran, and CIPA (International Scientific Committee for Documentation of Cultural Heritage). The intensive workshop aimed at conducting measurement sciences into the technological heritage

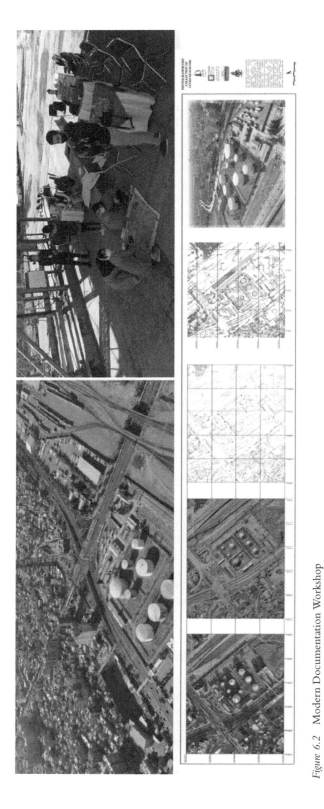

Figure 6.2 Modern Documentation Workshop

Students' activities during the modern documentation intensive workshop by means of drones and documented orthophotos created by the students.

documentation. The selected site for documentation was the oldest petroleum depository in both Mashhad and Iran, constructed in 1925 and abandoned in 2001.

As the first initiative to document the works of the modern movement in Iran, the workshop aimed to increase awareness of modern architectural heritage, incorporate modern technologies in surveying the built environment, and foster the development of ideas for adaptive re-use. In the course of five days of intensive on-site and campus work, the participants learned and practiced computerizing photogrammetric surveys of an industrial heritage site and practiced façade mapping by drone photogrammetry. In this workshop, the abandoned site of the Petroleum Reservoir of Mashhad (an area of approximately 5.5 hectares), including several mazut[5] tanks and industrial sheds, was documented by means of drone images. Through photogrammetric documentation, 3D models and a dataset for production of Building Information Model (BIM) models were created. These data-enriched samples could be used on a digital model for monitoring and operational purposes, with various potential applications for cultural-heritage conservation and restoration. This documentation system could be adopted by architects and urban planners for technical surveys and measurement of archeological sites, land plots, street façades, and topography. It could be seen as an alternative to traditional surveying tools (such as theodolite and level), which is a part of the current curriculum of architecture and urban planning programs in Iran.

The Iraqi and Afghan participants found drone documentation and photography interesting methods for surveying architectural and archeological ruins in unsafe and war-torn regions and proposed a similar method be applied in some zones of Iraq and Afghanistan. The speed, accuracy, and versatility of the data-enriched model creation (especially compared to vernacular documentation methods) had a substantial effect on the critical thinking of the students. The Iraqi and Afghan students claimed that the pedagogy in their home countries manifests a separation of education and technology. They highlighted that the surveying techniques they learned in their home countries, and later in the programs, were almost disconnected from high-tech facilities that could ease documentation, modelling, and design. They found such initiatives useful to fill the existing gap; however, a new combination of pedagogy and high-tech survey tools and advanced technologies is what they desired for their future fellows.

Lessons and Recommendations for Diversifying Programs via Internationalization

The international students participating in the two documentation intensive workshops were chiefly from countries with many endangered built heritage sites (vernacular and modern) due to uneasy political conditions or internal conflicts. The cultural landscape of many Middle Eastern countries (particularly Iraq and Afghanistan) has remained mostly unseen and unknown to the rest of the world due to security issues and lack of study and documentation. Organization of such workshops could highlight the importance of documentation of the built environment in conflict-prone regions as an initiative to safeguard endangered heritage.

Furthermore, the participants in the workshops were mostly from post-colonial Middle Eastern countries where the "developmentalism" rhetoric of the state is often reflected in large-scale renewal plans and infrastructure projects. This was also reflected by Iraqi and Afghan students when they spoke about architecture and urban-planning programs' curricula in their countries, where the main focus is on technical and structural issues (technical drawing, structural issues, infrastructure, land development, mapping, etc.). The two-decade presence of international (Western) military forces, consultants, volunteers, donors, and foundations in Iraq and Afghanistan has accelerated the developmentalism rhetoric—reflected in economic growth and competitiveness. Therefore, appreciation of indigenous fabrics and construction techniques as well as preservation of vernacular and modern heritage sites is often neglected. During the workshops, students were given time to think about their concerns and ideas for increasing vernacular and modern heritage awareness in their countries of origin. The final discussion highlighted the need to invest attention and capital in vernacular and modern heritage sites to attract sustainable income through tourism.

Both camps offered an atmosphere totally different from the mainstream studio work indicated by the official curriculum in Iran. While the typical design or planning studio is pre-planned with sets of instructions and assignments, working in the international workshops enhanced competencies and skills in different domains. Students learned to think out of the box, to see things differently, and to experience real issues and challenges. They also learned to be good observers and good listeners, abilities that they do not fully encounter in their campus studios. Importantly, international students could compare the values demonstrated during the field experiences to the value systems operating in their home countries, therefore drawing comparison lessons on how modern and vernacular heritage sites are recognized and treated in different contexts. Since the majority of international students in Iran return to their home countries after graduation, it is important for them to relate their knowledge to their place of origin through comparative learning. This is also in line with the findings of Yigitcanlar (2013) and Jones (2019) that international field trips and overseas learning experiences provide a valuable learning environment where students' cognitive learning is improved.

Organizing workshops and scientific camps for international students could contain various challenges in Iran. The challenges include securing sponsors to keep the workshops affordable to students; inviting guest instructors; establishing connections with professionals overseas, which, due to the international sanctions on Iran, have become an obstacle in recent years; and obtaining permissions from various state-controlled organizations. Despite these challenges, these two international intensive workshops could be a steppingstone to diversifying the architecture and urban planning curriculum at Ferdowsi University of Mashhad and to enhance the importance of cross-cultural learning in both disciplines. On the basis of the experiences available, the following recommendations are provided for the Faculty of Architecture and Urban Planning of Ferdowsi University of Mashhad in order to diversify the pedagogy with the focus on internationalization within the curriculum.

International Cooperation

International cooperation is to be achieved by establishing ties with counterpart academic institutions in Afghanistan and Iraq in order to develop mutual cooperation plans in teaching, research, exchange programs, and engagement activities of similar interests.

Diversifying Architecture and Urban-Planning Pedagogy

Understanding the depth and efficacy of architecture and urban-planning pedagogy at the faculty level should become a priority for diversifying the curriculum. To what extent have the program curricula and course contents in architecture and urban planning been adapted to fit the scope of internationalization by the faculty? Do the courses offered by the faculty meet the expectations and needs of the architecture and urban-planning job markets in Iran, Afghanistan, and Iraq?[26] What areas have been missed in the course curriculum that could have helped international students with their knowledge of the socio-political context of their country of origin? Future research should address these questions by critically revising the current curriculum.

The experience of the two workshops offered new perspectives on skills each architecture and planning student should be equipped with in order to relate knowledge to practice. This could be achieved by revising studio courses for both programs of architecture and urban planning at Ferdowsi

University of Mashhad. Currently, studios comprise the backbone of the architecture and urban-planning curricula with long hours of individual or team work on a subject ranging in scale from a building to a neighborhood to a city. The aim of the studio work is to enhance skills in presentation (visual, oral, written), design, planning, qualitative/quantitative analysis, and interpersonal communication. The experiences of the two workshops highlight the need to design strategies to incorporate critical-thinking skills into studio courses. This could be developed by assigning tasks and activities to include different methods of problem solving as alternatives to predefined standards (such as land use or building codes). Another strategy could be the integration of studio work with real challenges and issues in the city of Mashhad from architectural to a broad urban and regional scale. Off-campus field trips can enrich students' learning experiences, moving the learning out of campus studios into real spaces of the city where students can make connections to the way that the knowledge they are learning in the programs has real-world applications.

Since planning in Iran is largely a product of the state, much of the policy and practice that is taught by urban-planning departments is tailored to fit the professional planning context in Iran. However, the increase in the number of international students and their places of origin should be taken into consideration by the faculty. One strategy could be to include courses in the curriculum that have regional implications in order to expose students (both Iranian and international) to diverse contexts that enhance their learning, skills, and capabilities.

Establishing Ties With Public and Non-Governmental Institutions

Securing funds for organizing international workshops is one of the most important steps for managing this process. Establishing ties with municipalities, city councils, and other public institutions as well as NGOs could provide financial and administrative support for future international initiatives. Possible initiatives could include the organization of public exhibitions of student work or inviting public officials or NGO members to narrate their experience and expectations.

Intercultural Sharing Experiences

This can be achieved through organization of cultural events focusing on diversity and sharing intercultural experiences to integrate international students with their local peers. The point is to appreciate different local cultures, setting the stage for diversity and inclusiveness, possibly through such events as photography exhibitions, food-sharing, storytelling, and so forth.

Conclusion

This chapter focuses on internationalization as a way to promote diversity within architecture and urban-planning pedagogy. The increase in enrollment of international students in the architecture and urban-planning programs at Ferdowsi University of Mashhad indicates a need to diversify the pedagogy through cross-cultural learning initiatives. The experience of the two workshops provides a platform for the programs to diversify the pedagogy in three ways:

1) Incorporate concrete issues and challenges of the city of Mashhad into studio courses in order to enhance students' problem-solving skills.
2) Incorporate field experiences into the curriculum to enhance international students' competencies in comparing those experiences to the value systems of their home countries.
3) Incorporate into the pedagogy courses and content that have regional implications and that enrich students' cognitive learning through transcultural learning experiences.

However, the focus on internationalization as a way to promote diversity in architecture and urban-planning education must also be extended to various topics such as gender diversity in the future.

Notes

1. In the last decade, the number of female graduates and faculty members in the fields of architecture and urban planning has increased significantly in Iran, but despite this, women still have much less power in policy and decision-making structures.
2. "Faculty" describes a group of university departments concerned with a major division of knowledge.
3. At the time of writing (summer 2021), the ascendancy of the Taliban in the Afghan civil war was sure to substantially increase emigration and send fresh waves of refugees flooding across the border between the two countries; hence, the number of female Afghan students is predicted to increase considerably in the following academic years.
4. These values include construction techniques, materials, and the everyday life of villagers.
5. Heavy, low-quality fuel oil used in power plants and similar applications.
6. Afghanistan and Iraq have the most considerable cultural exchanges with Iran. Afghanistan shares a common language and long land border (the *Afghanistan–Iran border* is 921 km), while Iraq has a majority of Shi'ite Muslims, which is the official state religion in Iran, as well as a long land border *(the Iran–Iraq border* runs for 1,599 km).

References

Ali, A. K., & Doan, P. L. (2006). A survey of undergraduate course syllabi and a hybrid course on global urban topics. *Journal of Planning Education and Research*, *26*(2), 222–236. https://doi.org/10.1177/0739456x06291500

Anthony, K. H. (2008). *Designing for diversity: Gender, race, and ethnicity in the architectural profession*. University of Illinois Press.

Frank, A. (2006). Three decades of thought on planning education. *Journal of Planning Literature*, *21*, 15–67, https://doi.org/10.1177/0885412206288904.

Greenlee, A. J., Jackson, A., Garcia-Zambrana, I., Lee, C. A., & Chrisinger, B. (2018). Where are we going? Where have we been? The climate for diversity within urban Planning educational programs. *Journal of Planning Education and Research*. https://doi.org/10.1177/0739456X18815740

Jackson, A., Garcia-Zambrana, I., Greenlee, A. J., Lee, C. A., & Chrisinger, B. (2018). All talk no walk: Student perceptions on integration of diversity and practice in planning programs. *Planning Practice & Research*, *33*(5), 574–595. https://doi.org/10.1080/02697459.2018.1548207

Jones, P. (2019). The case for inclusion of international planning studios in contemporary urban planning pedagogy. *Sustainability*, *11*(15), 4174. https://doi.org/10.3390/su11154174

Kwitko, L., & Thompson, S. (2002). Issues of difference and diversity in planning education: A reflection on current Australian and New Zealand Practice. *Australian Planner*, *39*(1), 30–36. https://doi.org/10.1080/07293682.2002.9982278

Looye, J. W., & Sesay, A. (1998). Introducing diversity into the planning curriculum: A method for department-wide implementation. *Journal of Planning Education and Research*, *18*(2), 161–170. https://doi.org/10.1177/0739456X9801800208

Palazzo, D., Hollstein, L., & Diko, S. K. (2021). Urban planning as a career preference for students: Efforts to improve awareness about the profession. *Planning Practice & Research*, *36*(2), 174–192. https://doi.org/10.1080/02697459.2020.1782056

Sandercock, L., & Forsyth, A. (1992). A gender agenda: New directions for planning theory. *Journal of the American Planning Association*, *58*(1), 49–59. https://doi.org/10.1080/01944369208975534

Shilon, M., & Eizenberg, E. (2020). Critical pedagogy for the new planner: Mastering an inclusive perception of 'the other.' *Cities*, *97*, 102500. https://doi.org/10.1016/j.cities.2019.102500

Sweet, E. L., & Etienne, H. F. (2011). Commentary: Diversity in urban planning education and practice. *Journal of Planning Education and Research*, *31*(3), 332–339. https://doi.org/10.1177/0739456X11414715

Yigitcanlar, T. (2013). Cultivating the pedagogy of experience through international field trips. *SAGE Open*, *3*(2), 215824401348956. https://doi.org/10.1177/2158244013489560

7

A PATH TO RACIAL EQUITY

Representation and Youth Planning Education

Giovania Tiarachristie and Daphne Lundi

Urban planning influences so much of our everyday lives—where we live and play, how we move and interact with each other, and how we pass down resources to the next generation. Planners impact whose community needs are considered, and they navigate governance around whose perspectives are prioritized. Given this significant role, it is critical that the profession include perspectives that reflect the racial diversity within the communities that planners serve. Yet, across the country, there remains a vast underrepresentation of Black, Indigenous, and People of Color (BIPOC) in the planning profession. This underrepresentation of groups most negatively impacted by historically racist urban policies, alongside the overrepresentation of people already holding privilege and power, has continued to perpetuate the racial inequities that exist today. This chapter discusses the context of racial inequality in the United States and the state of representation in planning, summarizes the existing roadblocks and potential antidotes to the recruitment of BIPOC in the planning profession, and highlights youth planning education as a racial-justice tool that can address more equitable representation and civic engagement.

Racial Inequality in the United States

The beginning of the spread of COVID-19 in early 2020 amplified the deeply inequitable racial conditions in the United States and around the world. In the United States, BIPOC were hardest impacted by hospitalization and mortality. Today's racial disparities in health and wealth are deeply rooted in the country's underacknowledged racist origins, beginning with European colonization, enslavement, and genocide of Indigenous people, and the theft of Indigenous land and resources. It continued with 250 years of trade and chattel enslavement of African people brought over by Europeans and another 150-plus years of de facto segregation, neoliberal policies, and coded private practices that have perpetuated racist outcomes in the built and social environment. Urban planning has historically played a key role in affecting the inequitable distribution of services and resources across neighborhoods and thus the life outcomes of different racial and ethnic groups. Tools like zoning, ordinances, housing codes, and redevelopment projects have been used to carry out the exclusion, segregation, displacement, and disenfranchisement of BIPOC, and, conversely, to concentrate resources, wealth, and political power among White people. Planners have historically been "implicit in perpetuating racism" (Sweet, 2010, p. 230). Planning participation processes have been criticized over the decades for not representing various classes (Davidoff, 1965) and for ignoring gender inequalities (Milroy, 1991), disregarding gay and lesbian issues (Forsyth, 1995, 2001; Valentine, 1993), and perpetuating ableist spaces (Stafford, 2019).

The hard truths of our country's origins and development are barely discussed in urban planning classrooms, let alone the average American elementary or secondary school system. Segregation has limited our exposure to, and understanding of, each other's realities, shaping especially the privileges of White people that allow for ignorance and denial of the very existence of racial disparities. Yet this history and current realities are critical to understand, especially as planners, because if we're not actively being anti-racist and anti-oppressive in our approaches, we are perpetuating the systems in place and prolonging racist outcomes. But in the same way that our profession has the power to perpetuate racial inequity, we also hold the tools to help correct it and promote justice and healing.

Equitable Representation in Power as a Pathway to Justice

To achieve more just and equitable communities, planners need to better understand, represent, and advocate for the constituencies most affected by injustice and inequality. Planning scholar June Manning Thomas emphasizes, "If the urban planning profession cannot itself reflect commitment to social equity in the form of its own demographics, it could seem contradictory for professional planners to argue for social equity in society at large" (2008, p. 228). Improving diversity in planning, particularly better representation of low-income BIPOC communities in decision-making power, is central to achieving equity.

Several initiatives over the last 25 years have highlighted underrepresentation of BIPOC in the planning profession and have called for change. For example, the American Institute of Certified Planners has modified their Code of Ethics and Professional Conduct to note planners' responsibility to the public to seek social justice, the Planning Accreditation Board's strategic goals have emphasized the need to systematically approach diversity in curricula, and the American Planning Association's Diversity Committee (formerly Task Force) has hosted summits, created recommendations, and better highlighted diversity on their main website. Yet despite these efforts and more, across the country there continues to be a major disparity between what communities look like and who is doing the planning. According to the 2020 US Census, 40% of the population is made up of people of color—a likely undercount. But urban planners, who affect decision making on the built environment in these communities, are 73% White (US Census Bureau, 2018).[1]

Even in places with a more racially diverse population like New York City, there is still a major issue with underrepresentation. According to the 2020 US Census, the New York metropolitan area is made up of 68% people of color. Yet urban planners in the city are 64% White (US Census Bureau, 2020). Black people make up 24% of the population, but only 7% of planners are Black. Latinx communities make up 29% of the population, but only 12% of planners are Latinx (Table 7.1).

Table 7.1 2020 Race/Ethnicity in Overall Population Compared to Urban Planners

	NH White	NH Black	NH API	NH Native	Latinx
U.S. Population	60%	13%	6%	2%	18%
U.S. Urban Planners	73%	7%	6%	1%	10%
NYC Population	32%	24%	14%	1%	29%
NYC Planners	64%	7%	13%	<1%	12%

Note: NH indicates Non-Hispanic. Numbers are rounded to the nearest whole; other racial groups with numbers less than 1% were not included but does not negate their existence.

Source: US Census 2020; ACS 2014–2018 EEO Tabulations for occupation code 1840 "Other social scientists and related workers, including urban and regional planners"

This poor representation can be seen across public, private, and non-profit sectors, but the private sector is the least diverse, with only 2% of planners being Black (Tiarachristie, 2016). As communities have diversified over the decades, the planning profession has lagged, becoming less representative of communities today than in 1990 (Tiarachristie, 2016). Meanwhile, demographics continue to shift. In 2018, more than half of the US population of people under 15 years of age were Latinx, Black, Asian, Native, or mixed race (Frey, 2019). The census projects that by 2045, people of color will officially become the majority of Americans, outnumbering White people (Vespa et al., 2018).

Overcoming Barriers to Recruitment, Retention, and Advancement of Planners of Color

The problem of racial inequity and poor representation of BIPOC communities in planning can be overcome. It starts with acknowledging the harsh realities and intentionally applying equity practices that better recruit, retain, and advance historically marginalized groups in decision-making positions. To provide context for barriers to representation and share a spectrum of potential solutions, this section overviews some of the findings of "Elephant in the Planning Room: Overcoming Barriers to Recruitment and Retention of Planners of Color" by Giovania Tiarachristie (2016). This study collected data from more than 300 in-depth surveys, 11 focus groups, and 11 one-on-one interviews with planners and employers in the New York metropolitan area. It explores the state of diversity in the profession and documents the experiences of planners of color across a range of sectors and intersecting identities. The quotes shared in this chapter are courtesy of interviews and focus-group participants, who remain anonymous. Under each of the main barriers are example strategies for employers, planning schools, planning institutions, and everyday planners to use to help overcome these barriers to representation. It is recommended to refer to the main study for more detailed and complete information.

Strategies to Overcome Barriers to Recruitment

Strategy 1: Break Cycles of Poverty and Economic Injustice in BIPOC Communities

At the root of the lack of racial diversity in planning lies its unaddressed dirty history of racially and economically segregating communities and perpetuating systemic issues plaguing, in particular, Black, Indigenous, and Latinx neighborhoods. These neighborhoods have survived underfunded and segregated schools, food deserts, high rates of crime and violence due to extreme poverty and poor access to mental healthcare, as well as targeted policing and mass incarceration. These systemic issues have impact at the individual, household, and community levels and create additional barriers for many individuals to complete the degrees in higher education that are necessary to enter the planning profession. As one of the Latinx planners focus-group participants states,

> Educational attainment in the neighborhood that I grew up in was very low because of all the things you deal with living in poverty. It was hard to get through high school for many, let alone college or even graduate school.
>
> *(Latinx Planner in Non-Profit Sector)*

Example Strategies

- Apply a racial-equity lens to planning work and divert resources to improving the full spectrum of neighborhood resources, prioritizing the wellness of low-income BIPOC communities.

- Invest in housing, education, open space, healthy food, transportation, workforce development, criminal justice reform, as well as anti-displacement tactics, like local ownership- and wealth-building opportunities.
- Implement community-based participatory planning to amplify the voices and increase the role of historically marginalized, underrepresented groups in decision-making about neighborhoods and socioeconomic policies. This includes the engagement of young BIPOC.
- Continue learning about and acknowledging the violent history of systemic racism in the United States, and get involved in efforts to dismantle white supremacy to build a transformative, healing, anti-racist, and racially just system.

Strategy 2: Increase Early and Positive Exposure to Planning Career Paths

Of planners that participated in the study, 66% reported not hearing about planning until approximately their third year of college. Those that were exposed to the profession before college were majority White, largely due to advantages in social capital (e.g., someone they knew was a planner). Lack of diversity in the profession today limits exposure to planning as a career path in BIPOC communities. Further, many BIPOC communities have not had good relations with White-dominated government institutions, nor have they had exposure to how urban planning could be a tool to improve, rather than destroy, their communities. As one interviewee expressed: "If you grew up only seeing how the government destroys your neighborhood, and especially if that government doesn't look like you or act like they care about you, why would you ever want to be part of the government?" (Black Planner, Public Sector). Exposing young people of color to this career path is key to shifting representation. They often have deep insight into their families' and communities' needs yet are often systematically guided by media and racially biased institutions that see less potential in BIPOC children to pursue a very limited, and often racialized, set of career pathways (service positions, basketball players, etc.). Conversely, those considered gifted, with immigrant roots, or from more privileged backgrounds are often pushed to pursue more socially prestigious and better-paying careers, such as becoming a doctor, lawyer, or businessperson.

Example Strategies

- Implement workshops with youth in BIPOC communities, working with local schools or after-school programs, using urban planning to solve neighborhood problems they see. Gather their input for decision-making around real and active local projects. (Read more about examples of engaging youth in planning later in this chapter.)
- Develop a campaign working with underserved communities and local schools to raise awareness of planning as a respectable, well-paying career; its connection to social justice; and its career pathways.
- Develop mentorship programs with young people interested in planning careers.

Strategy 3: Prioritize Racial Equity Among Students, Faculty, and Curricula

In the New York metropolitan area, accredited planning schools remain majority White and male in both student body and faculty. An interviewee expressed a common sentiment, "I would look around and always notice that I was the only person of color in the classroom. And then I'd be the only person bringing up race in discussions" (Asian American Planner, Public Sector). Lack of racial diversity among faculty also contributes to the challenge of recruitment and retention of students of color, who often seek relatable mentors. Faculty of color also expressed feeling isolated and subject to unequal opportunities for growth and tenure compared to White peers, further contributing to faculty homogeneity. The high cost of planning programs can also pose a significant barrier for those from backgrounds with less familial wealth. Most programs in the area averaged well over $100,000 in tuition costs (excluding living expenses), while the median annual salary for a planner across the nation is $76,000 (US Bureau of Labor Statistics, 2020). Interviewees also noted that planning academia and practice do not centralize the social-justice narrative as much as urban policy, social work, and public health fields, thus it often attracts fewer BIPOC students and thus less racial diversity in the profession.

Example Strategies

- Target recruitment of BIPOC faculty, and more equitably support and promote their growth and visibility by encouraging and supporting them in publications, award nominations, tenure, etc., to address historic disparities.
- Mandate diversity and cultural-competency training, and center racial equity in the planning curriculum for graduation, ensuring students graduate with cultural humility and a sense of accountability to planning's racist history.
- Recruit graduates of community colleges in related fields with a social justice focus that may have attracted more students of color (e.g., sociology, American studies, culture and ethnic studies).
- Create programs to fast-track and reduce costs for BIPOC students. Work together with local firms and foundations to create scholarships.

Strategy 4: Make Access to Work Experience Equitable, and Acknowledge Lived Experience

Most employers interviewed said they tend to hire those that have interned with them. However, as most internships are unpaid, this enables those of wealthier backgrounds (who are more likely to be White) to gain experience and skills, while limiting opportunities for those that may come from less-privileged backgrounds and have family obligations (more likely to be people of color and womxn). Focus-group participants and interviewees challenged employers' notions of qualifications. While many White employers referred to qualifications as education pedigree and work experience, planners of color and managers with valued staff of color brought up the value of the lived experience—as a person of color, immigrant, parent, person with disabilities, and/or other historically marginalized identity—that cannot be gained through a prestigious degree. As one of the focus-group participants expressed, "I'm Black, I'm Latina, born and raised in New York City and experienced first-hand how certain policies affected my neighborhoods—shouldn't I have more street cred as a planner for the city than some White chick from Ohio?" (Afro-Latinx Planner, Public Sector). According to the survey, 81% of Latinx and 84% of Black planners are most likely to have grown up in similar environments to the communities that they serve as planners today (compared to 49% of White planners) yet are the two most underrepresented groups in the profession.

Example Strategies

- Go beyond performative diversity hiring for public relations, and shift the focus to having racial diversity among staff and leadership as key assets to achieving organizational mission and obligation to communities.
- Create partnerships between planning programs, local firms, and public agencies to develop full scholarship and paid fellowship cohort programs for BIPOC students that provide meaningful work experiences, professional development, and community.

Strategy 5: Break Unconscious Bias and Color Blindness in Hiring

In our society, we've internalized a particular image of competence (White, male, middle class) and are often unconsciously, systematically prejudiced against certain groups in the hiring process. One interviewee expressed, "People often look at me, see I am a Black woman, and already doubt that I am competent enough to do the job" (Black Planner, Private Sector). In describing difficulties with retention, surveyed employers often referred to a lack of "cultural fit" with some BIPOC planners, discrediting how people dress, wear their hair, or speak, and fall back to racial and gender stereotypes. Employers also talked about being color blind in their hiring—that race is not an important part of their workforce. But deeming race unimportant not only denies the influence of unconscious bias, but also can limit employers from understanding that people have different cultural norms and needs and that there are important assets and necessary changes that a racially diverse staff can bring to planning processes and outcomes.

Example Strategies

- Promote, mentor, and recruit for racial and ethnic diversity at all levels, especially managerial and senior levels, to correct for historic disparities. Both leadership and staff should represent the racial diversity of communities most negatively impacted and value equity as an asset.
- Proactively recruit staff of color from community colleges, HBCUs, and Tribal colleges. Provide meaningful training and mentorship to invest in the growth of a more racially diverse future workforce and leadership.
- Recruit from local diversity coalitions, committees, and organizations that work with a social-justice lens around the built environment and community development.

Strategies for Overcoming Retention and Advancement

Diversifying the planning profession requires strategies beyond just recruitment of new BIPOC planners, but also intentional strategies to better *retain* BIPOC. A participant in the Queer Planners of Color group expressed, "I changed jobs because I didn't want to be the only person of color. It's isolating culturally" (Black Planner, Private Sector). Many BIPOC planners interviewed expressed frustration and spoke of leaving or avoiding sectors altogether due to microaggressions and discrimination fatigue, isolation and self-doubt, being assigned less meaningful and less visible work, being skipped over for promotions compared to White colleagues, and being turned off by very White, male-dominant planning rhetoric and spaces. Thus, it is critical to incorporate strategies to train the existing workforce and leadership to be ready to receive and nurture racial diversity in the workplace, conduct assessments to identify inequities in pay and promotion, and train, promote, and hire BIPOC in senior positions, and compensate them well. The problem with lack of diversity is rooted in the actions of White people, and thus the burden of educating and making changes to address inequalities should not fall on the shoulders of BIPOC. Engagement of BIPOC requires fair compensation for the emotional labor and workplace traumas they experience from environments that are majority White and male. Most importantly, planning rhetoric needs to shift from the predominantly White, male, top-down approach it has traditionally taken. Planning must value and amplify the voices and lived expertise of BIPOC communities and commit to shifting the racial imbalance of power in this country.

We each move through this world subjectively, with limited, biased perspectives based on personal experiences. The coming together of people from different backgrounds, representing those most negatively impacted, enables an overall deeper awareness and understanding of the role of race, ethnicity, gender, ability, and class in social inequity and people's everyday lives. Ultimately, it can lead to more equitable processes and outcomes for historically marginalized communities. The involvement of young people, whose futures we as urban planners are helping to build, is especially critical.

Prioritizing Youth Perspectives in Planning

Early exposure to planning concepts not only exposes young people to new career pathways and is critical for improving representation within the field, but also provides spaces for young people to use their lived experience to reimagine their communities and advocate for change. According to the 2020 census, almost one in four people in the United States (73.1 million people) is under the age of 18. Globally, approximately 29% of the population is under 18 (CIA World Factbook, 2021). While young people represent a significant constituency locally and globally, they have little presence in planning and policymaking. Typical planning processes relegate the needs of young people to school and playground projects (Frank, 2006). The ways in which young people interact with the built environment differently from adults are rarely considered. Planners are trained to consider the needs of all people in the communities they serve, but on a regular basis roughly one-quarter of the community is not at the table. Implementing planning projects often takes years or even decades to complete. In that time, the young people who weren't at the table become young adults that must grapple with a previous generation's planning decisions and mistakes.

The lack of youth perspectives in planning and governance is particularly troubling when considering the overrepresentation of older adults in government: the average age of a US congressperson is 57.6 years, and 62.9 years for the Senate (Library of Congress, 2020). In local governance systems, such as community boards or civic associations, organizations are often overwhelmingly older and whiter than the general population (Kilgannon, 2016). Much has been written about the perceived apathy of young people to civics, citing lower voter turnout (Holbein, 2020) and involvement in civic organizations (Webster et al., 2021). But missing from these narratives is the fact that much of existing civic engagement does not consider the needs of young people, nor speak to the increasing urgency and anxiety that young people feel about the future (Center for Information and Research on Civic Learning and Engagement, 2013).

Even while young people are not consulted in urban planning, they are acutely aware of their physical environments and the disparities that exist. The 2014 *Well-Being of Adolescents in Vulnerable Environments* (WAVE) study examined the perception of adolescents in Baltimore (US), Ibadan (Nigeria), Johannesburg (South Africa), New Delhi (India), and Shanghai (China) with relation to health and well-being. While there were differences in perspectives because of built form variety across the cities, interviewees sophisticatedly identified planning topics such as housing, environmental health, and infrastructure as impacting their health (Mmari et al., 2014). Without an understanding of how and why neighborhood disparities exist, a young person may internalize that their community is to blame, instead of placing blame on racist policies that have marginalized Black, brown, and working-class communities. Introducing young people to urban planning can address the dearth of youth perspectives and expertise in community development, the lack of transparency around urban planning decision making and governance structures, and the lack of diversity in the planning profession.

Effective Youth Planning Education and Engagement

The American Planning Association New York Metro Area's Diversity Committee (DivComm) Youth Planning Engagement Team, which the authors of this chapter have led, has been engaging young people in planning since 2015. DivComm partners with elementary, middle, and high schools, as well as after-school programs and community colleges, to co-create curricula and lead interactive planning workshops in the classroom. Each class often begins with engaging young people to reflect on what makes up a city and what they see in their neighborhoods, connecting it to planning and/or the classroom subject, and inviting them to design and build their dream city. While there are different approaches to youth planning education, the following four principles have been shown to be successful from the teams' experience:

Respecting Lived Experience and Making Connections to Planning

Ethnography and participatory research have shifted to recognize young people as having unique perspectives and opinions that should be heard and respected, and that how they navigate the built environment is fundamentally different from adults (Davidson, 2017). From how young people travel to school or other places in their community, to what places they can safely linger and socialize, and how they choose to spend their leisure time, differs from how adults see and navigate space (Davidson, 2017). Engaging with young people in urban planning requires that adults make the space to actively listen to the experiences of young people. Asking thoughtful questions about themselves not only helps to create a rapport, but also can set the stage for young people to see the connections between their experiences and how they relate to urban planning. Table 7.2 provides examples of questions that can create connections to larger urban planning issues:

In asking questions about how young people feel in certain places, it is very likely that complicated feelings they have about their neighborhoods or cities may surface, especially if they come from marginalized communities. Asking about safety in place might lead to conversations about housing insecurity, gender-based violence, or over-policing. It is crucial to enter these conversations with empathy and sensitivity.

Connecting Urban Planning to Existing School Curricula

Given the role urban planning plays in shaping communities, a natural place to locate it in youth education could be a civics curriculum. However, there's a dearth of thorough civics education in K–12 schools. Nationwide, only 9 states require one year of civics, 30 require half a year, and 11 have no requirement (Shapiro & Brown, 2018). Furthermore, the structure of coursework tends to focus on US government history with minimal focus on public participation. A potential way to circumvent these gaps is to create planning experiences that are connected to foundational school curricula. For instance, a science class about ecosystems can also be an opportunity to talk about the different systems within a city or a neighborhood and how they are interconnected. An English-literature class could be an opportunity to examine the stories about young people in cities, such as *Brown Girl, Brownstones* (Marshall, 1959) or *A Tree Grows in Brooklyn* (Smith, 1943), and what they might tell us about the state of a city, the issues young people faced at that time, and how they compare to the issues young people face today. A math or home-economics class could be a pathway to talk about

Table 7.2 General Questions With Urban Planning Themes

Question	Urban Planning Themes
How did you get to school today, and how long did it take you?	Transportation planning and equity
What's your favorite place in your city, and how does that place make you feel?	Principles of good urban design, accessibility, and land use
Are there places in your city that you don't like or avoid?	Hostile architecture, exclusionary zoning, and nuisances
Have you ever felt unwelcomed in a place?	Surveillance and the history of loitering laws

Source: Created by Daphne Lundi (2022)

A Path to Racial Equity

city budgets and how or why certain projects or policies are valued over others. A history class can be a place to talk about urban renewal and the evolving state of cities, and so on.

Promoting Arts-Based Urban Planning

Engaging with young people presents an opportunity to step away from traditional modes of community engagement, such as charettes or surveys, to engagement that is grounded in art-based practices. Arts and culture play a significant role in shaping community identity. Art expression using collage, building with found objects, or storytelling can create the space for young people to share experiences of their communities and visualize alternative realities (Nonko, 2019). The Place-It! method, developed by urban planners James Rojas and John Kamp, is an art-based participatory planning process wherein participants use simple found objects to create physical representations of their communities. The artmaking creates an outlet for participants to imagine their communities interactively and creatively, both in their current conditions and future states (Rojas, 2013). The process of making art can also create a joyful space, allowing for more open and free dialogues (Korza et al., 2005).

Gamifying Planning Tools for a Younger Audience

For many planners, *SimCity*™ was the first place they came across urban planning concepts (Roy, 2019). The realms of video games and board games have vastly expanded since the original days of

Figure 7.1 High-School Students in Cobble Hill

High-school students in Cobble Hill create ideal cities using found objects in a workshop coordinated by the APA New York Metro Chapter Diversity Committee.

Source: Photo by Daphne Lundi (2019).

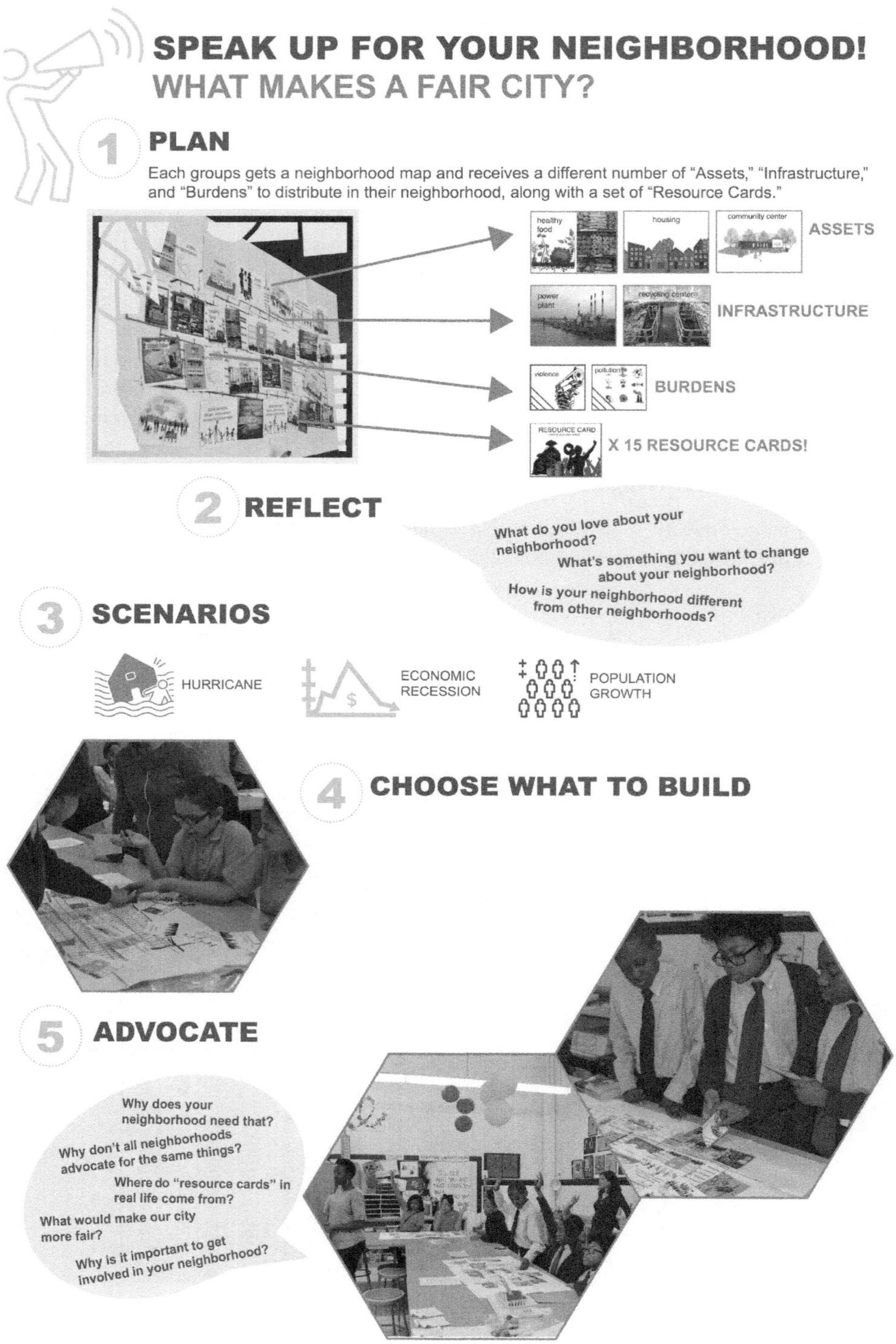

Giovania Tiarachristie and Daphne Lundi

Figure 7.2 Overview of *Speak Up for Your Neighborhood!*
Source: Kate Selden (2019).

SimCity™. Many current games, such as *Minecraft*™, can be useful mediums for exploring planning themes (Westerberg et al., 2015). Board and role-playing games can also be helpful for exploring different perspectives in urban planning. One example is the game *Speak Up for Your Neighborhood*, developed by planner Kate Selden, wherein players take on the roles of residents in different neighborhoods that each have varying degrees of economic and social stability. As players cycle through the game and are faced with different environmental and social challenges, they must decide how best to use their limited resources and how to advocate to elected officials for additional support.

The Center for Urban Pedagogy (CUP), a civic-design non-profit based in New York, has developed several games that help translate land-use policy in New York City into accessible language and graphics that help everyday New Yorkers understand the implications of zoning and the Uniform Land Use Review Procedure (ULURP). In the "What is ULURP?" activity, sandwiches are proxies for building development. Participants represent different roles in the rezoning process (mayor, community board, developer, city council, etc.) and collectively decide on the types and number of sandwiches they want in their community (Gaspar et al., 2017).

Beyond crafting youth-focused engagement strategies, planning professionals can also look for opportunities to embed youth engagement within neighborhood planning and development writ large. In *Urban Planning in The Classroom: The Intersection of Youth Participation in Planning and K–12 Education*, Kate Selden (2017) outlines strategies for youth participation in New York:

- Apportion a certain percentage of every neighborhood study to conducting outreach to young people.
- Community organizations, agencies, and other groups commissioning planning studies should incorporate a requirement for engaging young people into their requests for proposal (RFPs).
- Community boards should partner with local schools and planning programs to include young people in the creation of the yearly district needs assessment document.
- City council districts should partner with local classrooms to involve classes in the participatory budgeting process.

There are many creative ways to engage young people in planning. An important value that underlies these principles is acknowledging youth as a critical constituency to inform present and future decision-making. Engaging them in planning frameworks at an early age can help build the capacity of youth to become more civically engaged, empower them to pursue careers that expand their communities' decision-making powers, and help professionals design and plan futures that better serve the people who will inherit them.

Building Youth and BIPOC Power to Shape a More Equitable Future

The systems of inequality that exist today, as well as the barriers to racial diversity in the profession, are systemic and structural. Inaction to address these changes, or refusing to acknowledge the disparities that exist, only perpetuate planning to remain a predominately White profession with inequitable outcomes and damaging consequences for BIPOC communities. To address this, it is critical that BIPOC communities most negatively impacted by this history have meaningful representation in fields that make decisions around the built and social environment. Practitioners, schools, and planning institutions must work together to prioritize intentional, holistic strategies to better recruit, retain, and advance BIPOC in planning. Engaging young people as part of these strategies is particularly critical and powerful to both cultivate a new generation of more racially representative planners and also ensure the youth who inherit the future are part of building it today. The strategies included in this article are neither revolutionary nor exhaustive, but rather are tangible small steps and approaches that call for all stakeholders in the planning field to take shared responsibility in efforts to make our profession accountable to its past and its future. White privilege and power rely on the continued marginalization and oppression of BIPOC. But if urban planning has had the capacity to perpetuate systems of racism and oppression, then it also has the power to establish systems of justice, healing, and liberation for all.

Note

1 Estimates published by the US Census Bureau's Equal Employment Opportunity Tabulation tables for industry code 1840, based on the American Community Survey 2014–2018 five-year estimate, the most recent data set published in the EEO Tabulation. While there are more recent one-year ACS national estimates on race and the industry, the five-year ACS estimates reflect a lower margin of error due to greater sample size, and also allow comparison between the national and regional levels.

References

Center for Information and Research on Civic Learning and Engagement. (2013). *All together now: Collaboration and innovation for youth engagement.* https://circle.tufts.edu/sites/default/files/2020-01/all_together_now_commission_report_2013.pdf

Central Intelligence Agency. (2021). *The world Factbook.* www.cia.gov/the-world-factbook/countries/world/#people-and-society

Davidoff, P. (1965). Advocacy and pluralism in planning. *Journal of the American Institute of Planners, 31*(4), 331–338. https://doi.org/10.1080/01944366508978187

Davidson, E. (2017). Saying it like it is? Power, participation and research involving young people. *Social Inclusion, 5*(3), 228–239. https://doi.org/10.17645/si.v5i3.967

Forsyth, A. (1995). Diversity issues in a professional curriculum: Four stories and some suggestions for change. *Journal of Planning Education and Research, 15*(1), 58–63. https://doi.org/10.1177/0739456X9501500105

Forsyth, A. (2001). Nonconformist populations and planning sexuality and space: Nonconformist populations and planning practice. *Journal of Planning Literature, 15*(3), 339–358. https://doi.org/10.1177/08854120122093069

Frank, K. I. (2006). The potential of youth participation in planning. *Journal of Planning Literature, 20*(4), 351–371. https://doi.org/10.1177/0885412205286016

Frey, W. H. (2019, June 24). Less than half of U.S. children under 15 are white, census shows. *The Brookings Institution.* www.brookings.edu/research/less-than-half-of-us-children-under-15-are-white-census-shows/

Gaspar, C., & Torrey, M. (2017). *What is ULURP?* Center for Urban Pedagogy. https://citylimits.org/zonein/ulurp-explained/

Holbein, J. (2020, March 11). Why so few young Americans vote. *The Conversation.* https://theconversation.com/why-so-few-young-americans-vote-132649

Kilgannon, C. (2016, January 29). Greater diversity sought for New York city's community boards. *The New York Times.* www.nytimes.com/2016/01/30/nyregion/greater-diversity-sought-for-new-york-citys-community-boards.html

Korza, P., Assaf, A., & Bacon, B. (2005). *Inroads: The intersection of art & civic dialogue.* Americans for The Arts. www.animatingdemocracy.org/sites/default/files/documents/reading_room/INROADS%202.28.05.pdf

Marshall, P. (1959). *Brown girl, brownstones.* Random House.

Milroy, B. M. (1991). Taking stock of planning, space, and gender. *Journal of Planning Literature, 6*(1), 3–15. https://doi.org/10.1177/088541229100600101

Mmari, K., Lantos, H., Brahmbhatt, H., Delany-Moretlwe, S., Lou, C., Acharya, R., & Sangowawa, A. (2014). How adolescents perceive their communities: A qualitative study that explores the relationship between health and the physical environment. *BMC Public Health, 14,* 349. https://doi.org/10.1186/1471-2458-14-349

Nonko, E. (2019, October 16). NYC teens share how criminal justice system impacts their communities. *Next City.* https://nextcity.org/urbanist-news/nyc-teens-share-how-criminal-justice-system-impacts-their-communities

Rojas, J. (2013). Children are natural-born urban planners! *Journal of Applied Research on Children: Informing Policy for Children at Risk, 4*(2), 22. https://digitalcommons.library.tmc.edu/childrenatrisk/vol4/iss2/22

Roy, J. (2019, May 5). From video game to day job: How 'SimCity' inspired a generation of city planners. *The LA Times.* www.latimes.com/business/technology/la-fi-tn-simcity-inspired-urban-planners-20190305-story.html

Selden, K. (2017). *Urban planning in the classroom: The intersection of youth participation in planning and K-12 education* (Master's thesis). Pratt Institute Libraries. https://cat.pratt.edu/record=b1226533

Smith, B. (1943). *A tree grows in Brooklyn*. Harper.

Shapiro, S., & Brown, C. (2018, February 21). *The state of civics education*. Center for American Progress. https://americanprogress.org/article/state-civics-education/

Signe, C. (2020). *116th United States congress: A survey of books written by members*. Library of Congress. https://guides.loc.gov/116th-congress-book-list

Stafford, L. (2019, October 15). *Ableism and the struggle for spatial justice*. Open Democracy. www.opendemocracy.net/en/transformation/ableism-and-struggle-spatial-justice/

Sweet, E. (2010). Strategies for achieving diversity in urban planning: A case study at the university of Illinois. In N. A. Neville, M. B. Huntt, & J. Chapa (Eds.), *Implementing diversity: Contemporary challenges and best practices at predominantly white universities* (pp. 225–243). Center on Democracy in a Multicultural Society at University of Illinois at Urbana-Champaign.

Thomas, J. M. (2008). The minority-race planner in the quest for a just city. *Planning Theory, 7*(3), 227–247. https://doi.org/10.1177/1473095208094822

Tiarachristie, G. (2016). *Elephant in the planning room: Overcoming barriers to recruitment and retention of planners of color* (Master's thesis). Pratt Institute Libraries. https://cat.pratt.edu/record=b1224835

US Bureau of Labor Statistics. (2020, May). *Occupational employment and wages. 19–3051 Urban and regional planners*. www.bls.gov/oes/2020/may/oes193051.htm

US Census Bureau (2018). *Equal employment opportunity tabulation data tables, 2014–2018 American community survey 5-year estimates*. www.census.gov/data/tables/time-series/demo/eeo/acs-2014-2018.html

US Census Bureau. (2020). *Racial/ethnic population*. www.census.gov/quickfacts/fact/table/US/POP010220

Valentine, G. (1993). (Hetero)Sexing space: Lesbian perceptions and experiences of everyday spaces. *Environment and Planning D: Society and Space, 11*(4), 395–413. https://doi.org/10.1068/d110395

Vespa, J., Medina, L., & Armstrong, D. (2018). Demographic turning points for the United States: Population projections for 2020 to 2060. *U.S. Census Bureau Current Population Reports*. www.census.gov/content/dam/Census/library/publications/2020/demo/p25-1144.pdf

Webster, D., Dunne, L., & Hunter, R. (2021). Association between social networks and subjective well-being in adolescents: A systematic review. *Youth & Society, 53*(2), 175–210. https://doi.org/10.1177/0044118X20919589

Westerberg, P., & Heland, F. (2015). *Using Minecraft for youth participation in urban design and governance* (Report No. HS/088/15E). UN-HABITAT. https://unhabitat.org/sites/default/files/download-manager-files/Using%20Minecraft%20for%20Youth%20Participation%20in%20Urban%20Design%20and%20Governance.pdf

8
BUILDING PLANNING EDUCATION AT A HISPANIC-SERVING R1 INSTITUTION

Challenges in Diversity and Recruitment

Lauren Ames Fischer, Laura Keyes, and Abraham David Benavides

Historically in the United States, urban planning was a subject primarily taught in graduate professional design schools rather than in undergraduate social-science programs (Krueckeberg, 1985). In response to the needs of the growing profession, undergraduate degrees in urban planning increased tenfold in the United States between 1960 and 1975, producing almost 500 graduates annually (Krueckeberg, 1985). In the last 20 years, a focus on practice-oriented education and a desire to diversify degree offerings for undergraduates has led to an increase in undergraduate planning programs (Planning Accreditation Board, 2019). As of 2019, there were 16 accredited undergraduate programs in urban planning in the United States; however, the increase in degree programs has coincided with a decrease in the number of students enrolled in undergraduate planning programs (Palazzo et al., 2021). Between 2008 and 2019, the number of Planning Accreditation Board (PAB) accredited bachelor's degree programs increased from 14 to 16 while the total number of students enrolled decreased by more than 200, from 1,343 to 1,128 (Planning Accreditation Board, 2021).

The expansion of undergraduate educational offerings in planning has not necessarily increased the diversity of the profession. Indeed, as a field, planning struggles to produce inclusive educational programs and workplaces that reflect the diversity of the communities we serve (Lowe et al., 2016; Solis, 2020). Between 1960 and 1980, planning programs in the United States increased their gender diversity but fell short on racial and ethnic diversity (Thomas, 1996). Examining more recent data on students enrolled in urban planning programs, the Joint Task Force of American Planning Association (APA), American Institute of Certified Planners, Association of Collegiate Schools of Planning, and the PAB (2016) found that enrollment dropped among underrepresented demographic groups and that there is minimal improvement in the number and proportion of underrepresented faculty members. The analysis also showed that the most notable gains in diversity in the past decade have come from foreign students, whose enrollment in undergraduate PAB programs increased from 2% to 6% between 2008 and 2015 (ibid.).

Across PAB-accredited undergraduate programs, the racial diversity of students appears to be decreasing. In 2008, only 46% of students identified as White, whereas in 2015, 65% of students enrolled in PAB-accredited undergraduate programs identified as White. The opposite trend is observed in graduate education where the percentage of students identifying as White decreased from 60% to 51% between 2008 and 2015 (Joint Task Force, 2016). Overall, the undergraduate profile of PAB-accredited programs is whiter than graduate programs and, since 2009, the number of Black or African American students in undergraduate planning degree programs has fallen considerably and disproportionately in the United States (Lowe et al., 2016).

One potential influence on student diversity is the diversity (or lack thereof) of program faculty. While there was a notable increase in minority faculty members in US-based planning programs over the second half of the 20th century, partially due to the strengthening of diversity requirements in the PAB guidelines, only a third of graduate planning programs had specific goals related to faculty diversity (Ozawa et al., 2019). In recent years, there has been minimal change in racial and ethnic composition of planning faculty; in 2019, most full-time faculty at PAB-accredited programs (66%) identified as White, 12% identified as Asian, 8% as Black or African American, and 5% as Hispanic/Latino (Planning Accreditation Board, 2019). Though academic departments attempt to increase faculty diversity through a variety of efforts, including interest groups and specific training for minority faculty, they come up against institutional hiring practices that may dampen efforts to diversify (Ozawa et al., 2019). In the last four years of PAB site evaluations for 53 graduate and undergraduate planning programs, faculty diversity was the category with the highest cumulative number of citations, and student diversity was the second most common problem area (PAB, 2021).

While lack of diversity in planning programs is well documented and on the radar of many planning academics, there are institutional factors that undermine attempts to increase diversity. In this chapter, we provide a case study on the development of a new undergraduate degree in urban planning at the University of North Texas (UNT), a public, R1 research university, a Hispanic Serving Institution (HSI), and Minority Serving Institution (MSI) located in the Dallas–Fort Worth metroplex in the United States. In this case study, we document the origins of the new degree and review strategies employed by faculty and university leadership to promote faculty and student diversity. Our analysis is guided by several questions. Given the declining enrollment in undergraduate planning programs over the last decade, why did UNT create a new undergraduate degree in urban planning? How did concerns about faculty and student diversity shape the new program? What lessons can be learned from the UNT experience? We conclude with insights on current student demographics and a discussion of how to increase diversity and awareness about urban planning at other Hispanic Serving R1 and Minority Serving Institutions.

Undergraduate Planning Education in North Texas

Overall population growth pressures and regional demand for planning professionals set the context for the new degree proposal in 2016. From 2000 to 2015, the Dallas–Fort Worth (DFW) region increased by 1.9 million people, raising the population to 7.1 million residents, and making it the fourth largest metropolitan area in the United States (US Census, 2019). Population growth in the DFW region has also altered community demographics in favor of greater racial and ethnic diversity. In 2000, the populations of suburban Collin and Denton counties were both about 75% non-Hispanic White, but by 2019, the percentage had decreased to 55% and 57.6%, respectively. Over the last 20 years, both counties experienced increases in the percentage of Black, Asian, and Hispanic residents. In Collin County, the percentage of Black residents increased from 4.8% to 10.3%, Asian residents from 6.9% to 16.3%, and Hispanic residents from 10.3% to 15.5%. Denton County experienced similar trends, with a shift from 5.9% to 10% Black, 4% to 10.7% Asian, and 12.2% to 19.6% Hispanic residents. Increasingly, the growing suburban municipalities and counties reflect the diversity of the entire metropolitan region. In 2019, the demographics of the DFW population was 45.6% non-Hispanic white, 15.6% African American, 7% Asian, and 22% Hispanic (US Census, 2019).

For at least a decade, the faculty in the Department of Public Administration at UNT have had a desire to increase their undergraduate degree offerings. In fall 2016, the departure of the existing undergraduate degree in emergency management and disaster science to support a new independent department provided an opportunity. Building on the department's strengths in local government management, the faculty proposed two degree programs in nonprofit leadership and urban studies that would serve as feeders to the department's Master of Public Administration (MPA) program. By mid-2017, the Bachelor of Nonprofit Leadership Studies degree was approved by the Texas Higher Education Coordinating Board (THECB), and faculty turned their attention to building the urban studies degree.

In July 2017, support and enthusiasm from the newly hired provost, Dr. Jennifer Cowley, also a certified planner, provided continued momentum and financial support to create the urban-focused degree. As the department chair at the time recalls, the provost's guidance to the faculty was clear: "I see a significant market demand for this program, and it would be important to establish this program soon as we consider overall enrollment growth." During the degree-development process, several aspects of the vision changed. Rather than focusing on local government management, the curriculum expanded to include technical and urban-planning-specific topics, including a course on population demographics and another on land use and transportation. The degree name was also changed to Bachelor of Urban Policy and Planning (UPOP) to reinforce the technical and professional focus of the degree.

In fall 2019, the UPOP degree began accepting students. As a university with a large percentage of first-generation students (or students who are the first in their families to pursue a higher education degree) and students from lower income households, the faculty took several strategies to ensure student success in the program.

- *Minimize course pre-requisites* to make the degree more accessible to transfer students and to accommodate a wider range of student schedules and needs.
- *Establish a full-time undergraduate coordinator position* to manage student recruitment and retention, build community and professional relationships in North Texas, and teach core undergraduate courses. The department hired an AICP-trained planner with substantial practical experience and strong connections to professional planning organizations—having served as the chair of a state chapter of the American Planning Association—to fill this position. The coordinator has been instrumental in the degree's initial success by allowing the department to offer professional networking and development opportunities for students, in identifying volunteer and service opportunities for students to pursue individually, and for making connections between local stakeholders and new planning faculty members.
- *Provide financial support for new faculty to join and engage with professional organizations*, including the APA and Urban Land Institute, which are important for connecting students with non-academic employment and professional opportunities.
- *Hire two visiting assistant professors* with advanced degrees in urban planning and experience teaching at the undergraduate level.

It's important to note that student and faculty diversity didn't emerge as an explicit concern during the degree formation or faculty hiring processes. Though the university has a long history of serving minority and first-time-in-college (FTIC) students, UNT only achieved HSI and MSI status in 2020.[1] Though universities must apply to receive HSI or MSI status, these designations at UNT were primarily a result of changing regional demographics rather than a strategy to recruit Hispanic students. Since 2016, UNT has been a Tier 1 research institution, a designation given to higher-education institutions with high research productivity in the United States. The program plans to apply for PAB accreditation in the coming years pending adequate resources to meet the requirements, which may help with recruiting and marketing the degree and enhance graduates' entry into the field without obtaining a graduate degree.

Faculty Recruitment: Opportunities and Challenges

The UPOP degree was enabled by the hiring of two new urban-planning faculty—starting in fall 2019—who were brought on under the university's new Program for Enrollment Growth (PEG) intended to provide a "venture capital" approach to creating and justifying new degree programs. The PEG program required all new degree programs to hire new core faculty as visiting assistant professors for a minimum of three years, with the agreement that these lines would convert into tenure-track if the department, college, and university achieved a series of student growth and retention goals. Faculty hired under the PEG didn't receive the typical start-up package and had a higher teaching load than regular tenure-track faculty. The Bachelor of Urban Policy and Planning was the first beta test for the PEG program, and the two visiting UPOP positions were converted into tenure-track faculty lines in fall 2021, three years after the program was created.

The major items that were prioritized in faculty selection were the potential for a robust externally funded research program and the willingness to contribute to student recruitment and degree building activities that go beyond the traditional expectations of tenure-track faculty. This framework resulted in the hiring of two White, non-Hispanic faculty with substantial expertise in the subfield of land use and transportation. This outcome is reflective of the tradeoffs often encountered in R1 tenure-track hiring processes. While there is a general desire for faculty members that reflect the diversity of the student body, faculty searches tend to prioritize planning subfields that can attract external funding. These search constraints can severely limit the pool of potential candidates. While this approach helps solidify R1 status, it can also undermine diversity goals. In the wake of 2020's mobilization for racial equity, UNT faculty have become acutely aware of the need to explicitly confront racial disparities and exclusion in all aspects of higher education, including faculty diversity. As the department prepares to hire a third tenure-track position in urban planning, it remains unclear how racial diversity will be integrated into the hiring process. Although the university has a goal to "increase diversity of new faculty and staff hires" (Smatresk, 2020), the delegation of specific hiring decisions to departments and programs, combined with the intense focus on maintaining R1 status, may be a barrier to implementation (Ozawa et al., 2019).

Like most new degree programs, curricular development for the new planning degree has moved in stages. At the onset of the degree creation, the focus was on leveraging the existing assets of the department to expand undergraduate curricular options for students. The second phase of curriculum development has centered more on building a competitive undergraduate planning program that is distinct from the public affairs and urban studies majors commonly offered at the undergraduate level. UNT's competitive edge includes the ability to expose students to a range of viewpoints and experiences through diverse guest speakers and professional networking opportunities (see Keyes et al., Chapter 4 in this book), as well as opportunities to work closely with faculty on research and planning projects.

This phased approach has had several benefits. First, it allowed the department to craft a plan for action that could be accomplished without additional resources by embedding the core planning courses in existing departmental strengths and expertise. Second, it provided new faculty with considerable agency to shape courses and curriculum to fit the university and region's needs and priorities. Third, it enabled curriculum and faculty expertise to adjust to important real-time changes and emerging concerns in the field. To ensure that the planning faculty continue to provide students with diverse viewpoints and experiences, however, will require a purposeful and strategic plan of action that centers faculty diversity as a means of increasing the diversity of students who choose urban planning as a profession.

Student Recruitment: Opportunities and Challenges

A strategy for student recruitment was developed in tandem with the new degree proposal and executed by the department's undergraduate coordinator. Face-to-face interactions with newly admitted and existing students was the primary focus of initial recruitment in 2018 and 2019. Today, the face-to-face approach is three pronged: prospective student events, existing student events, and newly admitted student events. Faculty actively participate in university-wide events such as fall and spring admission events, transfer debuts, and summer orientations to personally engage students who are planning to attend the university. When asked about their current degree-seeking interests, students indicate preferences for degrees promoted by high-school counselors such as chemistry, biology, political science, or health administration, among others. Face-to-face interactions allow faculty to influence student interest by explaining how a degree in urban policy and planning could help them achieve their education and career goals. This direct engagement with faculty is incredibly important, as many university staff and counselors working in admissions have limited knowledge of urban planning and are often unable to explain its relevance. Face-to-face interactions are complemented by more traditional forms of outreach, including distributing course flyers at new and current student events and putting yard signs throughout campus to advertise the new degree program.

As the program has grown, the department has relied heavily on social media to recruit students by building a narrative around it. Daily content helps inform potential students about course information, student successes, and research experiences with faculty, as well as internship and career opportunities. We also use these platforms to share media stories on current events related to urban planning and policy, further illustrating how the degree can connect students with real-world problems and prepare them to develop novel solutions. Promotion of high-performing posts and student testimonials, along with strategic hashtags of UNT dorms, programs, clubs, and area high schools, help promote the UPOP brand and broaden connections with current and prospective students.

We have also used student testimonial videos to highlight student successes that help promote the educational and social culture of the program while also showcasing the diversity of students enrolled in the program. We did not target specific groups of underrepresented students in our initial recruitment efforts, choosing to focus on connecting the degree to professional opportunities and skill development while profiling the experiences of a diversity of students. With the university's new status as an HSI, the department is revising its recruitment strategy to target Hispanic students and has hired an undergraduate student to assist with developing a new, culturally responsive social media and outreach campaign in spring 2022.

During 2020, the COVID-19 pandemic required a transition from face-to-face to virtual recruiting activities that had an increased emphasis on using social media. In the future, we expect to offer both in-person and virtual recruiting events that will use student testimonials; as well as direct faculty and student contact at resource fairs, transfer debuts, and undergraduate open houses. We also hope to partner with student organizations and other academic departments to expand awareness about urban planning as a course of study and a professional endeavor.

The recruitment of a diverse student body is central to the UPOP program's growth strategy, and faculty have recognized the need to expand recruitment efforts to include high-school students. In 2019, faculty started building relationships with administrators at a magnet high school in the Dallas Independent School District called City Lab. City Lab is a selective, application-based public high school that prepares students to be future leaders in the urban development fields. The department has sponsored events at the high school, had faculty volunteer at virtual seminars, and had three undergraduates participate in a collaborative mentoring program with high-school students organized by the Urban Land Institute. To date, these efforts have had minimal success. While other universities in the region, such as the University of Texas at Arlington, have agreed to accept credit for City Lab courses in place of core classes in architecture or urban planning, UNT doesn't have this same arrangement. This highlights the limitations of department-based recruitment efforts at UNT—and perhaps other institutions—where recruitment at high schools occurs independently through the office of admissions with limited consultation of academic programs.

Due to the enduring nature of the COVID-19 pandemic, getting in front of prospective students remains a challenge, as does illustrating the value of a UPOP degree to underrepresented students. This book elaborates on a variety of approaches we, and others, are using to connect minority students with the urban-planning profession and planners of color. We will continue to use multimedia to highlight current student activities and experiences, and we plan to return to pre-pandemic support for faculty and student involvement in local and state planning conferences. These experiences are critical to helping raise awareness about the program's key role in supporting a student's career trajectory. Course syllabi and pedagogical approaches are also important marketing tools reflecting the continuum of practice-oriented opportunities.

Lessons Learned

Importance of University Leadership

The UPOP degree was initiated and conceived by faculty in the Department of Public Administration but was importantly shaped and championed by administrative leadership. Lacking any full-time faculty with expertise in urban planning, existing faculty relied on the guidance and advice of provost Jennifer Cowley, a practicing and academic urban planner. The department also depended on the undergraduate coordinator, another experienced planning professional. Lessons for other programs include engaging the relevant local chapter of the American Planning Association in degree formation (including details such as course titles, internship requirements, etc.) and consulting with urban-planning faculty at other universities.

In the case of UNT, university leadership also shaped the faculty selection process by emphasizing the importance of meeting R1 metrics (including research expenditures). The university's PEG program which provides new faculty with a higher teaching load and less job security than a traditional tenure-track position may have also shaped faculty recruitment by making the job less attractive to competitive candidates who were unwilling or unable to accept a temporary position. Going forward, the University's HSI and MSI status and a heightened concern with racial equity and disparities may help prioritize faculty diversity in future hiring processes.

Recruiting Diverse Faculty

The UPOP faculty selection process prioritized skills the faculty viewed as key to creating and sustaining a new degree program, including administrative skills, ability to work with others, and a record of accomplishment balancing scholarship with teaching and student engagement. As a new program at an R1 institution, the focus on student interactions was on par with the ability to have an externally funded research agenda. Racial and ethnic diversity of faculty wasn't a driving concern. As a result, the inaugural planning faculty for the new degree didn't increase the racial or ethnic diversity of the department. This illustrates how the multifaceted expectations of faculty search processes produce tradeoffs and competing incentives that make prioritizing faculty diversity a major challenge. As UNT prepares to hire for a third tenure-track position in planning, we hope to integrate several suggestions identified in the PAB Diversity Task Force Report (2019), including drafting a broad job announcement and reviewing professional references prior to reviewing resumes (Ozawa et al., 2019).

Tenure-track openings are only one method of increasing diversity among faculty and instructors. Given the infrequencies and uncertainty of university hiring, academic planning programs must find other ways to emphasize faculty and departmental commitment to diversity in the field of planning and to create a work environment that is inclusive for a diverse range of potential colleagues. At UNT, our strategies have included showcasing faculty and student research related to racial equity and highlighting community-based research and service projects in underserved neighborhoods. Active recruitment of minority practitioners for studio and practicum courses is another strategy that our department could use to diversify faculty teaching in the planning program with the caveat that adjunct salaries rarely compensate professionals appropriately.

Recruiting Diverse Students

The first wave of urban-planning students enrolled in the new UNT program mirrored the demographic makeup of the student body. As of November 2020, there were 60 declared urban-planning majors: 15% identified as Black, 28.3% as Hispanic, and 50% as Non-Hispanic White. Compared to an overall student body that is 48% Non-Hispanic White, 22% Hispanic, and 14% Black, the UPOP program appears to be recruiting a representatively diverse group of students. Racial diversity is a metric the department plans to track going forward to ensure that our program provides a pathway to planning careers for a range of students with the goal of helping promote diversity in the planning profession.

The recruitment of diverse students to the UPOP program—and increasing knowledge about the field of urban planning on campus more generally—is also bolstered by student activities. Current UPOP students that are affiliated with the urban planning student organization host collaborative events with other student groups that have shared interests, such as Future Without Poverty,[2] give presentations in their non-UPOP courses about the student group, organize meetings with professional planning interest groups in the region, and present their research at interdisciplinary campus-wide events. Faculty give advice and support to the student group, but they operate independently of the department and with limited resources. Going forward, our department needs to consider how to effectively and equitably leverage student networks, passions, and resources to support the recruitment of diverse students in ways that do not disproportionately burden existing students.

Changing Priorities

When the UPOP degree was conceived in 2016 and 2017, racial equity and faculty diversity were not major concerns at the University of North Texas. UNT only achieved HSI and MSI status in 2019 as a result of changing regional demographics rather than a purposeful enrollment strategy. The rarity of tenure-track faculty hires in urban-planning programs (and higher education more broadly) means that faculty hiring decisions made under one set of priorities (such as external funding) will shape program and degree development for years to come with few chances to augment faculty in favor of greater diversity. Going forward, planning programs should strategically engage their university leadership on the importance of diversifying the profession of urban planning and the role that faculty diversity can play in student recruitment and retention to support this goal.

Conclusion

In conclusion, increasing racial and ethnic diversity of professional planners begins with raising awareness about the field at all levels of education, including undergraduate. Urban planning, and the built-environment fields more generally, are not well-known professions or fields of study for many undergraduates, especially those identifying as first-generation or minorities. Social-media campaigns highlighting the diversity of current students and collaboration with student organizations and affiliated academic fields are two methods that have been successful at raising awareness about urban planning at UNT. Increasing faculty diversity has been a greater challenge due to institutional and departmental hiring practices that have historically emphasized external research funding and best-fit metrics that don't prioritize racial or ethnic diversity. As an HSI and MSI, UNT's urban policy and planning program has an opportunity—and a moral obligation—to recruit and train the next generation of diverse planners to serve an increasingly diverse region.

Notes

1 Minority Serving Institution (MSI) and Hispanic Serving Institution (HSI) are designations made for postsecondary educational institutions by the US Department of Education. MSI is a blanket category that includes colleges and universities that serve minority populations, as defined by § 365(3) of the Higher Education Act (HEA) (20 U.S.C. § 1067k(3)). HSI refers to an MSI that has at least 25% or more full-time enrollment of undergraduate students who identify as Hispanic. Other types of MSI designations are Historically Black Colleges and Universities (HBCUs), Tribal colleges and universities (TCUs), and Asian American and Pacific Islander Serving Institutions (AAPISIs).
2 Future Without Poverty is an international organization with a student chapter at the University of North Texas that aims to promote health equity through local and international projects.

References

Joint Task Force of American Planning Association, American Institute of Certified Planners, & Association of Collegiate Schools of Planning. (2016). *Joint task force on enrollment report.* www.planningaccreditationboard.org/wp-content/uploads/2021/04/2016EnrollmentRpt.pdf

Krueckeberg, D. A. (1985). The tuition of American planning: From dependency toward self-reliance. *The Town Planning Review*, 421–441. www.planningaccreditationboard.org/wp-content/uploads/2021/04/TheTuitionOfAmericanPlanning.pdf

Lowe, J., Chakraborty, A., Forsyth, A., Giusti, C., Goldsmith, W., Sandoval, G., & Thompson, M. (2016). *Report on race, ethnicity, and foreign origin data for ACSP, 2016* (p. 15). Association for Collegiate Schools of Planning (ACSP). www.planningaccreditationboard.org/wp-content/uploads/2021/04/2016Diversity.pdf.

Ozawa, C., Schwartz, S., & Johnson, J. (2019). Diversity Task Force Report. Planning Accreditation Board. www.planningaccreditationboard.org/wp-content/uploads/2021/03/2019DiversityReport.pdf

Palazzo, D., Hollstein, L., & Diko, S. K. (2021). Urban planning as a career preference for students: Efforts to improve awareness about the profession. *Planning Practice & Research*, 36(2), 174–192. https://doi.org/10.1080/02697459.2020.1782056

Planning Accreditation Board. (2019). *Student and faculty composition in PAB-accredited programs.* www.planningaccreditationboard.org/wp-content/uploads/2021/06/2019AR.pdf

Planning Accreditation Board. (2021). *Trouble areas and frequencies, 2017 standards, site visit team evaluation of 32 programs (2018–2020).* www.planningaccreditationboard.org/wp-content/uploads/2022/03/Trouble2017Stds.pdf

Smatresk, N. (2020). *Moving forward together: UNT's action plan for improving diversity and inclusion on campus.* https://president.unt.edu/sites/default/files/2020_Moving%20Forward%20Together%20Plan.pdf

Solis, M. (2020). Racial equity in planning organizations. *Journal of the American Planning Association*, 86(3), 297–303. https://doi.org/10.1080/01944363.2020.1742189

Thomas, J. M. (1996). Educating planners: Unified diversity for social action. *Journal of Planning Education and Research*, 15(3), 171–182. https://doi.org/10.1177/0739456X9601500302

US Census Bureau. (2019). *ACS demographic and housing estimates (5-year estimates) (Table DP05).* United States Census Bureau.

SECTION II

Planning Awareness Among Children and Youth

Varied factors create the conditions that shape the career preferences of children and youth. The immediate family environments and broader communities or societies in which children and youth grow build interest in and often shape their decisions to pursue specific career goals. In addition, the school environment engenders interactions and exchanges of information that enable children and youth to have ideas about different careers and pathways. It is for this reason that many studies identify parents' occupations, socioeconomic status, teachers, counselors, and peers as important factors molding the career choices of children and youth.

Whether in the family, broader community, school environment, or what children and youth see on television, one key observation is that their interactions and experiences in these spaces influence how they think, act, and make decisions about their future careers. To create similar interactions and experiences, career-development programs often initiate activities to raise awareness around specific professions, serving as springboards for developing the interest of children and youth in specific professions. This is particularly important for lesser-known and understood professions like urban planning. High school teachers, guidance counselors, students, parents, and the public are generally unfamiliar with the profession. It is therefore imperative to intentionally develop programs that engender urban planning experiences to serve as influential contexts to shape children-and-youth career preferences for the planning profession.

Such intentional programs, which we call Design and Planning Language Programs (DPLPs), are the focus of Section II of this book. DPLPs are programs or a set of activities often initiated by universities' urban planning programs and their home departments—or other planning-related organizations—to create awareness of planning issues and different career pathways related to urban planning. These programs are warranted because they can generate the necessary conditions to influence children-and-youth awareness of urban planning and its many facets to potentially choose it as an educational path and eventually as a career.

This section comprises nine such initiatives—across the United States, Japan, Australia, Egypt, United Arab Emirates, and Fiji. While there are no overarching commonalities in the structure of these programs, the DPLPs discussed in this section share the common aim of introducing urban planning to children and youth by engaging them in experiential activities that allow them to immerse themselves in specific urban planning issues and processes. The majority of DPLPs discussed are administered entirely by universities' urban planning programs or departments—often led by faculty and students—in collaboration with other community actors or entities.

DOI: 10.4324/9781003254003-11

The opening chapter by Leah Marie Hollstein, Stephen Kofi Diko, and Danilo Palazzo addresses two questions on how to increase professional planning awareness among youth and children—what factors influence career awareness, and how planning schools can influence career awareness through effective collaborations with high schools—by providing insights from the University of Cincinnati School of Planning's Activate Community Empowerment (ACE) outreach program. Beyond the case study, the chapter provides the underpinning literature on career choices and preferences among children and youth to set the tone for this section.

Deborah McKoy and David Hernandez Garcia reflect on the Youth-Plan, Learn, Act, Now (Y-PLAN) program from the University of California, Berkeley. Dating back to 2000, it is one of the oldest DPLPs administered by a planning program in the United States. Y-PLAN is a unique community engagement studio that adds a transformative learning experience to UC Berkeley's Department of City and Regional Planning. The program teams Berkeley students with low-income Black, Latinx, and Asian high-school students to tackle problems within their local communities. In this chapter, Deborah McKoy—the creator of Y-PLAN—and David Hernandez Garcia—an alumnus of the program—review the history of the program and its long-term effects on Berkeley planning students, participating high school students, and their neighborhoods.

Seth Asare Okyere, Lisa Ueno, Mowa Ebashi, Motoki Shimoda, Hiroshi Tsuji, and Michihiro Kita's chapter offers insights on a DPLP that focuses on elementary-age students from the Kaizuka West Elementary School Machizukuri Club in Japan. The DPLP is an awareness-focused planning education initiative by Osaka University, in conjunction with staff from the local government and a private real-estate company. Designed around the Japanese concept of Machizukuri, which means community planning, students and faculty from the Urban Planning and Design Lab of the Division of Global Architecture work with teachers and students of a local Machizukuri Club. This DPLP, set within the Japanese primary education system, demonstrates that it is possible to customize DPLPs and embed them within a range of educational systems and cultures.

Following Okyere et al.'s chapter, Bartlett Warren-Kretzschmar and Carlos V. Licon describe the use of the geodesign process with ninth graders as a hands-on planning experience-*cum*-educational tool for high-school students, suggesting that it is a potential avenue for introducing students to the planning profession. K. Meghan Wieters's subsequent chapter shares information about a 2013 initiative dubbed the NeighborWalk program that the Neighborhood Alliance of Central Oklahoma and City of Oklahoma City staff initiated with the University of Oklahoma to prepare learning modules for fifth graders to introduce them to urban planning.

Aya Elkhouly and Doha Eissa provide lessons from a DPLP for children between six and 15 years old in Egypt, UAE, and China between 2017 and 2020. They use their version of DPLP to propose a hybrid model that promotes a comprehensive urban planning awareness experience for children and youth. This is followed by Isabel Virgona and Simon Pinnegar's explanation of how a transformation in secondary school geography curriculum by integrating urban and regional planning can induce potential impacts on students' understanding of urban dynamics and their ability to engage in urban planning processes. Following this chapter is Robyn G. Mansfield's contribution, which demonstrates that one way to increase diversity in planning and students of planning education is by understanding the barriers to engaging children in urban planning processes occurring in vulnerable settings.

The last chapter of this section comes from Evangeline Linkous, Melissa Zornitta, and Melissa Dickens. The contributors draw on two initiatives—the Future Leaders in Planning (FLiP) program and the Mentor a Planning Student (MAPS) program—to demonstrate that raising awareness about planning education and careers can be achieved by building and enhancing relationships between faculty and students of urban planning programs and departments, as well as residents of their host communities. They emphasize a town-and-gown framework as critical for professional planning awareness among children and youth.

Indeed, the contributions from this section substantiate three observations by Palazzo et al. (2021). Firstly, DPLPs are intentional endeavors that enable urban planning educators and professionals to create activities and conditions that provide influential and vital proximal contexts to expose children and youth to urban planning, with the potential to also influence their career preferences for urban planning. Secondly, the DPLPs demonstrate the need to immerse children and youth around problem-solving activities relating to urban planning issues that they are familiar with and/or are of interest to them. Such real-world activities make urban planning real to children and youth and engender an interest in being part of solutions to the problems that confront communities and cities. Lastly, insights from the contributions confirm the daunting challenge of sustaining DPLPs. Unlike the Y-PLAN that has been in existence since 2000, many of the initiatives were one-off programs or lasted only a few years. This makes understanding and learning from what works to increase awareness about the urban planning profession challenging because they are not implemented long enough to offer lessons about their long-term effects. Furthermore, while most of the DPLPs discussed in this section are housed within academic institutions, others are created and staffed by individuals, groups, or non-profit organizations. Although these programs lack the institutional backing and structure that a university can lend to a DPLP, they also enjoy benefits from being located outside of these structures—including increased flexibility, nontraditional approaches, and short startup times, among other advantages.

Overall, Section II provides insights into the saliency of DPLPs in creating the necessary proximal contexts to raise awareness about the urban planning profession. Indeed, they demonstrate the need to be intentional about creating professional planning awareness through the different versions of these initiatives. The multiple jurisdictions where these DPLPs were implemented and their unique approach to engaging children and youth offer important understanding for adoption and adaptation by planning programs and departments, professional organizations, and non-profits interested in introducing the urban planning profession to children and youth.

Reference

Palazzo, D., Hollstein, L., & Diko, S. K. (2021). Urban planning as a career preference for students: Efforts to improve awareness about the profession. *Planning Practice & Research*, *36*(2), 174–192. https://doi.org/10.1080/02697459.2020.1782056

9

BECOMING ACTIVATED

Professional Awareness Through the Activate Community Empowerment Outreach Program[1]

Leah Marie Hollstein, Stephen Kofi Diko, and Danilo Palazzo

Career preferences of children and youth are often made based on their parents' occupations, television, real-life role models, socioeconomic status, and teachers, as well as perceptions of gender roles in society—making the immediate family environments, school environments, and community environments (Howard et al., 2015) important arenas for intervention when it comes to career-development initiatives. More often than not, career preferences of children and youth are influenced by multiple factors, with family and friends being the most impactful influencers, followed by college and high-school counselors (Kenny & Bledsoe, 2005; Hutchison et al., 2014; Gallup-Strada, 2017).

While children are often more exposed to the known careers in their family, school, and community environments, the same cannot be said of the urban planning profession. Families, friends, and high-school and university counselors are often unaware of the profession (Rodriguez, 2009; Tiarachristie, 2016)—and when they are, they often have an erroneous perception about what the profession is. The awareness challenge is aggravated by the lack of clarity on the academic home of urban planning programs, variations in academic curricula, and misconceptions about its employment prospects (see the "Introduction" of this book for a wider consideration of these issues). These issues engender an environment where many children and youth will probably miss out on the opportunity to know about and subsequently choose the urban planning profession as a career preference (Palazzo et al., 2021).

Despite the efforts of national planning associations such as the American Planning Association (APA), the Canadian Institute of Planners, and the Royal Town Planning Institute to help raise awareness of the planning profession and its related concepts among children and youth, there continues to be a need for more efforts to confront this challenge (Palazzo et al., 2021). Hence, the actions of planning schools around the United States and internationally are vital to addressing this missing cohort of students who are unaware of the planning profession and/or might be interested in choosing the profession as a career path (APA, 2022).

Against this backdrop, the School of Planning (SOP) at the University of Cincinnati (UC) developed ACE (Activating Community Empowerment), a high-school outreach program. Through ACE, faculty and students—ranging from bachelor's to PhD-level—initiated a series of Power Lunches and designed charettes to introduce concepts as disparate as community engagement, democratic participation, environmental analysis, networking, leadership, physical design, and public speaking to students at a public high school near the UC campus. A student-identified problem on their campus was adopted as the focal issue of a four-day design workshop intentionally aimed at empowering high-school students to engage with, and make changes to, the urban places in which they live.

Using the ACE program as a case study, this chapter's aim is to answer two main questions: (1) What factors influence career awareness among children and youth? and (2) How can planning schools influence career awareness through collaborations with high schools? The chapter also explores challenges and opportunities that can form the basis for improving ways to encourage high-school students to become community change agents and potential future urban planners.

Career Awareness and Preferences

This section focuses on the extant literature on career preferences among children and youth. It begins with the factors that influence children and youth career preferences, followed by how these factors often change over time. This section ends with a review of the role of higher education institutions and counseling programs in children and youth career awareness and preferences.

Proximal and Distal Factors

Career choices among children and youth are influenced by a number of factors. Families, friends, teachers, role models, and experiences at school, in their communities, at home, or while watching television often influence their career choices (Howard et al., 2015). Specifically, experiences during their school years become translated into career choices. This subsequently makes schools a strong influencing context for their career choices and preferences (Lent et al., 1994). A survey by Gallup in 2017 revealed that informal sources in students' communities (e.g., friends, family, and community leaders), at school (college staff, professors, high-school teachers, coaches), and at work (employers, coworkers, experienced professionals, the military) play larger roles than students' counselors—constituting 55% of the sources of information influencing their career choices. Clearly, informal environments and channels are becoming germane factors influencing children and youth career choices, as compared to formal channels such as high-school and college counselors and the media (Gallup-Strada Education Network, 2017).

In the mid-1980s, Bandura (1986) argued that behavioral outcomes of people—how they think, act, and the choices they make—are based on interactions with other people and the environments in which they find themselves. Schoon and Parsons (2002) suggest further that proximal factors and contexts are critically influential. Proximal factors such as interests, goals, and actions of children and youth; parents and their aspirations for them; and the socioeconomic circumstances they are raised in often influence their career choices and preferences (Vondracek et al., 1986; Caspi et al., 1998; Shavit & Muller, 1998; Lent et al., 2000; Schoon & Parsons, 2002; Dietrich & Kracke, 2009; Strom et al., 2014). Additionally, distal factors such as the social class of children and youth, the workplaces of their parents, and social norms and customs influence not only career choices, but also the attainment of those careers and education (Schoon & Parsons, 2002). In effect, the personal agency of children and youth about their career choices are often influenced by their immediate, as well as broader, environments.

This is not to suggest that the abilities and capacities of children and youth to self-regulate their career choices through their ambitions and aspirations are not important (Rogers et al., 2008; Ashby & Schoon, 2010). Lent et al. (1994) direct attention to the role cognitive abilities play in how children and youth appreciate and place importance on these influencing factors. The roles played by self-regulation and cognitive abilities of children and youth in their career choices and preferences can be traced to how they learn, the people they interact with, contextual factors or subjective influences, the expected outcomes of career choices and preferences, or whether certain career choices and preferences will eventually pay off in the future (Bandura, 1986; Krumboltz & Nichols, 1990; Lent et al., 1994; Wiesner et al., 2003).

Furthermore, studies on the determinants of career choices among children and youth also point out the evolutionary nature of the process as well as the role of proximal and distal factors and contexts (Wiesner et al., 2003; Kenny & Bledsoe, 2005; Rodriguez, 2009; Hutchison et al., 2014; Howard et al., 2015). Wiesner et al. point to the fact that "early adult career pathways clearly were linked to academic, personal, and interpersonal characteristics during childhood and adolescence" (2003, p. 324). Their study notes that temporary influencing factors are as important as those factors that may seem constant or permanent in the lives of children and youth. Furthermore, proximal factors, which may also be transient, are deemed as stronger influencing factors on career choices than distal factors among children and youth. Subsequently, understanding the influencing factors and contexts that mold children and youth's career preferences is imperative for creating intentional initiatives necessary to not only raise awareness about specific careers but also to effectively guide them with the appropriate information to make an informed decision about their career pathways.

Evolutionary Nature of Children's Career Choices

Children and youth are normally exposed to activities that may inform their career choices, which often develop as they grow, making the factors that influence career choices and preferences evolutionary (Ferreira et al., 2007). Furthermore, interactions with people, experiences with multiple contexts, and even engaging in some career-related activities can potentially create pathways leading to their career of choice and preference (Lent et al., 1994; Ferreira et al., 2007). They often develop an array of potential careers that eventually form part of their decision-making processes (Gottfredson, 1981). Cook et al. (1996) and Vondracek et al. (1999) argue that children and youth often have an awareness of the different jobs that they can potentially do, as well as the social contexts that shape them—awareness often gained from both proximal and distal factors. Schoon and Parsons (2002) thus conclude that children and youth sometimes end up choosing careers that are compatible with their personalities and familiar environments. Goyette and Mullen (2006) conclude their data analysis on the relationship between social background and selection of vocational or arts-and-science majors at college by affirming that: "low-SES [socioeconomic status] students are more likely to choose vocational majors [. . .] High-SES students choose A&S majors" (page 501), a conclusion also confirmed by Ma (2009).

Critically, the evolutionary nature of career development suggests it's a learning process occurring throughout the lives of children and youth (Collin & Watts, 1996; Mitchell & Krumboltz, 1996; Watson & McMahon, 2005). The source of learning converges with proximal factors—individual interests, goals, actions, family, school, society, peer group—and distal factors—community, social norms and customs, and the labor market context (Lent et al., 2000). For this reason, children and youth can be expected to have an interest in and awareness of certain careers. By understanding what and how children learn, and how their learning changes over time—that is, proximal and distal factors and contexts and the evolutionary nature of their career choices—career-development programs for children and youth can be made more intentional and tailored to ensure such career choices are targeted. Studies show that career education plays an important role in career-development learning and career preferences among children and youth (Caspi et al., 1998; Gillies et al., 1998; Watson & McMahon, 2005). In some cases, such career education helps reduce career stereotyping (Bailey & Nihlen, 1990; Bigler & Liben, 1990).

Career Education and Counseling

For many schools, career education is increasingly becoming an integral part of their curricula and sometimes included as career-counseling programs mandated by state departments (Withington et al., 2012). In addition, different approaches are adopted to make information about career choices and preferences available to children and youth. One-stop counseling centers, online-counseling services, mentoring and coaching programs, and career fairs are some examples of interventions dotted across many schools and communities (Amundson, 2006; Tien, 2007). However, with changing contexts and influential factors, career education needs to expand and incorporate new ways of introducing career opportunities to children and youth and help them make informed career choices (Amundson, 2006).

One way to do this is for career education and counseling efforts to recognize that career choices are both a lifelong process and are also influenced by informal sources. Career education and counseling should also come from different perspectives (Amundson, 2006). They must not only target children and youth but the broader social and informal contexts within which they grow. In view of this, such education and counseling programs can make provisions for educating parents and guardians, and even the general community, about the different career opportunities that they may not be aware of or familiar with.

Efforts to increase awareness of specific careers among specific groups are often undertaken through counseling activities and programs initiated by higher-education institutions. Tsui (2007) notes that to increase the representation of minority groups in science, technology, engineering, and mathematics (STEM) education, many higher-education institutions in the United States adopt pre-college summer and mentoring programs. These programs expose children and youth to the potentials and prospects of the fields, help build interest where interest is lacking, dissolve any potential fears, and offer targeted career counseling to children and youth who participate in these programs (Stipanovic & Stringfield, 2013).

These programs often complement counseling efforts that may be missing in proximal environments such as families, friends, and even teachers and high-school counselors who may have no knowledge about STEM fields, their job prospects, or the way to attain such careers. Good et al.'s (2002) study, for instance, showed that African American engineering students who remain in engineering majors were influenced by prior interactions with professionals in the field. A Campbell-Heider et al. (2008) study on the recruitment of minority teens into nursing revealed several barriers which existed as a result of misconceptions about the career. Partnerships with local school counselors and teachers to talk to teens about the profession and answer their questions were able to break barriers and help increase interest. In the accounting profession, Jackson and Bruns (2011) identified an absence of role models, lack of education about the career, misconceptions regarding existing opportunities for career advancement, and fear as barriers to attracting minorities. Schams et al. (2022) also showed the efficacy of a class-level intervention in decreasing students' career indecision, while Bounds (2017) explored the relevance of career-development programming, particularly among African American adolescents, in fostering their careers.

Even though these examples are not within the context of the urban planning profession, the conditions identified similarly affect children, youth, and even adults'—parents, other family members, teachers, and counselors—perceptions, familiarity with, and understanding of the urban planning profession. Rodriguez (2009) confirms this observation. In a quite recent study about diversity in the planning profession, the only research of its kind for the urban planning profession to the best of our awareness, Tiarachristie (2016) identified that inequality and poverty served as barriers to educational attainment among many African American children and youth that may potentially have an interest in urban planning.

In addition, the absence of opportunities for many African Americans to be active change agents in their neighborhoods, the potential to be exposed to the urban planning profession through good planning, "the late, or lack of, exposure of the planning profession in communities of color, largely due to limited social capital," and low levels of diversity in urban planning schools are among several barriers to recruiting and retaining people of color in the New York metropolitan area (Tiarachristie,

2016, p. 49). This only gives a glimpse of a broader challenge for the profession in North America, especially as New York City hosts a larger number of design-related education outreach projects to students than any other city in the United States (Palazzo et al., 2021). Furthermore, the planning literature provides cases of how children and youth, particularly those from low-income households and youth of color, are not engaged in urban planning processes (Severcan, 2015; Mansfield et al., 2021). These situations not only deprive children and youth from articulating their interests and aspirations in the urban planning process (McKoy et al., 2015; Derr & Kovács, 2017), but also create conditions where they are not exposed to the urban planning profession (McKoy et al., 2015; Palazzo et al., 2021).

These barriers provide an impetus for rethinking how particular interventions can be initiated to intentionally introduce the profession to children and youth and make them part of the proximal factors shaping their career preferences and choices. For the recruitment of minorities into urban planning programs, the challenge may be greater. However, Mateo and Smith's (2001) suggestion to increase workforce diversity in health care organizations provides a starting point for the strategic-rethinking process. Their suggestions include understanding the dynamics of the community's demographics, setting diversity goals, identifying barriers, and ensuring strong leadership support for diversity strategies.

Herein lies the immense responsibility of higher-education institutions with urban planning departments and programs to understand the awareness challenge of the planning profession among children and youth, and to formulate and implement strategies to address the challenge (Good et al., 2002; Campbell-Heider et al., 2008). Planning educators and researchers can tap into their community engagement toolkits as one way to address the professional awareness challenge. As McKoy and Vincent's (2007) study of youth participation in planning has shown, engaging children and youth in urban planning processes can shape the career paths of participating children as well as mentors.

ACE: Activating Community Empowerment In-School Workshop

This section describes the ACE initiative implemented at the UC's School of Planning. It begins with a background into the declining enrollment challenge at the school that informed the initiative followed by an in-depth description of the structure of the ACE initiative and its outcomes.

Challenge of Declining Enrollment

In the United States, the Planning Accreditation Board (PAB) has observed declines in overall student enrollment of accredited planning programs since 2008 (APA, 2016; Palazzo et al., 2021), particularly among domestic populations and populations of color (JTF, 2016). Between 2008 and 2020, the PAB observed a decline of 16.4% in overall student enrollments (PAB, 2020, 2021).

This national-level challenge also occurs at the School of Planning (SOP) in the College of Design, Architecture, Art and Planning (DAAP) at the University of Cincinnati (UC). In the 2012–2020 period, the number of enrolled students in both of the School of Planning's accredited planning programs declined.[2] Although enrollment has declined, racial diversity has slightly increased but is still quite low. Over the same period, with an average student enrollment of 120 in the Bachelor of Urban Planning program, and an average of 13 international students, 16.3% of citizens and residents students are non-White. In the Master of Community Planning program, in the same period, with an average student enrollment of 33, 21 of which were international students, 30.9% of citizens and residents declared themselves non-White (AROD-PAB, 2021).

In 2015, when the declining student enrollment became a central concern on the SOP policy agenda, the SOP developed an outreach program to address it. The premise of this program (further discussed in subsequent sections) was informed by general feedback of unawareness of and/or unfamiliarity with the urban planning profession among high-school counselors and students in the Cincinnati Public Schools.

Design and Planning Language Programs

Programs using design and planning language to engage students in outreach, community engagement, professional awareness, and student development exist throughout the United States. Most of them, noted hereafter as design and planning language programs (DPLPs), are supported by professional organizations associated with the built environment, like the American Institute of Architects (n.d.); Cooper-Hewitt, Smithsonian Design Museum (n.d.); Frank Lloyd Wright Trust (n.d.); and the Center for Architecture (n.d.). A smaller number are supported by academic institutions including the University of California, Berkeley and Florida State University. A surprising number of DPLPs have been developed by individuals or by local chapters of national organizations, crafting initiatives targeted to the specific needs of students in their communities (Palazzo et al., 2021; see Chapters 9 through 17 in this book for examples of DPLP initiatives undertaken by universities [University of California, Berkeley; Osaka University; Utah State University; University of Oklahoma], individuals [In-class and co-learning activities undertaken in China, Egypt, UAE] and groups [Hillsborough County City-County Planning Commission]).

The University of Cincinnati's School of Planning has developed two separate DPLPs. The first is a pilot, three-week-long workshop with students at Hughes High School—located in the proximity of the University of Cincinnati campus—called Activating Community Empowerment (ACE); the second, City Transformers, is a weeklong summer camp held from 2017 to 2019 intended to be offered annually (though suspended in 2020 and 2021 due to the COVID-19 pandemic). This chapter will recount the details associated with the ACE program; an in-depth description and discussion of the City Transformers activity can be found in Palazzo et al., 2021. ACE was developed and implemented by SOP faculty and students with dual aims: to empower students at Hughes High School to have a voice in their community and to potentially consider urban planning as a career choice, both achieved through a series of community-engagement activities.

Response to the Challenge

The SOP has developed a series of initiatives to stem enrollment decline and increase diversity in the undergraduate population, in particular African Americans who, despite representing 42% of the Cincinnati population, were represented at SOP in the period 2012–2020 by only 4% of the student population. Since 2015, these activities have involved the Cincinnati Public School system high-school counselors, teachers, principals, and students, along with SOP alumni, faculty, and current students. Both ACE and City Transformers have been implemented in the Cincinnati area, as a large percentage (between 80–90%) of UC's undergraduate population is local, a condition that, due to the geographic position of Cincinnati in southwest Ohio, also includes students from a select number of counties in Northern Kentucky and Eastern Indiana. As a result of these initiatives, two issues related to the decline in student numbers became apparent. To be clear, the following issues are not data-proof, as this was not the primary intention of the initiatives, but they are based on the outcomes of meetings, gatherings, and interactions with different people.

First, a large number of high-school counselors met with the SOP faculty during a general meeting organized in April 2015 by the Cincinnati Public Schools, the College of DAAP, and the SOP. During this meeting, it became evident that most of the high-school counselors were not as familiar with planning as they were with other potential career paths available at DAAP, such as architecture, art, and design. Some were completely unfamiliar with planning as an education program or career.

A second issue is that some counselors familiar with planning admitted that, in many cases, they did not suggest planning as a potential career, especially to first-generation college students in inner-city high schools, due to two common misunderstandings. The first of these is that the College of DAAP's programs are known to have admission requirements higher than other programs at the University of Cincinnati, leading counselors to preemptively quash applicants who might otherwise prove to be excellent SOP students. Secondly, a false axiom had been created and propagated—that since planning is in DAAP with creative-related programs like art, architecture, and design, it is an arts-related program. This assumption makes SOP programs harder to market to inner-city high-school students and their families, particularly first-generation college students, due to a perceived lack of professional opportunities once the program is successfully completed.

In addition to the aforementioned issues, which are particularly impactful upon the SOP's matriculation rate, high-school students are rarely exposed to planning-related issues in their courses. In only a few US states might students' social-studies curriculum include at least one unit of geography (often together with world history), where students can be exposed to the understanding of geography and spatial thinking or the implication of spatial arrangements and their connections with economic developments, social structures, and governmental authorities (Education Commission of the States, 2019). Topics related to urban planning and/or urban issues can also be covered in advanced-placement (AP) courses in environmental science, where scientific principles, concepts, and methodologies are taught "to understand the interrelationships of the natural world, to identify and analyze environmental problems both natural and human-made, to evaluate the relative risks associated with these problems" (Ohio Higher Education, 2021, p. 7), or human geography, where they can become familiar with "systematic study of patterns and processes that have shaped human understanding, use, and alteration of Earth's surface. Students employ spatial concepts and landscape analysis to examine human social organization and its environmental consequences" (Ohio Higher Education, 2021, p. 9). These few courses and curricula aside, most students do not encounter planning or planning-related topics in the course of their standard high-school curriculum. (See Chapter 15 for a study of the introduction of urban planning to a restructured high-school geography curriculum in New South Wales, Australia.) The resulting lack of student understanding of planning is compounded and reflected by their family's inability to consider it as a potential career path.

The SOP, through a series of activities, is trying to invert the national and local trends in planning-program enrollments by developing a larger local awareness of planning among youth and children. Among the initiatives, the one most specifically designed to address awareness of urban planning was a three-week-long workshop with high-school junior students at Hughes STEM High School (HSTEMHS) called Activating Community Empowerment (ACE).

HSTEMHS was chosen because it is one of the core academic programs of the University of Cincinnati Center for Community Engagement. The program was established "to strengthen . . . the relationship between the University of Cincinnati and HSTEMHS through reciprocal partnerships that benefit all involved" (University of Cincinnati, 2016). Hughes is located in the immediate vicinity of the main campus of the University (Figure 9.1). As a Cincinnati public school, they serve students in grades 7–12 from all across the city. According to data published by Cincinnati Public Schools (Ohio Department of Education, 2016), of the 944 enrolled students, 90.7% are Black-Non-Hispanic, 3.6% Multiracial, and 4.8% White-Non-Hispanic. The student population has 938 students (or 99.5% of the student population) who are considered to be economically disadvantaged, while 24.8% have disabilities. The four-year graduation rate is 74.5% (one out of four students does not graduate in four years), while the district's graduation rate is 83%. One factor in which HSTEMHS does exceed state averages is in the number of general education teachers for 1,000 students. At HSTEMHS this number is 52.2, while at the state level it is 46.4. Additionally, the number of HSTEMHS career and technical education teachers for every 1,000 students outnumbers the Ohio state average by more than 200%: 7.4 per 1,000 at HSTEMHS compared to the state average of 2.3.

Activating Community Empowerment

In November 2015, two SOP alumni were invited as guests to a Power Lunch at HSTEMHS designed to bring students and local professionals together to spark interest, mentorship, and collaboration between the school and community. After the lunch and a brief presentation, Power Lunch guests, including SOP students and faculty, engaged participating students in a short exercise to activate an interest in the built environment around their school. The majority of students, divided into teams, suggested that one immediate issue students faced was the state of their detached sports field (Coy Field) and the long path they had to walk to reach it (Figure 9.1).

ACE's subsequent March 2016 program was built around these initial reactions from students. It consisted of five meetings spanning three weeks. In coordination with classroom teachers and the school's principal, an activity was designed with the intention of empowering students' ability to engage with, and make changes to, the urban places in which they live. Forty-four 11th graders were guided through a process to investigate the urban environment around their school, identify problems, engage the wider community of students, recognize the decision processes needed to solve problems, explore areas of improvement, propose solutions, and present them to decision-makers.

As the student body of HSTEMHS is predominantly African American, it was important to those running the workshop that a diverse assembly of faculty, staff, and students was represented. The hope was that by demonstrating a wide range of people involved in planning, we would model an inclusive profession for the students. The University of Cincinnati participants were a combination of two full-time faculty (one White European male, one White female), one DAAP academic director (Asian American female), one PhD student (African male), three master's students (one Latin American female, one Hispanic female, one White female), and three undergraduate students (two White female, one White male). Workshop leaders developed a comprehensive teaching plan and facilitated the students through four two-hour sessions, with the support of the student's engineering teachers. A two-hour meeting with the two junior classes that joined the initiative took place on Monday and Tuesday afternoons. This was to enable students and teachers to have time during the rest of the week to work on the assignments before they met with the SOP team again. The initiative culminated with a final presentation to the school and community leaders.

The ACE Process and Outcomes

The activity was divided into four phases: process, knowledge, proposal, and presentation, almost evenly divided across four meetings. The team decided not to use the word *planning*. The reasons were to ensure ACE focused on activities and skills that students were developing and to focus discussion on familiar issues that mattered to the students. Instead, the team used words and concepts like community empowerment and engagement, plan (with the meaning of organizing and thinking in advance), design issues, and urban conditions, among others, which seemed easily understood at the students' level.

The process phase introduced students to concepts like time management, teamwork, and phasing. The SOP team and the students worked together using large whiteboards to elaborate a plan and contents for the whole task, with the goal to give a public presentation in three weeks. In the introduction to this phase, the SOP team described the importance of knowing the place, community, decision-makers, and decision-making process.

In the knowledge phase, a map of the area was provided to each student before a field trip to the sports field later that day. Students were asked to take notes on the map as well as pictures of the path

Becoming Activated

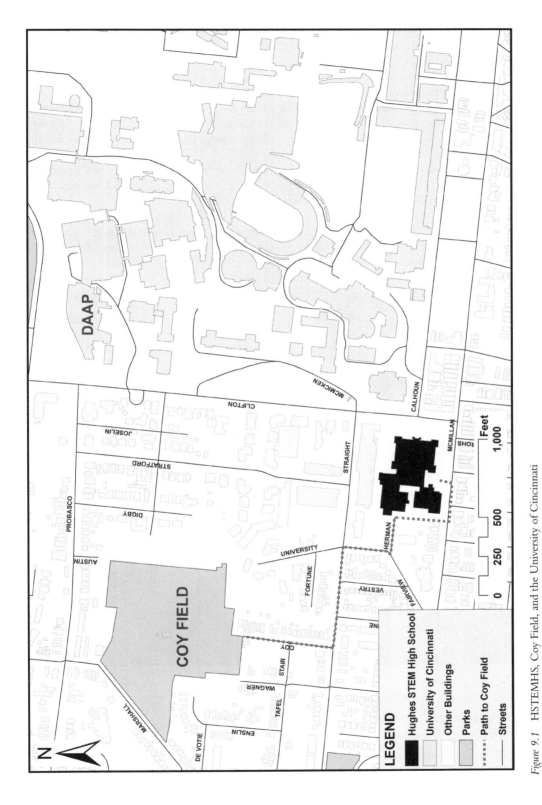

Figure 9.1 HSTEMHS, Coy Field, and the University of Cincinnati

This map shows the location of HSTEMHS, Coy Field, the path between the two, and proximity of HSTEMHS to the University of Cincinnati main campus.

and of the sports field to substantiate and support their claims. The students were also introduced to the meaning of community and how to involve community members through questionnaire administration.

On day two, the students were divided into two main groups to continue working on the knowledge phase. One group, divided into two teams, had the goal of mapping the problems related to the path and the sports field. The other group was asked to build an interview form and questionnaire to involve the larger community of HSTEMHS students and to recognize the key players at their own school or at higher levels to whom they could present their proposals or those who could make the needed decisions to affect the changes they wanted.

On day three, two teams worked on drawing proposals on maps while another two worked on creating an Excel file and graphs using the answers from the community survey that was conducted in the time between the second and third meetings.

On day four, the teams worked on their presentations. A week later, the students, in front of an audience comprising the HSTEMHS associate principal, the sports facility manager, and some teachers, made three presentations: one on the process, one on the path to the sports fields, and one on the improvement of the sports-field facilities (Figure 9.2). As a final act, the SOP team thanked the students and teachers and revealed that the activity they were involved in for almost three weeks was actually an urban planning activity; then they invited students to consider planning for their education and career.

Figure 9.2 Students Working and Final Presentation

(a) Students preparing a presentation with the aid of a UC PhD student.

(b) Students giving a presentation.

(c) HSTEMHS associate principal giving feedback to students.

(d) Students engaged in active listening.

Initial reactions of the classes to the initiatives were a combination of indifference, apathy, curiosity, and interest. The two HSTEMHS teachers helped the SOP team to keep the students attentive. This was crucial because, for most of the students, this type of activity and topic area was new, and initial interest was low. Evidence of low interest was shown as they focused on their phones, listened to music, or talked to each other in smaller groups. The control exerted by the teachers, especially in larger sessions when all of the students were together in one crowded room, was critical in drawing the students' focus toward the activities. Some students, from the onset of the meetings, were very outspoken. Others answered only if questions were individually directed to them, and yet others stayed embedded in their small clusters with little to no interest in participating.

The ACE initiative received good reactions about student accomplishments from the teachers and administrators of HSTEMHS. One of the two teachers, in an email sent to the DAAP academic director, said:

> [I] Wanted to follow up and express my thanks again for working with us at Hughes last quarter, I know that a majority of the students really learned a lot and were inspired. [We] . . . will use some of your ideas and strategies next year with our students.
>
> *(Teacher 1)*

The ACE initiative thus created a platform that provided awareness among both students and teachers. HSTEMHS teachers became more familiar with planning and understood the contributions they make to changing the built environment. In addition, the aim of empowering students to become change agents by identifying problems and finding ways to manage or mitigate these problems was achieved. The teacher further explained:

> Also, I wanted to let you know that our plant operator stopped me last week and wanted me to know that the graffiti and trash problem at Coy Field was taken care of and is all cleaned up.
>
> *(Teacher 1)*

Most importantly, teachers saw the need to integrate planning into the school's curriculum. They called for further collaboration and efforts realizing that there are many other subjects that can be enriched with planning knowledge and understanding. The teachers even became more aware that some of the skills they sought to impart to students from other disciplines, such as architecture and engineering, are better suited to planning. Consequently, the teachers themselves became more disciplinarily enlightened about planning. The teacher put it this way:

> I would love to find a time to talk to you . . . about the possibility of adding a Plan Reading and/or an additional architectural design course. I would love your feedback and which one you feel is a better fit for us.
>
> We are considering changing the name of our engineering pathway to something more specific and concrete to accurately describe what we offer and teach here [at Hughes STEM High School].
>
> *(Teacher 1)*

ACE aspires to evolve into a program capable of being carried out in different Cincinnati-area high schools during the school year, as a summer camp, or as a spring intersession activity. ACE was not intended to focus students solely on planning but was designed to get them engaged in their community and become active in making changes in their environment and in their community as they aspire to a better future. Consequently, ACE became a great avenue that created the needed proximal context for children and youth (in this case, high-school students) to be exposed not only to the planning profession but also to professionals who can serve as role models.

Though it can't be said that the DPLP initiatives that the University of Cincinnati School of Planning has undertaken—ACE or City Transformers (see Palazzo et al., 2021)—have had any significant role in enrollments between 2016 and 2020, there was during that time, however, an increased number of freshmen coming straight from high school–a large increase in 2018 which remained steady into 2019 (with dramatic effect due to the COVID-19 pandemic in 2020 and 2021)—but, it has to be noted, without any effect on diversity. Overall, we conclude that the primary effective goal of the University of Cincinnati initiatives is to produce awareness of planning as a profession among youth. A secondary goal, relevant and vital for the university organizers, is to increase enrollment in planning programs.

Conclusion

From the onset, this chapter has attempted to provide some responses to two main questions: (1) What factors influence career awareness among children and youth? and (2) How can planning schools influence career awareness through effective collaborations with high schools? To conclude, we revisit these questions.

Findings from literature show that DPLPs can shape career choices and preferences of children and youth in these programs by providing vital proximal contexts for awareness and influence. These proximal contexts then become avenues that expose children and youth to planning and design activities, and professionals who may end up becoming role models. Critically, they are avenues to help tackle some of the professional challenges that Rodriguez (2009) and Tiarachristie (2016) lament, such as a lack of professional awareness and interaction with urban planning professionals.

Proximal factors such as family, neighbors, and trusted advisors, such as high-school teachers and counselors, are highly influential in children's career choices. Through the ACE program, we became aware of the lack of knowledge among many of these influential individuals about the field of planning. The format of the program enabled us to directly address this lack of knowledge by educating high-school teachers about planning and making parents aware of the field by involving them in their children's activities through take-home materials and stories of school activities. Ideally, the in-school presentation to school administration would have been followed up by a presentation involving parents and other community members, as making a community more aware of the field of urban planning is also a way to support long-term career-choice influence.

DPLPs such as ACE also attempt to address potentially influential distal factors by attempting to impact social norms and customs among students and their communities. It is possible that they, or their families, have had few positive interactions with municipal functions such as planning. Programs giving young people the ability to be heard and influence their surroundings can change the relationships between these students, their communities, and the municipal government, establishing that it is possible to have a collaborative, positive relationship. In this way, ACE was an attempt to address the absence of opportunities for many African Americans to be active change agents in their neighborhoods. Though it was a one-off initiative, it confirms Wiesner et al.'s (2003) observation that temporary experiences are powerful and impactful in injecting formative ideas and interests in children and youth.

DPLPs also provide opportunities to expose children to the skills undergirding the urban planning profession. Public speaking, policymaking, budgeting, negotiation, research, critical thinking, writing, and others are skills DPLPs aim to develop among the students with whom they engage. Many of these skills directly align with the planning professions, compared to other professions that promote these DPLPs. They are often the core tasks of urban planners. The awareness from the reactions of one teacher after the ACE initiative consolidates this observation. Initiatives for children and youth often embody the principles and practices of planning, but unfortunately, they are propagated by other disciplines. As a result, the planning profession ends up being co-opted into these different disciplines. Even worse, it can get lost entirely. The ACE initiative provides some evidence that a professional demystification is needed for planning to engender greater awareness about the profession among children and the general public.

This demystification is paramount in directing interested students to further develop planning-related skills. The planning profession, at its core, teaches and trains students to use these skills to become active change agents. Schools of planning have an immense role to play in consciously making children and youth aware of planning as a career choice that deals with these skill sets. As the ACE initiative shows, creativity is needed to educate high-school students outside their K–12 core curricula. By connecting students to real problems relating to their experiential environments, students build interest and create experiences with which they can easily relate. Student engagement in the identification of these proximal problems is critical and helps to connect children and youth to the things they are passionate about and those that are part of their everyday experiences.

Akin to the professional practice of planning, the process must be informed by conscious efforts and proper diagnosis of the problem. Engagement with the Cincinnati Public Schools—students and partnerships with HSTEMHS teachers—SOP alumni, faculty, and students were critical factors supporting the ACE initiative by helping the team build trust and navigate engagement barriers at Hughes High School. This subsequently feeds into the second issue this chapter raises: a low level, and in some cases absence, of awareness about the planning profession among teachers, students, and school counselors. Sadly, research demonstrates that planning schools who train planning professionals do not exert much attention to increasing awareness about the profession as few initiatives originate from planning schools (Palazzo et al., 2021).

Career education is so vital in the career-development process that it is negligent of organizations like the American Planning Association, Planning Accreditation Board, Association of Collegiate Schools of Planning, and American Institute of Certified Planners to assume that the field is well known and open to the diverse body of students that will be needed to enter the field in the near future. At the national level, these organizations can advocate for policy changes to make geography and urban planning part of the standard high-school curricula across the 50 states. Additionally, there is a need to take intentional actions to increase planning-profession awareness among high-school students and teachers. Given that planning schools are the conduit for urban planning professionals, the chapter recommends they initiate and implement DPLPs as part of their outreach activities. This will contribute to creating the needed proximal contexts necessary for planning profession awareness among youth and children.

Furthermore, planning schools need to provide clarity and effectively communicate matriculation requirements among high schools. In other words, it is necessary to ensure that high-school counselors have knowledge of matriculation requirements and understand how planning is related to, but different from, both other creative-related disciplines as well as liberal-arts disciplines such as geography. A way to approach this is to constantly engage high-school counselors to understand their familiarity with the planning field. Such engagement should include an education element and direction to critical resources that provide information about the planning profession and its economic prospects.

Notes

1. This chapter builds on and has intersections with an earlier publication on professional awareness: Palazzo et al. (2021). As a result, some of the information and arguments can also be found in that publication.
2. The School of Planning has two accredited planning programs, the Bachelor of Urban Planning and the Master of Community Planning. It is also the home of the Master of Landscape Architecture (Landscape Architectural Accreditation Board Candidacy Status), Bachelor of Science in Urban Studies, Bachelor of Science in Horticulture, and PhD in Regional Development Planning.

References

American Institute of Architects. (n.d.) *AIA K-12 initiatives: Architecture resources for educators*. AIA.org. www.aia.org/pages/6323337-educators

American Planning Association (APA). (2016). *Reversing the decline in planning school enrollment*. American planning association. Retrieved June 1, 2022, from www.planningaccreditationboard.org/wp-content/uploads/2021/04/Mitchell.pdf

American Planning Association (APA) (2022). *All accredited programs*. Retrieved February 24, 2022, from www.planningaccreditationboard.org/accredited-programs/all/

Amundson, N. (2006). Challenges for career interventions in changing contexts. *International Journal for Educational and Vocational Guidance*, 6(1), 3–14. https://doi:10.1007/s10775-006-0002-4

AROD-PAB. (2021). *Annual report online database-planning accreditation board*. Retrieved June 10, 2022, from www.planningaccreditationboard.org/resources-publications/student-faculty-data/

Ashby, J. S., & Schoon, I. (2010). Career success: The role of teenage career aspirations, ambition value and gender in predicting adult social status and earnings. *Journal of Vocational Behavior*, 77(3), 350–360. https://doi.org/10.1016/j.jvb.2010.06.006

Bailey, B. A., & Nihlen, A. S. (1990). Effect of experience with nontraditional workers on psychological and social dimensions of occupational sex-role stereotyping by elementary school children. *Psychological Reports* (66), 1273–1282. https://doi.org/10.2466/pr0.1990.66.3c.1273

Bandura, A. (1986). *Social foundations of thought and action: A social cognitive theory*. Prentice-Hall.

Bigler, R. S., & Liben, L. S. (1990). The role of attitudes and interventions in gender- schematic processing. *Child Development* (61), 1440–1452. https://doi.org/10.2307/1130754

Bounds, P. S. (2017). Contextual factors related to African American adolescent career development. *Career Development Quarterly*, 65(2), 131–144. https://doi.org/10.1002/cdq.12087

Campbell-Heider, N., Sackett, K., & Whistler, M. P. (2008). Connecting with guidance counselors to enhance recruitment into nursing of minority teens. *Journal of Professional Nursing*, 24(6), 378–384. https://doi.org/10.1016/j.profnurs.2008.10.009

Caspi, A., Wright, B. R. E., Moffitt, T. E., & Silva, P. A. (1998). Early failure in the labor market: Childhood and adolescent predictors of unemployment in the transition to adulthood. *American Sociological Review* (63), 424–451. https://doi.org/10.2307/2657557

Center for Architecture. (n.d.). *K-12 Education*. Center for Architecture. www.centerforarchitecture.org/k-12/

Collin, A., & Watts, A. G. (1996). The death and transfiguration of career–and of career guidance? *British Journal of Guidance & Counselling*, 24(3), 385–398. https://doi.org/10.1080/03069889608253023

Cook, T., Church, M., Ajanaku, S., Shadish, W., Kim, J., & Cohen, R. (1996). The development of occupational aspirations and expectations among inner-city boys. *Child Development*, 67(6), 3368–3385. https://doi.org/10.2307/1131783

Cooper-Hewitt, Smithsonian Design Museum. (n.d.). *Educator resources*. Learninglab.si.edu. https://learninglab.si.edu/cooperhewitt?

Derr, V., & Kovács, I. G. (2017). How participatory processes impact children and contribute to planning: A case study of neighborhood design from Boulder, Colorado, USA. *Journal of Urbanism: International Research on Placemaking and Urban Sustainability*, 10(1), 29–48. https://doi.org/10.1080/17549175.2015.1111925

Dietrich, J., & Kracke, B. (2009). Career-specific parental behaviors in adolescents' development. *Journal of Vocational Behavior*, 75(2), 109–119. https://doi.org/10.1016/j.jvb.2009.03.005

Education Commission of the States. (2019). *High school graduation requirements (50-state comparison)*. Retrieved June 11, 2022, from https://reports.ecs.org/comparisons/high-school-graduation-requirements-01

Ferreira, J. A., Santos, E. J. R, Fonseca, A. C., & Haase, R. F. (2007). Early predictors of career development: A 10-year follow-up study. *Journal of Vocational Behavior*, 70(1), 61–77. https://doi.org/10.1016/j.jvb.2006.04.006

Frank Lloyd Wright Trust. (n.d.). *School programs*. Frank Lloyd Wright Trust. https://flwright.org/education/schooloutreach

Gallup-Strada Education Network. (2017). *On second thought: U.S. Adults reflect on their education decisions*. Gallup.

Gillies, R., McMahon, M. L., & Carroll, J. (1998). Evaluating a career education intervention in the upper elementary school. *Journal of Career Development* (24), 267–287. https://doi.org/10.1177/089484539802400401

Good, J., Halpin, G., & Halpin, G. (2002). Retaining black students in engineering: Do minority programs have a longitudinal impact? *Journal of College Student Retention*, 3(4), 351–364. https://doi.org/10.2190/A0EU-TF7U-RUYN-584X

Gottfredson, L. S. (1981). Circumscription and compromise: A developmental theory of occupational aspirations. *Journal of Counseling Psychology* (28), 545–579. https://doi.org/10.1037/0022-0167.28.6.545

Goyette, K. A., & Mullen, A. L. (2006). Who studies the arts and sciences? Social background and the choice and consequences of undergraduate field of study. *Journal of Higher Education*, 77(3), 497–538. https://doi.org/10.1353/jhe.2006.0020

Howard, K. A. S., Flanagan, S., Castine, E., & Walsh, M. E. (2015). Perceived influences on the career choices of children and youth: An exploratory study. *International Journal for Educational and Vocational Guidance*, 15(2), 99–111. https://doi.org/10.1007/s10775-015-9298-2

Hutchison, B., Spencer, N. G., & Trusty, J. (2014). Career development in schools: An historical perspective. In T. Eliason, Grafton, J. L. Samide, & Patrick, J. (Eds.), *Issues in career development: Career counseling across the lifespan: Community, school, and higher education*. Greenwich, CT: Information Age Publishing.

Jackson, C., & Bruns, S. M. (2011). A new strategy for cultivating diversity: Ideas for attracting minority students to the profession. *The CPA Journal*, 81(3), 68.

Joint Task Force (JTF) of American Planning Association, American Institute of Certified Planners, Association of Collegiate Schools of Planning & Planning Accreditation Board. (2016). *Joint task force on enrollment report. American planning association*. Retrieved June 1, 2022, from www.planningaccreditationboard.org/wp-content/uploads/2021/04/2016EnrollmentRpt.pdf

Kenny, M. E., & Bledsoe, M. (2005). Contributions of the relational context to career adaptability among urban adolescents. *Journal of Vocational Behavior*, 66(2), 257–272. https://doi.org/10.1016/j.jvb.2004.10.002

Krumboltz, J. D., & Nichols, C. W. (1990). Integrating the social learning theory of career decision making. In W. B. Walsh & S. H. Osipow (Eds.), *Career counseling: Contemporary topics in vocational psychology* (pp. 159–192). Erlbaum.

Lent, R. W., Brown, S. D., & Hackett, G. (1994). Toward a unifying social cognitive theory of career and academic interest, choice, and performance. *Journal of Vocational Behavior*, 45(1), 79–122. https://doi.org/10.1006/jvbe.1994.1027

Lent, R. W., Brown, S. D., & Hackett, G. (2000). Contextual supports and barriers to career choice: A social cognitive analysis. *Journal of Counseling Psychology*, 47(1), 36–49. https://doi.org/10.1037/0022-0167.47.1.36

Ma, Y. (2009). Family socioeconomic status, parental involvement, and college major choices—gender, race/ethnic, and nativity patterns. *Sociological Perspectives*, 52(2), 211–234. https://doi.org/10.1525/sop.2009.52.2.211

Mansfield, R. G., Batagol, B., & Raven, R. (2021). "Critical agents of change?" Opportunities and limits to children's participation in urban planning. *Journal of Planning Literature*, 36(2), 170–186. https://doi.org/10.1177/0885412220988645

Mateo, M. A. & Smith, S. P. (2001). Workforce diversity: Challenges and strategies. *Journal of Multicultural Nursing and Health* (7), 8–12.

McKoy, D. L., Stewart, J., & Buss, S. (2015). Engaging students in transforming their built environment via Y-PLAN: Lessons from Richmond, California, *Children, Youth and Environments*, 25(2), 229–244. https://doi.org/10.7721/chilyoutenvi.25.2.0229

McKoy, D. L., & Vincent, J. M. (2007). Engaging schools in urban revitalization: The Y-PLAN (youth-plan, learn, act, now!), *Journal of Planning Education and Research*, 26(4), 389403. https://doi.org/10.1177/0739456X06298817.

Mitchell, L. K., & Krumboltz, J. D. (1996). Krumboltz's learning theory of career choice and counseling. In D. Brown & L. Brooks (Eds.), *Career choice and development* (3rd ed., pp. 233–280). Jossey-Bass.

Ohio Department of Education. (2016). *2015–2016 Report card for Hughes stem high school*. Retrieved September 25, 2016, from http://reportcard.education.ohio.gov/Pages/SchoolReport.aspx?SchoolIRN=011609

Ohio Higher Education. (2021). *Advanced placement course credit alignment recommendations*. Retrieved June 11, 2022, from www.ohiohighered.org/sites/default/files/uploads/transfer/policy/AP_Alignment_Recommendations_11.18.21.pdf

Palazzo, D., Hollstein, L., & Diko, S. K. (2021). Urban planning as a career preference for students: Efforts to improve awareness about the profession. *Planning Practice & Research*, 36(2), 174–192. https://doi.org/10.1080/02697459.2020.1782056

Planning Accreditation Board. (2020, July 9). *Student enrollment in PAB-accredited Programs 2008–2019*. Retrieved June 1, 2022, from www.planningaccreditationboard.org/wp-content/uploads/2021/05/StudEnroll2019.pdf

Planning Accreditation Board. (2021, June). *Student and faculty composition in PAB-accredited programs: 2020 Annual report*. Retrieved June 1, 2022, from www.planningaccreditationboard.org/wp-content/uploads/2021/06/2020AR.pdf

Rodriguez, M. A. (2009, September 24). Let's teach children planning. *Planetizen*. Retrieved June 1, 2022, from www.planetizen.com/node/40827

Rogers, M. E., Creed, P. A., & Ian Glendon, A. (2008). The role of personality in adolescent career planning and exploration: A social cognitive perspective. *Journal of Vocational Behavior*, 73(1), 132–142. https://doi.org/10.1016/j.jvb.2008.02.002

Schams, S., Fouad, N. A., Burrows, S. G., Ricondo, K., & Song, Y. (2022). Effect of a class-level intervention on career indecision variables. *Career Development Quarterly*, *70*(2), 162–171. https://doi.org/10.1002/cdq.12292

Schoon, I., & Parsons, S. (2002). Teenage aspirations for future careers and occupational outcomes. *Journal of Vocational Behavior*, *60*, 262–288. https://doi.org/10.1006/jvbe.2001.1867

Severcan, Y. C. (2015). Planning for the unexpected: Barriers to young people's participation in planning in disadvantaged communities. *International Planning Studies*, *20*(3), 251–269. https://doi.org/10.1080/13563475.2014.985195

Shavit, Y., & Muller, W. (Eds.). (1998). *From school to work: A comparative study of educational qualifications and occupational destinations*. Oxford University Press.

Stipanovic, N., & Stringfield, S. (2013). A qualitative inquiry of career exploration in highly implemented career and technical education programs of study. *International Journal of Educational Reform*, *22*(4), 334. https://doi.org/10.1177/105678791302200404

Strom, P. S., Strom, R. D., Whitten, L. S., & Kraska, M. F. (2014). Adolescent identity and career exploration. *NASSP Bulletin*, *98*(2), 163–179. https://doi.org/10.1177/0192636514528749

Tiarachristie, G. G. (2016). *Elephant in the planning room: Overcoming barriers to recruitment and retention of planners of color* (Thesis). School of Architecture, Pratt Institute. Retrieved June 1, 2022, from www.nyplanning.org/wordpress/wp-content/uploads/2016/08/Tiarachristie-Thesis_Elephant-in-the-Planning-Room_080716.pdf

Tien, H. S. (2007). Practice and research in career counseling and development—2006. *Career Development Quarterly*, *56*(2), 98–140. https://doi.org/10.1002/j.2161-0045.2007.tb00025.x

Tsui, L. (2007). Effective strategies to increase diversity in STEM fields: A review of the research literature. *The Journal of Negro Education*, *76*(4), 555–581. www.jstor.org/stable/40037228

University of Cincinnati. (2016). *Hughes STEM high school*. Retrieved September 15, 2016, from www.uc.edu/cce/student/hughes.html

Vondracek, F. W., Lerner, R. M., & Schulenberg, J. E. (1986). *Career development: A life-span developmental approach*. Erlbaum. https://doi.org/10.4324/9781315792705

Vondracek, F. W., Silbereisen, R. K., Reitzle, M., & Wiesner, M. (1999). Vocational preferences of early adolescents: Their development in social context. *Journal of Adolescent Research*, *14*(3), 267–288. https://doi.org/10.1177/0743558499143001

Watson, M., & McMahon, M. (2005). Children's career development: A research review from a learning perspective. *Journal of Vocational Behavior*, *67*(2), 119–132. https://doi.org/10.1016/j.jvb.2004.08.011

Wiesner, M., Vondracek, F. W., Capaldi, D. M., & Porfeli, E. (2003). Childhood and adolescent predictors of early adult career pathways. *Journal of Vocational Behavior*, *63*(3), 305–328. https://doi.org/10.1016/S0001-8791(03)00028-9

Withington, C., Hammond, C., Mobley, C., Stipanovic, N., Sharp, J. L., Stringfield, S., & Drew, S. F., Jr. (2012). Implementing a statewide mandated career pathways/programs of study school reform model: Select findings from a multisite case study. *International Journal of Educational Reform*, *21*(2), 138–158. https://doi.org/10.1177/105678791202100204

10
WHY PLAN? A TWO-DECADE EXPLORATION INTO HOW AND WHY TO ENGAGE YOUNG PEOPLE IN CITY PLANNING AND DIVERSIFY THE PLANNING PIPELINE

Deborah McKoy and David Hernandez Garcia

It was Monday, March 9, 2020. Students slowly entered UC Berkeley's Wurster Hall, room 106, with a rather bewildered look, but soon settled into the circle of seats. The chancellor had just announced there would be no in-person classes after today due to the spreading COVID-19 pandemic. Students started asking each other, "What are we going to do?" and "Is fieldwork canceled?" This was a particularly international cohort of UC Berkeley undergraduate and graduate students, a third from outside the United States. Many were considering getting on the next plane home. But on the minds of students was, "How are we going to work with our student planning partners at Oakland High School?"

Spring 2020 was a momentous time for many reasons, not just because of the global pandemic. It was also the 20th anniversary of UC Berkeley's Y-PLAN studio, which centers on the engagement of young people in authentic local city planning projects. That semester, we were working with the Oakland Housing Authority (OHA) to engage youth in reimagining the future of an East Oakland community challenged by years of high crime, poverty, and disinvestment. As Y-PLAN mentors contemplated next steps in their own lives, they were also concerned with leaving their school partners high and dry. "They were just beginning to trust us. If we don't show up it will prove that their caution, their distrust of us in January when we first arrived in their classrooms, was warranted," one student mentor insisted.

The UC Berkeley Y-PLAN studio was midway through the semester, and the participants had finally started opening up—trusting that their ideas, concerns, fears, and hopes for the future would mean something to their client: authorities at OHA. In the process, Berkeley students were also learning more about the need for diversity in the pipeline of future planners.

Six weeks earlier, the chief operating officer (COO) at OHA presented the studio class with their project question: How can the Oakland Housing Authority increase access to stable, affordable housing, offering all residents a safe, opportunity-rich community and quality of life? The studio was to focus specifically on the Lion Creek Crossings redevelopment project in East Oakland—a neighborhood whose history is rich with culture and diversity as well as pain and disorder caused by years of neglect, gentrification, and displacement.

Serving as the studio client, OHA's COO shared the current goals of this redevelopment project and his own personal history as a Latino man whose upbringing, like many of the young people in the development, was shaped by the inequitable distribution of resources. He expressed his excitement about being there, and then he spoke about the importance of involving local high-school students in the project. He saw this work as a new opportunity to rethink the community engagement strategy while recognizing the tension from rapid gentrification that this East Oakland development faced. As a man who had found a professional home in affordable-housing development, he knew the importance of being a role model and introducing the field of planning and development to a new generation—at both local schools and in higher education.

As in years past, the studio-class process nurtured authentic dialogue and discussion among UC Berkeley students, local housing professionals, community leaders, and high-school students. Everyone shared opinions, insights, and struggles as they listened to and learned from one another, forming a powerful intergenerational community of practice (McKoy et al., 2022). Given the COVID-19 pandemic, the UC Berkeley studio mentors began to problem-solve ways to continue their work online. All 20 students chimed in, strategizing on what they could do. One of our students led the charge to support the high-school classrooms we had partnered with: "I don't care if Berkeley is closed down, I am still going to the high school tomorrow. If the kids are there, I want to be there too."

As the reality of the digital format settled in, another mentor who had already returned to China piped up on FaceTime. "I can still help from here. We have to write down all their good ideas from this week's charrette, so OHA and the community knows what they want, what they are afraid of, what they hope for." Grappling with an uncertain future, the Y-PLAN mentors saw and recognized the power and importance of planning through new and powerful lenses. Working with local high-school students deepened their understanding of place and the promise of city planning to challenge, and improve, the status quo.

Amazingly, nearly three hours of studio class time passed quicker than ever. To close the day, we engaged in a community-building activity—the web of connection—in which we tossed a ball of long red yarn to each other in order to express ourselves. Many Y-PLAN mentors shared their fears and ideas for what might come. Most importantly they reflected on how they would stay connected to each other, to the work, and to the young high-school planners just beginning to believe their input could help reimagine and rebuild the future of East Oakland. To Y-PLAN mentors, this understanding reaffirmed the critical role of professional planners learning to work with young people to build inclusive and equitable cities for all.

This scene depicts a planning studio at UC Berkeley, called CP 268 Y-PLAN (Youth—Plan, Learn, Act, Now). This vignette reveals how future city planners are learning to address specific local issues by bringing together disparate groups as equal participants to plan and lead cities. Via Y-PLAN, young people[1] from communities marginalized by historic segregation and disinvestment collaborate with professional adult practitioners—educators, city planners, designers, civic leaders, community activists—alongside students and faculty from colleges and universities. This distinctive studio class brings fresh insights to community engagement by using rigorous professional methods that empower students to grapple with challenges and build upon existing community assets.

This approach positively impacts both young people as well as broader planning practices in their communities and cities. It prepares young people to voice their critical perspectives, unique ideas, and actionable proposals for change. Embedding public schools and young, low-income, Black, Indigenous, and People of Color (BIPOC) into the planning ecosystem harnesses their vital contributions to the struggle to solve the most vexing challenges of our time. Over time, the accumulation of these contributions has convinced cities to actively seek out children and youth as contributors in city planning processes across the country. These systems-level changes are increasingly evident in cities such as the San Francisco Planning Department's Child and Youth Engagement Strategy. After more than ten years as a Y-PLAN client and project partner, the department officially committed to incorporate children and youth as agents to ensure an equitable, inclusive, and sustainable city (Garcia, 2021; San Francisco Planning Department, 2021). Looking forward, the city also hopes to inspire diversification of the field at large with this work.

How the Y-PLAN Studio Class Began

Established in 2000, the Y-PLAN course offers a unique model for authentic civic learning for both higher-education and K–12 schools, partnering UC Berkeley mentors with local public-school students charged by local planners and/or civic leaders to tackle municipal challenges such as affordable housing and transportation access. As K–12 students research these issues, acting as consultants for change, they become more prepared for college, careers, and civic life. They also gain an understanding of and interest in planning through authentic participation in planning issues in their community. Over the past two decades, Y-PLAN has engaged over 10,000 young people and hundreds of schools, teachers, and city planning partners across the United States and around the globe, from Tohoku, Japan to Berkeley, California.[2] Through this process young people are exposed to the planning field, often for the first time, and ignited by the notion that planning makes the processes of local change visible and attainable.

The Y-PLAN studio was inspired by a talk its founder and co-author, Deborah McKoy, gave in 1999 to the UC Berkeley Department of City and Regional Planning (DCRP) practicum class that was working with local schools in Oakland. While impressed by the students' passion, McKoy identified high levels of frustration from graduate planning students who were eager to simply reach out and work with local schools. The key question emerged: Why was it so difficult to bring together urban planning and public education when these fields had so many shared interests, goals, and people at their heart?

After that initial talk, McKoy was confronted by daunting questions such as: Is it not time to change all this? Is it not time city planners learned more about public schools and public schools more about city planning? In response, she proposed a new interdisciplinary course to the deans of city planning and education, building upon her experiences both in public housing in New York City and global-education initiatives. While skeptical of there being enough interest among planning students, the deans recognized the importance of collaboration between these fields. Thus, the CP 268/190 Y-PLAN class was born. Over the next 20 years, the Y-PLAN initiative would grow to inspire and shape a generation of more than 500 UC Berkeley students, hundreds of educators and city planners, and thousands of K–12 students. This unprecedented, global community of practice has co-constructed city planning work grounded in social justice.

As this initiative began to build steam, UC Berkeley students, particularly those from Berkeley's urban studies undergraduate major, Master of City Planning Program, and the Graduate School of Education, began to recognize how creating safe spaces for young people is a critical aspect of their city planning education. UC Berkeley students gained hands-on experience by fostering transformative community engagement experiences that encourage participants to discuss how and why unequal systems exist. Inviting high-school students to ask the simple yet powerful question of "*Why?*" leads to further questions of, "Why is one city street so much more dangerous than another? Why don't all young people have access to good schools, healthy food, and affordable housing?" While this inquiry process may seem natural to planning professionals, for many K–12 students, considering the root causes that shape their communities is empowering and helps them explore the systems that have shaped and driven unequal investment across their cities.

How Y-PLAN Operates: Five-Step Methodology

The Y-PLAN studio's community engagement strategy follows a flexible, but well-structured, process of critical inquiry that aligns with both core best practices for participatory planning and 21st-century learning skills such as communication, collaboration, critical thinking, and more. Professional planning and academic standards guide students, teachers, and civic partners through the collaborative planning and policymaking process. Curriculum steps are sequential and highlight both expected outcomes for each phase of work as well as the career- and college-readiness skills that participating students develop. Each step is accompanied by objective-driven lesson plans aligned to core career- and college-readiness skills and knowledge with activities and milestones designed to demonstrate evidence of student understanding.

While activities can be adapted, there are five key benchmarks and steps to a Y-PLAN process (also see Figure 10.1):

1) "Start Up" includes meeting the project client, deepening understanding of the project questions being posed to the Y-PLAN student scholars, and beginning to build a team by getting to know one another and each other's strengths and unique abilities. The final activity is to collectively create a project roadmap so expectations for all participants—members of this intergenerational community of practice—are clear and compelling.
2) "Making Sense of the City" engages students in a set of data gathering and community-based research activities designed to deepen one's understanding of the project site and area of focus. This includes several key activities such as mapping the neighborhood, interviewing local residents and project stakeholders, conducting online research, and working as a team to analyze the data and tell the story of what they now understand to be their planning project site.
3) "Into Action" leads K–12 students, university mentors, community partners, and clients through a professional charrette brainstorm and proposal-development process. Together they gather and review sources of inspiration, brainstorm possible solutions, and create a vision and plan for change.
4) "Going Public" has student teams present their ideas and proposals to a panel of the civic client, community partners, and adult allies. For years, these presentations were conducted at local city halls or other civic venues. During the COVID-19 pandemic, when Y-PLAN projects shifted to a digital format, students presented online using Zoom. While missing the in-person experience, online formats for final presentations and client roundtables allowed significantly more civic partners and community members to attend.
5) "Looking Forward and Back" is the culminating step, encouraging all members of an intergenerational community of practice to reflect on what their process has accomplished and to discuss future action. If Step 4 was the climax of presenting ideas, this phase provides high-school students, Y-PLAN mentors, and civic partners a moment to pause and deepen their own understanding of the planning and personal impacts that this has had on them. UC Berkeley Y-PLAN mentors incorporate their experience into research papers that often serve as final capstone reports. K–12 students work with their university mentors and teachers to reflect on the overall experience through activities such as writing a letter to the client on what they learned or preparing a college essay based on this work. Building on the Y-PLAN reciprocal engagement process, clients often do the same by writing letters to the students about how the student's ideas and recommendations will be used to further their work and future project plans.

Why Plan? How and Why to Engage Young People in City Planning

Y-PLAN Roadmap to Change

 Youth - Plan, Learn, Act, Now

Figure 10.1 Y-PLAN Roadmap

Key Components of Y-PLAN Projects

The most effective and meaningful Y-PLAN projects are characterized by four core components:

1) They have a strong, relevant social justice and health equity focus. Students take on projects focused on improving their own public-transportation systems, access to green space, public art and civic space, healthy eating, active living options, and more.
2) They connect young people with an authentic civic client from a local city and/or community that has the authority to actually implement student proposals. This relationship fundamentally strengthens democracy as students see firsthand how government works and civic leaders actively bring young people into local decision-making.
3) They follow the five-step action research methodology described earlier, which builds critical thinking and college/career-readiness for youth and deepens adult professionals' ability to plan for healthy, equitable, and joyful cities.
4) They use a range of publicly available and easily adaptable Y-PLAN curriculum activities and lesson plans that closely align with contemporary K–12 school reform initiatives and curriculum, such as the Common Core. As a result, Y-PLAN can come to life in settings ranging from government to physics classes. This alignment with core curriculum is important to ensure project partnerships do not create an additional burden to teachers but instead support their core academic work and fundamental goals.

The Y-PLAN process is implemented in different ways. Some teachers choose to do an intensive workshop daily for two weeks, while others spread the experience over a semester, working for one hour per week. In addition, having university student mentors working directly with local K–12 students during the school day, rather than in afterschool programs or extracurricular activities, helps to ensure that K–12 students do not simply self-select into Y-PLAN projects. By embedding Y-PLAN in the school day and core classrooms, far more students are able to participate in city planning projects.

Outcomes

Today, Y-PLAN has grown into a classroom-based educational strategy that uses the community as a text for learning to authentically engage young people in city planning and policymaking. Grounded in more than two decades of research, Y-PLAN's five-step, solution-oriented methodology demonstrates a double bottom line of positive outcomes for students and communities along with civic partners and planners. Y-PLAN is a reciprocal strategy that both builds the capacity of young people to effectively contribute youth-driven data and insight and also prompts civic leaders to value and use these recommendations to create more healthy, sustainable, and joyful places for everyone.[3]

Bringing students and planning professionals into more horizontal relationships through Y-PLAN projects redefines expectations of who can offer expertise on planning issues, thereby challenging traditional definitions and formal understandings of who a city planner is. Students assume their roles as change agents, as cities generate partnerships with marginalized community members. In addition to civic clients and K–12 students, these partnerships include a critical third component: institutions of higher learning that facilitate the dialogue and reflective practice needed to underpin fruitful partnership. In addition, they offer invaluable technical and pedagogical expertise. While this has historically been UC Berkeley and the Center for Cities and Schools (CC+S) staff, recent efforts to expand have led to a higher-education strategy in which faculty at universities such as Cal Poly Pomona, UC Davis, and San José State University have committed to lead their own iterations of this model.

Y-PLAN in Action: Oakland 2030 Equitable Climate Action Plan

The City of Oakland, located in the San Francisco Bay area, has served as a committed Y-PLAN partner since its beginning. In 2019, Y-PLAN facilitated a partnership between city leaders working on the Oakland 2030 Equitable Climate Action Plan (ECAP) and the Oakland Unified School District (OUSD) to engage youth on issues that profoundly affect their experiences as residents of Oakland today and tomorrow. Building a relationship between the City of Oakland and OUSD took time and dedication from Y-PLAN and Oakland city leaders, as well as contributions from K–12 students and UC Berkeley mentors. What began as one-on-one connections between individuals interested in transforming the relationships between cities and schools gradually became more systemic (McKoy et al., 2022).

Project Problem Statement

The City of Oakland asked students at Skyline High School to analyze climate issues impacting Oakland residents and to make recommendations for how the city can better support youth and their families. Through an equity lens, students researched topics from low-carbon mobility to adaptation and climate-education strategies. With UC mentors, students took on the challenge of addressing these questions: How can the City of Oakland equitably engage local youth in the Climate Action Plan process? What recommendations can youth propose that would uniquely advance equitable climate action through specific strategies such as low-carbon mobility, adaptation, and climate education for all residents?

Figure 10.2 Skyline Y-PLAN Students Presenting Final Projects to Civic Partners

Methods

In addition to conducting site visits and community observations, students created and distributed an online survey that gathered 174 responses. UC Berkeley mentors supported students by helping them refine their survey questions and guiding students as they implemented the survey and analyzed the results.

Student Recommendations

The essential role of young people in resiliency planning has been documented in recent years (McKoy et al., 2019). Some of the more specific project recommendations included the following:

- Reduce gas emissions by encouraging residents to walk to destinations and use more electric cars through culturally appropriate messaging.
- Prepare the Oakland public for wildfires by increasing water supply near high-risk locations.
- Open accessible cooling centers for extreme-heat seasons, which can double as warming centers during rain.
- Reduce flooding through regenerative design and development at the water's edge.
- Plant more trees and edible gardens in Oakland's urban communities.
- Install vertical wall gardens on residential apartments, commercial buildings, and school sites.
- Support low-income families to install solar panels on their homes.

Next Steps and Accountability for 2030 ECAP

The City of Oakland's sustainability department, working to update the 2030 ECAP, engaged with Y-PLAN students throughout the semester, visiting their classes many times. Their team continued to be in conversation with the Center for Cities and Schools and teachers to incorporate student ideas into a new draft of the ECAP currently guiding Oakland's energy policies and local measures to mitigate the impact of climate change and preserve local ecosystems. Programs and partnerships such as this often deepen over time as city leaders increasingly recognize the power and promise of youth, especially those from BIPOC communities (Eppley et al., 2021).

Making Space for Youth at the Planning Table

Engaging youth in planning and urban policy-making appears to be a mutually beneficial experience for all. It is not, however, sufficient to simply make space at the planning table; authentic child and youth engagement means making sure young people are full participants with sufficient skills, knowledge, and preparation to critically engage with adults.

Yet, as this work continues to grow across the United States, other scholars are beginning to conduct important research on potential challenges and pitfalls of such youth engagement strategies. Mansfield et al. (2021) recently conducted an extensive literature review of 87 relevant papers to better understand conditions that support and/or inhibit youth participation in city planning. Its authors call on researchers to deepen their tracking and analysis of such processes, cautioning that "children's participation in urban planning processes is still poorly understood, and they remain marginalized in this field" (p. 1). The authors also reflect on how, despite some movement in the field toward engaging youth, "Children have little agency in urban planning processes, and when they exercise the little they have, it is interpreted as problematic, reinforcing their vulnerability in the urban environment. A lack of incentive ensures ongoing exclusion that reinforces vulnerability" (Mansfield et al., 2021, p. 13).

The Y-PLAN course and global initiatives recognize this cautionary research. While many positive outcomes have been realized, we have faced a surprising number of challenges and obstacles. Following are three core challenges found by Y-PLAN students and civic partners:

- *Skepticism throughout city agencies regarding the capacity and legitimacy of the analysis and recommendations provided by young people in their final presentations.* One example was found in New York City, where Y-PLAN was implemented in more than 20 high schools over six years. Student proposals were grounded in both qualitative data (e.g., community stakeholder interviews) as well as quantitative data from extensive community surveys. Some of their adult partners were skeptical of the process, occasionally pointing to minor errors in order to dismiss the students' arguments. Empowered by the evidence they had collected, students were able to push back against these adults who sought (consciously or not) to marginalize students' ideas that challenged what they were expecting to hear.
- *Structural siloes that inhibit collaboration between city planning departments and school district leaders.* Without careful scheduling, timelines between the education and planning fields can be incongruous. Planning processes are long-term, multi-year affairs, whereas schools abide by rigid annual and daily schedules. In addition, differences in professional jargon used in planning and education fields frequently pose challenges and obstacles to collaboration. The issue of siloed work can also exist within organizations. For example, various planners in the San Francisco Planning Department had worked for years on isolated child and youth engagement efforts without a unifying strategy. This made Y-PLAN's partnerships with the department even more complex.
- *Potential for co-optation of young people in planning projects.* Consideration of spaces combined with forms of communication and discourse in city planning are generally framed and defined by adults. Thus, channeling the participation of young people through these traditional frameworks limits their ideas, enacting a managerial subterfuge of ideas, imagination, and people that could radically challenge the systems in which young people exist in cities (Clay & Turner, 2021). This was exemplified on an earlier project in West Oakland during the redevelopment

of a historic, yet dilapidated, train station that developers sought to tear down and rebuild. This angered community members and local labor unions who wanted to preserve not only the building but also the living memory of being the terminus of the Pullman Porters, the African American train car workers that provided a pathway to the middle class and the first Black labor union. The developer's implicit agenda in youth washing[4] their plan to gain broader support prompted reflection and action. In order to preserve the integrity and independence of youth input, Y-PLAN program leaders returned the funds provided to them by the developers. Breaking a formal funding partnership ensured that there was no conflict of interest or manipulation of the students' voices and proposals for change.

Recognizing the systemic nature of these challenges has helped shape the Y-PLAN initiative and studio course approach to empowering youth leaders to have agency in their own communities and shape their surroundings. Y-PLAN employs a long-term, two-pronged strategy: first, illustrating and sharing the benefits of incorporating youth voices in city planning aimed at current adult professionals; and second, changing the training and composition of future city planners through transformational, experiential learning opportunities.

In terms of planning instruction in higher education, this has required building departmental and academic bridges at the intersection of education and city planning. The primary vehicle for this strategy has been the Y-PLAN studio course at UC Berkeley, which has influenced more than 500 future leaders in city planning, education, and related fields. This course is one option to fulfill a master's graduation requirement and also serves as an upper division urban studies undergraduate course. Overcoming initial, institutional resistance as well as doubts over legitimacy of youth contributions, the Y-PLAN initiative evolved into a studio course at UC Berkeley that focuses on continuously moving the field of community engagement forward through each cohort's work as a community of practice. We've found that UC Berkeley mentors embrace a more inclusive view of city planning and continue to involve young people throughout their careers (Eppley & McKoy, 2020). Alumni have gone on to involve young people in professional-planning practices in local city government, community development non-profit organizations, and elected office.

Opportunities for critical formation of UC Berkeley students as future planners allows each of them to experience a paradigm shift by witnessing first-hand the extensive expertise and profound insights that young people have to offer the field.

Three Key Policy Recommendations Moving Forward

Y-PLAN continues to demonstrate that the definition of planner can indeed encompass those who have been systematically excluded by their age, race, ethnicity, or socioeconomic status. The following recommendations provide paths for the field of city planning to consider more perspectives and experiences.

1) Map the trajectory of higher education in city planning for undergraduates and graduate students to identify multiple entry points to the planning field. The goal is to learn about and support their journeys to engage with planning our cities.

    a) Key strategies:
        i) Collaborate with student organizations that specialize in creating community and supporting greater participation of students from marginalized communities.
        ii) Incorporate discussions of how to pursue planning education as a part of K–12 partnerships.

b) Examples from Y-PLAN at UC Berkeley:

　　i) Close collaboration with the College of Environmental Design Students of Color, Planning Students Association, and other student organizations.

　　ii) Integration of college and career readiness and informal information sharing, which allow students to build skills for leveraging their Y-PLAN experiences in preparing college application essays and future career plans.

2) Engage with BIPOC communities intentionally. Be critical and self-aware of what diversity means.

　a) Key Strategies:

　　i) Integrate relevant authors, experts, and practitioners who are also part of these racialized communities into the syllabus, course sessions, and opportunities to engage with young people.

　　ii) Recognize and seek out diverse perspectives and experiences in instructional and program teams.

　b) Examples from Y-PLAN at UC Berkeley:

　　i) Incorporation of a racial equity lens into the UC Berkeley studio course through course material, BIPOC guest speakers, and intentional discussions of issues of intersectionality and power dynamics in planning practice.

　　ii) Incorporating client roundtables into step four of the Y-PLAN methodology where young people present and discuss findings and recommendations with city leaders, thus providing a platform that empowers Y-PLAN students and Y-PLAN mentors, particularly those from BIPOC communities.

3) Embrace research to track change over time and ensure we go beyond peripheral changes to address structural issues in higher education and the professional field of city planning.

　a) Key Strategies:

　　i) Document the impact of intentional planning education for immediate and long-term timeframes.

　　ii) Build institutional consciousness and strategies within higher-education departments of planning and related fields about the opportunities for integrating young people.

　b) Examples from Y-PLAN at UC Berkeley:

　　i) Close collaboration with the department chair from the Department of City and Regional Planning to support the Y-PLAN initiative and transform it into a full studio course.

　　ii) The Center for Cities and Schools is documenting recommendations through project briefs and other key data points from every Y-PLAN project over 20 years and using this data to support extensive research and publications.

　　iii) Sharing insights and outcomes from more than 20 years of Y-PLAN students and partners through various publications (McKoy et al., 2022 and e.g., *Voices from The Field: A Glimpse Behind the Scenes at the Team That Has Shaped and Been Shaped by 20 Years of Y-PLAN*, Eppley & McKoy, 2020).

Closing

The COVID-19 pandemic laid bare the structural inequalities that have shaped our cities and educational systems, along with the specific burdens that young people faced when their lives and futures were upended. Growing calls for social justice, epitomized by the Black Lives Matter movement, will continue to inform how cities can address long-standing inequities. We must not allow entire populations to be silenced. This includes our future leaders—our young people.

Y-PLAN has operated in the planning landscape for 20 years by advancing an equity lens that focuses on young people from marginalized communities. During this time, the Y-PLAN Studio and global research initiative have reshaped planning education throughout the Department of City and Regional Planning at UC Berkeley. In 2019, UC Berkeley began to work with other universities such as San José State, Cal Poly, and UC Davis that are interested in adopting the Y-PLAN methodology. Moreover, this unique studio has changed the perspectives of planning professionals, educators, and young people themselves on what is possible when young people's civic participation is supported. As one long-time city manager and Y-PLAN client partner in Richmond, California said,

> Y-PLAN offers an important and powerful understanding of a critical part of our community—the youth. While working in this community for many years never before did I hear about "the two Richmonds" as I did here today—making visible the painful divide seen by high school students of the wealthier waterfront areas and their own home communities. This isn't just unfair, it's bad planning.

Y-PLAN is not a static methodology but rather a dynamic framework that transforms perspectives and places based on the local contexts, partners, and young people involved. The uncertainties and inequities that our cities and education systems face will only continue. Yet this precarity is the very reason why cities, as well as higher-education planning programs, must recognize and engage different voices to ensure that we diversify the planning pipeline for the future. By learning from young people of all backgrounds, city planners have the chance to uncover unexpected, creative solutions to our cities' most vexing challenges. The future of planning education must recognize the pedagogical power from opportunities to involve young, diverse people in planning courses and planning practices alike. What is clear is that bringing young people to the table as agents of change, with the appropriate support and preparation, is beneficial—if not transformative—to all.

Notes

1 There are differing definitions of what ages refer to children, youth, and young people (see United Nations For Youth www.un.org/en/sections/issues-depth/youth-0/index.html). The Center for Cities and Schools, where Y-PLAN is based, refers to children as birth to 11 years (largely elementary school), youth as 12–24 (including secondary school and college), and young people as a more all-inclusive term reflective of all ages under 24.
2 Y-PLAN has been implemented in more than 36 cities in the United States and nine countries worldwide. For more details see the Y-PLAN website: https://y-plan.berkeley.edu/
3 Learn more about Y-PLAN double bottom-line outcomes here: https://y-plan.berkeley.edu/what-is-y-plan
4 Youth washing "refers to young people's voices being used in a performative way without paying attention to them or acting on concerns raised by this group" (Brown, 2021).

References

Brown, H. (2021, November 4). "COP 26 is a youth-washing project", according to young activists participating in the conference. *The Scotsman*, 6:51 PM. https://www.scotsman.com/news/environment/cop-26-is-a-youth-washing-project-say-young-activists-3445764

Clay, K. L., & Turner III, D. C. (2021). "Maybe you should try it this way instead": Youth activism amid managerialist subterfuge. *American Educational Research Journal*, *58*(2), 386–419. https://doi.org/10.3102/0002831221993476

Eppley, A., Gamez-Djokic, B., & McKoy, D. L. (2021). Cultivating inclusion: Belonging and agency in young black men through civic action research. *Canadian Journal of Action Research*, *21*(2), 72–90. https://doi.org/10.33524/cjar.v21i2.513

Eppley, A., & McKoy, D. (2020). *Voices from the field: A glimpse behind the scenes at the team that has shaped and been shaped by 20 years of Y-PLAN*. UC Berkeley Center for Cities + Schools. http://y-plan.berkeley.edu/uploads/Y-PLAN_Voices_20_in_2020.pdf

Garcia, D. H. (2021). *Reframing for empowerment and development: Consolidating the San Francisco planning department's child and youth engagement strategy*. UC Berkeley Center for Cities + Schools.

Mansfield, R. G., Batagol, B., & Raven, R. (2021). "Critical agents of change?" Opportunities and limits to children's participation in urban planning. *Journal Of Planning Literature*. https://doi.org/10.1177/0885412220988645

McKoy, D., Eppley, A., & Buss, S. (2019). The critical role for young people in resilience planning. *Community Development Innovation Review. Federal Reserve Bank of San Francisco*, *14*(1), 127–135. www.frbsf.org/community-development/wp-content/uploads/sites/3/15_McKoy-Eppley-Buss.pdf

McKoy, D., Eppley, A., & Buss, S. (2022). *Planning cities with young people and schools: Forging justice and generating joy*. Routledge Press.

San Francisco Planning Department. (2021). *Child and youth engagement strategy project page*. San Francisco Planning Department. https://sfplanning.org/project/child-and-youth-engagement-strategy

11
ENGAGING ELEMENTARY SCHOOL PUPILS IN COMMUNITY AWARENESS AND PLANNING

Insights From the Kaizuka Machizukuri Club, Osaka

Seth Asare Okyere, Lisa Ueno, Mowa Ebashi, Motoki Shimoda, Hiroshi Tsuji, and Michihiro Kita

Residents' awareness and engagement in community planning is essential for creating environments that respond to their needs and aspirations. Across the diverse but interrelated disciplines of the built environment, there's a growing demand for more engagement of more people in the planning and management of local spaces (Wates, 2014). Over the last three decades, this idea has been entrenched in planning practice (Sanoff, 2007), and the extant literature is replete with diverse methods and tools that emphasize the ethical and social responsibilities of practitioners to engage local people as important constituents of human settlements (Dong et al., 2013; Sanoff, 2000; Wates, 2014). Whether framed in the context of community design (Toker, 2007), participatory design (Sanoff, 2007), co-design (Rosen & Painter, 2019), or even collaborative planning (Healey, 2010), community engagement in planning and design is considered by some to be the best way (Wates, 2014, p. 2) to ensure that communities become safer, stronger, and more sustainable—that planning interventions are fit for purpose (Aboelata et al., 2011).

This chapter contributes to ongoing discussions on engaging local communities in planning from the perspective of planning education. It follows the Dong et al. (2013) proposition that information (planning awareness) and knowledge (of planning processes, tools, etc.) are important components of building local peoples' capabilities to engage in the planning and design of their communities. These fundamentals, as they suggest, imply the need for educational activities and initiatives to enhance understanding of planning and its goals. Unfortunately, recent scholarship suggests that school-based planning and design programs that engage the community, particularly youth and children, as part of planning processes and awareness are few (Derr, 2015; Derr et al., 2017). This premise, the occasion of this edited volume, points to a potentially new epoch in planning education; that is, a practical knowledge hub for planning departments and schools to better engage communities for professional awareness (Palazzo et al., 2021). This discourse also offers opportunities to enhance the ability of local people to shape their living environments in more informed and capable ways.

This chapter suggests that planning schools and departments can serve as conduits through which such knowledge is acquired to generate interest and enhance planning capabilities for sustainable outcomes. It provides a descriptive narrative of primary school club activities designed by the Urban Planning and Design Lab within the Division of Global Architecture at Osaka University. The program, originally designed to increase pupils' awareness about their own communities and develop interest in planning them, envisages that such an approach can, in the immediate term, generate awareness about the rudiments, goals, and processes of planning. In so doing, pupils, as the future generation, can acquire the interest and capabilities needed for shaping the built environment now and in the future.

The rest of the chapter is structured as follows. The next section presents a brief local context of the Machizukuri approach to urban planning and student club activities in Japan. Next, the school-engagement program is described in terms of its origins, activities, actors, and processes. The last section of this chapter reflects on the program's implications for planning education and practice.

Machizukuri and Community Engagement in Japan

The term *Machizukuri* is composed of two Japanese words, namely "machi" and "zukuri." *Machi*, which loosely translates as town, is rather distinct and encompassing in the sense that it denotes the physical environment in which social activities occur. It also includes both material and non-material aspects of a community (Satoh, 2019, 2020). On the other hand, *zukuri* translates as "to make." In this context, to make, as Satoh (2019, p. 128) puts it, "does not simply mean to make inanimate things; rather, it means, connotatively, to cultivate things with full effort, heart, and soul while participating in the lengthy process of making and animating them." Machizukuri is the making and management of a town that both creates new things and enhances the existing through an incremental process where the original essence of community is kept (Okyere et al., 2019; Satoh, 2019). Furthermore, Watanabe (2007) stresses that, in planning terms, machi represents a community—the object of Machizukuri activities—while zukuri concerns the method of Machizukuri activities. Either way, Machizukuri can be conceptualised as a community-situated process where local-administration officials, experts, and community members work together to improve the living environment in a way that reflects local values and lifestyles (Aoki, 2018; Kusakabe, 2013; Okyere et al., 2019; Watanabe, 2012).

Historically, the term emerged in the 1960s and '70s from citizen environmental movements against public environmental pollution and its damaging effects on mental, socioeconomic, and living conditions (Satoh, 2020). In particular, industrial expansion was accompanied by emissions from chemical industries and refineries, which were considered responsible for public hazards and damages such as asthma and bronchitis (Kurokawa, 2010). Thus, Machizukuri became rooted in creative ways that groups of residents, through their own initiatives, achieved environmental improvements through efforts termed as Machizukuri plans. These citizen-improvement efforts later found their way into other community-improvement actions (Machizukuri plans) aimed at neglected, high-density, built-up wooden areas that were common in Tokyo and other large Japanese cities at the time (Ito, 2007; Satoh, 2019). Such community improvement actions were largely considered as anti-disaster solutions given that Japan's high frequency of earthquakes made dense urban fabric largely consisting of wooden houses highly susceptible to destruction. Within the context of urban planning, citizen movements, working hand in hand with experts, developed alternative Machizukuri plans to oppose the centralised and project-oriented nature of Japanese city planning that was considered to be harmful to the historical and natural environment (Mavrodieva et al., 2019).

Today, Machizukuri practices have become entrenched in urban planning and community development in Japan by emphasising area and community management through a common agreement among diverse stakeholders on comprehensive solutions to problems. Particularly after the Greater

Hanshin-Awaji Earthquake in Kobe in the late 1990s, Machizukuri activities received legal backing with the introduction of the Non-Profit Organisations Law in 1998, granting more autonomy and opportunities for local organisations to support citizen actions and movements (Okyere et al., 2019). As Evans (2001) has noted, though localised, it's a nationwide phenomenon that works across multiple scales and disciplines. Indeed, there are numerous examples of its role in post-disaster reconstruction and recovery (Aoki, 2018; Sugita, Kawasaki et al., 2020), preservation and restoration of green infrastructure (Kusakabe, 2013), shopping-district revitalisation (Sugita, Iida et al., 2020), community historical awareness (Nunokawa, 2007), urban regeneration (Murayama, 2018), and housing improvement (Hsiao, 2021).

In spite of this, the future of Machizukuri practice is challenged (Mavrodieva et al., 2019; Satoh, 2020) on two fronts. First is the notion of old-people centredness, that is, citizen-action groups for community planning are largely made up of the elderly (to a lesser extent the middle-aged) compared to younger cohorts (Sorensen & Funck, 2007). Second is the challenge of elevating the practice to the whole citizenry, that is, to "glocalise" Machizukuri and open it to the world through the accumulation of practices, as well as the development of methods and techniques, through planning education (Satoh, 2019, p. 140). Addressing both challenges is the central argument of this chapter, submitting that planning education that engages elementary schools can contribute to opening up local citizen-planning to diverse groups (e.g., schoolchildren) who have not characteristically been part of planning activities. Furthermore, engaging pupils through school-based learning of community planning, pupils can be exposed to the rudiments of planning methods and tools for enriching local action while generating awareness of the goals and purposes of planning, and eventually expand the demographic makeup of the people primarily involved in Machizukuri activities.

Against this brief local context, the next section of this chapter presents an elementary school Machizukuri-club activity—an educational activity organised by the Urban Planning and Design Lab of Osaka University.

The Kaizuka West Elementary School Machizukuri Club

Kaizuka is a small town located in the Osaka Bay area and the southwestern part of Osaka Prefecture. The town, like several Japanese municipalities, is confronted with the challenge of improving the quality of the living environment of municipal-housing areas. Municipal housing formed part of the massive public-housing supply promoted by mid-20th-century Japanese government-housing policy. However, market-oriented housing policy reforms in recent decades have meant that while the private real estate sector has become dominant and the quality of private housing has improved—in terms of energy efficiency, disaster resilience, and suitability to changing lifestyles—many municipalities are grappling with improving public-housing quality, rising vacancy within housing units, and overconcentration of the elderly population (see Kobayashi, 2016). In search of solutions to improve municipal housing and its surrounding areas, the Kaizuka municipality decided to embark on a private-finance initiative (PFI) to work with the corporate sector as a strategy for area planning revitalisation.

In 2018, the head of the Urban Planning and Design Lab (UPDL) at the Division of Global Architecture, Osaka University (Japan), who is also a member of the Kaizuka Municipal Planning Board, proposed that the PFI initiative should include elementary schoolchildren to introduce them to existing community issues, integrate their ideas into local initiatives, and generate awareness about planning and its processes. The crux of this proposal was that it was necessary for pupils to be informed and included in community planning and community initiatives through planning education. This proposal was accepted by the municipality.

To actualise this, the UPDL decided to engage schoolchildren by introducing a Machizukuri (community planning) club activity in the Kaizuka West Elementary School. Club activities are common in Japanese schools, where pupils join clubs either as curricular (science clubs) or extracurricular (e.g., swimming, basketball, music, etc.) activities. Rather than the more regular extracurricular activities, it was introduced as a class-based curriculum to provide an educational platform that actively engaged pupils in the knowledge and practice of community planning. This required extensive discussions with the school principal, teachers, and the municipality. Teachers were initially anxious about it in terms of their roles and workloads, as it was unfamiliar and differed from existing club activities. There was also the issue of how to maintain pupil enthusiasm. Academic staff and graduate students from UPDL held discussions with teachers and assured them that the UPDL would coordinate and manage the project as a club activity. Responsibilities would be shared, and the UPDL team would steer the program. The program was organised to give participating pupils a sense of accomplishment after every activity session—one that they could share with their parents. The project was positioned as a university-led pupil-engagement activity from the perspective of community planning and planning education. With the cooperation and support of all participants, the project is still ongoing, and the next section describes implemented activities, actors, and key milestones.

Actors

The club activity is composed of four main actors, including the UPDL, the Kaizuka City Office (Architectural Housing Division), a real estate developer (Next Axis Ltd.), and the Kaizuka West Elementary School.

Urban Planning and Design Lab

As mentioned earlier, the UPDL initiated the project and currently is the coordinator and managing entity. Graduate students (eight) from the lab steer and facilitate activities using topical discussions, workshops, and community surveys with pupils and selected elementary school teachers. Earlier in the project, academic staff from UPDL organised a workshop and discussions where teachers and pupils were introduced to basic community planning goals, principles, and tools. The eight graduate students from UPDL who are actively involved in the project are organised into three teams—nature, open space (e.g., playgrounds), and culture (e.g., festivals)—in line with the thematic aspects of the project. One graduate student leads each of the three UPDL teams while academic staff perform responsibilities such as supervision and monthly review of activities. At least one graduate student takes responsibility for documentation and producing reports as scholarly records.

Kaizuka Municipality

The Kaizuka municipality is represented in the project by two staff members from the Architectural Housing Division. The staff participates in monthly workshops held at the elementary school, supports field visits, and provides information related to municipal-planning activities. The staff also provides practical guidance to pupils, including feedback on their surveys and proposals.

Elementary School Teachers

Two teachers constitute the main support staff from the Kaizuka West Elementary School. They help the pupils to clearly grasp learning activities introduced in the program through teaching aids and assist students in fieldwork such as plotting, mapping, photographs, and recordings. They also help students to navigate the community using base maps.

Elementary School Pupils

There are 18 pupils from grades four through six who are engaged in the project. The pupils are organised into six groups of three members each. As the main beneficiaries of the project, they participate in discussions and monthly workshops, undertake field visits, and communicate their ideas, impressions, and proposals with support from teachers, UPDL graduate students, and municipality staff. So far, pupils have actively participated in all monthly workshops by joining a thematic area of interest—nature, open space, or culture. The workshops are supposed to provide a participatory and fun educational platform for the pupils. They are introduced to relevant planning issues—tailored to children's needs—and are required to take notes, ask questions, and identify issues to look out for during the field visits.

Pupils conduct spatial analysis through field visits, observation, and mapping of spatial features (e.g., children's playgrounds, open spaces, walking routes, etc.), including their characteristics and conditions. In combination with classroom-based workshops, students make proposals using their understanding, learning experiences, and feedback from the graduate students, municipality staff, and their own teachers.

Real Estate Company

Next Axis, a real estate company, is the main business partner of Kaizuka municipality in the PFI initiative for the replanning and revitalisation of the municipal housing area. They are responsible for the housing revitalisation, business development, and management of municipal housing or residential areas. For this project, however, the company was expected to participate in the workshops to provide practical information to pupils on the development financing component of community planning. They also supported site visits to the housing area and provided simple but practical explanations on housing improvement and community design. Additionally, they were expected to provide feedback on pupils' proposals from the perspective of planning feasibility and implementation.

Club Activities and Accomplishments

This section describes the main Machizukuri-club activities carried out since 2018 as part of the engagement of schoolchildren in community awareness and planning. To enrich pupils' understanding from both an educational and experiential perspective, three main activities have been implemented—map work, field surveys, and proposal development.

Map Work

One of the first engagements with schoolchildren in this project was the mapping exercise. As a foundation, graduate students and faculty, with the support of elementary school teachers, introduced topical discussions with pupils on "what is a map," "what are the features of a map," and "how to read maps" using illustrations and other teaching aids. Students were then presented with a map of Kaizuka to identify noticeable features and elements based on their earlier understanding. Following this basic foundation exercise, they were presented with a base map of Kaizuka on which they were to develop their own maps with reference to specific themes. For example, in one activity pupils mapped the walking or travel routes from their homes to the school grounds and indicated the main features of routes using colour codes as markers and identifiers. In order to foster an engaging process that is attentive to the learning needs of the students, the mapping exercise is organized into smaller groups under the guidance of at least one graduate student from UPDL and the elementary school teachers (Figure 11.1, top). Peer learning is promoted by different groups sharing ideas and

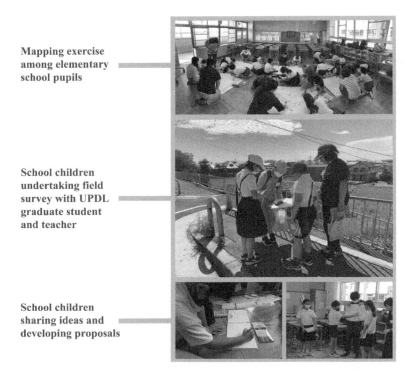

Figure 11.1 Images Depicting the Three Main School Club Activities

supporting each other. At the end of each mapping exercise, each group presents their map as a poster that they then discuss with their colleagues for feedback and clarification. Graduate students, faculty, and municipal staff also share comments to help pupils fine tune their work, including remarks on the connection between the exercise and understanding community and planning in general.

Field Surveys

Field surveys in Kaizuka town, including the municipal housing area and its surroundings, form one of the practical aspects of this school-based community planning club project. Pupils, together with teachers and graduate students, undertake transect walks, plotting, and observations. In line with their area of interest (e.g., nature, children's playgrounds, etc.), pupils identify major spatial elements as they walk through the town and plot them on the map (Figure 11.1, middle). For instance, those who belong to the nature thematic area locate green spaces or parks by plotting or updating the base map, while documenting conditions with field notes and self-taken photographs. Here also, schoolchildren are assisted by their teachers and UPDL graduate students.

Beyond class-based mapping, pupils obtain a practical understanding of the spatial distribution of material elements within the built environment in addition to their use and conditions. This exercise enables the schoolchildren to have the ability to pay particular attention to some of the important physical elements of their community and to reflect on their usefulness in their lives. The community field surveys provide children an opportunity to enhance awareness of their community and to reflect on its future through proposals or ideas.

Proposal Development

The third major activity in this project provides pupils the opportunity to propose ideas and strategies based on the results of the field-survey exercise. Having been introduced to the rudiments of planning coupled with practical exposure to community planning issues through fieldwork, children presented a set of proposals at a community improvement workshop. For the purposes of this chapter, two of the proposals by the elementary school pupils are briefly presented.

The first proposal is related to the theme of water park. The pupils in the nature group had noticed that the Kogi River (Figure 11.2), which flows through their community, had become a divider rather than a natural element supporting children's recreational and social activities. They therefore proposed to enhance community members' relationship with the river by creating a water park for the community, especially children, to play. Their proposal seeks to develop a new park along the river to encourage residents to use the adjoining land for relaxation and playful activities. The proposal comprises three main aspects: (1) the provision of amenities such as tables and chairs to encourage social gathering, (2) a fishing spot for recreational fishing, and (3) a sand pit along the river for children to play. For the most part, the project seeks to improve the landscape along the river to encourage social gatherings and cultural events. Additionally, a plaza, to be located in the middle of the park, would house shops selling products from the community to boost the local economy.

The construction of a community specialty market was the theme of the second proposal. The essence of this project was to provide a space to sell unique and popular goods from Kaizuka to serve the purposes of boosting the local economy and attracting people from other cities. Like many regional municipalities in Japan, the town suffers from an ageing, declining population and a

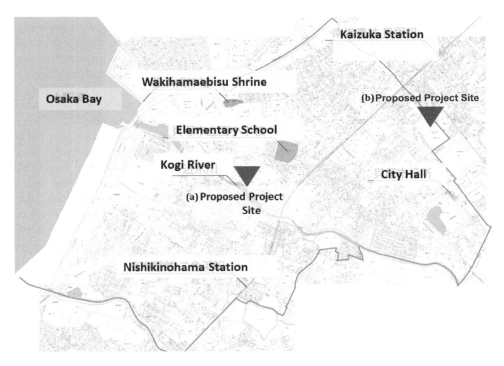

Figure 11.2 Location of Pupil's Proposals: (a) Water Park (b) Specialty Market

consequent weakening of the local economy. The proposed specialty market would be structured with two floors: the first for trading locally produced products that are unique to Kaizuka town and the second as a food court for tasting delicacies from the city. Generally, this entails providing a commercial space to market community produce through exhibitions and cultural events connected to the town festival.

Reflections and Takeaways for Planning Education

Children form an important demographic group in the use of spaces within the built environment. Their engagement in planning education offers immense opportunities for generating awareness of planning and interest in community development. This is particularly relevant in Japanese regional communities, where the challenge of an ageing and declining population is more pronounced than anywhere in the world. This chapter has provided a brief account of an ongoing elementary school club activity established by the UPDL at Osaka University as a means to engage local elementary school pupils to be more aware of their community and also to introduce basic community planning principles and tools through classroom learning.

Although it's still too early in the project to evaluate community awareness among elementary school pupils, this chapter reveals how an initial collaboration has been created that allows children to understand their community's planning issues and to confront them through their own ideas and proposals. In particular, the two proposals from the pupils indicate that students have become aware of how natural elements such as the river can be used as an ecological resource to promote child-friendly community spaces. Interestingly, this awareness finds support in recent research on landscape planning topics such as blue and green infrastructure, which indicates that water-sensitive urban design can contribute to the public realm and the sociability of communities—for both children and adults (Lamond & Everett, 2019; Pedrosa et al., 2021; Pedrosa et al., 2022). Additionally, by emphasizing the community specialty market as an avenue to promote locally made products and revitalize the local economy, the children's ideas correspond to community development planners' calls to use community resources (e.g., food produce, farmers' markets) for local economic development (Hughes & Isengildina-Massa, 2015; Rand et al., 2003). Together, these proposals go a long way toward demonstrating children's awareness of some of the key topics in planning, such as preservation of blue and green spaces, improving sociability of public spaces, and the sustainable development of the local economy through community resources and competitive advantage.

Nonetheless, key challenges exist. For one, the role of the private real estate company has been limited to occasional participation in the workshops without a strong connection between the club activity and the actual urban-renovation project that informed the club activity in the first place. This was, perhaps, due to failure on the part of the team members to clearly define roles and expectations in line with stakeholder interests. This is a major challenge that future schoolchildren-engagement projects must consider at an early stage, given that the private sector often needs to be persuaded, through time-consuming discussions, to actively participate in such programs. The role of municipality staff has also been passive, mainly in the form of feedback at two workshop sessions.

Despite these challenges, the ability to bring different stakeholders together around a shared interest in enhancing children's awareness of community planning and improvement is a useful starting point. In addition, school pupils' exposure to basic planning tools and principles for understanding and improving current community conditions is a notable accomplishment given initial reservations from the elementary school staff and municipality. Although the project is in its early phase, we suggest that planning schools and departments can bring planning closer to schoolchildren in two ways: (1) by identifying issues in their surrounding communities that are of relevance to planning functions and target communities, especially parents and schoolchildren; and (2) by developing learning-based programs jointly with schools (elementary or middle) using simple planning principles and tools that are fun and effective in exposing children to planning functions and roles. Going forward, future research should follow up with the pupils to examine the impact of this club activity on their awareness of planning tools, interest in the planning profession, and overall commitment to building sustainable and inclusive future communities.

References

Aboelata, M. J., Ersoylu, L., & Cohen, L. (2011). Community engagement in design and planning. In A. L. Dannenberg, H. Frumkin, & R. J. Jackson (Eds.), *Making healthy places* (pp. 287–302). Island Press. https://doi.org/10.5822/978-1-61091-036-1_19.

Aoki, N. (2018). Sequencing and combining participation in urban planning: The case of tsunami-ravaged Onagawa Town, Japan. *Cities, 72*, 226–236. https://doi.org/10.1016/j.cities.2017.08.020

Derr, V. (2015). Integrating community engagement and children's voices into design and planning education. *CoDesign, 11*(2), 119–133. https://doi.org/10.1080/15710882.2015.1054842

Derr, V., Malinin, L. H., & Banasiak, M. (2017). Engaging citizens and transforming designers: Analysis of a campus-community partnership through the lens of children's rights to participate. *Journal of Community Engagement and Scholarship, 9*(2), 6. http://jces.ua.edu/wp-content/uploads/2017/04/06_JCES-9.2-Engaging-Citizens-and-Transforming-Designers.pdf

Dong, A., Sarkar, S., Nichols, C., & Kvan, T. (2013). The capability approach as a framework for the assessment of policies toward civic engagement in design. *Design Studies, 34*(3), 326–344. https://doi.org/10.1016/j.destud.2012.10.002

Evans, N. (2001). Discourses of urban community and community planning: A comparison between Britain and Japan. *Sheffield Online Papers in Social Research, 3*. www.sheffield.ac.uk/polopoly_fs/1.71434!/file/evans.pdf

Healey, P. (2010). *Making better places: The planning project in the twenty-first century*. Macmillan International Higher Education.

Hsiao, H.-W. (2021). Using participatory-planning-based cooperative housing approaches as housing improvement solutions for Xizhou indigenous squatter settlements in New Taipei City, Taiwan. *City, Culture and Society*, 100370. https://doi.org/10.1016/j.ccs.2020.100370

Hughes, D. W., & Isengildina-Massa, O. (2015). The economic impact of farmers' markets and a state level locally grown campaign. *Food Policy, 54*, 78–84. https://doi.org/10.1016/j.foodpol.2015.05.001

Ito, A. (2007). Earthquake reconstruction machizukuri and citizen participation. In C. F. A Sorensen (Ed.), *Living cities in Japan: Citizens' movements, machizukuri and local environments* (pp. 157–171). Routledge.

Kobayashi, M. (2016). *The housing market and housing policies in Japan* (p. 558). https://ssrn.com/abstract=2752868 or http://dx.doi.org/10.2139/ssrn.2752868

Kurokawa, C. (2010). Social frameworks for civil society in Japan: In search for a Japanese model. I In H. Vinken, Y. Nishimura, B. White, & M. Deguchi (Eds.), *Civic engagement in contemporary Japan. Nonprofit and civil society studies* (pp. 41–64). Springer. https://doi.org/10.1007/978-1-4419-1504-7_3

Kusakabe, E. (2013). Advancing sustainable development at the local level: The case of machizukuri in Japanese cities. *Progress in Planning, 80*, 1–65. https://doi.org/10.1016/j.progress.2012.06.001

Lamond, J., & Everett, G. (2019). Sustainable blue-green infrastructure: A social practice approach to understanding community preferences and stewardship. *Landscape and Urban Planning, 191*, 103639. https://doi.org/10.1016/j.landurbplan.2019.103639

Mavrodieva, A. V., Daramita, R. I. F., Arsono, A. Y., Yawen, L., & Shaw, R. (2019). Role of civil society in sustainable urban renewal (Machizukuri) after the Kobe Earthquake. *Sustainability, 11*(2), 335. https://doi.org/10.3390/su11020335

Murayama, A. (2018). Reconsidering urban planning through community-based initiatives. I In B. Müller & H. Shimizu (Eds.), *Towards the implementation of the new urban agenda* (pp. 223–233). Springer. https://doi.org/10.1007/978-3-319-61376-5_18

Nunokawa, H. (2007). Machizukuri and historical awareness in the old town of Kobe. In A. Sorensen & C. Funck (Eds.), *Living cities in Japan: Citizens' movements, machizukuri and local environments* (1st ed.). Routledge.

Okyere, S. A., Diko, S. K., Abunyewah, M., & Kita, M. (2019). Toward citizen-led planning for climate change adaptation in urban Ghana: Hints from Japanese 'machizukuri' activities. In P. Cobbinah & M. Addaney (Eds.), *The geography of climate change adaptation in urban Africa* (pp. 391–419). Palgrave Macmillan. https://doi.org/10.1007/978-3-030-04873-0_14

Palazzo, D., Hollstein, L., & Diko, S. K. (2021). Urban planning as a career preference for students: Efforts to improve awareness about the profession. *Planning Practice & Research, 36*(2), 174–192. https://doi.org/10.1080/02697459.2020.1782056

Pedrosa, E. L. J., Okyere, S. A., Diko, S. K., & Kita, M. (2022). Informal greenspaces in peripheral Luanda, Angola: Benefits and challenges. In P. B. Cobbinah & M. Addaney (Eds.), *Sustainable urban futures in Africa*. New York Routledge.

Pedrosa, E. L. J., Okyere, S. A., Frimpong, L. K., Diko, S. K., Commodore, T. S., & Kita, M. (2021). Planning for informal urban green spaces in African cities: Children's perception and use in peri-urban areas of Luanda, Angola. *Urban Science*, 5(3), 50. https://doi.org/10.3390/urbansci5030050

Rand, G. E. D., Heath, E., & Alberts, N. (2003). The role of local and regional food in destination marketing: A South African situation analysis. *Journal of Travel & Tourism Marketing*, 14(3–4), 97–112. https://doi.org/10.1300/J073v14n03_06

Rosen, J., & Painter, G. (2019). From citizen control to co-production: Moving beyond a linear conception of citizen participation. *Journal of the American Planning Association*, 85(3), 335–347. https://doi.org/10.1080/01944363.2019.1618727

Sanoff, H. (2000). *Community participation methods in design and planning*. John Wiley & Sons.

Sanoff, H. (2007). Special issue on participatory design. *Design Studies*, 3(28), 213–215. https://doi.org/10.1016/j.destud.2007.02.001

Satoh, S. (2019). Evolution and methodology of Japanese machizukuri for the improvement of living environments. *Japan Architectural Review*, 2(2), 127–142. https://doi.org/10.1002/2475-8876.12084

Satoh, S. (2020). *Japanese machizukuri and community engagement: History, method and practice*. Routledge.

Sorensen, A., & Funck, C. (2007). *Living cities in Japan: Citizens' movements, machizukuri and local environments*: Routledge.

Sugita, M., Iida, T., Kita, M., Tsuji, H., Shimoda, M., Matsubara, S., & Okyere, S. A. (2020). A study on area's context of city center in which sequential redevelopment projects have been implemented. Analysis of economic system among proprietors and companies in Takamatsu Marugamemachi shopping street. *Journal of Architecture and Planning (Transactions of AIJ)*, 85(775), 1943–1953. https://doi.org/10.3130/aija.85.1943

Sugita, M., Kawasaki, E., Kita, M., Shimoda, M., Tsuji, H., Matsubara, S., & Okyere, S. A. (2020). Comprehension of area context in rehabilitation from disasters. A case study on land readjustment project of reconstruction from Great Hanshin-Awaji Earthquake in Matsumoto district, Hyogo ward, city of Kobe. *Journal of Architecture and Planning (Transactions of AIJ)*, 85(772), 1183–1193. https://doi.org/10.3130/aija.85.1183

Toker, Z. (2007). Recent trends in community design: The eminence of participation. *Design Studies*, 28(3), 309–323. https://doi.org/10.1016/j.destud.2007.02.008

Watanabe, S.-I. J. (2007). Toshi Keikaku vs machizukuri: Emerging paradigm of civil society in Japan, 1950–1980. In A. Sorensen & C. Funck (Eds.), *Living cities in Japan: Citizens' movements, machizukuri and local environments* (1st ed., pp. 39–55). Routledge.

Watanabe, S.-I. J. (2012). *The historical analysis of the 'Kunitachi Machizukuri movement': Its nature and the role of Professor Shiro Masuda*. Paper presented at the 15th International Planning History Society Conference.

Wates, N. (2014). *The community planning handbook: How people can shape their cities, towns and villages in any part of the world*. Routledge.

12
LEARNING ENVIRONMENTAL PLANNING WITH GEODESIGN
A Case Study in Cache Valley, Utah

Bartlett Warren-Kretzschmar and Carlos V. Licon

Planning decisions involve an understanding of different views about the importance of natural and built systems competing for land and resources. Furthermore, such decisions are complex and contain uncertainty about future development. For citizens to accept these decisions, the planning process must be transparent and comprehensible (Bruening et al., 2014). Participatory planning, that is, participation in decision-making about the future of a community, can promote an understanding of the planning processes, decisions, and their consequences. Realistically, however, most citizens do not or cannot participate in the planning process in their community. Ideally, planning concepts, approaches, and processes should be explained to citizens, most logically as part of civic education in schools.

Examples of educational opportunities for planning have been developed by the American Planning Association (APA). Through the APA Ambassadors workshops, such as Box City, elementary school children learn about the city planning process (APA, 2020). In addition, computer games, such as SimCity™, offer gamified approaches to simulating the objectives and constraints of planning communities (Minnery & Searle, 2014; Gaber, 2007). In both approaches, students develop plans for fictitious communities and employ theoretical planning ideas and strategies. However, the true challenges become apparent when planning ideas are transformed into concrete plans in specific locations. At this point, the complexity of the issues and consequences of planning decisions on the future community and environment become apparent—this is where the true learning opportunity lies. Situations that allow students to use their personal experience and knowledge to develop a vision for their own community offer an educational experience that illustrates the key aspects of planning decisions: knowledge, analysis, and tradeoffs (Derr, 2015).

One planning approach that offers a collaborative process to propose change and develop scenarios for future development is geodesign (Steinitz, 2012), an iterative planning approach in which interdisciplinary groups of experts and stakeholders collaboratively develop planning scenarios. Geodesign uses geospatial modeling to support informed design decisions and impact analysis. The geodesign process incorporates real-time feedback and negotiation among stakeholders to build a consensus around holistic planning and design proposals (Foster, 2016).

A digital version of the geodesign process is embodied in the Geodesignhub software and online platform developed by Dr. Hrishikesh Ballal (2014), which enables the rapid generation of georeferenced diagrams to illustrate projects and policies for future development. It enables negotiation among different stakeholder groups to build consensus around proposals to address growth and preservation efforts. Past case studies show that the use of the Geodesignhub in workshop settings

DOI: 10.4324/9781003254003-15

successfully supports interdisciplinary groups of experts, planners, and university students to develop scenarios for future change, as well as negotiation and decision-making among participants (Rivero et al., 2015). However, can Geodesignhub be used to teach young people who are not planning students or professionals about complex environmental issues in their communities and collaborative decision-making in the planning process? Can it help them think like planners, imagine the future of their communities, and even consider planning as a future career?

Geodesign Case Study: Cache Valley, Utah

The following case study explores the usability of the cloud-based Geodesignhub software and the geodesign process as a learning module in secondary education as a one-day workshop. More specifically, the case study examines whether the Geodesign learning module had an impact on students' environmental attitudes, their understanding of the future impacts of planning decisions on their community, and their awareness of the planning profession.

A Confluence of Planning Dilemmas

Cache Valley is a rural, agrarian landscape surrounded by the dramatic Wellsville and Bear River mountain ranges of northern Utah in the western United States. The valley was settled in 1856 by Mormon pioneers (Christensen et al., 2020). During the following years, homesteaders established farm communities together with an extensive canal system for irrigation, transforming the arid landscape into a rich agricultural landscape. The Mormon settlers also laid out towns in a grid system known as the Plat of Zion. Today the historic town centers throughout the valley are experiencing rapid and poorly controlled growth. The conversion of farmland into subdivisions and commercial growth in the form of strip development threatens the rural identity of the valley.

At the time of the workshop, the population of Cache Valley was approximately 116,000 people, with half of the population under 25 years of age (US Census, 2015). Population growth, expected to double in the next 25 to 30 years, challenges the preservation of the rural character of Cache Valley and the recreational and natural resources of the surrounding mountains. Surveys of Utah residents show that their top environmental concerns are loss of agricultural land, water availability, and air pollution (Envision Utah, 2015). While residents would like to retain viable agricultural land and preserve the rural character, climate change and drought in the western landscape make water a scarce and controversial resource. Furthermore, the topography of the valley promotes atmospheric inversions, which often produce dangerous air quality during the winter months. In the face of the expected doubling of the population, local planners and politicians must guide future development to address these and other issues in Cache Valley. The study area is located in the southern half of Cache Valley because this area is expected to experience the most pressure of urban expansion over the next 20 years.

Preparing a Geodesign Learning Module

The geodesign learning module used in this case study originates from a one-day workshop at Utah State University in October 2015 that employed Geodesignhub software. The workshop addressed the question of how population growth in Cache Valley can be accommodated while retaining the rural, agricultural character of the valley.

Under the direction of Professor Carl Steinitz, local planners, stakeholders, faculty, and graduate students from Utah State University proposed projects and policies to improve ten natural and built systems (see Figure 12.1). Using these projects and policies, participants designed different future scenarios in six stakeholder groups that embodied their respective priorities and objectives.

In order to create the learning module for the secondary school students, the workshop was simplified by reducing the number of stakeholder groups to five and focusing on the five systems that were most significant for future planning of the valley: biodiversity, water, commercial development, agriculture, and residential. In addition, we divided the one-day workshop into three shorter sessions that could be incorporated into the schedule and curriculum of the students.

High-School Students Use Geodesign

The geodesign learning module was tested in two ninth-grade geography classes, with a total of 55 students, at the InTech Collegiate Academy in North Logan, Utah. The school provided students with laptops and Wi-Fi access to the Internet, that is, the Geodesignhub platform. Researchers ran the workshop in three 90-minute sessions. Graduate students from the Master of Bioregional Planning program at Utah State University, who participated in the initial geodesign workshop, assisted in the classroom as team leaders of groups with approximately five high-school students per team.

In the first session, students were introduced to the Geodesignhub software, the study area, and the evaluation models of the natural and human systems (see Figure 12.1). The evaluation models identified the vulnerability and attractiveness of the landscape for promoting each of the five systems. Furthermore, these models formed the information base for the students' analyses and planning decisions. The high-school students were then grouped into five "system" teams (see Figure 12.2) in which they developed ideas about projects and policies that would improve their system in the study area. They used the Geodesignhub software to draw diagrams that showed the size and location of projects and the areas where specific policies could be adopted. For example, the Agriculture System team created farmland preservation policies for areas of prime productivity that need protection from development. These diagrams, which represent projects and policies, could be shared with everyone in the class over the Geodesignhub platform, and they formed the building blocks for developing scenarios in the next session.

In the second session, the high-school students were regrouped into five "stakeholder" teams: developers, young people, old people, environmentalists, and farmers. They were asked to role-play the character of their stakeholder group. All students received the problem statement: "The population of Cache Valley will double in the next twenty-five years. Locate residential housing for the new residents while protecting water, wildlife, and agricultural land." The graduate students, acting as team leaders, helped the high-school students collaboratively develop scenarios for future development of the study area. Each group first prioritized the importance of the systems, then selected the projects and policies created in the first session that supported the objectives and goals of their stakeholder group. At the end of the second session, each stakeholder group produced a scenario that best fulfilled their future needs and wishes.

The last session was attended by the software developer Dr. Hrishikesh Ballal, who joined the discussion on videoconference from Ireland. Each stakeholder group had five minutes to present and explain their preferred scenario for the future of Cache Valley. Other stakeholder groups were asked to rate how well they could work with the presenting group. In the ensuing discussion, the teams began to identify alliances and similarities among the scenarios of the different stakeholder groups that could support a planning consensus.

Evaluation of the Geodesign Learning Module

A mixed-method approach was used to evaluate the impact of the Geodesignhub software and workshop on the students' environmental attitudes and knowledge. The study employed the New Ecological Paradigm (NEP) survey instrument to measure those attitudes (Dunlap et al., 2000). The

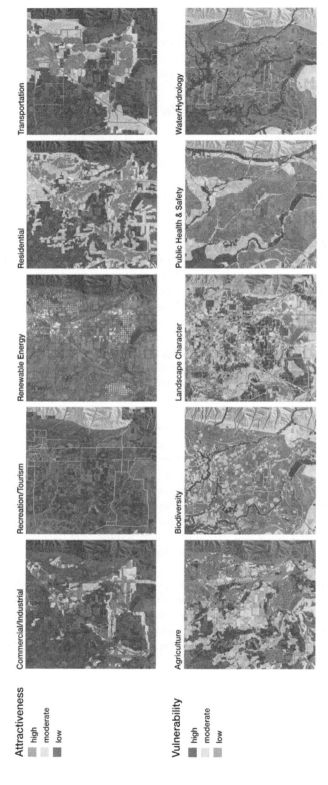

Figure 12.1 Evaluation Models Developed for the Cache Valley Geodesign Workshop

The models include five models of attractiveness (suitability): Commercial/Industrial, Recreation/Tourism, Renewable energy, Residential, and Transportation. Maps are rated using three categories: highly attractive, moderately attractive, and low attractive land. Five models of vulnerability (sensitivity) include Agricultural land, Biodiversity, Landscape character, Health and Safety, and Water/Hydrology. The rating of these maps shows highly vulnerable land, moderately vulnerable land, and low vulnerable land. In general, highly vulnerable and low attractive areas should be changed minimally, while low vulnerable and highly attractive areas could be changed.

Learning Environmental Planning With Geodesign

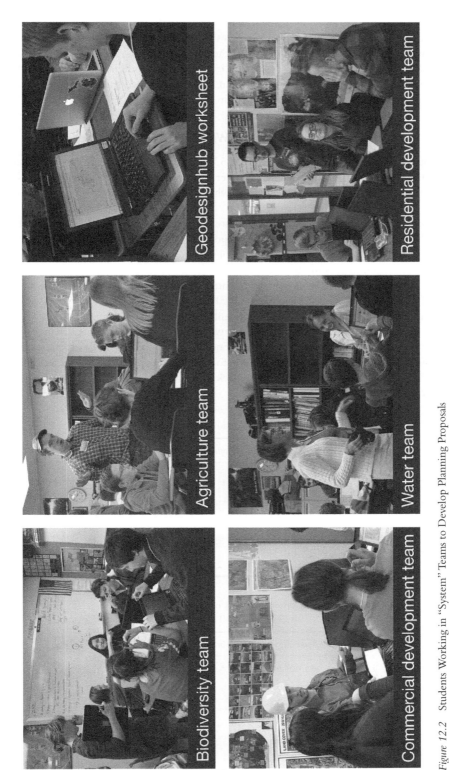

Figure 12.2 Students Working in "System" Teams to Develop Planning Proposals

Six frames showing students working in small teams. Some students discussing and some working with Geodesignhub software in their laptops.

survey was administered to the students pre- and post-workshop. In addition, the change in student attitudes about the planning and environmental issues facing the study area were also captured in separate pre- and post-workshop questionnaires. In the post-workshop questionnaire, students also evaluated the Geodesignhub software and planning experience. A content analysis of their comments identified themes in their responses. The researchers also recorded students' comments about the planning profession during and after the workshop.

Empowering Young Planners With Geodesign Software

Of the students who participated in the workshop, 53 responded to both surveys. The follow-up survey showed that about half of the students considered the software easy or very easy to use (see Table 12.1). In fact, when the students were asked what they liked best about the workshop, they mentioned the software most often.

In the workshop, a large majority of students mastered the functions of the Geodesignhub software, with 80% of the students creating project and policy diagrams on their own. In fact, the first class of students created diagrams for 97 different projects and policies, while the second class produced 115 diagrams, both in 90-minute sessions.

Students' comments about the workshop highlighted the software and the learning experience (see Table 12.2). They made comments such as, "I liked experimenting with the software," or "It was fun to collaborate with my classmates." Finally, students expressed feeling empowered. "We got to help influence something," or even "I really liked this workshop because it gives us a chance to really stop and think about what our future will be like." Furthermore, students' self-assessments showed that they considered themselves to be good collaborators (a mean score of 7.83 on a scale of 1 [low] to 10 [high]). The most frequent criticism was the lack of time, which is not surprising considering the constraints of the curriculum.

Table 12.1 Students' Evaluation of the Software (n = 53)

How easy was the Geodesign software to use?	
Very easy	21%
Easy	28%
Neither	17%
Difficult	15%
Very difficult	2%
No response	17%

Table 12.2 Content Analysis of the Post-Workshop Survey Reveals Five Themes (n = 53)

What did you like about the Workshop?	
Using the software	24%
The learning experience	23%
Working in groups	20%
The student empowerment	18%
The visioning process	9%
No response	6%

Geodesign Experience Influences Attitudes About Community Issues

The influence of the geodesign learning module on environmental attitudes of the students was not conclusive. Results do not show a statistically significant change in overall scores on the NEP survey pre- and post-workshop. However, the post-workshop NEP survey reveals that most students changed their minds about three of the NEP statements (see Table 12.3). Only one third did not change their initial views about these statements. NEP statement four describes an optimistic view of humans' ability to maintain a livable planet. One third of students increased their agreement with this statement while another third disagreed more. Interestingly, statement 11, which describes a very different view—that the planet has limited resources—shows the same split. Possibly, the majority of students may have become more adamant about their ideas after the geodesign experience. However, for a third, the planning experience was not sufficient to affect their environmental attitudes. Potentially, this group could be influenced with additional interaction with planning professionals and more exposure to the real-life planning process. These results deserve more in-depth study because they may illuminate how students are processing the dilemmas of planning decisions.

Furthermore, the students were asked to rate the importance of 11 issues in Cache Valley before and after the geodesign experience (see Table 12.4). Results show that the experience had a statistically significant effect on how the students rated the different issues ($p = 2.1e-9$, $chi^2 = 81.5$). Clean air and water, as well as renewable energy, remained consistently important

Table 12.3 New Ecological Paradigm Survey Statements That Show a Change in Response (n = 53)

NEP Statement	Disagree more	Unchanged	Agree more
4. Human ingenuity will ensure that we do not make the earth livable.	31%	36%	33%
6. The earth has plenty of natural resources if we just learn how to develop them.	36%	38%	26%
11. The earth is like a spaceship with very limited room and resources.	32%	33%	31%

Table 12.4 Students Rated the Importance of Planning and Development Issues in Cache Valley

Issues Ranked Pre-Workshop	Issues Ranked Post-Workshop
Clean air quality	Protect biodiversity and habitats *
Protect biodiversity and habitats	Enough clean water*
Enough clean water	Clean air quality
Safe living environment	Develop renewable energy*
Develop renewable energy	Preserve agricultural land*
Create new businesses	Safe living environment
Preserve agricultural land	Build new homes*
Build new homes	Develop recreation*
Preserve rural character	Create new businesses
Develop recreation	Preserve rural character
Improve public transportation	Improve public transportation

* Indicates increase in ranking post-workshop.

to them. However, after the workshop, the students considered building new homes to be slightly more important, which may reflect the challenge of the problem statement. Furthermore, the importance of environmental protection and water-related issues increased after the workshop. Overall, the responses were more equally divided among the issues in the post-workshop survey, indicating that the students developed a more comprehensive and insightful view of the systems and related planning issues.

Students Recognize the Importance of Planning

The survey results indicate that the geodesign learning module helped students understand the future impacts of planning decisions on their community. After the workshop, approximately 66% of the students better understood how they wanted Cache Valley to develop, while 24% remained unsure. Their comments revealed an understanding of the impact of planning as well as recognition of their potential role in decisions about the future of their community. For example, they commented that they learned, "What we do will affect the future," or "We can change the future if we plan it right." The students also recognized the complexity and consequences of planning: "What to do with land [is] complicated, takes a lot of discussing and is confusing," as well as the difficulty of building a consensus in planning: "Different people care about different things," and "The conflict [exists] between sharing the environment and new development."

The Geodesign Learning Experience: A Reflection

The survey results confirm that geodesign can be successfully employed as a learning module in a school setting to develop knowledge-based solutions to planning questions that concern the future of the local community. The students' visions for Cache Valley were not abstract; rather, they were concrete proposals that incorporated their local knowledge, attitudes, and experience. With the Geodesignhub software, the students were quickly able to draw and locate specific projects, share their ideas with others, receive feedback, and rework their ideas with the software, which reflects the typical iterative process of the design profession.

In "system" teams, the high-school students acquired knowledge about the study area and were able to develop informed proposals to improve their system under the guidance of a graduate student. Thereby, the students not only exercised an analytical approach to problem solving but also were able to visualize their ideas about the future. In addition, the graduate students had the opportunity to practice communicating their professional knowledge to a lay audience.

In the second session, the role-play in stakeholder groups required the students to assume a perspective different from their own. Although role-playing was not always easy, such an exercise promotes empathy and an understanding of other points of view, which are essential for communication and planning. For example, one student commented that "different people care about different things." Moreover, the students developed a common proposal for the future of their community that fulfilled the objectives of their stakeholder group. This task required the students to collaborate and negotiate a consensus within the group, which are also essential skills in planning. After the negotiation, a student identified "the conflict between sharing the environment and new development" as the most important thing he learned.

The NEP survey did not show a significant impact of the geodesign learning module on the students' environmental attitudes after a single intervention. However, the post-workshop survey revealed that the experience influenced their attitudes about the importance of different systems and their ideas about the future development of Cache Valley. Their survey responses about local issues reflected a growing awareness that planning involves many options and potentially conflicting objectives. Discussions within the small groups also revealed that the students did not seek a single right answer; rather, they weighed tradeoffs between competing interests and systems. For example, when students realized that doubling the population meant locating double the housing, they recognized the conflicts that would arise with the natural systems in the valley. The survey comments showed that the students had gained insight into the conflicts and consequences of planning decisions and the challenges that planners face. For example, students commented that they learned "how policies and projects interact with each other." Furthermore, the students' comments indicate that the geodesign learning experience also helped them to understand the potential of the planning profession. They liked that "as the future generation of this area, we have the option and the power to decide on our future home." Furthermore, they commented: "We enjoyed how seriously we were treated and that our opinion mattered."

The experience gave students a sense of empowerment, that is, their opinion matters, and enlightened them about the ability of planners to form the future and to make a difference. In fact, at the end of the workshop, several students commented that they had never heard of the planning profession, but they could now imagine becoming planners.

Practically, it was possible to execute the geodesign workshop in three sessions; however, the students considered the time to be too short. Alternative formats, such as unsupervised homework, could be incorporated into the learning module, as Geodesignhub supports distributed access and online collaboration. The developer of the software, used primarily as a communications platform for project negotiations, encourages innovative use in the educational setting. Furthermore, the significant supervision and input of graduate students as group leaders was central to the learning experience and success of the workshop. The workshop provided graduate students with the opportunity to mentor and teach their professional knowledge to a lay audience. In the future, this role could be filled by local planners and representatives of local organizations.

The Geodesign Experience in Planning Education

We found that high-school students embraced the technology and the Geodesignhub software. The active, hands-on interaction with the software kept the students engaged and promoted group discussion. The software required them to be specific about recommendations and enabled them to document and share their proposals. The ability to view and interact with the specific proposals supported debate and consensus-building about how to plan Cache Valley.

In the context of planning education, the geodesign learning experience offered students the opportunity to practice planning skills, such as giving ideas concrete form, considering different viewpoints, building consensus, and decision-making. The learning module provided a learning-by-doing experience that not only engaged students with real local issues but also illustrated how the planning profession finds solutions. The exercise helped the students think critically about planning decisions (Kwartler & Longo, 2008) and understand the relevance of the planning profession. The case study demonstrates that the geodesign learning module offers an opportunity to invest in the planning education of local students. The students were able to contribute their ideas about their own community, and they owned the final proposal. Hopefully, this sense of empowerment will ignite interest in and understanding of the planning profession in their future.

Acknowledgments

The authors are especially thankful to the InTech Collegiate Academy high-school students, their professor John Hernandez, Dr. Hrishikesh Ballal, and Utah State University graduate students Emmet Pruss, Lyndi Perry, Connor White, Scott McComb, and Thomas Terry.

References

American Planning Association. (2020). *In your community: APA ambassadors.* www.planning.org/ambassadors/

Ballal, H. (2014). *Geodesign Hub.* www. Geodesignhub.com

Bruening, A., Fayles, K., Oostema, C., & Thompson, A. (2014). *A guide to regional visioning: Mapping the course for successful community engaged scenario planning.* Envision Utah.

Christensen, L. B., Hall, W. J., Maughan, R. H., & Cooper, L. (2020). *Wellsville, gateway to cache valley: History.* www.wellsvillecity.com/history/

Derr, V. (2015). Integrating community engagement and children's voices into design and planning education. *CoDesign, 11*(2), 119–133. https://doi.org/10.1080/15710882.2015.1054842

Dunlap, R. E., Liere, K. D. V., Mertig, A. G., & Jones, R. E. (2000). Measuring endorsement of the new ecological paradigm: A revised nep scale. *Journal of Social Issues, 56*(3), 425–442. https://doi.org/10.1111/0022-4537.00176

Envision Utah. (2015). *Your Utah, your future survey results.* www.envisionutah.org/projects/your-utah-your-future/item/346-results

Foster, K. (2016). Geodesign parsed: Placing it within the rubric of recognized design theories. *Geodesign—Changing the World, Changing Design, 156*, 92–100. https://doi.org/10.1016/j.landurbplan.2016.06.017

Gaber, J. (2007). Simulating planning: SimCity as a pedagogical tool. *Journal of Planning Education and Research* (27), 113–121. https://doi.org/10.1177%2F0739456X07305791

Kwartler, M., & Longo, G. (2008). *Visioning and visualization: People, pixels, and plans.* Lincoln Institute of Land Policy.

Minnery, J., & Searle, G. (2014). Toying with the City? Using the computer game SimCity™4 in planning education. *Planning Practice & Research, 29*(1), 41–55. https://doi.org/10.1080/02697459.2013.829335

Rivero, R., Smith, A., Ballal, H., & Steinitz, C. (2015). *Promoting collaborative geodesign in a multidisciplinary and multiscale environment: Coastal Georgia 2050, USA.* Paper presented at the Digital Landscape Architecture, Anhalt University of Applied Sciences.

Steinitz, C. (2012). *A framework for geodesign: Changing geography by design.* Esri Press.

US Census Bureau. (2015). *FactFinder ACS demographic and housing estimates.* http://factfinder.census.gov/faces/tableservices/jsf/pages/productview.xhtml?src=CF.

13
PLANNING WITH CHILDREN
Implications for the Planning Profession and Active Citizens

K. Meghan Wieters

A key component of planning is community engagement. Planners seek new and better ways to inform the community about trends, problem-solve issues, and obtain meaningful input from all members of the community, but we do not systematically involve children in these planning efforts.

In the 1990s, research began to explore how to include children in civic engagement and legitimize the content received from them (Breitbart, 1995; Hart, 1979, 1992, 2013; Ärlemalm-Hagsér & Davis, 2014). Processes found to be effective included experiential and observational activities as compared to standard methods such as surveys (Breitbart, 1995). When researchers observe children and how they use elements within the built environment, the data is direct and can inform design and policy options. Additionally, direct questions to children about their experiences are preferable to secondary sources such as a parents' perceptions of their children's needs or ideas (Balseviciene et al., 2014; Bridgman, 2004). Models that surveyed parents about their children's perceptions were less effective and nullified the autonomy and individual contributions the children could provide more directly (Balseviciene et al., 2014). The use of drawing, cognitive mapping, and active play can provide insight useful to policy and planning as it relates to children (Breitbart, 1995; Freire, 2000; Scardamalia & Bereiter, 1991).

Roger Hart, a professor of environmental psychology with a focus on children's environments, was instrumental in taking Sherry Arnstein's ladder of citizen participation and incorporating comparable levels of engagement by children (Arnstein, 1969; Hart, 1992). The approach outlined the difference between relegating children to a photo op as opposed to being actual participants in a process (Hart, 1992). This level of integration of children into planning processes is atypical in planning, but giving agency to children in decision-making is part of the early childhood development discipline (Mayne et al., 2018; Ärlemalm-Hagsér & Davis, 2014; Scardamalia & Bereiter, 1991; Larson & Angus, 2011). Within this framework, where children can participate with tools and activities designed with them in mind, the NeighborWalk project emerged.

Engaging Children in Their Built Environments

Engaging children in planning has various impacts on projects, communities, and children themselves. Planning for communities is, inherently, planning for the future. When children are included as part of the process, they can illuminate aspects about a project that resonate with them. This is also a mechanism to build active citizens who will take this role of participation into adulthood.

To explore how children can and want to be involved in their communities, this chapter explores the NeighborWalk project in Oklahoma City from 2013–2015. The various partners on the project had many different goals and objectives, both stated and unstated. From the academic perspective, the goals included increasing exposure to and involvement by children in urban planning, understanding what elements of concern and benefit children perceive within the built environment, and increasing awareness of the planning profession for youth, with an emphasis on children of color. From the perspective of the City of Oklahoma City (OKC), as discussed in their 2014 report on the project, they indicated the project was an opportunity for "an interactive walkability and local government education program designed for elementary students and teachers to encourage neighborhood involvement, participation in public processes, and making healthy choices, like biking and walking" (Oklahoma City Office of Sustainability, 2014, p. 4). Neighborhood Alliance, a non-profit that works with city staff on community issues, had multilevel goals, with a main focus for this project to facilitate communicating neighborhood infrastructure needs and lack of funding to the city council.

Perspectives of children can be eye-opening and lack the adult filter that often clouds discussions and impedes the ability to address core issues. Examples of children's insight have been part of my planning practice work for more than 20 years. In the late 1990s, a commercial corridor-planning project was being developed in Austin, Texas. As part of that process, regular meetings and workshops were held and also included invitations to the students from Lively Middle School (formerly named Fulmore Middle School) to participate. The junior high school was located with frontage on the corridor, and thus their input on perceptions and needs for the corridor was particularly relevant. The students who attended were able to succinctly and directly state their concerns about design elements of the streetscape that made them feel safe or unsafe. Additionally, with clarity and lack of guile, these same students commented on their feelings of insecurity and disapproval about having to walk by an adult-oriented movie theater with patrons walking in and out as they walked to and from school.[1] Many of the adults had politely danced around the issue of such businesses on the corridor because of the tangled legal issues involved with having them removed.

Another example of children's participation and insight in planning projects is found within the neighborhood-planning program in Austin. As part of our work, typical activities included workshops and meetings with scenarios for improvements and land-use mapping activities. Additional parallel materials were often prepared to keep children of participants engaged while their parents worked through concepts during the meeting. This effort was primarily to overcome the barrier of child care by parents. However, the children were often able to mark on the maps provided to them places where they enjoyed going, places where they felt unsafe (e.g., loud dogs, trash, broken glass, scary sounds), and what they wished was in their neighborhoods. This provided insight into things adults also experienced and informed action items for the plan. The missed opportunity was that it was conceptualized more as child care, rather than a regular source of input to the plans.

With the NeighborWalk program, the focus on tools, modules, and activities included maintaining a spirit of discovery and revealing how the students' voices could be heard now and in the future. It was important to give the students the room to provide insights, free from adults' hasty reframing of the intent of the children's ideas. The nature of the program was centered around how the students viewed and interacted with the built environment. Care was taken in the teaching modules to show the students that, as users of the built environment, they were inherently experts on how those spaces did or did not work for them.

The goal to empower, rather than just instruct, was essential for this program to give possibilities to the children involved. The NeighborWalk program drew on concepts from the literature indicating that children are capable participants in planning projects. It furthered goals held by planners concerned about promoting the discipline to under-represented groups through exposure to the profession at a young age in these targeted schools. The key was to increase the inner feelings of

Inclusion and Promotion in Underserved Areas

Generally, when asking a room full of high-school or undergraduate students if they've heard of urban planning, the number of raised hands is few. Within planning schools across the United States there is a growing understanding that the profession lacks the diversity of professionals necessary to represent the communities we serve (Sweet & Etienne, 2011; Sweet, 2018; Greenlee et al., 2018; Thomas, 1996; Lee et al., 2020). However, there are paths to increase diversity of cultures, races, gender identities, and sexual orientations in the profession. One of the foci of the NeighborWalk program included increasing student exposure to planning in schools that have higher percentages of students of color. In Table 13.1, the schools included in this program, as compared to state averages, have higher percentages of Hispanic and Black students. Involving children in these schools was intended to plant the seed that professions within the built environment, specifically planning and landscape architecture, are jobs that could use their interests and skills.

Further, based on the literature, students in lower-income populations are more likely to lack exposure to career choices beyond the career paths by their parents or teachers (Wodtke et al., 2011; Sharif et al., 2019; Tang et al., 2008). Limited exposure to career paths may be due to a wide variety of causes. In Table 13.2, eligibility for lunch-program assistance gives some indication of economic status for the families of the children attending these schools. Lower-income families tend to have less discretionary income and time to assist their children in exploring possible opportunities for their future. Exposure to the planning profession and increasing the scope of career options to these students was combined with encouraging potential first-generation college graduates.

Additionally, lower-income families often live within areas where compounding impacts of infrastructure neglect, lack of familiarity with political processes, and lack of power within the city setting may decrease quality of life. The selection of these schools and neighborhoods was also chosen with a secondary goal of elevating these infrastructural gaps within OKC neighborhoods. It was anticipated that the city manager and city council would be more supportive of requests for improvements from children who provided the observations and voiced the needs of the community.

Table 13.1 Study Schools Race/Ethnicity Profile

School	Amer. Indian	Asian	Hispanic	Black	White	Two or More Races
State Average (OK)	14%	2%	17%	9%	49%	9%
Eugene Fields	2%	2%	67%	13%	11%	5%
F.D. Moon Academy	2%	n/a	7%	77%	3%	11%
Marcus Garvey Leadership Charter (closed 2014)	2%	1%	1%	96%	n/a	n/a
Hayes	3%	8%	57%	9%	13%	10%
Edgemere	5%	5%	19%	30%	29%	12%
Edwards	1%	n/a	61%	n/a	36%	2%
Prairie Queen	4%	n/a	71%	12%	9%	4%

Seven column table with school, American Indian, Asian, Hispanic, Black, White, and Two or More Races as headers. Schools listed from NeighborWalk program with relative percentages as compared to the Oklahoma State Average Race/Ethnicity percentages.

Source: Public School Review. Data is for 2018, except for Marcus Garvey Leadership Charter School, which is for 2013. www.publicschoolreview.com/

Table 13.2 Eligibility for School Lunch Programs

School	Eligible for Free Lunch	Eligible for Reduced Lunch
State Average (OK)	55%	10%
Eugene Fields	100%	5%
F.D. Moon Academy	100%	2%
Marcus Garvey Leadership Charter	84%	7%
Hayes	100%	6%
Edgemere	100%	9%
Edwards	38%	11%
Prairie Queen	100%	6%

Three column table with Schools, Eligible for Free Lunch, and Eligible for Reduced Lunch as headers. Schools listed from NeighborWalk program with relative percentages as compared to the Oklahoma State Average for these School Lunch programs.

Source: Public School Review. Data is for 2018, except for Marcus Garvey Leadership Charter School, which is for 2013. www.publicschoolreview.com/

Process to Develop Curriculum and Coordination

Neighborhood Alliance of Central Oklahoma is a non-profit organization that works to address affordable housing and access to businesses, health services, and green spaces within the community. With the Neighborhood Alliance's continued mission to address community needs, a subcommittee was selected to attend the 2012 NeighborWorks America Community Leadership Institute in Orlando, Florida, for training to empower and work with neighborhoods (Oklahoma City Office of Sustainability, 2014). Through this training, along with local interest by other community members, city staff, and business organizations, this alliance developed a plan for working in OKC neighborhoods. One of the action items included applying for a grant to create a program with schools to improve the visibility of needs in disadvantaged communities with elected officials (Oklahoma City Office of Sustainability, 2014). Staff from the Neighborhood Alliance contacted the University of Oklahoma (OU) and the OKC to begin to outline this project connecting built-environment needs with children as the voices for the community. University of Oklahoma faculty and graduate students met with the Neighborhood Alliance and the committee members to craft how a graduate class could develop teaching modules on the built environment, professional paths for the students, and ways for the youth to communicate with local officials about identified needs within the neighborhood.

From the academic side, the graduate students created a work plan to lay out tasks needed to complete the materials for the scheduled three-day interactive sessions planned for May 2013. Each session was scheduled for about half of the school day in a fifth-grade classroom with 25–30 students. Each session included a teaching component, interactive discussion, and activity. The graduate students outlined essential teaching concepts for the children highlighting planning, landscape architecture, and basic city functions. The graduate class developed and refined the materials, and these materials were reviewed and edited by staff at the OKC and the Neighborhood Alliance. The final session in the program was focused on performing a built-environment audit of the surrounding area to each school. The activity was for four to five students with an adult volunteer to perform audits for segments or paths that led to the school. A segment or path was approximately one block or 300 feet. All adult volunteers completed a required school background check in order to be a guide with the children. This background check typically takes between one to two weeks to process and ensures basic safety of adults interacting with children. Each student would be a lead investigator and assessor for a segment. The built-environment audit tool assessed sidewalk conditions, traffic, shade, comfort levels, and observed elements along the segment.[2] When the audit forms were completed, the teams returned to the classroom to code their responses with icon stickers on the map to provide a visual representation of positive and negative elements in the neighborhood. The goal was to use this map to present to city staff and city council the reflected needs within the community.

In 2013, the first year of the program, the curriculum and activities were pilot tested at three schools: Eugene Field, F.D. Moon Middle School, and Marcus Garvey Leadership Academy. For the second year of the program, additional review of the materials and activities was done collaboratively with the Neighborhood Alliance, OKC, and OU faculty and students meeting twice monthly from January to May 2014 (Oklahoma City Office of Sustainability, 2014). Additional partners were included in the 2014 program, including connections with the OU Health Sciences Center College of Public Health. The culmination of the program was a field trip to city hall by two of the elementary schools, with the third writing letters to their council representative (Oklahoma City Office of Sustainability, 2014). In 2015, new schools were selected for the final year of the program: Edgemere, Edwards, and Prairie Queen Elementary.

Teaching and Learning by Doing

The curriculum focused on how the built environment was connected to improved health, feelings of safety, and a strong sense of community. Layered within this was exposure to the different professions that help plan, design, build, and maintain these features in the community. The curriculum for day one evolved over the three years. Initially the first day included content on city functions. This involved defining city infrastructure and discussing major elements of the city, including housing, transportation, environment, jobs, and schools. Students were involved in discussing how these functions were part of their lives. The discussion moved to different professions that work within cities and included guest speakers from the city from planning, engineering, and police departments. The activity for this day was a visual preference survey that encouraged participation by the students to select images that reflected comfortable spaces, safe spaces, and preferred spaces. For subsequent years, some of the initial discussion on city functions and professions was refined and edited for time to maintain engagement with the children.

For day two, the focus was on engaging the students with how they see the city and how they might imagine improving it. The content included land-use, urban design, planning, and landscape architecture disciplines. The activity for the students was intended to actively inspire the students to improve a streetscape. A streetscape with building outlines was plotted out at a large poster size (36" × 48"). Students were given markers, glue, and scissors to create elements to glue onto the streetscape to create their vision of a fun, active space. For the second and third year of the program, the activities and content from the first two days were merged into the first day of a two-day event. The shift to a two-day format was due in part to school needs, such as time required for certain subjects and scheduling. Also, upon review of the first year of the program, combining the more educational materials of day one on city functions with the more active creation of a streetscape was deemed a better approach.

For day three, the focus was on the built-environment audit. The goal was to perform the audit on the street segments near and connecting to the elementary school. Prior to going outside, an overview about maps, a safety briefing, and passing out clipboards and safety vests began the day. Students were broken into small groups of four to five by the teacher, who was aware of good mixes of students. At least one adult led each group, and each student had their own segment to take the lead on recording observations and audit information.

The audit form included recording perceived weather conditions, date, sidewalk conditions, car traffic, shade, comfort level, and other observations such as broken glass, litter, or scary people. For sidewalk conditions, photos of No Sidewalk, Poor Sidewalk, Fair Sidewalk, and Good Sidewalk were provided for their comparison with the segment they were assessing. Traffic was evaluated based on the child's perception of how many cars had passed while at that segment. Shade assessment also used photos of No Shade, Some Shade, A Lot of Shade, or No Shade Due to Weather/Season. Comfort level was determined by the child—who could also ask their group for input—as to whether or not they would feel comfortable walking on that segment alone and explaining why. The other observations allowed the child to circle elements they observed along the segment, but they could also add items. Items included on the form included speeding cars, slow moving cars, scary houses, scary people, litter, broken glass, heavy traffic, loud cars, loud music, cars blocking the sidewalk, loose dogs, and graffiti.

When the small groups finished their assessment of each segment, they returned to the classroom to record the results on a large map of the area. For elements in the audit form, corresponding stickers were used (Figure 13.1). The stickers were color coded to express if the element was good (green), fair (yellow), or red (poor) for each element. This allowed a quick visualization of areas for improvement and positive areas in the community.

This fieldwork activity took careful planning to assess reasonable segments to review, appropriate distances that each group could travel to and back to the school, and timing for recording observations on a shared map. The maps were shared with city staff and the city manager. In 2014, we were able to schedule the field trip to city hall where two of the elementary schools were able to present their findings to the city manager. This field trip was only able to be accomplished one of the three years of the program. For the other years, students sent letters to the city council and city manager with their suggestions for improvements to the neighborhood based on the class modules and mapping work completed in the NeighborWalk program.

Reflection on Strategy and Implementation

The goals for the program were to engage children with professions often not included in standard curricula, target children in historically disadvantaged communities in order to give everyday tools of

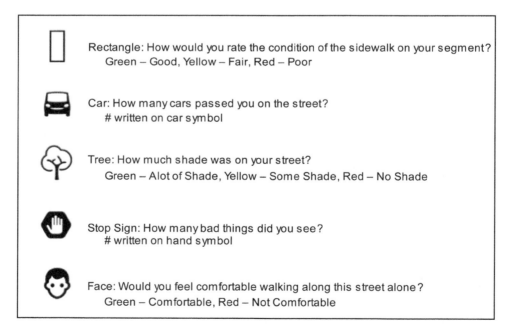

Figure 13.1 Symbols Used for Mapping Field Audits

empowerment in governance, and promote safe, active built environments. While this program was limited to three years, some anecdotal evidence shows glimmers of the potential this work can have:

- Kids reporting burned-out lights and potholes to the city's Action Line.[3]
- Active engagement in modules by kids whose teacher indicated they had difficulty paying attention to standard class activities.
- Kids expressing interest and demonstrating that they were unaware of potential jobs where they could draw, map conditions, address infrastructure needs, or discuss action steps with the community.
- Excitement at being listened to by adults.

This NeighborWalk program was not set up to measure long-term outcomes or track individual student paths or actions. The goals and structure of the program were more modest than a rigorous research program; however, the consistent engagement and excitement level of students with the material over the three years by new cohorts was promising. This program did not continue after 2015 due to lack of continued funding and changes in departmental staff at the city to help champion this atypical program. As with many service-learning programs, identifying long-term funding and sustained leadership is critical to become an established program. Additionally, gaining more buy-in from political leadership to support a longer-term effort for such a program is also important.

Some of the critical elements to engaging children within a planning program or project include the same things needed with adults. First, we analyze the best ways for a group of participants to digest the information and provide meaningful feedback. The creativity we need to engage adults is simply reframed for younger minds. Second, we value the input we receive and connect it to action with the project or process. This includes highlighting ideas raised by children and showing them how to share that with decision makers with letters, maps, or their voices. Third, we use graphics, photos, and language that is easily understood and connect it with hands-on experience, learning, and expression of ideas.

There are logistical elements that differ when planning for children versus adults. They can include the following:

- Increasing the amount of time to allow for concepts to be fully understood.
- Providing additional adult volunteers to act as guides for small-group activities or fieldwork.
- Implementing background checks and training for all adults working with the children.
- Providing safety precautions and training for the children when working in the field (e.g., safety vests for visibility).
- Allotting time for activity and content during the school day.
- Getting permission from parents via the school for off-campus activities.
- Gathering photo releases from parents for any photos taken of activities or use of other protocols to obscure children's faces for privacy.

The value children can provide to planning projects is underestimated and undervalued. For the planning profession, increasingly exposing children and teenagers to the skills and varied work planners do is essential to broadening the profession and addressing increased diversity and representation in the discipline.

Recommended Programs or Activities to Engage Children With Planning and Built-Environment Professions

Capturing the enthusiasm of an initial or temporary funding source to perform a program like this is important, but taking time to brainstorm ways to track success could be advantageous to gaining sustained funding. This program lacked the annual budget and assigned staffing needed to sustain it. At the conclusion of the grant funding and the departure of the key staff person, continuing the program was not feasible. With changes in political environment, budget cuts, and attrition of staff, programs like these can be seen as pet projects and easily set aside. Creating a service-learning contract between all related groups can identify roles and responsibilities as well as longer-term engagement options to rotate champions for the program.

A lesson learned from this program was that it missed out on connecting with parents in the community with a more formalized connection to the parents of the children in the classes. Parents were informed of the program and the field trip in the neighborhood. They were asked if they wished to serve as volunteers during the walking audits, and a few participated at one of the schools. However, having an alternative date in the evening or weekend to encourage the parents to do a similar audit activity and overview of how to engage in governmental and community issues would have made for a more complete program.

Additionally, from the urban planning academia perspective, increasing the role of academic planning departments in longer-term service-learning commitments to targeted areas of the community could assist with sustaining programs like those discussed here. Shorter programs or activities within the disadvantaged communities can also yield benefits in terms of immediate attention to address various planning issues, lead to longer-term commitments from three to five years, and avoid problems of researchers coming in to study disadvantaged areas lacking follow-up or implementation. This would allow university departments to carry some of the load for championing improvements and education within the community. It would also further the goal of exposing more youth, particularly in communities of color, to professions like urban planning with the hope of encouraging more diversity in the profession.

Acknowledgments

There are many people who were involved as volunteers over the three-year project. Specifically, Madeleine Wiens (OKC), John Tankard (OKC), T.O. Bowman (OKC), and Georgie Rasco (Neighborhood Alliance) were instrumental to this joint project. I am immensely grateful they approached me and my students to work on this project.

Notes

1 The adult-oriented theater had been open at that location prior to the school's development and was a grandfathered use. Shortly after the completion of the plan for this area, a community member purchased it with the intention to close it and ultimately reopen it as a business that fit in with the context of the corridor.
2 The built-environment audit tool was developed within the University of Oklahoma graduate course. It was based on several audit forms viewed on the Robert Wood Johnson Active Living website. The developed tool used similar questions or question types from established tools but reframed them for fifth graders with icons and photos to assist in identifying conditions in the built environment. The tool was a paper audit form where one segment of the sidewalk in the neighborhood was delineated for the fifth graders to record observations. Robert Wood Johnson Active Living tools can be found at: https://activelivingresearch.org/toolsandresources/all
3 Action Line is an information line and website for the Action Center that the City of Oklahoma City has used to allow citizens to log maintenance issues such as potholes, light fixture outages, or damaged sidewalks.

References

Ärlemalm-Hagsér, E., & Davis, J. (2014). Examining the rhetoric: A comparison of how sustainability and young children's participation and agency are framed in Australian and Swedish early childhood education curricula. *Contemporary Issues in Early Childhood*, *15*(3), 231–244. https://doi.org/10.2304/ciec.2014.15.3.231

Arnstein, S. R. (1969). A ladder of citizen participation. *Journal of the American Institute of Planners*, *35*(4), 216–224. https://doi.org/10.1080/01944366908977225

Balseviciene, B., Sinkariova, L., & Andrusaityte, S. (2014). Do green spaces matter? The associations between parenting stress, child mental health problems and green spaces. *Procedia—Social and Behavioral Sciences*, *140*, 511–516. https://doi.org/10.1016/j.sbspro.2014.04.462

Breitbart, M. M. (1995). Banners for the street: Reclaiming space and designing change with urban youth. *Journal of Planning Education and Research*, *15*(1), 35–49. https://doi.org/10.1177/0739456X9501500103

Bridgman, R. (2004). Criteria for best practices in building child-friendly cities: Involving young people in urban planning and design. *Canadian Journal of Urban Research*, *13*(2), 337–346. www.jstor.org/stable/44321120

Freire, P. (2000). *Pedagogy of the oppressed*. Continuum Publishing Company.

Greenlee, A. J., Jackson, A., Garcia-Zambrana, I., Lee, C. A., & Chrisinger, B. (2018). Where are we going? Where have we been? The climate for diversity within urban planning educational programs. *Journal of Planning Education and Research*. https://doi.org/10.1177/0739456X18815740

Hart, R. A. (1979). *Children's experience of place* (pp. xxv, 518). Irvington.

Hart, R. A. (1992). Children's participation: From tokenism to citizenship. In *Papers* (inness92/6; Papers). Innocenti Essay. https://ideas.repec.org/p/ucf/inness/inness92-6.html

Hart, R. A. (2013). *Children's participation: The theory and practice of involving young citizens in community development and environmental care*. Routledge.

Larson, R. W., & Angus, R. M. (2011). Adolescents' development of skills for agency in youth programs: Learning to think strategically. *Child Development*, *82*(1), 277–294. https://doi.org/10.1111/j.1467-8624.2010.01555.x

Lee, C. A., Chrisinger, B., Greenlee, A. J., Garcia Zambrana, I., & Jackson, A. (2020). Beyond recruitment: Comparing experiences of climate and diversity between international students and domestic students of color in U.S. Urban planning programs. *Journal of Planning Education and Research*. https://doi.org/10.1177/0739456X20902241

Mayne, F., Howitt, C., & Rennie, L. (2018). Rights, power and agency in early childhood research design: Developing a rights-based research ethics and participation planning framework. *Australasian Journal of Early Childhood*, *43*(3), 4–14. https://doi.org/10.23965/AJEC.43.3.01

Oklahoma City Office of Sustainability. (2014). *NeighborWalk: 2014 Youth walkability program report*. Oklahoma City Office of Sustainability

Scardamalia, M., & Bereiter, C. (1991). Higher levels of agency for children in knowledge building: A challenge for the design of new knowledge media. *The Journal of the Learning Sciences*, *1*(1), 37–68. https://doi.org/10.1207/s15327809jls0101_3

Sharif, N., Ahmad, N., & Sarwar, S. (2019). *Factors influencing career choices* (SSRN Scholarly Paper ID 3431911). Social Science Research Network. https://papers.ssrn.com/abstract=3431911

Sweet, E. L. (2018). Cultural humility: An open door for planners to locate themselves and decolonize planning theory, education, and practice. *Public Affairs*, *7*(2). www.ejournalofpublicaffairs.org/cultural-humility/

Sweet, E. L., & Etienne, H. F. (2011). Commentary: Diversity in urban planning education and practice. *Journal of Planning Education and Research*, *31*(3), 332–339. https://doi.org/10.1177/0739456X11414715

Tang, M., Pan, W., & Newmeyer, M. D. (2008). Factors influencing high school students' career aspirations. *Professional School Counseling*, *11*(5), 2156759X0801100502. https://doi.org/10.1177/2156759X0801100502

Thomas, J. M. (1996). Educating planners: Unified diversity for social action. *Journal of Planning Education and Research*, *15*(3), 171–182. https://doi.org/10.1177/0739456X9601500302

Wodtke, G. T., Harding, D. J., & Elwert, F. (2011). Neighborhood effects in temporal perspective: The impact of long-term exposure to concentrated disadvantage on high school graduation. *American Sociological Review*, *76*(5), 713–736. https://doi.org/10.1177/0003122411420816

14
PROMOTING URBAN PLANNING AWARENESS FOR CHILDREN

An Overview of Multifaceted International Case Studies and Community Outreach Initiatives

Aya Elkhouly and Doha Eissa

The career aspirations of children are set at a young age and are heavily influenced by their socio-economic backgrounds, genders (Chambers, 2019), and role models (MacCallum et al., 2002; Shah et al., 2010). Exposure to training and work experience provides a deeper understanding of different disciplines and helps them make better-informed university and career choices (Gutman et al., 2008). The fact that 68% of the world population will live in cities by 2050 highlights the implications of urban planners' work on citizens' lives and health (Barton & Tsourou, 2013).

Urban planning is the discipline of shaping the physical public realm, manifested in urban form and shape, as well as infrastructure, roads, buildings, and the spaces in between (Tranter & Sharpe, 2007). Nevertheless, urban planning as a discipline is rarely made attractive to children and youth as they consider their career preferences. One reason may be the limited initiatives taken to raise awareness of urban planning and its career options. This reinforces parents' misperceptions and students' unfamiliarity with the profession (Palazzo et al., 2021).

In this chapter, we present case studies of approaches to resolve this gap and raise children's awareness of urban planning. The case studies follow two approaches. First, an in-class education approach (ICE) that teaches general urban planning concepts with abstract drawings and physical models; and second, a contextualised professional co-learning approach (PCL) that provides children with first-hand local urban planning experience.

Both approaches combine theoretical teaching and practical work. Theoretical education is generally pursued through classes, and discussions, targeting the understanding of basic knowledge related to a given field. Practical education is usually deeper and more specific to a certain topic. It gives students hands-on work experience (Riyad et al., 2020), promotes cooperation and integration between team members, and enhances communication and problem-solving skills (Nováková & Giertlová, 2016).

The ICE approach described here took the form of a series of workshops moderated by a planning expert and delivered to groups of six-to-eight children between the ages 10–15. The workshops were held in civic-activity centres, university classrooms, and online during the COVID-19 lockdown. Workshops were structured around a theoretical discussion on a given urban planning topic followed by the application of an individual or group physical model. The PCL initiative was delivered in situ through engaging children in a real urban planning project to transform the

Mingdong area of Ningbo, China, into a child-friendly neighbourhood (International Society of City and Regional Planners, 2019).

In all cases, initiatives widened participants' understanding of urban planning. By the end of the workshops, some participants expressed their interest in more-advanced workshops on urban planning and design. Feedback from some mothers also included children working on their own physical models from recycled materials at home or asking their parents for city-building toys.

ICE Approach

DIY City Workshop, Egypt and UAE

The DIY City is an experimental workshop that first took place in 2012 to raise awareness of urban planning among middle-school and high-school students. The need for such an initiative emerged when an assistant professor of planning, who later moderated the workshop, observed that first-year students enrolled at the school of architecture and planning at Cairo University have misconceptions about their chosen field of study. The workshop was designed to raise awareness at an earlier stage among children and high-school students curious about the field and considering it as a career option. Each workshop familiarises participants with the steps and processes of urban planning and discusses career aspirations. It was a simple model with limited stakeholders that included the instructor, students, and a host. In our case, hosts included community centres in Dubai (UAE), the Sharjah International Book Fair 2017 (UAE), and winter camps in Cairo (Egypt). The instructor usually provided the required materials for model-making or provided parents with a supply list beforehand.

Workshops were often adapted to fit the available time, but the sequence of activities remained the same. The class started with a theoretical discussion on an urban-related topic. Then, participants experimented with materials and applied learned concepts on a three-dimensional model of their design. Class activities went as follows:

1) A discussion of participants' acquaintance with urban planning, as well as their likes and dislikes about their cities and neighbourhoods. The moderator then defined the scope of urban planning and its role in shaping the built environment with reflections on different cities around the world, particularly the participants' home cities.
2) A discussion of basic topics of urban planning such as infrastructure, road networks, land use, human-made features such as buildings, and open spaces versus natural features such as mountains or rivers. Students applied those concepts by designing a two-dimensional base map for their neighbourhood with natural features, street networks, and assigned land uses. Physical models were individual or group work, depending on the workshop's duration (Figure 14.1).
3) A discussion on constituents of the built environment. Discourse ran about public and private buildings and different building typologies, landmarks, vertical versus horizontal expansion of buildings, open spaces, landscape design of parks, sidewalks and pedestrian walkways, and ecological footprint (Figure 14.1). Students then experimented with various materials to develop their base maps into 3D physical models featuring buildings, street furniture, and landscape elements (Figure 14.2).
4) Finally the DIY City workshops concluded with a general discussion and feedback on the presented designs (Figure 14.1).

These activities were sometimes adapted to fit into a single two-hour session with a group project or expanded over multiple sessions with individual projects that built up over time. This flexibility made it easy to tailor workshop content and projects according to the attendees' level of interest and age. Finally, running workshops with a limited number of participants and hosting them in private

  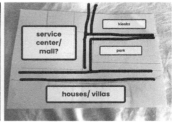

Figure 14.1 Examples of Workshop Outcomes
From right to left: A 2-D base map, neighborhood model (individual-work) and a city model (group-work).

learning centres exempted them from official approval and red tape, which reduced preparation and facilitated implementation.

Online DIY City Workshop

During the COVID-19 lockdown, face-to-face workshops were substituted with virtual workshops hosted on Zoom or Google Meet. Online workshops followed the same outline and sequence of activities as the face-to-face versions. Online workshops brought the advantage of having participants from a variety of cities and cultures, increasing the programme's overall outreach. However, they also brought new challenges. Unlike face-to-face workshops where all attendees lived in the same city and shared the same urban context, online workshops dimmed the notion of a shared local context and required the moderator to be ready with examples relevant to the different home cities of the participants.

On a practical level, model-making was more challenging in online workshops for several reasons. First, craftsmanship is more difficult to teach virtually. To overcome this, a pre-recorded video was played explaining model-making techniques, which was then paused for questions and follow-up with participants. The instructor was also ready with model-making materials to pursue ideas live during the session.

The second challenge was the absence of the shared pool of materials like those offered by the moderator in the face-to-face session, which limited the participants' chances to experiment with new model-making materials. This could be addressed by providing participants with a tool kit or a supply list before the workshop begins.

Third, running online workshops requires more moderators to help follow-up with breakout rooms, which is not always feasible. Otherwise, a smaller number of participants would need to be admitted. Finally, intermittent Internet connections in some cases limited successful content delivery.

In general, both scenarios of the DIY City Workshop had some similarities. It was noticed that attendees both online and face-to-face tended to design cities with similar features to their home cities. This reflects the effect of the surrounding built environment on children's subconscious and the importance of diversifying the urban input to which they are exposed. The generic nature of this approach and the fact that workshops did not focus on real urban problems or given urban settings sacrificed reality in favour of imagination, which suggests that this approach may be more suitable for younger age groups. For instance, one 8-year-old participant designed a turtle city with a water stream for raising and watching turtles. Another participant who was 10 designed a unicorn city where unicorns were the main means of transportation, with supportive activities like a unicorn farm and an open farm market. This directs attention to an educational approach which, besides teaching basic concepts, gives more room for imagination.

Promoting Urban Planning Awareness for Children

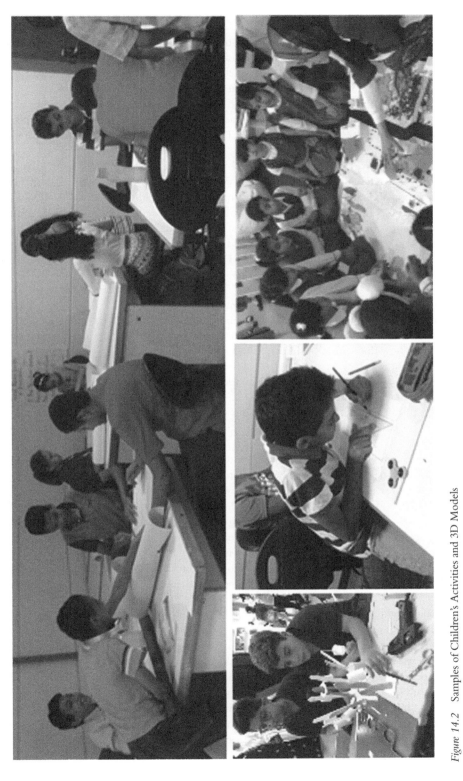

Figure 14.2 Samples of Children's Activities and 3D Models
This figure shows discussion and peer criticism of the children's activities and models for the ICE approach (2017–2020).

Children's University Workshop, Egypt 2017

The Children's University, or KinderUni, is an idea first adopted in 2002 in Tübingen, Germany, to introduce children to different university studies and career options. In 2011 the Academy of Scientific Research and Technology, Egypt (ASRT, 2020), became a part of this international initiative and in 2015, the academy introduced the initiative to the Egyptian community.

In 2017, the University for Modern Sciences and Arts (MSA) offered a programme for children with the intent of visiting and exploring different academic faculties (Elkhouly, 2020). Stakeholders were a blend of entities represented by the ASRT and MSA, along with children and parents of neighbouring communities.

The goals and objectives of the programme were to provide an interactive career-orientation experience to participants and engage parents in the educational and vocational choices of their children. The workshop also aimed to strengthen the bond between children and their neighbourhood universities by encouraging professors to volunteer in community service activities. Children spent two days in different departments with the faculty of engineering, including the school of architecture.[1] The introductory workshop on urbanism and architecture was delivered by four academics to 34 children over four hours (Elkhouly et al., 2021), during which they participated in four main activities consecutively:

1) Working individually to create discrete 3D forms (Figure 14.2).
2) Working in groups of three to five to create an imaginary 3D model of a city using the outcome of the previous activity (Figure 14.2). While participants were presenting their work, feedback was given on how the fields of architecture and urban planning work together to transform 3D forms into real projects.
3) Drawing 2D maps representing participants' journeys from home to school, then drawing a hypothetical image for their dream city.
4) Wrapping up the workshop with a discussion on the importance of urban planning and its impact on people's lives.

The programme was designed to introduce children to the field of architecture and urbanism, among other fields of expertise. Among the factors facilitating its implementation was the sponsorship of MSA. It helped with marketing for the programme, which expanded community outreach and provided needed support during the workshops, including venue, expert staff, and supplies. The short duration of the programme proved adequate during school semesters, unlike extended workshops which need scheduling according to students' school breaks. However, the main disadvantage was also that children were exposed to different majors in a short period leading to a rather superficial understanding of each field. For instance, some misconceptions about urban planning emerged, such as linking their aptness in urban planning and architecture to their drawing and art skills. A frequently asked question was, "What if I am not good at sketching, would I still fit in the career?" Other questions were mainly inquiries about the difficulty of the educational field and prospective salaries.

The workshop was composed of the four activities described previously, some of which reflected students' perception of their urban context or their innate aptitude for urban planning, while others reflected increased planning awareness. Children's drawings of their trips from home to school reflected awareness of their urban environment, while drawings of their dream cities showed their aspirations toward it. It was in the fourth activity when children's interest in the field became most apparent as they started to analyse and explain their projects through a role-playing discussion. Children also became aware that urban planning is key to designing projects like a university campus or an amusement park and that, through this profession, they could improve things they did not like about their built environment.

PCL Approach: Mingdong Community Development Initiative, China 2019

This case study involved the exposure of young people to urban planning careers through a workshop by the Young Planning Professionals (YPP). This workshop was held in the city of Ningbo, China, with the intent to turn the Mingdong district into a child-friendly neighbourhood (ISOCARP, 2019). The workshop incorporated a wide range of stakeholders including the United Nations Children's Fund (UNICEF), China Association of City Planning (CACP), Ningbo Bureau of Nature Resources and Planning (NBNRP), Ningbo Urban Planning and Design Institute (NBPI), International Society of City and Regional Planners (ISOCARP), and Centre for Urban Excellence. Participating stakeholders also included local coordinators, 18 young planning professionals (six of whom were international), volunteer students from university and high schools, parents, and above all, 15 children between the ages of 6 and 12 from the community's primary and middle schools.

The workshop aimed at engaging children as real stakeholders in a real urban-development project to turn Ningbo into a child-friendly city (Figure 14.3). It aimed at advocating children's rights and getting their insights for how to make the community child friendly (United Nations, 2018). As a by-product, children were introduced to urban planning, and professional awareness was fostered.

Mingdong, a neighbourhood of Ningbo, was selected as a pilot study due to its high percentage of children from low- and middle-income families, as well as children of migrant workers (Yinzhou Government, 2019). Mingdong presented features that make it a typical representative neighbourhood of Ningbo, increasing the interest in which kinds of child-friendly planning solutions could be adopted across the city.

The workshop was advanced as a competition in which YPPs would be divided into teams in cooperation with experts, planning institutions, governmental representatives, and neighbouring communities. Activities went as follows:

1) *Site survey and reading urban maps.* Participants marked the route from home to a given destination in their neighbourhood on a map while allocating landmarks on this route. This activity was supported with child-led explorative walks in the neighbourhood.
2) *Analysis of current urban situation.* Using colour codes, participants located spots of urban problems and urban potential on maps.
3) *Synthesis, packaging, prioritisation, and statement.* The children evaluated and discussed with experts the problems highlighted in the previous stage and prioritised them for intervention.
4) *Strategy development.* Participants collaborated with experts in focus groups to propose solutions and intervention strategies.
5) *Presentation of ideas.* Adult professionals helped participants present their intervention proposals, through sketches and videos, first to the workshop community (professionals, community non-governmental organization, and planning institutions), then to the community residents.

With these activities in the workshop, the children were exposed to various urban experiences which raised their awareness of urban planning and their understanding of the role of urban planners in resolving real urban challenges. Most young participants were extremely excited to know more about the profession. However, some challenges were faced, for example, being an international workshop that incorporated multiple stakeholders necessitated abiding by a pre-set, inflexible schedule, unlike the in-class approach. Finally, this workshop was based on a professional participatory call and was funded by the municipality and international organisations with an interest in implementing urban-development strategies for child-friendly cities (Aerts, 2018). As much as this format facilitated the workshop's coordination and implementation, it's not a reliable way of educating children about the profession because such calls are not often repeated. For a more-frequent

Aya Elkhouly and Doha Eissa

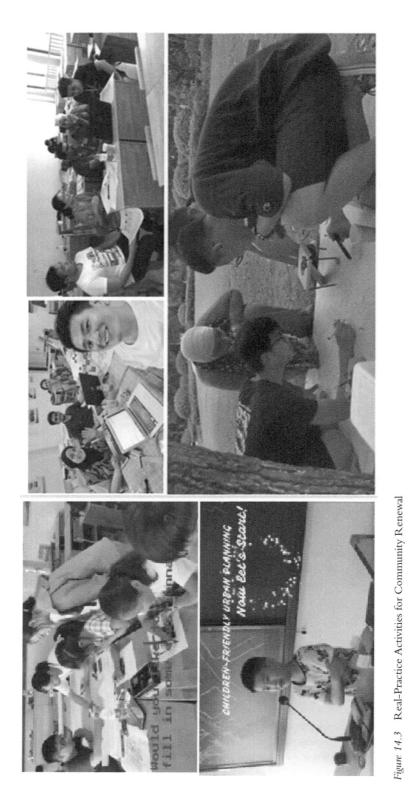

Figure 14.3 Real-Practice Activities for Community Renewal

This figure shows children engaging in different phases of the community renewal process, creating alternatives with YPP teams using the participatory workshops PCL approach (ISOCARP, 2019).

Table 14.1 Enabling and Inhibiting Factors of Planning-Awareness Workshops

Case Study	Enabling Factors	Inhibiting Factors	Recommendations
ICE: DIY City Face-to-Face	• Minimal stakeholders • Simple coordination • Flexible content and timing make it easy to tailor workshops to participants' needs • Could work with only one instructor • Materials provided by instructor and shared by participants	• Publicity depends on individual efforts like word of mouth, which decreases community outreach • No funding or sponsorship, so participants must pay enrolment fees	• Increase number of moderators and students per workshop • Collaborate with sponsors for funding and marketing to increase community outreach • Multiple site visits could be incorporated for a more grounded, real-life experience
ICE: DIY City Online	• The availability of free hosting platforms decreases the running costs of the workshop • Diversity of participants' backgrounds enriches outcomes and relevant discourse	• More instructors are needed to follow-up with participants in different breakout rooms, who are not always available • Unfeasibility of sharing material • Unfeasibility of group projects • Unpreparedness of participants with insufficient materials for making models • Difficult to mentor participants' model-making technicalities • Absence of shared local context	• Instructors send participants tool kits or supply lists beforehand • Train planning students to deliver the content and moderate the workshop to cover shortage of instructors
ICE: Children's University	• Sponsors facilitated required support, covered supplies, and marketed the workshop • Short duration encouraged enrolments during the school semester	• Dissimilar motor skills of participants in group model-making required attentive moderation	• Decrease ratio of moderators to students • Increase frequency • Target different types of children
PCL: Mingdong Community Development	• Sponsors facilitated required support, covered supplies, and marketed the workshop • Designing a child-friendly neighbourhood deals with children as natural stakeholders in the process and provides an interesting topic for them	• Real urban planning projects are not synchronized with school breaks which may decrease enrolment rates • Urban experts are not always interested in mentoring children • The occasional frequency and long time span of urban development projects makes it an unreliable approach for spreading urban planning awareness on a large scale	• Mimic real urban planning projects through urban planning school and urban educators to provide a more flexible experience that is more tailored to students' circumstances

and more-adaptable model, the co-learning experience could be simulated under the sponsorship of local urban planning associations or local universities.

This case study exemplifies how active urban participation helps introduce children to the process (Hart, 1992). In this workshop, awareness of the profession came as a by-product of the child-friendly community development project. The workshop succeeded in exposing participating children and young people to real-life urban practices and connected them to urban problems in their local contexts (Figure 14.3).

After the workshop ended, more social and political achievements followed. The overall experience elevated the social bond between residents of the neighbourhood. Ningbo Urban Planning and Design Institute (NBPI) published a newsletter—"Amazing Newsletter"—in English and Chinese which provided domestic and foreign readers with an overview of the YPP event in Ningbo (ISOCARP, 2019), and in 2020, the Ningbo municipal government issued a Three-Year Action Plan for Old Community Renewal (2020–2022).

Similarities and Differences Between Approaches

The case studies show two approaches that raised awareness of the urban planning profession among young people and children: the in-class education (ICE) approach (Figure 14.4) and the professional co-learning (PCL) approach (Figure 14.5). They were developed with different intents and consequently led to different learning outcomes.

Initiatives using the ICE approach were designed to introduce urban planning to middle and high-schoolers and help them as they consider their career options, while the PCL approach began

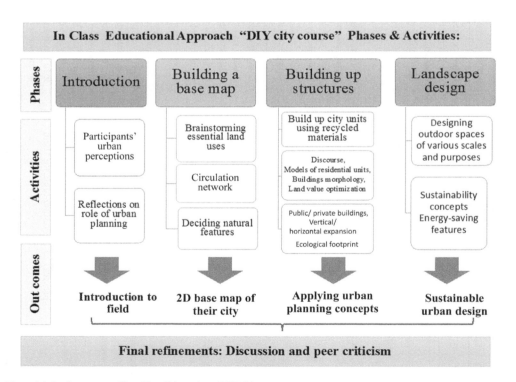

Figure 14.4 Structure of In-Class Education, DIY City

This figure shows the structure of the in-class education activities and phases for the DIY city course.

Promoting Urban Planning Awareness for Children

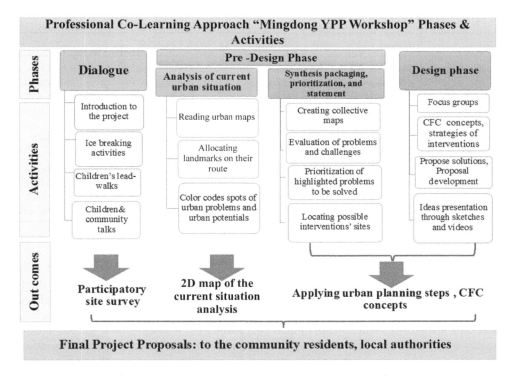

Figure 14.5 Structure of Professional Co-Learning, Mingdong Community Development

This figure shows the structure of the professional co-learning approach adopted for the Mingdong YPP workshops, including the activities and phases for the DIY city course.

to resolve a real urban challenge. Children were invited as stakeholders rather than students to turn Mingdong into a child-friendly neighbourhood. Hence, their urban planning awareness was raised as a by-product of their participation in the project.

Connection to Local Context

Each initiative connects differently to the local context. PCL is structured around the process of urban development with reference to an actual urban site, while ICE is about knowledge transfer of generic urban planning concepts, unbound to a specific context. Hence it is important in the latter to relate participants to their local environment through discussions, reflections, and relevant examples.

Specificity of Acquired Knowledge

PCL follows an in-depth approach as it focuses on problems relevant to a specific urban environment and develops appropriate strategies tailored to those problems. This implies that the acquired knowledge, tackled issues, and discourses are outlined by the givens of the urban context under study. ICE is characterised by a generic nature. It offers a breadth of knowledge that is adaptable according to the participants' ages, backgrounds, interests, and learning pace.

Table 14.2 Comparison of ICE and PCL

	ICE Approach	PCL Approach
Concept	• Simple model that requires limited stakeholders, tools, and coordination	• Multi-layered model that is based on the existence of a real urban planning project
Opportunities	• Easily attainable and flexibly arranged • Limited permissions and funding needed • Flexible time frame	• Engaging children and youth enriches knowledge transfer and provides a comprehensive educational experience
Obstacles	• Limited community outreach if held individually • Not realistic so might not interest teenagers	• Development projects may not be adequately frequent or abundant • Multiple stakeholders from various entities imply less flexibility and require more coordination • Security permissions and funding needed

Theoretical Versus Practical Education

Working on a real project in the PCL approach as opposed to a hypothetical scenario in the ICE approach has pros and cons. ICE gives students room for imagination, which is favourable at a younger age. This, nevertheless, requires a variety of available model-making supplies to induce participants' imaginations and respond to their aspirations. PCL provides a more grounded experience that is more reflective of the real profession. One limitation of the PCL approach, however, is that working on an actual site may require prior awareness of this site among the participants, and achieving this may require narrowing down participants to local inhabitants. In such case, students do not necessarily get introduced to concepts surpassing their direct context or project objectives. However, they might get to see their proposals realised, which inevitably would have a positive impact.

Hybrid Model for Promoting Awareness Among Children

Both the ICE and PCL approaches follow a similar sequence which is structured around four main stages. First is the community outreach stage. This is the marketing stage at which the programme is announced to target participants through social media, community centres, schools, and so on. The outline of the programme, profile of target participants, fees (if any), and structure of the workshops should be outlined at this stage. The second stage is the introductory phase offering a brief explanation of the programme that may include simple activities such as map reading in the PCL approach or sketching a dream city in the ICE approach. The third is the core stage in which the educational experience and engagement level reach their climax. In the PCL approach, this stage includes activities of data analysis, strategies proposals, and criticism, while in the ICE approach, it is when students integrate all the learned lessons into a 3D model. Finally, a conclusive stage recaps the whole process and discusses the proposals and outcomes of previous stages.

Our suggested model, shown in Figure 14.6, offers a road map of those stages with corresponding activities for both approaches. Activities of both could be conducted discretely or merged to support each other. For instance, at the introductory level, an urban walk inspired by the PCL approach to allocating road networks and land uses on a map would support creating a base map in the ICE approach.

We suggest the involvement of urban planning schools in designing, facilitating, and implementing this hybrid model. Their involvement would catalyse direct interactions between youth—our awareness target—and senior urban planning students, professors, experts, and different stakeholders

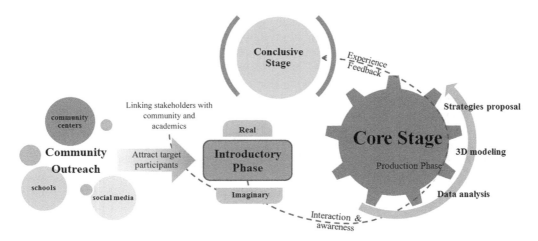

Figure 14.6 Suggested Model Promoting Planning Awareness for Children

This figure illustrates the suggested model based on the experiences from the two case studies on how planning awareness for children can be promoted.

in the planning profession. Moreover, urban planning schools could take part in real participatory community projects or even mock simulations of community development projects. For the latter scenario, child-friendly cities is put forward as a theme for hypothetical development projects. It serves our mission by nature because it not only tackles a topic of specific relevance to children, but also deals with them as essential stakeholders.

Conclusion

Raising awareness about different professions helps young people understand different disciplines and make better-informed career choices. As reported in the literature, the planning profession is not familiar to children and young people, which makes it an unlikely career choice. Here we showcased initiatives to raise awareness among youth about a planning career. The initiatives discussed are categorised under two approaches: an in-class educational approach (ICE) and a professional co-learning approach (PCL). Both support the main argument of using community outreach and child engagement as means of raising awareness about the urban planning profession.

The ICE approach is characterised by its academic nature. Knowledge transfer takes place in class or online between one facilitator or instructor and a group of participants. The facilitator teaches participants about generic urban concepts such as land use, land value, road networks, landscape, and so on. The content is adaptable in response to participants' age, interests, and learning pace.

In the PCL approach, students engage with urban development experts on a real project where they get in-situ, hands-on experience. They tackle concepts of urban development and use tools tailored to the project's objectives. Hence, the acquired knowledge and discourses are primarily tailored to the givens of the project rather than the participants' backgrounds or the moderator's vision. The study concludes in a phasing model that puts forward a systematic road map for promoting urban planning awareness among children. The phasing model divides the activities into four stages: community outreach and publicity, introduction, core, and conclusion. The model also breaks down each stage into several activities with corresponding learning outcomes. Those activities could be employed by urban planning schools or associations to design programmes for raising urban planning awareness among young people.

Some notes were also observed when applying those initiatives. Since the approaches target students at the primary and secondary school levels, synchronising workshops' duration and timing with school breaks is essential for successful community outreach and engagement. Unfortunately, this synchronisation is not always easy with the PCL approach as it relies on real urban-development projects that proceed on a timeline set by the entities and stakeholders involved. A suggestion of mimicking those PCL initiatives and facilitating them through urban schools was proposed to make up for the inflexibility of real projects. Also, our model suggests some activities that are imaginative and others that are more practical. This variety would suit different age groups of children and therefore expand the outreach of the awareness programme.

Outcomes from both approaches, whether physical models, participants' feedback, or discussions, suggested that children are aware of and affected by their urban environment. For instance, when asked about interesting features they would like to incorporate in their future cities, common replies of participants from Cairo included a river, boat marine, and zoo. This shows how children are impacted by the key features of their cities.

On the other hand, replies from children living in Dubai were shopping malls, high-rise towers, and highways. In one of the workshops, it was not until the 19th child that a park or public library was mentioned.

After explaining concepts of walkability, energy saving, and sustainable urban planning, participants started to incorporate elements such as shaded pedestrian walkways, roof gardens, and windmills in their models. This reveals how they not only grasped urban planning concepts but also were capable of interpreting their aspirations into urban planning projects and engaging in proposing viable solutions. This proves that raising awareness about urban planning among children, young people, and the public is a viable approach to making them appreciate its importance. It also urges young people to consider the discipline as a career which, in the long run, might have a positive effect on enrolment rates in urban planning programmes.

Note

1 In Egypt, planning and architecture are treated as disciplines of the engineering profession.

References

Aerts, J. (2018). *Shaping urbanization for children: A handbook on child-responsive urban planning.* UNICEF. www.unicef.org/reports/shaping-urbanization-children

ASRT. (2020). *Academy of scientific research and technology (ASRT).* www.asrt.sci.eg/

Barton, H., & Tsourou, C. (2013). *Healthy urban planning.* Routledge. https://doi.org/10.4324/9780203857755

Chambers, N. (2019, January 22). Our children's career aspirations have nothing in common with the jobs of the future. *The World Economic Forum.* www.weforum.org/agenda/2019/01/childrens-career-aspirations-jobs-of-future/

Elkhouly, A. (2020). *Planning for quality of child urban life: An assessment tool applied on greater Cairo communities* (Unpublished doctoral dissertation). Cairo University.

Elkhouly, A., Shawkat, I., & M. Ahmed, M. (2021). Child friendly cities between theoretical conceptualization and real perception: Capturing the children's perspectives to the city; A pilot case study in GCR. *VFC, Journal of Architecture, Arts and Humanistic Science.* www.academia.edu/72521786/Child_Friendly_Cities_between_theoretical_conceptualization_and_real_perception_Capturing_the_childrens_perspectives_to_the_city_a_pilot_case_study_in_GCR

Gutman, L., & Akerman, R. (2008). Determinants of aspirations. *Wider Benefits of Learning Research Report No. 27.* Centre for Research on the Wider Benefits of Learning, Institute of Education, University of London. https://discovery.ucl.ac.uk/id/eprint/1541614

Hart, R. A. (1992). *Children's participation: From tokenism to citizenship.* Innocenti Essay no. 4. UNICEF. www.unicef-irc.org/publications/100-childrens-participation-from-tokenism-to-citizenship.html

ISOCARP. (2019). *Young planning professionals' workshop—Ningbo, China 2019*. https://isocarp.org/ypp-ningbo-2019/.

MacCallum, J., & Beltman, S. (2002). *Role models for young people: What makes an effective role model program*. Australian Clearing House for Youth Studies, Hobart, Tasmania. https://researchrepository.murdoch.edu.au/id/eprint/9492/

Nováková, K. S., & Giertlová, Z. (2016). New models of theoretical and practical education in urban environment (on example of experience-based pedagogy in Slovak Towns). *Procedia—Social and Behavioral Sciences, 228*, 305–310. https://doi.org/10.1016/j.sbspro.2016.07.045

Palazzo, D., Hollstein, L., & Diko, S. K. (2021). Urban planning as a career preference for students: Efforts to improve awareness about the profession. *Planning Practice & Research, 36*(2), 174–192. https://doi.org/10.1080/02697459.2020.1782056

Riyad, M., Pramana, C., Munakib, & Maseleno, A. (2020). Theoretical education vs practical education. *Test Engineering and Management, 82*, 5074–5081. www.researchgate.net/publication/338831615

Shah, B., Dwyer, C., & Modood, T. (2010). Explaining educational achievement and career aspirations among young British Pakistanis: Mobilizing "ethnic capital"? *Sociology, 44*(6), 1109–1127. https://doi.org/10.1177/0038038510381606

Tranter, P., & Sharpe, S. (2007). Children and peak oil: An opportunity in crisis. *International Journal of Children's Rights, 15*(1), 181–197. https://doi.org/10.1163/092755607X181748

United Nations. (2018, May 16). *68% of the world population projected to live in urban areas by 2050, says UN*. Department of Economic and Social Affairs. www.un.org/development/desa/en/news/population/2018-revision-of-world-urbanization-prospects.html

Yinzhou Government. (2019). *Yinzhou people's government*. www.nbyz.gov.cn/art/2019/4/24/art_1229120956_862306.html

15
FOR MUTUAL BENEFIT? INTRODUCING URBAN PLANNING TO HIGH SCHOOL GEOGRAPHY STUDENTS IN NSW, AUSTRALIA

Isabel Virgona and Simon Pinnegar

As seen in many jurisdictions around the world, New South Wales (NSW)—Australia's most populous state—faces the challenge of meeting demand from both the public and private sectors for a robust pipeline of university educated urban planners, particularly in the fast-growing, global city of Sydney. With the metropolitan population expected to reach eight million over the next 30–40 years, it might seem that urban planning as a potential career—and an engaged interest in urban issues and future development of the city amongst young Sydneysiders—would be apparent. While student demand for planning degrees remains relatively robust (notwithstanding more structural challenges facing higher education in these current times), along with both undergraduate and postgraduate planning qualifications being offered by many of the city's universities, NSW and Australia share wider international concerns about making the profession more visible to the next generation.

Urban planning programs and planning professionals alike often share an optimistic view that if only high-school kids were more aware of city and regional planning as a career and the rich, interesting diversity it entails, we would all be run off our feet. However, the logical pathways from high-school classrooms to lecture theatres have narrowed rather than widened, particularly given a structural decline in the number of students completing Year 11–12 geography—traditionally planning's principal feeder subject—in NSW schools. Whether through broader high-school curriculum redesign, revised education-policy emphasis on STEM, or through changing student preferences, geography needed a major refresh by the mid-2010s. A new curriculum was delivered in 2018, and as part of this restructure and reinvigoration, greater awareness of urban and regional planning has been introduced, notably in Year 9, through the "Changing Places" course.

This chapter is based on research undertaken in the first full year of the new curriculum's rollout. It draws upon teacher and student perspectives concerning its potential impact on students' understanding, interest, and engagement in planning processes.[1] Interviews with education specialists and teachers and short surveys with Year 9 geography students across four secondary schools in the Greater Sydney region were conducted. Findings highlight a broadly positive response by both students and teachers to the relevance of the content, with a good level of interest generated among students both in wider community and urban planning-related issues, and the built-environment professions as a potential future career. It remains at an early stage in determining whether urban planning content and engagement has helped re-energise and make geography more relevant in the classroom, and how in turn this may provide a catalyst to ensure a strong pipeline of future urban planners in NSW and beyond.

Importance of Geography in Shaping Planning Futures

In 2004, the Planning Institute of Australia (PIA) held an inquiry to investigate the capacity for education to help address issues such as appropriate skills and currency in the modern professional-planning field. The PIA's general motivation for this inquiry was the need for skilled and credible planners. The Planning Education Discussion Paper (Gurran et al., 2008) that followed further highlighted the need to produce more planning graduates, with an international shortage of urban and regional planners. The research acknowledged that active engagement of the profession in shaping and providing guidance to secondary education in the field had been somewhat ad hoc (Gurran et al., 2008, p. 31) and considered ways that the PIA and university planning schools could have more active involvement with the curriculum. Heywood supports the wider role that schools play, not only funnelling students into undergraduate planning degrees but shaping broader consciousness on which professional programs are ultimately based (Heywood, 2006, p. 1).

Though prospective planning students demonstrate diversity in the subjects taken in their final years of secondary schooling, geography provides a number of strong synergies, with the nexus between the two fields (Phelps & Tewdwr-Jones, 2008) highlighting a shared interdisciplinary nature with problem solving at their core. In content as well as application, there is an overlapping interest in "critically thinking about space and place making" (RTPI, 2004) and use of an inquiry-based learning approach where students are encouraged to ask questions about real and hypothetical challenges. As such, planning—both as a discipline and profession—has a crucial interest not only in how these shared interests are engaged with in the school classroom as a means of helping students consider planning as a future study or career option but also in helping support the underlying health of geography as a subject more generally. This is particularly so in helping strengthen geography's relevance and appeal in the final years of secondary school and encouraging students to take the subject as part of completion of their High School Certificate (HSC) in Year 12.

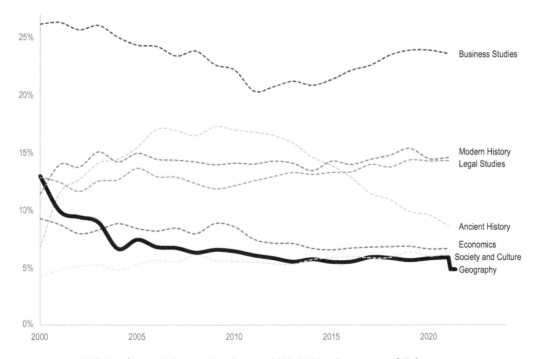

Figure 15.1 HSC Enrolments in Humanities Courses 2000–2021 as Percentage of Cohort
Source: Board of Studies Teaching and Educational Standards (BOSTES; 2021)

In this regard, geography's decline—and more recent stagnation—in NSW classrooms over the past 25 years has been of understandable concern, and for university urban planning programs, translates into a smaller pool of a key cohort of prospective students. Back in the 1990s, geography retained a relatively strong level of popularity. In 1995, 17% of all HSC students took the subject (10,298/61,551 total students) and in 2019, just 6% (4,189/75,006). Geography has continued to slip down in terms of subject popularity, with enrolments in 2019 placing it just 26th and putting it behind other humanities subjects such as economics, ancient history, legal studies, and modern history. Much of this decline came in the early 2000s following the arrival of the "new" HSC and associated changes to subject options. Since 2010, enrolment numbers have settled around the low- to mid-4000s, accounting for 6–7% of total subject enrolments (Pluss, 2020).

Enhancing Experiential Learning Through Curriculum Reform

In 2015, planning education was formally introduced to the compulsory K–10 Australian geography curriculum and endorsed through the NSW Geography K–10 Syllabus. As stated in the curriculum, geography is the study of places and the relationships between people and their environments (BOSTES, 2015, p. 9). It also intends to enable students to become active, responsible, and informed citizens, able to evaluate opinions of others and express their own ideas and arguments (ibid.). Alignment with principles of experiential learning—a purposeful process of engaged, active learning in which the student acquires knowledge, and skills of value through direct experiences in real world contexts (Kassem, 2007, p. 2)—can be clearly seen, with the subject refresh designed to provide students' active participation in community life, a commitment to sustainability, the creation of a just society, and the promotion of intercultural understanding and lifelong learning (ibid.).

Experiential learning, community-based learning, and *fieldwork* are all terms that are founded upon the theory of situated cognition (Vygotsky, 1978) whereby knowing, understanding, and thinking happen in sociocultural contexts (Lave & Wenger, 1991, p. 25). Experiential learning occurs in a setting where the learner experiences something firsthand. It involves the whole person, combining their thoughts, feelings, and actions to focus on the present moment. It involves self-reflection and can bring personal growth (Tyson & Low, 1987). Kolb embellished the concept and argued that learning is best conceived as the process where knowledge is created through the transformation of experience (Kolb, 1984, p. 38). Several academics have highlighted the advantages of experiential learning and fieldwork in planning education (Balassiano, 2011; Ives-Dewey, 2009; Eyler et al., 1997). Experiential learning promotes a deep learning approach because of its real-world orientation which focuses on a dialectic transfer of theory into practice (Baldwin et al., 2014). Fieldwork is central to the teaching and learning of geographical concepts (Dummer et al., 2008; Ives-Dewey, 2009). It provides exposure to practical applications of geographical concepts, gives students experience with team dynamics, and provides real-world experience (Ives-Dewey, 2009). With regards to planning, students are challenged to apply theories and concepts to complex and uncertain real-world problems, reinforcing the ethos of reflective practice and the public good (Roakes & Norris-Tirrell, 2000; Sletto, 2010).

The benefits of experiential learning, and use of urban planning-related topics and subject matter as an important vehicle, can be seen in the redesign of the NSW geography curriculum. The key geographical concepts of place, space, environment, interconnection, scale, sustainability, and change are explored throughout the program, in stages which progress with each year of study. In Stage 3 (Years 5 and 6), "Factors That Shape Places," students are asked to identify ways that people can influence places and contribute to sustainability. In Stage 4 (Years 7 and 8), "Place and Liveability," they must explore place and liveability and how this relates to access to services, environmental quality, and community, and they are asked to propose strategies to improve liveability. In Stage 5 (Years 9 and 10), "Changing Places," students discuss causes and consequences of urbanisation, as well as investigate settlement patterns, migration, and population growth (BOSTES, 2015, p. 30). Under each topic, teachers receive a set of outcomes, key inquiry questions, and content to guide the lessons. The addition of these topics to the curriculum supports an enhanced approach to instilling early understanding of how planning shapes the natural and built environment.

Experiencing "Changing Places" in the Classroom

The research reported upon in this chapter was conducted in 2018 during the first year of the full rollout of "Changing Places" in the NSW Year 9 geography curriculum. Four high schools (Schools A–D) within Sydney were selected as case studies, determined by seeking a geographical spread across the metropolitan area and across schools within the government and private systems. For each, the lead teacher responsible for design and delivery of the "Changing Places" course in their school was interviewed (Teachers A–D) and an in-class survey (administered by the teacher) was conducted with students undertaking the course. Across the four classes, a total of 91 pupils completed the questionnaire, answering a range of questions capturing their thoughts on "Changing Places," their broader interest in urban planning and larger built environment issues, and what impact and influence undertaking the course might have had in helping them consider future career directions. As well as the four teachers at each of the case-study schools, interviews were also held with the education manager of Australia's planning-accreditation body, the PIA, and a leading educator (Educator A) who had played a key role in stewarding through changes to the NSW geography curriculum.

When interviewed, all teachers welcomed the new curriculum and the flexibility it provided to design relevant and contemporary learning opportunities of urban planning. Each of the participating schools in different areas of Sydney were able to weave local experiences and issues related to planning into their teaching, making their lessons more accessible and interesting for students:

> We are always looking for ways to make geography more engaging and more relevant to their world and I think the new syllabus has done that . . . it's about making these projects real.
>
> *(Teacher A)*

Fieldwork, encouraging direct engagement with live issues in students' neighbourhoods and suburbs, was recognised as fundamental in helping students gain insight beyond the limitations of the classroom and making connections with issues shaping their everyday lives, from public transport access and provision of public space through to perceived loss of social cohesion and sense of community:

> Classroom activities are fairly limited in their capacity to explore, but field work does open some kind of window. The kids could actually examine what's going on, what planning is taking place and how that looks on the ground. We would ask the kids questions like "would you live here?"
>
> *(Teacher C)*

Another example shared was students engaging local businesses in a survey designed to identify the services and infrastructure required to satisfy the needs of the users. The result was a more relevant, real-world, and substantive experience for the students that they could refer to in class throughout the project (Teacher B). Fieldwork also helped students engage with real-world issues through experiencing places and situations that they learn about in class. A number of our teacher interviewees noted that their students were able to build empathy and appreciation for other people living in and visiting their parts of the city, helping them expand personal awareness beyond their regular day-to-day activities:

> Young students are still quite egocentric, so prompting them to think about how the elderly lady who lives next door might have different challenges in living in a place to what the student does, it does take a bit of maturity and a bit of digging in the students' research. But there's been a lot of light bulb moments after their survey or interview and [they] are so excited about their insights. It's about bringing them out of their bubble to have more empathy for people living around them.
>
> *(Teacher A)*

Subjects explored through fieldwork promoted student appreciation for council, services, and public entities when planning is well considered, and encouraged them to form opinions about what and why other cases have gone wrong and, crucially, where planning makes a difference:

> When the students see a block of units or a park redesign, we encourage them to ask the question: Why? Why are we changing this? Or creating something new? It's a necessary understanding of the students to not just straightaway think, oh no more development but why is this? Is it because there's a train station here, or general population growth for example?
>
> *(Educator A)*

"Changing Places" also provides the opportunity to bring policy makers and industry into the classroom, helping broaden students' awareness of planning as a professional industry as well as their participation in planning processes as a legitimate role for young people. At two of our case-study schools, teachers invited planning and built-environment professionals into the classroom to facilitate a more substantive experience for their students (Teacher A and Teacher B). One school arranged a panel of stakeholders and industry professionals to judge student assignments at an exhibition and found the students to be accountable and responsible to the real-world nature of the project. Another organised that the highest-performing students would be rewarded with an excursion to a leading demography firm.

So What Did the Students Think?

Students were asked an overarching question in the survey to gauge whether "Changing Places" had engaged them as intended. Different approaches, activities, and assignments were used to deliver the curriculum, but the results were promising across all four schools, with approximately two-thirds to one-third responding favourably when asked "Do you enjoy learning about planning issues in your area or city as part of your geography class?" (70% [n = 64] yes, and 30% [n = 27] no). In all schools a clear net positive can be seen, with a particularly strong positive response seen in School B, where more than 80% (n = 22) of students reflected on an enjoyable and informative class (Figure 15.2).

Previous research has highlighted that students often like their geography studies for their interest and relevance, enhanced by opportunities for practical fieldwork, allowing them to express their own opinions (Biddulph & Adey, 2003). When asked why students enjoyed learning about planning issues in their area, the quotes drawn out here capture an increased awareness of their natural

Introducing Urban Planning to High School Geography Students

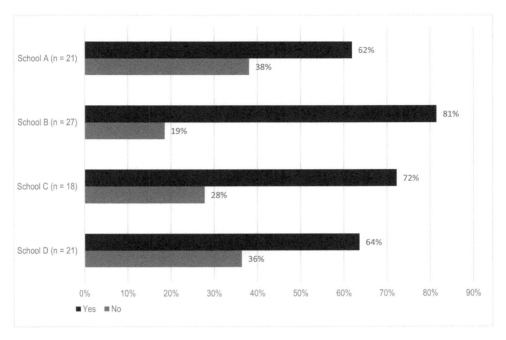

Figure 15.2 Do You Enjoy Learning About Planning Issues in Your Local Area as Part of Your Geography Class?

and built environment, the relevance of the content to their everyday lives, and the future-oriented nature of planning:

> These issues concern my area and will probably affect my day-to-day life. I have enjoyed learning about sustainable infrastructure.
>
> *(School A)*

> The holistic view of multiple parts of society e.g., roads, traffic, buildings and how they function together. I find this big picture view quite interesting, and I want to learn more about how they are interrelated.
>
> *(School C)*

It was not a universal hagiography, however. Among students less enamoured by their introduction to urban planning issues in geography, the most frequent negative response reflected a lack of interest in the content (73%) with comments such as, "it's boring and I just don't find it interesting" (School D). Some students interpreted it to be purely vocational and did not find this useful as they were not intending on pursuing a career in urban planning. Other students hinted that a lack of empowerment was a barrier to their interest in the topic—one participant noted, "because I have very little say in what occurs in my local community, as a minor, it can sometimes be hard for me to be interested in these issues" (School A). This sentiment touches on Malone (1999) and Cunningham et al.'s (1996) work, that children have been denied the right to make decisions about matters affecting them on the basis of their moral incompetence, inexperience, and lack of capacity to be rational.

When asked "What do you think a town planner does?" the four key themes identified by students included design (31%), land use (23%), liveability (23%), and infrastructure (22%). Keywords that students used to describe planners were "design" (21 comments) and "layout" (15 comments). While some student responses were short and sharp, for example, "plans towns," more often they offered insightful interpretations as shown here:

> Organises layout of community, involving public transport, community centres, green spaces, residential etc. caters for community needs.
>
> *(School A)*

> Looks at and studies statistics and problems an area experiences and then constructs plans to solve these problems with a focus on interconnection and liveability.
>
> *(School B)*

Students demonstrated an awareness of planning issues affecting their local area, with 22% recognising public transport and 12% noting traffic congestion as issues. Those students that held emotive views on major infrastructure projects usually attended schools in close proximity to recent projects. For example, students had knowledge of a new major motorway and new hospital being developed in Sydney were present in surveys by students attending schools nearby:

> Traffic, interruption to lifestyles, people forced out of their homes due to the destruction. Relocation of these people [is] poor—not given enough money to buy a house in the same area.
>
> *(School A)*

> The light rail on Anzac parade often causes many disruptions including re-routing bus routes, cutting down trees and generally complicating congestion; I feel that these issues were not communicated to their full extent.
>
> *(School D)*

At this stage, students are most familiar with city projects affecting areas that they know and are attached to. Comments suggest students are protective of their neighbourhoods and concerned regarding urban change as a result of planning decisions. Some identified planning issues beyond transport, such as water, open space, and housing for recently arrived migrants. Our findings demonstrate the importance of expanding awareness for students, to gear them with a foundational knowledge of urban planning from which to base judgement. When asked "What skills have you learnt or explored from "Changing Places?" responses frequently included critical thinking and analysis of demographics to understand the needs of communities (36%). Many students also recognised their increased understanding of liveability and sustainability (22%):

> I have learnt about management, critical thinking and developing complex solutions to problems.
>
> *(School C)*

> How to make use out of each space you have such as multi-purpose buildings, and how to make an area more attractive and more sustainable.
>
> *(School B)*

Students identified tangible skills that they had acquired; however, we can assume that they also expanded skills associated with fieldwork, which provides exposure to practical applications of geographical concepts and experience within a team dynamic (Ives-Dewey, 2009). Chawla and Heft (2002) also comment on the outcomes of engaged-learning experiences being twofold—material and personal. While students reflect mostly on the material outcomes, they less explicitly identify skills such as presentation, speaking with local stakeholders, and learning to consider perspectives other than their own.

Beyond Curriculum and Classroom

As part of the research, we were also keen to understand whether exposure to the subject and profession translates into more far-reaching interest, both in terms of thinking more broadly about planning issues and their impact upon their local area and the city and, indeed, whether "Changing Places" has sparked their interest in planning as a potential career. Results from the survey are modestly positive in this regard. Across our four classes, 56% (n = 51) stated that they had become more interested and aware of urban planning issues in their local area, while 42% (n = 38) said not (2% were undecided).

The syllabus intends to enable students to become active, responsible, and informed citizens, able to evaluate opinions of others and express their own ideas and arguments (BOSTES, 2015, p. 9). Since learning about planning at school, a small majority (n = 51) identified being more aware of activities such as construction and seeing evidence of planning in their community had increased their motivation to learn at school. A greater appreciation for the complexity of planning was also noted by some students:

> I have been much more aware of the processes urban planners go through and the issues they must resolve to improve various areas.
>
> *(School B)*

> Designing is fun and it gives a further insight into how our infrastructure works. Also, planning issues always spark heated debate. That's fun!
>
> *(School A)*

> The course has taught me about many instances of urban planning. My interest has followed on from that, because I now know more facts relating to the topic and so can form more informed opinions.
>
> *(School D)*

Perhaps understandably, translation of this interest into examples of engagement in local planning issues was less apparent. When asked whether they had ever "gotten involved," just 9% (n = 8) said yes, with the large majority (91%, n = 83) stating no. In cases where students had been involved, they tended to relate to local public spaces, such as completing a survey on the redevelopment of a local skate park (School B). In one response, the student had protested with his neighbours where a pocket park had been earmarked for redevelopment into a car park by their local council. This student also gave a speech at a council town meeting (School D). A small number commented on being consulted regarding a local development.

When asked about engagement from a different direction, the inverse was seen: 88% (n = 80) agreed that they felt it relevant to "participate in planning issues that will affect you and your family," with just 12% (n = 11) responding no. Students commonly referred to notions of democracy in this regard. This current generation have been encouraged to see themselves as key conduits of change, particularly in relation to sustainability. These sentiments are seen in the survey responses—that students want to have the opportunity to speak on changes and issues that will affect themselves and their families:

> No matter how small/insignificant a person is, it is important that if something affects you, you should seek to change that.
>
> *(School C)*

A secondary theme raised by students highlighted that their local knowledge could provide better insight for planners to be more informed in decision-making (16%). This demonstrates strong notions of place attachment, and an intricate knowledge of their neighbourhoods. It looks beyond *having* their say to *what* they would say and add to improve a project:

> Because it provides another perspective on planning issues—the more ideas that can be taken into account and planned for, the better.
>
> *(School D)*

Survey responses also highlighted a number of barriers, notably in relation to age: 17% (n = 16) of students felt they were too young to contribute or make any impact on their local areas:

> Urban planning doesn't really interest me at the moment since I'm young and cannot be involved in decisions regarding this.
>
> *(School A)*

All teachers interviewed felt a responsibility to encourage students to think differently about their environments and to feel empowered that they can influence decision-making. "They tend to be quite blind to it . . . but then a few kids start to make the connections" (Teacher D). Over time, teachers expressed the hope that young people would want to engage more with their environment, particularly at a local scale (Teacher C). Teacher A further describes the role of teachers as facilitators in broadening awareness:

> I feel that it's a real shame that more students don't feel empowered to influence those debates in trying to find solutions on issues. The starting point is awareness and education so that's my imperative—you need the awareness but also the confidence to articulate these issues.
>
> *(Teacher A)*

But does this enhanced interest influence students' deliberations on their future study and career options? As one respondent reflected, "the best show of activism, is that a student is so interested in making a change that they enrol in a built environment related career" (Educator A). When asked "Would you consider studying urban planning, architecture or landscape architecture at university?" 36 students responded yes. Interestingly, planning itself did not lead the pack, with architecture coming out on top among those responding yes (61%), with planning following with 26%, and landscape architecture at 13%.

Concluding Discussion

How to interest high-school students into considering urban planning for university study and, in turn, planning as a future career has been a focus of attention for both universities and planning-accreditation bodies for a number of years. While domestic enrolments in Greater Sydney universities have remained strong (and indeed went through a significant surge in the case of the

University of New South Wales from 2017; Bagshaw, 2017), in recent years, the picture nationally—and internationally—is less rosy, with a structural decline, particularly at the undergraduate level (Planning Accreditation Board, 2019; Palazzo et al., 2021). Inevitably, myriad factors come into play in this regard, for example, more structural changes in terms of secondary school student numbers coming through the system (the overall pool of potential applicants), changes to university funding and flow-through in terms of the status of urban planning degrees and their fees relative to other degree options, and shifts in real and perceived future-employment prospects—often tied to wider market cycles and/or government-planning "reform."

Although high-school geography has struggled to retain its place as a mainstream subject offering in NSW in recent years, there remains a resilient base, often driven by dedicated teachers at many public and private schools tasked with ensuring viable numbers to run classes in the final senior years and offer the subject at HSC. The curriculum refresh has provided a means whereby the inherent qualities of the discipline—and how students learn about space and place—have been further fleshed out and valorised to help make geography's real-world relevance more explicit and, crucially, demonstrate how subject matter relates to built-environment subjects as future-career options. In doing so, the structure and design of modules such as "Changing Places," making use of case studies and fieldwork activity, draw upon a shared commitment to, and characteristics of, experiential learning as a means to connect.

The findings highlight opportunities for improvement in the delivery of the program to further expand its impact. More formalised, joined-up programs to bring industry practitioners into the classroom would reduce the burden on teachers to personally initiate and form relationships with industry, smoothing the way for more robust experiential learning opportunities, while elevating the vocational opportunities of geography. Connections to industry can be value adding in myriad ways: preparation of syllabus-relevant content to support learning in the classroom, experiential learning outside of the classroom to validate learning, and exposing students to community consultation in a safe and protected environment, allowing them to gain a sense of competency through authenticity which could enhance student accountability for their work through purpose.

While our research offers only a small point-in-time snapshot of pupils' responses to "Changing Places" in its inaugural teaching year—and highlights inevitable variations seen across our case-study schools—the results offer promising signals. Not all students were transformed into budding planners, and for many, a more general interest in planning issues failed to ignite. For a good minority, an interest in studying subjects related to the built environment at university was identified. Even if students don't pursue this career path, they gained heightened awareness of their communities and empathy for the complexities involved in the planning process. The feedback also indicates that urban planning provided generally well-received subject matter among the geography students in all four schools, and although a number of teachers felt a little out of their depth teaching the material for the first time, the response among our small sample was also positive.

Note

1 Ethical considerations for children's involvement in the research were central to the design of the methodology. Student surveys were administered by the geography teacher, not the researcher, and emulate customary language teachers use with students on an everyday basis. No identifiable information was sought or collected from participants.

References

Bagshaw, E. (2017, January 21). Sydney growth pushes students to UNSW city planning degree. *The Sydney Morning Herald*. www.smh.com.au/education/uni-offers-2017-sydney-growth-pushes-students-to-unsw-city-planning-degree-20170120-gtv4o5.html

Balassiano, K. (2011). Tackling wicked problems in planning studio courses. *Journal of Planning Education and Research, 17*(3), 21–29. https://doi.org/10.1177%2F0739456X11415282

Baldwin, C., Harwood, A., Rosier, J., & Slade, C. (2014). Baseline survey of current experiential learning practice in Australian and New Zealand planning schools, *Australian Planner, 52*(2), 103–113. https://doi.org/10.1080/07293682.2014.926280

Biddulph, M., & Adey, K. (2003). Perceptions v. reality: Pupils' experiences of learning in history and geography at key stage 4, *The Curriculum Journal, 14*(3), 291–303. https://doi.org/10.1080/0958517032000137621

BOSTES (Board of Studies, Teaching and Educational Standards Authority NSW). (2015). *Geography K-10 syllabus*. Retrieved October 10, 2021, from https://educationstandards.nsw.edu.au/wps/portal/nesa/k-10/learning-areas/hsie/geography-k-10

BOSTES (Board of Studies, Teaching and Educational Standards Authority NSW). (2021). *HSC facts and figures*. Retrieved October 10, 2021, from https://educationstandards.nsw.edu.au/wps/portal/nesa/11-12/hsc/about-HSC/HSC-facts-figures

Chawla, L., & Heft, H. (2002). Children's competence and the ecology of communities: A functional approach to the evaluation of participation. *Journal of Environmental Psychology, 22*(1–2), 201–216. https://doi.org/10.1006/jevp.2002.0244

Cunningham, C., Jones, M., & Barlow, M. (1996). *Town planning and children: A case study of Lismore, New South Wales, Australia*. Department of Geography and Planning, University of New England.

Dummer, T., Cook, I., Parker, S., Barrett, G., & Hull, A. (2008). Promoting and assessing 'deep learning' in geography fieldwork: An evaluation of reflective field diaries. *Journal of Geography in Higher Education, 32*(3), 459–479. https://doi.org/10.1080/03098260701728484

Eyler, J., Dwight, G., & Branxton, J. (1997). The impact of service-learning on college students, *Michigan Journal of Community Service Learning* (4), 5–15. Retrieved October 25, 2021, from http://hdl.handle.net/2027/spo.3239521.0004.101

Gurran, N., Norman, B., & Gleeson, B. (2008). *Planning education discussion paper, planning institute of Australia, ACT: Kingston*. Retrieved April 20, 2018, from www.planning.org.au/policy/education

Heywood, P. (2006). Educating Australia's future planners. *Australian Planner, 43*(4), 28–31. Retrieved October 26, 2021, from https://eprints.qut.edu.au/7940/

Ives-Dewey, D. (2009). Teaching experiential learning in geography: Lessons from planning. *Journal of Geography, 107*(4), 167–174. https://doi.org/10.1080/00221340802511348

Kassem, C. (2007, March 28). *Task force on experiential learning. report to faculty assembly executive council*. Ramapo College of New Jersey.

Kolb, D. (1984). *Experiential learning: Experience as the source of learning and development*. Prentice Hall. Retrieved October 25, 2021, from www.researchgate.net/publication/235701029_Experiential_Learning_Experience_As_The_Source_Of_Learning_And_Development

Lave, J., & Wenger, E. (1991). *Situated learning: Legitimate peripheral participation*. Cambridge University Press.

Malone, K. (1999). Growing Up in cities as a model of participatory planning and 'placemaking' with young people. *Youth Studies Australia, 18*(2), 17–33. Retrieved October 26, 2021, from www.academia.edu/4224696/Growing_Up_in_Cities_as_a_model_of_participatory_planning_and_place_making_with_young_people

Palazzo, D., Hollstein, L., & Diko, S. K. (2021). Urban planning as a career preference for students: Efforts to improve awareness about the profession. *Planning Practice & Research, 36*(2), 174–192. https://doi.org/10.1080/02697459.2020.1782056

Phelps, A., & Tewdwr-Jones, M. (2008). If geography is anything, maybe it's planning's alter ego? Reflections on policy relevance in two disciplines concerned with place and space, *Transactions of the Institute of British Geography New Series, 33*(4), 566–584. Retrieved October 26, 2021, from www.jstor.org/stable/30135334

Planning Accreditation Board. (2019). *Student enrolment in PAB-accredited programs 2008–2018*. Retrieved October 25, 2021, from www.planningaccreditationboard.org/index.php?s=file_download&id=567

Planning Institute of Australia (PIA). (2004). *National inquiry into planning education and employment, planning institute of Australia, ACT: Kingston*. Retrieved March 10, 2018. www.planning.org.au/policy/national-inquiry

Pluss, M. (2020). Geography effect: Two decades of change. *Geography Teachers Australia Bulletin, 52*. Retrieved October 5, 2021, from www.gtansw.org.au/wp-content/uploads/2020/11/GTA-Special-Edition-Bulletin-2020-3-88-15-19.pdf

Roakes, S., & Norris-Tirrell, D. (2000). Community service learning in planning education: A framework for course development. *Journal of Planning Education and Research, 20*, 100–110. https://doi.org/10.1177%2F073945600128992636

Royal Town Planning Institute. (2004, January). *Policy statement on initial planning education*. RTPI.

Sletto, B. (2010). Educating reflective practitioners: Learning to embrace the unexpected through service learning, *Journal of Planning Education and Research*, *29*(4), 403–415. https://doi.org/10.1177%2F0739456X10362771

Tyson, B., & Low, N. (1987). Experiential learning in planning education. *Journal of Planning Education and Research*, *7*(1), 15–27. https://doi.org/10.1177%2F0739456X8700700102

Vygotsky, L. (1978). *Mind in society*. Harvard University Press.

16
CAN CHILDREN'S PARTICIPATION INSPIRE A NEW GENERATION OF PLANNERS?

Robyn G. Mansfield

Children's participation in urban planning processes is uncommon, even though global policy supports their participation, recognizing that children have specific needs in the urban context and a right to participate in decisions affecting them. This position is articulated in Article 12 of the Convention on the Rights of the Child (United Nations General Assembly, 1989). Sustainable Development Goal 11 Target 3 further supports children's participation in human-settlement planning and management (United Nations, 2020). Recent literature reviews on the topic, however, demonstrate that children continue to be excluded from such processes for a range of reasons despite well-documented positive and negative impacts of their participation or exclusion (Ataol et al., 2019; Mansfield et al., 2021). Though numerous studies demonstrate a broad range of benefits from children's participation in urban planning, the impact participatory processes have on children's understanding of the urban planning field and subsequent career choices is poorly understood and under-researched in the urban planning field.

Children have a unique and generally closer connection to their physical environments than adults (Beckett & Shaffer, 2005; Chatterjee, 2005; Freeman, 2019; Sancar & Severcan, 2010; Spencer & Woolley, 2000). This makes them both experts in the urban environment while also vulnerable to poor planning decisions, with the impacts of the latter resulting in outcomes detrimental to the health and well-being of children worldwide, particularly in vulnerable settings, and a major contributor to premature deaths (Bartlett et al., 1999; Chawla, 2015; Ellis et al., 2015; Kylin & Stina, 2015; Oliver et al., 2011). Meaningful participation of children in these processes positively impacts urban planning outcomes and provides mutually beneficial opportunities to both planning experts and children (Chawla, 2002, 2015; Chawla & Heft, 2002; Malone, 2015; McKoy et al., 2015; Tsevreni, 2011). From a professional-planning perspective, meaningful participation of children has the capacity to greatly improve planning outcomes that benefit entire communities (Derr & Kovács, 2017; Lúcio & l'Anson, 2015; Nordström & Wales, 2019). From children's perspectives, it exposes them to lesser-known career paths with the potential for them to carry these experiences into adulthood and, ultimately, the prospect of entering the planning profession (McKoy et al., 2021). This, in turn, has a potentially greater chance of carrying the value of children's participation into a reiterative cycle in planning education and the subsequent practitioner process (McKoy & Vincent, 2007). With concerns over the decline in enrollment and diversity in planning in North America (Palazzo et al., 2021), children's participation in planning may provide opportunities to improve understanding of the profession and career aspirations for young people. Research into children's participation in urban planning processes, however, lacks a focus on examining the impact of children's participation on children's career choices, or the impact of planning education on supporting children's participation.

Impact of Children's Participation in Urban Planning

Literature on children's participation is dominated by studies that are project specific and focus on singular components of the projects (Mansfield et al., 2021). The key purpose of the research studies identified in Mansfield et al.'s literature review (2021) was generally to test participatory methods or to generate an outcome such as a design or an evaluation of a public space (ibid.). General studies into the impact of children's participation tend to focus on built outcomes, social behavior, and the impact on children's relationships with adults in their communities (Bartlett et al., 1999; Derr et al., 2018; Driskell, 2002; Freeman, 2019; Kranz-Nagl & Zartler, 2009). Mansfield et al.'s (2021) semi-systematic literature[1] review identified that research into barriers and enablers to children's participation in planning tends to focus on structural and procedural conditions with a general theme of political and socio-cultural conditions identified as key impediments. One study provided a comprehensive list of barriers specific to their project (Severcan, 2015), while others scrutinized political institutions and perceptions of children's capacities and capabilities (Mansfield et al., 2021). Planning education was not examined, and none of the studies or key texts identify the impact of children's participation on their desire to pursue a career in urban planning.

Malone and Hartung (2010) demonstrate that the theoretical background and models for children's participation is limited, noting that children's participation is narrowly defined, adult led, or co-opted, and dominated by practical projects without an understanding of why children's participation occurs and what its impacts are. The "ladder of children's participation" (Hart, 1997, p. 41) provides guidance for how children might participate to support the realization of the Convention on the Rights of the Child. While Hart (1997) cautioned that it was not to become a manual for template approaches, it has dominated participatory practice (Malone & Hartung, 2010). Hart himself has since criticized use of the ladder, noting that it is limited in its understanding of the myriad ways in which children already participate in their communities and that the image of a "ladder" is problematic in its implied hierarchy of levels of participation (Hart, 2008).

Criticisms of the ladder have fueled further research into the complexity of children's participation. Botchwey et al. (2019) revised the ladder model based on examination of three case studies, splitting the ladder to acknowledge different processes that occur when children seek to participate versus being invited. Francis and Lorenzo (2002) propose an alternative to the ladder entirely, identifying seven realms of children's participation based on a study of how children have historically participated in city design with a proposal—the seventh realm—for a more proactive approach to involving children in planning and design. A final example is Shier's (2015) model, "the participation tree," which proposes that the tree grows from the seed where children first learn to participate in the family home followed by the community. Each of these models, and many others, are helpful for prompting debate on how children might be included in projects and programs. What they fail to mention, however, is the impact that participation has on children, and the value and influence adults may bring to children's lives and future career paths.

Rinke et al.'s (2014) study on the impact of students' experiences on their career paths to teaching demonstrates that experiences with professionals as a child can impact career choices. This "apprenticeship of observation" (p. 93) manifests through mentoring, practice, or empowerment of students. However, the study also serves as a warning of the limitations of this approach as it may serve to reinforce social inequalities (ibid.). Lave and Wenger (1991) attempt to theorize apprenticeship learning as a form of "legitimate peripheral participation," which presents a way of understanding the lesser-understood social-engagement style of learning as newcomers join "communities of practice" (p. 29). They caution that while historical forms of apprenticeship have operated as a form of control, this model must be practiced through meaningful participation at a level appropriate to the apprentice or newcomer's practice (ibid.). Tummons (2018) critiques this model for its refuting of formal institutional learning pedagogies; however, noting that along with "communities of practice" models, there is room for drawing on these theories as an educational model. O'Donnell and Tobbell's (2007) research into adult participation in higher education further demonstrates that meaningful inclusion and participation in communities of practice greatly impacts who participates in tertiary education.

Literature in different disciplines suggests that children's participation in discipline-focused activities in and out of school, and interactions with professionals, impacts children's knowledge of and predisposition to career paths (Kolne & Lindsay, 2020; Rinke et al., 2014; Rochera et al., 2019). For instance, Rinke et al. demonstrate that disciplinary, mentoring, and empowering practices can influence secondary school students to pursue subject-specific types of teaching professions (Rinke et al., 2014). Kolne and Lindsay (2020) suggest that participating in science and technology activities outside school may impact development of further interest in those fields, and Rochera et al.'s (2019) systematic literature review demonstrated that children and youth with disabilities were more likely to pursue a STEM career after participating in interventions specifically designed to engage youth in these fields. These examples indicate that children's meaningful participation in planning with associated professionals may impact their choice of a career path into urban planning, and there is a need to understand both how to improve their participation as well as the potential impact of planning education.

How Children's Participation Impacts Their study and Career Paths

The information for this chapter was collected as part of a broader research study[2] examining the mainstreaming of children's participation in planning for vulnerable settings. This chapter includes two key case studies involving children's participation in urban planning processes and interviews with 40 participants across the case studies.[3] Due to the work in the case studies occurring in settlements and the informality of some activities, it is unknown how many children have participated in the work implemented in each case study. However, interviewees have noted children of all ages have been involved in different aspects of their programs, including babies in Case Study 1.

The particularly interdisciplinary nature of Case Study 1 resulted in many disciplines working together on various aspects of the urban planning process. Disciplines include but are not limited to urban planners, landscape architects, and engineers working on the design and construction process with microbiologists, economists, and ecologists working on human and environmental health and well-being outcomes of the infrastructure, to name a few. Case Study 2 is dominated by disciplines associated not only with public art, but also with social work, and they work with international NGOs to deliver a range of outcomes such as public health and community cohesiveness. The words used by interviewees have been transcribed exactly without grammatical corrections in order to preserve the integrity of people's voices.

For the purposes of this study, the term "urban (and territorial) planning" is defined "as a decision-making process aimed at realizing economic, social, cultural and environmental goals through the development of spatial visions, strategies and plans and the application of a set of policy principles, tools, institutional and participatory mechanisms and regulatory procedures" (United Nations Human Settlements Program, 2015, p. 2). The case studies involve a range of disciplines working together to achieve urban planning goals in vulnerable settlements and include built-environment outcomes, such as urban public art, which support health messaging and community cohesiveness, WASH (water, sanitation, and hygiene) infrastructure, land tenure, land-use planning, pedestrian access, and impacts of the built interventions on health, wellbeing, and environmental impacts. The implications are that a range of disciplines responsible for urban planning need to be included in recommendations for future research to support urban planning disciplines as a disciplinary career path for children.

Case Study 1: Revitalising Informal Settlements and Their Environments (RISE)

Case Study 1 is the Revitalising Informal Settlements and Their Environments program (RISE). RISE's vision is to improve human, environmental, and ecological health in informal urban settlements through a novel approach to water management (RISE, 2017). It comprises a randomized control-group research program trialing a water-sensitive approach to water and sanitation management in 24 informal settlements in Makassar, Indonesia, and 12 settlements in Suva, Fiji (ibid.). The program is a transdisciplinary planning program focused on planetary health through revitalizing water, sanitation, and hygiene (WASH) infrastructure by incorporating community participation. While children's participation in design activities is not specified, they have participated in a range of infrastructure design and education activities through targeted activities or inadvertently. They are also key targets for gathering health and well-being data for measuring the impact of interventions (RISE, 2017). Qualitative interviews were conducted between November 2020 and May 2021 with 32 academic staff, professional-specialist staff, city actors, and other RISE researchers on the factors that impacted children's participation in their work in RISE.

While interview questions were focused on eliciting the barriers to children's participation in planning processes in RISE, several interviewees noted specific impacts of their participation as a child on their career choices. In addition to this, some interviewees also identified that some children who participated in the RISE program engaged in career discussions with RISE staff and supporters based on the field work they became involved in. Some respondents also demonstrated their own experience with participation as a child that influenced their career choices or how they practiced their chosen career.

Case Study 2: Artolution Projects

Case Study 2 focuses on Artolution, a US-based not-for-profit organization that develops participatory urban-art projects in refugee and IDP (internally displaced person) settlements in Jordan, Bangladesh, Colombia, and Uganda. Eight semi-structured qualitative interviews were conducted with key decision-makers who worked for Artolution or supported their work through funding or governance such as board members. The types of questions varied slightly to those associated with the RISE project, with a focus on what had influenced them to found, work for, support, or fund child participatory Artolution projects. The responses to questions provided information on the impact of their work on children's career choices and presented additional information on what influenced interviewees' own career choices.

Creating Future Planners?

Emerging in the interviews was the identification of conversations with children that led to discussions about future career options. The conversations generally emerged as a result of children observing RISE and Artolution staff working in the field within their communities, sparking curiosity and opening up opportunities for children to participate. Some interviewees recognized that involving children in their work may lead to them entering a similar field, and the way they engaged with children further supported children's interest in the field.

Planners Supporting School Curricula

In the following examples, interviewees connected their work to specific school curricula either through activities or discussions with children, supporting both school curricula and student career study pathways. For example, a RISE city actor identified the opportunity to discuss career options through school field excursions:

> Teachers have excursions, so they thought it would also be a good opportunity to enlighten students on coming into the treatment plant and seeing what we do. Apart from that, it also gives them a heads-up on what they want to do when they grow up, because we get to show them, "okay, if you want to be a water engineer you can do this particular subject."
>
> *(RISE city actor #14)*

Another RISE city actor identified participatory activities as important opportunities for attracting children to particular fields. They noted that it was important to bring them into these activities early to ensure they develop an interest and understand how to pursue such a career:

> We'd tell them right then, "This is something that you have to work towards, this is the type of studies that you will need to take, if you want to become something like what we do."
>
> *(RISE city actor #15)*

A RISE build team member noted it was important for children to participate in formal co-design activities:

> What I observed on one of the days during the workshop was one adult encouraging the secondary school students to attend, because it would be an eye-opener for them. They would learn a lot of things and get ideas about career opportunities as part of the RISE co-design workshop.
>
> *(RISE build team #4)*

These respondents demonstrated an interest in sharing their own career path with children, seeing these activities as an opportunity to inspire children's study and career paths.

Children Demonstrating Interest in Planning Projects

Several interviewees identified children as the future caretakers of water infrastructure in the RISE program, noting that their participation was critical since they would be responsible for the ongoing management of the water systems. When they observed children showing interest in the development of infrastructure, they focused their interactions on upskilling children in construction and maintenance of the systems. A RISE build team member noted that children's participation in the design process generated interest:

> [The children] would come after the workshops and then they start asking questions. "Oh, if I want to build these things, I should be doing these subjects right?" We noticed that they were really interested, so they're also thinking about their career. I think that's how impressed they were with the system.
>
> *(RISE build team #7)*

Further to this, the RISE build team member identified an unexpected outcome from using children as interpreters when their interpreter was unexpectedly absent. As part of their interpreter roles, the children were given the co-design book to study in advance of the workshop to assist with their interpreting into Hindi. The team member stated:

> Coming back, they started getting interested as they dove into the book, getting to understand it. So, the girl was really interested to becoming an engineer. And I said "Go for it." There's very little women engineers in Fiji, let alone engineers in Fiji. It's a career to go for here, so you've got something here that is your destiny, getting you understanding it now, and as part of your community. It's something that you can also give back; useful for you.
>
> *(RISE build team #7)*

These conversations demonstrate the importance of professionals associated with urban planning engaging with children, through participatory processes, to generate an interest in urban planning and related disciplines as career options.

Urban Planners as Ambassadors for Urban Planning

The language specialists use, and how they engage in a way that resonates with children, proved to be important for generating interest. Some interviewees noted the fun children have when they engage. One RISE researcher noted:

> A pair of rubber gloves is an amazing thing for making a kid feel like a scientist. I think we lost more rubber gloves than anything else because they were helping.
>
> *(RISE researcher #21)*

This comment highlighted how children connect with props associated with professions. This is further demonstrated by another RISE researcher's comments:

> I noticed there were lots of kids and they were very interested in what we were doing and why we were there, and during those initial stages, I brought some equipment along . . . and the kids were really interested . . . and they all crowded around to see what I was doing and they were really interested and engaged with that, so that was kind of cool.
>
> *(RISE researcher #25)*

RISE researcher #21 observed RISE researcher #25 working with the children and highlighted that children's connections to these props developed into improving and sharing their knowledge of that particular profession:

> Having the kids follow him around as he's teaching them, you know, like, "Do you know what these are?" . . . At least a couple of kids went and showed their—went and grabbed a parent. We ended up with a couple of parents there and he ended up talking to them . . . and the kids of course, they're really proud showing . . . you could see the way the knowledge transferred up.
>
> *(RISE researcher #21)*

These examples demonstrate that engaging children in activities as helpers, or other forms of participation, combined with an open and respectful dialogue, provides opportunities to educate children on urban planning career options that can spark their interest, particularly when activities are fun, engaging, and enjoyable.

Urban Planners Increasing Diversity in Planning

Children's participation in urban planning projects has the added benefit of exposing career opportunities, skills, and knowledge development to extremely vulnerable children who generally lack opportunities to engage with professionals. RISE and Artolution expose children from extremely vulnerable environments to career paths that may normally be out of reach.

In this general conversation, a RISE build team member invited one of the older children in an informal settlement to look at the RISE infrastructure. They encouraged children from the informal settlements to continue studying and demonstrated the connection with the development of RISE infrastructure:

> I just asked him, "Do you do science? What is your favorite subject?" I said, "You know you might be able to do something like this as real work?" He was like, "Oh, okay." He goes like, "True?" and I'm like "Yeah, you can do it. So, when we come, if you're free, you should come out and have a look."
>
> *(RISE build team #9)*

An Artolution staff member noted an incident where a child who participated in a project was inspired and encouraged to continue pursuing their interest in urban art:

> They told me after years, "Hey, you remember [name]?" "Yeah, he was one of the sharpest kids." He has saved up [money] which is about two hundred bucks and he wants to buy a second-hand camera because he's been taking pictures on his cell phone . . . he said, "I want to be able to take better pictures. I want to understand this more."
>
> *(Artolution team member #34)*

Artolution team member #34 then described how several of the urban planning specialists continued to support the career development of this child due to their interest in pursuing this field.

These examples demonstrate that participatory processes create an environment for professionals in a variety of urban planning and related disciplines to act as ambassadors for their professions. They further demonstrate that participatory processes can allow urban planning professionals to connect with children, articulate and demonstrate what their discipline entails, generate interest, outline an educational and career path, and potentially provide ongoing mentoring.

Childhood Experiences Influencing Interviewees' Career Choices

Despite interviewees demonstrating little-to-no understanding of their own potential for educational and mentoring impact on children, they occasionally reflected upon influences on their own career choices and what their early experiences mean for how they practice their chosen profession.

Impact of Participatory Processes as a Child

A RISE researcher was quite specific that their participation as a child impacted their decision to become a specialist in the urban planning field—describing in detail the process they had been involved in when they were under the age of 12 and the successful impact of the broader community's participation: "When I was a child, my parents used to take us to local council planning sessions around public space in our neighborhood." They then followed with the comment, "maybe that has influenced my perspectives of who and how people should be engaged, or at least my transition into [urban planning specialist] certainly" (RISE researcher #17). Another RISE researcher identified an immersive experience as a child that influenced their involvement in a similar program as an urban planning specialist:

> So basically, I went there as a teenager . . . it works very differently than the school works . . . it's full of imagination, experimentation . . . you really learn a lot of things in that way that is really close to nature and really close to science. . . . I think maybe if I didn't have that, maybe I would have a different relationship with this [RISE].
>
> *(RISE researcher #23)*

These examples demonstrate that participatory experiences as a child had a profound impact that inspired these interviewees to enter urban planning disciplines and adopt participatory practices. This was true in the case of RISE researcher #23 who identified the impact their experience had on the way they currently operate as an urban planning specialist.

Impact of Mentors as a Child

Other interviewees' responses were less direct, but still identified key childhood memories as influencing their careers, either as a disciplinary choice or how they operated in their chosen discipline. Interaction with adults in positions of power such as teachers factor here. Here, the advice and support from adults like teachers helped them to develop the confidence to pursue something different. A RISE community fieldworker identified the impact a teacher had on her career choices:

> You can become a teacher, a nurse or a lawyer, that's like a common career in our culture. . . . I had this favorite teacher of mine who I—almost every day, she'll see me coming to her office because I liked to get advice from her . . . so, that was like a big boost for me and I'm happy that at some point in life we get to cross paths with the people that really help us get through in life.
>
> *(RISE community fieldworker #11)*

An Artolution staff member highlighted the role of connecting with a particular person as they reflected on their own experience with a teacher who had a profound impact on their career choice:

> This guy was like the coolest guy ever. Right, he'd wear cut offs and like cool band shirts and painting glasses and funky colored socks and Vans shoes. Very, very cool art teacher. He'd wear like a lab coat covered in paint, just the coolest dude ever and I looked at him as a high schooler, I was like 16, just turned 16, newly 16, I'd just had my sixteenth birthday a couple of months after that, and I met him, and I just idolized him. I was like this guy's the coolest guy ever, he had tattoos on his legs. Wow, like it was cool. Had a sleeve or whatever, I was like "I didn't know an art teacher could look like that." . . . And we painted and it was beautiful and I was like "I want to do this for the rest of my life. This is it. I want to be like [my teacher] and I want to do this. This is awesome."
>
> *(Artolution team member #35)*

The detail respondents provided in describing the impact of their mentors demonstrated the profound impact adults can have on children's fields of study and chosen careers.

Enabling Environments

Some interviewees described the importance of an enabling environment from which to pursue their subject-matter interests. An Artolution supporter continues to support children's participation based on their ability to pursue their childhood passion:

> I think that art was meaningful in my own childhood. Although I'm not especially talented at it, I spent a lot of time and I was drawn to it as a child and adolescent.
>
> *(Artolution supporter #38)*

A RISE researcher highlighted the importance of parents and open discussion of interests:

> [My dad's] just one of that generation where, you know 16, go out and get a job sort of situation and so absolutely loves STEM, absolutely loves science. . . . So, I think when he had a [child] who was interested in STEM it was like "Great, I have someone to talk to."
>
> *(RISE researcher #21)*

For some interviewees like RISE researcher #21, these experiences encourage them to pass this passion on to children through their own work. These interviewees identified that they had been free to discuss or pursue their interests in an enabling environment, which gave them freedom to follow their discipline. It also demonstrated the impact of parents who support children pursuing career paths.

These examples highlight that encounters with key adult figures can have long-term impact on children's future career choices or their own professional philosophy and practices in their chosen profession. It also demonstrates the potentially limited understanding children may have of future career options when other professions may be less visible or complicated to understand.

The Role of Urban Planning Education?

Interviewees' responses suggest that children's participation in planning processes may impact their career choices. Several interviewees noted that they first encountered the notion of children's participation in their tertiary studies, which had some bearing on the types of urban planning projects they then practiced, their participatory philosophies, and, in some cases, demonstrated a change in direction in their chosen disciplinary fields. A RISE city actor noted the following:

> So I did a WASH research on a particular community, and on looking at their knowledge, attitude and practice—because my target group were young children between the ages 5–19 and also looking at the adults, so it was 20 years and above . . . so in terms of the responses I got from the younger children from the ages 5–19, comparing to the ones of the adults, I was so interested in the children because they had a lot to give me.
>
> *(RISE city actor #14)*

A RISE researcher noted that their design school emphasized involving all stakeholders on design projects, including children, which has impacted their career focus and how they now teach participation in their discipline at a tertiary level:

> I think with any type of design that you do, even if it's not this type of project, but at least what we learned in the design school in grad school, they were saying that you have to do all the information-gathering with the key stakeholders that you're designing for.
>
> *(RISE researcher #31)*

A RISE build team member also attributed their belief in children's participation in the RISE program to their tertiary studies and explained that they ensure children participate in their work based on the focus on participation in their tertiary education:

> I was doing a bachelor in public health. We did community engagement school projects. . . . [O]ne of our learnings back then was we need to empower these children because children were the future of these communities.
>
> *(RISE build team #8)*

The broad range of disciplines studied by interviewees demonstrate the critical need to embed research into children's participation across multiple disciplines that support the urban planning fields. A number of interviewees entered the urban planning field from other disciplines, such as public health, and their work on transdisciplinary programs requires collective understanding of the impact they can have on children's career choices through participatory processes.

Where to From Here?

Results of these interviews demonstrate that children participating in planning processes can influence children's fields of study, career aspirations, career choices, or how they practice in chosen careers. This study is limited due to the original focus of the interviews and limited number of responses specifically pertaining to discussions on careers. What it does provide however, is some insight into possible methods for attracting future urban planning students and serves as a reminder that children are the future generation that will be tasked with tackling complex human settlement planning. Generating interest in how urban planning can make a difference will help to equip children with the knowledge and skills to positively impact the urban environment.

The responses across the diverse disciplines involved in urban planning processes in these projects provide clues as to how urban planners and practitioners in associated disciplines might influence children to pursue careers in urban planning based on both their childhood experiences, which influenced their own career choices, and the language and activities that sparked children's discussion of career possibilities in the field. Highlighting urban planning as a career option and demystifying the field needs greater participation of children in all aspects of urban planning, including the higher-education sector. As some interviewees suggested that higher education may influence practitioners to involve children in their work, there is scope for incorporating children's participation in higher-education teaching.

Research into children's participation in planning processes needs further focus on the impacts of participatory processes on their career aspirations. It also needs a deeper understanding of the influences on career planners that led to them entering the profession. While further research is needed to develop robust changes in planning education, some initial, simple, and practical recommendations for both practitioners and educators to present urban planning disciplines as a career path for children are as follows:

- Draw on specialists in children's participation in urban planning to support teaching of planning. Specialists in children's participation without an urban planning background can also be used to assist in curricula design in collaboration with urban planning specialists.
- Encourage higher education research into children's participation in all aspects of urban planning.
- Clarify what urban planning professions entail by developing fun, accessible, engaging methods of communication through schools, local councils, and planning processes.

- Use planners as ambassadors for the next generation of planners by ensuring children can easily connect with material components of participatory processes, including language, fashion, cultural aspects, and props.
- Include children in urban planning projects as helpers or drivers of the projects.
- Educate the broader adult population by championing children's participation and the impacts this can have on shaping the urban environment, for example, through industry bodies and mainstream media.
- Provide ongoing mentoring for children interested in pursuing a career in planning.
- Use the many practical manuals for including children in urban planning work.
- Above all, ensure that all people and practices adhere to child-protection policies.

Notes

1 A semi-systematic review (a narrative review using systematic methods) was used to present a condensed summary of a broad range of literature on this topic and generate a deeper understanding of the state of current knowledge resulting in a critical perspective that creates an agenda for further research (Green et al., 2006; Snyder, 2019).

The study used this approach to utilize the benefits of the interpretive approach of a narrative review beyond simply an accumulation of knowledge but incorporating systematic practices to improve transparency and create a replicable approach (Bryman, 2012; pp. 109–111; Snyder, 2019). The study also used the method to determine critical themes and ultimately a research agenda (Green et al., 2006; Mansfield et al., 2021).

2 The doctoral research study seeks to identify the core problem leading to children's exclusion from planning processes for vulnerable settings and examines this through a series of case studies chosen to best identify, examine in detail, and present recommendations for a way forward. Qualitative interviews have been conducted with urban planning decision-makers to determine the factors that lead to the inclusion or exclusion of children in the development of the built environment in case studies spanning post-disaster reconstruction, informal settlements, refugee, and IDP settlements. The locations of settlements for which respondents are responsible include Australia, Ecuador, Fiji, Bangladesh, Uganda, Colombia, and the United States. Ultimately, the research is designed to position children as active citizens in civil society, as well as to propose recommendations to mainstream their participation and agency in urban planning processes for vulnerable settings to achieve Sustainable Development Goal 11.

3 Where the identification of a specific discipline might reveal the identity of an interviewee, their discipline has been changed to RISE build team, RISE city actor, RISE researcher, RISE community fieldworker, Artolution team member, and Artolution supporter to preserve their anonymity, using terms as per the ethics approval application.

References

Ataol, Ö., Krishnamurthy, S., & van Wesemael, P. (2019). Children's participation in urban planning and design: A systematic review. *Children, Youth and Environments*, *29*(2), 27–47. https://doi.org/10.7721/chilyoutenvi.29.2.0027

Bartlett, S., Hart, R. A., Satterthwaite, D., de la Barra, X., & Missair, A. (1999). *Cities for children: Children's rights, poverty and urban management*. Earthscan.

Beckett, K. L., & Shaffer, D. W. (2005). Augmented by reality: The pedagogical praxis of urban planning as a pathway to ecological thinking. *Journal of Educational Computing Research*, *33*(1), 31–52. https://doi.org/10.2190%2FD5YQ-MMW6-V0FR-RNJQ

Botchwey, N. D., Johnson, N., O'Connell, L. K., & Kim, A. J. (2019). Including youth in the ladder of citizen participation: Adding rungs of consent, advocacy, and incorporation. *Journal of the American Planning Association*, *85*(3), 255–270. https://doi.org/10.1080/01944363.2019.1616319

Bryman, A. (2012). *Social research methods* (4th ed.). Oxford University Press.

Chatterjee, S. (2005). Children's friendship with place: A conceptual inquiry. *Children Youth and Environments*, *15*(1), 1–26. www.jstor.org/stable/10.7721/chilyoutenvi.15.1.0001

Chawla, L. (2002). "Insight, creativity and thoughts on the environment": Integrating children and youth into human settlement development. *Environment & Urbanization*, *14*(2), 11–22. https://doi.org/10.1177%2F095624780201400202

Chawla, L. (2015). Benefits of nature contact for children. *Journal of Planning Literature*, *30*(4), 433–452. https://doi.org/10.1177%2F0885412215595441

Chawla, L., & Heft, H. (2002). Children's competence and the ecology of communities: A functional approach to the evaluation of participation. *Journal of Environmental Psychology*, *22*(1–2), 201–216. https://doi.org/10.1006/jevp.2002.0244

Derr, V., Chawla, L., & Mintzer, M. (2018). *Placemaking with children and youth: Participatory practices for planning sustainable communities*. New Village Press. https://doi.org/10.2307/j.ctvwrm51q

Derr, V., & Kovács, I. G. (2017). How participatory processes impact children and contribute to planning: A case study of neighborhood design from Boulder, Colorado, USA. *Journal of Urbanism: International Research on Placemaking and Urban Sustainability*, *10*(1), 29–48. https://doi.org/10.1080/17549175.2015.1111925

Driskell, D. C. (2002). *Creating better cities with children and youth: A manual for participation*. Earthscan.

Ellis, G., Monaghan, J., & Mcdonald, L. (2015). Listening to "generation Jacobs": A case study in participatory engagement for a child-friendly city. *Children, Youth and Environments*, *25*(2), 107–127. https://doi.org/10.7721/chilyoutenvi.25.2.0107

Francis, M., & Lorenzo, R. (2002). Seven realms of children's participation. *Journal of Environmental Psychology*, *22*(1–2), 157–169. https://doi.org/10.1006/jevp.2001.0248

Freeman, C. (2019). *Children and planning*. Lund Humphries.

Green, B. N., Johnson, C. D., & Adams, A. (2006). Writing narrative literature reviews for peer-reviewed journals: Secrets of the trade. *Journal of Chiropractic Medicine*, *5*(3), 101–117. https://doi.org/10.1016/S0899-3467(07)60142-6

Hart, R. A. (1997). *Children's participation: The theory and practice of involving young citizens in community development and environmental care*. Earthscan and Unicef.

Hart, R. A. (2008). Stepping back from 'the ladder': Reflections on a model of participatory work with children. In A. Reid, B. Jensen, J. Nikel, & V. Simovska (Eds.), *Participation and learning: Perspectives on education and the environment, health and sustainability* (pp. 19–31). Springer. https://doi.org/10.1007/978-1-4020-6416-6_2

Kolne, K., & Lindsay, S. (2020). A systematic review of programs and interventions for increasing the interest and participation of children and youth with disabilities in stem education or careers. *Journal of Occupational Science*, *27*(4), 525–546. https://doi.org/10.1080/14427591.2019.1692692

Kranz-Nagl, R., & Zartler, U. (2009). Children's participation in school and community. In B. Percy-Smith & N. Thomas (Eds.), *A handbook of children and young people's participation: Perspectives from theory and practice* (pp. 164–173). Routledge.

Kylin, M., & Stina, B. (2015). A lawful space for play: Conceptualizing childhood in light of local regulations. *Children, Youth and Environments*, *25*(2), 86–106. https://doi.org/10.7721/chilyoutenvi.25.2.0086

Lave, J., & Wenger, E. (1991). *Situated learning: Legitimate peripheral participation*. Cambridge University Press.

Lúcio, J., & l'Anson, J. (2015). Children as members of a community: Citizenship, participation and educational development—an introduction to the special issue. *European Educational Research Journal*, *14*(2), 129–137. https://doi.org/10.1177%2F1474904115571794

Malone, K. (2015). Children's rights and the crisis of rapid urbanisation: Exploring the United Nations post 2015 sustainable development agenda and the potential role for UNICEF's child friendly cities initiative. *The International Journal of Children's Rights*, *23*(2), 405–424. https://doi.org/10.1163/15718182-02302007

Malone, K., & Hartung, C. (2010). Challenges of participatory practice with children. In B. Percy-Smith & N. Thomas (Eds.), *A handbook of children and young people's participation: Perspectives from theory and practice*. Routledge.

Mansfield, R. G., Batagol, B., & Raven, R. (2021). "Critical agents of change?" Opportunities and limits to children's participation in urban planning. *Journal of Planning Literature*, *36*(2), 170–186. https://doi.org/10.1177%2F0885412220988645

McKoy, D. L., Eppley, A., & Buss, S. (2021). *Planning cities with young people and schools: Forging justice, generating joy*. Routledge.

McKoy, D. L., Stewart, J., & Buss, S. (2015). Engaging students in transforming their built environment via Y-PLAN: Lessons from Richmond, California. *Children, Youth and Environments*, *25*(2), 229–244. https://doi.org/10.7721/chilyoutenvi.25.2.0229

McKoy, D. L., & Vincent, J. M. (2007). Engaging schools in urban revitalization: The Y-PLAN (Youth—plan, learn, act, now!). *Journal of Planning Education and Research*, *26*(4), 389–403. https://doi.org/10.1177/0739456X06298817

Nordström, M., & Wales, M. (2019). Enhancing urban transformative capacity through children's participation in planning. *Ambio*, *48*(5), 507–514. tps://doi.org/10.1007/s13280-019-01146-5

O'Donnell, V. L., & Tobbell, J. (2007). The transition of adult students to higher education: Legitimate peripheral participation in a community of practise? *Adult Education Quarterly*, *57*(4), 312–328. https://doi.org/10.1177%2F0741713607302686

Oliver, M., Witten, K., Kearns, R. A., Mavoa, S., Badland, H. M., Carroll, P., Drumheller, C., Tavae, N., Asiasiga, L., Jelley, S., Kaiwai, H., Opit, S., Lin, En-Yi, J., Sweetsur, P., Barnes, H. M., Mason, N., & Ergler, C. (2011). Kids in the city study: Research design and methodology. (Study protocol)(Report). *BMC Public Health*, *11*, 587. https://doi.org/10.1186/1471-2458-11-587

Palazzo, D., Hollstein, L., & Diko, S. K. (2021). Urban planning as a career preference for students: Efforts to improve awareness about the profession. *Planning, Practice & Research*, *36*(2), 174–192. https://doi.org/10.1080/02697459.2020.1782056

Rinke, C. R., Mawhinney, L., & Park, G. (2014). The apprenticeship of observation in career contexts: A typology for the role of modeling in teachers' career paths. *Teachers and Teaching, Theory and Practice*, *20*(1), 92–107. https://doi.org/10.1080/13540602.2013.848517

RISE. (2017). *Revitalising informal settlements and their environments*. www.rise-program.org/

Rochera, M. J., Merino, I., Oller, J., & Coll, C. (2019). Children's and adolescents' specific interest in science and technology, participation in out-of-school activities and inclination to become scientists. *Journal of Science Education and Technology*, *28*(4), 399–413. https://doi.org/10.1007/s10956-019-09776-w

Sancar, F. H., & Severcan, Y. C. (2010). Children's places: Rural–urban comparisons using participatory photography in the Bodrum peninsula, turkey. *Journal of Urban Design*, *15*(3), 293–324. https://doi.org/10.1080/13574809.2010.487808

Severcan, Y. C. (2015). Planning for the unexpected: Barriers to young people's participation in planning in disadvantaged communities. *International Planning Studies*, *20*(3), 251–269. https://doi.org/10.1080/13563475.2014.985195

Shier, H. (2015). Children as researchers in Nicaragua: Children's consultancy to transformative research. *Global Studies of Childhood*, *5*(2), 206–219. https://doi.org/10.1177/2043610615587798

Spencer, C., & Woolley, H. (2000). Children and the city: A summary of recent environmental psychology research. *Child: Care, Health and Development*, *26*(3), 181–198. https://doi.org/10.1046/j.1365-2214.2000.00125.x

Snyder, H. (2019). Literature review as a research methodology: An overview and guidelines. *Journal of Business Research*, *104*, 333–339. https://doi.org/10.1016/j.jbusres.2019.07.039

Tsevreni, I. (2011). Towards an environmental education without scientific knowledge: An attempt to create an action model based on children's experiences, emotions and perceptions about their environment. *Environmental Education Research*, *17*(1), 53–67. https://doi.org/10.1080/13504621003637029

Tummons, J. (2018). *Learning architectures in higher education: Beyond communities of practice*. Bloomsbury Academic.

United Nations. (2020). *Sustainable development goals knowledge platform: Goal 11*. https://sustainabledevelopment.un.org/sdg11

United Nations General Assembly. (1989). *Convention on the rights of the child, 1577 C.F.R.* General Assembly resolution 44/25. www.ohchr.org/en/instruments-mechanisms/instruments/convention-rights-child

United Nations Human Settlement Program. (2015). *International guidelines on urban and territorial planning*. https://unhabitat.org/international-guidelines-on-urban-and-territorial-planning

17
TOWN AND GOWN PARTNERSHIPS FOR YOUTH ENGAGEMENT AND DIVERSITY IN THE PLANNING PROFESSION

Evangeline Linkous, Melissa Zornitta, and Melissa Dickens

The Tampa Bay region—located in south-central Florida along the Gulf Coast—is an important center for planning and development activities and professionals. Planning is integral to the success of the community because it is one of the fastest-growing regions in the country. The Hillsborough County City-County Planning Commission (hereafter Plan Hillsborough) is the lead public agency charged with long-range planning for the greater Tampa area, including Hillsborough County, the City of Tampa, Plant City, and the City of Temple Terrace. The leading professional-planning membership organization in the area is the Sun Coast Section of the Florida Chapter of the American Planning Association (APA Sun Coast), the largest section of the APA in Florida with approximately 600 members. The major university in the Tampa Bay area is the University of South Florida (USF). USF started its Master of Urban and Regional Planning (MURP) program in 2009, which earned accreditation with the Planning Accreditation Board (PAB) in 2020. The MURP program enjoys strong support from the Tampa Bay professional planning community, who value a local graduate planning program as an important resource for filling talent needs.

These organizations—Plan Hillsborough, APA Sun Coast, and USF MURP—regularly collaborate to support regional planning initiatives and are especially active in efforts to foster greater and more-diverse engagement around community planning and development topics. This chapter focuses on two town-and-gown partnerships—defined here as university and community collaborative initiatives—specifically targeted toward growing planning education awareness. One is the Future Leaders in Planning (FLiP) program, an educational-enrichment summer program for high-school students that highlights planning as a career opportunity while providing broad exposure to planning activities in Tampa Bay. The second is the Mentor a Planning Student (MAPS) program for USF MURP students that provides graduate planning students with exposure to professional planners and their work environments while growing awareness of, and relationships between, the USF MURP program and professional planning organizations in the community.

This chapter presents information about program design, implementation, and outcomes of these approaches to expanding awareness about planning education. It provides replicable models of successful programs for elevating the knowledge of planning within a community. The chapter also demonstrates how such initiatives are mutually beneficial, forging rewarding alliances that enhance local planning institutions, grow diverse engagement with the profession, and foster interest in planning as an educational objective and career choice. The collaborative spirit that supports these initiatives is also expressed in this chapter's authorship, which represents current and past leaders from USF MURP, Plan Hillsborough, and APA Sun Coast.

Future Leaders in Planning (FLiP)

In 2015, planning commissioners for Plan Hillsborough challenged its staff to broaden the agency's award-winning public-education program with a goal of increasing its community presence and enhancing awareness about what the organization does. Given this charge, staff recognized an opportunity to provide outreach that was not project specific and could give back to communities in the county. In addition, Plan Hillsborough did not have a program designed to reach out to youth in the community and saw an opportunity to get input from a different segment of the population.

In response, Plan Hillsborough launched the Future Leaders in Planning (FLiP) program, designed to introduce high-school students to planning as a community resource and a potential career pathway. FLiP is a summer enrichment program organized around an intensive series of speakers, interactive planning activities, and tours on foot, bus, streetcar, and boat. It provides participants with the opportunity to network and learn from planning professionals, connect with other students who share a passion for creating communities, and gain exposure to planning from multiple perspectives, including environmental, historic preservation, community redevelopment, transportation, and more. In order to ensure that the program is accessible to students from all backgrounds, FliP is free to participants.

The program started small with nine high-school students taking part in a two-day program in 2016. In its second year, the program doubled the number of participants and added a third day of programming. By 2018, it grew to 21 students and four days—an approach that continued in 2019. The COVID-19 pandemic forced the cancellation of FliP in 2020, but it resumed in virtual form in 2021. FLiP program highlights in recent years include the following (adapted from Merenda, 2019):

- USF campus master plan and sustainability walking tour, with presentations about USF planning educational pathways from USF MURP faculty and the USF Center for Urban Transportation Research.
- APA Sun Coast presentation on APA student membership and activities.
- Walking tours of City of Tampa parks, including WaterWorks Park, Julian B. Lane Riverfront Park, and Riverwalk Park—winner of the American Planning Association's Great Places in America: People's Choice Award.
- Behind-the-scenes baggage-handling tour of Tampa International Airport with a discussion of the airport's economic development, sustainability efforts, and master plan.
- Tampa TECO Line Streetcar rides, plus a streetcar expansion-study presentation (first time for many on public transit).
- City of Plant City walking tour highlighting planning for a small city.
- Environmental Protection Commission air, water, wetlands, and waste division employee talks with tours of air, benthic, and chemistry labs.
- Port Tampa Bay master plan and economic development boat tour.
- MacDill Air Force Base planning tour.
- Historic Ybor City Then, Now and Tomorrow walking tour.
- Urban Land Institute (ULI) Tampa Bay Building Healthy Communities presentation and interactive planning exercise.

As is evident, the program relies on partnerships with numerous local organizations. Critically, these partners provide the financial and in-kind support that enable Plan Hillsborough to offer the program free of charge to youth participants. Hillsborough County Public Schools oversees the

Figure 17.1 FLiP Participants Tour Tampa's Historic Ybor City

student application and selection process and provides transportation to program destinations not served by public transportation. Private planning firms, as well as professional organizations like APA Sun Coast and ULI Tampa Bay, provide programming and sponsorship support. As part of their outreach efforts, staff from the area's local governments and agencies offer tours and talks. Although Plan Hillsborough administers FLiP through coordination of these various activities, this partnership-based approach minimizes the staffing burden and ensures a rich mix of activities that expose high school students to the rich diversity of the planning field.

Parents are invited to attend the program's closing planning activity conducted in partnership with ULI Tampa Bay. Typically organized as a charette, ULI Tampa Bay volunteers lead students in identifying potential planning solutions for real-world planning problems. Most recently, students developed concepts for integrating a new baseball stadium within Tampa's historic Ybor City neighborhood. This hands-on final activity allows students to work in teams, collaborate with planning professionals, prepare a final presentation, and hone their public-speaking skills. In addition to providing an opportunity for students to showcase their newly acquired planning abilities, this event connects parents to local planners and community initiatives. Everyone leaves knowing what a comprehensive plan and long-range transportation plan are and how to engage with the local planning process. Upon completion of the program, students evaluate each phase of the program and comment on whether they are considering a career in planning.

Several elements are integral to ensuring FLiP is sustainable and successful. Foremost is the team of partners who provide program content, transportation, and financial support. Second, it is important to involve young professionals with whom students can relate to as chaperones and activity facilitators. Plan Hillsborough involves its USF MURP student interns, who offer relatability and

Figure 17.2 FLiP Participants at ULI Tampa Bay-Led Charette Activity

insights about planning education. Third, inviting parents to student presentations extends the program's reach. Finally, participants need snacks, good meals, comfortable shoes, water, and sunscreen. With these elements in place, the FLiP program yields numerous impacts: networking and presentations skills are honed, public transit is tried, friendships are made, mentorships emerge, citizen participation in communities is encouraged, passion for planning ignited, and young lives are forever impacted.

FLiP's success has resulted in recent efforts to extend the model to younger audiences. In 2019, Plan Hillsborough was approached to assist the Tampa Heights Junior Civic Association (THJCA) with youth summer camps. THJCA is a community organization that works to connect residents and youth in a historically African American neighborhood to community resources and opportunities. To create a fun and engaging educational experience for the mostly elementary and middle-school youth participating in THJCA summer camps, Plan Hillsborough staff used a Box City exercise—a curriculum model that engages students in city design by decorating and strategically placing boxes to form a neighborhood. Billed as FLiP Jr., the summer camp also introduced students to land use, community planning, and the Vision Zero safety program. This collaboration was very successful, and Plan Hillsborough is working with THJCA to make the FLiP Jr. program a permanent partnership offered as part of THJCA summer enrichment camps in three locations, expanding FLiP's reach to additional communities that THJCA is active in. It will be open to youth ages 6–16 and serve approximately 40 students.

Youth are major stakeholders in planning. They have a unique perspective on their communities and are often among the populations most impacted by local planning initiatives. Education of young people about planning is important to help them have a voice in the planning process and build their civic and community awareness. The commitment of the Plan Hillsborough staff to the goal of increasing awareness among youth about planning has been the key success factor for FLiP and FLiP Jr. Additionally, leveraging community partners, who serve as invaluable speakers and sponsors to the program, has allowed these programs to grow and thrive.

Figure 17.3   FLiP Jr. Participants Share Their Model Cities

Mentor a Planning Student

In 2014, USF MURP launched a mentorship program to match graduate planning students to area planning professionals. The decision to launch a mentorship program responded to several driving factors. First, MURP students regularly indicate that the aspects of the program they value most are those that prepare them for, and provide linkages to, career opportunities. Many USF MURP students enter the program with a passion for being part of community and environmental solutions but lack the role models and support networks in the professional-planning world that help smooth the transition to practice. Though committed to planning careers, many students have questions about which discipline within the field they will enjoy working in, whether to go into public or private practice, and similar career-readiness concerns. Although internships and community-engaged coursework provide students with exposure to the working world, students know that they may be evaluated both for grades and future employment in these forums. USF MURP recognized the need to provide students with an opportunity to build relationships, ask questions, and feel out their career path in a more informal context.

Second, USF MURP sought to provide a resource that could address broader efforts within the planning profession to promote a diverse and inclusive community of practice. The APA offers a set of recommendations for increasing diversity in the planning profession, which includes the creation of mentoring programs and making planners from diverse backgrounds more visible so that young people can see more people like themselves in leadership positions (Vazquez, 2002). USF MURP is home to a diverse group of students, including many who are first-generation college students, BIPOC, LGBTQ+, veterans, and non-traditional students. USF MURP faculty felt that a mentorship program could respond to the APA's guidance and help support students interested in cultivating relationships with professional planners with similar backgrounds.

Finally, MURP faculty recognized there was limited awareness about the still-young USF MURP program among area planning professionals—a dynamic that could limit program recruitment, job and internship placements, and engaged learning opportunities. A mentorship program provides a platform for an ongoing town-and-gown dialogue. Professional planners value the opportunity to better understand and connect to what's being taught in planning programs and interact with emerging planning professionals. Through a mentorship model, the professional community better understands, values, and participates in planning education. Fostering these shared values helps forge new institutional capacities and engagement in support of planning education that expand opportunities for students, planning organizations, and employers alike.

With these factors in mind, MURP faculty reached out to the Florida Chapter of APA to bring their Mentor a Planning Student (MAPS) program to USF. First launched at Florida State University (FSU), the goals of MAPS are as follows (American Planning Association, Florida Chapter, 2021):

- To expose students to the actual work environments, responsibilities, and interactions of professional planning positions in Florida.
- To bring students into a mentor relationship with a practicing public- or private-sector planner in the region.
- To help planning students begin to develop their professional career networks.
- To further facilitate the relationship between university planning programs, APA Florida sections, and planning professionals.

The Florida Chapter of APA helps Florida universities with planning-education programs to work with their local APA sections to implement MAPS. The USF MAPS program operates as a partnership between USF MURP and APA Sun Coast, relying in large part on volunteer time. Students apply for the program via MURP, and MURP faculty work with volunteers from APA Sun Coast to identify volunteer mentors that match student interests. The USF MURP program launches each year in September once students are settled into the new academic year. At that time, students apply for the program via an online application that identifies their goals and interests. Faculty then work with APA Sun Coast volunteers to identify mentor matches. APA Sun Coast also issues an annual call for mentors in their marketing materials. Mentors must be practicing planners with at least three years of experience. MURP faculty reach out to potential mentors to inform them about the program and gauge their interest in participating.

At USF, the MAPS program is designed to run for one academic year, and MURP students may repeat the program and apply for a new mentor in their second year. The program has been modified slightly over the years, most recently as a result of the COVID-19 pandemic, but it essentially incorporates two core requirements. The first is for mentors to review mentee resumés and cover letters, as well as offer professional-development guidance. The second is that mentors and mentees must meet at least three times during the academic year. Although typically these meetings were encouraged to be in person, the pandemic resulted in the increasing use of virtual meetings—a convenient option in a large metropolitan area like Tampa. Though meetings should be tailored to the interests and opportunities particular to each mentor–mentee match, USF MURP suggests an initial "coffee" meeting to get to know each other and establish goals. A second meeting may be an in-office shadowing experience demonstrative of a typical workday. A third meeting may include an out-of-office shadowing experience that highlights fieldwork or engagement with stakeholders or clients.

In addition to these core requirements, mentors and mentees are encouraged to participate in a program kickoff and complete a year-end program evaluation. The program kickoff includes both mentors and mentees, providing an overview of MAPS while creating a structured setting for a first meeting between mentors and mentees. At this time, mentors and mentees are encouraged to identify preferred communication modes and begin drafting a basic work plan for the year. For mentors, the kickoff also provides an opportunity to meet MURP faculty, learn about the USF MURP program, and review MAPS program expectations. At the end of the academic year, participants complete a program-evaluation survey. Mentors are recognized at APA Sun Coast's annual awards ceremony and in APA Sun Coast's newsletters.

USF MURP's MAPS program launched during the 2015–16 academic year and has continued to operate since. Like FLiP, MAPS operates primarily through volunteer participation and in-kind support. MURP faculty and APA Sun Coast volunteers collaborate to review applications, Plan Hillsborough provides space for the kickoff event convenient to area planning professionals, and APA Sun Coast members volunteer their time as mentors.

Implementation of MAPS has yielded valuable lessons about creating and enhancing successful mentorship programs. First is that mentors must lead the experience. Mentees recognize that mentors are potential future employers, as well as busy, important professionals in the field they aspire to work in. This power dynamic means mentees may be sensitive to perceived disinterest or aloofness on the part of the mentor. For this reason, the MURP program encourages mentors to take the lead in reaching out to mentees first and regularly, touch base at least once a month, and take an active role in scheduling meetings.

Second, mentors and mentees should be reminded that, although the program aims to grow student awareness of and networks with the local professional-planning community, it's not a guaranteed pathway to employment. Mentors may not require or encourage students to work as part of the program. Likewise, students should not expect the mentoring relationship to directly yield employment.

A third lesson relates to the importance of emphasizing program boundaries. Both mentors and mentees are busy with professional and personal activities, and the program is intentionally designed to be approachable and workable for those with full plates. The program's clear structure can launch productive working relationships that extend beyond the formal constraints of the program, but also establishes limits where participants can freely move on.

A fourth lesson is that mentees have multiple needs and interests. Although all students are interested in MAPS for professional development, students look to MAPS to help navigate various career concerns. Some seek exposure to different planning disciplines or work environments. Some are new to planning, looking for introductory experiences, while others are homing in on specific jobs to apply for as they prepare for graduation. The USF MURP application asks students to clearly indicate discipline, organization, public/private, and geographic preferences for matches if applicable, but also indicates that general exposure is a great option for the undecided. The application also allows students to indicate if they seek a match for diversity and inclusivity issues such as BIPOC, LGBTQ+, and women in planning. MURP faculty educate both mentees and mentors about the many roles the MAPS program can play in supporting student professional development, and the application encourages students to voice their particular interests so that a suitable match may be identified.

A fifth set of lessons relates to mentor recruitment, retainment, and recognition. USF MURP works with APA Sun Coast to recruit mentors through calls to action in newsletters and on social media. This promotes broad awareness of and participation in the program. However, personal outreach is also essential for success. The ongoing partnership of APA Sun Coast to help identify and reach out to mentors matching student needs is critical for productive relationships among mentors and mentees. Mentors will burn out after a few years of service, so regularly involving new mentors is key to program sustainability. Finally, mentors should be recognized for their contribution to the planning profession. USF MURP works with APA Sun Coast to acknowledge mentors at annual events and in marketing materials.

Finally, the divergent experiences of USF and FSU implementing MAPS indicates that planning mentorship programs can be tailored to different university contexts and resource constraints. For example, FSU is a larger, more established program with a curriculum that encourages students to progress in first- and second-year cohorts. It's based in Tallahassee, a college town with a relatively small, centralized professional-planning sector. FSU indicates it can be challenging for their program to identify a sufficient pool of mentors given their relatively large student body and smaller local planning community. In response to these conditions, the MAPS program at FSU is offered to first-year students only as part of a required course. Because FSU includes MAPS as part of a required course, dedicated faculty time to administer the program is also ensured.

USF and APA Sun Coast adapted MAPS to fit the USF and Tampa Bay context but retained the overall program goals and design. In contrast to FSU, USF MURP has a relatively small student body with a flexible curriculum aimed in part at working professionals and thus not organized by cohort. USF and APA Sun Coast serve the sprawling Tampa Bay area, so students and professionals come from numerous organizations spread across a large metropolitan area. USF opted to make its program voluntary, open to students who want to take advantage of the opportunity, while allowing flexibility for students who are already working in planning, challenged by long commutes, or otherwise want to forgo participation. MURP's relatively small size, combined with strong support for the program from the large planning sector in the area, means the program can be offered to students in more than one year. This option appeals to students who seek to gain insights from professionals with experience in diverse planning disciplines, and to find out more about planning experiences across public and private sectors. At USF, MAPS relies on volunteers from faculty and APA Sun Coast. The large local professional base in the Tampa Bay area helps makes this model work in terms of the mentor volunteers. However, as USF MURP continues to grow, the program is looking at models where faculty service can be better supported, such as through incorporating MAPS into a class or internship.

In the exit survey for the program, both mentors and mentees report that the MAPS experience is valuable and educational. Mentors value the program for connecting them to new ideas and future talent, and for the intangible rewards of mentoring. A few exceptional MAPS mentors have participated each year since it started. The program also regularly attracts new mentors, providing a valuable way to connect the MURP program with the local planning community on an ongoing basis. In recent years, MURP alumni who were mentored in the program's early years have become eligible to serve as mentors. Perspectives from mentors and mentees are featured in Box 17.1.

Box 17.1 Mentor and Mentee Perspectives on MAPS

Mentee

My MAPS mentorship irrevocably integrated me into Tampa Bay's planning scene and eventually helped me secure a position on the Citizens Advisory Committee at the county planning commission. Although my mentor's knowledge was extensive—and great to call upon as I was going through school—the experience benefited me most because of the connections and network it provided. I was able to become acquainted with public servants and consultants, and that has helped me significantly in job hunting, winning work, and cooperating publicly. I hope to one day inspire young planners in the MAPS program and serve as a connection the way my mentor served me, and I look forward to encouraging them to "aim high in hope and work," to quote Burnham.

The MAPS program showed me the wide variety of roles a planner can play in the field. My mentors included a county transportation planner and, in a separate year of the program, a transportation planner with a nonprofit. Both worked in transportation, but their roles and responsibilities were very different. That kind of insight is valuable when considering the path you'd like to take in the profession. The MAPS program was my first experience with planning outside of the classroom, and it really opened my eyes to what the profession looked like on a daily basis. It also helped foster wonderful connections to professional planners. I'm happy to say that I now work under my former mentor at her agency, so the program facilitated my desire to explore the public side of planning.

Mentor

As a planner with over 30 years of public service, I have found the enthusiasm and fresh perspectives these students bring to an issue to be of equal value to the knowledge we are able to bestow to them about our profession. It gives me great solace that the next generation of planners will be better educated and trained, have improved tools and—in part as a result of this program—the needed experience to achieve the development goals of our local communities and hometowns. As such, I have found it to be a greatly rewarding experience to mentor students in USF's MAPS program.

The USF MURP MAPS program has helped my firm and I stay connected with up-and-coming planners. As a mentor, it has been interesting to find connections between what is currently being taught in graduate planning schools and the types of projects planners are working on in their day-to-day experience. It has also been a nice way to introduce mentees to topic areas they might not traditionally learn in school such as freight planning. I hope that this program continues, and I am always happy to support it as a mentor!

Mentee as a Student and Mentor as Alumni

As someone who has played the role of both mentee and mentor in the USF MAPS program, I have only amazing things to say about it. As a mentee who was still trying to discover what field of planning I wanted to pursue, being connected to planning experts in my areas of interest was instrumental in helping me determine my path. Now I serve as a mentor myself and am thoroughly enjoying the experience and benefiting greatly from staying connected to the USF MURP program through its motivated and passionate students.

Although job matching and placement are not parts of the program, MAPS enhances the networks of both planning students and professionals, which can assist with future employment opportunities for students and recruitment for employers. The program introduces students to major area employers—a benefit valued by all students and one that can open new doors for the many USF MURP students that are first-generation college students lacking an established professional circle. Employers are also able to get to know students and learn more about the forthcoming talent pool of emerging planners.

MAPS has garnered recognition and served as a model nationally. APA featured the MAPS program in a blog post and video series, as well as a 2019 national-conference presentation. Other state chapters of APA and universities have reached out to USF MURP faculty and APA Sun Coast leadership for guidance on creating similar programs in their states. The program has also expanded in Florida, with Florida Atlantic University launching its own MAPS program in 2017 in partnership with the Broward and Treasure Coast Sections of the APA.

Finally, although MAPS is not solely a diversity initiative, it is an integral part of creating opportunities for emerging planners from all backgrounds and exposing them to the value of the profession. A USF MURP class of 2022 student shared how being mentored through MAPS created a foundation for her work supporting the FLiP Jr. program working as an intern with Plan Hillsborough (see Box 17.2).

> **Box 17.2   USF MURP Class of 2022 Student Experience**
>
> After graduating with my bachelor's, I was looking for work and was feeling lost in my career direction. I found my mentor on LinkedIn, and we ended up having a meeting where he convinced me to pursue planning and to apply to the MURP program at USF! As luck would have it, he ended up becoming my mentor in the MAPS program! Through the MAPS program, not only did I get the opportunity to learn more about him and his work, but he also helped me to explore my own interests as well. Together we volunteered every week at a local community garden where we had conversations that ended up catalyzing my passion for food system work. Because of this program, I not only got priceless networking experience and knowledge, but also learned a lot about myself and my own path.
>
> Because of my mentor through the MAPS program, I truly became more confident and enthusiastic about the work I am doing. He showed me that planning work doesn't stop when you leave the office, and the importance of continually engaging with the local community. I really put this newfound knowledge to work with my participation in the FLiP Jr. Program. I was able to become a mentor myself for children that were coming from neighborhoods that have been historically disadvantaged. The first couple of weeks in the program were a challenge in finding ways to connect to children who were dealing with serious issues that were honestly bigger than planning. But, because we were there consistently at least once a week, the children began to open up and become engaged. I think the most impactful portion of the program, for both myself and the kids, was the beautification project we did at the Tampa Heights Junior Civic Association. The children planted and painted flower boxes, did some landscaping, and worked together to paint a beautiful mural of one of the girls in the program. Even the older kids were so invested and didn't want to stop when time was up! We also took the kids on a field trip to County Center to meet Plan Hillsborough planners. Before we left for the trip, we showed the kids how to be advocates through collaborating in small groups to come up with reasons why they would like the trolley to expand into their neighborhood. We ended up riding the trolley to county center where the kids were able to speak to our Executive Director to tell her the reasons they had come up with to expand the trolley. It was a great exercise to show the children the power that they have as citizens and residents of their community. Overall, I am extremely grateful for being a part of the MAPS program as it has really helped to create who I am as a planner and individual today.

Related Efforts

USF MURP, APA Sun Coast, and Plan Hillsborough are involved in several related initiatives that complement FLiP and MAPS to support planning education awareness and growing engagement with the profession.

Based on the successful launch of MAPS, APA Sun Coast developed the Career Advancement for Mid-Level Planners (CAMPs) program. CAMPs supports the ongoing advancement of planning skills through targeted coaching of planners with five or more years of professional experience. CAMPs participants aim to grow their careers and have diverse objectives such as enhancing leadership capabilities, increasing their network size and quality, or becoming a more effective planner. CAMPS coaches are recognized area planning leaders identified by APA Sun Coast leadership. Less structured than MAPS, CAMPS requires the mid-level planner to identify a viable goal for the program, and coaches commit to supporting that goal through collaboratively identified activities. Now in its fourth year, the CAMPs program has matched 18 mid-career planners and coaches for a total of 36 participants. Though geared at those already in the profession, CAMPs provides a model approach to retaining community planning talent, supporting planners who are underrepresented within the profession, and affirming the importance of role models and service in support of planning education.

At the state level, APA Florida goes beyond the MAPS program to support planning education for youth. Another APA Florida youth planning education initiative was the development of a set of teaching guides that are available for download and use from their website. Designed to educate kindergarten through high-school students about how communities are planned, they help planners reach out to educators and prepare materials for classroom use. The guides include an agenda and step-by-step curriculum linked to grade-appropriate Common Core educational standards, with materials including PowerPoint presentations, handouts, posters, and games. Some specific lessons and activities include how to make a map, creating a book about community assets, and participating in a mock-planning commission. The guides come in four versions: Kindergarten–Grade 2, Grades 3–5, middle school, and high school. Both APA Sun Coast members and Plan Hillsborough staff regularly use these materials as part of the Great American Teach-In—a day where professionals share information about their careers with school children—as well as at other educational outreach efforts.

As part of its mission to ensure that planning professionals are knowledgeable about and engaged with planning education, MURP launched an advisory committee in 2019. The MURP Advisory Committee Guidelines (University of South Florida Master of Urban and Regional Planning Program, 2020) identify four purposes for the group:

- Periodically and objectively review and advise the MURP program on curriculum and professional development activities.
- Provide advice and support to the MURP program director, faculty, staff, and students on issues relating to program education, strategic vision, and research.
- Serve as a voice, advocate, and ambassador for MURP to its various constituents and stakeholders, including the planning community, research sponsors, agencies, industry, alumni, and colleagues.
- Help identify and connect MURP with new potential programming sponsors and prospects for philanthropic support that would provide additional resources to enhance student success such as scholarships and enhancements to current environments and infrastructure.

Membership includes representatives from area planning agencies, alumni, and community stakeholders. Members serve for two-year terms, renewable one time—a rotation that ensures that new voices are being heard and that a broad cross-section of the community takes part in the mission of increasing awareness about the importance of planning education.

MURP faculty meetings with the MURP Advisory Committee have created productive, informative exchanges. The Advisory Committee has indicated an especially strong interest in better understanding how engaged-research collaborations work, a call that MURP faculty are responding to through efforts to provide information about the semester schedule cycle and creation of a more robust planning studio program. Such efforts continue to grow interactions and awareness building about planning education in the community. In 2021, the advisory committee launched a fundraising effort to support a diversity scholarship for a MURP student with preference given to diverse students from historically underrepresented or marginalized groups.

Finally, USF MURP students have developed two fun platforms that foster awareness about planning education and the planning profession. Both are efforts of the Student Planning Organization, which is open to any USF undergraduate, graduate, or non-degree-seeking students. Though USF's planning program is a master's-only program, the Student Planning Organization works to involve the broader USF student community in planning-related social and educational initiatives. The first is the Dine-and-Learn series, launched in 2016 to enhance student awareness of professional-planning opportunities and support networking. The Student Planning Organization uses USF student-organization funds to invite area planning professionals to dinner on campus, where students can informally engage with them about their careers. Professional participants report enjoying the opportunity to meet with MURP students and learn about the program. During the COVID-19 pandemic, this popular program was necessarily on hiatus, prompting students to innovate and create a new online-interview series through which the Student Planning Organization identifies area planning professionals to be interviewed by MURP students. The interview series is open to the public and promoted on social media, allowing for broader community reach. It helps maintain fresh relationships between community planning professionals and graduate students, enhances recruitment efforts, and raises awareness about planning education and professional opportunities.

Conclusion

This chapter highlights the collaborative work of three Tampa Bay area planning organizations—the USF MURP program, Plan Hillsborough, and APA Sun Coast—to address the challenge of increasing community engagement around planning education and the profession. The strategies discussed here create an effective foundation for planning-education awareness among youth, prospective planning students, the community, and professional planners. These collaborative efforts also underscore how the work of diverse planning institutions provides critical value and synergies that go beyond any one organization. The recruitment efforts of universities help create stronger professional-planning associations and agencies, while the outreach efforts of those organizations provide meaningful experiences that augment planning-education programs. These efforts also highlight the importance of volunteerism and partnerships when resources to support such initiatives may be limited within a single organization. Such collaborations communicate to youth and emerging planners that there is a rich and inclusive pathway in the planning field, one that can change lives in the community just as it creates personal opportunities.

Acknowledgements

The authors would like to thank Lynn Merenda for her valuable insights about the FLiP program.

References

American Planning Association, Florida Chapter. (2021). *Mentor a planning student.* https://florida.planning.org/career-center-professional-resources/maps/

Merenda, L. (2019, Spring). How Hillsborough's high school students have FLiPped over potential planning careers. *Florida Planning*, 16–17. https://planhillsborough.org/wp-content/uploads/2019/07/How-Hillsboroughs-High-School-students-have-FLiPped-over-potential-planning-careers-FLPlanningAPANewletter-Spring2019.pdf

University of South Florida Master of Urban and Regional Planning Program. (2020). *MURP advisory committee guidelines.* University of South Florida Master of Urban and Regional Planning Program.

Vazquez, L. (2022, July 22). Diversity and the planning profession. *Planners Network.* www.plannersnetwork.org/2002/07/diversity-and-the-planning-profession/

SECTION III

Planning Education Awareness

Cultivating urban planning awareness in children and youth through Design and Planning Language Programs (DPLPs) establishes an avenue to create interest in planning as a potential college focus and eventually as a career. Such programs, some of which have been rendered in Section II, not only plant seeds of interest in potential students but also educate their relatives, teachers, counselors, and the general public on the need for urban planning professionals. The programs often provide information to those individuals who might have direct or indirect roles in advocating, recommending, or endorsing future educational and professional choices for children and youth.

While children, youth, and high schoolers are center stage for these activities, other groups, such as college students, might also take advantage of compelling initiatives promoting the significance of planning. Many professionals and academics can relate to how difficult it can be to attract students into planning programs or simply explain to current college students what urban planners can achieve. This difficulty makes it challenging to offer prospective and current college students an informed knowledge of the profession to help them choose planning for their careers. This final section covers experiences and reflections around the issue of planning awareness in several international academic environments—from the United States, Nigeria, Namibia, and India—in addition to a self-reflection on how planners, through contradictions and conflicts, perceive their roles in our current society.

The opening chapter by Savis Gohari explores awareness of the planning profession and the role of urban planners in substantiating its current and potential relevance and impacts on society. To get authentic insights, contribute to current and future advancements, and enhance public awareness about the urban planning profession, the author uses the free, voice-based social-media app Clubhouse to elicit opinions about the profession. Participants suggest that urban planning overlaps with many disciplines, and to be able to survive, it needs to create added value. Here, planning education can contribute to preparing future planners to decide which role they want to play in the built environment by developing a deeper understanding of their field, adopting a reflective and critical approach, and seeing problems and solutions in context.

The chapter by Dohyung Kim explores undergraduate planning students' motivations for and perspectives on planning education and the profession by surveying undergraduates in the department of Urban and Regional Planning at California State Polytechnic University, Pomona, in the United States. The survey data confirms general observations such as students' late exposure to urban planning and financial barriers to postbaccalaureate education. It also identifies planning subjects that align with younger generations' interests, students' preference for public-sector jobs, and bachelor's degree programs as the pipeline for master's programs. Identified opportunities for increasing interest include scholarships for youth, visibility on media that youth are familiar with, and recruitment events for community college and university students. This chapter also emphasizes faculty diversity and mentorship programs as important for students' career development.

Carlton Basmajian and Francis Owusu explore the changes introduced at Iowa State University's undergraduate planning program to tackle declining enrollment and lack of student engagement. In 2012, the Community and Regional Planning department took steps to expand the number of students studying planning, including increasing points of entry into the program, streamlining the curriculum, developing new introductory courses, establishing new minors, and building advising relationships with other departments. The result was increased enrollment in the program and individual courses, high levels of engagement among students, and lessons for other programs desiring increased program awareness.

Kwame N. Owusu-Daaku and Mackenzie Devine assess the extent to which an introductory urban planning course offered to environmental science students at the University of West Florida department of Earth and Environmental Science influenced their consideration of urban planning as a field of study and/or career choice. Among other factors, participating in a real-life team-based course project positively influenced respondents' considerations of becoming urban planners. The authors used survey responses and follow-up interviews and found that respondents expressed interest in taking additional planning courses after the introductory one. Hence, planning educators in non-planning programs can use their courses to raise awareness of planning as a graduate discipline or future profession.

The Alabama City Year Program (ACYP), managed by the Master of Community Planning program at Auburn University in the United States, provides an integrated framework of community engagement, offering experiential learning to planning students and benefiting local communities while serving the program's outreach mission. Binita Mahato, Sweta Byahut, and Jay Mittal describe how ACYP helps increase planning awareness in underserved communities, generates interest among students via active learning, and benefits student recruitment. The initiative provides an adaptable framework for small planning programs. The chapter discusses the opportunities and challenges of the evolving ACYP and describes a way forward for establishing a successful service-learning initiative that benefits all stakeholders.

David S. Osiyi and Victor U. Onyebueke examine the career choices of university applicants in Nigeria with a comparative focus on urban planning vis-à-vis contemporary popular courses. They use national and university data to understand and interpret students' career preferences, planning awareness, and enrollments in Nigeria. The results show a student-application ratio of 1:31 for planning against the most popular courses. This gap stems from perceived differences in employment prospects, job internationalization, social prestige, and so forth. Imaginative approaches for rejuvenating interests in planning and increasing enrollment are recommended.

Eric Yankson discusses how spatial-planning education awareness can be enhanced in sub-Saharan Africa based on observations from Namibia. He asserts that networking among planners, public engagement, marketing of planning programs, and accreditation by national or international experts are all pivotal. The involvement of current students in community-based projects and the impacts of planners on local development are also crucial. Finally, the author stresses the importance of internationalization in Namibian planning education—particularly from cross-border countries. Overall, the chapter articulates the creation of planning-education awareness as a multifaceted endeavor encompassing diverse actors, including academics, planning professionals, communities, and non-governmental organizations.

Bhargav Adhvaryu and Bhavesh Joshi provide a context for, and a brief historical overview of, urban planning in India. The authors establish the need for planners, explain the role of planners in the Indian context, and discuss desirable skills for planners and planning education in India.

Strategies to create and increase public awareness of planning and to make planning more mainstream are discussed, starting with a case study. Two interviews with expert planning practitioners who have extensive experience in the Indian context support the general discourse.

As the chapters in Section III suggest, it is important to have enough educated professionals to tackle the current and emergent challenges of cities. Therefore, improving the attractiveness of planning programs is pivotal. A broader appreciation of what urban planners do to deal with the challenges that cities and communities face today and those that will emerge in the future is imperative. Addressing the need for planning professionals and broader appreciation of the profession will not happen without explicit dedication and interventions to increase cognizance of it. Since the profession isn't well known among children and youth, and not well appreciated by college students and the general population, promoting awareness about the profession—both in practice and education—will require tremendous efforts. These interventions need to start with the agents who provide the space for imparting urban planning knowledge to the next generation—city and regional planning departments and their regulating bodies, such as national associations and accreditation boards.

18
SHAPING AWARENESS ABOUT PLANNING BY HELPING PLANNERS TO BECOME MORE MINDFUL AND CRITICAL ABOUT THEIR IDENTITY, ROLE, AND CONTEXT

Savis Gohari

The challenges of our modern society, such as poverty, poor air and water quality, inequality, climate change, and high energy consumption, exacerbated by increasing urban populations, underscore the need for the urban planning profession to direct and manage the development of cities. Unfortunately, the profession is not well known among the general population, and youth usually do not consider it as a potential career path (Palazzo et al., 2020). On the other hand, planning is a unique profession that cannot be explained in a single and narrow definition fitted into a single entity or category. People can't fully agree on what it really is (Abukhater, 2009). Environmentalists, architects, civil engineers, advocates, or even developers can call themselves planners—and their interests can be varied or contradictory. This happens because there is an overlap between planning and other disciplines. There is also some confusion about the purpose, role, and task of planning as a profession because planning tends to borrow ideas and principles from other practices (Allmendinger & Tewdwr-Jones, 2002). Moreover, planners experience difficulties in asserting themselves effectively because they serve in a variety of conflicting roles, representing different constituencies—often functioning as staff member, analyst, arbiter, and/or advocate (Peiser, 1990). For the survival of the planning discipline, planners need to express how their profession contributes to the improvement and development of their communities, that is, what their added value and societal impacts are. While mapping the realms that planning intersects is a crucial step to take, planning educators and practitioners also need to engage in a broader discussion of what urban planners' role is in the new and emerging economy (Ozawa & Seltzer, 1999) and urbanism (Watson, 2007).

The discourse over the role of the planner has a long history in the planning field. It is affected by changing societal needs as well as planners' changing perceptions of the role of planning in addressing these needs (Burchell & Sternlieb, 1978; Briassoulis, 1999). As Faludi (1973) argued, understanding the nature of planning is also a challenge of constructing an image of the role of planners. Connell (2010) also finds in his study on the nature of underlying differences among contemporary schools of planning that the envisioned role of the planner often stands out as the defining feature of different planning schools. Howe (1980) discussed that the planner's role is mainly categorized as a technical or political role. Technical planners rely on technical solutions and usually take on value-neutral adviser roles to serve the public interest without promoting policy positions. They see planning as a rational, scientific effort about control and prediction. However, political planners take a more value-committed role, usually representing the interests of unheard voices and helping to contribute to meaningful engagement—they consider planning as a bridge between social justice and urban development.

Adopting a particular role shows how a person understands planning issues and how that person acts accordingly. Sager (1994) argues that it's common for urban planners to experience a mismatch between their own values and the planning style of the agency or country within which they are working. They may solve this mismatch by putting away their own values and adopting a neutral planning role. A planners' task is usually to satisfy a client's need within a defined time and space, which may force planners to shift their concerns from broader public interests to what is important to their client. Therefore, they may put aside professional and personal values to adopt values important to their clients, particularly market values. Therefore, planners may be turned into a silenced profession fearful of speaking their minds. Grange (2013) persuasively argues that planners nonetheless play an important role in co-constructing their own identities through the ways in which they seek to legitimize their abilities, authorities, and roles. By adopting particular roles, planners also hold the power to co-construct their own identities.

Since the 1980s, planning, especially in western-European countries, has shifted from hierarchical, rule-based systems to new forms of collaborative planning involving citizens, interest organizations, and private actors. This has changed the traditional perception about the capacity of planners to steer and regulate urban-development processes (Sehested, 2009). Many theorists, such as Healey (1998), believe the participatory form of planning is essential for the development of pluralist democratic practices for governance in our unequal, culturally diverse, and conflict-ridden societies. In this regard, it is important to investigate the experiences and perspectives of urban planners in different sectors and inject them into the ongoing debate and policymaking in education and practice. Since planning takes place in multiple settings, public, private, and non-profit sectors have different influences on the skills deemed valuable for planners. It is reasonable to expect that skills needed in an entrepreneurial planning environment differ from those in more rule-based, bureaucratic settings.

Burchell and Sternlieb (1978) defined two principal groups of skills for urban planners—substantive and procedural. The first includes scientific and technical skills that relate to knowledge about spatial, social, economic, political, and environmental systems of the city, while the second comprises a selection of communication, mediation, and practical (soft) skills. As most development problems are tackled within multidisciplinary contexts, a basic scientific and technical education is necessary to permit planners to communicate with other professionals meaningfully and make substantive contributions to plan making. As Dawkins (2016) discusses, planners rely on a range of skills in practice, reflecting the generalist nature of planning work, and should be able to integrate perspectives from a number of specializations. Without substantive and technical knowledge, planners will not be able to use procedural skills, and without communication, mediation, and practical procedural skills, planners cannot put their scientific and technical knowledge to use. Dawkins (2016) also presents evidence that the substantive skills and technical knowledge that are acquired in schools are mainly underused in practice, further noting a divergence between the rates of acquisition and use for these skills. One possible reason for this discrepancy is a divergence between planning education and planning practice, which are influenced by different contextual factors (Myers & Banerjee, 2005). In this regard, the necessity of acquiring a wide range of skills and the varied contexts of planning practice can be reasons why the perception of urban planners and planning among the general public is not well known.

In order to enhance public awareness of the urban planning profession, to redefine the concept of planning and the planner's role, and to contribute to improvements in planning education, this chapter tries to understand how different planning practitioners, educators, and overlapping disciplines define urban planning and perceive the roles and necessary skills that are needed for future urban planners. Asking for actual roles that planners adopt and use in practical situations can reveal the real demands for a planner's knowledge, skill, and competence as well as the tensions planners face in trying to improve the welfare of people and the quality of their communities. Such development depends on the economic, environmental, and social success of urban areas, the improvement of which is the core principle underpinning planning. This chapter also identifies requisite skills and training for the planning profession that should be included in planning education. Asking these questions helps to understand whether planners' valued skills are part of a broader pattern of job skills needed in contemporary society or whether planners, in some ways, are unique in job competencies. The hope is that the responses will inform a cross-discipline of education and training that reinforces the notion that urban planners, by what they do and seek to address, are part of a discipline fundamentally different from others (Guzzetta & Bollens, 2003).

Clubhouse as a Tool for Gauging Perceptions

To reflect on awareness challenges and understand how planning and planners' roles are defined by different disciplines, and what skills they think are needed for future urban planners, the author needed a platform in which planners and other professionals from different contexts and sectors could come together and share their insights. In this regard, Clubhouse was a reasonable tool. It is a free, audio-chat social-network app that was created during the COVID-19 pandemic (fall 2019). On February 1, 2021, Clubhouse had an estimated 3.5 million downloads globally (Perez, 2021). Its environment is similar to an online audio-only conference or seminar on Zoom that everyone can join, depending on their interest in topics. When people join a discussion room, their followers will be notified, so they can also join the room.

Two discussion rooms were organized and scheduled in two different clubs. First, in the Sustainable Futures Club with the topic "What is urban planning and who are urban planners?" Second, in the Future of Cities Club, with the topic "Building urban planners today for the future of cities." Both events were announced on LinkedIn, Facebook, and Twitter 14 days in advance. Twenty-five people participated in the first room, among which ten joined as speakers. In the second one, 58 people participated, and 35 of them joined as speakers. The 35 speakers included 12 architects, ten urban planners, four urban activists, four entrepreneurs, two environmentalists, two engineers, and one other that shared their opinions. In both, the author, together with the administrators of the clubs, acted as moderators. After a brief introduction to the objectives and rules of the room, participants were invited to introduce themselves and share insights about how they define planning, how they see the role of planners, and which skills they think are necessary for future planners. Both rooms targeted urban planners and the general public. Two different clubs were chosen to reach wider groups of people. Since the aim of both rooms was the same, their findings are presented together, under the same topics and questions.

The use of Clubhouse has some benefits for this study: (1) accessibility to a large volume of users from across the world, (2) time and cost-efficiency, and (3) possibility to connect with participants for follow-up questions or discussions.

Insights of planners and other professionals were sought since they are valuable for enhancing the interest and awareness about the planning profession. In addition, having both planners and other professionals in the same space increased the possibility of sharing meaningful feedback and questions. This possibility was enhanced by choosing a topic and question that could attract both planners and the general public. Subsequently, the author targeted people who were interested in the topic of sustainable development.

Complex and Interdisciplinary Nature of Planning

These questions ("What is urban planning and who are urban planners?") received varied but interesting responses from participants. For instance, one participant responded:

> Planning is a set of activities intended to improve the quality of decisions for a community and help the community to be prepared for the future. Planning deals with many aspects and should make some systematic use of information to create images of the future and strategies to reach them.
>
> *(urban planner, private sector, Spain)*

Almost all speakers pointed to the difficulty of defining urban planning due to its broadness and multifaceted nature. According to one of the speakers:

> Many people do not know what urban planning means. It is like asking what sustainability is. People may have heard about it many times, but do not really understand it. They may think, planning is about building cities in a human-centric way, but it is more than that.
>
> *(urban activist, NGO, Finland)*

Nonetheless, consensus emerged around what planning entails as many speakers agreed with an observation by an urban planner from Austria. The participant noted:

> Planning is very broad and cross sectoral profession. Planners can work in different sectors and levels of organizations while contributing towards the same mission. And that's why technically, anyone who works in a city, at some level can contribute to the urban planning process.
>
> *(urban planner, public sector, Austria)*

Planning as a Context-Dependent Process

The rest of the speakers defined planning in light of their contextual understanding of the dominant global political economy within which planning operates. One reason for the difficulty of defining planning explicitly was the lack of clear boundaries for the profession. Participants noted that planners need to recognize and solidify their identity to be able to take appropriate actions for the many problems confronting them. In addition, defining the boundaries of planning can chart a distinctive path for both planning education and practice, and for filling the existing gap between them. Since it was difficult to clearly define urban planning (and planners), it was agreed that pointing to the major problems that participants face in their communities can add great value to the discussion. Hence, as noted by a participant:

> It only makes sense to discuss planning in relation to defined contexts. The complexity of the contexts and tasks urban planners involve can make it difficult to answer the question adequately. This requires basic conceptual repertoire and methodological tools that appropriate education can provide.
>
> *(urban planner, academia, United States)*

It was also apparent that context, as per participants' discussions, transcended professional-planning practice in their respective countries to also include country-specific development characteristics and educational systems for training planning professionals.

Many arguments surrounded the idea that what planners do to yield desirable future conditions is done with little reference to contextual differences confronting them. For example, one participant believed that many planners' and architects' work has become an imitation of known architects' and designers' projects in other contexts. Therefore, the next generation of planning should not only concentrate on the transferable parts of urban planning, but also to reinforce local identity and contribute to diversity and inclusion.

The participant described earlier tried to explain that culture should be positioned in the discourse as one of the contextual factors. Different attempts to this effect have already been made to elaborate on the essential role of culture in planning (Evans, 2002; Gibson & Stevenson, 2004; Hawkes, 2001). However, Skrede (2016) argues that the value of culture appears to be narrowed down to an economic asset because culture hasn't been properly defined or taught. Thus, the lack of comprehension of what culture means may cause neoliberal (re)interpretations of economic sustainability to be given more attention than culture itself. However, different approaches and preferences of planners to promote social-cultural or economic sustainability can affect their choice of action (ibid.). As Knieling and Othengrafen (2009) argue, planning culture refers to values, attitudes, mindsets, and routines shared by those taking part in planning. This influences the perceived planning tasks, the behaviors in groups or communities, and the pursuit of particular interest therein.

Another speaker supported the integration of cultural-contextual aspects into the planning field by bringing evidence from other contexts:

> Many of our public spaces and buildings in Africa are becoming westernized, with English signs, which has destroyed the local culture, local narrative and social mobility. The reason is that they often hire international urban planners and architects, and not the local one.
> *(urban activist, NGO, Africa)*

Planners' Role in the Face of Complexity and Power

Another issue that was brought up after discussing the importance of context in planning was the role of planners. According to one participant, the political and complex nature of planning requires continuous evaluation of the physical, social, financial, and environmental conditions, which has exacerbated the complexity of defining planners' role:

> Urban planning is interdisciplinary. The role of urban planners is also tightly intertwined with politics, reflecting the asymmetrical power relations in confronting diversity of interest, which makes their responsibility ambiguous.
> *(urban planner, academia, Norway)*

The previous statement was followed by a discussion about interests planners should protect in a pluralistic planning world, and the values that direct their activities. According to one of the participants, planning cannot be devoid of opinions and values about social issues:

> I really feel for the urban planners because they know if they stand in the way of their governments, they're just not going to work in that country again. And if not urban planners, then who's going to do the right thing? How can we change things, when the poor or powerless cannot speak? Is there a public interest and, if so, how do we recognize it? If not, which values should we represent? How can we resolve conflicts? How does one find out what social values are? And what if they conflict with our values?
> *(fashion entrepreneur, Africa)*

Many studies deal with the dilemmas of urban planning regarding the role of planners in the face of politics, power, and conflict that were discussed in the Clubhouse rooms (Forester, 1982; Auerbach, 2012; Forester, 2013). These studies affirm that pluralistic planning redefines the role of the planner to advocate the client's preferences while doing the actual planning, taking part in the process of policy and decision-making, and being involved in politics. However, it is often not clear who the planners' client is or should be—the government, developers, entrepreneurs, or the general public? While many participants tried to reemphasize the role of planners in today's societies, some participants had more pessimistic opinions, believing that planners have less impact on city planning than many actors such as developers. For example, an experienced architect and urban planner mentioned:

> For me, those planners whose goal is to contribute to the physical improvements in the way that cities look and function better, are disillusioned. Planning does not have as much influence over built environment as they think it does. It is primarily developers who determine what actually gets built and when it gets built. It is developers, who work within existing political and economic institutions, and not planners.
>
> *(architect and urban planner, private sector, Malaysia)*

In light of the political nature of planning, existing conflicts of interest, and values among different groups, one participant mentioned the ethical aspect of planning, which requires planners to have specific morality and ethics:

> I think urban planners need to have a specific kind of personality. We need altruistic people as urban planners; we need people who care about the needs and happiness of the other people; who want to do things to help people, even if it brings no advantage to themselves.
>
> *(urban planner, public sector, Iran)*

The majority of participants linked questions of what planning is and who planners are to the roles of planners, about which participants had different opinions. Many believed that planners should take a leadership role, while others believed that planners should play a mediatory role, negotiating different interests to resolve existing conflicts. As being a mediator requires neutrality, not everyone agreed. According to one participant:

> Planning is becoming increasingly entrepreneurial and facilitative of private development interests. Thus, planners need to be alert about the ideological shift from a planning position of advocacy to an entrepreneurial one. If planners see themselves as mediators, who should bring about more balanced planning outcomes? A mediatory role may fail to give sufficient attention to the importance of economic power in shaping [balanced] outcomes.
>
> *(entrepreneur, private sector, Sweden)*

Another participant, an urban activist from Africa, drew attention to the reality of politics and corruption in Africa and some parts of Asia and suggested that:

> Planners must become more vocal of the institutional and political barriers that may prevent them from acting in accordance with their own professional judgements.
>
> *(urban activist, NGO, Africa)*

Participants' opinions about the role of planners were quite different, mainly derived from their various approaches toward the power and politics of the environments they came from, including their countries, sectors, and organizations. These have seemingly shaped their personal and professional values as well as the complex nature of planning itself.

Substantive and Procedural Skills of Future Planners

The outcome of these discussion sessions was consistent with Albrechts's (1991) point of view. Albrechts saw urban planners as having specific skills or being armed with adequate tool kits to steer developments in desired directions. Based on the discussions on what planning is and what role planners play, and regarding the development direction of modern planning and governance, participants identified different substantive knowledge that can enable future planners to understand, synthesize, and deploy knowledge from other disciplines in the planning process. Some suggested substantive knowledge that, according to the participants, is missing from most planning curricula, including innovation and economy, technology and technical tools, data and new methods, sustainability issues and sustainable-development goals, and the interplay between different contexts and planning. Therefore, a cross-disciplinary education in planning was suggested. According to one of the participants:

> The entrepreneurial process is what we [planners] don't study in university. Future planners should learn how to facilitate startups in a city or in a community and discover which tools are needed to bring real economy to the startups, procurement processes, and different partnerships. They should learn how to become economic drivers and to foster innovation, by bringing all the actors together.
>
> *(urban planner, academia, Sweden)*

The previous statement indicates a need for supplementary tools, knowledge, or skills in order to put substantive economic knowledge into practice. Another participant suggested design-thinking as a tool that can allow planners to gain valuable public input and undertake thorough analysis of cultural and social situations. Another tool that was proposed was ethnographic analysis, which can allow planners to study urban spaces to inform decision-making. Participants noted that adopting these tools in planning practice can be ensured if practitioners maintain a connection with universities providing planning education. This will then allow such universities to adjust to the dynamics of planning within changing institutional and physical contexts.

Participants also agreed that planning education generally provides little guidance on how to achieve diverse and contradictory goals in practice, and which role or strategy should be taken to resolve the dilemmas that planning practices pose. As De Neufville (1983) argued, to fill the void between the world of practice and what is formally taught, people need to agree on what planning is explicitly about. For this reason, and the interdisciplinary nature of urban planning, planning education should help students to be able to distinguish the planning profession and discipline from other fields. Understanding how these aspects influence an urban context can strengthen their perceptions of how they should do planning in their own context, as well as how they can exchange experiences with other stakeholders in other contexts.

It is also important that students learn from other contexts, not only theoretically but practically, to immerse themselves in other values, religions, languages, and traditions. Participants argued that for students to be recognized as expert planners, they must learn how to bring some added value to the planning process. Thus, urban planning education should be about more than teaching substantive skills. It should evoke urban planners' better selves (Forester, 2004, p. 243), encouraging them to change things for the better. Participants further reasoned that planning education usually doesn't provide a mindset that can guide planners effectively in their behavior and the different roles they might play in the future, such as advocate, facilitator, mediator, manager, or entrepreneur.

Hence, the mindset and approach of planners are also important tools that form their beliefs, attitudes, and feelings about their societal roles. In this regard, it is critical that planning education provides the right training and coaching programs to create adaptive, flexible, and self-reflexive planners who have critical, systematic, strategic, and life-cycle mindsets. This will, in turn, engender planners to become drivers and/or initiators of positive changes and processes, instead of playing passive and/or neutral roles. In this regard, due to the unique position of planners in a governance system, they should be equipped with some soft, practical, and procedural skills and be guided toward a new type of critical and reflective practice that is both ethical and creative. As one of the participants mentioned:

> We need to teach students to discover their voice, and to have some meaningful impact. They must rethink who they are serving, what are their social and cultural value?
> *(urban activist, NGO, United States)*

Regarding the importance of procedural skills, some of the participants discussed that future planners do not need to have all the substantive knowledge if they know how to collaborate with others, consider overlaps, and understand interdisciplinarity. Recalling a shift toward a more network-based plan making, the participants discussed that planners need to learn how to collaborate, communicate, negotiate, delegate responsibility, manage conflict, build trust, share value, and create mutual interest.

Implications for Awareness and Future of Planning

The essence of this work was distilled from the general agreement that there is a lack of awareness about the planning profession. This chapter tries to contribute to this by first reflecting on the existing challenges and then collecting recommendations on how planning education can play a role in shaping awareness about the profession. Due to the methodological barriers encountered during COVID-19, Clubhouse, an app that was created in the pandemic to give people a virtual platform to connect and have meaningful conversations, was used. The aim was to reach out to both urban planners and the general public to gather them together in the same rooms, asking about their perceptions on what planning is and what planners do. The participating planners' experiences and perspectives informed discussion on how to develop future planning, and how planners should contribute to increasing the curiosity, awareness, and knowledge of the non-experts (general public) that were in the rooms. All those people that joined the events had a chance to participate in debates and express their opinions. Some joined as speakers, while others preferred to be just listeners. Since the majority of participants did not leave the room, we hoped that the discussions could partially help to increase the knowledge of the audiences.

Urban Planning Is a Complex Concept

Regarding the question about what people think about planning and planners, even though almost all of the participants defined planning as an interdisciplinary, pluralist, and political process, nobody could offer an explicit, single, and narrow definition. The inability to define planning stems partially from the dynamic and multilayered nature of urban systems within which many interconnected component parts, existing at multiple scales, contribute toward the overall functionality of the system. The overlap and confusion between planning and other fields calls for a sound and independent definition of planning. A consensual definition can serve as a vehicle to build a joint understanding about planning for planners, thereby advancing the public awareness.

Divergence of the Planner's Role

According to Potts et al. (2014, p. 164), planning practice is shaped largely by the "ebb and flow of power," and planners cannot be "the omnipotent gatekeeper" of the planning system. Many planners are attracted to this profession with the aim of protecting the environment; advocating for the poor and powerless; building better, sustainable, human-centric, inclusive, diverse, and nature-based cities; and contributing to improving the world. However, many have also lost faith that they can influence the political world through planning. The challenge of planning in the face of power has affected planners' choices of action and perceptions about the roles they should play in society. Depending on contextual conditions, planners adopt different roles that may challenge, maintain, or reinforce existing power imbalances in the planning system (Fox-Rogers & Murphy, 2016). The results also reveal existing conflict between planners' self-perception about their roles and the reality of practice, as well as a lack of congruence between their goals and their achievements. Accordingly, a lack of unanimity of evidence and opinions on the role of planners can be another factor that has challenged the public awareness.

Planning as a Context-Dependent Profession

Results suggest that context plays a crucial role in shaping planners' identities, approaches, and choices of action. Therefore, future planners should be equipped with sufficient knowledge, skills, and tools to enable them to recognize and respond to the cumulative influences of the broad political, social, economic, and cultural aspects of the context that shapes their identities as well as the context within which they plan.

Recommendations

To overcome urban planning's professional challenges, there was consensus among the Clubhouse discussion rooms about the need to prepare students to deal with the full complexity of planning by defining ethical planning and establishing typologies of settings in which planning takes place in different contexts. While these efforts exist somewhat in many planning programs (Silva, 2004; Connell, 2010), they aren't comprehensive enough to chart a path that allows future planners to attain cogent expertise for practice. In this regard, the accumulated opinions and sources suggest that planning education needs to combine diverse planning traditions and methods into a distinctive body of knowledge to distinguish different planning traditions from other unrelated paradigms. In addition, it must show several existing alternatives to students to make them critically aware of the varied roles of planners in society. This will enable them to make informed decisions about the roles they should adopt, where, and when.

An education system that meshes with the realities of practice can also serve as a vehicle to enhance the ability of planners to address important practical issues based on a holistic understanding of the larger picture within which planning issues are often generated and evolve. In addition, future planners need to become more critically aware of the roles they play in supporting the existing political and economic power base of the different societies where they work. This also highlights the importance of teaching planning in different national contexts in planning education. Therefore, it is suggested that future planning education offer overseas fieldwork and study visits to showcase international issues, cultural differences, and barriers. Many European planning schools, such as the master's degree program of Urban Ecological Planning at Norwegian University of Science and Technology, and the University of Dundee School of Town and Regional Planning, are structured around overseas fieldwork. The European Erasmus Programmes have also proven to be very successful and cost-efficient as they have opened up the world to so many young professionals at relatively little cost (Verschure, 2021).

References

Abukhater, A. B. E.-D. (2009). Rethinking planning theory and practice: A glimmer of light for prospects of integrated planning to combat complex urban realities. *Theoretical and Empirical Researches in Urban Management, 4*(2, 11), 64–79. www.jstor.org/stable/24872421

Albrechts, L. (1991). Changing roles and positions of planners. *Urban Studies, 28*(1), 123–137. https://doi.org/10.1080/00420989120080081

Allmendinger, P., & Tewdwr-Jones, M. (2002). *Planning futures: New directions for planning theory*. Routledge.

Auerbach, G. (2012). Urban planning: Politics vs. planning and politicians vs. planners. אופיקוגרפיה, 49–69. www.jstor.org/stable/23718581

Briassoulis, H. (1999). Who plans whose sustainability? Alternative roles for planners. *Journal of Environmental Planning and Management, 42*(6), 889–902. https://doi.org/10.1080/09640569910885

Burchell, R. W., & Sternlieb, G. (1978). *Planning theory in the 1980's: A search for future directions*. Center for Urban Policy Research, Rutgers University New Brunswick.

Connell, D. J. (2010). Schools of planning thought: Exploring differences through similarities. *International Planning Studies, 15*(4), 269–280. https://doi.org/10.1080/13563475.2010.517286

Dawkins, C. J. (2016). Preparing planners: The role of graduate planning education. *Journal of Planning Education and Research, 36*(4), 414–426. https://doi.org/10.1177/0739456X15627193

De Neufville, J. I. (1983). Planning theory and practice: Bridging the gap. *Journal of Planning Education and Research, 3*(1), 35–45. https://doi.org/10.1177/0739456X8300300105

Evans, G. (2002). *Cultural planning: An urban renaissance?* Routledge.

Faludi, A. (1973). *Planning theory*. Pergamon Press.

Forester, J. (1982). Planning in the face of power. *Journal of the American Planning Association, 48*(1), 67–80. doi:10.1080/01944368208976167

Forester, J. (2004). Reflections on trying to teach planning theory. *Planning Theory & Practice, 5*(2), 242–251. https://doi.org/10.1080/1464935042000225292

Forester, J. (2013). *Planning in the face of conflict: The surprising possibilities of facilitative leadership*. APA.

Fox-Rogers, L., & Murphy, E. (2016). Self-perceptions of the role of the planner. *Environment and Planning B: Planning and Design, 43*(1), 74–92. https://doi.org/10.1177/0265813515603860

Gibson, L., & Stevenson, D. (2004). Urban space and the uses of culture. *International Journal of Cultural Policy, 10*(1), 1–4. https://doi.org/10.1080/1028663042000212292

Grange, K. (2013). Shaping acting space: In search of a new political awareness among local authority planners. *Planning Theory, 12*(3), 225–243. https://doi.org/10.1177/1473095212459740

Guzzetta, J. D., & Bollens, S. A. (2003). Urban planners" skills and competencies: Are we different from other professions? Does context matter? Do we evolve? *Journal of Planning Education and Research, 23*(1), 96–106. https://doi.org/10.1177/0739456X03255426

Hawkes, J. (2001). *The fourth pillar of sustainability: Culture's essential role in public planning*. Common Ground Publishing Pty Ltd in association with the Cultural Development Network (Vic). www.theHumanities.com.

Healey, P. (1998). Collaborative planning in a stakeholder society. *The Town Planning Review, 69*(1), 1–21. www.jstor.org/stable/40113774

Howe, E. (1980). Role choices of urban planners. *Journal of the American Planning Association, 46*(4), 398–409. https://doi.org/10.1080/01944368008977072

Knieling, J., & Othengrafen, F. (2009). *Planning cultures in Europe: Decoding cultural phenomena in urban and regional planning*. Ashgate Publishing, Ltd.

Myers, D., & Banerjee, T. (2005). Toward greater heights for planning: Reconciling the differences between profession, practice, and academic field. *Journal of the American Planning Association, 71*(2), 121–129. https://doi.org/10.1080/01944360508976687

Ozawa, C. P., & Seltzer, E. P. (1999). Taking our bearings: Mapping a relationship among planning practice, theory, and education. *Journal of Planning Education and Research, 18*(3), 257–266. https://doi.org/10.1177/0739456X9901800307

Palazzo, D., Hollstein, L., & Diko, S. K. (2020). Urban planning as a career preference for students: Efforts to improve awareness about the profession. *Planning Practice & Research*, 1–19. https://doi.org/10.1080/02697459.2020.1782056

Peiser, R. (1990). Who plans America? Planners or developers? *Journal of the American Planning Association, 56*(4), 496–503. https://doi.org/10.1080/01944369008975453

Perez, S. (2021). *Report: Social audio app clubhouse has topped 8 million global downloads.* Retrieved December 7, 2021, from TechCrunch.

Potts, R., Vella, K., Dale, A., & Sipe, N. (2014). Exploring the usefulness of structural–functional approaches to analyse governance of planning systems. *Planning Theory, 15*(2), 162–189. https://journals.sagepub.com/doi/full/110.1177/1473095214553519.

Sager, T. (1994). *Communicative planning theory.* Ashgate.

Sehested, K. (2009). Urban planners as network managers and metagovernors. *Planning Theory & Practice, 10*(2), 245–263. https://doi.org/10.1080/14649350902884516

Silva, C. N. (2004). Urban planning and ethics. *Public Administration and Public Policy, 311.*

Skrede, J. (2016). What may culture contribute to urban sustainability? Critical reflections on the uses of culture in urban development in Oslo and beyond. *Journal of Urbanism: International Research on Placemaking and Urban Sustainability, 9*(4), 408–425. https://doi.org/10.1080/17549175.2015.1074603

Verschure, H. (2021). Lessons learned from 55 (or more) years of professional experience in urban planning and development. *Urban Planning, 6*(2), 218–224. https://doi.org/10.17645/up.v6i2.3980

Watson, V. (2007). *Urban planning and twenty-first century cities: Can it meet the challenge?* Global Urban Poverty.

19
UNDERGRADUATE URBAN PLANNING STUDENTS' AWARENESS OF AND MOTIVATIONS FOR PLANNING EDUCATION AND PROFESSION

Dohyung Kim

There has been a steady decline in college enrollment in the United States, in both undergraduate and graduate programs, from 2011 to 2017 (Fain, 2017). The decline is more significant in the areas of the social sciences and the humanities, due to perceptions like lack of clear purpose or direction for these majors, as well as concerns about career development (Nietzel, 2019). Urban planning programs are no exception to this trend. According to the Planning Accreditation Board (PAB), the number of students in accredited planning programs declined between 2008 and 2018, from 1,343 to 1,109 in bachelor's programs, and from 4,986 to 4,049 in master's programs (Planning Accreditation Board [PAB], 2019). It is noteworthy that the number of both bachelor's and master's programs increased during these years and that the number of foreign students in the programs likewise increased during this period. Thus, the enrollment decline challenge was predominantly caused by domestic students.

In addition to the enrollment decline, another significant challenge that urban planning programs confront is student diversity. Although planning schools and the profession both acknowledge that promoting diversity is essential to advancing planning scholarship and the knowledge base (Thomas, 1996), students from underrepresented populations often face exceptional barriers to enrolling in planning programs (Joint Task Force of APA, AICP, ACSP, and PAB, 2016). This prevents diverse populations from developing a clear career path and pipeline into the planning field, which is critical to the long-term stability, relevance, and effectiveness of the profession.

Enrollment declines and student diversity in planning programs are multi-layered issues. Some planning scholars have tried to address these complicated issues by shedding light on the climate for diversity (Greenlee et al., 2018; Lee et al., 2020). Some scholars have paid attention to enhancing awareness of urban planning as a discipline and a profession through youth and children (Palazzo et al., 2021). However, research on undergraduate planning programs from the perspective of student recruitment in the face of current enrollment declines has remained relatively unexplored, primarily due to conventional planning education that emphasizes a master's degree. Undergraduate planning programs can lead students into an early career path and pipeline for master's programs and professions. Thus, undergraduate planning students' motivations for their selection of the college major, along with their perspectives on planning education and the profession, can be keys to developing countermeasures against the enrollment decline. Recognizing the unique situations and demands of students from underrepresented populations can also help to promote student diversity in planning programs.

This chapter explores undergraduate students' motivations for choosing urban planning programs by surveying students in the department of Urban and Regional Planning (URP) at California State Polytechnic University, Pomona. The survey attempts to find answers to four primary questions: (1) When and how do undergraduate planning students get to know urban planning as a professional field and college major? (2) What are their motivations to select urban planning as a college major? (3) What are their career prospects in the planning profession? and (4) What are their perspectives on pursuing a planning master's degree? The large, diverse student body of URP produced a rich data set that facilitates the exploration of answers to the questions not only by a large number of students but also by diverse students in terms of ethnicity, gender, first-generation college students, transfer students, and first-time freshmen. The findings from this survey will assist planning programs in fostering outreach and recruiting programs that attract diverse students to their programs. It will also allow them to set appropriate advising strategies that support a student's preparation for their career development.

Study Context

This chapter is based on a survey targeting students in the Bachelor of Urban and Regional Planning program (BURP) at Cal Poly Pomona, one of the largest and most diverse undergraduate planning programs in the United States. During the 2020–21 academic year, approximately 230 students were enrolled in BURP, and diverse ethnic groups are represented. About 53% are Hispanic/Latino; Asian students (21%) are the second-largest ethnic group, followed by White (12%) and Black/African American (4%). The student body also represents those from socially and economically underrepresented populations. A large group of BURP students is first-generation college students (61%) and transfer students (57%). Unlike the national trend of enrollment decline, the student body of BURP has grown from 172 to 230 between the academic years 2017–18 and 2020–21. Therefore, a large, diverse group of students in BURP provides an opportunity to research students' motivations and perspectives on urban and regional planning as a college major and as a professional career.

The survey was conducted from February 4 to March 9, 2021, and deployed through an online survey platform, Google Docs. The URL of the online survey was delivered to only undergraduate students through the department's email list. The survey consisted of a total of 19 questions in three sections, "Planning as a College Major as a Prospective Student," "Planning Career Prospects," and "Personal Profile." The six questions in the "Planning as a College Major as a Prospective Student" category ask students their age when they chose planning as a professional field and college major, the other majors they considered when applying to college, and the subject matter that they expected to learn from their planning education. In the "Planning Career Prospects" category, seven questions address the students' future professional career development and interest in pursuing a planning master's degree. The "Personal Profile" category consists of six questions about students' personal information, including their class, ethnicity, gender identity, whether they are first-time freshmen (FTF) or transfer students, and if they are first-generation college students.

Approximately 47% of BURP students, 107 total, responded to the survey (see Table 19.1). This sample represents the population well. The respondents' distribution in ethnicity, FTF/transfer, and first-generation students is quite similar to the composition of all the students in the program as described earlier.

Awareness of Urban and Regional Planning

The professional awareness challenge is one of the most significant obstacles that urban planning schools and departments experience. A previous study pointed out that the lack of professional

Table 19.1 Profile of Survey Respondents

Profile	Cohort	Count	%
Ethnicity	Hispanic/Latino	58	54.2
	White	18	16.8
	Asian	22	20.6
	African American	3	2.8
	Others	6	5.6
Sexual Orientation	Female	45	42.0
	Male	57	53.3
	LGBTQ+	5	4.7
	Prefer not to say	0	0.0
Class	1st Year	47	43.9
	2nd Year	26	24.3
	3rd Year +	34	31.8
FTF/Transfer	FTF	45	42.1
	Transfer	62	57.9
First-Generation Student	Yes	62	57.9
	No	45	42.1

awareness of urban planning has directly contributed to the decline in student enrollment in undergraduate planning programs (Palazzo et al., 2021). The survey results confirm this finding. Students learned about the professional field of urban planning for the first time at an average age of 19.6 years. The age they learned about urban planning as a college major for the first time was at an average of 20.1 years. This late exposure to urban planning is shared by all students, regardless of their ethnicity, gender, and status as first-generation college students, indicating a large number were exposed to urban planning by a college or community college. The average seems to be skewed by transfer students, but FTF are not necessarily exposed to urban planning early. The average age that FTF learned about urban planning as a professional field and a college major were 16.8 and 17.2 years, respectively, which is approximately the 10th or 11th-grade level. It is, therefore, reasonable to suppose that students discovered the field of urban planning at a time close to submitting their college applications.

Students' late exposure to urban planning is reflected in how they selected it as a college major. The primary resource from which students learned about the planning major was during their college research, mostly through the Internet. About 40.1% of students relied on this resource. Students' professors and counselors are also important resources (20.4%). This is followed by 13.6% of students who learned about the major from their peers and friends. While some of them heard about the major from their family members (11.7%), the contribution of high schools to the provision of this information is very limited (4.9%).

The survey results indicate the positive role colleges and community colleges play in introducing urban planning as a college major, but most high-school students are not exposed to planning or planning-related topics. As a result, they miss the opportunity to learn about and choose it as a career preference. It is thus critical to increase the visibility of urban planning in high school, but it's also a difficult challenge. Current high-school curricula do not introduce planning-related topics (Education Commission of the States [ECS], 2020). Although high-school counselors and teachers play major roles in shaping student career preferences (Howard et al., 2015), in general, the planning profession is an unfamiliar area for them as well (Tiarachristie, 2016). In the long term, it would be ideal to introduce the value and principles of urban planning in high-school curricula by introducing planning-related topics in subjects such as history, geography, economics, and social science.

Scholarship programs for high-school students can be a model to increase the visibility of urban planning in high schools. For example, a federally designated Metropolitan Planning Organization (MPO), the Southern California Association of Governments (SCAG), has awarded a scholarship to high-school students who plan to pursue their college majors and career paths in transportation-related fields. It expects the scholarship to draw students interested in transportation and that preparing a scholarship application will be an opportunity for them to research and learn more about transportation. Many local American Planning Association (APA) chapters are already active in developing and awarding scholarships, but eligibility for them is typically limited to students enrolled in planning degree programs. Following SCAG's model, it will be worthwhile to consider scholarship programs designed to attract high-school students into planning or related majors.

The fact that the primary source of information about the urban planning major is the Internet raises an important question. Do planning program websites provide the information that prospective students, especially high-school students, are looking for? In addition to the departmental information, an introduction to the profession and planning disciplines on the webpage would be valuable for high-school students. Such an introduction would increase general familiarity with the profession. This is not limited to planning programs' websites. The common goal of four organizations—Association of Collegiate Schools of Planning (ACSP), American Planning Association (APA), American Institute of Certified Planners (AICP), and Planning Accreditation Board (PAB)—is to raise awareness about the planning profession. Although these organizations publicize videos and content via online platforms and social media such as YouTube and Facebook, it is questionable if these materials can attract Generation Z (those born after 1997), whose behavior is facilitated by technological advances including entertainment products (e.g., realistic videogames), greater 24–7 access to social networks, and greater mobility in devices (e.g., mobile phones) (Wood, 2011). Therefore, these organizations need to consider developing and disseminating content that appeals to the younger generations via the new media with which they are familiar.

The younger generations' exposure to the information about a discipline will help create a bridge between the profession and college major selection. Once they become aware of a profession, young people expand their interest in it by searching for information about the field. When their interest becomes mature enough, they will select a college major related to the profession. Typically, there is a natural time lag between when a student learns of a profession and the selection of their college major. According to the survey, however, there is only a five-month gap between the time BURP students learned about urban planning as a profession and their selection of a college major. Due to their late exposure to the urban planning profession, they are not able to take enough time to build mature interests in the urban planning profession and make a smooth transition to the selection of an urban planning major. Therefore, the role of APA, ASCP, AICP, and PAB in raising the visibility of the profession is an important means for attracting youth to planning undergraduate programs.

Perspective on Planning as a College Major

The survey showed leading motivations for students selecting urban planning as a major were service to communities (23.6%), interest in physical design (22.8%), and job-related practical reasons—job security and job diversity (14.9%; see Figure 19.1). Other factors identified in the survey include attentiveness to environment/sustainability (7.9%); contribution to social justice, advocacy, and civic engagement (7.1%); and interests in transportation (2.4%). This suggests that prospective students view urban planning as a college major that contributes to producing knowledge and solutions to urban problems while providing opportunities to build stable career paths.

Overall, it seems the disciplines and values of urban planning are appreciated by prospective students. Their concerns about and service to their communities motivated them to choose an urban planning major. Relating to these concerns becomes an important strategy to attract underrepresented

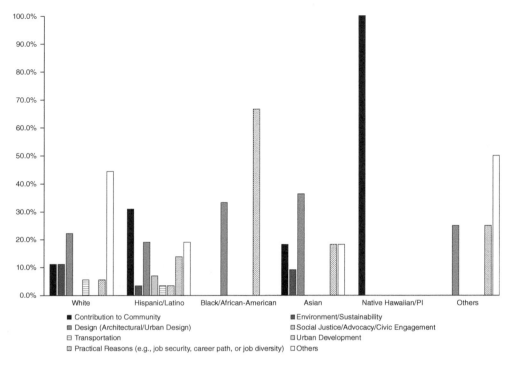

Figure 19.1 Students' Motivation in Selecting Urban Planning as Major by Ethnicity

students to urban planning programs. This is because the motivation of students for serving communities is well matched with the goals of urban planning. Therefore, serving communities needs to be emphasized in recruiting events or information sessions, such as open houses, promotional videos, and the programs' web pages. Consideration should also be given to supporting high school clubs that focus on community engagement and service. By collaborating with these clubs on community engagement projects, it is possible to effectively introduce urban planning disciplines to students in those clubs.

Motivations vary by student cohort. Motivation for community service of ethnic minority students, including Hispanic/Latino (31%) and Asian (18.2%) students, is stronger than for White students (11.1%). Similarly, the percent of female (31.1%) students who selected urban planning as their major due to service to communities is higher than the percentage of male students (15.8%). A higher percentage is also found in FTF (30.6%) in comparison to transfer students (15.6%). Interests in physical design were popular motivations of Asian (36.4%) and transfer (27.4%) students.

The motivation of students who selected urban planning as their major is also associated with other college majors they considered. A large number of students considered design disciplines, such as architecture (33%) and landscape architecture (18.7%), as their college major. Urban studies (13.7%), civil (and construction) engineering (13.7%), and geography (10.4%) were also popular disciplines considered. Students' motivations and interests in design-oriented disciplines are an interesting point. A group of students who are not admitted to an architecture program[1] tend to select a Bachelor of Urban Planning as their second choice, since they think urban planning is somewhat similar to architecture. Thus, BURP students' interests in physical design are found, but this phenomenon is common in many undergraduate planning programs. To satisfy the demands of this group of students, urban planning programs might consider emphasizing interdisciplinary education by collaborating with architecture and landscape architecture programs (such as hosting design studios where students from those design-oriented programs could work together).

Listing various subjects in planning discipline, a survey question asked, "Did you expect to learn the subjects below before joining the URP program?" The respondents were asked to choose one of five Likert scale answers from "very unlikely" to "very likely." Surprisingly, social justice, equity, diversity, and inclusiveness are less recognized as planning subjects than others (Figure 19.2). Compared to physical design and sustainability, students had lower expectations regarding learning these social-context topics. The recent (2020–21) movements of Black Lives Matter (BLM) and anti-Asian hate crimes raised the awareness of these topics among younger generations like millennials and Generation Z (Bellan, 2020). Their active involvement in these movements stems from their familiarity with race-related inequality. Their racial awareness reflects the fact that 48% of Americans under 21 identify as non-White (Horowitz et al., 2019). Thus, it is important to emphasize urban planning's emphasis on social justice, inclusiveness, and equity when reaching out to youth about urban planning as a career path. Therefore, planning communities and professional organizations need to raise their voices on these social movements. In this respect, faculty diversity needs to be emphasized. Increasing the diversity of planning faculty is one of the most important factors in attracting and maintaining a diverse student body (Sweet & Etienne, 2011). Since diverse students tend to easily build connections with diverse faculty and resonate with their advising, increasing faculty diversity can contribute to attracting students who are interested in inclusiveness and equity.

In the same vein, it is a positive that students expect to learn a subject like sustainability from planning programs. Alongside physical design and community development, sustainability is one of

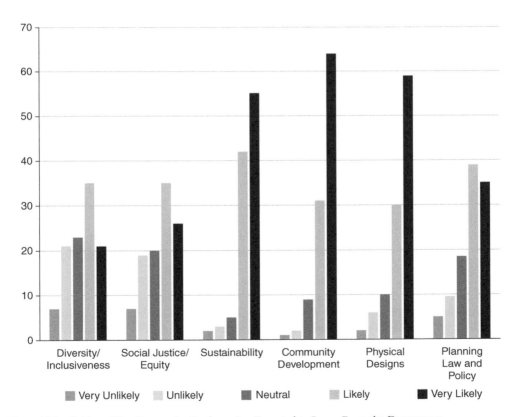

Figure 19.2 Subjects That Prospective Students Are Expected to Learn From the Department

the subjects that students highly expect to learn. Generation Z and millennials are more likely than their older counterparts to say climate change is caused by human activity (Parker & Igielnik, 2020). Thus, planning communities and professional organizations need to advertise and inform prospective students about planning programs' specialties in teaching and researching these subjects.

According to the National Center for Education Statistics, about 80% of students in the United States end up changing their major at least once. Within three years of initial enrollment, about 33% of undergraduates in bachelor's degree programs who declared a major had changed it at least once (National Center for Education Statistics [NCES], 2017). Introducing the diverse aspects of urban planning disciplines to college students who are interested in changing their major is one of the strategies to increase the number of students in planning programs. Arefi and Ghaffari (2020) introduced an approach that attracts undergraduate students in non-planning majors to a planning graduate program through classes that familiarize students with the interdisciplinary nature of planning. It was found that this approach resonated with the students. In the same vein, offering planning courses as general education courses and planning minor programs will help to expand the attractiveness of a planning major at the university level.

Planning as a Professional Career

Urban planning education is a steppingstone that allows students to develop their planning professional careers based on planning knowledge and skill sets learned during their education. Therefore, a good understanding of undergraduate students' career prospects after their graduation can be a starting point to build a solid pipeline into the planning professions. To address this, the survey included a question asking which area of urban planning students want to work in. Reflecting the interests of students in physical design, the area of urban design is the most popular area of planning (33.3%), followed by environmental planning (28.1%) and community development (20.8%).

In response to a question about the sector in which students want to work, 27.2% expressed their preference for the public sector, while 18.4% preferred the private sector. Another 31.1% of the students stated that they would be fine with either the public or private sector; 23.3% answered, "Do not know yet." Surprisingly, none preferred non-governmental/non-profit organizations. As expected, there were different preferences among student cohorts. The transfer (30.6%) and first-generation (35.5%) students' preferences for the public sector were much higher than FTF (20.0%) and non-first-generation students (13.3%). Another outstanding point is that the percent of Hispanic/Latinos (27.6%) who answered with "Do not know yet" was much higher than Whites (16.7%) and Asians (13.0%). As expected, there was a clear distinction between those in different class years. While second- (30.8%) and third- or later-year (20.0%) students' preference for the private sector was higher than first-year students (8.5%), 75% of second-and first-year students did not know their preferable sectors yet. Their uncertainty can be improved with internship experiences. It was observed that a large number of third- or later-year students undertake internships and that the internship experience contributes to students' career-path development and career-preference decisions.

The students' greater preference for the public sector is understandable. It is the conventional employment area for those with a planning major. The preference of underrepresented students, like transfer and first-generation students, for the public sector can be interpreted as their willingness to have opportunities for community service and their interest in better job security. However, this conventional framework is not always accurate. It is important to provide diverse opportunities for students to learn a wide range of career tracks and job opportunities that will use their planning knowledge and skill sets. Potential avenues include faculty advising, career fairs, internship opportunities, networking with alumni and professionals, professional conferences, and so forth.

Students of color and first-generation college students are less likely to have reliable advisors or mentors among family or close peers (Ishitani, 2006). This may contribute to Hispanic/Latino students' indecisiveness in their preference of job sector. Therefore, the role of planning programs in providing those guidance opportunities is especially valuable, such as building mentoring relationships between students and alumni of color. Through these relationships, students of color and those from underrepresented populations gain a sense of belonging and connection, as well as help navigating the career-development experience if the students are connected with a mentor who went through a similar situation.

Consideration of an Urban Planning Master's Degree

In general, conventional planning education centers on a master's degree, with master's programs welcoming students from many academic backgrounds. Since students with a bachelor's degree in urban planning are educated with important values and knowledge about the field, they have the potential to be successful planning master's students. At the same time, they may think a bachelor's degree is good enough to build their professional planning careers, or they may pursue a master's degree other than urban planning to avoid redundancy. Since the preference of undergraduate planning students for a planning master's degree remained unexplored, the survey asked the students' their thoughts about a planning master's degree.

About 38.8% of respondents expressed interest in a planning master's degree, and the same number of them were undecided. Only 23.4% of them were not interested in a master's degree. The interest of transfer students (29%) and first-generation college students (35.5%) was much lower than FTF (51.1%) and non-first-generation students (42.2%). Since transfers and first-generation college students are often from socially and economically disadvantaged families (Whitley et al., 2018), this results in inequities in post-baccalaureate planning programs. Variations among students of different ethnicities are also noteworthy. Asian students' interest (50%) in a planning master's degree and White students' non-interest (38.9%) are clear, while a large number of Hispanic/Latino students are indecisive (43.1%). Another interesting finding is that interest among freshman and sophomore-level students (45.2%) is much higher than junior and senior-level students' (25.3%).

These findings are consistent with the barriers that discourage students from proceeding to an urban planning master's program. Of four possible barriers listed—financial burden, redundant subject matter, confidence with a bachelor's degree for a professional career, and interest in a master's degree of another discipline—respondents chose financial burden as the greatest barrier, followed by interest in a master's degree of another discipline, redundant subject matter, and confidence with a bachelor's degree for a professional career. The students interested in a planning master's program prefer to continue their education right after graduation (41.3%) or after having a short professional experience (one or two years) (40.0 %), rather than after having a longer job experience of more than one or two years.

Some students preferred a master's program that is different from but related to urban planning subject matter. Their top choice was architecture (25.2%). Another design discipline, landscape architecture (14.4%), was also popular. This reflects consistent interests in physical design and recognition of urban planning as a design discipline from the perspective of prospective students. Other notable disciplines include public administration (14.4%), urban studies (13.9%), civil engineering (8.9%), and geography (6.9%).

Overall, the survey results confirm that urban planning undergraduate programs can be a solid middle part of the pipeline that directs youth to planning master's programs. The respondents seem to observe a planning master's degree as a valuable educational opportunity. The biggest challenge that the master's programs confront is how to reduce students' financial burden. Financial burden disproportionally impacts underrepresented students, as the interest of transfer students and first-generation college students is much lower than their counterparts. Their financial situations may discourage them from interest in earning a master's degree. It is not easy to find effective resolutions for this challenge, but being aware of it and putting forth consistent efforts surrounding it is important. Expanding scholarship programs for diverse students, especially those not traditionally the beneficiaries of generational wealth and social capital, is an option. Evening master's programs can also be a viable option to help them pursue a master's degree without giving up their jobs.

The pattern of students' perspectives on a planning master's degree is quite similar to students' preference for professional career development. Hispanic/Latino students are much more indecisive about pursuing a planning master's degree. It also indicates that students lose interest in the master's degree when they become upper-division students. Thus, the strategies described in this chapter, and other chapters in this book, can help guide students' pursuit of master's degrees. Faculty advising also becomes particularly important; they can play a major role as accessible mentors by cultivating and maintaining students' motivations for master's degrees. Students' classroom learning experiences can also inspire motivation for post-baccalaureate education. Furthermore, like mentorship programs between students and alumni of color, diverse students tend to easily build connections with diverse faculty and resonate with their advising.

Conclusion

The challenges of urban planning education are complex, including but not limited to the low visibility of urban planning as a discipline and profession, recent enrollment decline, and the lack of student racial diversity. To overcome these challenges, planning academia and the planning profession need to build a pipeline that directs youth from underrepresented populations into the planning education and professions. However, primarily due to conventional planning education that centers on a master's degree, the roles of undergraduate planning programs in the pipeline are relatively underestimated. This chapter provides rich data that enhances the understanding of undergraduate planning students' awareness of and motivation to select their major as prospective students, their career prospects in the planning profession, and their perspectives on pursuing a planning master's degree. The data confirms general observations, such as students' late exposure to urban planning and financial barriers to post-baccalaureate education. It also identifies equity issues, such as students from underrepresented populations (transfer and/or first-generation students) abandoning the idea of pursuing a master's degree. Based on this understanding, this chapter discussed a few alternatives to attract diverse students into planning degree programs and to help them build their professional career paths or pursue planning master's degrees. In summary, they include the following:

- Raising youth awareness of urban planning by offering scholarship programs and disseminating information about planning education and the profession via the media with which that younger generation is familiar.
- Advertising the discipline's scholarly/professional emphasis on the topics in which younger generations are interested (e.g., social equity, sustainability, and climate change).
- Organizing recruitment events that invite community college students (e.g., college fairs, open houses, or meetings with university ambassadors/recruiters).
- Enhancing the visibility of the planning major in universities for students who have not decided on a major or are interested in changing their major (e.g., planning courses as general education courses or a planning minor degree).
- Increasing faculty diversity to enhance mentorship with students of color and socially, economically underrepresented students.
- Developing mentorship programs between students and alumni/professionals, especially for students of color with alumni of color.
- Developing financial support programs like scholarships and fellowships for the post-baccalaureate planning education of students of color and underrepresented students.

However, the intention of this chapter is not to conclude this discussion with these suggested alternatives but to open the discussion to explore more alternatives. Hopefully, the data will motivate planning departments and schools to develop customized alternatives that fit with their circumstances by considering the complexity of diverse students' demands and perspectives. Diversity is a much more complex matter than racial diversity. Not all students of color are from disadvantaged backgrounds. The attention that students from working-class and poor populations need differs from that of students of color, while low-income students of color may still represent a large portion of disadvantaged populations. Thus, the first step for building a pipeline that leads diverse youth and children into planning education and professions is a good understanding of their demands and motivations.

Note

1 The architecture program is an impacted program, but BURP is not. Impact means that there are more applications from qualified applicants than available spaces in a program. An impacted program can require higher standards for admitting students.

References

Arefi, M. & Ghaffari, N. (2020). Five episodes of urban discovery as a student recruitment strategy in planning. *Journal of Planning Education and Research*. https://doi.org/10.1177/0739456X20903362

Bellan, R. (2020, June 12). Gen Z leads the Black Lives Matter movement, on and off social media. *Forbes*. www.forbes.com/sites/rebeccabellan/2020/06/12/gen-z-leads-the-black-lives-matter-movement-on-and-off-social-media/?sh=6d60b0b19a88

Education Commission of the States (ECS). (2020). *50-state comparison: High school graduation requirements*. www.ecs.org/high-school-graduation-requirements/

Fain, P. (2017, December 20). Enrollment slide continues, at slower rate. *Inside Higher Ed*. www.insidehighered.com/news/2017/12/20/national-enrollments-decline-sixth-straight-year-slower-rate

Greenlee, A. J., Jackson, A., Garcia-Zambrana, I., Lee, A. C., & Chrisinger, B. (2018). Where are we going? Where have we been? The climate for diversity within urban planning educational programs. *Journal of Planning Education and Research*. https://doi.org/10.1177/0739456X18815740

Horowitz, J. M., Brown, A., & Cox, K. (2019). *Race in America 2019*. Pew Research Center. www.pewresearch.org/social-trends/wp-content/uploads/sites/3/2019/04/Race-report_updated-4.29.19.pdf

Howard, K. A. S., Flanagan, S., Castine, E., & Walsh, M. E. (2015). Perceived influences on the career choices of children and youth: An exploratory study. *International Journal for Educational and Vocational Guidance*, 15(2), 99–111. https://doi.org/10.1007/s10775-015-9298-2

Ishitani, T. T. (2006). Studying attrition and degree completion behavior among first-generation college students in the United States. *Journal of Higher Education*, 77, 861–885. www.jstor.org/stable/3838790

Joint Task Force of American Planning Association (APA), American Institute of Certified Planners (AICP), Association of Collegiate Schools of Planning (ACSP) & Planning Accreditation Board (PAB). (2016, April). *Joint task force on enrollment report*. www.planningaccreditationboard.org/wp-content/uploads/2021/04/2016Enrollment Rpt.pdf

Lee, A. C., Chrisinger, B, Greenlee, A. J., Garcia-Zambrana, I., & Jackson, A. (2020). Beyond recruitment: Comparing experiences of climate and diversity between international students and domestic students of color in U.S. urban planning programs. *Journal of Planning Education and Research*. https://doi.org/10.1177/0739456X20902241

National Center for Education Statistics (NCES). (2017). *Data point: Beginning college students who change their majors within 3 years of enrollment*. (NCES 2018-434). https://nces.ed.gov/pubs2018/2018434.pdf

Nietzel, M. T. (2019, January 7). Whither the humanities: The ten-year trend in college majors. *Forbes*. www.forbes.com/sites/michaeltnietzel/2019/01/07/whither-the-humanities-the-ten-year-trend-in-college-majors/?sh=25ac794164ad

Palazzo, D., Hollstein, L., & Diko, S. K. (2021). Urban planning as a career preference for students: Efforts to improve awareness about the profession. *Planning Practice & Research*, 36(2), 174–192. https://doi.org/10.1080/02697459.2020.1782056

Parker, K. & Igielnik, R. (2020). *On the cusp of adulthood and facing an uncertain future: What we know about Gen Z so far*. Pew Research Center. www.pewresearch.org/social-trends/2020/05/14/on-the-cusp-of-adulthood-and-facing-an-uncertain-future-what-we-know-about-gen-z-so-far-2/

Planning Accreditation Board (PAB). (2019). *Student enrollment in PAB-accredited programs 2008–2018*. www.planningaccreditationboard.org/wp-content/uploads/2021/05/StudEnroll2019.pdf

Sweet, E. L., & Etienne, H. F. (2011). Commentary: Diversity in urban planning education and practice. *Journal of Planning Education and Research, 31*(3), 332–339. https://doi.org/10.1177/0739456X11414715

Thomas, J. M. (1996). Educating planners: Unified diversity in social action. *Journal of Planning Education and Research, 15*(3), 171–182. https://doi.org/10.1177/0739456X9601500302

Tiarachristie, G. G. (2016). *Elephant in the planning room: Overcoming barriers to recruitment and retention of planners of color* (Unpublished masters' thesis). Pratt Institute.

Whitley, S. E., Benson, G., & Wesaw, A. (2018). *First-generation student success: A landscape analysis of programs and services at four-year institutions*. Center for First-Generation Student Success, NASPA Student Affairs Administrators in Higher Education, and Entangled Solutions. https://firstgen.naspa.org/files/NASPA-First-generation-Student-Success-Exec-Summary.pdf

Wood, S. (2011). *Generation Z as consumers: Trends and innovation*. NC State University, Institute for Emerging Issues. https://iei.ncsu.edu/wp-content/uploads/2013/01/GenZ Consumers.pdf

20
INCREASING PLANNING EDUCATION AWARENESS AND ADDRESSING ENROLLMENT CHALLENGE IN URBAN PLANNING SCHOOLS

The Iowa State University Experience

Carlton Basmajian and Francis Owusu

In the United States, instruction in urban planning mostly occurs at the graduate level. Indeed, from the moment of its entrance into the academy, urban planning, largely, has been a master's-level curriculum. More recently, over the last five decades or so, a handful of undergraduate programs have appeared. These programs tend to be small, and only a few are accredited by the Planning Accreditation Board (PAB), the agency that oversees planning education in the United States.

Iowa State University (ISU) (2022) has offered graduate planning education since the 1940s, making it one of the oldest programs in the United States. Beginning in the late 1970s, the university began offering a fully accredited undergraduate planning degree, which by the mid-1990s had become the larger of the department's two degree programs. Like other planning-degree programs, the Community and Regional Planning (CRP) department at ISU has seen its enrollment ebb and flow over time. Some of these changes can be traced to broader economic trends that shape the popularity of different fields of study. Others, however, are internal to the institution, a result of visibility and perception among students. This is especially the case with the undergraduate planning program.

When enrollment in the undergraduate program began to decline in the late 2000s, faculty in the department became concerned and took action to try to reverse this slide and rebuild student numbers. In this chapter, we'll review the process by which CRP faculty at ISU developed and implemented strategies to address enrollment challenges facing the undergraduate planning-degree program. We begin by describing how the program began losing enrollment and the analysis the faculty undertook to understand the problem. Then, we discuss a series of steps the department took to make the undergraduate program more accessible and appealing to a wider variety of students. Finally, we recount some of the outcomes generated by these changes.

Iowa State University (ISU)

Iowa State University (ISU) is a large public university in the midwestern United States. Founded in the middle of the 19th century, it is one of the oldest of the nation's land-grant universities (Iowa State University College of Design, 2022a). The Carnegie Corporation classifies ISU as a very high research-activity institution, placing it among the 131 most research-intensive universities in the country (The Carnegie Classification of Institutions of Higher Education, 2022).

Honoring its formal name, the Iowa State University of Science and Technology, much of the institution's energy is directed toward instruction and research in science, technology, engineering, and mathematics (STEM). This orientation is reflected in the distribution of overall research expenditures, in the ranks of faculty, and in student enrollments (undergraduate and graduate). While the university houses a range of humanities and social-science departments, these programs primarily provide courses to satisfy distributional requirements for undergraduate students majoring in STEM disciplines. They have small enrollments and offer a limited number of graduate degrees. The number of students majoring in the humanities and social sciences remains a fraction of the university's overall student population. Different from most other research-intensive universities, ISU primarily is an undergraduate-serving institution. More than 85% of the student body is enrolled at the undergraduate level. Graduate education occupies a comparatively small footprint on campus.

College of Design (COD)

Outside of the university's STEM departments, ISU houses one of the largest design colleges (by total enrollment) in the United States. The College of Design (COD) comprises seven departments (Architecture, Art and Visual Culture, Community and Regional Planning, Graphic Design, Industrial Design, Interior Design, and Landscape Architecture) that range across the different scales of design, from small objects to large places. Like the rest of the university, the COD focuses almost exclusively on undergraduate education. More than 90% of the approximately 2,000 students enrolled in the college are in bachelor's degree programs. The emphasis on undergraduate education includes the Department of Community and Regional Planning (CRP), one of the constituent departments of the COD.

Like many design colleges around the country, the College of Design at ISU limits the number of students allowed to enter its undergraduate programs. These restrictions are in place due to the studio-based instructional model of most design disciplines and the demands of accreditation, which requires a minimum amount of physical space per student and a low student–faculty ratio. These factors in turn control the number of students who can be enrolled in each cohort of each program.

The public universities in Iowa are required by state law to admit every Iowa resident who meets a basic threshold on the Regent Admission Index (RAI), which is based on combined high-school grade point average and standardized-test scores (Board of Regents State of Iowa, 2022). For many years, the COD had regularly admitted more students than it could accommodate in its most in-demand undergraduate-degree programs (architecture and graphic design). At first, the individual departments handled student enrollment independently, but the absence of a central process for managing student demand proved cumbersome. To better accommodate student interests, the college adopted an enrollment management system (EMS) to control the size of its undergraduate programs and ease the path for transfer between programs.

This system, implemented in 2005, created an internal, secondary application process through which students must pass to enter the undergraduate majors in the college. Upon matriculation, all new students are classified as having an open-option major during their first year in the college. During this open year, students are required to take a set of four design-based, general-education courses (known as the design core). These courses provide an integrated introduction to design, including three-dimensional studio design and freehand drawing, as well as design history, theory, and criticism. Students use their remaining first-year credits to complete the university's general-education requirements (Iowa State University College of Design, 2022c).

At the end of their first year, students apply to join their preferred undergraduate-degree program. The application consists of an internal transcript and a design portfolio. The transcript includes grades from all the courses a student takes during their first year, while the portfolio showcases design projects completed within the design-core courses. In submitting the application, students use a ranked-choice technique where they name their top program choice followed by their second, third, fourth, and fifth choices. Their choices are one of the college's undergraduate-degree programs: architecture, landscape architecture, community planning, interior design, graphic design, industrial design, and studio art. Each program reviews and scores the applications that include that program as a ranked choice. Based on the programs' evaluations of their applications, students are then matched to the program that ranks them highest that also matches their highest rank. Thus, high-performing students (in terms of grade point average and portfolio quality) are typically assigned to their first-choice programs, less high-performing students their second choice, and so on down to the lowest-performing students who can end up in their third, fourth, or fifth-choice program.

Community and Regional Planning (CRP) Department

Within the COD, the Community and Regional Planning (CRP) department has, since the late 1970s, maintained accredited undergraduate and graduate (master's) degree programs. The planning department is the second smallest program in the COD, in terms of student enrollment and faculty count. It currently has 13 tenured/tenure-eligible faculty and enrolls around 80 undergraduate students, as well as 25 graduate students, each year. It houses several minors and certificate programs, including geographic information systems (GIS), urban studies, and heritage preservation.

Like other programs in the COD, the undergraduate program is the primary educational focus of the CRP faculty, and most of the department's instructional effort goes toward undergraduate courses. These courses tend to be large (averaging around 30 students) in terms of enrollment and draw students from within the program as well as from other programs around campus. The department maintains a separate core curriculum for the graduate program, but most elective courses are shared with undergraduates.

Problem

When the enrollment management system in the COD was instituted in 2005, CRP was included along with the college's other departments. Under the EMS, all students entering the college were tracked into a common first year, known as open-option design. Students would complete their entire first year as open option. At the end of that year, students would apply to the major of their choice. By requiring students to complete a set of common design-core courses prior to choosing a major, the EMS program was a major change to the way students entered the college. Prior to EMS, students entered individual majors as freshmen. Popular majors, like architecture, used an internal set of courses to cull excess students to match enrollment to the number of available seats. Most students would end up staying in their initial choice, but others would migrate among degree programs; some came to CRP.

Under the EMS, students could no longer enter design programs as freshmen. Every program required first-year students to complete the design core. In theory, this put CRP on level with other programs. College staff tried to market the undergraduate planning degree to design students as an alternative to architecture or landscape architecture (the two most content-adjacent programs). Planning was effectively pitched as an urban-design degree (Gunder, 2011). In practice, however, the EMS experience was less salubrious for CRP.

The design core was premised on the idea that a common language and skill set exists among all designers. Hence the core courses were structured to be broadly applicable to students with a range of interests, from fine arts to architecture. This shaped the character and content of the design-core courses and the pedagogy employed by the instructors, which had the effect of narrowing the idea of what constitutes design. Programs like architecture were presented as exemplars of design, while programs like CRP were seen as the place where less-talented designers ended up.

Thus, despite the effort to market CRP as equivalent to other programs, planning came to be perceived as an outlier by undergraduate design students. Most saw planning as something other than design, as a social science or even an engineering field, and thus a far less-desirable alternative to architecture or landscape architecture (McClendon et al., 2003; Palazzo et al., 2021). For entering students interested in planning but not other aspects of design, the design core became a barrier. An unknown number may have selected other majors (e.g., political science or sociology) and matriculated into a different college on campus. An equally large number of potential transfer students could have been deterred by the prospect of having to complete the design core, and never applied to join the program.

As a result of these factors, the number of students coming into CRP through the EMS began to decline not long after it was instituted. The leading indicator was a decrease in the number of new students who named CRP as their first or second choice. Early on, students entering CRP through the EMS were a mix of those who had identified CRP as a first or second choice (typically behind architecture or landscape architecture); however, by 2009, the number who picked CRP first or second had declined, and by 2012, virtually none picked CRP as a first choice, and few had it as a second choice (see Figure 20.1). While this was happening, the number of students entering CRP from the EMS dropped so much that intake from the EMS into the program all but ceased. This contributed to overall enrollment in CRP reaching a nadir in 2013.

Over time, the impact of the enrollment management program and its attendant shaping of the composition of student cohorts fueled a decline in enrollment in the undergraduate CRP program. With full implementation of the EMS, undergraduate enrollment in the planning curriculum

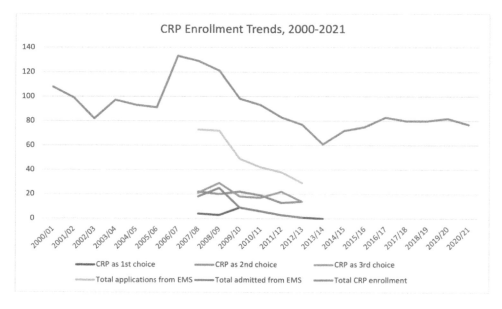

Figure 20.1 CRP Enrollment Trends Before, During, and After Enrollment Management

continued to decrease. In the five years prior to the adoption of the EMS (2000–2005), the total number of CRP majors averaged 95. From 2009 to 2013, the years when the full impact of enrollment management was most evident, the total number of students in the program decreased from 102 to 61, a drop of 50%.

Perhaps most perniciously, the shrinking enrollment affected student morale and engagement. Many students sustained an interest in the discipline after enrolling and became passionate about their coursework and the possibility of a career as a planner. Quite a few, however, regarded the program as disjointed, and not what they had expected from a major in the College of Design. After spending a year in CRP, some retook the design-core courses to improve their grades and revise their portfolios to apply for a different major. Some simply left the program and the college, realizing that planning held little interest for them. And some stayed in the program nursing their disappointment. The decline in enrollment and morale was notable because it happened during a period when overall enrollment at ISU was growing (Iowa State University Office of the Registrar, 2022).

Solutions

Recognizing that a declining program in an expanding university could endanger the long-term viability of the CRP department, the faculty undertook a somewhat-urgent review of the undergraduate program beginning in 2012, including a look at admissions, advising, learning outcomes, and curriculum. The premise motivating the review was that the undergraduate program was underperforming, in terms of student numbers and student engagement. The goal was to identify potential barriers that hinder enrollment and devise ways to remove them. Proposed changes would support improved student engagement and morale. The faculty set a goal for the undergraduate program of enrolling 35 to 45 new students per cohort, per year, which would move the total undergraduate enrollment in the major back toward 100 students.

Entry and Curriculum

The first step was examining the program's participation in the college's enrollment management program. Based on an analysis of enrollment data and reports from exit interviews with graduating students, in the spring of 2012, departmental faculty voted to remove the CRP major from the enrollment management program. This change included removing the requirement that students complete the design-core curriculum or submit a ranked-choice application to join the major. With this change, CRP would function like most majors on campus, open to any student regardless of background. With this change, a path would be open for students to declare planning as their major at any point during their time at the university.

Next, the department embarked on a comprehensive review of the undergraduate curriculum, which had not been done in many years. The curriculum-review process included analyzing student exit-survey data, consultation with the department's alumni stakeholders, mapping the curriculum against PAB accreditation criteria to identify gaps and excessive overlaps, and a series of departmental conversations. The review's objective was to (1) streamline and simplify the requirements so that students could complete the CRP major in four years, three years, or two years, depending on the number of credit hours they have completed upon entering the program; (2) provide opportunities for motivated students to complete the CRP major along with a second major simultaneously, within the span of eight semesters; (3) remove curricular barriers that discourage students from transferring to CRP from other majors within the COD, other colleges at ISU, and community colleges around the region; (4) allow CRP majors to take advantage of ISU's extensive study abroad programs outside the COD's Rome program; and (5) gradually increase enrollment in the Bachelor of Science CRP major from the current cohort size of 25 to a cohort size of 35–40.

The review revealed several issues, including redundancy in courses, rigidity of requirements, and relatability of topics covered. The number of required courses had, over the years, ballooned, such that mandatory classes comprised well over half the curriculum. There were required courses with substantial overlaps in content. There were two different sets of planning electives, the difference between them hard for students to gauge. There was little room for electives outside of planning. Finally, there were several emerging topics in planning that were absent from the curriculum.

In response, a set of recommended curricular changes were devised. The total number of credit hours of core coursework required for the undergraduate degree was reduced from 28 to 24, which included combining several existing required courses. The total number of required planning-elective credit hours was also reduced, and the list of planning electives was streamlined to eliminate outdated courses, which created new space for more open electives determined by students themselves and drawn from any program on campus. The revised curriculum created an even balance between core courses, planning electives, and open electives. This restructuring of the degree program not only allowed planning students to add a second major (or multiple minors) more easily, but also allowed students in other degree programs to add planning as a second major while completing their primary degrees within a four-year calendar.

A key part of the revised curriculum was the replacement of the existing introductory courses in history and methods. Two existing courses that covered the history of planning were combined into one new course. Similarly, a planning methods mini-sequence (two courses) was combined into a single methods course. Accompanying these new core courses was the creation of, for the first time, a clear sequence of core courses (history, environment, theory, methods, law, studio). The sequencing was intended to create a consistent pathway through the degree program that supported the development of more cohesive cohorts of students.

The new history course would serve as a gateway course for the department. This course, designated as CRP 201 (The North American Metropolis), would fulfill several tasks and serve multiple audiences simultaneously. Topically, the course would introduce the history of cities and city planning in the United States (and to a lesser extent, modern Europe). It would be required for all students majoring in CRP. The course would also fulfill a general social-science elective for students in other programs as well as the university's US diversity requirement.

The new four-credit methods course, CRP 301 (Urban Analytical Methods), would focus on a narrow set of quantitative methods important for planning. An existing introduction to environmental-planning course (CRP 293) was added to the core. This course had long attracted students from across the university, including students in environmental studies, environmental science, and global resource systems, and would now also be required of all CRP students.

Further curricular revisions included removing almost all prerequisites for elective courses. This step was taken because many of the elective courses that the department offers on an annual basis are considered upper level by the university (designated as 400-level course numbers). Removing prerequisites from those courses would make it easier for students from other programs to register for planning electives more easily.

Finally, the department made the decision to offer, on a yearly basis, a slate of the same four introductory courses—CRP 201 (US Planning History), CRP 251 (GIS), CRP 291 (International Planning), and CRP 293 (Environmental Planning)—that were geared both to students majoring in CRP and students seeking elective credits. These courses provide different points of introduction to the study of planning. They fulfill general-education requirements as social sciences for students from different disciplinary backgrounds and provide content appropriate for beginning-level planning students.

In 2013, the department adopted these curricular changes as a package.

Minors

After the adoption of the revised undergraduate curriculum, the department established two new minors based in planning: geographic information systems (GIS) and urban studies. Both were designed to draw mostly from existing courses without the need to create new classes. They represented areas of strength for the department in terms of faculty capacity. The goal for both was to offer clearly defined pathways for students to learn about planning that were coherent in terms of knowledge but flexible enough to meet the needs of different interests. The minors would not be so untethered as a random selection of electives but also not so rigid that completing the requirements would be difficult. They would be open to students from any department on campus, including those in the COD and CRP.

The GIS minor was first offered in 2016. The minor is anchored by introductory (CRP 251) and intermediate (CRP 351) GIS courses developed in 2016. CRP 251, intended for beginning undergraduates, was designed to introduce students to GIS in an accessible way. From the time of its first being on offer, 251 has grown to average 50 students per semester (it is offered in both autumn and spring). Approximately 60% of these students come from outside planning, but the course has helped generate interest in GIS and helped increase enrollment in other GIS courses offered by CRP.

The urban studies minor was also first offered in 2016. The minor has experienced significant growth in enrollment since its introduction, with most of the students joining from the other programs in the COD. As enrollment in both minors has grown, they have contributed to the larger uptick in enrollment in other CRP courses.

Outreach

In conjunction with revising the undergraduate curriculum, the CRP department initiated steps to publicize the study of planning among undergraduates at ISU. This was seen as a corollary step to the curriculum changes given the lack of recognition of the existence of planning as a field by many students. Under EMS, marketing and outreach had been centrally coordinated by the college's advising staff. There was a single message about the college's undergraduate-degree programs, which emphasized their common roots and the single path into the programs (through the core curriculum and EMS). CRP was marketed as a standard design program that required the same kind of preparation, skills, and interests as architecture, landscape architecture, or any other major in the college. After exiting the EMS system, the revised marketing plan emphasizes planning as an interdisciplinary major, grounded in design but extending into the social and natural sciences. Outreach among campus partners now focuses on multiple paths of entry, the absence of the design-core requirement, and the program being outside the enrollment management system.

Upon adopting the new curriculum, faculty and staff in the planning department reached out to other departments on campus, particularly those that had sent large numbers of students to enroll in planning courses as electives. Targeted programs included environmental science, sociology, anthropology, world languages, political science, global-resource systems, civil engineering, and forestry. The goal of this communication was to reemphasize awareness of the planning program to faculty and advisors who influence student decisions about elective coursework.

Targeting key departments was part of an outreach strategy to begin developing collaborative advising relationships between CRP and other programs. The hope was that these relationships would extend the reach of the planning program to create visible pathways for a wide range of students to find their way into planning courses, a minor, or a second major. It is the quiet work of academic advisors that directs students to courses and programs that fit their interests, advice that tends to be taken to heart by most undergraduates. For instance, the CRP department organized lunch-and-learn sessions for academic advisors in selected programs. By reaching out to advisors, CRP hoped to encourage them to recommend planning to students who showed an interest in the field.

As part of the outreach, CRP representatives met with staff from the university's undergraduate office of admissions. University admissions officials had previously reported being unfamiliar with ISU's planning program and, in some cases, even unaware that the program existed. Over a series of meetings, CRP faculty provided a detailed overview of the undergraduate planning curriculum and information about the kinds of topics and skills that the program offers, as well as ideas and language for talking to prospective students and parents about planning as a field of study.

ISU annually accepts a large number of transfer students from the state's community colleges. These students arrive at different stages in their education and land in programs across campus. Yet their presence in the COD has long lagged behind other colleges, due in part to the enrollment management system. As part of its outreach strategy, CRP developed a set of articulation agreements with the largest community colleges in Iowa. Those articulation agreements were designed to ease the transfer process for community college students to migrate to the CRP program and complete a bachelor's degree (Iowa State University College of Design, 2022b).

These agreements provided a defined path for transfer students who would be able to complete pre-identified courses while enrolled in community college that could be transferred to the planning program. If they completed an associate of arts or science degree prior to enrolling at Iowa State, they could finish a bachelor's degree with only two extra years of study. In effect, these agreements would allow students to complete a bachelor's degree in planning at ISU within the space of four years, regardless of where they began or when they transferred.

The most tightly focused outreach around CRP was initiating an annual guest lecture to first-year students in the environmental science and environmental studies undergraduate learning community (Iowa State University Learning Communities, 2022). This group held particular interest not only because environmental science is a popular program at ISU, but also because it has long shared several cross-listed courses with CRP, and it was common for students to move between the two programs to take courses. Increasing the visibility of planning among these students was expected to bring a critical mass of environmental students into undergraduate planning courses, expanding the study of environmental planning at a critical moment and, eventually, seeing more of those students adding planning as a second major.

Finally, when the department left the enrollment management system, a concerted effort was made to publicize to new design students that CRP had become an open major, one that did not require completion of the design core or a supplementary application and could be combined with other design-degree programs. Part of this new communication about the program included pushing the college to hire an undergraduate academic advisor who could speak knowledgeably about planning to potential undergraduate students. The result was onboarding an alumnus of the CRP program as the CRP academic advisor. The academic advisor assumed responsibility for advising all undergraduates in the CRP program, but also would serve as a planning-knowledge resource for other advisors in the COD, explaining the field to curious students and directing those showing interest in planning to one of the entry level planning courses.

Outcomes

Implementation of these steps has unfolded over several years, beginning in the autumn of 2013 when the new curriculum took effect and the department officially withdrew from the college's enrollment management system. This was also the academic year when the new gateway course, CRP 201, and new methods course, CRP 301, were first offered, and the new sequence of core courses was implemented.

Several metrics reveal how enrollment subsequently changed. At the initial offering of CRP 201, course enrollment was 29 students, virtually all CRP majors. Over the next five years, enrollment in the course ticked sharply upward. In 2014 it grew to 46; in 2018 it reached 80, and in 2020, it rose to 99 (Table 20.1). During the same period, enrollment in CRP 251, the introductory GIS course, grew from 55 to 87. Enrollment in CRP 291 went from 26 to an average of 50. Enrollment in CRP 293, which had long been the department's largest course, remained strong, drawing around 90 students each autumn. The increases in enrollment in the department's four 200-level courses has brought a new level of stability to the undergraduate program (Table 20.1).

As hoped, increased enrollment in lower-level courses has begun to translate into greater enrollment in upper-level courses as well. The department offers a slate of electives each semester, which cover a range of more-specialized topics within planning. These courses are primarily at the 400 level, indicating their appropriateness for advanced (third or fourth year) undergraduates, yet they do not have prerequisites, meaning that students can move directly from a 200-level introductory course to a 400-level elective.

Pushed by higher low-level course enrollments, the average size of each cohort in CRP has slowly increased from 25, where it sat in 2012/13 when the plan for increasing enrollment was put into place, to a little more than 35 at present (2021/2022). This gradual increase in student intake has bumped the total enrollment of students majoring in CRP from 61 to right at 90.

Perhaps most importantly, the new pathways for students entering CRP have changed the level of student engagement. By leaving enrollment management, the program has been thrown open to the campus. Students can simply declare CRP as a major, no different from sociology, chemistry, or English. No longer are students tracked into the program after failing to gain admission to architecture or landscape architecture.

Students who now enter CRP are self-selected. Routes by which students reach the major have multiplied. As before, the number of students arriving in the COD as new freshmen with a self-declared major of CRP remains in the single digits (averaging four to six per academic year). Those students can start taking classes in the major during their first semester at ISU; however, the number of students who complete the COD core but fail to gain admission to another program within the college and then end up in CRP has declined significantly. There are now typically fewer than five such students each year. In fact, most years the department enrolls only a small handful of students who complete the full design core.

The biggest shift has come from students transferring into the major from other programs on campus. At this point, these students represent the largest block of CRP majors. The points of origin for these students are disparate. Since the adoption of the new curriculum in 2013, students have arrived from a wide array of other majors. In fact, most students majoring in CRP now originate in a college other than the College of Design.

Table 20.1 CRP 200-Level Course-Enrollment Trends Post EMS

Year	CRP 201	CRP 251-Fall	CRP 251-Spring	CRP 291	CRP 293
2014/15	46	XXX	XXX	26	75
2015/16	57	21	34	40	62
2016/17	73	24	35	Not offered	90
2017/18	80	36	32	51	85
2018/29	69	50	50	49	85
2019/20	92	49	47	48	88
2020/21	99	49	38	51	93

In addition to internal transfers, the program has seen an increase in the number of students choosing CRP as a second major or minor. They bring a variety of interests to the program and help build connections between planning and other programs, which helps pave the way for other students to undertake similar programs of study. By the autumn of 2021, the number of students in the two minors housed in CRP had increased to 57 (29 in urban studies and 28 in GIS).

Conclusion

The experience of the planning department at ISU offers several lessons for other institutions, particularly those with substantial undergraduate programs. Facing declining enrollment, lack of student engagement (the result of a restrictive internal-admissions process), a rigid program of study, and virtually no effort devoted to student recruitment, the Community and Regional Planning department took a series of steps, beginning in 2012, to expand the number of undergraduate students engaged in the study of planning at Iowa State University. The changes included increasing points of entry into the program, streamlining the curriculum, developing new introductory courses, establishing new minors, and building advising relationships with other departments on campus.

We can draw five key lessons from the ISU experience. First, messaging around planning as a field of study was critical. The interdisciplinary nature of planning became the headline description of the field as an academic subject in the university. As faculty and advising staff shifted their language, the common refrain became that planning, by virtue of its topical diversity around a common interest in the built environment, could accommodate many kinds of interests. This made it easier for students to find their own connection to the program, which helped bring new students to CRP courses and eventually into the degree programs.

Second, streamlining the curriculum with an eye toward flexibility proved to be a way to support students from a wide range of backgrounds. This allowed students from different backgrounds to join the planning program in a way that built on their existing interests and previous coursework and helped them extend their studies in new directions. It also made the task of completing curricular requirements simpler so that students could combine planning with another major in the typical span of a four-year bachelor's degree and enter planning at different points in their studies.

Third, restructuring broad-based introductory courses allowed the department to simultaneously serve students already enrolled in the planning undergraduate program as well as students from other majors with no prior knowledge of the field. These courses offer a means of exposing students to planning who otherwise might never encounter it. When well taught, introductory courses can become a draw in themselves, introducing students to the field of planning and then pulling them into more-advanced planning courses. This has an upward effect, driving enrollment in electives and, increasingly, the likelihood that a student will end up adding planning to their program of study.

Fourth, the introduction of minors for undergraduates proved useful for providing additional entry points for students interested in planning adjacent issues but who do not see planning as a primary focus. A minor gives students a chance to explore a new subject without the burden or expectations that come with a second major in the field. Structuring minors with these students in mind so that courses from a range of disciplines can be counted for credit has proven to be important. It has allowed students from different disciplines to add minors without sacrificing their primary interests.

Fifth, building relationships with advisors across campus was critical to creating institutional awareness of planning as a field of study. Most undergraduates navigate curricular choices by relying on advice from advisors in their home discipline. Providing those advisors with basic information about planning, including lists of courses to which they can direct students based on interests, makes it easy for them to recommend those courses. Once relationships are established, advisers can become partners in terms of providing pathways for bringing new students into planning courses and, later, into minors and the major.

These changes provided a needed lift to the ISU undergraduate planning program. Individually, none would have been enough to reverse the decline of the program, but together they provided sufficient force to issue a course correction. Since the changes were instituted, enrollment in CRP has rebounded somewhat. Student numbers in entry level courses have steadily increased. The total number of students majoring in CRP is up. The number of students adding planning as a second major has increased as well. Subscriptions to the department's elective courses are up, measured by head counts in individual courses but also averaged over all the courses offered in any given semester. Alongside an uptick in the number of planning majors, enrollment in the department's slate of minors has reached a critical mass.

These changes reversed the decline in the number of undergraduate planning students and over time increased the number of student credit hours the CRP department delivers. More importantly, the changes have improved the character of the department, as students who choose to study planning are now primarily self-identified and self-motivated. Engagement and morale are up, among both students and faculty. The department's enrollment is now on a path to return to its historic norms.

References

Board of Regents of the State of Iowa. (2022). *Regent admission index*. www.iowaregents.edu/institutions/higher-education-links/regent-admission-index

Carnegie Classification of Institutions of Higher Education. (2022). *Standard listings*. https://carnegieclassifications.iu.edu/lookup/standard.php#standard_basic2005_list

Gunder, M. (2011). Commentary: Is urban design still urban planning? An exploration and response. *Journal of Planning Education and Research, 31*(2), 184–195. https://doi.org/10.1177/0739456X10393358

Iowa State University. (2022). *About Iowa State*. https://web.iastate.edu/about

Iowa State University College of Design. (2022a). *History & organization*. www.design.iastate.edu/college/organization/

Iowa State University College of Design. (2022b). *Future undergraduates*. www.design.iastate.edu/future-students/future-undergraduate/transfer/

Iowa State University College of Design. (2022c). *Undergraduate students core design program*. www.design.iastate.edu/current-students/undergraduate-students/core-design-program/

Iowa State University Learning Communities. (2022). www.lc.iastate.edu/

Iowa State University Office of the Registrar. (2022). *Enrollment by major or department*. www.registrar.iastate.edu/resources/enrollment-statistics/enrollment-by-major-or-department

McClendon, B., Erber, E., McCoy, M., & Stollman, I. (2003). A bold vision and a brand identity for the planning profession. *Journal of the American Planning Association, 69*(3), 221–232. https://doi.org/10.1080/01944360308978016

Palazzo, D., Hollstein, L., & Diko, S. (2021). Urban planning as a career preference for students: Efforts to improve awareness about the profession. *Planning Practice & Research, 36*(2), 174–192. https://doi.org/10.1080/02697459.2020.1782056

21
FACTORS INFLUENCING CONSIDERATIONS FOR URBAN PLANNING AS A FIELD OF STUDY AND/OR CAREER CHOICE AMONG ENVIRONMENTAL SCIENCE STUDENTS

Kwame N. Owusu-Daaku and Mackenzie Devine

The ability of introductory or general-education courses to influence non-majors to become majors in the discipline of the introductory course has received a fair amount of attention. Literature exists on the topic of introductory courses' influence on recruiting non-majors within academic disciplines such as computer science, geology, and of course urban planning. For example, a study focusing on enrollment trends in computer science noted that initial experiences with introductory computer-science courses have been connected to students' intent to major in computer science following course completion (Sax et al., 2017). Within the field of geology, the impacts of introductory course components on the recruitment of geology majors demonstrated an observed increase in major declarations after the administration of surveys during the semester of the course (Hoisch & Bowie, 2009). This finding provides evidence that different course components have the potential to impact the individuals enrolled in a course and their decisions to take additional courses on the subject. Broadening the range of topics or skills learned in introductory courses for non-majors might also improve the accessibility of such courses. For example, redesigned introductory computer-science courses for non-majors that did not solely focus on programming enabled non-majors to find the subject more accessible (Ahmad & Gestwicki, 2013). Some studies also show that courses that expose students to a variety of career paths within subject areas are beneficial to students enrolling in more courses in the subject area and potentially declaring a major (Estaville et al., 2007; Hoisch & Bowie, 2009). For example, an urban planning course attempted to recruit non-planning majors into the field through an immersive city-based field course. The results of this study were that 27% of students enrolled in the course stated they would consider pursuing a graduate degree in planning (Arefi & Ghaffari, 2020).

Despite these findings in the literature, it is unfortunately not evident from practice how many, or to what extent, planning programs use general-education or introductory courses to influence the choice of urban planning as a field of study or profession. Anecdotal evidence and extant literature speak to the ability of planning programs to use general-education and/or introductory courses to recruit majors. For example, a question posed to an informal online group of planning educators and scholars about which urban planning programs offer general-education or introductory courses to non-majors[1] (Owusu-Daaku, 2021) yielded the following results. The department of Urban and Regional Planning at California State Polytechnic University, Pomona, offers lower-division (typically first- and second-year students) general-education courses that welcome majors and non-majors, and an upper-division (typically third, fourth-, and fifth-year students) general-education course for non-majors. The department also offers a minor (Urey, 2021). Although the urban planning program at the University of Kansas does not have an undergraduate major, the program offers a 200-level course on sustainability, a 300-level course as an introduction to planning, and two 500-level sustainable land use/environmental methods courses all majors can take (Johnson, 2021). The Department of Geography, Planning, and Sustainability at Westfield State University offers about three sections a semester of an introduction to community planning course as a general-education course which fulfills a social-understanding requirement (Bristow, 2021). In New Zealand, most undergraduate core planning courses are available as options for other majors (Hamish, 2021). For example, an environmental management professor at the University of New Zealand teaches a third-year environmental planning course that is taken by landscape architects, agricultural scientists, and environmental policy students. Although this professor does not teach lower-level planning courses, such courses are not closed to other majors (Hamish, 2021).

Other avenues, such as the North American Planning Accreditation Board (PAB), provide minimal comment on general-education or introductory course offerings in planning programs. For example, the Innovative Practices section under Curriculum and Delivery of the 2018 PAB report stated that East Carolina University offered a general-education course taught by a planner-in-residence (PAB, 2018). We attempted an online review of accredited planning programs to identify such introductory or general-education courses; however, the information we were looking for was either difficult to find, or, when we did find said information, it was difficult to identify whether the course was a general education one.

The earlier discussion highlights how some planning programs are recruiting prospective planners through introductory and general-education courses. Required introductory and general-education courses possess the potential to increase the diversity of people and disciplines in urban planning because such courses are often more racially, ethnically, and disciplinarily diverse than other courses in a college or university due to their required status.

Thus, a question we pose is, "How, and in what ways, can professors who teach planning courses and professors with planning degrees in non-planning programs also use their courses to recruit prospective planners?" The courses of such professors might typically be at an introductory level or otherwise specialized to only one field of planning—depending on the nature of the department or program and its curriculum. As such, these courses might provide enough of an overview of the planning discipline to non-majors to interest them in further planning courses or a future planning career. Our response to such a question is important if, indeed, we want to recruit a range of both people and disciplines into urban planning.

In answering our research question, our hope is that the information we provide in this chapter can support college-level planning educators in non-planning departments to effectively articulate the utility of their courses in influencing student consideration of urban planning as a field of study and/or ultimate career choice, as well as the specific strategies in such courses that can prove particularly effective for such considerations.

Brief Overview of this Case Study's Introductory Urban Planning Course

Urban Planning, offered every fall semester by the University of West Florida (UWF) department of Earth and Environmental Sciences (EES), is an upper-level undergraduate elective course that is also cross-listed as a graduate elective. UWF does not offer Urban Planning as a major course of study or degree program. Also, because the course is offered by EES, a majority of the students who enroll are majoring in environmental science, with the occasional non-environmental-science student who may major in history, communication, or economics—and may or may not be minoring in environmental science. The course, which is a three-credit-hour course that meets twice a week for 75 minutes each, is taught by the first author, Kwame N. Owusu-Daaku, who started teaching it in 2017. The learning goal of the course is that, upon completion of the course, students will have a better understanding of how the field of planning has evolved, the topics that urban planners study, and the type of work urban planning practitioners engage in. Weekly course meetings are structured around lectures and discussions based on the textbook for the course, which between 2017–20 was *Contemporary Urban Planning* (11th edition) by John M. Levy. Between 2017–19, the students submitted multiple reading reflections on selected chapters from the textbook. For the same semesters, the instructor required students to complete an assignment called the Planning Pathways and Theory assignment, which we will explain further in a later section of this chapter. The course also features a real-life team-based project. The projects have varied each semester, but they have always been team-based and have all had a real-life component of either engaging with a real-life client or analyzing a real-life issue.

Methodology for Addressing Our Research Question

We emailed a survey to approximately 70 students, all of whom had completed the introductory Urban Planning course offered by UWF EES in the Fall semesters of 2017, 2018, 2019, and 2020, receiving a total of 36 responses. The survey instrument was a modified Student Assessment of Learning Gains (SALG) survey. The SALG survey is a free, standardized, modifiable survey that enables instructors to evaluate students' learning gains made in a course or their progress toward achieving course learning outcomes (About SALG, n.d.). As a result, many of the survey questions ask respondents to assess the learning gains they made relative to the topic of the question. For gains questions, the categories ranged in order of increasing gains made as follows: no gains, a little gain, moderate gain, good gain, great gain. We assumed any losses were captured under no gains. We also asked specific questions related to whether the students, at any point during or after the course, considered becoming an urban planner and what aspects of the course contributed to this consideration. For aspects of the course that influenced considerations, the categories ranged in order of increasing influencing as follows: none, a little, some, a fair amount, a great deal. We assumed any negative influences were captured under none. All questions were independent; no respondent had to answer a specific question before they could see or respond to another.

We analyzed survey responses using simple counts and percentages as well as culled insightful comments from the short-answer sections of the survey for each question. We also analyzed the results of four former students who responded to requests for follow-up interviews based on their indication in the survey that they had taken actions toward the planning profession beyond merely considering planning as a field of further study or career path. The survey indicated that these actions could range from applying (or planning to apply) to graduate school in urban planning, completing (or planning to complete) an urban planning internship, or working (or applying for a job) as an urban planner. These interviewed respondents were asked questions related to their current involvement in the planning profession, the ways in which specific course components influenced their decisions to enter the field, and whether they would have engaged with urban planning earlier if they had had the option to.

When Considerations of Planning as a Career Occurred

In response to the question, "Did you at any point during this course consider becoming an urban planner?" (n = 30), 70% of respondents stated they did, while the remaining 30% expressed they did not. In a related question of what this consideration of becoming an urban planner was like *after* the course had ended (n = 30), 53.3% stated that they had made this consideration again post course, while the remaining 46.7% stated they had not. The difference does not necessarily suggest that respondents changed their minds about the prospect of urban planning as a career but rather that they considered this prospect less post course than while taking it. This decline in consideration during and after the course indicates that planning educators should ramp up their consideration-of-planning-as-a-career appeals during a course and not necessarily before or after because, from this sample at least, students are more open to urban planning as a field while they are immersed in urban planning content and practice. This finding is in line with the extant literature (Hoisch & Bowie, 2009; Sax et al., 2017).

Influence of Specific Course Components

We wanted to know responses to the respective influences of the specific course components (i.e., course lectures and discussions, readings and reading reflections, Planning Pathways and Theory assignment, and real-life team-based project) on students' considerations to become an urban planner.

First, for course readings and/or reading reflections (n = 23), 34.8% of respondents considered them to have a fair amount of influence on their considerations to become an urban planner. Those who considered them to have a great deal and some influence were both 26.1% (Figure 21.1a). Overall, responses suggest that about 60.9%—from a fair amount to a great deal—think that readings and/or reading reflections influenced their considerations.

Second, concerning lectures and discussions (n = 23), approximately 74% of respondents stated that course meetings (both in person and via Zoom), lectures, and/or discussions influenced them a great deal in their considerations to become a planner (see Figure 21.1b). These course meetings were a combination of lectures using slides and discussions based on the readings and prompts that the instructor provided within the slides.

Third, the Planning Pathways and Theory assignment (n = 21) asked students to articulate a specialization or subfield of planning they would like to be engaged in, why they want to engage in this specialization, the requisite skills they would need to succeed in their chosen specialization, and a road map for the next five years to move them closer to their desired specialization.[2] Even though only 14.3% of respondents stated that the assignment influenced their considerations to become an urban planner a great deal (Figure 21.1c), more than half (57.1%) rated the assignment as having a fair amount of influence on their considerations. These two ratings collectively account for a 71.4% influence to become an urban planner.

For the real-life team-based project (n = 23), more than half (52.2%) reported that the real-life team-based project influenced them a great deal in their considerations to become an urban planner. This percentage was followed by 34.8% stating that the real-life team-based project influenced them a fair amount. Therefore, collectively the real-life team-based project had an 87% influence (either a great deal or a fair amount) on considerations to become an urban planner (Figure 21.1d). The following comment is illustrative of this influence: "The group work helped me the most, allowing me to work together with people on big and important projects. It helped me with teamwork as well as interaction with peers."

From the survey, the lectures and/or discussions (n = 23) reported the highest "great deal of influence" (73.9%), followed by the real-life team-based project (52.2%), readings and/or reflections (26.1%), and the Planning Pathways and Theory assignment (14.3%). Although in this course the

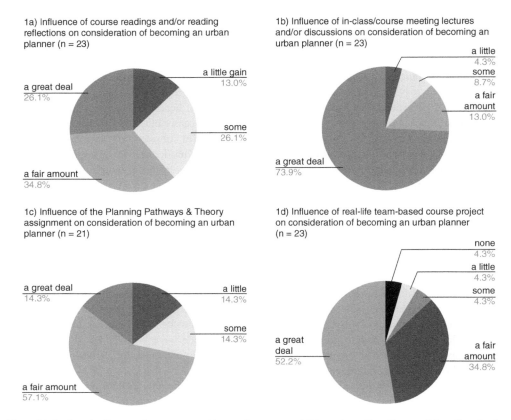

Figure 21.1a, b, c, d Survey Outcomes on Course Lectures and Discussions, Readings and Reading Reflections, Planning Pathways and Theory Assignment, and Real-Life Team-Based Project

Source: Authors

point of the readings and reflections was to assist with the ability to productively engage in course discussions and answer questions on the lecture slides, respondents seemed more interested in passively listening to lectures or engaging in discussions rather than reading and reflecting on what they had read via writing. Lectures and/or discussions also probably had the highest "great deal of influence" because the content of planning as a field was the most novel aspect of the course to students (we discuss the confirmation of this by an interviewee later in this chapter) more so than the opportunity to work as a team on a real-life project or complete a career-pathways assignment. Regardless, planning educators of non-majors should convey course content in a stimulating way—whether that be through interactive lectures or spirited discussion. The real-life team-based project ranked second highest as far as a "great deal of influence." From this sample, if planning educators of non-majors give opportunities to experience the work of planners and/or apply the concepts learned in-class, students may be more likely to consider planning as a prospective career as the literature suggests (Arefi & Ghaffari, 2020).

Learning Gains From the Course

The following subsections consider what gains all these course components made on students' further consideration of the discipline and profession of urban planning. Figure 21.2 illustrates these respective gains.

Interest in Taking Additional Planning Courses

In response to the following question, "As a result of your work in this course, what gains did you make in your interest in taking or planning to take additional planning courses?" (n = 34), a combined total of 91.2% of respondents stated they made some gains (i.e., ranging from a little gain to great gains) in their interest/plans to take additional planning courses. Figure 21.2a shows the breakdown of all responses to this question. Figure 21.2a illustrates the potential for students to make gains in their desire to learn more about the subject and profession of urban planning following the completion of an introductory class.

Integration of Learning

The following question sought to assess any gains respondents had made in their ability to integrate their urban planning learning with other coursework or related situations: "As a result of your work in this course, what gains did you make in applying what you learned to other situations?" Figure 21.2b highlights the responses and illustrates that 100% of respondents stated they made some form of gains (from a little gain to great gain) in integrating what they had learned in urban planning with other situations, with great gain accounting for 52.9% of respondents. One comment from a respondent illustrative of this integration is as follows: "[I have] Gained teamwork and presentation

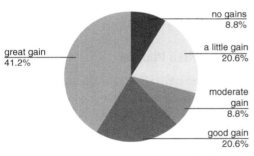

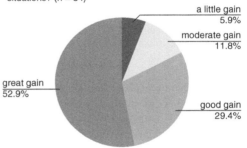

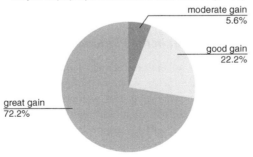

Figure 21.2a, b, c Interest in Taking Additional Planning Due to Course Work, Potential Application on What Learned to Other Situations, and Gains Obtained in This Course to Help Address Real World Issues

Source: Authors

skills that can be integrated into other classes and projects." Results suggest that, should planning educators of non-majors emphasize the applicability of planning coursework to other courses or situations, students could potentially consider planning as a future academic or career option because of planning's integrative and connective abilities.

Addressing Real-World Issues

All (100% of) respondents stated they had made gains (moderate gain to great gain) in response to the following question: "As a result of your work in this course, what gains did you make in your understanding of how studying this subject helps people address real-world issues?" (n = 36). Figure 21.2c presents the breakdown of these gains according to moderate gain, good gain, and great gain. A few comments illustrative of this increased understanding are as follows:

> This class opened up my mind to numerous world issues I did not think about previously. I now look at world issues different and with what I learned in this class in mind.
>
> This course allowed for a multidimensional view of structural issues that surround the framework for environmental improvement rather than just straight science or theory. This class was more real-world than most of the other classes I took.

From these results, for planning to have appeal to non-majors, planning educators should highlight the ability of planning to address real-world issues. This suggestion is supported by the literature on how such real-world application improves the accessibility and thus reach of a course to non-majors (Ahmad & Gestwicki, 2013). All students in the sample responded to this particular question, and all respondents stated they made moderate gains and higher.

Actions Toward Becoming an Urban Planner

Following the survey, from the respondents who stated they had taken some action toward their consideration to become an urban planner, four of them agreed to a follow-up interview. The following subsections will discuss their experiences and comments. Themes discussed are current involvement in the planning profession, specific course components that influenced their decisions to take further actions to enter the planning profession, course elements they currently use in their education or career, potential for an introductory urban planning course taken earlier on in their education to have had a greater impact on their career trajectory, and desire to have taken urban planning as an undergraduate degree.

Involvement in the Planning Profession

One interviewee worked directly in an environmental-planning department and had conducted planning for the military and aerospace fields, while two others either worked in planning departments or in connection with planners (zoning and wastewater management respectively). Two interviewees were in a master's program for urban and regional planning—one after taking urban planning courses at the undergraduate level (this respondent took the UWF planning course as a graduate student) and the other as a result of taking this urban planning course as an undergraduate. The general sentiment from interviewees was that they are striving to make practical changes (to both themselves and society) through a career and the planning profession or planning-related work offered them that opportunity.

Course Components Influencing Decisions

Three out of the four interviewees mentioned the real-life team-based project as having the greatest influence in their decisions to further engage with the planning profession. These projects were noted for helping students realize that planning was a viable career choice through the hands-on experience the project provided, and networking exposure via working and communicating with local professionals. From this sample, any planning education for non-majors should involve an opportunity for real-world application in teams—as having "a why" early on (as one interviewee stated) seems influential and clearly beneficial.

For the Planning Pathways and Theory assignment, even though the assignment was not ranked highly as having a great deal of influence for survey respondents (14.3%; refer to Figure 21.1c), for the two interviewees who did go to planning graduate school following the course, this assignment still held utility. This benefit is because a portion of the assignment asks students to consider what specific graduate school they would want to apply to if they decided that going to graduate school was essential to their five-year career pathway.

Alternative course activities that interviewees suggested included job fairs, implementing a planning group at the university that could work with other departments (engineering, landscape architecture, etc.), and establishing government agency/urban planning liaisons with the program to provide opportunities for guest speakers and job-shadowing days. Another interviewee also suggested having alumni from the program who are involved in the planning field come back to speak about how they took their degrees and applied their learning in different ways.

Course Elements Employed in Education and Careers

Three of the interviewees noted that they either directly or indirectly use elements of the course in their education and/or careers. Specific examples were philosophies of planning, zoning concepts, and the history of planning. Additionally, interviewees mentioned the ability to analyze data and communicate (verbally and written) clearly and effectively. An illustrative comment of this employment is as follows:

> I think the history of urban planning is one of the most important things I learned in my academic career, period. I fall back on that foundational knowledge more often than I do most things that I learned [in my master's program]. It's an incredibly intersectional place that many other things are born from. Urban planning is how do we make a city safe and equitable? How do we make this environment manageable and accessible? The historical component that [this course] teaches is useful and this component's ability to make intersectional ties are some of the most important things that need to be in the curriculum.

Influence of Earlier Exposure to Planning on Careers

In response to the question, "Do you think your career path would have been influenced (or changed completely) by taking an introductory or general education planning course early in your educational career?" the general consensus for this question was that yes, taking an introductory course earlier in their education would have more greatly influenced interviewees' career paths into the planning profession. All of the interviewees took this particular urban planning course within the last year of their respective academic programs. One interviewee noted how the course might be best taught at different times for different people, reemphasizing the influence an introductory urban planning course can have on career trajectories despite being offered later on in one's education (Hoisch &

Bowie, 2009; Sax et al., 2017). Another interviewee confessed that higher advanced-placement testing scores impacted the number of general-education courses they took during their first two years of college—implying that even if urban planning had been offered as a general-education credit at the time, they would not have been able to take the course. This realization suggests identifying ways of conveying planning knowledge to students who might test out of general education or introductory courses. Interviewees also suggested having urban planning become a facet of another course, like history, which may expose students to the field earlier. A notable comment that illustrates not just potential but actual influence is the following:

> I had all of this intense scientific knowledge [from a natural resources undergraduate degree] but I didn't have an application avenue. You understand all of these concepts, but you don't know why it matters, how do you apply them, and what do they look like when you externalize them to the real world. Urban planning was that for me. It was perfect timing for me because I was looking for something to connect these avenues that I knew were intersectional, but I just didn't quite know where they intersected. I think that for some people [urban planning] would set up the reason why a lot sooner.

Interest in Urban Planning as an Undergraduate Degree

Two interviewees were currently enrolled in master's programs for urban and regional planning, and one had nearly completed an environmental science master's degree. Three of the four interviewees indicated they would have been interested in urban planning undergraduate degrees if they were offered by their institutions as undergraduate degrees. One current graduate student noted that being able to minor in planning might be beneficial in addition to being able to major in it and noted that a majority of their current cohort peers had not discovered urban planning until late in their undergraduate degrees and that the discipline or degree is not something enough people know about. A comment illustrative of the collective responses to this question is as follows:

> Yes, on the condition that I had some kind of idea of urban planning before entering the field. I didn't even start as an environmental science major until I took an introductory environmental science class that opened my eyes. I don't know of any young person that wants to build a city—that doesn't happen without some introductory knowledge of it. After taking urban planning, I was definitely saying this would be something I would do and if it was offered as an undergraduate degree and I had taken an introductory class, it would have been my major.

This quote demonstrates the importance of introducing the subject of urban planning early in the academic setting in order to increase the potential for students to enroll in more courses and/or pursue the subject as a major. This quote also demonstrates the need for increased awareness of planning among the general population as a potential field of study and possible career paths associated with the subject.

Conclusion

This study confirms a few findings in the literature. The first is that initial experiences of students within introductory courses do connect with students' intent to major in the discipline following course completion (Sax et al., 2017; Arefi & Ghaffari, 2020), as evidenced by the two interviewees who explicitly stated that they went on to graduate school in urban planning as a direct influence of completing this course.

The second is that exposing students to the content of a planning course in a variety of ways has been shown to be beneficial for recruiting students into enrolling in more courses and potentially declaring planning majors (Estaville et al., 2007; Hoisch & Bowie, 2009; Arefi & Ghaffari, 2020) as evidenced by 74% of survey respondents stating that course lectures and discussions influenced them a great deal to consider becoming a planner. This great deal of influence was closely followed by the real-life team-based course project (i.e., 52% of survey respondents).

More importantly though, beyond merely confirming literature, this study demonstrates and validates some ways in which professors who teach planning-related courses (or with urban planning degrees) in non-planning departments (and thus to non-planning majors) can still use their courses to open up students to the possibilities (and wonders) of planning as a profession. These ways include delivering planning content in a stimulating, engaging manner and exposing students to the work of planners by providing opportunities for real-world applications of planning skills and content. These possibilities are, of course, not unique to this case study. However, this case study provides further evidence of the practicality of these strategies for recruiting non-majors (in this case environmental science majors) into the planning profession.

Notes

1 The group in question is the Planners 2040 Facebook group for academics who teach and research planning issues to engage in dialogue and share resources with each other. The first author who is a member of the group posed the following question to the group on January 31, 2021. "Hi All. Please forgive this seemingly impossible question. Does anyone know how to figure out how many Urban Planning programs offer general education or introductory planning courses to non-majors? Or who would be a possible clearinghouse for such information? Thanks in advance for any and all suggestions." He received six responses.
2 The reason students did not complete reading reflections or the Planning Pathways and Theory assignment in 2020 was that the instructor did not have a teaching assistant to assist with grading that semester.

References

About SALG. (n.d.). *Student assessment of learning gains (SALG)*. https://salgsite.net/about
Ahmad, K., & Gestwicki, P. (2013). Studio-based learning and app inventor for android in an introductory CS course for non-majors. *Association for Computing Machinery Technical Symposium on Computer Science Education, USA*, 287–292. https://doi.org/10.1145/2445196.2445286
Arefi, M., & Ghaffari, N. (2020). Five episodes of urban discovery as a student recruitment strategy in planning. *Journal of Planning Education and Research*. Online first, 1–10. https://doi.org/10.1177/0739456X20903362
Bristow, R. [Robert Bristow]. (2021, January 31). *Westfield State University, department of geography, planning and sustainability offers GPS0105, intro to community planning, a social understanding gen ed.* [Comment on the online forum post Owusu-Daaku, K.N., 2021. Facebook www.facebook.com/groups/planners2040/posts/3780563715336816/
Estaville, L., Brown, B., & Caldwell, S. (2007). Geography undergraduate program essentials: Recruitment. *Journal of Geography*, *105*(1), 3–12. https://doi.org/10.1080/00221340608978654
Hamish, R. [Rennie Hamish]. (2021, January 31). *In NZ most undergrad core planning courses are available as options for other majors. My third year environmental planning paper* [Comment on the online forum post Owusu-Daaku, K.N., 2021. Facebook]. www.facebook.com/groups/planners2040/posts/3780563715336816/
Hoisch, T. D., & Bowie, J. I. (2009). *Assessment of factors that influence the recruitment of majors from introductory geology courses*. American Geophysical Union. https://ui.adsabs.harvard.edu/abs/2009AGUFMED13C0613H
Johnson, B. [Bonnie Johnson]. (2021, January 31). *At the University of Kansas we do not have an undergrad major but we have a 200 level course on* [Comment on the online forum post Owusu-Daaku, K.N., 2021. Facebook]. www.facebook.com/groups/planners2040/posts/3780563715336816/
Owusu-Daaku, K.N. [Kwame Ntiri Owusu-Daaku]. (2021, January 31). *Hi all. Please forgive this seemingly impossible question. Does anyone know how to figure out how many urban planning programs* [Online forum post]. Facebook. www.facebook.com/groups/planners2040/posts/3780563715336816/
Planning Accreditation Board [PAB]. (2018). *Innovative practices–curriculum & delivery*. www.planningaccreditationboard.org/wp-content/uploads/2021/05/InnovCurriculum.pdf

Sax, L., Lehman, K., & Zavala, C. (2017). Examining enrollment growth: Non-CS majors in CS1 courses. *Association for Computing Machinery SIGCSE Technical Symposium on Computer Science Education, USA*, 513–518. https://doi.org/10.1145/3017680.3017781

Urey, G. [Gwen Urey]. (2021, January 31). *Cal poly Pomona offers lower division GE courses that welcome both majors and non majors* [Comment on the online forum post Owusu-Daaku, K.N., 2021. Facebook]. www.facebook.com/groups/planners2040/posts/3780563715336816/

22
ALABAMA CITY YEAR PROGRAM

Binita Mahato, Sweta Byahut, and Jay Mittal

University urban planning programs worldwide face challenges of providing quality and real-world planning exposure to their communities, particularly underserved ones. Most programs employ one of two distinct approaches in this effort—Design and Planning Language Programs (DPLPs) or service learning to deliver information about their core curricula. DPLPs are offered at an early age—to children and youth—to expose them to the discipline and encourage them to choose planning as a career (Palazzo et al., 2021). Service-learning programs focus on community partnerships to engage students in real-world planning issues, primarily raising planning awareness and providing high-quality experiential learning opportunities (Forsyth et al., 2000). However, for smaller planning programs,[1] both can be challenging. This chapter presents a case study of the Alabama City Year Program (ACYP), managed by the Master of Community Planning (MCP) program at Auburn University in the United States, as an initiative for experiential learning, planning awareness, and recruitment via community engagement. This chapter first presents the challenges of planning recruitment and awareness as pertinent to small planning programs. Second, the chapter discusses lack of planning awareness in Alabama to establish the context within which the ACYP operates. Finally, the case of ACYP as an adaptable framework to address the planning awareness and recruitment challenges of small planning programs is presented. The chapter concludes with the prospects and constraints of the ACYP and proposes a way forward for a successful integrated DPLP and service-learning initiative.

Planning Recruitment and Awareness Challenges

Urban planning has long struggled to raise its awareness as an established discipline. Being a multidisciplinary field, lack of originality and uniqueness renders planning a field without a strong, distinct disciplinary identity (Pinson, 2004). Challenges include theoretical and philosophical contradictions within the field, conflicting multidisciplinary interpretations, and variations of the discipline's name used by different programs (Evans, 1993; Pinson, 2004; Davoudi & Pendlebury, 2010). This lack of recognition often affects student recruitment in planning schools. In the United States, student enrollment declined by 10% in accredited planning programs between 2012–20 (Planning Accreditation Board, 2013, 2014, 2015, 2016, 2017, 2018, 2019, 2020). Low enrollment could also be attributed to lower entry-level salaries than other higher-paying professions of engineering, medicine, business, or law. Further, in professional appointments, a planning degree is preferred but often not a requirement for a planning job (Evans, 1993; Willson, 2017). And, unlike other professional disciplines, planners do not require licensure to practice (Willson, 2017). The challenges with lack of disciplinary recognition, low remuneration, and lack of recognition of the degree have limited the discipline's popularity as a promising career field for young professionals.

As a profession, planning contributes to better management of urban areas, addresses future challenges in cities, provides for planned development, and impacts a large percentage of the population. Yet, its service to society has often been criticized as biased, especially toward marginalized groups. Planning practices supporting economically and racially privileged populations (Goetz et al., 2020), and lack of diversity in the planning profession and education, render negative connotations of the field to minority and marginalized populations, thus affecting its popularity.

In the United States, the planning profession is dominated by non-Hispanic Whites (75.9%) followed by Asians (7.82%) and African Americans (5.42%) (Data USA, 2019). A similar pattern can be observed in student enrollment in planning schools. Figure 22.1 shows the racial and gender composition of students enrolled in planning programs in the United States from 2013–20. Whites represent most of the student body in planning programs, while other racial minorities have very little representation. In terms of gender, male planners dominate the workforce by 59.4% (Data USA, 2019) as well as planning education. However, the ratio of female students has been increasing since 2013 (Figure 22.1), mostly among minority groups, demonstrating their increased interest in the discipline and echoing the national drive for increasing diversity in education and the profession. The need and demand for student-body diversity urges planning education toward more attainable actions to create a campus climate and learning context that supports diversity (Evans & Chun, 2007; Sweet & Etienne, 2011). The challenge is to attain and maintain diversity in planning education while structurally adjusting course content and curricula to develop a more diverse, equitable form of education that creates "just" planners and raises the awareness of the field to common people.

Urban Planning Practice and Education in Alabama

The southern United States has long been characterized by a "lack of planning" and as "chaotic" without "conscious form and design" approaches (Cummings, 2018). While several southern cities witnessed a strong tradition of urban planning in the 18th century, such as Savannah, Georgia, and Charlotte, North Carolina, southern urban planning in the 19th century was just a desperate attempt to address the rapid urbanization of that period (Cummings, 2018). During the industrialization era, more organized urban planning in southern cities can be witnessed in the 20th century. Between the late 19th century and 20th century, many southern cities grew rapidly from small towns to big economic centers of the country. Scholars, such as Brownell (1975), Preston (1979), Goldfield (1982), and Hanchett (1998), however, criticize such growth for being dominated by business-improvement measures rather than alleviating the living conditions of the public (Goldfield, 1982) and for being aligned with the "white business elites" (Brownell, 1975) with little or no planning undertaken for lower-income and racial-minority groups. Segregation of neighborhoods and urban parks, such as in Charlotte (Hanchett, 1998), racially inspired zoning regulations, such as in Atlanta (Preston, 1979), and unjust urban-renewal plans of the 1960s dominated the urban planning practice in southern cities and towns.

Today, many cities in the South, including those in Alabama, lack progressive-planning practices and have absent or outdated comprehensive plans. While large or medium-sized cities have planning departments that offer planning services to the local community, smaller communities lack the institutional structure for systematic planning. Alabama has 12 regional councils of government, which serve multijurisdictional regional communities in the state. Of the eight public state universities, only two—Auburn University (Master of Community Planning) and Alabama A&M University (Bachelor of Science in Urban Planning and Master of Urban and Regional Planning)—offer planning degrees accredited by the North American Planning Accreditation Board (PAB). With small

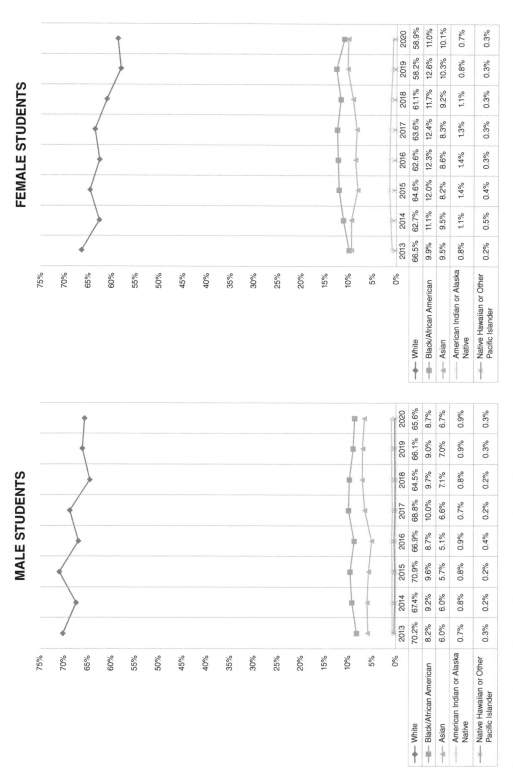

Figure 22.1 Graduate and Undergraduate Planning Enrollment (Full-Time and Part-Time) by Gender and Race

Source: Planning Accreditation Board Annual Reports (2013 to 2020)

numbers of planning graduates in the state, smaller communities rely on an array of small planning-related training programs. The Alabama Planning Institute (API), co-sponsored by the Alabama Chapter of the American Planning Association (AL-APA) and the Alabama League of Municipalities (ALM), offers some training programs to local officials and staff responsible for planning and zoning practices in their communities. The ALM represents around 450 incorporated cities and towns in Alabama and strengthens municipal governance statewide. Despite these efforts, several Alabama communities are underserved by professional, quality, and equitable planning services. University planning programs, in such contexts, can serve their planning needs through outreach programs.

Addressing Planning Awareness and Recruitment Challenges Through a Single Initiative

The challenges of planning awareness and recruitment, discussed previously, are prevalent in most planning programs, but it is most dire in smaller-sized programs in the South. For these programs, it is often challenging to assign budgets for outreach activities and maintain high student enrollment alongside diversity. With limited resources, one possible way to integrate outreach components into regular planning curricula is to adopt a single, yet integrated initiative that acts as a two-way tool for addressing both the planning awareness and recruitment challenges small planning programs face. Such initiatives can serve various objectives: marketing the planning discipline and promoting programs as potential career options, improving student enrollment, adding diversity, and expanding the curricular standards to provide exposure to real-world planning challenges to students via experiential learning.

The Master of Community Planning (MCP) program at Auburn University, housed in the Department of Political Science, is a small planning program with five core faculty, a few adjuncts, and a student body of about 45 graduate students. It has struggled to maintain its student numbers due to its small-town location and other challenges that the discipline faces. Not being a stand-alone planning department, school, or college also limits the program's abilities and budgetary resources to employ multiple outreach and service-learning initiatives to promote urban planning as a promising career choice for youth. To overcome these challenges, the MCP program established the Alabama City Year Program (ACYP) as a combined initiative for service-learning and outreach. The intent was to tackle the following concerns: How can planning programs address awareness and recruitment challenges through a single initiative? How can such an initiative benefit programs, students, and communities? How can small programs overcome institutional barriers such as funding and address faculty workload, keeping promotion and tenure (P&T) requirements in mind?

Alabama City Year Program (ACYP)

Auburn's MCP program has a long history of engagement serving local communities in Alabama. The program initiated the ACYP in 2016 to provide a structure to its community engagements. ACYP works as a two-way tool to address the challenges of professional-planning awareness and student recruitment via its community outreach initiative. The ACYP initiatives can be categorized into three types (Table 22.1). In Type A, the program works with small communities, towns, or villages with no professional-planning departments or staff. In such partnerships, smaller communities benefit the most from basic planning services offered via the ACYP compared to the students or the program. Thus, Type A projects fulfill planning-awareness goals more than recruitment goals.

Type B initiatives include collaborations on single or multiple planning projects with larger cities like Montgomery or Birmingham. Projects of this type vary from market to spatial analyses, supplementing existing plans and establishing standards. Although well equipped with planning staff, the partnering communities benefit from political neutrality, fresh ideas and options, and innovative

Table 22.1 Types of Initiatives, Alabama City Year Program

	Type A	Type B	Type C
Scale or Focus	Small communities, towns, or villages (population less than 15,000)	Single or multiple projects in a larger city (population 50,000 or more)	Topical focus in a small to a large city (no limit for population)
Community Resources	Lack of planning department/staff	Large planning department/staff	Medium to large planning department/staff
Service via ACYP	Comprehensive strategic development plans	Market, spatial, and socioeconomic analyses that complement planning	Limited topical focus (transportation, historic preservation, land-use planning, etc.)
Role of ACYP	Attempt to provide the services of a planning department	Work with planning staff, provide auxiliary planning services	Work with planning staff, provide innovative ideas
Community Engagement	Maximum—communities organize site visits, regularly attend project reviews, and provide community input	Intermediate to low—communities organize site visits, provide data, attend project reviews, and provide community input intermittently	Intermediate to high—communities organize site visits, provide data (if available), attend project reviews, and provide community input intermittently or regularly depending on project scope and commitment
Engagement Benefits	Planning awareness—provides planning services and resources to underserved communities	Planning recruitment—helps students build a professional network and find potential employees, an incentive that helps recruit potential students	Planning awareness and/or recruitment—provides specialized topical-planning services and resources to communities, and helps students build a professional network and find potential employees
Examples of ACYP Engagements	• *Brownfield Redevelopment Planning in Pell City in Synthesis Studio (Fall 2019) • *Community Health Assessment for Opelika in Synthesis Studio (Spring 2018) • *Comprehensive Plan for Loachapoka in Synthesis Studio (Fall 2018) • *Strategic Plan for Tuskegee in Synthesis Studio (Fall 2016)	• *Peacock Tract Revitalization Projects in Urban Design Studio • *Historic Interpretation Plans for Montgomery in Synthesis Studio (Spring 2020) • *Synthesis Studio II and *Urban Economics projects, *Highway 84 East Corridor Development Project in Dothan (Spring 2019, Fall 2018, and Spring 2018, respectively)	• MLK Drive Corridor Redevelopment Plan for Auburn in Urban Design Studio (Spring 2021) • *Pedestrian and Parking Management Plan for Prattville in Sustainable Transportation Planning (Spring 2017) • *Community and Regional Asset Mapping for LaGrange in Urban Economics (Fall 2016) • *Bike Master Plan for Auburn in Sustainable Transportation Planning (Fall 2015) • Historic Preservation Plans for Dauphin Island Parkway in Mobile in Historic Preservation Planning (Spring 2015)

*These student projects can be viewed on the ACYP website: www.alabamacityyearprogram.com (Figure 22.2)

Figure 22.2 Spring 2020 Urban Design Studio Field Visit, Montgomery

The project was showcased on the Alabama City Year Program website (www.alabamacityyearprogram.com), which helps ACYP to gain visibility and attract future community partners.

planning tools. The program benefits by building a professional network for experiential learning, and the students benefit by finding placement opportunities that provide incentives to attract potential students to the MCP program. In terms of commitment, both Types A and B are operated as full-phase projects incorporated into core-studio courses, such as Synthesis Studio 1 and 2^2 or Urban Design Studio.

Type C partnerships are topical. ACYP works with communities on special topics like transportation planning, historic preservation, local economic development, real estate, or land development. These projects (see Box 22.1 for a description of Type B and C projects) are less committed to communities as they aim to deliver within a limited scope. These topical projects are incorporated into elective or seminar courses where students apply conceptual principles, theories, and methods learned through these projects.

Box 22.1   ACYP Projects in Dothan, Alabama

Types B and C ACYP projects were undertaken in Dothan, Alabama, during a three-semester-long engagement with the city. The MCP program responded to a request from the city for student engagement on the Highway 84 East Corridor redevelopment project initiated in 2018. The Spring 2018 Sustainable Transportation Planning elective class worked on the plan alongside the city planning department and consultants. The student teams re-envisioned the corridor focusing on roundabout design, nodal redevelopment, connectivity, pedestrian and bike safety, parking, and recreational-trail enhancements. Student project ideas were reviewed by the city's engineering department and one of the student teams proposed a traffic roundabout on Highway 84 which was incorporated into the plan, and is now a central element in the detailed planning of a major project to revitalize the city center. In Fall 2018, students in the Urban Economics core class created potential economic-development strategies for Dothan to attract new businesses and investments by retaining local families and improving community assets while revitalizing specific areas. The following semester, in Spring 2019, student teams in the MCP program's Synthesis Studio worked on specific planning projects, including land-use-capacity analysis with a focus on housing and mixed uses, feasibility of using form-based code for historic preservation, rental housing study and analysis, rails-to-trails analysis and impact study, a wellness district (healthcare node) master plan, and a land-use study. These projects were conceptualized with Dothan planning staff and specifically responded to their planning needs. The city supported the projects by providing local travel and meals for students and organizing data sets, field trips, charrettes, and final presentations. Some costs were covered by the small-community outreach grants ($1,000) offered by the College of Liberal Arts. Dothan city has also offered to provide accommodations to students for future projects if needed. In each of these projects, students worked closely with city staff and other stakeholders and presented their work to the planning director, senior city officials, and city leaders, including the mayor. Since 2018, Dothan has hired several MCP students as interns every summer. The projects can be viewed online at https://www.alabamacityyearprogram.com/dothan-al

---

Table 22.2 shows the ACYP framework demonstrating goals and objectives for planning awareness and recruitment for its beneficiaries—students, programs, and communities. The framework also demonstrates the benefits of each initiative type for planning awareness and recruitment goals. For example, Type A projects benefit communities significantly by providing planning resources and services, while Type B and C projects provide low to moderate community benefits (Table 22.2). The ACYP framework helps integrate and distribute different types of projects into the curriculum.

Table 22.2 Framework Demonstrating ACYP's Goals and Objectives for Planning Awareness and Recruitment at the Levels of Students, Program, and Communities

Goal	Level	Objective	Type A	Type B	Type C
Planning Awareness	Students	Gain professional real-life experience in solving community planning problems with a real client	high	high	high
		Understand the complexity of urban problems	high	high	moderate
		Understand the multidisciplinary approach of urban planning	moderate	high	high
		Get exposed to equity and diversity issues of communities	high	high	low
		Opportunity to work with diverse and underserved communities	high	high	high
	Programs	Raise awareness of urban planning as a program and as a profession	high	moderate	high
		Potential marketing tool for program	moderate	high	high
		Develop community partnerships for future collaborations and data exchanges	high	high	low
		Service to the communities	high	high	high
		Align with departmental and collegial outreach expectations	high	high	high
		Gain local, state, and national-level recognition	high	high	high
		Maintain standards and accreditation compliances	high	high	high
	Communities	Get access to planning resources and services	high	low	high
		Develop partnerships with academic programs for innovative ideas	high	moderate	high
		Get exposed to challenges faced by underserved communities	high	high	high
		Receive specialized planning services: land-use planning, housing, real estate, urban design, transportation, historic preservation, GIS, etc.	high	high	moderate
		A multi-scale approach to planning: neighborhood planning, corridor planning, comprehensive planning, site planning, etc.	moderate	high	low
Planning Recruitment	Students	Find potential recruiter	high	high	low
		Build professional network	high	high	high
		Develop areas of interest and expertise	moderate	high	high
		Learn and apply necessary planning tools	high	high	high
	Programs	Placement of students	high	low	low
		Find potential recruiters for students	high	low	low
		Increase and/or maintain student numbers	high	low	low
		Maintain student diversities	high	low	low
		Groom students for the professional world	high	high	moderate
	Communities	Increase the visibility of planning as a future career path in the community	high	high	low
		Recruit proficient student interns and entry-level planners	high	low	low
		Obtain diverse, just, equitable planning perspectives	high	high	low
		Support student projects	high	high	moderate
		Maintain community and academic partnerships	high	high	high

Dark, medium, and light gray represent high, moderate, and low levels of benefit, respectively.

Especially for small planning programs, having a range of projects helps with feasibility and reduces the burden of outreach and service-learning for a small faculty. The different types of projects are distributed over several semesters and various course types—core classes, electives, studios, and seminars—to divide the workload among different faculty and offer a range of real-world experiences to students. This approach also creates possibilities for smaller underserved communities to obtain planning services at no cost. Varied options help larger communities attain a creative and innovative academic outlook and specialized services.

The MCP program, students, and communities are all beneficiaries and stakeholders in the ACYP. Faculty and students actively engage in understanding, analyzing, and addressing the planning challenges of partnering communities, and the ACYP projects are embedded into the class syllabus and larger program curriculum. Faculty meet in advance with the community partner to discuss and assess the need, formulate project details, and define the scope of work. The core classes with significant community outreach include Synthesis Studio, Urban Design Studio, and Urban Economics. Additionally, several elective courses, such as Historic Preservation Planning, Sustainable Transportation Planning, and Real Estate Principles, frequently collaborate with local communities. The funding mechanism of the projects also differs by their types. Bigger cities generally have funds to support expenses for student travel, materials, and printing costs for deliverables, as well as to organize field trips or charrettes. For small or underserved communities, the MCP program either bears the expenses internally or applies for internal grants. In either case, the availability of funding is vital, but for now, it is considered secondary to the primary goal of the ACYP to offer experiential learning and community outreach.

Initiation and Evolution

The ACYP was initiated by Auburn's MCP program to provide a platform for and structure to the community engagement its faculty undertakes to provide experiential learning in classes with communities in and around Alabama. A key objective of the ACYP was to provide students with multiple engagement opportunities to instill a richer and deeper understanding of complex planning issues. ACYP also furthered the outreach mission of Auburn University, a land-grant institution committed to improving local communities. In 2016, in its first strategic plan, the MCP program articulated the overall mission of the program, aligning it with Auburn University's land-grant mission, with community-based engaged learning a key focus:

> The centerpiece of the program is the opportunity for students and faculty to engage with underserved communities throughout Alabama and the Southeast through outreach, teaching, and engaged research. Through working on projects with communities throughout Alabama and the Southeast, students learn to help diverse and complex communities create and implement plans that improve and protect their quality of life, culture, diversity, resource base, built environment, natural environment, and economic vitality.

The MCP's strategic plan also identifies "Engagement—achieve distinction as a program that fosters learning through engagement" as one of its five primary goals. The ACYP was designed to provide a face to ongoing community engagement projects and formalize the program's future-engagement mission.

The ACYP is an evolving concept and was initially conceptualized to enable multiple classes to work simultaneously in the same city for a year to provide multi-perspective planning solutions to the community. From students' perspectives, this would have allowed studying one community more comprehensively from different topical angles. From a coordination standpoint, faculty could leverage established community partnerships, streamline the analysis, and avoid repetitive data collection. For example, Urban Design Studio and Sustainable Transportation courses worked with Phenix City, Alabama, in Spring 2022. While the studio worked on the revitalization of the city's downtown, the Sustainable Transportation elective focused on redesign of a major street corridor in the city. The classes collaborated to combine data collection and field trips. However, as the ACYP is gaining momentum, commitment to a single community for multiple courses is not always feasible due to the varied scope of courses and different faculty expertise and interests, which may not align with community needs. Logistical issues make it difficult to plan field visits (scheduled on different days of the week) and review presentations for different classes. Therefore, ACYP evolved to adopt a need- and relevance-based flexible approach. For example, the Urban Economics class worked in Mobile, while the Historic Preservation Planning class collaborated with Goodwater the same year. Similarly, the transportation class worked in Dothan and the Synthesis Studio in Tuskegee, even though two MCP classes subsequently did work in Dothan. In practice, synergies between different courses have been built through multiple engagements with specific communities (such as Dothan and Montgomery) in various classes spanning multiple semesters by one or more faculty. At the same time, other classes have focused on stand-alone projects in varied communities. MCP classes have occasionally also collaborated with Master of Landscape Architecture classes in the same community (Prattville and Pell City) at the same time. This flexibility has allowed community engagement projects to respond to specific requests from communities while meeting the needs and interests of the faculty.

ACYP Achievements

ACYP continues to evolve but offers insights to other small planning programs interested in expanding their outreach mission. The ACYP community engagement activities have raised the profile of Auburn University and its commitment to the land-grant mission, as well as helped maintain accreditation standards set by the PAB. While it was initially conceptualized as an outreach program, over the years ACYP has achieved many things—from community goodwill to benefitting the program, department, college, and university.

Serving Underserved Communities

Between 2016–21, Auburn's MCP classes have worked in at least 11 communities, including Auburn, Dothan, Loachapoka, Mobile, Montgomery, Pell City, Prattville, Prichard, Opelika, and Tuskegee in Alabama, and LaGrange in Georgia. Several of these partnerships are multiyear, multi-project engagements across multiple courses. These community engagement projects have been beneficial for the partnering communities, students, and the program. Through ACYP, the program has been able to help many underserved communities in Alabama that lack planning expertise. The Auburn University Community Planning program has gained goodwill among such communities across and beyond the state who frequently approach it for future engagements. The ACYP offers additional planning resources with a focus on improving the quality of life, culture, natural environment, local-resource base, built environment, and economic vitality in collaborating communities. The communities benefit from faculty expertise and students' help in generating baseline scenarios, data collection and analysis, new ideas, and alternative proposals. For providing a wide range of community engagement, the program has been recognized and praised by the Office of University Outreach via outreach grants and has been showcased in the university's outreach magazine *Beyond Auburn*.

Student Learning Outcomes

The MCP program uses two modes of assessment to evaluate student learning outcomes (SLOs)—graduating-student exit surveys and Synthesis Studio SLO evaluations. The exit survey is the self-assessment by students on the SLOs, while the Synthesis Studio SLO evaluation is completed by faculty, external reviewers, and participating communities and serves as a proxy for the ACYP.[3] The program also prepares its Annual Assessment Report for the university assessment office. The SLOs evaluate the ACYP projects based on parameters aligned with the PAB's disciplinary standards: general planning knowledge (purpose and meaning of planning, planning theory, planning law, human settlements and planning history, the future, and global dimensions of planning); planning skills (research, writing, oral, graphic communication, quantitative and qualitative methods, plan creation and implementation, planning-process methods, and leadership); and planning values and ethics (professional ethics and responsibility, governance and participation, sustainability and environmental quality, health and the built environment, growth and development, and social justice). Between the academic years 2016–17 and 2020–21, Synthesis Studio evaluations[4] show that the community projects significantly improved students' understanding of: planning law and its legal implementation; advanced written, oral, and graphic communication skills; leadership roles in developing plans while working with clients; and equity, diversity, and social-justice issues. Community partners have also consistently praised students' work. For instance, the City of Dothan noted the following:

> The City of Dothan could not be more pleased or impressed with the deliverables and insight provided by the Auburn Student Team in addressing technical design details for the Highway 84 Corridor.

In addition, the Student-Faculty Advisory Council (SFAC) meets at the end of every semester to create a two-way conversation platform between the students and the faculty. The students consistently praise the ACYP as being the most important component of the MCP program.

Planning Awareness

The ACYP serves as a tool to popularize planning ideas across the state, furthering the profession of planning, impacting communities and future planners, and consistently benefiting from greater recognition and goodwill within the planning community in the state. ACYP has improved planning awareness by increasing the visibility of the planning profession in the community as can be noted in this remark regarding an ACYP project:

> From my perspective as the campus sustainability director, one of the most important outcomes is that it extended and heightened a community conversation about the importance of sustainability in urban planning. It created a deeper understanding of the meaning and relevance of sustainability as well as its practical power to enhance the quality of life on campus and in the Auburn community. This may be the most significant and long-lasting outcome of all.

ACYP projects have been frequently presented at the annual Alabama Chapter of the APA (AL-APA) conferences, and both the students and program have received several Distinguished Leadership Awards. These initiatives have helped generate further interest among communities and helped the MCP program generate goodwill and expand its statewide footprint. Maintaining a website that documents these engagements (www.alabamacityyearprogram.com, Figure 22.2), using the ACYP experiences as a key feature in student-recruitment materials, and the visibility of the projects in local planning chapters have each triggered several partnership queries from communities.

Recruitment, Placement, and Student Diversity

ACYP also benefits student recruitment and placement. Though this wasn't an intentional aspect of the original design, the MCP program has been able to maintain its program strength due to the popularity of the ACYP. A significant number of prospective students mention ACYP as one of their key reasons for application in their statements of purpose. Serving the underserved community promotes the program and planning in general to the minority communities in the state. The MCP program has maintained a diverse student body, with an almost-equal distribution of male and female students, around 39% White, 4% Hispanic, 16% African American, and 41% Asian.[5] In 2019, the program was ranked sixth in the nation for its student diversity and tenth among small-city programs by Planetizen (2019). In 2018, ACYP was also noted as a noteworthy practice by the PAB.

ACYP also helps in student placement and internships. Students get opportunities to interact with planning officials, senior city staff, and leadership such as the mayor or city manager. These interactions help develop professional networks that often lead to internships and jobs and make graduates more competitive. MCP has an approximately 90–95% placement rate for planning students within a few months of graduation. This in turn helps with student recruitment.

Lessons Learned From ACYP

The next parts will examine some of the lessons learned from this experience.

Funding

As ACYP is still evolving, it does not have a dedicated budget. Projects are funded either through university grants or by the partnering communities—sometimes in cash but always in-kind. For example, projects in Dothan, Montgomery, and Opelika received internal university and college grants and awards. During the 2017–18 and 2018–19 academic years, faculty secured four university outreach grants and undertook five community engagement projects. Some projects have also been supported financially by community partners or stakeholders. In Fall 2019, the Alabama Department of Environmental Management (ADEM) sponsored the Synthesis Studio in Pell City as part of the Environmental Protection Agency's (EPA) small-grant program, where students developed planning strategies for brownfield redevelopment. Similarly, in 2016, a local real estate firm provided financial support for the student project in LaGrange, Georgia. More recently, in Summer 2020, two faculty members partnered with the Montgomery Housing Authority (MHA) and helped it secure a $450,000 HUD Choice Neighborhoods Initiative (CNI) planning grant. The MCP program faculty and students have been engaged with the MHA in the 2021–22 academic year with community projects that the grant will support. Instead of relying on case-based funding options, having a dedicated budget for ACYP would be beneficial for sustaining the program in the future.

Flexibility

The ACYP experience shows that maintaining flexibility in service-learning programs through various projects helps better manage faculty interests, course SLOs, and community expectations. ACYP's initial idea of working with a single city each year was ineffective, as students, faculty, and communities have varying needs and derive different benefits from DPLPs. Commitment to a single partnership might not sufficiently meet the needs of all these beneficiaries. For small programs like Auburn's MCP, it is more sustainable to opt for community partners and projects on a case-to-case basis. Programs need to balance these benefits by creating different scales and types of programs and distributing them over time. Selected projects under these initiatives can vary by size of selected cities, the scope of work, and project focus. The flexibility to choose projects is also beneficial considering the scope and expectations of different courses. Some courses, such as Synthesis Studio or Urban Design Studio, incorporate a full-scale project in a semester. In contrast, other elective or special-topic courses, such as Transportation Planning or Historic Preservation, may commit to a limited scope to meet the course SLOs and requirements. Flexibility also allows faculty to select projects of interest and relevance to their courses without any obligation. Presently, the MCP faculty reviews requests and selects projects as per their interest and course needs to maintain their respective workloads, which have minimal outreach components. While working with a single city on multiple projects might be a good model of service-learning from students' perspectives, flexibility allows serving more communities, especially underserved ones, and incorporating a range of planning topics. Given the opportunity and resources, ACYP's success greatly depends on flexibility of project selection, scale, partner-community commitment, and focus area.

Faculty Workload

Lack of faculty workload adjustment to account for outreach activity has been a key barrier to implementing ACYP. For small programs with low budgetary autonomy, outreach and service-learning initiatives could become a burden to the faculty if they're not incorporated into Promotion and Tenure (P&T) and workload requirements. Smaller planning programs are often not stand-alone departments, but part of larger departments with related but multiple and varied disciplines. It is challenging for such departments to recognize and value outreach work and account for it systematically in the annual faculty workload distribution. Auburn's MCP program is part of the Department of Political Science. While outreach is an important and significant part of Auburn University's land-grant mission and the MCP program incorporates it well in its strategic mission, it is not reflected in the department's mission, which considers outreach activities optional. Moreover, classes with or without significant outreach components are considered similar in the faculty workload—lectures, studios, or seminar classes have the same credit hours regardless of varied or absent outreach commitment. While the MCP program's ACYP is the program's hallmark and is well-known throughout the state, faculty with significant outreach agendas do not receive compensation or a course reduction for additional outreach work. Such barriers could become a potential future threat for programs like the ACYP. Existence of such programs depends largely on the goodwill of the faculty and their interest in increasing experiential learning, planning awareness, and recruitment. To balance faculty workload and make outreach sustainable, small planning programs may consider integrating outreach initiatives internally through co-teaching or extending the same projects in multiple studios (such as integrating Synthesis Studios 1 and 2).

The Way Forward

ACYP continues to evolve in response to challenges and opportunities. It's a collaborative initiative bridging the knowledge gap between three stakeholders—faculty, students, and partnering communities. It has the potential to disseminate research, as well as share new ideas and best practices among local communities. For underserved and small communities, programs like ACYP are perhaps the primary way of getting professional-planning services. Working with minority communities also helps maintain the diversity of the student body, as recruitment and retention of planners of color remain barriers to just and equitable planning in the country (Tiarachristie, 2016). Initiatives like

ACYP are useful to practice-oriented planning programs as they connect classroom learning to the challenges of the field. Both students and faculty benefit from this experiential learning. The faculty stays current with professional practice, while students learn about complex planning issues, approaches to handling them, insights from practitioners, technical and conceptual ideas from their peers and faculty, and professional networks for jobs and internships. However, the benefits of initiatives like ACYP come at a cost for the faculty of small planning programs (Forsyth et al., 2000). The MCP program faculty initiated ACYP without measurable support or funding from the department, college, or university. As a way forward, ACYP could aim for more substantial integration and value faculty contributions by receiving outreach credit in P&T requirements and workload assignments. Increasing publications through ACYP is a key way to receive P&T acknowledgment for research through outreach and teaching. Currently, the faculty does conference presentations on ACYP projects and is restructuring the teaching load within the MCP program to give more credit to ACYP-project work. ACYP may also consider allocating a dedicated budget for the program instead of relying on small grants or inconsistent community contributions to support student and faculty travel, materials, presentation costs, conference participation, and faculty time. With such modifications, ACYP can continue to increase planning awareness and serve communities in Alabama and the Southeast region and, in turn, help increase student recruitment for the program and maintain diversity.

Notes

1. This designation is according to Planetizen's *Guide to Graduate Urban Planning Programs, 6th Edition,* which defines small planning programs as those with fewer than 55 students enrolled on average over three years with a small faculty body.
2. Synthesis Studio (capstone project) is offered both in Fall and Spring semesters as Synthesis Studio 1 and 2, engaging with two different ACYP projects. Second-year Master of Community Planning students need to take both Synthesis Studio 1 and 2 to graduate.
3. Every Synthesis Studio worked through the ACYP except for Fall 2020 and Spring 2021, since working with an actual community was not feasible due to the COVID-19 pandemic. During these semesters, Synthesis Studios resorted to hypothetical projects.
4. Synthesis Studio evaluations use the 15 parameters of the SLOs for evaluation of student apprehension post completion of each studio project.
5. Including both domestic and international Asian students.

References

Brownell, B. A. (1975). *The urban ethos in the South, 1920–1930.* Louisiana State University Press.
Cummings, A. S. (2018, March 26). The emergence of urban planning in the South, 1880–1930. *Tropics of Meta.* https://tropicsofmeta.com/2018/03/26/the-emergence-of-urban-planning-in-the- south-1880–1930/
Data USA. (2019). *Data USA: Urban & regional planners.* https://datausa.io/profile/soc/urban-regional-planners#demographics
Davoudi, S., & Pendlebury, J. (2010, November 1). The evolution of planning as an academic discipline. *Town Planning Review, 81*(6), 613. doi:10.3828/tpr.2010.24
Evans, A., & Chun, E. B. (2007). Are the walls really down? Behavioral and organizational barriers to faculty and staff diversity. *ASHE Higher Education Report, 33*(1), 1–139. https://doi.org/10.1002/aehe.3301
Evans, B. (1993). Why we no longer need a town planning profession. *Planning Practice & Research, 8*(1), 9. https://doi-org.spot.lib.auburn.edu/10.1080/02697459308722865
Forsyth, A., Lu, H., McGirr, P. (2000). Service-learning in an urban context: Implications for planning and design education. *Journal of Architectural & Planning Research, 17*(3), 236–258. www.jstor.org/stable/43030542
Goetz, E. G., Williams, R. A., & Damiano, A. (2020). Whiteness and urban planning. *Journal of the American Planning Association, 86*(2), 142–156. https://doi.org/10.1080/01944363.2019.1693907
Goldfield, D. R. (1982). *Cotton fields and skyscrapers: Southern city and region, 1607–1980.* Louisiana State University Press.

Hanchett, T. W. (1998). *Sorting out the New South City: Race, class, and urban development in Charlotte, 1875–1975*. University of North Carolina Press.

Palazzo, D., Hollstein, L., & Diko, S. K. (2021). Urban planning as a career preference for students: Efforts to improve awareness about the profession. *Planning Practice & Research, 36*(2), 174–192. https://doi.org/10.1080/02697459.2020.1782056

Pinson, D. (2004). Urban planning: An 'undisciplined' discipline? *Futures, 36*(4), 503–513. https://doi.org/10.1016/j.futures.2003.10.008

Planetizen. (2019, September 3). *The top schools for urban planners*. Retrieved June 1, 2022, from planetizen.com/topschools

Planning Accreditation Board. (2013). Student and faculty composition in PAB-accredited programs. *2013 Annual Report Data*. www.planningaccreditationboard.org/wp-content/uploads/2021/04/2013AR-data.pdf

Planning Accreditation Board. (2014). Student and faculty composition in PAB-accredited programs. *2014 Annual Report Data*. www.planningaccreditationboard.org/wp-content/uploads/2021/04/2014AR.pdf

Planning Accreditation Board. (2015). Student and faculty composition in PAB-accredited programs. *2015 Annual Report Data*. www.planningaccreditationboard.org/wp-content/uploads/2021/04/2015ARdata.pdf

Planning Accreditation Board. (2016). Student and faculty composition in PAB-accredited programs. *2016 Annual Report Data*. www.planningaccreditationboard.org/wp-content/uploads/2021/04/2016ARdata.pdf

Planning Accreditation Board. (2017). Student and faculty composition in PAB-accredited programs. *2017 Annual Report Data*. www.planningaccreditationboard.org/wp-content/uploads/2021/04/2017AR.pdf

Planning Accreditation Board. (2018). Student and faculty composition in PAB-accredited programs. *2018 Annual Report Data*. www.planningaccreditationboard.org/wp-content/uploads/2021/04/2018AR.pdf

Planning Accreditation Board. (2019). Student and faculty composition in PAB-accredited programs. *2019 Annual Report Data*. www.planningaccreditationboard.org/wp-content/uploads/2021/06/2019AR.pdf

Planning Accreditation Board. (2020). Student and faculty composition in PAB-accredited programs. *2020s Annual Report Data*. www.planningaccreditationboard.org/wp-content/uploads/2021/06/2020AR.pdf

Preston, H. L. (1979). *Automobile age Atlanta: The making of a Southern metropolis, 1900–1935*. University of Georgia Press.

Sweet, E. L., & Etienne, H. F. (2011). Commentary: Diversity in urban planning education and practice. *Journal of Planning Education and Research, 31*(3), 332–339. https://doi-org.spot.lib.auburn.edu/10.1177/0739456X11414715

Tiarachristie, G. (2016, August 9). The elephant in the planning room: Overcoming barriers to recruitment and retention of people of color in the planning profession. *American Planning Association New York Metro Chapter*. www.nyplanning.org/groups/diversity/elephant-planning-room-overcoming-barriers-recruitment-retention-people-color-planning-profession/

Willson, R. (2017, September 11). So . . . No planning degree? *American Planning Association*. www.planning.org/blog/blogpost/9133362/

23
CAREER CHOICES IN THE CENTURY OF URBANIZATION

A Comparative Study of Student Enrollments in Nigerian Universities From the Urban Planning Perspective

David S. Osiyi and Victor U. Onyebueke

More than 600 planning schools worldwide are providing undergraduate and/or graduate-level training (Frank & Silver, 2018). A closer look at the growth trends reveals "some correlation between the level and speed of urbanization and development that a nation experiences and the type of planning and ergo training and education for planning" (Frank, 2018, p. 135). This alludes to the notion of urbanization-planning elicitation, epitomizing the contemporary co-occurrence of global urbanization, rising city challenges, and the growing need for planning. For example, Nigeria is Africa's most populous country with an estimated population of about 208 million people in 2020 and a huge urban population of nearly 110 million growing annually at a rate of more than 4% (World Bank, 2022). The country hosts 18[1] (32%) out of some 57 African planning schools (Association of African Planning Schools [AAPS], 2021). In the present century of urbanization with more than 55% of the global population living in cities and towns (United Nations, 2019), the planning profession has garnered international strides and critical acclaim as a major city-building and -managing enterprise with established transnational education, trainings, and practices (Amirahmadi, 1993; Friedmann, 2005; Frank & Silver, 2018). The recent COVID-19 pandemic has not only amplified histories of contagious diseases in cities across the world but is renewing calls for active reengagement between urban planning and public health (Grant et al., 2017; UN-Habitat & WHO, 2020). This evolving arrangement, which is partly driven by the New Urban Agenda[2] on sustainable healthy cities, re-conceptualizes "city planning as preventive medicine, where interventions combine attention to physical, social, and institutional factors that shape urban health" (Corburn, 2015, p. 48).

These entrenched and shifting roles of planning are notable and appear to bring the planning profession to the limelight with expectations of improving its reputation and occupational prestige. Yet, awareness of the urban planning profession and student enrollments continue to decline in some countries in both the Global North and South (Osiyi & Jiburum, 2020; Palazzo et al., 2021; Nigerian Institute of Town Planners, 2021). Besides the apparent confusion attributable to scant research into the real reasons for these pervasive setbacks, the consequences for falling enrollments and diminishing chances of meeting enlarged planning demands are graver, especially for sub-Saharan Africa, where the discipline is largely under-resourced (UN-Habitat, 2013). Today, low or declining student enrollment in planning, irrespective of causes and consequences, has shifted from being the call-of-duty concern of professional-planning institutions and planning-school administrators to a front-burner issue in contemporary scholarship. Although enrollment downturns are not new, and in fact, occur in diverse disciplines (see Kiser & Hammer, 2016; Delcoure & Carmona, 2019; Aulck et al., 2020; Peterson et al., 2020), a focus on planning is warranted in the current situation. Besides being the chosen theme of this book, the exacerbated challenges facing cities in the 21st century, which border on the very survival of urban humanity, have ramifications for urban planning (UN-Habitat & WHO, 2020). In the Nigerian context, continued attention has been directed to low planning-student enrollment and career choice (Morenikeji & Shuaibu, 2006; Al-Hasan et al., 2013; Osiyi & Jiburum, 2020) as well as professional training and awareness creation (Wahab et al., 2014; Nigerian Institute of Town Planners [NITP], 2021). Amid numerous concerns and queries, one outstanding gap is the dearth of interdisciplinary enrollment comparisons, especially at the national level.

This chapter takes a comparative look at career-choice trends among fresh university applicants in Nigeria with a focus on urban planning using time series (enrollment) data—national UTME (Unified Tertiary Matriculation Examination) and university specific (University of Nigeria, Nsukka [UNN]) enrollment data. It investigates student enrollment in urban planning in relation to the popular or preferred course offerings in Nigeria. The specific objectives are to: (1) compare trends in the career choice of planning with those of the ten most popular courses,[3] (2) ascertain determinant factors of career choices and any variations between urban planning and the comparator courses, (3) explore the extent of manpower demand for planning, and (4) recommend workable measures for improving student enrollment, retention, and graduation in urban planning.

This chapter has five sections. The chapter began by elucidating the nexus between urbanization, planning, and planning education. The next section illuminates social cognitive career theory (SCCT) and reviews relevant literature on career awareness, motivations and/or influences, career preferences, and student enrollment. Furthermore, current manpower demands for urban planning are discussed to set the stage for the supply side (enrollment, training, and completion) in Nigeria and further afield. The third section is the research methodology segment, while the fourth section outlines the research results and discussions. The chapter concludes with recommendations for improving planning awareness and student enrollment.

Theories and Factors of Career Choice and Student Enrollments

This section discusses career choices in general and planners' demand in some African countries compared with the United States and the United Kingdom.

Social Cognitive Career Theory and Career Choice

Career guidance and counseling issues are universal and cut across different cultures and societies (Onoyeyan & Unegbu, 2019). In an era of global competitiveness, all people are affected by a range of occupational concerns, some of which may be peculiar to certain cultures or regions, while others may be common across many cultural and regional contexts (Leung, 2008). Several theoretical models on career development and decision-making processes, developed mostly in the United States, exist today. Leung (2008) has described them as the "big five career theories"[4] (p. 115). These models show different aspects and note how people–environment interactions help cultivate career interests as well as choice and adjustment mechanisms. Mostly, they form the basis for ascertaining factors of career-choice decisions, student enrollment, and course completion. Aspects of these theories and their numerous spin-offs are often deployed in enrollment-management strategies of many universities and tertiary institutions. Since SCCT espouses intricate interactions between the desires and aspirations of adolescents in their career determination and the external forces that influence them (Schaub & Tokar, 2005; Akosah-Twumasi et al., 2018), we shall take a closer look at this model (Figure 23.1). Originally based on the social-cognitive theory of Albert Bandura, the SCCT

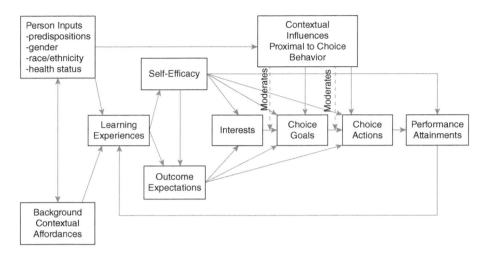

Figure 23.1 Elements of the Social Cognitive Career Theory
Source: Schaub and Tokar (2005, p. 305). Copyright [2021] Elsevier (reprinted with permission)

was developed mostly by Lent et al. (2002) and Lent (2005) to highlight the mutual interactions between individuals and their environments in career interests and choice determinations.

The SCCT, like the other career-decision theories, is reducible to person–work environment interactions in determining people's vocational interests and related adjustments. Amid extrinsic and intrinsic motivations (employment opportunities, salary, job security, satisfaction, etc.), contextual or third-party influences (environment, parents, family members, peer group, friends, counselors, etc.), and career-awareness learning experiences, the theory depicts detailed decision-making procedures and three interconnected career outcomes (and variables). These include how: (1) academic and vocational interests are developed (self-efficacy), (2) individuals make educational and career choices (outcome expectations), and (3) educational and career performance and stability are set and reached (personal goals). According to Lent (2005), self-efficacy signifies "a dynamic set of beliefs that are linked to particular performance domains and activities" (p. 104).

Active assimilation of self-efficacy is dependent on four main information sources—enactive mastery experience, vicarious learning, verbal and social persuasion, and physiological and affective states or emotions (Bandura, 1997). These elements are responsible for expanding or raising the awareness fields of prospective career entrants. Maddux's (2005) addition of a fifth source, imaginal experiences, addressing imagined role-plays in self-efficacy reinforcement, also deserves mention. Almost certainly an offshoot of physiological and affective emotions, we find connections between this element and the idea of playful public participation in urban planning induced by NextCampus, a gaming application, as highlighted by Poplin (2012, p. 195). Similarly, Terzano and Morckel (2017) showed how SimCity gaming software deployed as a pedagogical tool increased students' interest and perceptions of the planning discipline as being fun and creative. In other words, computer-simulated urban environments in SimCity gaming software and other city building games can stimulate imagined experiences of becoming urban planners in children and young people.

Professional Awareness, Career Choice, and Student Enrollment

Contemporary literature on the subject matter, drawn from both Global North and African contexts, is structured and summarized in line with the key tenets of SCCT in Table 23.1. Four main

Table 23.1 Determinant Factors in Career Choice and Development

	Key Factors of Career Choice	SCCT Elements	Context and Specification (Authors)
1	Professional awareness and career self-identification	Learning experiences	• Awareness challenges (students' unfamiliarity, parents' misperceptions, and non-recommendation by school counselors) of urban planning in North America and impacts on student enrollment and diversity (Palazzo et al., 2021) • Awareness of law librarianship is critical in determining its career-choice prospects among university undergraduates in Southwest Nigeria (Onoyeyan & Unegbu, 2019) • Awareness of pharmacy among secondary school students in Lagos, Nigeria (Ghazali et al., 2020) • Professional awareness (via relatives' and siblings' career occupations, related past experiences, among others) of estate management as a career choice in Nigeria (Ayodele, 2019)
2	Employment prospects and material expectations (financial rewards, independence, prestige, etc.)	Outcome expectations	• Journalism (mass communication) as respondents' hope for "dreams jobs upon graduation" (Emmanuel et al., 2021, p. 14) • Nursing students are motivated by high and rewarding job prospects amid individual aspirations and internationalization of the health sector (Angel, 2017) • Opportunity to set up private practice and undertake specialist training as a motivation for Nigerian medical students (Ashipa et al., 2017) • Chartered accountants and lucrative job prospects in Ghana (Zotorvie, 2016) • Medical students attested to a clearer sense of career aim, practical relevance, and preparation than other disciplines in German tertiary institutions (Piedmont & Robra, 2015)
3	Environmental or extrinsic factors, interpersonal influences by parents, peers, and teachers	Contextual factors	• Parents, guardians, and school environment (Okojide et al., 2018) • Parents' and teachers' influence on career decisions of students in Nigeria (Al-Hasan et al., 2013; Jamabo, 2014) • Influences of family, teachers, and students in South Africa (Shumba & Naong, 2012) • Funding, grants, and targeted scholarships (Alhassan & Lawal, 2015; Aulck et al., 2020) • Course marketing and outreach programs (Hayden et al., 2011; Rosi et al., 2016; Palazzo et al., 2021)
4	Personality traits, personal status, and interests (previous academic performance, health condition, etc.)	Self-efficacy	• Students' interest is vital to career decisions in Kenya, Nigeria, and South Africa (Shumba & Naong, 2012; Ayodele, 2019) • Personal interest in becoming a chartered accountant and job prospects (high earning expectations, prestige, etc.) as career motivations in Ghana (Zotorvie, 2016) • Students' academic attainments and performances, personal interests, and school environments (Okojide et al., 2018)

Source: Authors' literature review and analysis

career-choice factors are implicated, namely: (1) professional awareness and career self-identification; (2) employment prospects and material expectations (financial reward, independence, etc.); (3) environmental or extrinsic factors, interpersonal influences by parents, peers, and teachers; and (4) personality traits, personal status, and interests (previous academic performance, health conditions, etc.).

Relating these factors to the Nigerian context, four notable peculiarities are evident:

- Prior awareness of a course or discipline is critical to students' career decisions and consequent endeavors to accept particular course offerings in university admission.
- SCCT-designated outcome expectations—employment prospects, internationalization, material expectations, and social prestige—appear to account for the inherent differences between popular and unpopular courses. Notice the apparent convergence of work focusing on some of the most sought-after disciplines like medicine, nursing, journalism, and accounting in the same cell (Table 23.1).
- Influences and motivations (from parents, family members, guardians, peer groups, friends, role models, teachers, counselors, etc.) often combine with intrinsic attributes like personality traits and personal interests to determine students' career choices.
- In addition, contextual or environmental factors like awareness-raising programs and funding opportunities are a strategic stimulus to improving student enrollment in diverse disciplines.

Notwithstanding the foregoing, career "choice remains a worrisome problem among Nigerian students across the country as many students are dependent on chance and luck elements in career decisions making and are not aware of new career opportunities" (Onoyeyan & Unegbu, 2019, p. 1). Therefore, the content and context of the awareness-raising information to be deployed by promoting bodies is pivotal.

Best-practice interventions to increase student enrollment and ensure course retention and completion are applicable across disciplines and universities. These tools and techniques are often process-oriented and context-based and include, albeit are not limited to, five basic measures summarized in Table 23.2 with specific reference to their applicability to planning.

Since career paths extend beyond graduation, it is equally important to focus on the big picture—the labor market's demand-and-supply mechanisms and the education-employment interface (Fuertes et al., 2021). Before considering practical lessons that professional bodies and planning-school administrators could learn from existing awareness-creation and enrollment-improvement tools, let us explore the manpower demand for planning.

Manpower Demand for Planning and Student Enrollment

Globally, issues of professional demand and supply, in addition to competencies to manage rapid urbanization and resultant megacities, have remained on the agenda of planning scholars (Cevrić, 2011; Watson & Odendaal, 2012; Parker et al., 2020). Granting the current study's scope, explanations are limited to planning demand in order to highlight prospective opportunities for intended planning applicants. Table 23.3 compares the planners-to-population ratios and number of registered planners in four African Planning Association[5] (APA) member countries with the US and UK indices.

Since the number of planners registered in particular countries may not equate to those in actual domestic-planning practice,[6] there is a need for cautious interpretations. At least three facts are decipherable: (1) while national registers of planners appear to relate to population size, the planners-to-population ratio also mimics the point of intersection between planning demand and supply curves; (2) notwithstanding the clear ascendancy of the United States and United Kingdom in both absolute numbers and ratios of planners to population, the two origins of modern planning

Table 23.2 Tools and Techniques for Increasing Professional Awareness and Student Enrollment

	Measures for Increasing Professional Awareness and Student Recruitment	Evidence of Application	
		General/Specific Disciplines	Applicability to Urban Planning
1	Enrollment-management analytics and academic-support programs are known to increase enrollment and tuition revenue	University-wide enrollment and retention programs (Alhassan & Lawal, 2015; Kiser & Hammer, 2016; Aulck et al., 2020); college of business administration (Delcoure & Carmona, 2019)	Interdisciplinary and university-wide initiatives are operable in all regions of the world and therefore applicable to planning and the study context
2	Publicity and outreach programs to raise professional awareness (e.g., summer camps, advertisements, announcement, etc.)	A project to engage students and teachers to increase interest in STEM courses (Hayden et al., 2011); awareness as a career determinant for law librarianship (Onoyeyan & Unegbu, 2019)	Raising awareness of the planning profession among youth in North America via Design and Planning Language Programs (Palazzo et al., 2021); awareness-raising programs are applicable to planning in other regions and the study context
3	Curriculum relevance, career competence, skills, and employment prospects	Medical and nursing students, for example (Piedmont & Robra, 2015; Angel, 2017)	Curriculum reforms for planning schools consolidation, appropriate local knowledge production, and effective practice (Cevrić, 2011; Watson & Odendaal, 2012; Parker et al., 2020); applicable to planning in other regions and the study context
4	Targeted scholarships and bursaries through corporate social responsibility (CSR) initiatives	Optimizing scholarship allocation via machine learning (Alhassan & Lawal, 2015; Aulck et al., 2020); co-funding education as a CSR (Fusheini & Salia, 2021)	Interdisciplinary and university-wide initiatives instrumental to student enrollment, performance, and completion; applicable to planning and the study context
5	Technological tools like geographical information systems (GIS) and playful participation with game applications like SimCity	Early exposure to SimCity and geospatial information systems as a pathway to GIS-related careers (Poplin, 2012; Peterson et al., 2020)	Playful planning as a creative and exciting career inducement (Terzano & Morckel, 2017; Peterson et al., 2020); tools are compatible with planning and have high prospects for global application

Source: Authors' literature review

recorded marginal depreciations after nearly one decade; and (3) there are indications that Nigeria's current planning capacity is ostensibly half and three-quarter of those of South Africa and Zimbabwe, respectively.

In the year 2000, Adepoju Onibokun, the renowned planning scholar in Nigeria, estimated a capacity need of 10,000 trained planners for the country (Onibokun, 1981). Evidence repeatedly points to the imperative to staff the country's vast public-planning administration machinery, composed of the federal government, 36 states (plus Abuja, Federal Capital Territory, FCT), and 774 local governments. By the workings of two relevant legislations regarding land management

Table 23.3 Ratio of Registered Planners to Population in Selected Countries (2011 and 2021)

Country	2011* Pop. (million)	2011* No. of Registered Planners	2011* No. of Planners per 100,000	2020/21 Pop. (million)**	2020/21 No. of Registered Planners***	2020/21 No. of Planners per 100,000	2011–20/21 Change (No. of Planners per 100,000)
Nigeria	162.5	2,333	1.44	211.4	4,753[i]	2.25	+0.81
South Africa	50.8	1,690	3.33	60.0	2,677[ii]	4.46	+1.13
Zimbabwe	12.7	262	2.06	15.1	449[iii]	2.97	+0.91
Kenya	41.6	194	0.47	55.0	296[iv]	0.54	+0.07
United States	304.1	38,830	12.77	332.9	40,000[v]	12.02	−0.75
United Kingdom	61.1	23,000	37.63	68.2	25,579[vi]	37.51	−0.12

Source: *UN-Habitat (2013, p. 22); **UNFPA (2021); ***Planning institutions of various countries

[i] Guardian: https://guardian.ng/property/toprec-inducts-139-as-nitp-plans-summit/
[ii] South African Council for Planners (2021)
[iii] Obtained figures from Mr. MacDonald M. Mugwazeni, the Honorary Secretary of Zimbabwe Institute of Urban and Regional Planners (ZIRUP) by email (19/08/2021)
[iv] The Kenya Gazette (15th May, 2020)
[v] American Planning Association (2021). A Brief History of the American Planning Association. www.planning.org/aboutapa/
[vi] Royal Town Planning Institute (2021). Membership by Gender. www.rtpi.org.uk/membership/about-rtpi-membership/about-our-members/

and planning development (Nigerian Land Use Act of 1978 and Nigerian Urban and Regional Planning Law of 1992), these public departments—not to mention many contiguous ministries and parastatals, or quasi-public agencies—hold diverse employment opportunities for planners (Al-Hasan et al., 2013). Demand for planning expertise, especially for those with advanced degrees and international exposure, is also motivated by growing private practices, as well as a need for planning teachers, urban activists, and urban researchers in Nigeria and abroad (Onibokun & Faniran, 2013). This is not to say, however, that university admissions, consequent professional training, and career trajectory are essentially a direct and consecutive path (UN-Habitat, 2013).[7]

Furthermore, the ongoing reengagement of planning with its historical roots in public health has potential both to expand planning jobs and improve the likelihood of attaining healthy city futures (Corburn, 2015; WHO, 2016). This global/national/city goal implies aligning planning practice with the integrated health interventions and impact assessment in keeping with the UN's 17 Sustainable Development Goals (SDGs), in particular, SDG 3 (good health and wellbeing) and SDG 11 (sustainable cities and communities) (UN-Habitat & WHO, 2020). In spite of these evolvements of urbanization-planning elicitation, precedents have shown that the vast majority of students (between 92% and 98%) who enroll in planning programs as a fallback option often come to terms with the decision and proceed to finish the course (Morenikeji & Shuaibu, 2006; Al-Hasan et al., 2013).

Enrollment Dynamics: A Note on Methodology

To assess the relative trends in student enrollment in urban planning in Nigeria, this research made use of the national-level UTME dataset (2012–17) and the University of Nigeria, Nsukka (UNN) university-specific supplementary admission information (2015–20), along with other secondary data. While the former dataset was obtained from the Joint Admissions and Matriculation Board (JAMB) in June 2018, comprising the top 15 first-choice courses with the highest overall applicants

Table 23.4 Applications to Ten Most-Popular Courses vs. Planning in Nigeria (2012–2017)

Popular Courses and URP	2012	2013	2014	2015	2016	2017	Average
Medicine and Surgery	106,153	121,327	129,925	135,728	140,108	118,474	**125,286**
Economics	91,740	100,743	90,854	69,547	69,715	61,178	**80,630**
Mass Communication	70,737	81,592	76,028	68,249	71,175	79,900	**74,614**
Business Administration	76,842	87,799	75,488	64,617	64,077	67,756	**72,763**
Accounting	60,112	96,357	121,268	72,413	72,349	N/A	**70,417**
Computer Science	57,733	77,759	73,352	64,357	67,362	76,744	**69,551**
Microbiology	47,078	56,275	57,264	58,226	65,319	74,664	**59,804**
Political Science	54,567	63,186	61,322	55,125	58,850	61,478	**59,088**
Law	54,452	60,059	57,814	55,369	57,763	55,755	**56,869**
Nursing and Nursing Science	N/A	52,997	62,519	68,009	75,981	80,618	**56,687**
Urban and Regional Planning	2,489	2,677	2,154	1,984	2,089	2,665	**2,343**

Source: Joint Admission and Matriculation Board (JAMB; 2018)

and the urban planning equivalent, the latter is essentially enrollment shortfalls[8] that occurred during primary admission. For the purposes of this study, only the top ten were used (Table 23.4). The popular, crowd-pulling, and more-competitive courses are those disciplines or programs most attractive to pre-university Nigerian students. The latter dataset consists of admission shortfalls in various faculties and departments of UNN published annually on the university website. We have categorized affected unpopular or less-popular courses as separate from their highly subscribed and popular equivalents. Candidates who were not admitted to their first-choice courses are given a second chance to choose from courses with enrollment deficits (Table 23.4). While our UTME dataset shows the ten most subscribed, and therefore highly competitive, courses in the primary admission cycle over corresponding years in the country, the UNN secondary or supplementary admission (or its equivalent in other universities) are shortfall statistics. It lists close to 58 less-subscribed courses or departments (urban planning inclusive) from 12 faculties in five years. The collected multi-layered datasets were organized and analyzed through summation, tallying (in absolute and percentage values), and codification to obtain the research results.

Career Preferences and Student Enrollment: A Comparative Analysis

This section examines the enrollment trends in planning compared to other more popular courses in Nigeria.

Planning Enrollments Versus Popular Courses at the National Level

The enrollment trend in planning is examined relative to those of the top-ten popular courses (by gross number of applicants) at the national level. The leading courses among pre-university students in Nigeria vary slightly from year to year as shown in Table 23.4. With an average national figure of about 2,343, urban planning applicants represent an infinitesimal proportion (4.13%) of the average applicants to the bottom contender in the list (nursing/nursing science). When the median figures for applicants to planning (2,343) and the ten crowd-pulling popular courses (72,571) are compared, it reveals a yawning student applicants' ratio of 1 in 31.

Nigeria's 172 public and private universities have an estimated total admission quota or capacity—the perceived maximum number of students that available infrastructure and personnel can cope with—of around 500,000 (Akinpelu, 2020). According to Yusuf Akinpelu, out of about two million UTME applicants in 2019, approximately 1.7 million scored above the pass mark of 140 (out of 400), but a mere 612,557 (around 36% of candidates with passing grades) were offered admissions into the nation's tertiary institutions—universities (444,947), polytechnics and monotechnics (96,423), colleges of education (69,810), and innovation-enterprise institutions (1,377).[9] The admission procedure is guided by a JAMB quota system based on diverse criteria like merit, catchment areas, carrying capacity of the department, candidate's state of origin, as well as environmental and educationally disadvantaged areas with a view to national diversity.[10] In general, only a mere one-third of UTME applicants get admitted in the primary admission, while the remaining two-thirds (about 64%) that did not succeed would have to settle for one of the following options: exploit supplementary admission opportunities at various universities, retake the entrance examination the ensuing year(s), explore other vocational options, or seek admission abroad. Another option, albeit for very limited spaces, is to pursue direct entry admission after obtaining A-Level (Advanced Level) passes in three required subjects or a National Diploma certificate from a polytechnic. In essence, the potential market for further student recruitment into undersubscribed courses can be exploited by different universities during remedial or supplementary admission as we shall see in the next section.

Table 23.4 shows at least five major patterns. One, medicine and surgery remained the leading contender among these popular courses all through the six years under review. Two, nursing and nursing science represents the highest gainer, rising from apparent obscurity in 2012 to the number two position in 2017. Three, accounting peaked to the second position in 2014 but decreased steadily afterward, eventually falling out of the top-ten list in 2017. Four, microbiology experienced progressive increments in the number of applicants throughout the six years. Applications for the other eight popular courses fluctuated throughout the period. Five, urban and regional planning remained undulating in the same period—albeit in a comparatively diminished enrollment zone. Overall, some trends tend to raise critical questions. Why are these ten courses preferred by pre-university students, and what factors accounted for their popularity (or professional awareness)? In particular, how was nursing and nursing science able to attain the enrollment height it did within just five years? Are there lessons here for planning regarding professional awareness-raising and enrollment-improvement measures?

The apparent convergence of these top-ten course offerings around employment prospects, financial expectations, as well as social prestige (refer to Table 23.1, second row) speaks for itself. Put differently, clamors to study medicine, nursing, journalism (mass communication), accounting, and other leading courses in Nigeria are connected with students' personal traits and outcome-expectation attributes. Over and above the hope of getting dream jobs after graduation, close influencers (parents, peers, teachers, counselors, etc.) play determinant roles. Other motivations include social prestige as well as monetary and salary considerations (Ashipa et al., 2017; Emmanuel et al., 2021). For instance, the dominance enjoyed by medicine and surgery, the recent sharp rise in popularity of nursing and nursing science, and to some extent, microbiology, can be attributed to the internationalization of the health sector with widening opportunities for qualified doctors, nurses, and other health workers abroad (Angel, 2017; Ashipa et al., 2017).

By implication and akin to the health sector, the planning profession has great potential and yet-to-be-exploited scope for internationalization. This is because the responsibility to strengthen community resilience in post-COVID-19 cities heralds a new dawn for planning (UN-Habitat & WHO, 2020). The changing urban environment continues to exert overarching influences on both individual and collective aspirations and has been the single instigating agency in the evolution of cross-disciplinary fields like urban studies and urban science (Hannigan & Richards, 2017; Acuto et al., 2018). Equally, the same narrative has benefited city destination branding and marketing programs in the tourism industry (Rosi et al., 2016).

Figure 23.2 Ahmadu Bello Way and Democracy Avenue, Abuja, FCT, Nigeria
The urban environment emblematizes urban planning and the need to plan.
Source: Sani, D.J. (2021, December 15)

Planning and Less-Popular Courses at the University of Nigeria, Nsukka

One perceptible difference between popular and unpopular courses is that while the former are mostly oversubscribed and account for most of the enrollment spillovers, the latter (including planning) contend with perennial shortfalls. At the local-university level, the affected departments in conjunction with their admissions units resort to remedying shortfalls through supplementary admissions targeted at the spillover candidates. Our case study, the UNN, has a total of 17 faculties, 118 departments, and about 12 specialized institutes (University of Nigeria, Nsukka, 2021). Out of these establishments, 12 faculties (70.59%) and roughly 58 departments (49.15%) have regularly been featured on supplementary admission lists in descending order of magnitude (Table 23.5). This is really huge and portends impending enrollment crises for the affected programs in the university if care is not taken. Could this be the same for other Nigerian universities? The implicit rationale of enrollment management is to ensure that admitted shortfall candidates go through the program and eventually graduate (see Alhassan & Lawal, 2015; Delcoure & Carmona, 2019).

Table 23.5 Enrollment Shortfalls at UNN (2015–2020)

Faculty	2015/16[i]	2016/17[ii]	2017/18[iii]	2018/19[iv]	2019/20[v]	Total Number	%
Agriculture	359	259	480	329	458	**1885**	**21.38**
Physical Sciences	238	166	192	420	329	**1345**	**15.25**
Education	102	135	188	243	354	**1022**	**11.59**
Biological Sciences	220	73	220	213	217	**943**	**10.69**
Engineering	124	75	190	218	195	**802**	**9.10**
Social Science	165	158	123	184	129	**759**	**8.61**
Environmental Studies	115	29	109	182	169	**604**	**6.85**
Vocational Technical Education	54	71	188	108	177	**598**	**6.78**
Arts	76	59	65	68	126	**394**	**4.47**
Basic Medical Sciences	94	120	Nil	19	21	**254**	**2.88**
Business Administration	52	8	35	45	37	**177**	**2.01**
Veterinary Medicine	11	Nil	Nil	13	11	**35**	**0.40**
Total	1610	1153	1790	2042	2,223	**8,818**	**100.01**

Source: [i] *New Update on Shopping for Advertised Courses for 2015/2016 Admissions* <www.unn.edu.ng/application-for-advertised-courses-for-20152016-admissions/>
[ii] *Application for Advertised Courses for 2016/2017 Admissions* <www.unn.edu.ng/application-for-advertised-courses-for-20162017-admissions/>
[iii] *Application for Advertised Courses for 2017/2018 Admissions* <www.unn.edu.ng/application-for-advertised-courses-for-20172018-admissions/>
[iv] *Application for Advertised Courses/"Shopping" for 2018/2019 Admissions* <www.unn.edu.ng/application-for-advertised-coursesshopping-for-20182019-admissions/>
[v] *Application for Advertised Courses/Shopping for 2019/2020 Admissions* <www.unn.edu.ng/application-for-advertised-coursesshopping-for-20192020-admissions/>

The Faculty of Environmental Studies (FES) comprises four departments: Urban and Regional Planning, Architecture, Estate Management, and Geoinformatics and Surveying. In five academic sessions under review, FES accounted for a mere 6.85% of the total shortfall figures. Consequently, FES is ranked seventh on the UNN shortfall list—outcompeting six faculties (Agriculture, Physical Sciences, Education, Biological Sciences, Engineering, and Social Science, in that order). Although five faculties are ahead of FES (see Table 23.5), it can be construed as a comparatively competitive faculty.

A closer look at the host faculty shows a time-series graph of divergent shortfall trends in the four departments over the last six years (Figure 23.4). Urban and Regional Planning has the highest enrollment shortfall, or deficit, in FES while Architecture has the least deficits. By extension, Architecture is considered the most preferred course in the faculty.

A recent cross-national survey, using national admissions data, has confirmed admission shortfalls are a perennial problem in several planning schools in Nigeria, and they are heavily dependent on supplementary admissions to make up student quotas (Osiyi & Jiburum, 2020). They isolated limited or poor awareness as the dominant cause of falling enrollment in planning. Quite recently, the national president of the Nigerian Institute of Town Planners, Olutoyin Ayinde, noted that "overwhelming ignorance about the profession is preponderant even amongst the elites, which is why it is not surprising that those at the helm of affairs politically also mistake physical planning for a revenue generation tool" (NITP, 2021, p. 3). This lack of planning awareness is both crosscutting and wide-ranging as it encompasses students, parents, and career counselors along with the general public.

Career Choices in the Century of Urbanization

Figure 23.3 Planning Students Busy With Studio Work

Even shortfall candidates admitted into planning out of happenstance typically come to terms with the discipline.

Source: Sodangi, A.B. (2021, December 16)

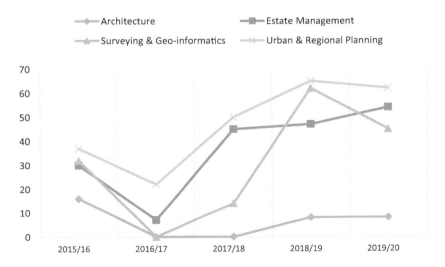

Figure 23.4 Enrollment Shortfalls in the Faculty of Environmental Studies, UNN (2015–2020)

Strategies for Rejuvenating Interest and Enrollment

Ever since its origin around the turn of the 21st century, urban planning owes its steady strides and growth partly to the awareness elicited by the urban environment and partly to the related tasks of taming and harnessing the city. In recent times, compelling pieces of evidence are pointing to falling or slowing student enrollment in planning, which ostensibly portends approximate reductions in planning capacity in affected regions. We examined student enrollment in urban planning relative to the ten most preferred or popular courses in Nigeria—Africa's most populous and rapidly urbanizing country. Both national-level UTME and university-specific primary and secondary (supplementary) admissions information was used to explore multidisciplinary career-choice trends and their determinant factors with a view to learn from apparent successes of the comparator courses vis-à-vis professional awareness-raising and improved student enrollment. By structuring extant literature on the subject matter with SCCT, we confirm that career decisions and students' preferences as they relate to diverse course offerings are a product of people's professional awareness and career self-identification (learning experiences), employment prospects and material expectations (outcome expectations), environmental or extrinsic factors (contextual influences), as well as personality traits, personal status, and interests (self-efficacy attributes).

Current knowledge of, interest, and enrollments in planning, compared to crowd-pulling or popular disciplines in Nigeria, feature at comparatively lower levels. Over the six years under review, planning applicants in Nigeria constituted about 3% of the average number of applicants compared to the top ten programs, a trend that runs counter to the prevailing high spate of urbanization and its presumed correlate of intensifying planning demand. Even though application trends in planning have undulated over the years, this underperformance presumably stems from a mixture of low awareness, uncomplimentary influences (from parents, peers, and teachers), and uncertain employment prospects as per material expectations. However, the fact that the case-study university datasets together with hints from some planning schools in the country show that planning surpasses at least 30 other departments does paint a reassuring and fairly optimistic picture for the future.

As a recap, the general elements of professional awareness creation with potential to present planning as a viable career path and improve student enrollments include, but are not restricted to, the following:

- Targeted awareness, publicity, and outreach programs to be undertaken regularly by professional planning institutions (NITP and Town Planning Registration Council of Nigeria) and planning schools (see Palazzo et al., 2021).
- Transition toward more people-centered and friendly planning practice through the promotion of bottom-up planning, public-private-community participation, adapting curriculum to local environments, etc. (see Parker et al., 2020).
- Dedicated scholarships and bursaries as an indispensable booster for improving student enrollment across disciplines and universities (Aulck et al., 2020), since urban planning discipline in Nigeria, a country with very high poverty regimes, can benefit immensely from such financial supports.
- Enrollment-management analytics via all sorts of academic support services tailor-made to enable planning schools not just to admit study-ready students, but also to ensure their retention and graduation (see Delcoure & Carmona, 2019).
- Early exposure of children and young adults to planning through involvement in playful planning is essential, but also quite critical is the need to expand the target spectrum to include their closest influencers (Peterson et al., 2020).

In order to create a harvest of passionate, unswerving planning students and enduring career interests in Nigeria and elsewhere, we propose interventions and outreach programs that are multifaceted and targeted in nature. Concerted efforts of planning schools, professional-planning associations, and the public/private sector are required to initiate awareness-raising programs in the form of workshops, community engagement visits, and the use of conventional and social media.

Cities and the urban environment continue to feature as a stimulus and springboard for the advancement of evolving disciplines (urban studies and urban science), as well as city destination branding and marketing programs. Taking advantage of the influential and overarching agency of this urban leitmotif will naturally open awareness and enrollment doors for the planning discipline, especially if its intrinsic public-health linkages are also exploited. We recall that it is not only medical and health-practice jobs that are globalizing; to a certain extent urban planning (planning education, associations, and consultancies) has equally experienced, and is still experiencing, analogous international openings and opportunities. How much more now, with the COVID-19 pandemic, is the discipline's moniker as "preventive medicine" (Corburn, 2015, p. 48) being put to an empirical test? Although job availability, including employment prospects and material expectations of prospective students, is outside the scope of this very work, it is imperative for future studies to explore career-mobility prospects for urban planners across local and international scales.

Commitment and hard work are required to drive these outreach programs, although the problem of financing and a few other inhibiting factors might also crop up. In conceiving prospective outreach manuals for planning schools and professional planning associations, attention should be placed on content, context, and up-to-date information. The Nigerian planning context is endowed with the requisite opportunities and strengths: the high ambition and strong motivations to advance the planning profession by the current NITP leadership (see NITP, 2021), a large youthful population with better computer and Internet-savvy skills, and rapid urbanization amid globalizing urban futures and fresh planning mandates.

Notes

1 Besides the 18 planning schools in Nigeria affiliated with AAPS, there are at least 31 others. Watson and Agbola (2014) recounted a total of 49 planning schools (31 in Polytechnics and Colleges of Technology, and 18 in universities) were present in the country as of 2014.
2 The New Urban Agenda is the flagship of Habitat III, the 2016 United Nations Conference on Housing and Sustainable Urban Development that was held in Quito, Ecuador. This resolution agenda marked the global commitment to sustainable-urbanization targets with emphasis on achieving sustainable cities and communities (SDG 11).
3 In this chapter, courses refer to university degree programs that students enroll in to complete a structured curriculum that allows them to attain competencies in a discipline or specialization in the discipline.
4 (1) Theory of work adjustment, (2) Holland's theory of vocational personalities and work environments, (3) self-concept theory of career development, (4) Gottfredson's theory of circumscription and compromise, and (5) social cognitive career theory.
5 The African Planning Association (APA) is to planning institutions what AAPS is to planning education. Established in 2002, this forum aims to unite and coordinate planning institutions and professional practice in Africa. By 2012, APA had planning institutions across 26 out of 54 African countries as affiliate members.
6 For example, the American Planning Association and Royal Town Planning Institutes have members located in approximately 90 and 88 countries, respectively.
7 Planning graduates (like some graduates of other courses) may eventually not work in the planning sector. Also, it is worth noting that employment search and destinations of new planning graduates are concerns not considered in this chapter since these issues are outside the remit of this study.
8 Enrollment shortfalls denote deficits in admission quotas of specific departments or faculties. The higher the shortfall, the higher the admission offers. And so, departments with no shortfalls at all or lower shortfalls are considered more competitive than those with higher shortfalls.
9 Such capacity figures apply mostly to primary admissions and are therefore not definite caps. Though further opportunities open during secondary admissions, university enrollments, as far as diverse contending course offerings are concerned, remain somewhat a zero-sum game in which gains by some departments appear to translate into equivalent losses by others.
10 Unlike in the US, for example, where diversity in student enrollment has to do with racial and socio-cultural representation/participation, the Nigerian case is much more multifarious.

References

AAPS, Association of African Planning Schools. (2021). *Member schools*. Retrieved May 20, 2021, from www.africanplanningschools.org.za/member-schools

Acuto, M., Parnell, S., Seto, K. C., Contestabile, M., Allen, A., Attia, S., & Zhu, Y. (2018). Science and the future of cities, report of the international expert panel on science and the future of cities. *Nature Sustainability, 1*(1), 3–60. https://sites.nationalacademies.org/cs/groups/depssite/documents/webpage/deps_191052.pdf

Akinpelu, Y. (2020, June 20). 2019 UTME: Two in three students who applied for admission into Nigerian institutions not admitted. *Premium Times* (Nigeria). www.premiumtimesng.com/news/headlines/398679-2019-utme-two-in-three-students-who-applied-for-admission-into-nigerian-institutions-not-admitted.html

Akosah-Twumasi, P., Emeto, T. I., Lindsay, D., Tsey, K., & Malau-Aduli, B. S. (2018, July). A systematic review of factors that influence youths career choices—the role of culture. *Frontiers in Education, 3*, 58–73. https://doi.org/10.3389/feduc.2018.00058

Alhassan, J. K., & Lawal, S. A. (2015). Using data mining technique for scholarship disbursement. *International Journal of Information and Communication Engineering, 9*(7), 1741–1744. https://citeseerx.ist.psu.edu/viewdoc/download?doi=10.1.1.975.1686&rep=rep1&type=pdf

Al-Hasan, Z. A., Momoh, S., & Ugbonakhena, O. O. (2013). Town planning education: A survey of students' entrance, performance and prospects in Auchi Polytechnic, Nigeria. *International Journal of Scientific & Technology Research, 2*(8), 273–279. http://citeseerx.ist.psu.edu/viewdoc/download?doi=10.1.1.436.3027&rep=rep1&type=pdf

Amirahmadi, H. (1993). Globalization and planning education. *Environment and Planning B: Planning and Design, 20*(5), 537–555. https://doi.org/10.1068/b200537

Angel, E. (2017). *Motivating factors influencing nursing as a career choice: An analysis of domestic and international nursing students' motivation, self-concepts, and cultural orientation* (Doctoral Dissertation). Western Sydney University. https://researchdirect.westernsydney.edu.au/islandora/object/uws:50379/datastream/PDF/view

Ashipa, T., Akinyinka, M. R., & Alakija, W. (2017). Motivation, career aspirations and reasons for choice of medical school among first year medical students in Ogun state, Nigeria. *Journal of Advances in Medicine and Medical Research, 22*(7), 1–14. https://doi.org/10.9734/JAMMR/2017/33750

Aulck, L., Nambi, D., & West, J. (2020). Increasing enrollment by optimizing scholarship allocations using machine learning and genetic algorithms. In A. N. Rafferty, J. Whitehill, V. Cavalli-Sforza, & C. Romero (Eds.), *Proceedings of the 13th international conference on educational data mining (EDM 2020)* (pp. 29–38). https://educationaldatamining.org/files/conferences/EDM2020/papers/paper_44.pdf

Ayodele, T. O. (2019). Career choice of real estate students in Nigeria: The explaining influences in comparative perspective. *Property Management, 37*(1), 154–176. https://doi.org/10.1108/PM-02-2018-0013

Bandura, A. (1997). *Self-efficacy: The exercise of control*. W. H. Freeman/Times Books/Henry Holt & Co.

Cevrić, B. (2011). Evolution of Botswana planning education in light of local and international requirements. *Spatium* (25), 30–38. https://doi.org/10.2298/SPAT1125030C

Corburn, J. (2015). City planning as preventive medicine. *Preventive Medicine, 77*, 48–51.10.1016/j.ypmed.2015.04.022

Delcoure, N., & Carmona, J. S. (2019). Enrollment management analytics: A practical framework. *Journal of Applied Research in Higher Education, 11*(4), 910–925. https://doi.org/10.1108/JARHE-10-2018-0209

Emmanuel, N. O., Okoro, N., & Ukonu, M. O. (2021). Beyond classroom-newsroom gap: Why do Nigerian students study journalism in the age of convergence? *Media Practice and Education, 22*(2)104–123. https://doi.org/10.1080/25741136.2021.1876513

Frank, A. I. (2018). Adapting, shifting, defining new roles: Education for a maturing professional field. In A. I. Frank & C. Silver (Eds.), *Urban planning education* (pp. 131–145). Springer. https://doi.org/10.1007/978-3-319-55967-4

Frank, A. I., & Silver, C. (2018). Introduction. In A. I. Frank & C. Silver (Eds.), *Urban planning education* (pp. 1–7). Springer. https://doi.org/10.1007/978-3-319-55967-4

Friedmann, J. (2005). Globalization and the emerging culture of planning. *Progress in Planning, 64*(3), 183–234. https://doi.org/10.1016/j.progress.2005.05.001

Fuertes, V., McQuaid, R., & Robertson, P. J. (2021). Career-first: An approach to sustainable labour market integration. *International Journal for Educational and Vocational Guidance, 21*, 1–18. https://doi.org/10.1007/s10775-020-09451-2

Fusheini, K., & Salia, H. (2021). The contribution of corporate social responsibility (CSR) initiatives to student enrollment and performance in Ghana. *International Journal of Educational Management, 35*(3), 606–620. https://doi.org/10.1108/IJEM-07-2020-0348

Ghazali, Y., Okeke, A., & Okoya, F. (2020). Impact assessment of pharmacy awareness campaigns conducted in selected high schools across Lagos, Nigeria. *Heliyon, 6*(7), e04380.1–5. https://doi.org/10.1016/j.heliyon.2020.e04380

Grant, M., Brown, C., Caiaffa, W. T., Capon, A., Corburn, J., Coutts, C., Crespo, C. J., Ellis, G., Ferguson, G., Fudge, C., Hancock, T., Lawrence, R. J., Nieuwenhuijsen, M. J., Oni, T., Thompson, S., Wagenaar, C., & Ward-Thompson, C. (2017). Cities and health: An evolving global conversation. *Cities & Health, 1*(1), 1–9 https://doi.org/10.1080/23748834.2017.1316025

Hannigan, J., & Richards, G. (Eds.). (2017). *The SAGE handbook of new urban studies*. Sage. https://doi.org/10.4135/9781473982604

Hayden, K., Ouyang, Y., Scinski, L., Olszewski, B., & Bielefeldt, T. (2011). Increasing student interest and attitudes in STEM: Professional development and activities to engage and inspire learners. *Contemporary Issues in Technology and Teacher Education, 11*(1), 47–69. www.learntechlib.org/p/35368/

Jamabo, T. (2014). Relationship between parental socio-economic variables and adolescents vocational aspiration. *Journal of Education and Practice, 5*(13), 169–172. www.iiste.org/Journals/index.php/JEP/article/download/12761/13070

The Kenya Gazette. (2020, May 15). *Kenyan institute of planners: Membership and categories*. https://kip.or.ke/wp-content/uploads/2018/02/Vol.CXXII-No_.87_.pdf

Kiser, M., and Hammer, E. E. (2016). Need to increase enrollment: A successful academic provisionary program. *Journal of College Student Retention: Research, Theory & Practice, 18*(2), 217–233. https://doi.org/10.1177/1521025115584749

Lent, R. W. (2005). A social cognitive view of career development and counseling. In S. D. Brown & R. T. Lent (Eds.), *Career development and counseling: Putting theory and research to work* (2nd ed., pp. 101–127). John Wiley & Sons.

Lent, R. W., Brown, S. D., & Hackett, G. (2002). Social cognitive career theory. In D. Brown & Associate (Eds.), *Career choice and development* (4th ed., pp. 255–311). Jossey-Bass.

Leung, S. A. (2008). The big five career theories. In J. A. Athanasou & R. Van Esbroeck (Eds.), *International Handbook of Career Guidance*. Springer. https://doi.org/10.1007/978-1-4020-6230-8_6

Maddux, J. E. (2005). Self-efficacy: The power of believing you can. In C. R. Snyder & S. J. Lopez (Eds.), *Handbook of positive psychology* (pp. 277–287). Oxford University Press.

Morenikeji, W., & Shuaibu, S. (2006). Factors affecting students' choice and perception of urban and regional planning in Nigerian universities. *Nigerian Institute of Town Planners Journal, XIX*(1), 17–33. www.academia.edu/signup?a_id=32568060

Nigerian Institute of Town Planners, NITP. (2021, January 27). *First press conference by NITP president in 2021* [Press release]. www.nitpng.org/first-press-conference-by-nitp-president-in-2021/

Okojide, A., Adekeye, A., & Bakare, E. (2018). Factors influencing career choice among undergraduates in covenant university, Nigeria. *Proceedings of ICERI2018 Conference 12th-14th November 2018, Seville, Spain*. http://eprints.covenantuniversity.edu.ng/12265/1/INFLUENCING%20CAREER%20CHOICE%20AMONG.pdf

Onibokun, P. (1981). Planning, planners and planning education in Nigeria. *Journal of Nigerian Institute of Town Planners, 1*(1), 5–16.

Onibokun, A., & Faniran, A. (2013). *Urban research in Nigeria*. IFRA-Nigeria. https://books.openedition.org/ifra/534?format=toc

Onoyeyan, G. O., & Unegbu, V. (2019). Awareness as determinant of choice of law librarianship as a career among law students in South-West Nigeria. *SAGE Open*, 1–9. https://doi.org/10.1177/2158244019859086

Osiyi, S. D., & Jiburum, U. (2020). Students' enrollments in urban and regional planning programs and crossroad to career in planning in Nigerian universities. *Journal of Planning Education and Research*, 1–6. https://doi.org/10.1177/0739456X20927435

Palazzo, D., Hollstein, L., & Diko, S. K. (2021). Urban planning as a career preference for students: Efforts to improve awareness about the profession. *Planning Practice & Research, 36*(2), 174–192. https://doi.org/10.1080/02697459.2020.1782056

Parker, G., Wargent, M., Linovski, O., Schoneboom, A., Gunn, S., Slade, D., Odeleye, N., Maidment, C., Shepherd, E., Doak, J., Elliot, T., Nicholls, V., Street, E., Dobson, M., Platts, S., & Tasan-Kok, T. (2020). The future of the planning profession. *Planning Theory & Practice Journal, 21*(3), 453–480. https://doi.org/10.1080/14649357.2020.1776014

Peterson, E. G., Kolvoord, B., Uttal, D. H., & Green, A. E. (2020). High school students' experiences with geographic information systems and factors predicting enrollment in the geospatial semester. *Journal of Geography, 119*(6), 238–247. https://doi.org/10.1080/00221341.2020.1824009

Piedmont, S., & Robra, B. P. (2015). Theory and practice in medical education—expectations and development of skills experienced by students of human medicine compared with students in other disciplines. *GMS Zeitschrift für Medizinische Ausbildung, 32*(1), 1–30. https://doi.org/10.3205/zma000950

Poplin, A. (2012). Playful public participation in urban planning: A case study for online serious games. *Computers, Environment and Urban Systems, 36*(3), 195–206. https://doi.org/10.1016/j.compenvurbsys.2011.10.003

Rosi, M., Smole, J., & Potočnik-Topler, J. (2016). Raising awareness of urban environment development in primary schools. *Acta Economica et Turistica, 2*(2), 105–113. https://doi.org/10.1515/aet-2016-0009

Schaub, M., & Tokar, D. M. (2005). The role of personality and learning experiences in social cognitive career theory. *Journal of Vocational Behavior, 66*(2), 304–325. https://doi.org/10.1016/j.jvb.2004.09.005

Shumba, A., & Naong, M. (2012). Factors influencing students' career choice and aspirations in South Africa. *Journal of Social Science, 33*(2),169–178. www.tandfonline.com/doi/abs/10.1080/09718923.2012.11893096

South Africa Council for Planners. (2021, May 20). *Registered professional planners in South Africa*. https://sacplan.org.za/registered-planners/

Terzano, K., & Morckel, V. (2017). SimCity in the community planning classroom: Effects on student knowledge, interests, and perceptions of the discipline of planning. *Journal of Planning Education and Research, 37*(1), 95–105. https://doi.org/10.1177/0739456X16628959

UNFPA, United Nations Population Fund. (2021). *World dashboard*. www.unfpa.org/data/world-population/

United Nations, Department of Economic and Social Affairs, Population Division (2019). *World Population Prospects 2019: Highlights*. ST/ESA/SER. A/423. https://population.un.org/wpp/publications/files/wpp2019_highlights.pdf

UN-Habitat. (2013). *The state of planning in Africa: An overview*. UN Habitat. https://unhabitat.org/sites/default/files/download-manager-files/The%20State%20of%20Planning%20in%20Africa%20%2C%20An%20Overview%20.pdf

UN-Habitat & WHO. (2020). *Integrating health in urban and territorial planning: A sourcebook*. UN-HABITAT and World Health Organization. https://apps.who.int/iris/bitstream/handle/10665/331678/9789240003170-eng.pdf

University of Nigeria, Nsukka. (2021). *Academics*. www.unn.edu.ng/#

Wahab, B., Egunjobi, L., Gyuse, T., & Kadiri, W. (Eds.). (2014). *Regional planning and development in Nigeria: An overview* (pp. xi–xiv). Nigerian Institute of Town Planners and Town Planners Registration Council of Nigeria. www.researchgate.net/publication/318207576

Watson, V., & Agbola, B. (2014, March 29). Why Africa's cities need African planning. *ArchDaily*. https://www.archdaily.com/489181/why-africa-s-cities-need-african-planning

Watson, V., & Odendaal, N. (2012). Changing planning education in Africa: The role of the association of African planning schools. *Journal of Planning Education and Research, 33*(1), 96–107. https://doi.org/10.1177/0739456X12452308

World Bank. (2022). *Urban population- Nigeria*. Retrieved February 16, 2022, from https://data.worldbank.org/indicator/SP.URB.TOTL?locations=NG

World Health Organization, WHO. (2016). *Health as the pulse of the new urban agenda: United nations conference on housing and sustainable urban development, Quito, October 2016*. World Health Organization. https://apps.who.int/iris/bitstream/handle/10665/250367/9789241511445-eng.pdf

Zotorvie, J. S. T. (2016). Determinants of career choice among students of institute of chartered accountants (Ghana). *European Scientific Journal, 12*(31), 255–274. https://doi.org/10.19044/esj.2016.v12n31p255

24
ENHANCING PLANNING-EDUCATION AWARENESS IN SUB-SAHARAN AFRICA

Lessons From Namibia

Eric Yankson

This chapter assesses various ways to enhance spatial-planning education awareness in sub-Saharan Africa based on a case evaluation of Namibia. Spatial-planning education, as defined here, refers to formal training in academic institutions with the goal of equipping graduates to respond to the needs of regions, cities, and communities in professional or other settings. This is an area that could benefit from more attention in the existing literature as much of the prevailing research is focused on the Global North (particularly North America and Europe). A strong case can thus be made for an in-depth analysis on sub-Saharan Africa where planners are particularly pivotal for addressing the many development challenges experienced by regions, cities, and communities.

The rationale for focusing on Namibia is even more compelling given the fact that there appears to be little (if any) existing academic research on planning education in the country. Moreover, given the vestiges of urban inequality, poverty, and informality emanating from the apartheid era, the roles of planners in shaping local development and the built environment in general is very important. This chapter primarily relies on experiences of the author within Namibian academia and the urban planning profession, as well as interviews and document analysis, to make its assertions. It begins by reviewing relevant literature and concepts on planning education globally. It then zeroes in on the situation in sub-Saharan Africa and Namibia. The chapter subsequently evaluates lessons in enhancing planning-education awareness based on a case study of Namibia before concluding the discussion.

The Evolution and Conceptualization of Planning Education

Arguably, the origins of spatial planning date back to the founding of human settlements. This notwithstanding, formal planning education may largely be traced to the early parts of the 20th century when the emergence of the city planning movement created the need for an academic discipline responsive to the needs of an emerging profession. Three main phases can be observed in the evolution of this form of education (Silver, 2018). The first, from the early 1900s to 1940, was characterized by an Anglo-American influence that sought to shape the built environment in Europe and North America. It also aimed to transfer planning ideologies to colonies in Africa, Asia, and Latin America (Silver, 2018). This phase was associated with a modernist worldview that sought to redress the ills of the industrial revolution by creating a more orderly physical landscape devoid of problems such as slums (Watson, 2011).

During the second phase after World War II, planning education began to focus on post-war reconstruction as well as the promotion of indigenous concepts in former colonies (Silver, 2018). In places such as the United States, emphasis began to shift toward a knowledge-based social-science approach underpinned by concepts in disciplines such as economics, sociology, and political science (Frank, 2006; Watson, 2011). From the 1960s, there was a proliferation of planning programs within academic institutions in the United States and Europe. This emerged in response to the need to train professionals who could design land-use plans and urban-renewal strategies for local authorities. Moreover, as academic institutions began to enroll more students from the developing world, they started running some programs more relevant to the Global South (Frank, 2006; Watson, 2011). In the third phase from the 1990s, planning education was a post-socialist construction aimed at integrating places such as Eastern Europe and China into the global economy (Silver, 2018).

According to Roderiguez-Bachiller (1988), three major conceptualizations of planning education can be articulated. The traditional technical approach, originating from Europe and Britain, focuses on the spatial context of the discipline and how that is interlinked with the built environment, especially architecture (Diaw et al., 2002). The comprehensive integrated model, associated with Britain, entails elements of physical planning, urban management, and methodology. Moreover, the academic-postgraduate model, originating from the United States, has a strong social-science component, with the goal of serving the broad job market in public policy (Diaw et al., 2002).

In many parts of the world, planning education is shaped by context-specific national dynamics such as urbanization and the need for trained professionals to address a country's development needs. Simultaneously, there has been growing international collaboration as a way of sharing experiences and promoting global best practices (Frank & Silver, 2018). Thus, planning-education awareness can also be understood within the lens of internationalization in which universities across the world engage in exchange programs. Specifically, planning students can be exposed to different national contexts with the view of enriching their worldviews and informing them about alternative scenarios (Butt et al., 2013; Lee et al., 2020).

In places such as North America, a pattern of decreased student enrollment in planning programs has been observed over the years. This situation has been caused in part by a low level of awareness among high-school students about the profession, as well as the career prospects it offers. This emanates from the few courses offered at this level that expose students to concepts such as world regional geography and spatiality (Palazzo et al., 2021). Moreover, poor perceptions of the profession among parents and school counselors mean that they generally do not perform the necessary mentoring roles that can encourage students to enroll in these programs. Given these developments, more research is needed by universities and planning departments in their attempts to implement design and planning language programs that seek to create greater awareness about the profession (Palazzo et al., 2021).

Planning education is also confronted by challenges such as a lack of diversity. This could be partly explained by unequal power structures in academia, which imply that scholars are more likely to focus on works published by those within their own networks. Moreover, the dominance of certain schools of thought in planning discourse implies that alternative conceptualizations seeking to engender diversity and other novel ideas are less likely to gain traction within the profession (Sweet & Etienne, 2011). To change the status quo, it is important for planning programs to recruit more people of color onto their faculties. There is also the need for the content of planning programs to be broadened to include themes such as race, ethnicity, and gender (Sweet & Etienne, 2011).

Ultimately, arguments about planning education boil down to the content of the courses offered as well as their relevance to professional practice. For instance, it may be argued that planning theory has little relevance beyond the classroom. It should, however, be noted that this course offers useful conceptual insights that can inspire planning practice (Olesen, 2018). Moreover, the incorporation of content on sustainable development into practical modules in planning programs could be a way of enhancing students' employability after graduation (Dimitrova, 2014; Maruna et al., 2018).

Planning Education in Sub-Saharan Africa and Namibia

In the sub-Saharan African context, spatial planning education is strongly influenced by vestiges of colonialism as reflected, for instance, in the curricula. During the colonial era, this form of education was mostly aimed at training civil servants to enforce national-planning laws that were modeled along British and other Western models. Even in the postcolonial epoch, much of the planning curriculum is based on concepts adopted with little to no modification from educational systems in Europe and North America (Watson & Odendaal, 2012; Odendaal, 2012; Odendaal & Watson, 2018). This is undergirded by a modernist worldview in which emphasis is placed on the training of professionals adept at designing zoning and other land-use plans. Thus, there is relatively less focus on the socio-spatial context of African urbanism (Diaw et al., 2002).

The implication is that the profession has been less effective at dealing with contemporary challenges such as informality and inequality evident in cities across the continent (Watson & Odendaal, 2012). A postmodern approach to planning education is therefore critical for responding to contemporary shifts in the profession and addressing the power structures emanating from modernism. This may, for instance, entail more learner-centered and participatory or community-based approaches to course delivery (Lamb & Vodicka, 2021). The Association of African Planning Schools has been involved in initiatives to change planning education so that it is more responsive to present-day issues. These interventions include better networking and funding among planning schools on the continent with the goal of creating academic programs that are more relevant to contemporary needs (Watson & Odendaal, 2012; Odendaal, 2012; Odendaal & Watson, 2018).

Broadly speaking, planning education on the African continent comprises three main areas of focus. To begin with, some programs such as those at the University of Botswana have a bias toward physical planning and design. Second, other programs (e.g., at the Kwame Nkrumah University of Science and Technology in Ghana) that were originally oriented toward physical planning and design have now been shifting toward a greater focus on urban policy and management. The third category comprises programs such as those at Kenyatta University in Kenya with a geographical, regional, and environmental-science emphasis (Watson & Odendaal, 2012). In places such as Malawi, planning education is characterized by a dichotomy between the technical and socio-political underpinnings of the profession (Manda, 2013).

With specific reference to Namibia, the history of planning education may largely be understood within the context of university education. This dates to 1980 when the Academy for Tertiary Education was established as the first institution of higher learning in the country. The passage of the Academy for Tertiary Education Act 9 of 1985 empowered the Academy to create a university, a Technikon, and a college for out-of-school-training (Du Plessis & Keyter, 2019). Following independence in 1990, the Presidential Commission on Higher Education recommended that these three establishments should be replaced with two independent higher-educational institutions (Du Plessis & Keyter, 2019). This led to the emergence of the University of Namibia (UNAM) and the Polytechnic of Namibia (PoN, now the Namibia University of Science and Technology).

UNAM was created under the University of Namibia Act, 1992, Act 33. It has expanded over the years to offer programs in various disciplines, including the natural, health, and social sciences, as well as engineering and information technology. The PoN was established under the Polytechnic of Namibia Act, 1994, Act 33 (Du Plessis & Keyter, 2019). The institution (i.e., PoN) offered planning courses in the form of certificate programs by the Department of Land Management. Specifically, the following programs were offered: land measurement, land valuation, land registration, and land-use planning. These courses were primarily designed to address the capacity needs of the then Ministry of Lands, Resettlement, and Rehabilitation. They therefore had a bias toward land-use concepts and were couched in a modernist worldview. Also, many graduates went on to pursue further studies in South Africa and were thus able to specialize further in their areas of interest.

In 2010, the planning component of the Department of Land Management broke off and merged with a new architecture program to create the Department of Architecture and Spatial Planning (DASP). This period coincided with rapid urbanization in Namibia characterized by rural–urban migration and the proliferation of informal settlements. There was therefore the need for academic programs that were more responsive to these urban-development challenges. At the end of 2012, the government of Namibia identified the need to transform PoN into a university of science and technology with the goal of meeting the nation's ever-growing human-resource needs. Thus, the Namibia University of Science and Technology (NUST) formally became operational in 2015 following this transformation (Du Plessis & Keyter, 2019). In the recent past, there have been ongoing discussions regarding further institutional and departmental restructuring at NUST as part of measures to enhance administrative efficiency and cut down on costs. Thus, the possibility exists that DASP may be realigned or rechristened, while the nature of some spatial-planning programs offered at the university could change in the near future.

A number of degrees are currently awarded at the DASP under the restructured Faculty of Engineering and Spatial Science (created from a recent partial merger of the former Faculty of Engineering and Faculty of Natural Resources and Spatial Sciences). These include the Bachelor of Urban and Regional Planning, Bachelor of Regional and Rural Development, Bachelor of Urban and Regional Planning Honors, and Bachelor of Regional and Rural Development Honors. The bachelor's degrees are offered for three years, with an additional one year for the honors-level qualifications.[1] While there is currently no master's program in either degree program, students have a wide array of graduate options in cognate disciplines subject to their research interests and abilities to fulfill admission requirements. These include master's degrees in spatial sciences, urban design, architecture, and landscape architecture.

The importance of spatial planning to the development of Namibia (especially in the post-independence era) cannot be discounted. It essentially entails the need to reverse the legacy of inequality, poverty, and informality emanating from the apartheid era. The curriculum of planning education at DASP is thus a holistic one comprising physical, environmental, and socioeconomic planning. The goal is to train graduates who are equipped to respond to the ever-changing needs of the country, particularly at the regional, urban, and neighborhood scales. This is partly evident in the graduates from the DASP programs who are employed in various establishments such as village, town, and regional councils; government ministries, departments, and agencies; academia; as well as private consulting firms.

Conceptually, spatial-planning education in present-day Namibia may be regarded as emphasizing elements of both modernism and postmodernism. The modernist aspects are palpable in terms of the focus on physical planning, as evident in aspects such as land-use planning and layout drafting. While these technical aspects of the profession continue to receive considerable attention, there is also growing awareness of the need to plan for people and communities. Thus, emphasis on the socioeconomic context of planning has also received appreciable attention in the curriculum. Overall, planning education in Namibia reifies the comprehensive integrated model by focusing on the physical environment, institutional and regulatory contexts, as well as methodological issues in data collection and analysis. Going forward, there is the need to place more emphasis on indigenous aspects of Namibian urbanism to make an even bigger impact on local and national development. Thus, courses such as historic-preservation planning can be introduced during future curricula reviews.

Enhancing Planning Education Awareness: Lessons From Namibia

While Namibia has made significant progress in spatial-planning education over the years, some challenges remain. For instance, even though DASP is generally able to meet its annual enrollment targets, declining levels are still evident in student-registration numbers at higher levels. Thus, enrollment rates in the final year of the three-year bachelor's programs and the honors level tend to be lower than those in the first and second years. This occurs in part because students sometimes switch to other disciplines or institutions. The switch is due to various reasons, such as changes in professional or career interests, as well as negative perceptions regarding job prospects after graduation. There's also a paucity of awareness within the regional councils regarding the programs offered by DASP. This results in low hiring of graduates, thus portending negatively for the success of the programs. The regional councils are public or governmental entities responsible for overseeing spatial planning in Namibia's 14 administrative regions, providing a very practical platform for students to apply the skills they have acquired during their educational training. However, as noted, low awareness implies that the councils are sometimes unwilling or unable to recruit graduates from the planning programs offered by NUST. The situation occurs due to relatively few existing avenues such as public meetings or discussion forums where the councils are provided with information about the programs. Moreover, these programs are not widely known in rural areas and outside the borders of Namibia for similar reasons. Toward addressing these and related challenges, it is important to increase awareness regarding the country's planning-education system. Several approaches can be envisaged, and these are discussed as follows.

Networking

The key to enhancing planning-education awareness is continuous networking among planners in both academia and industry. This will increase the job prospects of planning graduates and enhance the general appeal of the profession (Manda, 2013). Within the Namibian context, this occurs through events such as the annual school of the Namibia Institute of Town and Regional Planners (NITRP), a conference event that brings together practicing professionals, academics, and stakeholders from the government sector. Moreover, the presence of both academics and practicing planners on the NITRP serves to facilitate regular interactions among the two groups. Networking also entails events where planners are exposed to university students with the goal of providing mentoring support and exposing them to potential employment opportunities after school.

Going forward, it is important to have regular social events where practicing planners (some of whom were trained in South Africa, as well as other places outside Namibia) and those in academia can interact on a regular basis. For instance, the NITRP can take a lead by organizing more such engagements in different parts of the country. The creation of online discussion platforms can also help reach out to more planners toward better networking. Additionally, DASP can organize periodic events that bring together planners toward pooling ideas for better delivery of planning programs in the department. The end goal of these interactions is to enhance awareness among planners regarding the programs offered in academia. This will increase the likelihood of employing more graduates from these programs, especially in entities such as regional councils.

Public Engagement

Public engagement remains a central defining feature of the planning process (Slotterback & Lauria, 2019). Perhaps, in recognition of this, the process of designing and revising academic programs in Namibia is an interactive one that involves engagement among various stakeholders both within and outside academia. Specifically, it comprises a program advisory committee made up of members from both academia and industry to solicit input from industry experts to produce graduates who are ready for the job market. In the case of spatial-planning programs, for instance, some of the external persons brought on board during the program-review process include professionals at town-planning consulting firms, as well as planners from the various regional councils and municipalities.

Going forward, public engagement in the design of academic programs must also incorporate input from local communities and their representatives. For instance, community leaders and persons from the Shack Dwellers Federation of Namibia (SDFN) can be included in the process as a way of incorporating their experiences on local development challenges, which contemporary spatial-planning programs must respond to. The SDFN is a non-governmental organization (NGO) promoting advocacy and mobilizing support for residents of informal settlements. These settlements are at the urban periphery with poor quality infrastructure and services, which spring up due to rapid urbanization. Besides the SDFN, engaging other NGOs through networking and public engagements will serve to enhance the design of academic programs. These NGOs include community-based and civil-society organizations. Additionally, more representation from government ministries, departments, or agencies would help DASP formulate programs, enabling graduates to be better attuned to the political processes and institutional frameworks within which planners perform their duties.

Marketing of Planning Programs

Marketing of academic programs is pivotal for increasing awareness among youth regarding the benefits and job prospects associated with them (Palazzo et al., 2021). In Namibia, this occurs through events such as the annual Windhoek Show, during which representatives from various establishments exhibit their programs or services to members of the general public. This serves to educate prospective university applicants about what various academic fields entail and implications for their career paths going forward. NUST and DASP need to maximize these opportunities for increasing awareness about planning programs by deploying the various program coordinators as exhibitors who would educate members of the general public about what they have to offer. Moreover, visits to secondary schools to interact with students can help to increase awareness about the choice of planning as a professional discipline.

The marketing of planning programs must also occur through media platforms such as newspapers and social media. Great potential exists for these forms of marketing due to the increased need to reach out to greater audiences vis-à-vis the ever-growing demand for planners to address the nation's development challenges. Social-media platforms in particular are very appealing to the youth; this is one area where NUST can take advantage to increase the appeal of their planning programs and the planning profession in general. Ultimately, enhancing the visibility of the department through its website will serve to increase awareness regarding the programs or courses it offers.

Accreditation of Planning Programs

The accreditation of planning programs should be undergirded by local and regional considerations while still embracing global best practices in teaching, research, and innovation (Cavrić, 2011). One way of attaining this is through the input of national and international experts to enhance the appeal of the profession for youth and members of the general public. In Namibia, this already occurs through the rigorous accreditation requirements of the National Council for Higher Education, which necessitate the accreditation-approval process be superintended by a team of national and international experts. This is a quality assurance mechanism that serves to ensure that academic institutions keep up with both national and international best practices.

It is therefore important for DASP to continue maintaining the accreditation of its spatial-planning programs to increase their appeal among the youth. Moreover, this must be communicated to potential applicants as a way of engendering their confidence in the qualifications they would earn should they enroll in the department. While the facilities available for delivering the spatial-planning programs are generally in good shape, some improvements would further enhance the accreditation process. For instance, the existing computer-lab facilities need to be expanded to accommodate more students at one time. Moreover, the use of software such as ArcGIS and SPSS should be better integrated into the various courses offered in the programs as a way of enhancing the analytical and problem-solving skills of students.

Involvement of Students in Community Projects and Internships

The involvement of students in projects with direct community benefits also serves to increase the public appeal of planners. Specifically, more community engagement by the youth enrolled in planning and other programs can help to improve public perceptions regarding the built-environment professions (Million & Heinrich, 2014). At NUST, for instance, students have over the years been involved in informal-settlement upgrading, as well as other community-based projects. These serve to elucidate their contributions to local development. The ripple effect is that it increases awareness among local communities regarding the importance of planning in promoting their well-being. The situation occurs because residents experience first-hand the benefits of planning in addressing challenges such as low-quality infrastructure and poor service delivery experienced in these locales. This could spark interest in the profession among the youth, ultimately resulting in higher levels of enrollment in planning programs.

Involvement of students in internships through the work-integrated learning module is another way of enhancing awareness about the programs offered at DASP, especially among practicing planners.[2] This can help students when it comes to their job prospects after graduation. In instances where internships entail elements of community engagement, students are particularly exposed to practical scenarios, which help to increase awareness about the profession among local communities.

Impacts of Planners on Local Development

Planners play critical roles in assisting communities to deal with current and emerging challenges (Picketts et al., 2012). Thus, the impacts of planners on local development emphasizes their crucial role in building communities and neighborhoods. These can occur in terms of their research outputs, which make recommendations that subsequently form the bases for government policies or interventions with community benefits. Moreover, planners can also be involved in various projects that entail community engagement. Currently, however, one mostly hears about planners in the newspapers only when they advertise rezoning notices or when issues about informal settlements and land servicing crop up.

Planners have a strong influence on local development, but communities hardly see the full scope of the work they do because much of this happens in offices. Also, the preponderance of socio-spatial inequality and urban informality even after the end of apartheid adds to the less-favorable public perceptions about the work of planners. These challenges notwithstanding, planners have made some impact, and the work they do should be given more coverage to promote public awareness about the profession. For instance, the various informal settlement upgrading projects spearheaded by planners at DASP should be celebrated to enhance the reputation of the profession. Also, the impact of planners in the orderly development of Namibian towns and cities should be highlighted. Another way in which the appeal of planners can be enhanced is through the creation of a planning digest or newsletter that regularly features work done by planners in both academia and industry. Moreover, radio announcements in various languages can be adopted to create more awareness about the work planners do.

Internationalization of Namibian Planning Education

As noted earlier, the internationalization of planning education helps to promote cross-cultural awareness and brings the global context to bear on course-delivery modules (Butt et al., 2013; Lee et al., 2020). Therefore, another avenue for increasing awareness about Namibian planning education is through its increased internationalization. To begin with, this can entail more involvement in activities of continental and regional-planning bodies. For instance, DASP can begin to play a more-active role in the activities of the Association of African Planning Schools. Moreover, it can start a program of collaboration with the South African Institute of Town and Regional Planners (under the auspices of its Namibian counterpart, i.e., the NITRP) as a way of enhancing the visibility of activities by professionals in Namibia.

Internationalization could also entail more-frequent engagements between DASP and planning departments in various countries within sub-Saharan Africa. Thus, visits in the recent past by staff from the University of Pretoria and students from the University of Botswana deserve commendation. Moreover, internationalization should involve enrollment in DASP programs by students from other countries, especially southern Africa. Admittedly, this should not occur at the expense of the core mandate of the department to train professionals primarily for the needs of Namibian industry. This mandate emerges because although plans are underway to establish similar departments in other institutions, DASP still remains the focal point for the delivery of spatial-planning programs in the country. However, allocating a few admission slots annually for international students will not upend this goal. While a relatively low demand exists for the planning program at NUST (i.e., when compared to institutions in South Africa), it has steadily been attracting interest from students in other southern-African countries such as Botswana in the recent past. Moreover, through the fees charged and networks established, admission of international students will help to mobilize more resources for the long-term sustenance of the program.

Conclusion

This chapter has evaluated ways of enhancing planning-education awareness in sub-Saharan Africa based on a case study of Namibia, which reveals this awareness can be created in five main ways. To begin with, stakeholder engagement is pivotal. This comprises persons in both academia and industry, as well as the public and private sectors. Such collaboration promotes knowledge exchange and pools synergies for the better delivery of such programs. The Namibian case study also reveals the importance of both formal and informal approaches to marketing planning programs. The formal strategies comprise official events where such awareness creation takes place. Also, the informal approaches entail person-to-person contacts, as well as social media and other platforms. Generally, the accreditation of planning programs (which currently largely occurs within the confines of general-education accreditation) makes it easier to market them. This is because potential students are motivated by the credibility of the certifications awarded, which has significant implications for their employability and ability to pursue further studies. Moreover, a community-based approach to the delivery of spatial-planning programs is important for building confidence regarding the roles of planners in society. Such interactions simultaneously expose students to real-world situations while enhancing the appeal of the profession especially among the youth. Also, the internationalization of Namibian planning education helps to increase its appeal beyond the nation's borders and promote cross-national exchanges among students and staff.

While these findings are mostly relevant in a sub-Saharan context, they also imply several general conceptual and empirical insights. Conceptually, the analysis reveals that spatial-planning education epitomizes how pedagogy results in transformation of the built environment through the input of planners, communities, and other stakeholders. Thus, it serves as a confluence of diverse perspectives and synergies. Moreover, the findings demonstrate how the dichotomy between modernism and postmodernism largely define the underlying schools of thought associated with contemporary spatial-planning education. This occurs because of the quandary between ensuring a more-orderly physical landscape versus addressing the inherent socioeconomic dynamics, which enhance livability.

Empirically, the findings reveal the nuances of the planning discipline, which call for the need to rethink traditional approaches to awareness creation and course delivery. This occurs due to the imperative to respond to the needs of regional, local, and national dynamics. Finally, this chapter articulates spatial-planning education as a product of historical context that simultaneously adapts to the contemporary needs of a society. The goal is to maximize relevance by addressing priority development matters borne out of temporal provenance.

Notes

1 All planning programs are accredited with the National Council for Higher Education. The bachelor's and honors programs are discrete qualifications, each with its own admissions criteria. For instance, a senior secondary school level certificate is generally the entry qualification for the bachelor's degree. Moreover, a completed bachelor's degree is a requirement for admission into the honors program, which is regarded as a more-advanced form of qualification. The honors degree helps students to hone their research skills through a mini thesis and better prepares them for the job market. It also qualifies those in the Bachelor of Urban and Regional Planning Honors stream for professional registration with the Namibia Institute of Town and Regional Planners.
2 Work-integrated learning aims to provide students with practical exposure to the planning profession through internships with planning firms, local authorities, government departments, or other entities.

References

Butt, A., Ratnayake, R., & Budge, T. (2013). Planning education and inter-cultural collaboration: Awareness, innovation, reflection and preparation for practice. *Bhumi: The Planning Research Journal*, *3*(1), 1–10. http://dl.lib.mrt.ac.lk/handle/123/10496

Cavrić, B. (2011). Evolution of botswana planning education in light of local and international requirements. *Spatium International Review*, *25*, 30–38. https://doi.org/10.2298/SPAT1125030C

Diaw, K., Nnkya, T., & Watson, V. (2002). Planning education in Sub-Saharan Africa: Responding to the demands of a changing context. *Planning Practice and Research*, *17*(3), 337–348. https://doi.org/10.1080/0269745022000005689

Dimitrova, E. (2014). The 'sustainable development' concept in urban planning education: Lessons learned on a bulgarian path. *Journal of Cleaner Production*, *62*, 120–127. https://doi.org/10.1016/j.jclepro.2013.06.021

Du Plessis, D., & Keyter, C. (2019). Capacity building through public institutions of higher learning: A case study of Namibia. *Africa Journal of Public Sector Development and Governance*, *2*(1), 70–83. https://journals.co.za/doi/pdf/10.10520/EJC-1a0fc8d44e

Frank, A. I. (2006). Three decades of thought on planning education. *Journal of Planning Literature*, *21*(1), 15–67. https://doi.org/10.1177/0885412206288904

Frank, A. I., & Silver, C. (2018). Introduction. In A. I. Frank & C. Silver (Eds.), *Urban planning education: Beginnings, global movement and future prospects* (pp. 1–7). Springer. https://doi.org/10.1007/978-3-319-55967-4_17

Lamb, T., & Vodicka, G. (2021). Education for 21st century urban and spatial planning: Critical postmodern pedagogies. In A. I. Frank & A. da Rosa Pires (Eds.), *Teaching urban and regional planning: Innovative pedagogies in practice* (pp. 20–38). Edward Elgar Publishing. https://doi.org/10.4337/9781788973632

Lee, C. A., Chrisinger, B., Greenlee, A. J., Garcia Zambrana, I., & Jackson, A. (2020). Beyond recruitment: Comparing experiences of climate and diversity between international students and domestic students of color in US urban planning programs. *Journal of Planning Education and Research*. https://doi.org/10.1177/0739456X20902241

Manda, M. (2013). Reflections on planning education in Malawi. *Education and Society in Southern Africa*, *1*(1), 58–74. www.academia.edu/download/35343090/REFLECTIONS_ON_PLANNING_EDUCATION_IN_MALAWI.pdf

Maruna, M., Rodic, D. M., & Colic, R. (2018). Remodelling urban planning education for sustainable development: The case of Serbia. *International Journal of Sustainability in Higher Education*, *19*(4), 658–680. https://doi.org/10.1108/IJSHE-07-2017-0102

Million, A., & Heinrich, A. J. (2014). Linking participation and built environment education in urban planning processes. *Current Urban Studies*, *2*, 335–349. https://doi.org/10.4236/cus.2014.24032

Odendaal, N. (2012). Reality check: Planning education in the African urban century. *Cities*, *29*(3), 174–182. doi:10.1016/j.cities.2011.10.001

Odendaal, N., & Watson, V. (2018). Partnerships in planning education: The association of african planning schools (AAPS). In A. I. Frank & C. Silver (Eds.), *Urban planning education: Beginnings, global movement, future prospects* (pp. 147–160). https://doi.org/10.1007/978-3-319-55967-4_17

Olesen, K. (2018). Teaching planning theory as planner roles in urban planning education. *Higher Education Pedagogies*, *3*(1), 302–318. https://doi.org/10.1080/23752696.2018.1425098

Palazzo, D., Hollstein, L., & Diko, S. K. (2021). Urban planning as a career preference for students: Efforts to improve awareness about the profession. *Planning Practice and Research*, *36*(2), 174–192. https://doi.org/10.1080/02697459.2020.1782056

Picketts, I. M., Curry, J., & Rapaport, E. (2012, June). Community adaptation to climate change: Environmental planners' knowledge and experiences in British Columbia, Canada. *Journal of Environmental Policy and Planning*, *14*(2), 119–137. https://doi.org/10.1080/1523908X.2012.659847

Roderiguez-Bachiller, A. (1988). *Town planning education*. Avebury.

Silver, C. (2018). The origins of planning education: Overview. In A. I. Frank & C. Silver (Eds.), *Urban planning education: Beginnings, global movement and future prospects* (pp. 11–25). Springer. https://doi.org/10.1007/978-3-319-55967-4_17

Slotterback, C. S., & Lauria, M. (2019). Building a foundation for public engagement in planning: 50 years of impact, interpretation, and inspiration from Arnstein's ladder. *Journal of the American Planning Association*, *85*(3), 183–187. https://doi.org/10.1080/01944363.2019.1616985

Sweet, E. L., & Etienne, H. F. (2011). Commentary: Diversity in urban planning education and practice. *Journal of Planning Education and Research*, *31*(3), 332–339. https://doi.org/10.1177/0739456X11414715

Watson, V. (2011, April). Inclusive urban planning for the working poor: Planning education trends and potential shifts. *WIEGO Working Paper (Urban Policies number 21)*. Women in Informal Employment Globalizing and Organizing (WIEGO). www.wiego.org/sites/default/files/publications/files/Watson_WIEGO_WP21.pdf

Watson, V., & Odendaal, N. (2012). Changing planning education in Africa: The role of the association of African planning schools. *Journal of Planning Education and Research*, *33*(1), 1–12. https://doi.org/10.1177/0739456X12452308

25
RAISING URBAN PLANNING AWARENESS IN INDIA

Bhargav Adhvaryu and Bhavesh Joshi

Urban planning is a relatively new profession. Cities existed before it was invented, so why do we need the profession? The answer is simple. The world has witnessed rapid urbanization and city growth post-industrialization. The complex multi-dimensional issues that arise due to unprecedented rapid urbanization can't be addressed using the traditional departmental approach wherein problems are approached in a compartmentalized manner. The current chaotic state of most Indian cities indicates this approach has been rendered redundant in solving modern-day issues. To address complex and highly interconnected urban issues, today's cities must have specialist professionals with interdisciplinary and evidence-based problem-solving skills backed by theoretical underpinnings of how cities evolve, grow, and function. The theoretical framework needs context-specific customization that draws from several disciplines such as architecture, urban design, economics, behavioral psychology, sociology, anthropology, public policy, geography, management, technology, engineering, and law. This ought to be the key goal of planning education and practice all around the world and ought to translate into planning practice.

After a brief historical overview of planning in India, we establish the need for planners and their desired skills compared with the current supply (i.e., the lack of it). Rajkot city is used as a case study to analyze the level of public awareness about planning and citizens' participation in the planning process. Based on that, we recommend strategies to increase planning awareness and make it more mainstream.

Historical Overview of Urban Planning in India

Human settlements in ancient India are well documented. For example, the Indus Valley civilization, with an estimated span of 2,000 years, was at its peak during BCE 2600–1900. Its largest cities—Mohenjo-Daro and Harappa—had an estimated population between 30,000–60,000. Archaeological excavations have revealed systematically laid out street-grid systems, well-designed drainage and water-supply systems, other civic infrastructure, and the presence of clustering of uses.

The roots of modern[1] urban planning in India can be traced to some complementary events during British colonial rule[2] (1757 CE–1947 CE), during which a variety of survey organizations were set up. For example, the Survey of India (established in 1767) aimed to map the country's physical territory. The Geological Survey of India (established in 1851) sought to appraise and predict underground resources. The Census of India (first completed in 1872) sought to uncover the demography of populations. The Archaeological Survey of India (established in 1871) was intended to catalog the large corpus of cultural monuments, and the Anthropological Survey of India (established in 1945) aimed to study cultural aspects. Since land revenue constituted a major part of imperial income, the British colonists paid special attention to land survey and planning (Kumar et al., 2020).

Aside from the need for law and order, the British colonial government saw planning and civic governance through the lens of public health and municipal sanitation. The outbreak of a fatal plague in Bombay (now Mumbai) in 1896, for example, prompted the creation of the Bombay City Improvement Trust as an administrative entity under the direct supervision of colonial administrators and engineers (Kumar et al., 2020). The Bombay City Improvement Trust was established in 1898, in the aftermath of the plague, as an administrative organization in charge of the city's general development, modeled after the Glasgow City Improvement Trust. The Trust's purpose was to address three key challenges of Bombay—dismally poor sanitation, lack of building codes leading to overcrowding, and lack of governance and accountability of city officials. It invoked the power of eminent domain, which entailed taking over private land in the public interest, using it for the creation of new streets, opening up crowded localities, and reclaiming land for expansion (Spodek, 2013). This could be considered the first instance of a coordinated and focused physical-planning effort in India. Other cities soon followed Bombay's example, namely the City of Mysore Improvement Act, 1903; Calcutta Improvement Act, 1911; United Provinces Town Improvement Act, 1919; Punjab Town Improvement Act, 1922; Nagpur Improvement Trust Act, 1936; and Rajasthan Urban Improvement Act, 1959.

During British colonial rule, many British urban-development concepts, practices, regulations, and laws were introduced in India. The Bombay Town Planning Act, 1915 (subsequently revised to the new Bombay Town Planning Act, 1954) had two major goals: improving Bombay's physical environment, which was widely viewed as unhygienic and causing public health problems, and regulating Bombay's future expansion through planned city extension or town-planning schemes. The administration also passed the Land Acquisition Act, 1894 as part of the wider land-governance paradigm that they established, which was later abolished in 2013 (Kumar et al., 2020). The first town-planning scheme[3] (under the Bombay Town Planning Act, 1915) was prepared for Jamalpur, Ahmedabad in 1917. We can argue that the year 1917 could be considered the birth year of modern-planning practice in India.

Some historically important planning-related events were the New Delhi Master Plan, made by the British architect Sir Edwin Landseer Luytens in 1912—based on the principles of Sir Ebenezer Howard's garden city movement—which was implemented in 1932. Also, between 1915–19, Sir Patrick Geddes, a Scottish town planner, produced a series of town-planning reports on at least 18 Indian cities. These were based on the place-work-folk principle, which was divergent from the then-prevailing engineering-based town-planning interventions (National Commission on Urbanisation, 1988). Geddes's idea of conservative surgery also gained a lot of traction, and in general, his principles are considered impactful in planning thought and theory as argued by Rao-Cavale (2017) and Home (1997). The Great Depression of the 1930s, and World War II, brought a hiatus to planning in India as it did elsewhere. The construction of New Delhi as a new national capital (inaugurated in 1931), which continued even through the Depression, was a major exception. Another important event from an urban planning standpoint was the report of the Health Survey and Development Committee published in 1946 under the chairmanship of Sir Joseph Bhore. The report recommended the creation of a ministry of housing and town planning in every province, well-equipped provincial directorates of town planning, the appointment of an expert in the central ministry of health to advise on and scrutinize town planning schemes, and creation of improvement trusts in all large cities (Ansari, 1977 as cited in Spodek, 2018). After the 1947 independence of India, Chandigarh became the first example of a designed city, which was led by the Swiss-French architect Le Corbusier and officially inaugurated in 1953. Subsequently, in 1962, the Master Plan for Delhi was the first example of a comprehensive master plan for a city in India, which was formulated based on the provisions of the Delhi Development Act, 1957, that entailed large-scale bulk land acquisition.

Following this, in 1966, the first Urban Development Plans Formulation and Implementation (UDPFI) Guidelines (Institute of Town Planners, India, 1996) were prepared and circulated to all the states and union territories by the Ministry of Urban Development (now the Ministry of Housing and Urban Affairs). Before these guidelines, most master plans were prepared along the lines of the 1962 Master Plan for Delhi. The UDPFI guidelines were more comprehensive and generic, allowing cities to plan according to their particular requirements. Economic liberalization started in India in the early 1990s. In subsequent years, India witnessed rapid urbanization that led to the haphazard growth of cities and overstressed infrastructure systems. To deal with this, some states prepared metropolitan-region plans to encourage the decentralization of economic activities. However, these were not implemented due to the lack of funding and support from the central government (Punekar, 1968). In 2005, the Jawaharlal Nehru National Urban Renewal Mission (JNNURM) was launched to encourage reforms and ensure planned urban development, which was succeeded by the Atal Mission for Rejuvenation and Urban Transformation (AMRUT) program in 2015. The Smart Cities Mission was also introduced in 2015 to improve core infrastructure and deliver a clean, sustainable environment.

At the national level, the Planning Commission (now called National Institution for Transforming India (NITI Aayog) was set up in 1951 as the apex body for economic planning. From 1951–2017, it produced 12 five-year plans. In most of these plans, there were several recommendations related to town-and-country planning, such as enacting town-and-country planning legislation in all states, emphasizing preparation of master plans and regional plans, setting up public health and engineering departments, setting up statutory boards for water supply and sewerage infrastructure improvement, improving public transport, formulating a long-term national urbanization policy, and building the capacities of urban local bodies, to name a few.

In general, urban planning proposals require land, and therefore, spatial planning assumes a significant component. However, some aspatial components like policies that draw from empirically established problems are also needed to make a master-development plan more comprehensive. In our opinion, planning in India is largely dominated by spatial planning, with little or no reference to context-based planning policies.

Need of Planners in the Indian Context

The importance of the role of planners is expected to increase over the next several decades. According to a 2011 report of an expert committee set up by the Ministry of Human Resources Development in the Government of India, there are only about 7,000 qualified town planners in India. Given that there are 7,935 cities (including towns) in India (Census of India, 2011), the report projects that India will need 160,000 planners by 2030. This amounts to India being able to produce 8,000 planners per year—6,000 expected from bachelors of planning and 2,000 from masters of planning programs (Meshram, 2020). Our experience indicates that this is a daunting requirement unlikely to be met by 2030.

As part of the National Urban Information System, the Indian government is making satellite imagery available in these 7,935 cities to help develop geographic information system (GIS) databases that will be able to inform the needs of these areas as they develop over the next few decades. Of all the cities and towns to think about and prepare for the future, approximately 24% have finalized master plans. The government is hoping that this push will bring that up to 100% within the next few years (Berg, 2012). The Town and Country Planning Organisation (TCPO), Ministry of Housing and Urban Affairs, Government of India estimates that out of the 7,935 cities in India, only 2,631 (33%) have statutory master plans, 85% of which are approved, and the remaining are under preparation (Kumar et al., 2020). Although both sources vary in their estimates, cities and towns without master plans range from 5,700–6,000. This leaves a huge scope for remaining towns and cities to produce master plans, which emphatically establishes the need for planners in India in the coming decades.

Desirable Skills for Planners in India

In the previous section, we discussed the need for planners and established it in the Indian context. In this section, we discuss three key skills desired from planners in India (and perhaps globally) related to negotiation, analysis, and urban economics, which draws from our experience and interviews with leading urban planning experts in India.

People Skills: Negotiation, Consensus Building, and Communication

Some of the most important skills a planner needs are people skills—the ability to negotiate with a wide variety of people and groups. What separates urban planning from architecture is that in architecture there is one landowner (or a unified group, e.g., a company), while cities have multiple landowners and stakeholders (B. Patel, personal communication, August 31, 2015). This makes pleasing all stakeholders extremely difficult. The role of the planner is to negotiate and build consensus, resolve conflicts, and articulate the merits of the proposal to the satisfaction of the landowners and stakeholders. In addition to landowners (that include residents and workers) as the prime stakeholders, there would be others, such as non-governmental organizations, lobbyists, community groups, business associations, and so forth. Bringing all stakeholders together and negotiating an acceptable outcome is therefore the most important skill.

When communicating with the public, creativity in imagining and visualizing alternative futures is very useful. People not trained as planners may not have the ability to think and visualize what they want. Planners can start from abstract ideas and then seek stakeholders' inputs or start from initial stakeholder ideas and refine as needed. In either case, stakeholder involvement is important. During the process of developing proposals, it's desirable to think from different perspectives, present innovative ideas, and think outside the box. For example, these must include perspectives of residents, local businesses, environmental groups, public transport operators, public infrastructure agencies, and so on. Ms. Ballaney[4] (S. Ballaney, personal communication, 26 July 2021), in addition to understanding the needs of the stakeholders, also emphasizes the ability to communicate and negotiate in a language they understand. This could be extended to not only the language but also to vocabulary that is non-technical and free of planning jargon.

Analytical and Problem-Solving Skills

Analytical skills cover a spectrum of skills such as data analytics, data visualization, and GIS skills. In a lot of instances, it is necessary to summarize large amounts of quantitative data to create lucid descriptive statistics and visualizations. Given that land records are gradually moving toward digitalization in India, using GIS software to create thematic and analytical maps would go a long way to save time and present better narratives for proposals supported by data-based evidence. At the core lies the ability of planners to be problem-solvers. Great analyses and visualizations not backed by viable solutions aren't likely to be accepted by stakeholders. As Ms. Ballaney (S. Ballaney, personal communication, 26 July 2021) maintains, problem-solving leading to acceptable, implementable solutions comes from the ability of the planner to understand and contextualize perspectives from various disciplines (e.g., sociology, engineering, urban design, travel behavior, environmental science, to name a few).

Urban Economics Skills

Last but not least, the understanding of how cities grow and function, and how firms and households make location decisions, is necessary. A planner without an understanding of how the land and labor markets function (or urban economics in general) is prone to have a lesser degree of success in making planning work. As Mr. Phatak[5] (V.K. Phatak, personal communication, 18 July 2021) says, planning in India is largely axiomatic and rarely evidence-based, and if planners do not understand markets, then provisions in the plans are very likely to fail. In other words, planners start from self-evident statements (axioms) or presumptions that become the basis for plan making and proposals. For example, a certain amount of green space per capita is needed, so the plan must provide that for a projected (future) population. However, such axioms are never questioned regarding their veracity and affordability.

These skill sets are extremely useful in planning work, as it's a profession that deals with both short- and long-term uncertainty. As Christensen (1985) puts it, if targets are known and not the process to achieve them, then planning becomes a learning process. Alternatively, if there is agreement on the process to achieve alternative targets, but not the targets themselves, planning becomes a bargaining process. If neither is known, then planning becomes a search for order in chaos. Several decades later, these principles hold; depending on the context, the approach to planning needs to be adapted.

Planning Education in India: A Brief History

Urban planning education started in India when the School of Planning in Delhi was established in 1954 by the then Ministry of Education, Government of India, which later became the School of Planning and Architecture, Delhi. In 2020, about 30 Indian universities offered planning programs at both postgraduate and undergraduate levels (Institute of Town Planners, India, 2021). As shown in Figure 25.1, there are about 50 planning programs, of which about 22 were added in the last

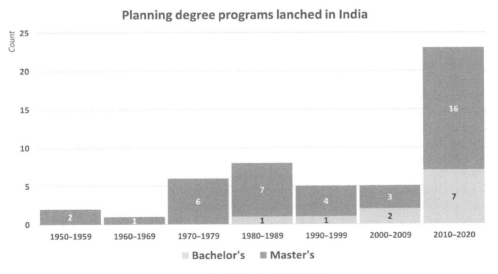

Figure 25.1 Planning Degree Programs Launched in India (1950–2020)
Only the start of the programs is shown; some of them are now closed.
Source: Based on Institute of Town Planners, India (2021)

decade. Most of these programs are housed in private universities, which operate for profit. This signifies that currently there is enough market demand for planners, which is very likely to increase over the next few decades.

Perspectives on Planning Curricula

The 50 or so planning programs offer specializations in various subfields, such as urban planning,[6] urban design, housing, regional planning, traffic and transportation planning, environmental planning, infrastructure planning, and so on. The program names and content change from time to time. At the core of the planning curriculum lies the domain of spatial planning. Most, if not all, planning programs in India will have a sizeable component of spatial planning and design. Though holders of bachelor's degrees in geography, sociology, and economics are allowed to enter a master's program in planning (in most universities), data from the CEPT University admissions office 2015–20 shows that 75% of applicants are architects, 15% are civil engineers, 5% planners (BPlan), and 5% others (e.g., economists, geographers, and sociologists). One of the main pedagogic tools for planning education is the studio, which attempts to simulate real-life situations. Students go through three or four studios during their two-year master's program, which focuses on various spatial scales or themes, providing them practical experience. In some universities, the last semester is either a studio or research- or project-based dissertation.

From the authors' observations and that of Mr. Phatak (V.K. Phatak, personal communication, 18 July 2021), planning education in India is moving toward specialization and super-specialization.[7] We think this isn't necessary, as it fragments key learning and reduces interdisciplinarity. Rather, planning curricula must focus on generalist education and development of the three key skills discussed previously. Using combinations of studios, lecture courses, and dissertation topics, students may develop major inclinations. Specialization and super-specialization are better gained on the job over a few years and/or by undertaking a second master's degree after work experience. On planning education, Ms. Ballaney (S. Ballaney, personal communication, 26 July 2021) emphasizes three very important points: first, that practicing planners must be involved in teaching various planning studios; second, that teachers must be updated with new knowledge and ideologies (which should reflect in the curriculum); and third, that data collection and collating by smaller spatial-planning units is needed, which eventually builds a larger picture.

The other criticism of the planning curriculum in India could be adherence to outdated and non-contextual standards. National-level guidance documents such as Urban and Regional Development Plans Formulation and Implementation (URDPFI) Guidelines (see, e.g., Town and Country Planning Organisation, 2015) present blanket guidelines that may or may not be appropriate for a city's context. For example, the guidelines propose land-use structure for a developable area by prescribing the percentage of area under land-use categories such as residential, commercial, industrial, recreation, and so forth, for different sizes of cities (Town and Country Planning Organisation, 2015, Table 5.2, p. 140). The objectives of such prescriptions are not clear, and therefore it is inconceivable that cities can or should follow such prescriptions—let cities develop plans on their own, rather than follow a central agency. A better approach would be to incorporate location behavior (market economics) through a land-use-transport interaction modeling framework (e.g., SIMPLAN, which demonstrates an Indian application, Adhvaryu, 2010). In the absence of data and resources to build mathematical models of cities to assist plan-making, the plans need to be robust enough to provide a generic framework for development, but flexible enough for course correction as required due to unforeseen circumstances. There is vast literature on the liberal approach to planning that strongly suggests respecting market forces (both real estate and labor markets), which are instrumental in shaping cities, and, if needed, allow government intervention to take care of vested interests that are not favorable to a city's development and growth.

From the authors' own experiences, we argue that, gradually, planning education in India must move away from the planners-play-God (traditional, top-down)[8] model to a more planners-facilitate model, which we call the liberal approach to planning. This would entail replacing the traditional predict-and-provide with provide-and-revise, replacing utopian ideals with more pragmatic planning that considers what the city can afford and announcing trunk infrastructure (roads, public transport, infrastructure utilities, etc.) well in advance (say 20–30 years). Of course, the trunk infrastructure provision will require some broad estimates for budgeting. However, committing to building it would be based on periodic monitoring of the development. Other components in a liberal-planning framework would include having minimal land-use zones, developing control regulations to address side-effects that otherwise cannot be solved efficiently by markets, and not creating unnecessary land-market distortions that outbid landowners (in the sense used by Alonso, 1964). The COVID-19 pandemic taught us how unpredictable the future is. Therefore, plans with long-term firm projections (except trunk infrastructure) can never be taken seriously. Plans that are robust enough to adapt to a dynamic world seem to be the need of the hour.

In general, we believe that the way forward for planning curricula in India should involve producing generalist planners with focus on imparting the necessary skills discussed earlier. Planners must be able to demonstrate a high aptitude for problem-solving and be able to work out cities' requirements from first principles rather than relying on outdated and axiomatic standards.

The Case Study of Rajkot

Rajkot comprises Rajkot Municipal Corporation (RMC), 162 square kilometers (appx. 100 sq. miles), with an estimated population of 1.5 million in 2021, and the wider metropolitan region called Rajkot Urban Development Authority (RUDA), that includes RMC, which is about 686 square kilometers (appx. 426 sq. miles) with an estimated population of two million. Population wise, Rajkot is the fourth largest city in Gujarat state and the 28th largest in India. It is an industrial, service-sector, and education hub for the Saurashtra region.

Key Duties of Planners

Both RMC and RUDA have positions for planners. RUDA planners are mainly involved in the preparation of the Development Plan (DP) and Town Planning Scheme (TPS) for the entire RUDA area and its execution outside the RMC area, whereas RMC planners assume the role of execution (as delegated by RUDA) of DP and TPS within the RMC boundary. However, often due to a shortage of personnel in RMC, qualified planners are not available, and therefore engineers are deputed for such posts. Their key duties comprise dealing with building- and development-plan approvals, illegal construction, building-completion applications, and land disputes. Extensive field visits are followed up with huge amounts of paperwork for issuing notifications and certificates. RUDA, the planning authority, has more qualified planners, but that too is inadequate given the quantum of work. Their main duties, in addition to preparation of DP and TPS, specifically deal with inviting objections, scrutinizing the objections and suggestions received, submitting proposals to the state government, and after approval, implementing the TPS. Often, implementation of the approved TPS is delayed several years (usually five to ten), mainly due to land disputes and encroachments by squatter settlements. In both cases, RMC or RUDA planners have limited time to think about the future of cities because, as discussed earlier, they spend their time mainly in day-to-day activities, even though they are the best people to undertake long-term planning, with their immense local knowledge and understanding of a city's problems at the grassroots level.

Public Awareness of the Planning Process

Cities in Gujarat, under the Gujarat Town Planning and Urban Development Act, 1974, each have an urban-development authority that is responsible for making a DP for the city and its environs for a 20-year horizon (revised after 10 years). As part of the plan-making process, the urban-development authority conducts a public-consultation process wherein it invites suggestions and objections to the proposed plan through a series of stakeholders' meetings. This process, with some variations, is usually followed in most Indian cities.

Our Rajkot experience has shown that only stakeholders who are directly affected attend such meetings. Affected stakeholders include those whose land plots and properties are impacted by road widening or whose plots are put under reservation.[9] Most citizens are not aware of the rights and amenities to which they are entitled under the act. For example, land parcels under a DP get the benefit of land zoning and appreciation in land value due to better accessibility. Citizens also benefit due to the development of social-infrastructure development in the plan area in reserved land like parks, gardens, schools, hospitals, and other physical-infrastructural facilities like water-supply networks, sewerage, and accessible-road networks.

The second revision of the Rajkot DP 2031 was initiated in August 2014 by RUDA. They conducted three rounds of stakeholders' consultation meetings between December 2014 and March 2015. In the first round, participation included experts' consultation, in which the stakeholders were involved through interviews and focus-group discussions to review and assess the current levels of urban services and infrastructure needs. The second round was more participatory and collaborative. A series of working group meetings were held, and stakeholders made more specific suggestions for improving the existing conditions. The third round was carried out to seek suggestions on various issues identified under each sector of the DP and discuss various feasible solutions for them. The objections and comments received from different groups of participants were around only 1,500 for the three rounds, which indicates very little involvement of the public given that RUDA-area population is about two million.

The DP is delivered by breaking up the area into smaller chunks varying from 100–200 hectares (appx. 250–500 acres), called the Town Planning Scheme (TPS). At this scale, more zoomed-in details are available for examination. In the recent past, for the TPS in Vavdi, there were a total of 64 landowners affected, of which only 40% participated in the process, submitting objections and suggestions. Similarly, in another TPS in Raiya, of the 79 landowners affected, only 60% participated. Typically, a TPS, directly and indirectly, impacts about 40,000 to 45,000 citizens. Given these participation numbers, even from those directly impacted, participation is lower than expected, and it is mainly related to their own plots (NIMBYism) and does not include broader area-level involvement suggestions.

A nationwide Smart Cities Mission was launched in June 2015 with its main objective to promote cities that provide core infrastructure, a clean and sustainable environment, and a decent quality of life for citizens through the application of smart solutions. The focus is on sustainable, inclusive development by the creation of replicable models that act as lighthouses to other aspiring cities. One hundred cities have been selected to be developed as Smart Cities through a two-stage competition. Rajkot was one of the cities and received ₹2.623 billion ($38.342 million US) in funding to implement 58 projects. As per the Smart City proposal report, the citizen engagement was nearly 70% of the population (Ministry of Urban Development, Government of India, n.d.). The Rajkot Smart City Cell (under RMC) tirelessly tried to increase public participation through various publicity strategies like social-media posts, radio advertisements, ward-committee public meetings headed by the respective municipal councilors, marathons, bicycling, painting competitions, flower shows, and so on. This gained huge public participation that was higher than that seen in the DP and TPS processes. However, based on one author's experiences on heading the Smart City Cell for three years, it can be argued that although the participation level was high, the feedback on the Smart City proposal was inadequate—it did not materialize into concrete and constructive suggestions. We attribute this to the lack of effectively communicating the impacts and benefits of the proposal to citizens of Rajkot.

Overall, in Rajkot, at all three levels of planning the DP (macro), the TPS (micro), and special projects (e.g., Smart Cities Mission), the level of participation observed is low. We believe that this is not likely to be very different for most other Indian cities.

Strategies to Increase Planning Awareness

The authors feel that promulgating a city's master-development plan must have the engagement of public relations and marketing professionals. It must be treated as a campaign designed to enhance public participation, with stakeholders identified for the various geographies, community groups, industry groups, non-governmental organizations, environmental lobbyists, and so on. Using the power of digital communications, all stakeholder groups must be sent information supported by clear infographics well in advance of the stakeholders' meetings. Putting up plans in a large town-hall room hoping that people will turn up and participate hasn't worked. Planners must also be able to explain the pros and cons of the plan to successfully negotiate consensus. In specific cases, we also recommend the public meetings be held on-site to provide a local context. More long-term recommendations include a mandatory course in school and university curricula on cities and the role of urban local bodies in shaping the future of cities, which are discussed in the next section.

Making Planning More Mainstream

In many social situations, planning professionals find themselves having to respond to the question, "So what do you do exactly"? Unlike an architect, engineer, or doctor, a planner often faces this situation—this says a lot about the social perception of planning. Ms. Ballaney (S. Ballaney, personal communication, 26 July 2021) opines that not many people are aware that cities are products of planned decisions. The social perception of planners could be higher.

There are several ways we propose to make planning more mainstream. One of the first things would be to introduce key topics related to cities as part of geography and civics curricula in high schools. The topics should address modern-day public infrastructure systems, such as water-supply systems, sewerage systems, solid-waste management, stormwater drainage, transport systems, and infrastructure. The complexity and the interconnectedness of these systems must be emphasized. Students should be made aware that cities need to be planned and managed for them to function well. The role and responsibilities of civic administrators should be clearly articulated. They must be able to appreciate the arduous tasks city planners and managers do on a day-to-day basis, complemented by various field visits.

Similar efforts must be made to address university students. For example, Ahmedabad University has a Foundation Programme with four studios, spanning a year, on democracy and justice, water, environment, and neighborhoods (Ahmedabad University, 2021). Regardless of the program discipline (arts, humanities, sciences, engineering, or management), these studios are mandatory for first-year undergraduates. The studios help them appreciate, among other things, the nuances of neighborhoods, how cities function, the key elements in their neighborhoods, key local issues, and possible solutions. We think more such hands-on project-based learning courses on cities must be made mandatory for all degree programs in universities across India for all disciplines.

The role of urban local bodies engaged in planning and related activities is very important. Marketing campaigns need to be designed wherein planning efforts and recent projects are exhibited to the public regularly. The local radio and TV stations must be involved in spreading the word about exhibitions and interviews with people, especially school and university students. Consistent efforts along these lines for three to five years are very likely to raise the awareness of urban planning among the public.

Lastly, it is important for Indian academics to develop a context-specific research agenda and conduct research that informs planning policy from an interdisciplinary perspective. However, in this regard, the national government could be more encouraging. For example, urban planning is hardly ever mentioned in research funding and grants announcements. While research funding for lifesaving drugs and vaccines, climate change, clean energy, and technology, to name a few, may seem more important, certainly urban planning should not be ignored.

Conclusion

In this chapter, we outlined the history of urban planning in India, which has evolved from the late 1910s on various fronts. The need for planners was discussed in the Indian context. We argue that the key skills needed by planners include people skills, analytical and problem-solving skills, and a good understanding of urban economics. Without these skills, planners would not be able to function effectively and deliver impactful plans and proposals. Planning education has also evolved since the first master's degree program in 1954. Some universities have created more super-specializations within planning, which we believe are unnecessary, while some have ventured into offering bachelor's degree programs in planning. The sheer number of planners required, with the right skills, by 2030 is going to be huge. Both publicly funded and private universities need to respond to this rising demand both in terms of curricula (i.e., providing the necessary skills) and the sheer number of planning-program seats that need to be increased. The discussion on the current level of planning awareness and how to raise it is examined via the case study of Rajkot city, leading to a more generic discussion on making planning more mainstream in India. Addressing this requires medium- to long-term strategies, such as city-related courses in school and university curricula, innovative publicity strategies for wider promulgation of plans and projects, a context-specific interdisciplinary research agenda in planning, and more funding from the national government to bridge the gap between research and practice.

Acknowledgments

We acknowledge the interviewees, Mr. Vidyadhar K. Phatak and Ms. Shirley Ballaney, for sparing their time and sharing their valuable experiences. Thanks to Ms. Amita Pathria and Mr. Sameer Kumar for their assistance.

Notes

1 The term *modern* in general is used to mean planning theory and practices that emerged after the mid-18th century (after industrialization and then later after the automobile was invented).
2 Includes the Company rule in India 1757–1858 and the British Raj 1858–1947.
3 Known in general as the land readjustment and pooling method. Instead of acquiring land from owners, land is brought together by pooling it from a group of owners, then the area is planned by readjusting and reshaping land parcels to provide regular shapes to original plots and use portions for roads, civic infrastructure, and public amenities. The key advantages of this method (over bulk land acquisition) are that the original owners are not displaced and, more importantly, the increment in land value accrues to the owners whenever the land is sold and developed for urban use. In addition, since the role of the government is more that of a facilitator, it is less likely to be subject to corrupt practices, as compared to the land-acquisition method (based on Ballaney, 2008).
4 Shirley Ballaney is an architect-urban planner with more than 25 years of experience. She practices as an independent consultant and is doing work for the World Bank, Asian Development Bank, DFID, NIUA, and

many private consulting firms. She is currently engaged in several statutory urban planning and research projects with an emphasis on transforming the planning practice in India to make it more effective in improving the quality of life in Indian cities. She has several accolades to her name. Noteworthy are the Hubert Humphrey Fellowship by the Department of States, US, to pursue the Special Program in Urban and Regional Studies at MIT, USA (2005–06); fellowships from the Netherlands Government (1997 & 2015), Swedish International Development Agency (2002) and United Nations University Japan (2000); and the Michael Ventris Memorial Award for Architecture from the Architectural Association, London (1992).

5 Vidyadhar K. Phatak is the former head of the Town & Country Planning Division at the Mumbai Metropolitan Region Development Authority (MMRDA) and has been at the center of several planning and development initiatives in Mumbai for more than four decades. He has been involved with the preparation of the last two plans for the Metropolitan Region of Mumbai and recently with the preparation of the Master Plan for Mumbai City. With a nuanced understanding of cities and their politics and mammoth experience in planning and development, he has been invited to advise several state and city governments across India. He was also Dean of the Faculty of Planning, CEPT University (2016–19).

6 In some universities the degree names are Master of Urban Planning, Master of Urban Transport Planning, and so on. In some other universities, the degree name is Master of Planning (MPlan), and the specialization is written in parentheses, e.g., MPlan (Urban), MPlan (Transport), MPLan (Infrastructure), and so on.

7 The terms *specialization* and *super-specialization* come from the field of medicine. In the context of planning, a master's degree in city planning along with a master's degree in transport planning or infrastructure planning could be considered a specialization and super-specialization, respectively.

8 This comes from the erstwhile socialist model of governance in India, wherein ownership, production, and distribution of goods and services rested with the government, which pervaded into urban planning. Post economic liberalization in 1991, the role of market forces has assumed more importance in urban planning.

9 Reservation means land reserved for public purposes such as utility infrastructure, e.g., water-treatment plants, sewage-pumping stations, public-health services, police stations, parks and gardens, and economically weaker section housing.

References

Adhvaryu, B. (2010). Enhancing urban planning using simplified models: SIMPLAN for Ahmedabad, India. *Progress in Planning*, 73(3), 113–207. https://doi.org/10.1016/j.progress.2009.11.001

Ahmedabad University. (2021, July 31). *Foundation programme*. Retrieved June 21, 2022, from https://ahduni.edu.in/ug-programme-related-links/foundation-programme/

Alonso, W. (1964). Location and land use. Toward a general theory of land rent. In *Location and land use. Toward a general theory of land rent*. Harvard University Press.

Ansari, J. H. (1977). Evolution of town planning practice and system of urban government in India. *Urban and Rural Planning Thought*, XX(1), 9–23. As cited in Spodek (2013).

Ballaney, S. (2008). *The town planning mechanism in Gujarat, India*. The World Bank Institute.

Ballaney, S. (2021, July 26). *Expert interview* [Email].

Berg, N. (2012, April 8). Master planning 7,935 Indian cities and towns. *Bloomberg CityLab*. Retrieved June 21, 2022, from www.bloomberg.com/news/articles/2012-08-03/master-planning-7-935-indian-cities-and-towns

Census of India. (2011). *Primary census abstract: Figures at a glance*. Government of India. Retrieved June 21, 2022, from https://censusindia.gov.in/2011census/PCA/PCA_Highlights/pca_highlights_file/India/5Figures_at_glance.pdf

Christensen, K. (1985). Coping with uncertainty in planning. *Journal of American Planning Association*, 51(1), 63–73. https://doi.org/10.1080/01944368508976801

Home, R. (1997). *Of planting and planning: The making of British colonial cities*. E & FN SPON.

Institute of Town Planners, India. (1996). *UDPFI: Urban development plans formulation and implementation guidelines (Volume 1)*. Ministry of Urban Affairs & Employment, Government of India. Retrieved June 21, 2022, from www.cmamp.com/CP/FDocument/Volume1UrbanDevelopmentPlansFormulationandImplementation.pdf

Institute of Town Planners, India. (2021). *Planning courses recognized by ITPI up to 2021*. www.itpi.org.in/uploads/pdfs/list-of-recognized-schools-or-institutions-upto-2021-17-june.pdf

Kumar, A., Vidyarthi, S., & Prakash, P. (2020). *City planning in India, 1947–2017* (1st ed.). Routledge.

Meshram, D. S. (2020). Energizing town planning education in India: Way forward. *Journal of Indian Town Planning Institute*, 17(2), 1–27. www.itpi.org.in/uploads/journalfiles/journal-17x2.pdf

Ministry of Urban Development, Government of India. (n.d.). *The smart city challenge stage 2: Smart city proposal (Rajkot)*. Retrieved June 21, 2022, from https://smartnet.niua.org/content/f459de96-6ad3-4a42-8940-23c308315719

National Commission on Urbanisation. (1988). *Report of the national commission on urbanisation* (I–VII). New Delhi.
Patel, B. (2015, August 31). *Personal interaction* [Unrecorded lecture].
Phatak, V. K. (2021, July 18). *Expert interview* [Video conferencing].
Punekar, S. D. (1968). Metropolitan regional planning. *Economic and Political Weekly, 3*(47), 1813–1816. www.epw.in/journal/1968/47/planning-uncategorised/metropolitan-regional-planning.html
Rao-Cavale, K. (2017). Patrick Geddes in India: Anti-colonial nationalism and the historical time of 'cities in evolution. *Landscape and Urban Planning, 166*, 71–81. https://doi.org/10.1016/j.landurbplan.2016.11.005
Spodek, H. (2013). City planning in India under British rule. *Economic and Political Weekly, 48*(4), 53–61. www.epw.in/journal/2013/04/special-articles/city-planning-india-under-british-rule.html
Spodek, H. (2018). *City planning in India under British rule*. IGNOU. Retrieved June 21, 2022, from https://egyankosh.ac.in/bitstream/123456789/44517/1/Unit-38.pdf
Town and Country Planning Organisation. (2015). *Urban and regional development plans formulation and implementation (URDPFI) guidelines (Volume 1)* (Volume I). Ministry of Urban Development, Government of India. Retrieved June 21, 2022, from http://mohua.gov.in/upload/uploadfiles/files/URDPFI%20Guidelines%20Vol%20I.pdf

CONCLUSION

A Clarion Call to Act Intentionally

Stephen Kofi Diko, Danilo Palazzo, and Leah Marie Hollstein

Historically, the urban planning profession has not been without controversies (Pinson, 2004) and is currently experiencing a dual-identity crisis. Internally, there has been controversy about whether the urban planning profession is rational, pluralistic, advocative, or incremental and whether its emphasis should be on the planning process or planning goals. Additionally, an external professional-identity challenge has often made it difficult to communicate effectively to the wider public what the urban planning profession is. Many a planner continues to find it difficult to explain to people the simple meaning of urban planning. Even when explanations are proffered, follow-up questions such as, "Is it related to engineering?" or "Is it related to architecture?" leave planners searching for the right way to position the saliency of the profession among the public. As the introduction to this book has illustrated, the challenge is not only about a lack of awareness about the urban planning profession but also that many children and youth, their relatives, teachers, school counselors, and mentors, often have no exposure to, and worse, have misconceptions about, the profession.

This is incredibly daunting given that the lived experiences of this urban century often illustrate that the future of cities will be increasingly more complex and complicated, surpassing our current awareness of how to tackle emergent and unknown challenges (UN DESA, 2018; Hurtado et al., 2022). For this reason, it is important to ensure that the urban planning profession, dedicated to making cities and their residents better, becomes mainstream among the public, most especially among children and youth as they are the future of the profession. More importantly, the multiplicity and variety of interests, values, people, races, ethnicities, genders, income levels, and community challenges confronting cities require recognition of the need to diversify the profession to ensure not only representation but also genuine participation in dealing with urban challenges.

Yet addressing diversity in the profession, and making it mainstream and familiar among children and youth, their relatives, teachers, and school counselors as well as the general public, cannot be achieved by only becoming aware of these professional challenges. Further steps need to be taken since there is a long way to go in both planning practice (Solis, 2020) and education (Greenlee et al., 2018; Jackson et al., 2018; García et al., 2021). As the various chapters of this book have illustrated, it requires intentionality on the part of all those interested in tackling the diversity and awareness challenges that confront the urban planning profession and education. The theme of intentionality follows from the advocacy of Palazzo et al. (2021), who emphasized the immense roles to be played by urban planning programs and schools, urban planning professional associations and accreditation boards, and urban planners themselves to be active and intentional in dealing with these professional challenges.

It is with great excitement that this book has provided a platform to engender a discourse around the diversity and awareness challenge of the planning profession and education. It takes the discourse further by critically providing a space for contributors across the world to share their experiences in tackling these challenges. In all, we have received 26 contributions on experiences from countries in Africa, Asia, Europe, and North America that provide an immense foundation to begin this discourse. The paragraphs that follow subsequently provide a synthesis of the various contributions of this book to identify key lessons for tackling the diversity and awareness challenges of the urban planning profession and education.

A Call to Action

The call for immediate, concerted efforts to address the dual challenges of diversity and awareness in the urban planning profession and education by the contributors to this book is grounded on the fact that taking action yields positive results. Though past and current efforts are not enough to ensure sustainable pathways for addressing these two germane challenges, nonetheless, the contributors provide valuable lessons for navigating the challenges, intensifying efforts, and charting a path for the future. For each theme, we summarize the relevant lessons.

Addressing Diversity in Planning

In recent years, national and global events, particularly in the United States, have engendered a heightened sense of the urgency for diversity in the urban planning profession and education. For our cities, these movements have revealed how underrepresentation of various demographics has caused disparities in the prosperity and opportunities that should be available to all, while also reflecting the ramifications of how the burdens of society are borne by sectors of our cities that have historically enjoyed less representation, power, and access to opportunities. Further compounding these issues are emergent factors such as urbanization, climate change, and health pandemics, including COVID-19, that have exposed the inequities in the various outcomes of planning in our cities. As a result, issues of justice, fairness, access, and opportunity cannot be discussed without diversity in planning.

Despite the relevance of diversity in planning, an emerging challenge arising in this book concerns the definition of diversity. As the contributions to Section I demonstrate, diversity can be defined or approached from multiple perspectives, making it a strength and a challenge. Responding to these multiple perspectives and definitions, diversity goals must be broadened to ensure wide representation and engagement of different demographics in the planning profession and education. Yet the multiple, possibly diverging, perspectives on diversity can result in some form of prioritization where some aspects of diversity are valorized over others. Additionally, it might happen, in fact, that some specific diversity goals may be achieved that result in the faulty presumption that all diversity challenges have been sufficiently tackled. Indeed, what is relevant in the urban planning profession and education is that no matter the perspective from which diversity is approached, it should embody actions that ensure transformation and genuine outcomes for a broad set of diversity goals focusing on achieving broader representation.

Indeed, in our attempt to emphasize diversity in the urban planning profession and education, it is important to move beyond the rhetoric of diversity, equity, and inclusion statements. While they are a step in the right direction, they must translate into real actions, impact, and transformation in planning outcomes in our cities and in the educational system that produces urban planners. For planning practices, we must be intentional, prioritizing efforts to tackle injustices and poverty in historically disinvested and disadvantaged communities by broadly and genuinely engaging the communities and demographics that have experienced these egregious actions. For the profession, we also need to be intentional about recruitment efforts and develop effective mechanisms to retain cohorts who are less represented in the profession. In this respect, breaking barriers and practices that engender underrepresentation—of races, ethnic groups, genders, and indigenous people—in our profession is imperative. Such intentional strategies are also necessary within the academy where there is a need to recruit and retain diverse students and faculty while creating an academic environment that valorizes diversity not only as a standard but also as an outcome of academic performance.

Contributions in Section I also emphasize the important roles of the various national academic and professional associations for planning, such as the American Planning Association, Association of Collegiate Schools of Planning in North America, Association of African Planning Schools, Association of European Schools of Planning, and Planning Accreditation Board, among others. For instance, despite diversity being a central concern for planning in the United States, it remains a critical area in the accreditation standards that many urban planning schools and departments often fail to attain. Given that many planning students and faculty, as well as the entire professional body, have an underrepresentation of people of color, diversity as a criterion in the accreditation standards should remain a priority. Also, historically Black colleges and universities, Hispanic-serving institutions, and minority-serving institutions in the United States have continually contributed to diversity efforts in the planning profession, but with diversity as a priority accreditation criterion, the onus thus will be expanded to include all planning schools and departments. Indeed, contributions to diversity in planning illustrate how this endeavor is surmountable. The experiences and efforts that planning schools and departments have implemented provide a basis for confidence that when we are intentional about moving beyond diversity, equity, and inclusion statements and plans, we can indeed have a diverse student body and faculty, and this will translate into diversifying our profession.

These are a few of the many recommendations advanced in this book that provide a rich set of strategies to tackle the diversity challenge in the planning profession and education. Across all the contributions, recruitment and enrollment are adduced as critical to diversifying the planning profession and education. Equally important is mentorship for students, faculty, and practitioners of color. Representation in the form of professional mentors and networks is vital, especially for those who do not see many professionals who come from similar backgrounds to their own. Their interests need to be sustained, and any barriers to practicing the profession need to be tackled. As the examples from our contributors illustrate, mentorship programs are thus necessary for diversity efforts in the urban planning profession and education.

Addressing the Planning-Awareness Challenge

Concerning this second theme, four main lessons emerge, namely the need to (1) engage children and youth in experiential learning, (2) integrate urban planning concepts and ideas into children-and-youth educational curriculum, (3) consider urban planning activities as children-and-youth extracurricular activities, and (4) position the urban planning profession in the global urban development agenda.

First, as we attempt to introduce the profession to children and youth, the problems that they care about in their immediate families, communities, environments, and/or important national issues with planning solutions need to be highlighted during our interactions with them. Creating experiential planning activities relating to issues that matter to them will allow children and youth to appreciate the relevance of the profession, its impact on their communities, and why it's needed to make the people and places dear to them better. In this way, we move the profession from an elusively abstract notion to one that speaks to the reality and practicality of everyday living, which urban planning can tackle—and that children and youth as well as their relatives, teachers, and school counselors are exposed to. This is apparent in all of the contributions to Section II. They illustrate how engaging children and youth in the planning process based on real-life community problems induced a realization that planning is a necessary profession dedicated to and relevant for addressing cities' and their residents' problems.

Reaching out to children and youth to engage them in real-world problem-solving activities via urban planning needs to consider the local context within which they live and thrive. For planning, this includes making conscious efforts to reach out to children in vulnerable settings to demonstrate to them how planning can transform and address their vulnerabilities. It also includes harnessing information communications technology (ICT) as an important tool to engage children and youth in urban planning (Westerberg & von Heland, 2015). Warren-Kretzschmar and Licon's chapter, for instance, provides evidence affirming the importance and effectiveness of using ICT such as geodesign to engage children and youth in order to raise awareness about the urban planning profession. Furthermore, the contributions of Section II demonstrate that there is no one way to develop these intentional experiential initiatives to create planning awareness among children and youth. This warrants rethinking what we already know, adapting existing approaches, and identifying new avenues to ensure that how we engage children and youth to make them aware of the urban planning profession, and inspire them to be urban planners, is innovative and effective.

Another way to tackle the awareness challenge is to make urban planning concepts and ideas part of children and youth's education curricula. For many children and youth, their first encounter with the profession is during their college education, which is late in their career-development trajectory. By integrating planning concepts and ideas into child-and-youth educational curricula, such as geography, economics, and social studies, they become aware of the relevance of the profession, its contribution to addressing societal challenges, and its economic prospects for them early on in their development. Early exposure to the profession also gives them time to build interest and understanding of qualification and enrollment requirements. As the contribution from Australia revealed, such efforts were impactful in addressing shortfalls in urban planning enrollments and building a generation that is interested in becoming community change agents even if not through the urban planning profession. Another aspect of making planning concepts and ideas part of children-and-youth educational curricula is by making them part of the set of extracurricular activities available to students. This not only creates experiential-learning opportunities but also becomes a fun avenue to introduce the profession to children early on in their development processes.

These initiatives require engaging with community partners. All the contributions emphasize the critical role different actors play in helping create and implement the Design and Planning Language Programs (DPLPs) discussed. Private-sector organizations, public institutions, non-profit organizations, teachers, and alumni, among others, all play a part in making sure awareness about the urban planning profession is achieved. For more sustainable pathways, Linkous et al. suggest town-and-gown partnerships that allow children and youth, their parents, schoolteachers, and counselors to feel the presence of urban planning departments and schools within their host communities. The example from Japan (Okyere et al.) consolidates this further as children solving real community problems and showcasing them to the public provides further impetus to the saliency of the profession and cogently inking its contributions to solving community problems in both children's and parents' minds. In all cases, the processes need to be intentional, engage partners from the onset in co-identifying the problem to be addressed by urban planning, and provide the necessary resources to support children and youth, as well as their facilitators, in making sure these initiatives are a success.

Nonetheless, increasing awareness about the profession is not only about implementing DPLPs for children and youth. It also involves making connections to the greater community within which children and youth live to reach out to their relatives, mentors, and others that shape their development. It also includes being innovative with our urban planning programs and courses. For instance, we need to build relationships with other departments and use general-education courses on urban planning within our universities—that may not be a standard approach under a department or school of urban and regional planning—to expose students to the profession. We can also modify matriculation requirements, streamline planning curricula, develop new introductory courses, establish new minors, and increase our service-learning or outreach initiatives with community partners. These are low-hanging fruits that we can use to increase awareness within the university setting—and not only among children and youth. These contributions thus emphasize the immense need for planning schools and departments to be innovative, flexible, and responsive to opportunities for reaching out to students within their universities and communities who may not be aware of, but could possibly be interested in, the urban planning profession.

For planning practitioners, it means being effective at our professional mandate to ensure that we continually engage communities in our planning processes, and make planning impactful and transformative for our cities and residents. Engaging broadly and genuinely is imperative as these avenues not only introduce the profession to the public but also garner interest, build confidence in its saliency, and present opportunities for parents to see their children potentially becoming change agents in their communities if they choose planning as a career. However, since the built environment is affected by various professions planners often interact with, it is necessary to articulate the unique value that urban planning offers communities and clearly distinguish it from other professions. To valorize and distinguish the profession also demands positioning its employment prospects among the general public to emphasize its social prestige and demystify any misconceptions. Another way to appraise the profession is to identify the role it plays in this urban century, demonstrating how urban planning has become germane to global development issues, including the sustainable development agenda, climate change, and health pandemics such as COVID-19. For instance, it is only through effective planning and management that our cities can be transformed into places for innovation, growth, economic prosperity, inclusion, and land development sensitive to our natural resources (UN-Habitat, 2020). Not surprisingly, the United Nations Sustainable Development Goal 11 Target 3 emphasizes the need to "enhance inclusive and sustainable urbanization and capacity for participatory, integrated and sustainable human settlement planning and management in all countries" (UN-Habitat, 2020, p. 8). Additionally, the UN's New Urban Agenda provides an impetus for urban planning efforts that is participatory, responsive, and sensitive to the varied demographics of urban areas, while emphasizing the need to train and build the capacity of urban planners to meet current and future urban challenges amid a century of uncertainty (United Nations, 2017). These goals can mostly be achieved by effective planning professionals at the city, regional, and national levels, thus consolidating the necessity for planning. Indeed, the need for urban planning professionals now and in the future is immense as most of the global population will continue to reside in urban areas of our cities. But neither the urban planning academy nor the practitioners can do all this alone. All efforts need to involve various stakeholders, have the requisite coordination and financial resources, be flexible, have effective instructors and facilitators, and ensure effective communication across stakeholders, children, and youth.

Furthermore, to ensure that the planning-awareness challenge is addressed, some key themes emerge including the importance of networking and stakeholder engagement; mentoring for children, youth, and students already enrolled in urban planning programs; ensuring that there is industry input in educational content; strong marketing strategies for urban planning programs (either through social media or in-person events); accreditation of planning programs; and internationalization of planning education. These are germane factors needed to ensure the success of urban planning-awareness initiatives. But above all, the process needs to be intentional with a clear objective to increase awareness about the urban planning profession if the awareness challenge is to be addressed.

There is a strong connection between the diversity and awareness challenges of the urban planning profession and education. Indeed, diversifying the profession requires that children and youth made aware of planning and enrolled in planning programs are mentored to sustain their interest. Diversity in the planning profession and education transcends awareness alone. Even more concerning is the multidimensionality of planning that can leave students confused and uncertain about what roles they can perform as planners after graduation. This can diminish their interest in practicing the profession. For this reason, creating DPLPs and implementing awareness strategies can serve as additional avenues to offer mentorship for young students or students already enrolled in planning programs to become aware of the practice of the urban planning profession, helping them to hone their interests early, and to gain practical experience in urban planning.

The Future of Planning Awareness and Diversity Discourse

The future we want is the future we create through our efforts today. If the planning diversity and awareness challenges are to be addressed, it depends on the actions that we take today. For this reason, we are happy that this book, following Palazzo et al. (2021), is championing the discourse to identify strategies that have been and can be implemented to address these imminent challenges. This is a sure way to cross-pollinate the ideas and move beyond rhetoric to action. The 26 contributions in this book are only a fraction of the experiences that exist globally. As we initiate this discourse, we anticipate more research and publications from the academy to capture more experiences and initiatives that exist across various countries.

We, the editors, hope that readers will find these contributions as insightful and beneficial as we have. The practical suggestions, the lingering questions, and the calls to action are all important reminders that we need to create the future we want for the planning profession and education. We invite our readers to not only glean from the knowledge collated in this book but to move a step further to adopt, adapt, and share this knowledge in formal and informal avenues. It is our hope and interest to further this discourse in other avenues and encourage our contributors and readers to do the same.

References

García, I., Jackson, A., Harwood, S. A., Greenlee, A. J., Lee, C. A., & Chrisinger, B. (2021). "Like a fish out of water" the experience of African American and Latinx planning students. *Journal of the American Planning Association*, *87*(1), 108–122. https://doi.org/10.1080/01944363.2020.1777184

Greenlee, A. J., Jackson, A., Garcia-Zambrana, I., Lee, C. A., & Chrisinger, B. (2018). Where are we going? Where have we been? The climate for diversity within urban planning educational programs. *Journal of Planning Education and Research*. https://doi.org/10.1177/0739456X18815740

Hurtado, P., Shah, S., DeAngelis, J., & Gomez, A. (2022). *2022 trend report for planners*. American Planning Association and Lincoln Institute of Land Policy. Retrieved July 5, 2022, from www.planning.org/publications/document/9228382/

Jackson, A., Garcia-Zambrana, I., Greenlee, A. J., Lee, C. A., & Chrisinger, B. (2018). All talk no walk: Student perceptions on integration of diversity and practice in planning programs. *Planning Practice & Research*, *33*(5), 574–595. https://doi.org/10.1080/02697459.2018.1548207

Palazzo, D., Hollstein, L., & Diko, S. K. (2021). Urban planning as a career preference for students: Efforts to improve awareness about the profession. *Planning Practice & Research*, *36*(2), 174–192. https://doi.org/10.1080/02697459.2020.1782056

Pinson, D. (2004). Urban planning: An 'undisciplined' discipline? *Futures*, *36*(4), 503–513. https://doi.org/10.1016/j.futures.2003.10.008

Solis, M. (2020). Racial equity in planning organizations. *Journal of the American Planning Association*, *86*(3), 297–303. https://doi.org/10.1080/01944363.2020.1742189

UNDESA. (2018). *World urbanization prospects: The 2018 revision (ST/ESA/SER.A/420)*. Retrieved June 21, 2022, from https://population.un.org/wup/Publications/

UN-Habitat. (2020). *Sustainable development goals: Monitoring human settlements indicators. A short guide to human settlements indicators goal 11+*. Retrieved June 21, 2022, from https://unhabitat.org/sites/default/files/2020/06/sustainable_development_goals_summary_version.pdf

United Nations. (2017). *The new urban agenda*. Retrieved July 5, 2022, from https://habitat3.org/wp-content/uploads/NUA-English.pdf

Westerberg, P., & von Heland, F. (2015). *Using Minecraft for youth participation in urban design and governance*. UN-Habitat. Retrieved July 5, 2022, from https://unhabitat.org/using-minecraft-for-youth-participation-in-urban-design-and-governance

INDEX

AAPS (Association of African Planning Schools) 272, 285–286, 298
Abuja 277, 281; Ahmadu Bello Way xii, 281; Democracy Avenue xii
access to funding for under-represented students 44
access to planning programs 38
accredited planning programs 2, 12, 15–17, 19, 21–23, 36, 105, 114
ACSP (Association of Collegiate Schools of Planning) xix, 12–13, 15–16, 23–24, 26–27, 95, 227, 233
African Planning Association 276, 285
African Planning Schools 272, 286, 288, 291, 296, 298
agencies xxi–xxii, 156–157, 198–199, 205, 207–208, 292
American Planning Association *see* APA (American Planning Association)
APA (American Planning Association) 8–13, 33–34, 46–49, 57, 113–115, 201–202, 222–224, 227
APA Florida xv, 202, 207
APA Sun Coast 197–198, 202–204, 206, 208
architecture xv–xix, 4, 19, 58–61, 65–67, 71–74, 162, 236–238
architecture programs 60, 65, 67, 69, 71–73, 228
Association of Collegiate Schools of Planning *see* ACSP (Association of Collegiate Schools of Planning)
Australia 5–6, 57, 66, 97, 172
awareness 2–7, 99, 103–105, 111–113, 129–131, 207–211, 293–298, 314–316; enhancing 65, 198, 224, 295; increasing 113, 200, 207, 294, 296; planning-education 208, 210, 290; planning-profession 113, 260; professional-planning 113, 260; raising 7, 94, 98, 169–170, 277
awareness challenges 215, 257, 275, 311–312, 315–316

barriers 1–2, 77, 104–105, 115–116, 185, 231, 269; curricular 239; financial 209, 232; identifying 105; institutional 49, 55, 260; potential 239; structural 65, 67
barriers to children's participation in planning 98, 187
best practices 28, 38, 44, 87, 120; global 290, 294; international 294
biases 21, 35, 49–50, 291; unconscious 80
BIPOC (Black, Indigenous, and People of Color) 13, 40, 75–77, 80, 85–86, 118
BIPOC communities 77–78, 80, 85, 124, 126
Black 24, 27, 31–33, 36–37, 75–77, 89, 94, 151; Indigenous, and People of Color (*see* BIPOC (Black, Indigenous, and People of Color))
Black/African American *see* Black
Box City 139, 200
bursaries *see* scholarships

Cache Valley xi, xiii, 139–142, 145–146, 148
career aspirations xxii, 157–159, 171, 184, 193; children's 170; teenage 114
career awareness 102, 273; factors influence 98, 102, 112; planning schools influence 102, 112
career choices 102–104, 112, 115, 187, 190–193, 210, 272–288
career choices and preferences of children and youth 8, 97, 112, 115, 233
career counseling 8, 104, 115–116
career development 42, 114–116, 224–225, 285, 287; professional 225, 232
career education 103–104, 113
career guidance 114, 273, 287
career interests 273–274, 293
career in urban planning 5, 177, 185, 193–194, 199
career opportunities 54, 92, 188, 197, 201
career options 158–159, 162, 166, 173, 187–189, 192–193

317

Index

career paths 78, 151, 185–186, 188, 190, 227–229, 253–254
career preferences 7, 9, 99, 101–103, 105, 271
careers 3–5, 97–98, 101–104, 187–189, 193–195, 206–209, 252–253, 275–277
children and youth 7–8, 97–99, 101–105, 112, 118–119, 194–195, 311, 313–315
children's participation in urban planning 115, 124, 128, 150, 157, 184–188, 193, 195
civic engagement 22, 25, 75, 137, 149
Civic Learning 81, 86, 119
climate for diversity 29, 34, 157, 224, 233
Clubhouse 215, 220–221
colonialism 289–291
community: awareness 129, 131, 133, 135–137, 200; engagement 31–32, 106–107, 129–130, 137–138, 148–149, 265–266, 295; planning 129, 131–133, 136–137, 197, 200; resilience xviii
Community Outreach Initiatives 158, 260
community projects 267–268, 295
counseling see counselors
counselors xxii, 102–104, 107, 274, 276, 287
courses 50–54, 61–62, 107, 236–237, 240–247, 254–255, 279–280, 290–292
COVID-19 pandemic 52, 92–93, 117–118, 120, 158, 160
CRP (Community and Regional Planning) xiv, xviii, 4, 18, 235–245
curricula 21, 48–49, 71–73, 153, 172–176, 239–242, 244, 291–292

data 1–3, 27, 53, 120, 151–152, 232–233, 258, 304
decisions xx, xxii, 97, 139, 246, 252–253
declining enrollment 2, 89, 105, 210, 244
demographics 28, 30, 76–77, 87, 89, 312
disciplines 186, 189–194, 231–232, 246–247, 257–258, 275–276, 283–285, 290–291
Diversity in Planning xxi–2, 10–13, 21–29, 31–35, 41–50, 54–67, 71–74, 311–313
Diversity in urban planning education and practice xvi, xxi, 58–59, 61, 63–64, 74
DPLPs (Design and Planning Language Programs) 5, 97–99, 106, 112–113, 209, 257, 314

education 1–5, 7–9, 23–25, 57–59, 252–253, 258, 286–287, 311–313
educational programs 18, 34, 48, 64, 74
Elephant 10, 77, 87, 116, 234
employment prospects 77, 79–80, 101–102, 201–203, 205, 275–277, 284–285
engage young people in city planning 98–99, 119, 121–123, 125, 127, 149
enrollment 3–6, 8–9, 20–22, 224–225, 237–239, 241, 243–245, 272–273
environment: living 69, 129–131, 138; physical 81, 86, 130, 292, 300
environmental planning xvi–xx, 230, 240, 242, 247
environmental science xv, xviii, 240, 242, 246, 248

equity xxii–xxiii, 10–13, 29–30, 37, 46, 55–57, 229, 312–313
ethics xiv, 57, 62, 218, 223
ethnic diversity 28, 32, 80, 88–89, 93–95
ethnicity xxiii, 1–2, 21, 27, 225–226, 228
expectations 47, 69, 72–73, 269, 272, 274–275
experiential learning 174, 181–182, 257, 260, 263, 265
experts 126, 130, 139–140, 163, 168
exposure 2, 5–6, 47–48, 78, 150–151, 178–179, 197, 201–203

faculty 21–24, 26–36, 38–44, 47–49, 65–67, 89–94, 265–270, 281–282; diverse 49, 229, 232
faculty and students 12, 59, 97–98, 101, 265
faculty composition 9, 20–21, 25, 36, 271
faculty diversity 89–91, 94, 210, 229
faculty members xiv, xvii, 31, 33, 49, 55
faculty of color 16, 25, 28, 30–31, 78
field trips 49–50, 153–154, 156, 263, 265–266
fieldwork 48–50, 52, 132, 135, 174–176, 178
first generation college student (FGCS) 48, 56, 107, 201, 225–226, 230–233
flexibility 159, 168, 175, 266, 268–269
funding 38, 40, 44, 165, 168, 268
futures 9, 81, 127, 271, 302

gender 9, 11–12, 59, 114–115, 225–226, 258–259
geodesign 139–148, 314
geography xviii, 107, 113, 172–175, 181–182, 255, 307
GIS (geographic information systems) xvii–xviii, 237, 240–242, 244, 277
graduates 17, 23, 28, 88–90, 236–237, 291–294
graduate students 125, 132–134, 140–141, 146–147, 152
guest speakers 48–50, 52, 54, 253

HBCUs (Historically Black Colleges and Universities) xiii, xix 11, 15–25, 28, 39, 95
health 81, 184, 186–187, 195–196, 287–288, 291
higher education 8, 46, 56–57, 115, 125–126, 195–196, 233–234, 297
high-school counselors 3, 101, 104, 106, 113
high-school students 92, 101–102, 112–113, 118–120, 141, 146–147, 197–198, 226–227
Hispanic/Latino 27, 32, 88–89, 94–95, 151, 231–232
Hispanic-serving institution see HSI (Hispanic-serving institution)
Historically Black Colleges and Universities see HBCUs (Historically Black Colleges and Universities)
HSI (Hispanic-serving institution) 13, 89–93, 95, 313

inclusion 12, 27, 32, 41–43, 46, 49–50, 55–57, 229
inclusiveness see inclusion
increasing diversity 30, 46, 57, 63, 93

318

Index

inequality 59, 62, 76, 85, 291–292
inequities 55, 80, 127, 231, 312
initiatives 41, 66–67, 97–99, 105–108, 111–113, 208–210, 260–261, 269–270
institutions 16–18, 22–23, 25–26, 37, 93, 104–105, 234–236, 296–297
instructors 52, 56, 159–160, 165, 169, 248–249
interdisciplinary 54, 94, 217, 220, 241
interdisciplinary nature 186, 216, 219, 230
internationalization 66–67, 71–74, 275–276, 280, 290, 296
international students 27–28, 32, 45–46, 60, 66–67, 69, 71–73, 296–297
internships 201, 204, 268, 270, 295, 297

jobs 47–58, 151, 153, 201, 203, 293–295
justice 11, 21, 76, 307, 312

K-12 82, 85, 113, 119–120, 122, 125

lack of diversity 2, 6, 35, 78, 80–81
landscape architecture 151–152, 180, 228, 236–238, 241, 243
Latinx 27, 34, 36–37, 76–77, 79
leadership xiv, 11, 13, 79–80, 267–268
local communities 205–206, 210, 258, 260, 265, 294–295
local contexts 127, 130–131, 166–167, 307, 314

marketing 23, 56, 162, 165, 294
master's programs 62, 224, 231, 252–254, 304
MCP (Master of Community Planning) 260, 263, 265, 267–270
mentoring 41–42, 78, 80, 104–105, 190–191, 200–206, 230–232, 313–316
minorities 13, 16, 22, 25, 90, 104–105
motivations 224–225, 227–228, 232–233, 273, 275–276, 286
motivations for planning education 225, 227, 229, 231, 233
MURP (Master of Urban and Regional Planning) 18, 197, 203–204, 206–207, 258

networking 48–49, 52, 54, 200, 293–294
non-majors xxiii, 246–247, 252–253, 255

outcomes 80–81, 105–106, 184–186, 218–219, 274–275, 312–313
outreach 40, 105–106, 198–199, 241–242, 260, 265–266, 269–270, 284–285
overcoming barriers to recruitment and retention of planners 10, 77, 87, 116, 234

PAB (Planning Accreditation Board) 2–3, 15–27, 31–37, 43, 45–47, 88–89, 224, 233–235
PAB-accredited programs xiii 35–38, 88–89, 95, 271
parents 101–102, 149–151, 155–156, 158–159, 162–163, 189–190, 199–200, 274–276

participatory 133, 182, 187, 306, 315
pedagogy 22, 25, 48–50, 52, 63–66, 71–74
people of color xix, 26, 30, 32, 76–77, 79
perceptions 62, 65, 149–150, 219–221, 287–288, 290
Planners of Color Interest Group *see* POCIG (Planners of Color Interest Group)
Planning Accreditation Board *see* PAB (Planning Accreditation Board)
planning awareness 97–99, 209–210, 257, 260–261, 263, 269–270
planning careers 44, 78, 94, 169, 201
planning courses 232, 241, 245, 247, 251
planning curriculum 48, 65, 74, 79, 304
planning departments 233, 237, 241, 244, 258, 260–261
planning discipline 24, 59, 213, 227, 229
planning education 55–59, 63–66, 182–186, 207–210, 219–222, 224–235, 285–292, 297–299
planning educators 210, 213, 247, 249, 252
planning field 35, 37, 119, 124–125, 213, 217
planning graduates xxiii, 56, 173, 285, 293
planning practice 126–127, 129, 214, 219, 221–222, 311–312
planning processes 11, 56, 129, 139–140, 192–194, 219
planning profession xxii–xxiii, 5–7, 75–77, 112–113, 147, 149–151, 252–253, 312–313
planning professionals xxi–xxii, 59, 119, 122, 198–199, 210–211
planning programs 12–13, 17–19, 34–42, 209–211, 224–225, 229–231, 290, 293–297; undergraduate 88–89, 224, 226, 228, 232, 235
planning schools xxii–xxiii, 1, 4–5, 113, 257–258, 284–285, 313
planning theory xviii, 47, 57, 59, 222–223
POCIG (Planners of Color Interest Group) xvi, 12–13, 16, 25–26, 29, 32–33
policies 11–13, 41, 61, 66, 73–74, 139–141
practitioners xxi–xxii, 27, 47–49, 193, 313, 315
professional awareness xxi, 1, 105–106, 112–113, 274–277, 280
professional development 47–50, 52, 54, 56, 203
professional networking 48, 52, 54, 90
professional organizations 51, 90, 99, 106, 229–230
prospective students 4, 92–93, 225, 227, 229–232
public awareness 209, 211, 214, 220–221, 295, 299

race 1–2, 21, 27, 45–46, 65, 80, 151
racial diversity 11–12, 15–16, 22–24, 26–27, 77–80, 232–233
racial equity 28, 35–38, 43, 45, 75–87, 93–94
racial inequality 33, 75
recruitment 12–13, 23–26, 34–35, 38–40, 44–46, 55–56, 77–78, 91–94
recruitment and retention *see* recruitment
recruitment strategies 23, 35, 38, 43, 92
regional planners 1, 3, 7–8, 76, 87

319

Index

regional planning xiv, xvi–xx, 172, 221–222, 252, 254
representation 11–13, 19–20, 26, 36–37, 77, 311–313
retention xxi, 16, 23–25, 34–35, 46, 55–56, 77–78
role models 102, 104, 112, 118, 201, 207

scenarios 63, 139–141, 150, 160, 290
scholarships 40, 44–45, 47, 79, 227, 275
skills 57, 72–73, 111–113, 173–174, 178–179, 214–215, 219, 221–222
social justice 32, 34, 76, 78, 227, 229
social media 92, 203, 208, 227, 294, 296
spatial planning 57, 61, 63, 292–293, 301, 304
strategies 11, 13, 37–38, 41–42, 44–46, 51, 80, 85
student body 12, 28–30, 94, 225, 258, 260; diverse 26, 28, 36, 39–40, 225, 229
student diversity 29, 34–35, 89, 91–92, 224–225, 268
student engagement 51, 93, 113, 239, 243–244
student enrollment 13, 105, 236–237, 257–258, 272–279, 284–286
student recruitment 90–92, 94, 268, 270, 277, 280
students of color 28–29, 32, 35, 78–79, 231–233
studios 50, 55, 125–126, 265–266, 304, 307
sustainability 152–153, 156–157, 174, 178–179, 198, 222, 229, 267

teachers 104, 110–113, 119–122, 132–134, 175–176, 180–181, 191, 275–277
technology 5, 196, 219, 221, 236, 291–292

tools 69, 75–76, 129, 131–132, 136, 149–150, 219, 276–277
trends 55, 60, 233–234, 273, 280, 284

undergraduates 2–3, 36–37, 54, 88, 92, 94, 236–237, 241–245
undergraduate students 92, 95, 225, 230, 237, 244
underrepresented students 33, 47, 52, 55, 92–93, 230–232
underserved communities xv, 2–3, 261, 264–266, 268
universities 24–26, 57–59, 90–93, 235–237, 239–240, 279–281, 290–292, 307–309
urban design xv, xvii, 261, 264, 302, 304
urbanization 272–287, 290, 300, 310, 312
urban planning education 1–2, 57, 59–61, 63–65, 286, 297–298
urban planning processes xvi–xvii, 98, 105, 124, 184, 186, 193–194
urban planning profession xxi, 6–7, 99, 101, 104–106, 213–214, 311, 313–316
urban planning programs 17–18, 97–98, 105, 224–225, 228, 247, 255, 314–315
urban planning schools xxi, 7, 104, 165, 168–169

women 16–17, 22, 24–25, 60, 67, 74
workshops 69, 71–73, 140–141, 144, 146–147, 158–160, 162–163, 165–166